TENTH EDITION

Entrepreneurship
THEORY, PROCESS, PRACTICE

Dr. Donald F. Kuratko

The Jack M. Gill Distinguished Chair of Entrepreneurship;
Professor of Entrepreneurship; Executive & Academic Director

Johnson Center for Entrepreneurship & Innovation
The Kelley School of Business
Indiana University–Bloomington

CENGAGE

Australia • Brazil • Canada • Mexico • Singapore • United Kingdom • United States

Entrepreneurship: Theory, Process, Practice, Tenth Edition
Donald F. Kuratko

Vice President, General Manager, Social Science & Qualitative Business: Erin Joyner

Product Director: Jason Fremder

Content Developer: Tara Singer

Product Assistant: Brian Pierce

Marketing Director: Kristen Hurd

Marketing Manager: Emily Horowitz

Marketing Coordinator: Christopher Walz

Art and Cover Direction, Production Management, and Composition: Lumina Datamatics, Inc.

Intellectual Property Analyst: Diane Garrity

Project Manager: Sarah Shainwald

Manufacturing Planner: Ron Montgomery

Cover Image: ©Dan Collier/Dreamstime.com

For product information and technology assistance, contact us at
Cengage Customer & Sales Support, 1-800-354-9706

For permission to use material from this text or product,
submit all requests online at **cengage.com/permissions**
Further permissions questions can be emailed to
permissionrequest@cengage.com

Library of Congress Control Number: 2015954157

ISBN-13: 978-1-305-57624-7

Cengage
200 Pier 4 Boulevard
Boston, MA 02210
USA

Cengage is a leading provider of customized learning solutions with employees residing in nearly 40 different countries and sales in more than 125 countries around the world. Find your local representative at **www.cengage.com/global**

To learn more about Cengage platforms and services, register or access your online learning solution, or purchase materials for your course, visit **www.cengage.com**.

Printed in the United States of America
Print Number: 03   Print Year: 2020

BRIEF CONTENTS

CONTENTS

PREFACE

Entrepreneurship is the most powerful economic force known to human kind! The entrepreneurial revolution that captured our imagination during the last three decades has now permeated every aspect of business thinking and planning. As exemplified by the dynasty builders of the previous decades, such as Sam Walton of Walmart, Fred Smith of FedEx, Bill Gates of Microsoft, Herb Kelleher of Southwest Airlines, Steve Jobs of Apple, Andy Grove of Intel, Larry Page and Sergey Brin of Google, and Mark Zuckerberg of Facebook, the applications of creativity, risk taking, innovation, and passion led the way to economic development far greater than anyone could imagine. Today we witness the immense impact of entrepreneurial companies such as Google, Amazon, Facebook, Twitter, and LinkedIn, which have produced technological breakthrough after breakthrough. As the second decade of the twenty-first century ends, we continue to encounter newer and sometimes more complex challenges and pressures than ever before in the form of green technologies, social entrepreneurship, sustainability, health care, and technological change. The entrepreneurial drive and determination of yet-to-be-discovered dynasty builders will be our greatest solution to all of these challenges.

The process of transforming creative ideas into commercially viable businesses continues to be a major force in today's world economy. Successful entrepreneurship requires more than merely luck and money. It is a cohesive process of creativity, risk taking, and planning. Students today need courses and programs that set forth a basic framework for understanding the process of entrepreneurship. I wrote this textbook to structure and illustrate the discipline of entrepreneurship in a manner that is as unique and creative as entrepreneurship itself. The text and online materials included in *Entrepreneurship: Theory, Process, Practice*, 10th edition, to bring together in one place the most significant resources for exploring the development of new and emerging ventures and to present them in an exciting, organized, and challenging manner.

ORGANIZATION

The chapter sequence in *Entrepreneurship: Theory, Process, Practice*, 10th edition, is systematically organized around the initiation, planning, growth, and development of new and emerging ventures. Each major part of the text contains chapters that specifically address these pertinent concepts of entrepreneurship.

Part 1 (Chapters 1–4) introduces the entrepreneurial mind-set and examines the entrepreneurial revolution that has taken root across the globe. In it, we address the individual characteristics that shape entrepreneurs and their thinking, the "dark side" of entrepreneurship, and the ethical perspective that impels entrepreneurs in the development of morally conscious approaches to business. From an organizational perspective we introduce the concept of corporate entrepreneurship as a strategy to foster innovation within larger domains. Finally, and perhaps increasing in significance, we focus on social entrepreneurship and the global environment.

Part 2 (Chapters 5–8) examines the initiation of entrepreneurial ventures. We begin with the pursuit of ideas, with opportunity recognition, with creativity, and with innovation. We then examine the methods for assessing new ventures and business opportunities (including the Lean start-up methodology and design thinking), and the pathways to ventures, whether starting a brand new venture, acquiring an existing firm, or purchasing a franchise. This part concludes with a thorough examination of the sources of capital formation available to entrepreneurs.

Part 3 (Chapters 9–12) focuses on the development of entrepreneurial plans. We begin with the legal perspective, the critical legal issues (proprietary protections, patents, copyrights, trademarks, and bankruptcy laws), and the structures of organizations (sole proprietorships, partnerships, and corporations). We then discuss the marketing issues that affect the preparing, planning, and operating of entrepreneurial start-ups (including social media marketing and mobile marketing) as well as the financial tools that entrepreneurs need. Finally, the development of a clear and comprehensive business plan is examined. A complete sample business plan appears in the appendix following Chapter 12.

Part 4 (Chapters 13–15) focuses on the growth, valuation, and harvesting of entrepreneurial ventures. The need for strategic planning, the challenge of managing entrepreneurial growth, and understanding the transition from the entrepreneurial to managerial are all discussed in this part. We then present the valuation process for an entrepreneurial venture as well as effective methods for valuation that need to be considered. Finally, we look at harvesting strategies available to entrepreneurial firms.

DISTINGUISHING FEATURES

Entrepreneurship: Theory, Process, Practice presents an organized, systematic study of entrepreneurship. Certain distinguishing features enhance its usefulness for both students and professors. Each chapter contains these specific learning items:

- **Opening Quotations.** Thought-provoking quotes titled "Entrepreneurial Thought" at the beginning of each chapter capture students' interest about the basic idea for the chapter.

- **Objectives.** A clear set of learning objectives provides a preview of the chapter material and can be used by students to check whether they have understood and retained important points.

- **Figures and Tables.** Numerous charts and tables illustrate specific text material, expand chapter ideas, or refer to outside source material.

- **Summary and Discussion Questions.** Each chapter closes with a summary of key points to be retained. The discussion questions are a complementary learning tool that will enable students to check their understanding of key issues, to think beyond basic concepts, and to determine areas that require further study. The summary and discussion questions help students discriminate between main and supporting points and provide mechanisms for self-teaching.

- **Key Terms.** The most important terms appearing in each chapter are shown in boldface where they first appear. A list of the key terms appears at the end of each chapter, and a complete glossary appears at the end of the book.

INNOVATIVE CONTENT IN THE 10TH EDITION

Producing a new edition is always an ambitious undertaking, but we always welcome the opportunity to refocus and, if necessary, redefine content that makes entrepreneurship clear and engaging for learners and future entrepreneurs.

- **MindTap Digital Learning Suite.** This digital learning solution helps instructors engage and transform today's students into critical thinkers. As a student using MindTap® you'll explore up-to-the-minute entrepreneurial methodologies with hands-on learning experiences. Find out what it's like to be an entrepreneur while building key skills you'll need to invent and launch your brilliant idea. All activities are written exclusively by author "Dr. K" as author Dr. Donald F. Kuratko's students call him and are designed for you to experience his famous "Spine Sweat" firsthand. Implement Design Methodology, the Lean Start-up Methodology, and the Business Model Canvas, and other frameworks within our exclusive learning suite, and gain an understanding of the most contemporary methods being employed in the marketplace.

- **The Entrepreneurial Process.** Short vignettes about the entrepreneurial process are included throughout the text to show how practicing entrepreneurs handle specific challenges and opportunities. Newer and updated process boxes reflect some of the more interesting stories on the various roads traveled by entrepreneurs, including entrepreneurial passion and entrepreneurial fear in Chapter 2, Procter and Gamble's entrepreneurial engine in Chapter 3, social enterprising and incentivizing entrepreneurs in Chapter 4, the Franchise Disclosure Document in Chapter 7, guerrilla marketing in Chapter 10, and valuing a venture in Chapter 14.

- **New Topics, Models, and Processes.** This edition contains the most recent topics, models, and processes developed by scholars in the entrepreneurship field. Some examples include cognition, metacognition, and grief recovery with failure, and ethical challenges for entrepreneurs (Chapter 2); new illustrations and a training program for corporate entrepreneurship (Chapter 3); sustainable entrepreneurship, shared value and triple bottom line thinking, benefit corporations, global entrepreneurs, and diaspora networks (Chapter 4); franchise disclosure documents (Chapter 7); bootstrapping and crowdfunding as sources of capital (Chapter 8); parody, issues with mobile devices, and other new legal concepts (Chapter 9); social media marketing, mobile marketing, and pricing in the social media age (Chapter 10); new tips on business plans and effective "pitches" (Chapter 12); strategic entrepreneurship (Chapter 13); and harvesting issues (Chapter 15).

- **New References and Citations.** In an effort to make *Entrepreneurship: Theory, Process, Practice* the most comprehensive text available, every chapter contains a wealth of endnotes located at the end of each chapter. These references have been carefully selected to provide professors and students with a thorough background of the latest research that relates to the entrepreneurship material being presented. The focus here is on the "theoretical" component of entrepreneurship.

- **Online Ethical Dilemmas in E-Commerce**
  Questions concerning the ethical challenges that now confront entrepreneurs in the social media age strike at the potential venture success, which is at stake in the hands of the social media reputation management sites. How should entrepreneurs proceed?

- **Social Impact Investing**
  This type of investing has started to bring opportunities to harness entrepreneurial ideas and capital markets to finance social initiatives. Increasing the funding capability of social entrepreneurship will increase the likelihood of more efficient, sustainable, and effective social initiatives.

- **The Contemporary Methodologies for Venture Evaluation**
  With newer movements taking shape in the ever changing entrepreneurial world, we provide sections that highlight some of the more contemporary methodologies being utilized for concept assessment and new venture evaluation.

  - **Design Methodology:** Design is now a hot topic in the business world. The demand is becoming so great that universities are now building programs that take a general approach to design rather than concentrating it in just technical schools like architecture and engineering. We present sections on:

  - Design and Learn

  - Design is a learning process that shapes and converts ideas into form, whether that is a plan of action, an experience, or a physical thing. *Learning from qualitative research—Learning from prototyping—Learning from feedback are all presented in this edition of the text.*

  - Design Development and Design Methodology

  - Taking an initial concept idea and developing a proof of concept that elicits feedback from relevant stakeholders. To accomplish this, several criteria must be met, including concept feasibility, concept desirability, and concept viability

  - Design-Centered Entrepreneurship

  - Researchers Michael G. Goldsby, Donald F. Kuratko, Matthew R. Marvel, and Thomas Nelson have introduced the concept of design-centered entrepreneurship with a conceptual model.

  - **The Lean Start-up Methodology:** Similar to design methodology, the Lean Start-up methodology provides a scientific approach to creating early venture concepts and delivers a desired product to customers' hands faster. The Lean Start-up methodology was first developed in 2011 by Eric Ries, founder of IMVU Inc., as a way to prevent waste in start-ups and ensure that the business plan remains a living document. We include Key Lean Startup Key Terminology in this section.

- **Peer-to-Peer Lending (P2P)**
  Peer-to-peer lenders are Internet-based sites that pool money from investors willing to lend capital at agreed-upon rates.

- **Crowdfunding**
  This practice seeks funding for a venture by raising monetary contributions from a large number of people, typically via the Internet. In the United States, legislation that is mentioned in the 2012 Jobs Act will allow for a wider pool of small investors with fewer restrictions following the implementation of the act.

- **Updated information on IPOs, Venture capitalists, Angel investors, B Corporations, and LC3s**

- **Business Model Canvas**
  The essential elements of the Business Model Canvas are presented and discussed in Chapter 12.

UPDATED AND ENHANCED SUPPLEMENTARY MATERIALS

The following resources and ancillaries have been created to support users of *Entrepreneurship*, 10th edition:

- **MindTap Digital Learning Suite.** Through paths of dynamic assignments and applications that you can personalize, real-time course analytics, and an accessible reader, MindTap helps you turn cookie cutter into cutting edge, apathy into engagement, and memorizers into higher-level thinkers. As an instructor using MindTap, you have at your fingertips engaging, challenging, rigorous learning activities written exclusively by Dr. Kuratko. Students learn firsthand what it's like to be an entrepreneur as they complete challenges that develop their creative and critical thinking skills. Give your students a powerful learning experience while saving time planning lessons and course structure using our exclusive interface designed to improve your workflow. All activities are written and produced exclusively by Dr. Donald F. Kuratko to help students and instructors experience his innovative teaching methodology first hand.

  Self-Assessments engage students by helping them make personal connections to the content presented in the chapter.

  Reading Quizzes assess students' basic comprehension of the reading material to help you gauge their level of engagement and understanding of the content.

  Video Case Activities engage students by presenting everyday businesses facing managerial challenges, placing concepts in real-world context and making for great points of discussion.

  Experiential Exercises challenge students to work in teams in our one-of-a-kind collaborative environment to create their own venture from concept to investor pitch. Carry out Dr. K's famous Spine Sweat Experience in your course for an extra challenge.

- **Instructor's Manual.** The Instructor's Manual contains chapter outlines, lecture outlines, answers to review and case questions, teaching notes for the comprehensive part cases, and similar content, as well as methods for incorporating the MindTap digital learning suite into your course. It is available on the text website at **www.cengagebrain.com**.

- **Cognero.** This program is easy-to-use test-creation software that is compatible with Microsoft Windows. Instructors can add or edit questions, instructions, and answers, and select questions by previewing them on the screen, selecting them randomly, or selecting them by number. Instructors can also create and administer quizzes online, whether over the Internet, a local area network (LAN), or a wide area network (WAN).

- **Test Bank.** Thoroughly revised and enhanced, test bank questions are linked to each chapter's knowledge objectives and are ranked by difficulty and question type. An ample number of challenging questions are provided that are tagged according to learning objectives, difficulty, and Bloom's Taxonomy.

- **LivePlan Business Software.** Students can create robust, polished business plans worthy of the most distinguished investor using the LivePlan business software.

- **PowerPoint® Slides.** PowerPoint presentations for instructors and students are colorful and varied, designed to hold students' interest and reinforce all of each chapter's main points. The PowerPoint presentations are available on text website at **www.cengagebrain.com**.

- **Website.** A dynamic, comprehensive website at **http://academic.cengage.com/management/kuratko** features an Interactive Study Center with quizzes that allow students to test and retest their knowledge of chapter concepts. In addition, the website features downloadable flashcards of key terms, additional sample business plans, and much more. Instructors can download resources including the Instructor's Manual, Test Bank, and PowerPoint® presentation slides.

ACKNOWLEDGMENTS

Many individuals played an important role in helping to write, develop, and refine the text, and they deserve special recognition. First, my wife, Debbie and daughters, Christina and Kellie, from whom I took so much time, deserve my deepest love and appreciation. Appreciation is extended to the staff at Cengage Learning, in particular Jason Fremder, Tara Singer, and Suzanne Wilder. The professionals who reviewed the manuscript and offered copious suggestions for improvement played a decisive role in the final result. I would first like to acknowledge the reviewers whose comments and suggestions have helped to shape this and all previous editions of *Entrepreneurship*. Solochidi Ahiarah, SUNY College at Buffalo (Buffalo State College); Mary Allender, University of Portland; James Almeida, Fairleigh Dickinson University; Jeffrey Alves, Wilkes University; Joseph S. Anderson, Northern Arizona University; Lawrence Aronhime, Johns Hopkins University; Kenneth M. Becker, University of Vermont; Ted Berzinski, Mars Hill College; Thomas M. Box, Pittsburg State University; Stephen Braun, Concordia University; Martin Bressler, Houston Baptist University; Debbi Brock, Berea College; John Callister, Cornell University; Don Cassidy, Inver Hills Community College; A. A. Farhad Chowdhury, Mississippi Valley State University; James J. Chrisman, Mississippi State University; John E. Clarkin, College of Charleston; Teresa A. Daniel, Marshall University; Judy Dietert, Texas State University–San Marcos; Barbara Frazier, Western Michigan University; Barry Gilmore, University of Memphis; Michael Giuliano, University of Maryland University, College Asia; James V. Green, University of Maryland, College Park; Judith Grenkowicz, Kirtland Community College; Stephanie Haaland, Linfield College; Peter Hackbert, Sierra Nevada College; David M. Hall, Saginaw Valley State University; Barton Hamilton, Olin School of Business, Washington University; Brenda Harper, Athens State University; Tim Hatten, Mesa State College; Daniel R. Hogan, Jr., Loyola University; Kathie K. Holland, University of Central Florida; Frank Hoy, University of Texas–El Paso; Rusty Juban, Southeastern Louisiana University; Ronald Kath, Life University; James T. Kilinski, Purdue University Calumet; Michael Krajsa, DeSales University; Stewart D. Langdon, Spring Hill College; Karl LaPan, Indiana University-Purdue University Fort Wayne; Hector Lopez, Hostos Community College/CUNY; Louis Marino, University of Alabama; Charles H. Matthews, University of Cincinnati; Todd Mick, Missouri Western State College; Angela Mitchell, Wilmington College; David Mosby, UTA; Lynn Neeley, Northern Illinois University; Charles Nichols, Sullivan University; Terry W. Noel, California State University–Chico; John H. Nugent, Montana Tech of the University of Montana; Don Okhomina, Alabama State University; Joseph C. Picken, University of Texas at Dallas; Paul Preston, University of Montevallo; J. Harold Ranck, Jr., Duquesne University; Christina Roeder, James Madison University; William J. Rossi, University of Florida; Jonathan Silberman, Arizona State University West; Cynthia Simerly, Lakeland Community College; Ladd W. Simms, Mississippi Valley State University; Marsha O. Smith, Middle Tennessee State University; Richard L.

Smith, Iowa State University; Marcene Sonneborn, Syracuse University; Timothy Stearns, California State University–Fresno; Charles Stowe, Sam Houston State University; Michael Stull, California State University San Bernardino; Jeffrey S. Sugheir, Boise State University; Thomas C. Taveggia, University of Arizona; Jill Thomas-Jorgenson, Lewis-Clark State College; Judy Thompson, Briar Cliff University; Charles N. Toftoy, George Washington University; Monica Zimmerman Treichel, Temple University; Henry T. Ulrich, Central Connecticut State University; Randall Wade, Rogue Community College; Michael Wasserman, Clarkson University; Joan Winn, University of Denver; Amy Wojciechowski, West Shore Community College; Nicholas Young, University of St. Thomas; Raymond Zagorski, Kenai Peninsula College/University of Alaska; and Anatoly Zhuplev, Loyola Marymount University.

I would also like to thank Justin K. Otani and Adam D. Johnson, creators of the "Hydraulic Wind Power, LLC" business plan that appears as the Appendix following Chapter 12. In addition, thanks to Andrew F. Vincent, author of "Drop to Me.Com," the Internet-based business plan located on the text website. Both individuals prepared excellent and comprehensive examples of business plans from which students are sure to benefit.

I would also like to express my deepest appreciation of my colleagues at the Kelley School of Business at Indiana University–Bloomington for their tremendous support. In particular, I thank the staff at the Johnson Center for Entrepreneurship & Innovation at the Kelley School of Business, Indiana University–Bloomington. A special thanks to Patricia P. McDougall, the Haeberle Professor of Entrepreneurship and former Associate Dean at the Kelley School of Business, Indiana University, and Jeffrey G. Covin, the Glaubinger Professor of Entrepreneurship at the Kelley School of Business, Indiana University, both of whom have always supported my efforts immensely. Finally, my continued respect and appreciation to Idalene (Idie) Kesner, dean of the Kelley School of Business, Indiana University, for her outstanding leadership and enthusiastic support.

Dr. Donald F. Kuratko
The Kelley School of Business
Indiana University–Bloomington

ABOUT THE AUTHOR

DR. DONALD F. KURATKO (known as "Dr. K") is the Jack M. Gill Distinguished Chair of Entrepreneurship; Professor of Entrepreneurship; Executive & Academic Director of the Johnson Center for Entrepreneurship & Innovation, at the Kelley School of Business, Indiana University–Bloomington. Dr. Kuratko is considered a prominent scholar and national leader in the field of entrepreneurship. He has published over 190 articles on aspects of entrepreneurship, new venture development, and corporate entrepreneurship. His work has been published in journals such as *Strategic Management Journal*, *Academy of Management Executive*, *Journal of Business Venturing*, *Entrepreneurship Theory & Practice*, *Journal of Operations Management*, *Journal of Product Innovation Management*, *Small Business Economics*, *Journal of Small Business Management*, *Family Business Review*, *Business Horizons*, and the *Journal of Business Ethics*. Professor Kuratko has authored 30 books, including one of the leading entrepreneurship books in universities today, *Entrepreneurship: Theory, Process, Practice*, 10th edition (Cengage/South-Western Publishers, 2017), as well as *Corporate Entrepreneurship & Innovation*, 3rd edition (South-Western/Thomson Publishers, 2011),
Innovation Acceleration (Pearson/Prentice Hall Publishers, 2012), and *New Venture Management* (Pearson/Prentice Hall Publishers, 2009). In addition, Dr. Kuratko has been consultant on corporate innovation and entrepreneurial strategies to a number of major corporations such as Anthem Blue Cross/Blue Shield, AT&T, United Technologies, Ameritech, Walgreens, McKesson, Union Carbide Corporation, ServiceMaster, SPX Corp., Molex Corp., and TruServ. Dr. Kuratko also serves as the Executive Director of the Global Consortium of Entrepreneurship Centers (GCEC), an organization comprising over 300 top university entrepreneurship centers throughout the world.

Under Professor Kuratko's leadership and with one of the most prolific entrepreneurship faculties in the world, Indiana University's Entrepreneurship Program has consistently been ranked as the #1 university for entrepreneurship research by the *Global Entrepreneurship Productivity Rankings*; the #1 University Entrepreneurship Program in the United States (public universities) by *Fortune*; and the #1 Graduate Business School (Public Institutions) for Entrepreneurship and the #1 Undergraduate Business School for Entrepreneurship (Public Institutions) by *U.S. News & World Report*. In addition, Indiana University was awarded the *National Model MBA Program in Entrepreneurship* for the MBA Program in Entrepreneurship & Innovation developed by Dr. Kuratko. Before coming to Indiana University he was the Stoops Distinguished Professor of Entrepreneurship and Founding Director of the Entrepreneurship Program at Ball State University. In addition, he was the Executive Director of the Midwest Entrepreneurial Education Center. Dr. Kuratko was the first professor ever to be named a Distinguished Professor for the College of Business at Ball State University and held that position for 15 years. The Entrepreneurship Program that Dr. Kuratko developed at Ball State University continually earned national rankings including: Top 20 in *Business Week* and *Success* magazines; Top 10 business schools for entrepreneurship research by the *Journal of Management*; Top 4 in *U.S. News & World Report* (including the #1 public university for entrepreneurship); and the #1 Regional Entrepreneurship Program by *Entrepreneur*.

Dr. Kuratko's honors include earning the Entrepreneur of the Year for the state of Indiana (sponsored by Ernst & Young and *Inc.* magazine) and being inducted into the Institute of

American Entrepreneurs Hall of Fame. He has been honored with the George Washington Medal of Honor; the Leavey Foundation Award for Excellence in Private Enterprise; the NFIB Entrepreneurship Excellence Award; and the National Model Innovative Pedagogy Award for Entrepreneurship. In addition, he was named the National Outstanding Entrepreneurship Educator by the U.S. Association for Small Business and Entrepreneurship and he was selected one of the Top Entrepreneurship Professors in the United States by *Fortune*. He has been honored with the Thomas W. Binford Memorial Award for Outstanding Contribution to Entrepreneurial Development by the Indiana Health Industry Forum and he was named a 21st Century Entrepreneurship Research Fellow by the Global Consortium of Entrepreneurship Centers. In his years at Ball State University he earned the College of Business Teaching Award for 15 consecutive years as well as being the only professor in the history of Ball State University to achieve all four of the university's major lifetime awards, which included the Outstanding Young Faculty Award, Outstanding Teaching Award, Outstanding Faculty Award, and Outstanding Researcher Award. Dr. Kuratko was honored by his peers in *Entrepreneur* magazine as one of the Top Entrepreneurship Program Directors in the nation for three consecutive years including the #1 Entrepreneurship Program Director in the nation. The U.S. Association for Small Business & Entrepreneurship honored him with the John E. Hughes Entrepreneurial Advocacy Award for his career achievements in entrepreneurship and corporate innovation and the National Academy of Management honored Dr. Kuratko with the Entrepreneurship Advocate Award for his career contributions to the development and advancement of the discipline of entrepreneurship. Professor Kuratko has been named one of the Top 50 Entrepreneurship Scholars in the world and was the recipient of the Riata Distinguished Entrepreneurship Scholar Award. He was the inaugural recipient of the Karl Vesper Entrepreneurship Pioneer Award for his career dedication to developing the field of entrepreneurship and in 2014 he was honored by the National Academy of Management with the Entrepreneurship Mentor Award for his exemplary mentorship to the next generation of entrepreneurship scholars and professors.

IN REMEMBRANCE

Dr. Richard M. Hodgetts (1942–2001)

On November 17, 2001, Dr. Richard M. Hodgetts passed away after a 3½-year battle with bone marrow cancer. The field of Management lost one of its most significant scholars and teachers.

Dr. Hodgetts earned a Ph.D. from the University of Oklahoma, an M.B.A. from Indiana University, and a B.S. from New York University. A prolific scholar and author Dr. Hodgetts published more than 125 articles on a variety of topics ranging from entrepreneurship to strategic management to total quality management. His articles appeared in a host of leading journals including the *Academy of Management Journal*, *Academy of Management Executive*, *Organizational Dynamics*, *Business Horizons*, *Personnel*, *Personnel Journal*, and the *Journal of Small Business Management*. He was also the editor of *Journal of Leadership Studies* and served on a number of editorial boards. He was the author or coauthor of 49 books. Some of the most recent include *International Business*, *International Management*, *Modern Human Relations at Work*, *Measures of Quality and High Performance*, and *Entrepreneurship, A Contemporary Approach*, which he wrote with Dr. Kuratko.

Dr. Hodgetts was an active Academy of Management member his whole career, serving as program chair in 1991, chair of the Management History Division, editor of the New Time special issue of *Academy of Management Executive*, and member of the Board of Governors from 1993 to 1996. For all of his dedicated service, he was inducted into the prestigious *Academy of Management Fellows*.

Besides his tremendous contributions to the knowledge base of management, Dr. Hodgetts was a truly outstanding teacher. He won every Distinguished Teaching Award offered at both his first job of 10 years at the University of Nebraska and his home school for 25 years at Florida International University, including Faculty Member of the Year by the Executive MBA students in the year of his passing. Some of his more notable honors included the Outstanding Educator Award from the National Academy of Management in 1999; the John F. Mee Management Contribution Award, from the Management History Division of the Academy of Management in 1998; the Professor Excellence Program Award from FIU in 1997, a Teaching Improvement Program Award from FIU in 1996; and an Excellence in Teaching Award from FIU in 1995.

Dr. Hodgetts consulted for a number of Fortune 500 firms and provided training for a wide variety of companies, including AT&T, Delco Electronics, Eastman Kodak, GE, IBM, Motorola, Texas Instruments, and Walmart. He has also lectured in Mexico, Venezuela, Peru, Chile, Jamaica, Trinidad, Denmark, Kuwait, and at a host of U.S. colleges and universities.

He literally developed thousands of students at all levels—undergraduate, MBA, executive development, and doctoral—and millions across the world were influenced by his texts and innovative distance education materials and courses. Simply put, he was the ultimate scholar and educator!

Dr. Hodgett's distinguished career as a scholar and educator was exemplified in his humor, his dedication to research, his genuine interest in his students, his compassion, and his true courage. Millions of students and practicing leaders have been, and will continue to be, influenced by his teaching and publications. His legacy will live forever!

INTRODUCTION

THEORY, PROCESS, AND PRACTICE

I have subtitled this book on entrepreneurship as *Theory, Process, Practice* for two specific reasons, of which one is emotional and the other is logical. First, I wanted to honor my former mentor, coauthor, and friend, Dr. Richard M. Hodgetts, in selecting a subtitle that he developed for one of his most successful management books decades ago. The sad loss of Dr. Hodgetts to cancer in 2001 will always leave a void for all of us who knew him and recognized his powerful influence on the entire field of management in business schools. (See my remembrance of Dr. Hodgetts located just after the Preface.) The second reason I selected this subtitle is its representation of the book's focus. I believe that students studying entrepreneurship must be exposed to the "theory development" of the field, the "processes" by which we now teach and study entrepreneurship, and the actual "practice" of entrepreneurship by those individuals and organizations that have been successful. Thus, in order to completely understand and appreciate this emerging discipline we call entrepreneurship, students must learn from theory, process, and practice. The subtitle represents the complete foundation of a discipline. Let's begin by briefly examining each facet.

THE THEORY OF ENTREPRENEURSHIP

Not too long ago the field of entrepreneurship was considered little more than an applied trade as opposed to an academic area of study. There was no "research" to be accomplished because it was thought that those who could not attend college would simply "practice" the concept of new business start-up. Yet our economy was actually based upon entrepreneurship, and history has proven that with each downturn in the economy it is entrepreneurial drive and persistence that bring us back. Thus, individual scholars began to examine entrepreneurship from a research perspective, and in doing so they initiated an academic field of scholarly pursuit. So we look back at some of the "believers" among the academic community, such as Arnold C. Cooper (Purdue University), Karl A. Vesper (University of Washington), Donald L. Sexton (Ohio State University), Robert C. Ronstadt (Babson College), and Howard H. Stevenson (Harvard University), who are all examples of the "pioneering" researchers in the embryonic days of entrepreneurship. Their wisdom, scholarship, and persistence guided the field of entrepreneurship from what was once considered a disrespected academic area to a field that has now gained unimaginable respect and admiration among business schools in the twenty-first century. Their willingness to delve into the research issues important to this developing discipline provided motivation for the next generation of scholars to pursue the entrepreneurship field with greater vigor.

Today we celebrate the immense growth in entrepreneurship research as evidenced by the number of academic journals devoted to entrepreneurship (44), the number of endowed professorships and chairs in entrepreneurship (more than 400), the development of the 21st Century Entrepreneurship Research Fellows by the Global Consortium of Entrepreneurship Centers, and the increasing number of top scholars devoting much of their valuable research time and efforts to publishing on aspects of entrepreneurship in the top academic journals. It is indeed gratifying to see *Academy of Management Journal*, *Academy of Management Review*, *Strategic Management Journal*, *Journal of Operations Management*, and the *Journal of Management* publishing more entrepreneurship research; this increase is in direct proportion to the change in the journals' editorial review boards to include more scholars in the entrepreneurship field. Finally, many universities are now including certain entrepreneurship journals in their lists of top journals for the faculty to publish in. Many of the top business schools in the United States have accepted the *London Times* list of the top 45 academic journals, which includes the *Journal of Business Venturing and Entrepreneurship Theory & Practice*. Additionally, a number of major academic institutions have developed programs in entrepreneurial research, and every year Babson College conducts a symposium titled "Frontiers in Entrepreneurship Research." Since 1981 the conference has provided an outlet for the latest developments in entrepreneurship.

In 1998 the National Consortium of Entrepreneurship Centers (NCEC) was founded for the purpose of continued collaboration among the established entrepreneurship centers, as well as the newer emerging centers, to work together to share information, develop special projects, and assist one another in advancing and improving their centers' impact. Today that organization has changed its name to the Global Consortium of Entrepreneurship Centers (GCEC) to better reflect the international growth of entrepreneurship centers. As mentioned earlier, this consortium also established the 21st Century Entrepreneurship Research Fellows, a growing collection of scholars in the field of entrepreneurship who have developed a mission to identify leading-edge research issues and domains and develop high-profile research initiatives that demonstrate the highest level of scholarship to entrepreneurship centers and the academic community at large. Research drives business schools. Today we see research in entrepreneurship as an accepted and respected part of this drive.

THE PROCESS OF ENTREPRENEURSHIP

Beginning with the "early adopters" of the discipline of entrepreneurship, such as the University of Southern California (USC), Babson College, Harvard University, and Indiana University, the number of schools teaching and researching entrepreneurship has exploded to more than 1,000 schools with majors in entrepreneurship, an additional 1,000 with concentrations in entrepreneurship, and at least one course in entrepreneurship now taught at over 3,000 universities worldwide! Some of the more prestigious research universities in the United States, such as Indiana University, Syracuse University, Oklahoma State University, University of Colorado, University of Louisville, and University of Washington, have developed Ph.D. programs in entrepreneurship in order to prepare the next generation of scholars and researchers. The academic field of entrepreneurship has evolved dramatically over the last 40 years! In the midst of this huge expansion of courses remains the challenge of teaching entrepreneurship more effectively.

It has become clear that entrepreneurship, or certain facets of it, *can* be taught. Business educators and professionals have evolved beyond the myth that entrepreneurs are born, not made. Peter Drucker, recognized as one of the leading management thinkers of the twentieth century, said, "The entrepreneurial mystique? It's not magic, it's not mysterious, and it has nothing to do with the genes. It's a discipline. And, like any discipline, it can be learned."[1] Additional support for this view comes from a 10-year literature review of enterprise, entrepreneurship, and small-business management education that reported, "Most of the empirical studies surveyed indicated that entrepreneurship can be taught, or at least encouraged, by entrepreneurship education."[2]

Given the widely accepted notion that entrepreneurial ventures are the key to innovation, productivity, and effective competition, the question of whether entrepreneurship can be taught is obsolete. Robert C. Ronstadt posed the more relevant question regarding entrepreneurial education: What should be taught, and how should it be taught? He proposed that entrepreneurial programs should be designed so that potential entrepreneurs are aware of barriers to initiating their entrepreneurial careers and can devise ways to overcome them. He contended that an effective program must show students how to behave entrepreneurially and should also introduce them to people who might be able to facilitate their success.[3]

Four years later, researchers Robinson and Hayes conducted a survey of universities with enrollments of at least 10,000 students to determine the extent of the growth in entrepreneurship education.[4] While significant growth was cited, two specific challenges were pointed out: developing existing programs and personnel, thus improving the quality of the field. There are several obstacles that need to be overcome to facilitate the development of quality in the field. At the heart may be the lack of solid theoretical bases upon which to build pedagogical models and methods, and the lack of formal academic programs, representing a lack of commitment on the part of institutions. Professors Robinson and Hayes believed that entrepreneurship education had come a long way in 20 years, yet there were several weak points in the field that were identified through their research. Of primary concern is the lack of depth in most of the programs that were then started. Further growth would depend upon how new programs were integrated with and nurtured by the established entrepreneurship education system. In the years that followed, we experienced a greater depth in the academic programs as well as newer initiatives to integrate entrepreneurship throughout the campuses.

In more recent times, researchers Solomon, Duffy, and Tarabishy conducted one of the most comprehensive empirical analyses on entrepreneurship education. In their review of entrepreneurship pedagogy, they stated, "A core objective of entrepreneurship education is that it differentiates from typical business education. Business entry is fundamentally a different activity than managing a business."[5] They concluded that pedagogy is changing based on a broadening market interest in entrepreneurial education. New interdisciplinary programs use faculty teams to develop programs for the nonbusiness student, and there is a growing trend in courses specifically designed for art, engineering, and science students. In addition to courses focused on preparing the future entrepreneur, instructional methodologies are being developed for those who manage entrepreneurs in organizations, potential resource people (accountants, lawyers, consultants) used by entrepreneurs, and top managers who provide vision and leadership for corporations, which must innovate in order to survive. Today's entrepreneurship educators are challenged with designing effective learning opportunities for entrepreneurship students.

The current trend in most universities is to develop or expand entrepreneurship programs and design unique and challenging curricula specifically designed for entrepreneurship students. One shining example of this expansionary trend is Dr. Michael H. Morris at the University of Florida, who developed one of the most powerful educational programs for faculty to learn how to teach entrepreneurship. Titled "The Entrepreneurship Experiential Classroom," this uniquely designed entrepreneurship program has touched the lives of over a thousand faculty members who have experienced the latest curriculum techniques and methods to enhance their own classrooms across the world. Another significant example is the national recognition now being given to the top entrepreneurial schools through awards such as the United States Association for Small Business and Entrepreneurship (USASBE) National Model Programs and the national rankings such as those done by *U.S. News & World Report* and *Fortune Small Business* magazine. This kind of experience is offered to students in innovative entrepreneurship programs recognized by the USASBE. Highlights of these programs can be found at **www.usasbe.org**. These awarded model programs include undergraduate majors and concentrations, graduate-level programs, innovative pedagogy, and specialized programs. All of these universities have produced entrepreneurship education that has had real impact on students and a lasting impact on the entrepreneurship field.

THE PRACTICE OF ENTREPRENEURSHIP

The final aspect of entrepreneurship is its application in practice. We have seen this exhibited by the thousands of successful entrepreneurs throughout the last 40 years. They and their new ventures have changed our world … forever! However, it is important to understand the differences between mere opportunistic moneymaking and the real practice of entrepreneurship. For example, in the late 1990s we experienced the dot-com frenzy in which everyone thought they were entrepreneurs simply because they put a business title on the Internet. As

I have pointed out many times, in the 1940s it cost $20 billion to invent the atomic bomb. It took another $20 billion to put man on the moon 20 years later. In 1999, the dot-coms burned right through $20 billion to achieve ... well, nothing really. The dot-com bust hurt more than the cash-burning Internet start-ups and the venture capitalists that funded them. This plague spread like wildfire, collapsing the true entrepreneurial spirit of building one's dream into an enduring entity. Our classrooms became infatuated with the drive for investment and liquidity, fast cash, quick exits, and no real commitment. We pursued an "investment mentality" rather than facilitating the search for an "enduring enterprise." We have survived that time, but it did leave us a legacy to *learn* from. We must again focus on the real goals of entrepreneurs and the motivation that permeates from them. We must educate our next generation of entrepreneurs to learn from the dot-com evaporation and return to the roots of business formation and development. Exit strategies are fine, but they should not dominate the pursuit of entrepreneurial opportunity. One author referred to the dot-com individuals as "opportuneurs" rather than entrepreneurs because they uncoupled wealth from contribution, replaced risk taking with risk faking, and exploited external opportunity rather than pursuing inner vision.[6]

It should be the mission of all entrepreneurship educators to teach the students of today about the *true* entrepreneur. It is the mission of this book to provide an integration of entrepreneurs and their entrepreneurial pursuits into the text material. I want to be sure that today's practicing entrepreneurs and their interesting stories are presented in order to illustrate the real problems and issues involved with their ventures. Students need the exposure to those entrepreneurs who have paid the price, faced the challenges, and endured the failures. I want the lessons learned from our experienced entrepreneurs to "make a difference." It is only by reading about and studying their practices that we can truly learn the real application of the entrepreneurial theories and processes.

FINAL THOUGHTS BEFORE VENTURING INTO THE TEXT

After reviewing the major facets of theory, process, and practice that are so integral to the study of entrepreneurship, the question remains: So how do I approach this subject? The answer is neither complex nor profound. The answer is really an appreciation for your abilities and recognizing that each one of us can make a difference if we try. Remember, the journey of 10,000 miles always starts with the first step! Let this book and your entrepreneurial course be your first step.

Entrepreneurship is the new revolution, and it's about continual innovation and creativity. It is the future of our world economy. Today, the words used to describe the new innovation regime of the twenty-first century are: *dream, create, explore, invent, pioneer,* and *imagine*! I believe we are at a point in time when the gap between what can be imagined and what can be accomplished has never been smaller. This is the challenge for all of today's entrepreneurship students. To paraphrase the late Robert F. Kennedy in a speech made more than 40 years ago: You are living in one of the rarest moments in education history—a time when all around us the old order of things is crumbling, and a new world society is painfully struggling to take shape. If you shrink from this struggle and the many difficulties it entails, you will betray the trust that your own position forces upon you. You possess one of the most privileged positions; for you have been given the opportunity to educate and to lead. You can use your enormous privilege and opportunity to seek purely your tenure and security. But entrepreneurial history will judge you, and as the years pass, you will ultimately judge yourself on the extent to which you have used your abilities to pioneer and lead into new horizons. In your hands ... is the future of your entrepreneurial world and the fulfillment of the best qualities of your own spirit.[7]

NOTES

1. P. F. Drucker, *Innovation and Entrepreneurship* (New York: Harper and Row, 1985).

2. G. Gorman, D. Hanlon, and W. King, "Some Research Perspectives on Entrepreneurship Education, Enterprise Education, and Education for Small Business Management: A Ten-Year Literature Review," *International Small Business Journal* 15 (1997): 56–77.

3. R. Ronstadt, "The Educated Entrepreneurs: A New Era of Entrepreneurial Education is Beginning," *American Journal of Small Business* 11(4) (1987): 37–53.

4. P. Robinson and M. Hayes, "Entrepreneurship Education in America's Major Universities," *Entrepreneurship Theory and Practice* 15(3) (1991): 41–52.

5. G. T. Solomon, S. Duffy, and A. Tarabishy, "The State of Entrepreneurship Education in the United States: A Nationwide Survey and Analysis," *International Journal of Entrepreneurship Education* 1(1) (2002): 65–86.

6. J. Useem, "The Risktaker Returns," *FSB* (May 2001): 70–71.

7. D. F. Kuratko, "The Emergence of Entrepreneurship Education: Development, Trends and Challenges," *Entrepreneurship Theory and Practice,* 29(5) (2005): 577–597.

PART 1

The Entrepreneurial Mind-Set in the Twenty-First Century

CHAPTER 1

Entrepreneurship: Evolutionary Development— Revolutionary Impact

LEARNING OBJECTIVES

1 To examine the historical development of entrepreneurship

2 To explore and debunk the myths of entrepreneurship

3 To define and explore the major schools of entrepreneurial thought

4 To explain the process and framework approaches to the study of entrepreneurship

5 To set forth a comprehensive definition of entrepreneurship

6 To examine the entrepreneurial revolution taking place today

7 To illustrate today's entrepreneurial environment

Entrepreneurial Thought

Most of what you hear about entrepreneurship is all wrong. It's not magic; it's not mysterious; and it has nothing to do with genes. It's a discipline and, like any discipline, it can be learned.

— **Peter F. Drucker** *Innovation and Entrepreneurship*

1-1 ENTREPRENEURS—BREAKTHROUGH INNOVATORS

Entrepreneurs are individuals who recognize opportunities where others see chaos, contradiction, and confusion. They are aggressive catalysts for change within the marketplace. They have been compared to Olympic athletes challenging themselves to break new barriers, to long-distance runners dealing with the agony of the miles, to symphony orchestra conductors balancing different skills and sounds into a cohesive whole, and to top-gun pilots continually pushing the envelope of speed and daring. Whatever their passion, entrepreneurs are the heroes of today's marketplace. They start companies and create jobs at a breathtaking pace. The global economy has been revitalized because of their efforts, and the world now embraces free enterprise as the most significant force for economic development. The passion and drive of entrepreneurs moves the world of business forward. They challenge the unknown and continuously create breakthroughs for the future.

One anonymous quote sums up the realities for entrepreneurs: "Anyone [can be an entrepreneur] who wants to experience the deep, dark canyons of uncertainty and ambiguity; and who wants to walk the breathtaking highlands of success. But I caution, do not plan to walk the latter, until you have experienced the former."[1]

1-2 ENTREPRENEURS VERSUS SMALL-BUSINESS OWNERS: A DISTINCTION

The terms *entrepreneur* and *small-business owner* sometimes are used interchangeably. Although some situations encompass both terms, it is important to note the differences in the titles. Small businesses are independently owned and operated, are not dominant in their fields, and usually do not engage in many new or innovative practices. They may never grow large, and the owners may prefer a more stable and less aggressive approach to running these businesses; in other words, they manage their businesses by expecting stable sales, profits, and growth. Because small firms include those purchased as already established businesses as well as franchises, small-business owners can be viewed as *managers* of small businesses.

On the other hand, entrepreneurial ventures are those for which the entrepreneur's principal objectives are innovation, profitability, and growth. Thus, the business is characterized by innovative strategic practices and sustainable growth. Entrepreneurs and their financial backers are usually seeking rapid growth and immediate profits. They may even seek the sale of their businesses if there is potential for large capital gains. Thus, entrepreneurs may be viewed as having a different perspective from small-business owners on the development of their firms.

In this book, we concentrate on entrepreneurs and the effective development of entrepreneurship, including the entrepreneurial mind-set in established organizations. Some of the particular points in this book may apply to both small-business owners and entrepreneurs; however, keep in mind that our focus is on the aspects of innovation and growth associated with entrepreneurs.

1-3 ENTREPRENEURSHIP: A MIND-SET

Entrepreneurship is more than the mere creation of business. Although that is certainly an important facet, it's not the complete picture. The characteristics of seeking opportunities, taking risks beyond security, and having the tenacity to push an idea through to reality combine into a special perspective that permeates entrepreneurs. As we will illustrate in Chapter 2, an entrepreneurial mind-set can be developed in individuals. The term, "entrepreneurial mindset" represents the cognition and commitment to view the world with an innovative perspective. This composes the entrepreneurial potential in every individual. This mind-set can be exhibited inside or outside an organization, in for-profit or not-for-profit enterprises, and in business or nonbusiness activities for the purpose of bringing forth creative ideas. Thus, entrepreneurship is an integrated concept that permeates an individual's business in an innovative manner. It is this mind-set that has revolutionized the way business is conducted at every level and in every country. It is clear that the world has embraced entrepreneurship and innovation, and the way we view business will never be the same. So it is. The entrepreneurial revolution has taken hold in an economic sense, and the entrepreneurial mind-set is the dominant force.

1-4 THE EVOLUTION OF ENTREPRENEURSHIP

LO5 Set forth a comprehensive definition of entrepreneurship

The word **entrepreneur** is derived from the French *entreprendre,* meaning "to undertake." The entrepreneur is one who undertakes to organize, manage, and assume the risks of a business. In recent years, entrepreneurs have been doing so many things that it is now necessary to broaden this definition. Today, an entrepreneur is an innovator or developer who recognizes and seizes opportunities; converts those opportunities into workable/marketable ideas; adds value through time, effort, money, or skills; assumes the risks of the competitive marketplace to implement these ideas; and realizes the rewards from these efforts.[2]

The entrepreneur is the aggressive catalyst for change in the world of business. He or she is an independent thinker who dares to be different amid a background of common events. The literature of entrepreneurial research reveals some similarities, as well as a great many differences, in the characteristics of entrepreneurs. Chief among these characteristics are personal initiative, the ability to consolidate resources, management skills, a desire for autonomy, and risk taking. Other characteristics include aggressiveness, competitiveness, goal-oriented behavior, confidence, opportunistic behavior, intuitiveness, reality-based actions, the ability to learn from mistakes, and the ability to employ human relations skills.[3]

Although no single definition of *entrepreneur* exists and no one profile can represent today's entrepreneur, research is beginning to provide an increasingly sharper focus on the subject. A brief review of the history of entrepreneurship illustrates this.

The world currently is in the midst of a new wave of business and economic development, and entrepreneurship is its catalyst. Yet the social and economic forces of entrepreneurial activity existed long before the new millennium. In fact, the entrepreneurial spirit has driven many of humanity's achievements.

Humanity's progress—from caves to campuses—has been explained in numerous ways. But central to virtually all of these theories has been the role of the "agent of change," the force that initiates and implements material progress. Today we recognize that the agent of change in human history has been, and most likely will continue to be, the entrepreneur.[4]

LO1 Examine the historical development of entrepreneurship

The recognition of entrepreneurs dates back to eighteenth-century France, when economist Richard Cantillon associated the "risk-bearing" activity in the economy with the entrepreneur. The Industrial Revolution was evolving in England during the same period, with the entrepreneur playing a visible role in risk taking and the transformation of resources.[5]

The association of entrepreneurship and economics has long been the accepted norm. In fact, until the 1950s, the majority of definitions and references to entrepreneurship had come from economists. For example, the aforementioned Cantillon (1725), the French economist Jean Baptiste Say (1803), and twentieth-century economist Joseph Schumpeter (1934) all wrote about entrepreneurship and its impact on economic development.[6] Since that time, researchers have continued to try to describe or define what entrepreneurship is all about. Following are some examples:

> Entrepreneurship . . . consists in doing things that are not generally done in the ordinary course of business routine; it is essentially a phenomenon that comes under the wider aspect of leadership.[7]

> Entrepreneurship, at least in all nonauthoritarian societies, constitutes a bridge between society as a whole, especially the noneconomic aspects of that society, and the profit-oriented institutions established to take advantage of its economic endowments and to satisfy, as best they can, its economic desires.[8]

> In . . . entrepreneurship, there is agreement that we are talking about a kind of behavior that includes: (1) initiative taking, (2) the organizing or reorganizing of social economic mechanisms to turn resources and situations to practical account, and (3) the acceptance of risk of failure.[9]

After reviewing the evolution of entrepreneurship and examining its varying definitions, Robert C. Ronstadt put together a summary description:

> Entrepreneurship is the dynamic process of creating incremental wealth. This wealth is created by individuals who assume the major risks in terms of equity, time, and/or career commitment of providing value for some product or service. The product or service itself may or may not be new or unique but value must somehow be infused by the entrepreneur by securing and allocating the necessary skills and resources.[10]

Entrepreneurship as a topic for discussion and analysis was introduced by the economists of the eighteenth century, and it continued to attract the interest of economists in the nineteenth century. In the twentieth century, the word *entrepreneurship* became synonymous—or at least closely linked—with free enterprise and capitalism. Also, it was generally recognized that entrepreneurs serve as agents of change; provide creative, innovative ideas for business enterprises; and help businesses grow and become profitable.

Whatever the specific activity they engage in, entrepreneurs in the twenty-first century are considered the heroes of free enterprise. Many of them have used innovation and creativity to build multimillion-dollar enterprises from fledgling businesses—some in less than a decade! These individuals have created new products and services, and have assumed the risks associated with these ventures. Many people now regard entrepreneurship as "pioneership" on the frontier of business.

In recognizing the importance of the evolution of entrepreneurship in the twenty-first century, we have developed an integrated definition that acknowledges the critical factors needed for this phenomenon.

> *Entrepreneurship is a dynamic process of vision, change, and creation. It requires an application of energy and passion toward the creation and implementation of innovative ideas and creative solutions. Essential ingredients include the willingness to take calculated risks—in terms of time, equity, or career; the ability to formulate an effective venture team; the creative skill to marshal needed resources; the fundamental skill of building a solid business plan; and, finally, the vision to recognize opportunity where others see chaos, contradiction, and confusion.*

1-5 AVOIDING FOLKLORE: THE MYTHS OF ENTREPRENEURSHIP

LO2 Explore and debunk the myths of entrepreneurship

Throughout the years, many myths have arisen about entrepreneurship—primarily because of a lack of research on the subject. As many researchers in the field have noted, the study of entrepreneurship is still emerging, and thus "folklore" tends to prevail until it is dispelled with contemporary research findings. Ten of the most notable myths (and an explanation to dispel each myth) are as follows.

1-5a   Myth 1: Entrepreneurs Are Doers, Not Thinkers

Although it is true that entrepreneurs tend toward action, they are also thinkers. Indeed, they are often very methodical people who plan their moves carefully. The emphasis today on the creation of clear and complete business plans (see the chapter on the Business Plan Process) is an indication that "thinking" entrepreneurs are as important as "doing" entrepreneurs.

1-5b   Myth 2: Entrepreneurs Are Born, Not Made

The idea that the characteristics of entrepreneurs cannot be taught or learned—that they are innate traits one must be born with—has long been prevalent. These traits include aggressiveness, initiative, drive, a willingness to take risks, analytical ability, and skill in human relations. Today, however, the recognition of entrepreneurship as a discipline is helping to dispel this myth. Like all disciplines, entrepreneurship has models, processes, and case studies that allow the topic to be studied and the knowledge to be acquired.

1-5c Myth 3: Entrepreneurs Are Always Inventors

The idea that entrepreneurs are inventors is a result of misunderstanding and tunnel vision. Although many inventors are also entrepreneurs, numerous entrepreneurs encompass all sorts of innovative activity.[11] For example, Ray Kroc did not invent the fast-food franchise, but his innovative ideas made McDonald's the largest fast-food enterprise in the world. A contemporary understanding of entrepreneurship covers more than just invention; it requires a complete understanding of innovative behavior in all its forms.

1-5d Myth 4: Entrepreneurs Are Academic and Social Misfits

The belief that entrepreneurs are academically and socially ineffective is a result of some business owners having started successful enterprises after dropping out of school or quitting a job. In many cases, such an event has been blown out of proportion in an attempt to "profile" the typical entrepreneur. Historically, in fact, educational and social organizations did not recognize the entrepreneur. They abandoned him or her as a misfit in a world of corporate giants. Business education, for example, was aimed primarily at the study of corporate activity. Today the entrepreneur is considered a hero—socially, economically, and academically. No longer a misfit, the entrepreneur is now viewed as a professional role model.

1-5e Myth 5: Entrepreneurs Must Fit the Profile

Many books and articles have presented checklists of characteristics of the successful entrepreneur. These lists were neither validated nor complete; they were based on case studies and on research findings among achievement-oriented people. Today we realize that a standard entrepreneurial profile is hard to compile. The environment, the venture, and the entrepreneur have interactive effects, which result in many different types of profiles. Contemporary studies conducted at universities across the world will, in the future, provide more accurate insights into the various profiles of successful entrepreneurs. As we will show in Chapter 2, an "entrepreneurial mind-set" within individuals is more understandable and realistic than a particular profile.

1-5f Myth 6: All Entrepreneurs Need Is Money

It is true that a venture needs capital to survive; it is also true that a large number of business failures occur because of a lack of adequate financing. However, money is not the only bulwark against failure. Failure due to a lack of proper financing often is an indicator of other problems: managerial incompetence, lack of financial understanding, poor investments, poor planning, and the like. Many successful entrepreneurs have overcome a lack of money while establishing their ventures. To those entrepreneurs, money is a resource but never an end in itself.

1-5g Myth 7: All Entrepreneurs Need Is Luck

Being in "the right place at the right time" is always an advantage—but "luck happens when preparation meets opportunity" is an equally appropriate adage. Prepared entrepreneurs who seize the opportunity when it arises often seem "lucky." They are, in fact, simply better prepared to deal with situations and turn them into successes. What appears to be luck is actually preparation, determination, desire, knowledge, and innovativeness.

1-5h Myth 8: Entrepreneurship Is Unstructured and Chaotic

There is a tendency to think of entrepreneurs as gunslingers—people who shoot from the hip and ask questions later. They are assumed by some to be disorganized and unstructured, leaving it to others to keep things on track. The reality is that entrepreneurs are heavily involved in all facets of their ventures, and they usually have a number of balls in the air at

THE ENTREPRENEURIAL PROCESS

The E-Myth

Michael E. Gerber has written a book titled *The E-Myth: Why Most Businesses Don't Work and What to Do About It*, in which he clearly delineates the differences among the types of people involved with contemporary small businesses:

- The *entrepreneur* invents a business that works without him or her. This person is a visionary who makes a business unique by imbuing it with a special and exciting sense of purpose and direction. The entrepreneur's far-reaching perspective enables him or her to anticipate changes and needs in the marketplace and to initiate activities to capitalize on them.

- The *manager* produces results through employees by developing and implementing effective systems and, by interacting with employees, enhances their self-esteem and ability to produce good results. The manager can actualize the entrepreneur's vision through planning, implementation, and analysis.

- The *technician* performs specific tasks according to systems and standards management developed. The technician, in the best of businesses, not only gets the work done but also provides input to supervisors for improvement of those systems and standards.

Understanding these definitions is important, because Gerber contends that most small businesses **don't work**—their owners do. In other words, he believes that today's small-business owner works too hard at a job that he or she has created for himself or herself rather than working to create a business. Thus, most small businesses fail because the owner is more of a technician than an entrepreneur. Working only as a technician, the small-business owner realizes too little reward for so much effort, and eventually, according to Gerber, the business fails.

The e-myth is that today's business owners are not true entrepreneurs who create businesses but merely technicians who have created a job for themselves. The solution to this myth lies in the owner's willingness to begin thinking and acting like a true entrepreneur: to imagine how the business would work without him or her. In other words, the owner must begin working **on** the business, in addition to working **in** it. He or she must leverage the company's capacity through systems development and implementation. The key is for a person to develop an "entrepreneurial perspective."

Source: Adapted from Michael E. Gerber, *The E-Myth Revisited: Why Most Businesses Don't Work and What to Do About It* (New York: Harper Collins, 1995, 2001) and personal interview.

the same time. As a result, they are typically well-organized individuals. They tend to have a system—perhaps elaborate, perhaps not—that is personally designed to keep things straight and maintain priorities. In fact, their system may seem strange to the casual observer, but it works.

1-5i Myth 9: Most Entrepreneurial Initiatives Fail

The common mythical statement is that 9 out of 10 new ventures fail. The facts do not support such a contention. The statistics of entrepreneurial failure rates have been misleading over the years. In fact, one researcher, Bruce A. Kirchhoff, has reported that the "high failure rate" most commonly accepted might be misleading. In 1993, Kirchhoff traced 814,000 businesses started in 1977 and found that more than 50 percent were still surviving under their original owners or new owners. Additionally, 28 percent voluntarily closed down, and only 18 percent actually "failed" in the sense of leaving behind outstanding liabilities.[12] More recent studies have supported the fact that new ventures do not fail at such an alarming rate.[13]

While many entrepreneurs do suffer a number of failures before they are successful, they follow the adage "If at first you don't succeed, try, try again." In fact, failure can teach many lessons to those willing to learn, and often it leads to future successes. This is clearly shown by the **corridor principle**, which states that, with every venture launched, new and unintended opportunities often arise.

1-5j Myth 10: Entrepreneurs Are Extreme Risk Takers

As we will show in Chapter 2, the concept of risk is a major element in the entrepreneurial process. However, the public's perception of the risk most entrepreneurs assume is distorted. Although it may appear that an entrepreneur is "gambling" on a wild chance, the entrepreneur is usually working on a moderate or "calculated" risk. Most successful entrepreneurs work hard—through planning and preparation—to minimize the risk involved and better control the destiny of their vision.

These ten myths have been presented to provide a background for today's current thinking on entrepreneurship. By sidestepping the folklore, we can build a foundation for critically researching the contemporary theories and processes of entrepreneurship.

1-6 APPROACHES TO ENTREPRENEURSHIP

To understand the nature of entrepreneurship and better recognize its emerging importance, it is important to consider some of its theory development. The research on entrepreneurship has grown dramatically over the years. As the field has developed, research methodology has progressed from empirical surveys of entrepreneurs to more contextual and process-oriented research. Theory development is what drives a field of study. Entrepreneurship theory has been developing for the last 40 years, and it is apparent that the field is growing. We need to understand some of that development to better appreciate the discipline of entrepreneurship. The study of the basic theories in entrepreneurship also helps to form a foundation upon which a student can build an understanding of the process and practice of entrepreneurship.

A *theory of entrepreneurship* is a verifiable and logically coherent formulation of relationships, or underlying principles, that either explain entrepreneurship, predict entrepreneurial activity (e.g., by characterizing conditions that are likely to lead to new profit opportunities or to the formation of new enterprises), or provide normative guidance (that is, prescribe the right action in particular circumstances).[14] It has become increasingly apparent in the new millennium that we need to have some cohesive theories or classifications to better understand this emerging field.

In the study of contemporary entrepreneurship, one concept recurs: Entrepreneurship is interdisciplinary. We outline, in the following sections, various approaches that can increase our understanding of the field.[15]

1-6a Schools-of-Thought Approaches to Entrepreneurship

LO3 Define and explore the major schools of entrepreneurial thought

A schools-of-thought approach divides entrepreneurship into specific activities, either macro or micro in viewpoint, but both address the conceptual nature of entrepreneurship. We further break down each of these two major views into six distinct schools of thought, three of which apply to the micro and three to the macro view (see Figure 1.1). Although this presentation does not purport to be all-inclusive, neither does it claim to limit the schools to these

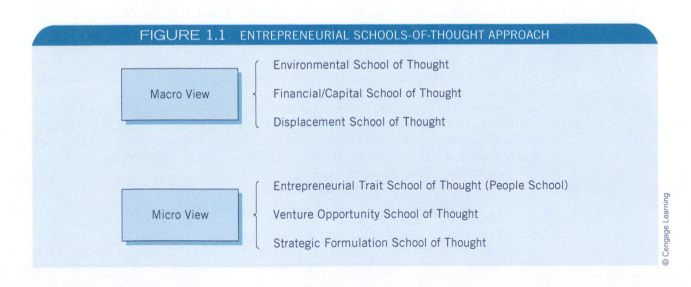

FIGURE 1.1   ENTREPRENEURIAL SCHOOLS-OF-THOUGHT APPROACH

Macro View
- Environmental School of Thought
- Financial/Capital School of Thought
- Displacement School of Thought

Micro View
- Entrepreneurial Trait School of Thought (People School)
- Venture Opportunity School of Thought
- Strategic Formulation School of Thought

© Cengage Learning

six, for a movement may develop for unification or expansion. Whatever the future holds, however, it is important to become familiar with these conceptual ideas on entrepreneurship to avoid the semantic warfare that has plagued general management thought for so many years.[16]

THE MACRO VIEW

The macro view of entrepreneurship presents a broad array of factors that relate to success or failure in contemporary entrepreneurial ventures. This array includes external processes that are sometimes beyond the control of the individual entrepreneur, for they exhibit a strong external locus of control point of view.

Three schools of entrepreneurial thought represent a breakdown of the macro view: (1) the environmental school of thought, (2) the financial/capital school of thought, and (3) the displacement school of thought. The first of these is the broadest and most pervasive school.

The Environmental School of Thought

The environmental school of thought deals with the external factors that affect a potential entrepreneur's lifestyle. These can be either positive or negative forces in the molding of entrepreneurial desires. The focus is on institutions, values, and mores that—grouped together—form a sociopolitical environmental framework that strongly influences the development of entrepreneurs.[17] For example, if a middle manager experiences the freedom and support to develop ideas, initiate contracts, or create and institute new methods, the work environment will serve to promote that person's desire to pursue an entrepreneurial career. Another environmental factor that often affects the potential development of entrepreneurs is their social group. The atmosphere of friends and relatives can influence the desire to become an entrepreneur.

The Financial/Capital School of Thought

The financial/capital school of thought is based on the capital-seeking process—the search for seed and growth capital is the entire focus of this entrepreneurial emphasis. Certain literature is devoted specifically to this process, whereas other sources tend to treat it as but one segment of the entrepreneurial venture.[18] In any case, the venture capital process is vital to an entrepreneur's development. Business-planning guides and texts for entrepreneurs emphasize this phase, and development seminars that focus on the funds application process are offered throughout the country on a continuous basis. This school of thought views the entire entrepreneurial venture from a financial management standpoint. As is apparent from Table 1.1, decisions involving finances occur at every major point in the venture process.

The Displacement School of Thought

The displacement school of thought focuses on the negative side of group phenomena, in which someone feels out of place—or is literally "displaced"—from the group. It holds that the group hinders a person from

TABLE 1.1 FINANCIAL ANALYSIS EMPHASIS		
Venture Stage	**Financial Consideration**	**Decision**
Start-up or acquisition	Seed capital Venture capital sources	Proceed or abandon
Ongoing	Cash management Investments Financial analysis and evaluation	Maintain, increase, or reduce size
Decline or succession	Profit question Corporate buyout Succession question	Sell, retire, or dissolve operations

advancing or eliminates certain critical factors needed for that person to advance. As a result, the frustrated individual will be projected into an entrepreneurial pursuit out of his or her own motivations to succeed. As researchers have noted, individuals fight adversity and tend to pursue a venture when they are prevented or displaced from doing other activities.[19] Three major types of displacement illustrate this school of thought:

1. **Political displacement.** Caused by factors ranging from an entire political regime that rejects free enterprise (international environment) to governmental regulations and policies that limit or redirect certain industries.

2. **Cultural displacement.** Deals with social groups precluded from professional fields. Ethnic background, religion, race, and sex are examples of factors that figure in the minority experience. Increasingly, this experience turns various individuals away from standard business professions and toward entrepreneurial ventures. In the United States minority businesses represented 15 percent of all businesses during the last 20 years.[20]

3. **Economic displacement.** Concerned with the economic variations of recession and depression. Job loss, capital shrinkage, or simply "bad times" can create the foundation for entrepreneurial pursuits, just as it can affect venture development and reduction. [21]

These examples of displacement illustrate the external forces that can influence the development of entrepreneurship. Cultural awareness, knowledge of political and public policy, and economic indoctrination will aid and improve entrepreneurial understanding under the displacement school of thought. The broader the educational base in economics and political science, the stronger the entrepreneurial understanding.

THE MICRO VIEW

The **micro view of entrepreneurship** examines the factors that are specific to entrepreneurship and are part of the **internal locus of control**. The potential entrepreneur has the ability, or control, to direct or adjust the outcome of each major influence in this view. Although some researchers have developed this approach into various definitions and segments, our approach presents the *entrepreneurial trait* theory (sometimes referred to as the "people school of thought"), the *venture opportunity* theory, and the *strategic formulation* theory. Unlike the macro approach, which focuses on events from the outside looking in, the micro approach concentrates on specifics from the inside looking out. The first of these schools of thought is the most widely recognized.

The Entrepreneurial Trait School of Thought

Many researchers and writers have been interested in identifying traits common to successful entrepreneurs.[22] This approach of the **entrepreneurial trait school of thought** is grounded in the study of successful people who tend to exhibit similar characteristics that, if copied, would increase success opportunities for the emulators. For example, achievement, creativity, determination, and technical knowledge are four factors that *usually* are exhibited by successful entrepreneurs. Family development and educational incubation are also examined. Certain researchers have argued against educational development of entrepreneurs, because they believe it inhibits the creative and challenging nature of entrepreneurship.[23] Other authors, however, contend that new programs and educational developments are on the increase because they have been found to aid in entrepreneurial development.[24] The family development idea focuses on the nurturing and support that exist within the home atmosphere of an entrepreneurial family. This reasoning promotes the belief that certain traits established and supported early in life will lead eventually to entrepreneurial success. (In Chapter 2, the concepts of entrepreneurial cognition and metacognition, which are beginning to take hold in the research on entrepreneurs, are discussed.)

The Venture Opportunity School of Thought

The **venture opportunity school of thought** focuses on the opportunity aspect of venture development. The search for idea sources, the development of concepts, and the implementation of venture opportunities are the important interest areas for this school. Creativity and market awareness are viewed as essential. Additionally, according to this school of thought, developing the right idea at the right time for the right market niche is the key to entrepreneurial success.[25]

Another development from this school of thought is the previously described *corridor principle*: New pathways or opportunities will arise that lead entrepreneurs in different directions. The ability to recognize these opportunities when they arise and to implement the necessary steps for action are key factors. The maxim that preparation meeting opportunity equals "luck" underlies this corridor principle. Proponents of this school of thought believe that proper preparation in the interdisciplinary business segments will enhance an entrepreneur's ability to recognize venture opportunities.

The Strategic Formulation School of Thought

George Steiner once stated that "strategic planning is inextricably interwoven into the entire fabric of management; it is not something separate and distinct from the process of management."[26] The strategic formulation school of thought approach to entrepreneurial theory emphasizes the planning process in successful venture development.[27]

One way to view strategic formulation is as a leveraging of unique elements.[28] Unique markets, unique people, unique products, or unique resources are identified, used, or constructed into effective venture formations. The interdisciplinary aspects of strategic adaptation are apparent in the following characteristic elements (and their corresponding strategies):

- **Unique markets. Mountain versus mountain gap strategies**, which refers to identifying major market segments as well as interstice (in-between) markets that arise from larger markets.

- **Unique people. Great chef strategies**, which refers to the skills or special talents of one or more individuals around whom the venture is built.

- **Unique products. Better widget strategies**, which refers to innovations that encompass new or existing markets.

- **Unique resources. Water well strategies**, which refers to the ability to gather or harness special resources (land, labor, capital, raw materials) over the long term.

Without question, the strategic formulation school encompasses a breadth of managerial capability that requires an interdisciplinary approach.[29]

SCHOOLS OF ENTREPRENEURIAL THOUGHT: A SUMMARY

Although the knowledge and research available in entrepreneurship are in an emerging stage, it is still possible to piece together and describe current schools of thought in the field. We can begin to develop an appreciation for the schools and view them as a foundation for entrepreneurial theory. However, just as the field of management has used a "jungle" of theories as a basis for understanding the field and its capabilities, so too must the field of entrepreneurship use a number of theories in its growth and development.

1-6b Process Approaches to Entrepreneurship

LO4 Explain the process and framework approaches to the study of entrepreneurship

Another way to examine the activities involved in entrepreneurship is through a *process approach*. Although numerous methods and models attempt to structure the entrepreneurial process and its various factors, we shall examine two of the more traditional process approaches here.[30]

First, we discuss the *integrative* approach, as described by Michael H. Morris, Pamela S. Lewis, and Donald L. Sexton.[31] Their model incorporates theoretical and practical concepts as they affect entrepreneurship activity. Then we explore the *dynamic states* approach based on a complex systems perspective developed by researchers Jonathan Levie and Benyamin B. Lichtenstein. Both of these methods attempt to describe the entrepreneurial process as a consolidation of diverse factors, which is the thrust of this book.

AN INTEGRATIVE APPROACH

A more integrative picture of the entrepreneurial process is provided by Morris, Lewis, and Sexton.[32] Presented in Figure 1.2, this model is built around the concepts of input to the entrepreneurial process and outcomes from the entrepreneurial process. The input component of Figure 1.2 focuses on the entrepreneurial process itself and identifies five key elements that contribute to the process. The first element is environmental opportunities, such as a demographic change, the development of a new technology, or a modification to current regulations. Next is the individual entrepreneur, the person who assumes personal responsibility for conceptualizing and implementing a new venture. The entrepreneur develops some type of business concept to capitalize on the opportunity (e.g., a creative approach to solving a particular customer need). Implementing this business concept typically requires some type of organizational context, which could range from a sole proprietorship run out of the entrepreneur's home or a franchise of some national chain to an autonomous business unit within a large corporation. Finally, a wide variety of financial and nonfinancial resources are required on an ongoing basis. These key elements then are combined throughout the stages of the entrepreneurial process. Stated differently, the process provides a logical framework for organizing entrepreneurial inputs.

The outcome component of Figure 1.2 first includes the level of entrepreneurship being achieved. As we shall discuss in more detail in the next chapter, entrepreneurship is a variable. Thus, the process can result in any number of entrepreneurial events and can produce events that vary considerably in terms of how entrepreneurial they are. Based on this level of "entrepreneurial intensity," final outcomes can include one or more going ventures, value creation, new products and processes, new technologies, profit, jobs, and economic growth. Moreover, the outcome can certainly be failure and thereby include the corresponding economic, psychic, and social costs.

This model not only provides a fairly comprehensive picture regarding the nature of entrepreneurship, it also can be applied at different levels. For example, the model describes the phenomenon of entrepreneurship in both the independent start-up company and within a department, division, or strategic business unit of a large corporation.

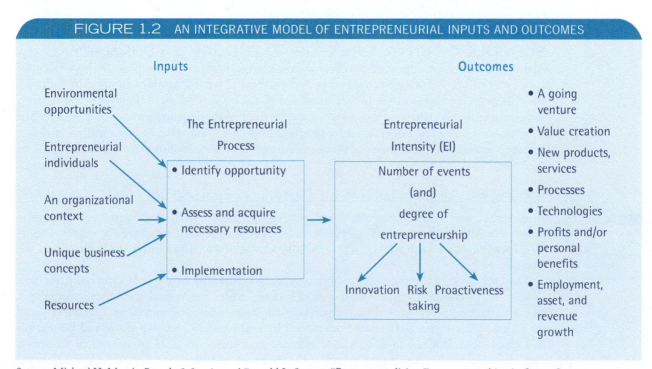

FIGURE 1.2   AN INTEGRATIVE MODEL OF ENTREPRENEURIAL INPUTS AND OUTCOMES

Source: Michael H. Morris, Pamela S. Lewis, and Donald L. Sexton, "Reconceptualizing Entrepreneurship: An Input-Output Perspective," Reprinted with permission from *SAM Advanced Management Journal* 59, no. 1 (Winter 1994): 21–31.

FIGURE 1.3   DYNAMIC STATES APPROACH

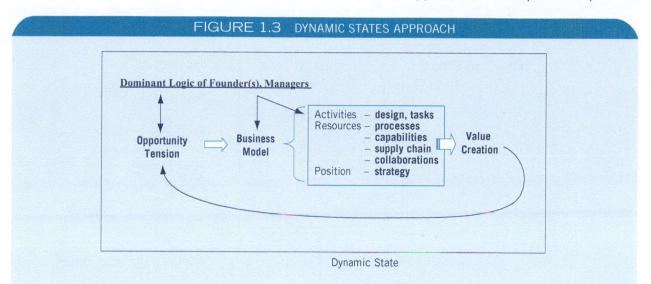

Dynamic State

Source: Jonathan Levie & Benjamin B. Lichtenstein, (2010). "A Terminal Assessment of Stages Theory: Introducing a Dynamic States Approach to Entrepreneurship," *Entrepreneurship Theory and Practice*, 34, no. 2 (2010): 332. Reproduced with permission of John Wiley & Sons Ltd.

DYNAMIC STATES APPROACH

Researchers Jonathan Levie and Benyamin B. Lichtenstein developed a **dynamic states model** that depicts ventures being dependent on their environment for survival. A dynamic state is a network of relationships and systems that convert opportunity tension into value for a venture's customers, generating new resources that maintain the dynamic state. This model is a more process-oriented view that incorporates an array of individual, organizational, and environmental elements. The strategy for value creation chosen by the firm is enacted by its business model which itself is derived from the emerging dominant logic of the firm. These elements of a dynamic states model are pictured in Figure 1.3. The dynamic states model is more optimistic for entrepreneurs suggesting that smaller and newer firms have more flexibility in making ongoing changes. Thus, it may be easier for new ventures to create a high degree of interdependence between themselves and their environment, enabling entrepreneurs to organize for the current and anticipated demands of their market.[33]

A FRAMEWORK OF FRAMEWORKS APPROACH

Researchers Donald F. Kuratko, Michael H. Morris, and Minet Schindehutte contend that theories or frameworks based on combinations offer a more dynamic view of the phenomenon of entrepreneurship. Much like the "multiple lens" approach that characterizes general management, the theories based on combinations can delve into some of the particular aspects of entrepreneurship with greater granularity.[34] As one researcher noted in regards to entrepreneurial decision making; "there are numerous opportunities for multilevel research to make a substantial contribution to the field of entrepreneurship (p. 419)."[35]

The schools of thought and the process approaches that exist in the field of entrepreneurship are based on a phenomenon that incorporate many diverse and heterogeneous dimensions that only a comprehensive framework approach might afford researchers the capacity to explore and expand the knowledge base. A sizeable body of research has developed that supports the individual frameworks through the schools of thought or through process models but the integration of previously disparate aspects of entrepreneurship may be particularly valuable to advancing the field of entrepreneurship. As such, greater knowledge could be gained from the extrapolation of particular insights from each of the frameworks presented in this approach. Thus a "**framework of frameworks**" that allows for the profession to move forward identifying the static and dynamic elements of new theories, typologies, or frameworks could be an important and distinguishing approach to grow the knowledge base of the field. Figure 1.4 depicts the framework of frameworks approach for entrepreneurship as the nexus of the major strands of entrepreneurship frameworks currently employed.

FIGURE 1.4 A FRAMEWORK OF FRAMEWORKS APPROACH

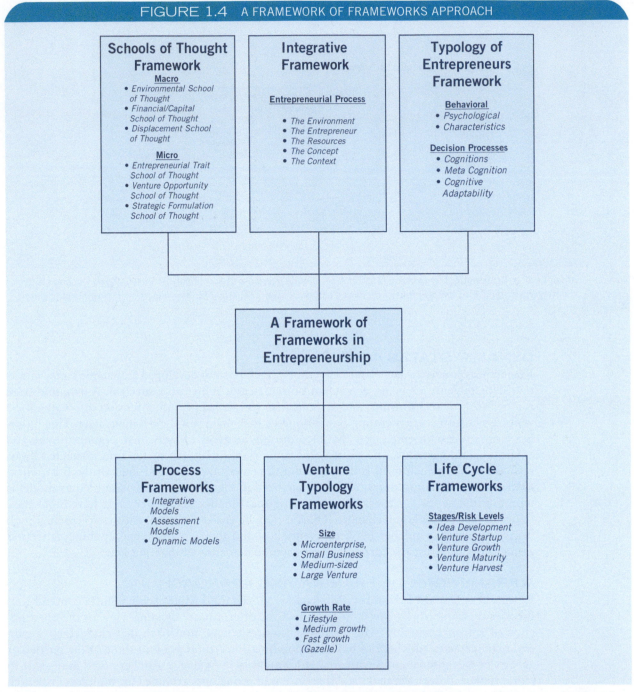

Source: Donald F. Kuratko, Michael H. Morris, and Minet Schindehutte, "Understanding the Dynamics of Entrepreneurship through Framework Approaches," *Small Business Economics*, 45, no. 1 (2015): 9. Berlin, Germany; Springer Publishing.

1-7 THE ENTREPRENEURIAL REVOLUTION: A GLOBAL PHENOMENON

LO6 Examine the entrepreneurial revolution taking place today

Entrepreneurship is the symbol of business tenacity and achievement. Entrepreneurs were the pioneers of today's business successes. Their sense of opportunity, their drive to innovate, and their capacity for accomplishment have become the standard by which free enterprise is now measured. This standard has taken hold throughout the entire world.

For example, starting with just 10 developed countries in 1999, the Global Entrepreneurship Monitor (GEM) has now grown to include over 70 economies and 100 countries by

2014. In 2013, people were surveyed in 70 economies which account for over 75 percent of the world's population and 90 percent of the world's GDP.

The GEM data has shown that 250 million people were involved in early stage entrepreneurial activity. Out of these individuals, an estimated 63 million people expected to hire at least five employees over the next five years, and 27 million of these individuals anticipated hiring 20 or more employees in five years. The latest GEM analyses shows that growth expectations and aspirations of early-stage entrepreneurs represent a key dimension of potential entrepreneurial impact and may be linked directly to many first-priority policy objectives around the world: to create more jobs. All of this illustrates the contribution of entrepreneurship and the entrepreneurial mindset to job growth across the globe.[36]

GEM groups the participating economies into three levels: factor-driven, efficiency-driven, and innovation-driven. These are based on the World Economic Forum's (WEF) *Global Competitiveness Report*, which identifies three phases of economic development based on GDP per capita and the share of exports comprising primary goods. According to the WEF classification, the factor-driven phase is dominated by subsistence agriculture and extraction businesses, with a heavy reliance on labor and natural resources. In the efficiency-driven phase, further development is accompanied by industrialization and an increased reliance on economies of scale, with capital-intensive large organizations more dominant. As development advances into the innovation-driven phase, businesses are more knowledge-intensive, and the service sector expands.

Lessons gleaned from the GEM studies included:

- Entrepreneurship does not impact an economy simply through higher numbers of entrepreneurs. It is important to consider quality measures, like growth, innovation, and internationalization.

- Entrepreneurship needs both dynamism and stability. Dynamism occurs through the creation of new businesses and the exit of nonviable ones. Stability comes from providing new businesses with the best chance to test and reach their potential.

- Entrepreneurship in a society should contain a variety of business phases and types, led by different types of entrepreneurs, including women and underrepresented age groups.

- Initiatives aimed toward improving entrepreneurship should consider the development level of the economy. With a strong set of basic requirements in place, efforts can turn toward reinforcing efficiency enhancers, and then building entrepreneurship framework conditions.

- An entrepreneurial mind-set is not just for entrepreneurs. It must include a variety of stakeholders that are willing to support and cooperate with these dynamic efforts. In addition, nonentrepreneurs with entrepreneurial mind-sets may indirectly stimulate others to start businesses. This indicates the value of broader societal acceptance of entrepreneurship.[37]

It is clear that we have experienced an Entrepreneurial Revolution across the world. This revolution will continue to be as important (if not more!) to the twenty-first century as the Industrial Revolution was to the twentieth century.

Entrepreneurs will continue to be critical contributors to economic growth through their leadership, management, innovation, research and development effectiveness, job creation, competitiveness, productivity, and formation of new industry.

To understand the nature of entrepreneurship, it is important to consider from two perspectives the environment in which entrepreneurial firms operate. The first perspective is statistical, providing actual aggregate numbers to emphasize the importance of small firms in the U.S. economy. The second perspective examines some of the trends in entrepreneurial research and education to reflect the emerging importance of entrepreneurship in academic developments.

1-7a The Impact of Entrepreneurial Ventures in the United States

The past 20 years have witnessed the powerful emergence of entrepreneurial activity in the United States. Many statistics illustrate this fact. For example, the U.S. Small Business Administration reported that, during the past 10 years, new business start-ups numbered over 400,000 *per year*. Although many of these incorporations may have previously been sole proprietorships or partnerships, the trend still demonstrates the popularity of venture activity, whether through start-ups, expansions, or development. More specifically, in the second decade of the new millennium, we have witnessed the number of businesses in the United States soar to more than 28 million, and that number is still growing at a rate of 2 percent annually. Let us examine some of the historical numbers supporting this phenomenon.

The United States consistently exhibits one of the highest entrepreneurship rates in the developed world. Entrepreneurship provides job options for those who see opportunities and those who need a *source* of income. They affect the U.S. economy as both current and future employers. Entrepreneurs additionally play key roles as suppliers, customers, and service providers for other businesses, creating value and employment beyond their specific organizations. According to the 2014 GEM Report on the United States, an estimated 25 million Americans were starting or running new ventures, and 7.7 million projected that they would employ six or more people in the next five years. In addition to these entrepreneurs, an estimated 14 million Americans were running established ventures with 3.2 million planning to employ six or more employees in the years ahead. 13 percent of the U.S. working age population was in the process of starting or running a new business—the highest entrepreneurship rate reported among the 25 developed economies that participated in GEM Global Study from North America, Europe, and Asia. The majority of entrepreneurs in the United States start businesses to pursue an opportunity; however, necessity-motives remain persistently higher than before the recession. The United States has the highest rate of entrepreneurship among 55–64 year olds in the 25 developed economies studied as they are more confident in their abilities to start businesses than those 18–44 years of age.[38]

According to the *Kauffman Index of Entrepreneurial Activity, 1996–2010*,[39] a leading indicator of new business creation in the United States, 0.34 percent of American adults created a business per month in 2010, or *565,000* new businesses representing the highest level of entrepreneurship over the past decade and a half. With the economic recovery period from 2011 through 2014, the new venture creation levels dipped to 0.28 percent signifying improving conditions for employment.

The U.S. Small Business Administration reports that smaller firms reached a record total of 28.2 million by 2014. Of these, approximately 6 million were employing firms, and they accounted for 49.6 percent of U.S. private-sector jobs. Small firms made up 99.7 percent of U.S. employing firms. Further, women- and minority-owned businesses increased. Minority-owned businesses numbered 5.8 million, a 45.6 percent increase over the last five years; women-owned businesses totaled 7.8 million, a 20.1 percent increase over the five-year span.[40]

In examining the age factor, 15 percent of the self-employed were less than 35 years old, yet older Americans are also more likely than before to be their own boss. The percent of the self-employed population who were between the ages of 55 and 64, for instance, grew from 16.4 percent in 2000 to 22.2 percent later in the decade. This trend is perhaps an indicator that more baby boomers have sought "lifestyle entrepreneurship" or a second career later in life.[41]

Entrepreneurs will continue to be the answer to any economic downturn, and they will continue to lead economic growth in several different ways. Entrepreneurs enter and expand existing markets, thereby increasing competition and economic efficiency. Entrepreneurs also create entirely new markets by offering innovative products. These new markets present profit opportunities to others, further spurring economic growth. Additionally, a full 14 percent of entrepreneurs who started a business claimed their product had no direct competitor—a clear indication of new markets being created by entrepreneurs.

Some of the reasons cited for the exceptional entrepreneurial activity in the United States include:

- The United States is a culture that supports risk taking and seeking opportunities.
- Americans are relatively alert to unexploited economic opportunity and have a relatively low fear of failure.
- The United States is a leader in entrepreneurship education at both the undergraduate and graduate levels.
- The United States is home to a high percentage of individuals with professional, technological, or business degrees, a group that registers at the highest entrepreneurial activity rate.

Overall, every study continues to demonstrate that entrepreneurs' ability to expand existing markets and create new markets makes entrepreneurship important for individuals, firms, and entire nations.[42]

1-7b The Impact of Gazelles

LO7 Illustrate today's entrepreneurial environment

New and smaller firms create the most jobs in the U.S. economy (and across the globe, for that matter). The facts speak for themselves: The vast majority of these job-creating companies are fast-growing businesses. David Birch of Cognetics, Inc. named these firms *gazelles*.[43] A gazelle, by Birch's definition, is a business establishment with at least 20 percent sales growth every year (for five years), starting with a base of at least $100,000.

The "gazelle factor" may be the most important finding in economic growth. Consider that, despite the continual downsizing in major corporations over the last decade, gazelles produced 5 million jobs and brought net employment growth to 4.2 million jobs. More recently, gazelles (which currently number about 358,000 or 4 percent of all ongoing companies) generated practically as many jobs (10.7 million) as the entire U.S. economy (11.1 million) during the same period.

Recent global studies are demonstrating consistent results about gazelles. For example, WEF analyzed *Inc.* magazine's "500 Fastest-Growing Private Companies in the US" from 2000 to 2009 and the *Fast Track 100* and *Tech Track 100* rankings of privately held British companies using revenues, revenue growth rates, and the year of incorporation. The WEF also examined the Deloitte Technology *Fast Company* rankings from 13 countries: the United States, Canada, the United Kingdom, Germany, France, Sweden, Norway, Israel, China, India, Japan, Australia, and New Zealand.

In the *Inc. 500* sample of U.S. companies, the top 1 percent account for 20.5 percent of revenue growth (approximating a 1/20 rule). The top 10 percent of the companies account for 56 percent of growth for the whole 500 companies. The United Kingdom sample in *Fast Track 100* was similar, with the top 1 percent responsible for 20.8 percent and the top 10 percent accounting for 55.2 percent. The *elite few* in the United Kingdom technology sample in *Tech Track* is even more noticeable, with the top 1 percent providing 31.4 percent of growth and the top 10 percent giving 60.3 percent.[44]

In another study focused on the United States, entitled *High-Growth Firms and the Future of the American Economy*, it was found that in any given year, the top-performing 1 percent of companies account for some 40 percent of jobs. Within that category, fast-growing *"gazelle"* companies (three to five years old) make up less than 1 percent of all businesses, yet account for approximately 10 percent of net new jobs in any given year. The "average" company in the top 1 percent generates an astounding 88 net new jobs annually, compared to the two to three net new jobs generated by the average firm in the economy as a whole.[45] Overall, the extraordinary performance and contribution of these gazelles warrants further recognition as a powerful factor in the economy.[46] (See Table 1.2 for myths associated with gazelles.)

GAZELLES AND INNOVATION

Gazelles are leaders in innovation, as shown by the following:

- New and smaller firms have been responsible for 55 percent of the innovations in 362 different industries and for 95 percent of all radical innovations.
- Gazelles produce twice as many product innovations per employee as do larger firms.
- New and smaller firms obtain more patents per sales dollar than do larger firms.

GAZELLES AND GROWTH

Note how these growth data indicate the current "Gazelle Factor":

- During the past 10 years, business start-ups have approached nearly 400,000 per year, according to the U.S. Small Business Administration.
- Of approximately 28 million businesses in the United States (based on IRS tax returns), only 17,000 qualify as "large" businesses.

TABLE 1.2   MYTHOLOGY ASSOCIATED WITH GAZELLES

Gazelles are the goal of all entrepreneurs. Creating a gazelle can be rewarding not only financially but professionally; however, not all entrepreneurs are suited to the high-stress environment that running a gazelle induces. The more successful a firm becomes, the more society scrutinizes the actions of the management. Once the world is watching, keeping a gazelle growing takes not only tenacity but composure under extreme pressure.

Gazelles receive venture capital. Although venture capital (VC) firms prefer to invest in gazelles, many gazelles have never received VC funding. With gazelles numbering close to 400,000, less than two percent of these companies have received funding, even in boom times.

Gazelles were never mice. By definition, gazelles are companies created with the intent of high growth and wealth creation, whereas *mice* are companies created with the goal of merely generating income and no intention of growth. Companies can be gazelles at birth; however, many businesses become gazelles later in life. As many as 20 percent of gazelles have been in operation for more than 30 years.

Gazelles are high tech. To be classified as a gazelle, a company must have grown sales by 20 percent for at least a five-year period, starting with a base of at least $100,000—which can include firms in any industry. This myth most likely stems from the high margins enjoyed by most technology-based companies; however, gazelles are commonly found in low-tech sectors. Two prevalent examples are Best Buy and Starbucks.

Gazelles are global. The scope of a business has no role in its distinction as a gazelle, so even though some gazelles are operating on a global scale, it is not a necessary characteristic. Making the decision to expand overseas prematurely can just as quickly lead to the death of a business as it can lead to its success. Beyond the risks, international trade accounts for more than $800 billion annually in economic activity—but without careful planning, going global could lead to going out of business.

© Cengage Learning

- The compound growth rate in the number of businesses over a 12-year span is 3.9 percent.
- Each year, about 14 percent of firms with employees drop from the unemployment insurance rolls, while about 16 percent new and successor firms—firms with management changes—are added. This represents the disappearance or reorganization of half of all listed firms every five years!
- In 2020, demographers estimate that 35 million firms will exist in the United States, up significantly from the 28 million firms that existed in 2014.

GAZELLES AND SURVIVAL

How many gazelles survive? The simple answer is "none." Sooner or later, all companies wither and die. The more relevant question, therefore, is: Over any particular interval, how many firms die, and to what degree is it a function of their age at the beginning of the period?

The common myth that 85 percent of all firms fail in the first year (or the first two years, according to some versions of the myth) is obviously not true. The origins of this myth have been traced by David Birch, formerly with the Massachusetts Institute of Technology (MIT) and later his own firm, Cognetics, Inc. to a perfectly accurate piece of research stating that 85 percent of all firms fail. This finding may have been extended to become "85 percent of all small start-up firms fail in the first year."

Whatever the origin of this myth, the more accurate statement is that about half of all start-ups last between five and seven years, depending on economic conditions following the start.

1-7c   Legacy of Entrepreneurial Firms

Fostering and promoting entrepreneurial activity has been, and will continue to be, an economic solution for recessions, downturns, and challenges. It is the most powerful economic force ever discovered on our planet, and its success has at least three entrepreneurial components.

First, large existing firms in mature industries that adapted, downsized, restructured, and reinvented themselves in the early 2000s are now thriving, having learned to become more entrepreneurial. As large firms have become leaner, their sales and profits have increased sharply. For example, General Electric, which cut its workforce by 40 percent over the same period, saw its sales increase fourfold, from less than $20 billion to nearly $80 billion. This goal was accomplished, in many cases, by returning to the firm's "core competencies" and by contracting out functions formerly done in-house to small firms.

Second, while large existing companies have been transforming themselves, new entrepreneurial companies have been blossoming. Thirty years ago, Nucor Steel was a small manufacturer with a few hundred employees. It embraced a new technology called thin-slab casting that allowed it to thrive, while other steel companies stumbled. Nucor grew to 59,000 employees, with sales of $3.4 billion and a net income of $274 million. Newer entrepreneurial companies—some of which did not exist 20 years ago—have collectively created millions of new jobs during the past decade. Among many notable examples, consider Facebook, Twitter, Google, LinkedIn, and YouTube.

Third, thousands of entrepreneurial firms have been founded, including many established by women, minorities, and immigrants. These new companies have footholds in every sector of the economy and can be found in every part of the country. Together they make a formidable contribution to the economy, as many, by hiring on one or two employees, have created most of the net new jobs in the last few years.

In summary, entrepreneurial firms make two indispensable contributions to the U.S. economy. First, they are an integral part of the renewal process that pervades and defines market economies. They also play a crucial role in championing innovations that lead to technological change and productivity growth. In short, they are about change and competition because they change market structure. The U.S. economy is a dynamic, organic entity, always in the process of "becoming," rather than having already arrived. It is about prospects for the future, not the inheritance of the past.

Second, entrepreneurial firms are the essential mechanism by which millions enter the economic and social mainstream of American society. Small businesses enable millions of people—including women, minorities, and immigrants—to access the American dream. The greatest source of U.S. strength has always been the dream of economic growth, equal opportunity, and upward mobility. In this evolutionary process, entrepreneurship plays the crucial and indispensable role of providing the "social glue" that binds together both high-tech and "Main Street" activities.[47]

New-business formation is the critical foundation for any net increase in global employment. All of our detailed information provides insight into why the global economic future may well lie in the development of our entrepreneurial abilities.

1-8 TWENTY-FIRST-CENTURY TRENDS IN ENTREPRENEURSHIP RESEARCH

As we continue our study of entrepreneurship, it is important to note the research and educational developments that have occurred in this century. The major themes that characterize recent research about entrepreneurs and new-venture creation can be summarized as follows:

1. *Venture financing*, including both venture capital and angel capital financing as well as other innovative financing techniques, emerged in the twenty-first century with unprecedented strength, fueling entrepreneurship throughout the world.[48]

2. *Corporate entrepreneurship* (entrepreneurial actions within large organizations) and the need for the entrepreneurial mind-set among employees have gained greater acceptance during the past few decades.[49]

3. *Social entrepreneurship* has emerged with unprecedented popularity among the new generation of entrepreneurs seeking innovative solutions to world problems.[50]

4. *Entrepreneurial cognition* (examining the ways that entrepreneurs think and act) is a wave of research on the psychological aspects of the entrepreneurial process.[51]

THE ENTREPRENEURIAL PROCESS

The Best Business Schools for Entrepreneurship

In examining the various rankings of entrepreneurship programs over the last five years the following universities have consistently been noted as among the very best in the world.

The Best Graduate Programs in Entrepreneurship	The Best Undergraduate Programs in Entrepreneurship
Indiana University–Bloomington**	Indiana University–Bloomington**
Stanford University	University of Pennsylvania
Harvard University	University of Southern California
Massachusetts Institute of Technology	University of Arizona**
University of California–Berkeley**	Babson College
Babson College	

**denotes public university

Source: Adapted from "Best Colleges for Aspiring Entrepreneurs," *Fortune Small Business* (2007); "Venture Education," *Fortune Magazine* (2010); and "Best Business School Rankings" *U.S. News & World Report (2007 through 2015).*

5. *Women and minority entrepreneurs* have emerged in greater numbers over the last two decades. They appear to face obstacles and difficulties different from those that other entrepreneurs face.[52]

6. The *global entrepreneurial movement* is increasing, judging by the enormous growth of interest in entrepreneurship around the world in the past few years.[53]

7. *Family businesses* have become a stronger focus of research. The economic and social contributions of entrepreneurs with family businesses have been shown to make immensely disproportionate contributions to job creation, innovation, and economic renewal.[54]

8. *Entrepreneurial education* has become one of the hottest topics in business and engineering schools throughout the world. It has even expanded across campuses to include almost every major discipline. The number of schools teaching entrepreneurship courses has grown from as few as a dozen 35 years ago to more than 3,000 schools offering majors or minors in entrepreneurship at this time.[55]

1-9 KEY ENTREPRENEURSHIP CONCEPTS

Before concluding our discussion of the nature of entrepreneurship, we need to put into perspective three key concepts: entrepreneurship, entrepreneur, and entrepreneurial management.

1-9a Entrepreneurship

Entrepreneurship is a dynamic process of vision, change, and creation that requires an application of energy and passion toward the creation and implementation of new ideas and creative solutions. This process of innovation and new-venture creation is accomplished through four major dimensions—individual, organizational, environmental, and process—and is aided by collaborative networks in government, education, and institutions. All of the macro and micro positions of entrepreneurial thought must be considered while recognizing and seizing opportunities that can be converted into marketable ideas capable of competing for implementation in today's economy.

1-9b Entrepreneur

As we demonstrated earlier in the chapter, the *entrepreneur* is an innovator or developer who recognizes and seizes opportunities; converts those opportunities into workable/marketable ideas; adds value through time, effort, money, or skills; and assumes the risks of the competitive marketplace to implement these ideas. The entrepreneur is a catalyst for economic change who uses purposeful searching, careful planning, and sound judgment when carrying out the entrepreneurial process. The entrepreneur—uniquely optimistic and committed—works creatively to establish new resources or endow old ones with a new capacity, all for the purpose of creating wealth.

1-9c Entrepreneurial Discipline

The underlying theme of this book is the **entrepreneurial discipline**, a concept that has been delineated as follows:

> Entrepreneurship is based upon the same principles, whether the entrepreneur is an existing large institution or an individual starting his or her new venture singlehanded. It makes little or no difference whether the entrepreneur is a business or a nonbusiness public-service organization, nor even whether the entrepreneur is a governmental or nongovernmental institution. The rules are pretty much the same, the things that work and those that don't are pretty much the same, and so are the kinds of innovation and where to look for them. In every case, there is a discipline *and* the techniques and principles of this emerging discipline will continue to drive the entrepreneurial economy in the twenty-first century.[56]

1-9d Entrepreneurial Leadership

Entrepreneurship represents the ultimate source of economic dynamism and empowerment and is transformative at the societal, organizational and individual levels. Researchers Donald F. Kuratko and Michael H. Morris use the metaphor of "fire in a bottle." From a leadership perspective, entrepreneurship has become the symbol of business tenacity and achievement. Entrepreneurs' sense of opportunity, their drive to innovate, and their capacity for accomplishment have become the standard by which true leadership is now measured. If leadership is the capacity to lead, and entrepreneurial relates to the pursuit of innovation, then combining the two capacities: the capacity to lead and the capacity to risk pursuing innovative opportunities results in **entrepreneurial leadership**. It is leadership in discovering new possibilities, opening up new horizons, promulgating a new vision, combining resources in new ways, and inspiring others while implementing new venture concepts. And it is leadership in dealing with the externalities and ethical dilemmas that surround entrepreneurial action. *Entrepreneurial leadership* may be one of the most significant phrases in the twenty-first century and it serves as the ultimate vision for this book.[57]

SUMMARY

This chapter examined the evolution of entrepreneurship, providing a foundation for further study of this dynamic and developing discipline. By exploring the early economic definitions as well as select contemporary ones, the chapter presented a historical picture of how entrepreneurship has been viewed. In addition, the 10 major myths of entrepreneurship were discussed to permit a better understanding of the folklore that surrounds this newly developing field of study. Contemporary research is broadening the horizon for studying entrepreneurship and is providing a better focus on the what, how, and why behind this discipline.

The approaches to entrepreneurship were examined from three different perspectives: schools of thought, process, and frameworks. Six selected schools of thought were presented, two approaches for understanding contemporary entrepreneurship as a process were discussed, and a framework of frameworks was proposed for future development of the field.

This chapter then attempted to provide a broad perspective on the Entrepreneurial Revolution that is occurring throughout the United States and the world. The chapter discussed important statistics that support our entrepreneurial economy. A description of gazelles and their impact on the economy was presented: Gazelles are business establishments with at least 20 percent sales growth every year for at least five years, starting from a base of $100,000.

The chapter concluded with definitions of three key concepts: entrepreneurship, entrepreneur, and entrepreneurial leadership.

KEY TERMS

better widget strategies
corridor principle
displacement school of thought
dynamic states model
entrepreneur
entrepreneurial discipline
entrepreneurial leadership
Entrepreneurial Revolution
entrepreneurial trait school of
    thought

entrepreneurship
environmental school of thought
external locus of control
financial/capital school of thought
framework of frameworks
gazelle
great chef strategies
internal locus of control
macro view of entrepreneurship
micro view of entrepreneurship

mountain gap strategies
strategic formulation school of
    thought
venture opportunity school of
    thought
water well strategies

REVIEW AND DISCUSSION QUESTIONS

1. Briefly describe the evolution of the term *entrepreneurship*.

2. What are the 10 myths associated with entrepreneurship? Debunk each.

3. What is the macro view of entrepreneurship?

4. What are the schools of thought that use the macro view of entrepreneurship?

5. What is the micro view of entrepreneurship?

6. What are the schools of thought that use the micro view of entrepreneurship?

7. What are the three specific types of displacement?

8. In the strategic formulation school of thought, what are the four types of strategies involved with unique elements? Give an illustration of each.

9. What is the process approach to entrepreneurship? In your answer, describe the dynamic states approach.

10. Describe the "framework of frameworks" approach to entrepreneurship.

11. Explain the predominance of new ventures in the economy.

12. Define a *gazelle* and discuss its importance.

NOTES

1. Jeffry A. Timmons and Stephen Spinelli, *New Venture Creation*, 7th ed. (New York: McGraw-Hill/Irwin, 2007), 3.

2. For a compilation of definitions, see Robert C. Ronstadt, *Entrepreneurship* (Dover, MA: Lord Publishing, 1984), 28; Howard H. Stevenson and David E. Gumpert, "The Heart of Entrepreneurship," *Harvard Business Review* (March/April 1985): 85–94; and J. Barton Cunningham and Joe Lischeron, "Defining Entrepreneurship," *Journal of Small Business Management* (January 1991): 45–61.

3. See Calvin A. Kent, Donald L. Sexton, and Karl H. Vesper, *Encyclopedia of Entrepreneurship* (Englewood Cliffs, NJ: Prentice Hall, 1982); Ray V. Montagno and Donald F. Kuratko, "Perception of Entrepreneurial

Success Characteristics," *American Journal of Small Business* 10, no. 3(1986): 25–32; Thomas M. Begley and David P. Boyd, "Psychological Characteristics Associated with Performance in Entrepreneurial Firms and Smaller Businesses," *Journal of Business Venturing* 2, no. 1(1987): 79–91; and Donald F. Kuratko, "Entrepreneurship," in *International Encyclopedia of Business and Management*, 2nd ed. (London: Routledge Publishers, 2002), 168–176.

4. Kent, Sexton, and Vesper, *Encyclopedia of Entrepreneurship*, xxix.

5. Israel M. Kirzner, *Perception, Opportunity, and Profit: Studies in the Theory of Entrepreneurship* (Chicago: University of Chicago Press, 1979), 38–39.

6. See Ronstadt, *Entrepreneurship*, 9–12.

7. Joseph Schumpeter, "Change and the Entrepreneur," in *Essays of J. A. Schumpeter* ed. Richard V. Clemence (Reading, MA: Addison-Wesley, 1951), 255.

8. Arthur Cole, *Business Enterprise in Its Social Setting* (Cambridge, MA: Harvard University Press, 1959), 27–28.

9. Albert Shapero, *Entrepreneurship and Economic Development* Project ISEED, Ltd. (Milwaukee, WI: Center for Venture Management, 1975), 187.

10. Ronstadt, *Entrepreneurship*, 28.

11. John B. Miner, Norman R. Smith, and Jeffrey S. Bracker, "Defining the Inventor-Entrepreneur in the Context of Established Typologies," *Journal of Business Venturing* 7, no. 2(1992): 103–113.

12. Gene Koretz, "A Surprising Finding on New-Business Mortality Rates," *Business Week* (June 14, 1993): 22.

13. Brian Headd, "Redefining Business Success: Distinguishing Between Closure and Failure," *Small Business Economics 21*, no. 1 (2003): 51–61.

14. Ivan Bull and Gary E. Willard, "Towards a Theory of Entrepreneurship," *Journal of Business Venturing* 8, no. 3 (1993): 183–95; Ian C. MacMillan and Jerome A. Katz, "Idiosyncratic Milieus of Entrepreneurship Research: The Need for Comprehensive Theories," *Journal of Business Venturing* 7, no. 1 (1992): 1–8; Scott Shane and S. Venkataraman, "The Promise of Entrepreneurship as a Field of Research," *Academy of Management Review* 25, no. 1 (2000): 217–26; Christian Bruyat and Pierre-Andre Julien, "Defining the Field of Research in Entrepreneurship," *Journal of Business Venturing,* 16 no. 2 (2001):165–80; Phillip H. Phan, "Entrepreneurship Theory: Possibilities and Future Directions," *Journal of Business Venturing* 19, no. 5 (September 2004): 617–20; Sharon A. Alvarez and Jay B. Barney, "The Entrepreneurial Theory of the Firm," *Journal of Management Studies*, 44, no. 7 (2007): 1057–1063; Brian L. Connelly, R. Duane Ireland, Christopher R. Reutzel, and Joseph E. Coombs, "The Power and Effects of Entrepreneurship Research," *Entrepreneurship Theory and Practice* 34, no. 1 (2010): 131–49; and Dennis P. Leyden and Albert N. Link, "Toward a Theory of the Entrepreneurial Process," *Small Business Economics* 44, no. 3 (2015): 475–84.

15. William B. Gartner, "What Are We Talking About When We Talk About Entrepreneurship?" *Journal of Business Venturing* 5, no. 1 (1990): 15–28; see also Lanny Herron, Harry J. Sapienza, and Deborah Smith Cook, "Entrepreneurship Theory from an Interdisciplinary Perspective," *Entrepreneurship Theory and Practice* 16, no. 3 (1992): 5–12; Saras D. Sarasvathy, "The Questions We Ask and the Questions We Care About: Reformulating Some Problems in Entrepreneurship Research," *Journal of Business Venturing* 19, no. 5 (September 2004): 707–17; Benyamin B. Lichtenstein, Nancy M. Carter, Kevin J. Dooley, and William B. Gartner, "Complexity Dynamics of Nascent Entrepreneurship," *Journal of Business Venturing* 22, no. 2 (2007): 236–61; Peter W. Moroz and Kevin Hindle, "Entrepreneurship as a Process: Toward Harmonizing Multiple Perspectives," *Entrepreneurship Theory and Practice* 36, no. 4 (2012): 781–18; see also: Michael H. Morris and Donald F. Kuratko, *Wiley Encyclopedia of Entrepreneurship* (NewJersey: Wiley & Sons, 2014.)

16. See Harold Koontz, "The Management Theory Jungle Revisited," *Academy of Management Review* 5, no. 2 (1980): 175–87; Richard M. Hodgetts and Donald F. Kuratko, "The Management Theory Jungle—Quo Vadis?" *Southern Management Association Proceedings* (November 1983): 280–83; Cunningham and Lischeron, "Defining Entrepreneurship"; MacMillan and Katz, "Idiosyncratic Milieus of Entrepreneurship Research"; Murray B. Low, "The Adolescence of Entrepreneurship Research: Specification of Purpose," *Entrepreneurship Theory and Practice* 25, no. 4 (2001): 17–25; and Johan Wiklund, Per Davidsson, David B. Audretsch, and Charlie Karlsson, "The Future of Entrepreneurship Research," *Entrepreneurship Theory and Practice* 35, no. 1 (2011): 1–9.

17. See Andrew H. Van de Ven, "The Development of an Infrastructure for Entrepreneurship," *Journal of Business Venturing* 8, no. 3 (1993): 211–30; Jeffrey G. York and S. Venkataraman, "The Entrepreneur-Environment Nexus: Uncertainty, Innovation, and Allocation," *Journal of Business Venturing* 25, no. 5 (2010): 449–63; and Linda Edelman and Helena Yli-Renko, "The Impact of Environment and Entrepreneurial Perceptions on Venture Creation Efforts: Bridging the Discovery and Creation Views of Entrepreneurship," *Entrepreneurship Theory and Practice* 34, no. 5 (2010): 833–56.

18. See David J. Brophy and Joel M. Shulman, "A Finance Perspective on Entrepreneurship Research," *Entrepreneurship Theory and Practice* 16, no. 3 (1992): 61–71; and Truls Erikson, "Entrepreneurial Capital: The Emerging Venture's Most Important Asset and Competitive Advantage," *Journal of Business Venturing* 17, no. 3 (2002): 275–90.

19. Ronstadt, *Entrepreneurship*; and Daniel V. Holland and Dean A. Shepherd, "Deciding to Persist: Adversity, Values, and Entrepreneurs' Decision Policies," *Entrepreneurship Theory and Practice*, 37, no. 2 (2013): 331–58.

20. Small Business Administration, *Office of Advocacy* (Washington, DC: Government Printing Office, March 2014); Matthew C. Sonfield, "Re-Defining Minority Businesses: Challenges and Opportunities," *Journal of Developmental Entrepreneurship* 6, no. 3 (2001): 269–76; and Lois M. Shelton, "Fighting an Uphill Battle: Expansion Barriers, Intra-Industry Social Stratification, and Minority Firm Growth," *Entrepreneurship Theory and Practice* 34, no. 2 (2010): 379–98.

21. Sara Carter, "The Rewards of Entrepreneurship: Exploring the Incomes, Wealth, and Economic Well-Being of Entrepreneurial Households," *Entrepreneurship Theory and Practice* 35, no. 1 (2011): 39–55.

22. Kelly G. Shaver and Linda R. Scott, "Person, Process, Choice: The Psychology of New Venture Creation," *Entrepreneurship Theory and Practice* 16, no. 2 (1991): 23–45; Ronald K. Mitchell, Lowell Busenitz, Theresa Lant, Patricia P. McDougall, Eric A. Morse, and J. Brock Smith, "The Distinctive and Inclusive Domain of Entrepreneurial Cognition Research," *Entrepreneurship Theory and Practice* 28, no. 6 (Winter 2004): 505–18; and Ha Hoang and Javier Gimeno, "Becoming a Founder: How Founder Role Identity Affects Entrepreneurial Transitions and Persistence in Founding," *Journal of Business Venturing* 25, no. 1 (2010): 41–53; and J. Robert Mitchell and Dean A. Shepherd, "To Thine Own Self Be True: Images of Self, Images of Opportunity, and Entrepreneurial Action," *Journal of Business Venturing* 25, no. 1 (2010): 138–54.

23. See Magnus Aronsson, "Education Matters—But Does Entrepreneurship Education? An Interview with David Birch," *Academy of Management Learning & Education* 3, no. 3 (2004): 289–92.

24. See Jerry A. Katz, "The Chronology and Intellectual Trajectory of American Entrepreneurship Education," *Journal of Business Venturing* 18, no. 2 (2003): 283–300; Donald F. Kuratko, "The Emergence of Entrepreneurship Education: Development, Trends, and Challenges," *Entrepreneurship Theory and Practice* 29, no. 5 (2005): 577–98; and Dean A. Shepherd, "Educating Entrepreneurship Students About Emotion and Learning from Failure," *Academy of Management Learning & Education* 3, no. 3 (2004): 274–87.

25. Dimo Dimov, "Grappling with the Unbearable Elusiveness of Entrepreneurial Opportunities," *Entrepreneurship Theory and Practice* 35, no. 1 (2011): 57–81; Jintong Tang, K. Michele (Micki) Kacmar, and Lowell Busenitz, "Entrepreneurial Alertness in the Pursuit of New Opportunities," *Journal of Business Venturing* 27, no. 1 (2012): 77–94; and Michael M. Gielnik, Hannes Zacher, and Michael Frese, "Focus on Opportunities as a Mediator of the Relationship between Business Owner's Age and Venture Growth," *Journal of Business Venturing* 27, no. 1 (2012): 127–42.

26. George A. Steiner, *Strategic Planning* (New York: Free Press, 1979), 3.

27. See Marjorie A. Lyles, Inga S. Baird, J. Burdeane Orris, and Donald F. Kuratko, "Formalized Planning in Small Business: Increasing Strategic Choices," *Journal of Small Business Management* 31, no. 2 (1993): 38–50; R. Duane Ireland, Michael A. Hitt, S. Michael Camp, and Donald L. Sexton, "Integrating Entrepreneurship and Strategic Management Actions to Create Firm Wealth," *Academy of Management Executive* 15, no. 1 (2001): 49–63; and Dimo Dimov, "Nascent Entrepreneurs and Venture Emergence: Opportunity Confidence, Human Capital, and Early Planning," *Journal of Management Studies* 48, no. 6 (2011): 1123–53.

28. Ronstadt, *Entrepreneurship*, 112–15.

29. Michael A. Hitt, R. Duane Ireland, S. Michael Camp, and Donald L. Sexton, "Strategic Entrepreneurship: Entrepreneurial Strategies for Wealth Creation," special issue, *Strategic Management Journal* 22, no. 6 (2001): 479–92.

30. See the special issue, dealing with models, of *Entrepreneurship: Theory and Practice* 17, no. 2 (1993); see also James J. Chrisman, Alan Bauerschmidt, and Charles W. Hofer, "The Determinants of New Venture Performance: An Extended Model," *Entrepreneurship Theory and Practice* 23, no. 1 (1998): 5–30.

31. Michael H. Morris, Pamela S. Lewis, and Donald L. Sexton, "Reconceptualizing Entrepreneurship: An Input-Output Perspective," *Advanced Management Journal* 59, no. 1 (Winter 1994): 21–31.

32. Ibid.

33. Jonathan Levie and Benjamin B. Lichtenstein, "A Terminal Assessment of Stages Theory: Introducing a Dynamic States Approach to Entrepreneurship," *Entrepreneurship Theory and Practice* 34, no. 2 (2010): 317–50.

34. Donald F. Kuratko, Michael H. Morris, and Minet Schindehutte, "Understanding the Dynamics of Entrepreneurship through Framework Approaches," *Small Business Economics,* 45, no. 1 (2015): 1–13.

35. Dean A. Shepherd, "Multilevel Entrepreneurship Research: Opportunities for Studying Entrepreneurial Decision Making," *Journal of Management,* 37, no.2 (2011): 412–20.

36. Jose Ernesto Amoros and Niels Bosma, *Global Entrepreneurship Monitor: Global Report*, Global Entrepreneurship Research Association (GERA), 2014.

37. Donna Kelley, Niels Bosma, and José Ernesto Amorós, *Global Entrepreneurship Monitor 2010 Global Report* (Wellesley, MA: Babson College, 2010); and Amoros and Bosma, *Global Entrepreneurship Monitor: Global Report*.

38. Donna J. Kelley, Abdul Ali, Candida Brush, Andrew C. Corbett, Thomas Lyons, Mahdi Majbouri, and Edward G. Rogoff, *Global Entrepreneurship Monitor: National Entrepreneurial Assessment for the United States of America* (Wellesley, MA: Babson College, 2013).

39. Robert W. Fairlie, *Kauffman Index of Entrepreneurial Activity, 1966–2014* (Kansas City, MO: Ewing Marion Kauffman Foundation, 2015).

40. *Small Business Advocacy* (Washington DC: U.S. Small Business Administration, Office of Advocacy, 2014).

41. Ibid.; and Fairlie, *Kauffman Index of Entrepreneurial Activity, 1996–2014*.

42. Maria Minniti and William D. Bygrave, *Global Entrepreneurship Monitor* (Kansas City, MO: Kauffman Center for Entrepreneurial Leadership, 2004); and Erkko Autio, *Global Report on High Growth Entrepreneurship* (Wellesley MA: Babson College and London, UK: London Business School, 2007).

43. David Birch's research firm, Cognetics, Inc., traces the employment and sales records of some 14 million companies with a Dun & Bradstreet file.

44. George Foster, Antonio Davila, Martin Haemmig, Xiaobin He, and Ning Jia, *Global Entrepreneurship*

and the Successful Growth Strategies of Early-Stage Companies: A World Economic Forum Report (New York: World Economic Forum USA Inc., 2011); see also Gideon D. Markman and William B. Gartner, "Is Extraordinary Growth Profitable? A Study of *Inc. 500* High-Growth Companies," *Entrepreneurship Theory and Practice* 27, no, 1 (September 2002): 65–75 and Magnus Henrekson and Dan Johansson, "Gazelles as Job Creators: A Survey and Interpretation of the Evidence," *Small Business Economics* 35, no. 2 (2010):227–44.

45. Dane Stangler, *High-Growth Firms and the Future of the American Economy* (Ewing Marion Kauffman Foundation, March 2010).

46. David Birch, Jan Gundersen, Anne Haggerty, and William Parsons, *Corporate Demographics* (Cambridge, MA: Cognetics, Inc., 1999).

47. "The New American Revolution: The Role and Impact of Small Firms" (Washington, DC: U.S. Small Business Administration, Office of Economic Research, 1998); and William J. Dennis, Jr., and Lloyd W. Fernald, Jr., "The Chances of Financial Success (and Loss) from Small Business Ownership," *Entrepreneurship Theory and Practice* 26, no. 1 (2000): 75–83.

48. Dean A. Shepherd and Andrew Zacharakis, "Speed to Initial Public Offering of VC-Backed Companies," *Entrepreneurship Theory and Practice* 25, no. 3 (2001): 59–69; Dean A. Shepherd and Andrew Zacharakis, "Venture Capitalists' Expertise: A Call for Research into Decision Aids and Cognitive Feedback," *Journal of Business Venturing* 17, no. 1 (2002): 1–20; Lowell W. Busenitz, James O. Fiet, and Douglas D. Moesel, "Reconsidering the Venture Capitalists' 'Value Added' Proposition: An Interorganizational Learning Perspective," *Journal of Business Venturing* 19, no. 6 (2004): 787–807; and Dimo Dimov, Dean A. Shepherd, and Kathleen M. Sutcliffe, "Requisite Expertise, Firm Reputation, and Status in Venture Capital Investment Allocation Decisions," *Journal of Business Venturing* 22, no. 4 (2007): 481–502.

49. Donald F. Kuratko, R. Duane Ireland, and Jeffrey S. Hornsby, "Improving Firm Performance Through Entrepreneurial Actions: Acordia's Corporate Entrepreneurship Strategy," *Academy of Management Executive* 15, no. 4 (2001): 60–71; Donald F. Kuratko and David B. Audretsch, "Clarifying the Domains of Corporate Entrepreneurship," *International Entrepreneurship & Management Journal*, 9, no. 3 (2013): 323–35; Donald F. Kuratko, Jeffrey S. Hornsby, and Jeffrey G Covin, "Diagnosing a Firm's Internal Environment for Corporate Entrepreneurship," *Business Horizons*, 57, no. 1 (2014): 37–47; Michael H. Morris, Donald F. Kuratko, and Jeffrey G. Covin, *Corporate Entrepreneurship and Innovation*, 3rd ed. (Mason, OH: Cengage/South-Western, 2011); R. Duane Ireland, Jeffrey G. Covin, and Donald F. Kuratko, "Conceptualizing Corporate Entrepreneurship Strategy," *Entrepreneurship Theory and Practice* 33, no. 1 (2009): 19–46; and Donald F. Kuratko, Jeffrey S. Hornsby, and James Hayton, "Corporate Entrepreneurship: The

Innovative Challenge for a New Global Economic Reality." *Small Business Economics* 45, no. 2 (2015): 245–253.

50. Ana Maria Peredo and Murdith McLean, "Social Entrepreneurship: A Critical Review of the Concept," *Journal of World Business* 41 (2006): 56–65; James Austin, Howard Stevenson, and Jane Wei-Skillern, "Social and Commercial Entrepreneurship: Same, Different, or Both?" *Entrepreneurship Theory and Practice* 30, no. 1 (2006): 1–22; Thomas J. Dean and Jeffery S. McMullen, "Toward a Theory of Sustainable Entrepreneurship: Reducing Environmental Degradation Through Entrepreneurial Action," *Journal of Business Venturing* 22, no. 1 (2007): 50–76; Desirée F. Pacheco, Thomas J. Dean, David S. Payne, "Escaping the Green Prison: Entrepreneurship and the Creation of Opportunities for Sustainable Development," *Journal of Business Venturing* 25, no. 5 (2010): 464–80; Bradley D. Parrish, "Sustainability-Driven Entrepreneurship: Principles of Organization Design," *Journal of Business Venturing* 25, no. 5 (2010): 510–23; and Dean A. Shepherd and Holger Patzelt, *Entrepreneurship Theory and Practice* 35, no. 1 (2011): 137–63.

51. Jill Kickul and Lisa K. Gundry, "Prospecting for Strategic Advantage: The Proactive Entrepreneurial Personality and Small Firm Innovation," *Journal of Small Business Management* 40, no. 2 (2002): 85–97; Robert A. Baron, "The Role of Affect in the Entrepreneurial Process," *Academy of Management Review* 33, no. 2 (2008): 328–40; and Robert A. Baron, Keith M. Hmieleski, and Rebecca A. Henry, "Entrepreneurs' Dispositional Positive Affect: The Potential Benefits – and Potential Costs – of Being 'Up,'" *Journal of Business Venturing* 27, no. 3 (2012): 310–24.

52. Lisa K. Gundry and Harold P. Welsch, "The Ambitious Entrepreneur: High Growth Strategies of Women-Owned Enterprises," *Journal of Business Venturing* 16, no. 5 (2001): 453–70; Anne de Bruin, Candida G. Brush, and Friederike Welter, "Towards Building Cumulative Knowledge on Women's Entrepreneurship," *Entrepreneurship Theory and Practice* 30, no. 5 (2006): 585–94; Dawn R. DeTienne and Gaylen N. Chandler, "The Role of Gender in Opportunity Identification," *Entrepreneurship Theory and Practice* 31, no. 3 (2007): 365–86; Francis J. Greene, Liang Han, and Susan Marlow, "Like Mother, Like Daughter? Analyzing Maternal Influences Upon Women's Entrepreneurial Propensity," *Entrepreneurship Theory and Practice* 37, no. 4 (2013): 687–711; Susan Marlow and Maura McAdam, "Analyzing the Influence of Gender Upon High-Technology Venturing Within the Context of Business Incubation," *Entrepreneurship Theory and Practice* 36, no. 4 (2012): 655–76; and Alicia M. Robb and John Watson, "Gender Differences in Firm Performance: Evidence from New ventures in the United States," *Journal of Business Venturing* 27, no. 5 (2012): 544–58.

53. Shaker A. Zahra, James Hayton, Jeremy Marcel, and Hugh O'Neill, "Fostering Entrepreneurship During International Expansion: Managing Key Challenges,"

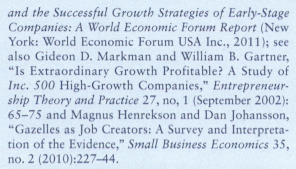

European Management Journal 19, no. 4 (2001): 359–69; Erkko Autio, Gerard George and Oliver Alexy, "International Entrepreneurship and Capability Development—Qualitative Evidence and Future Research Direction," *Entrepreneurship Theory and Practice* 35, no. 1 (2011):11–37; Nicole E. Coviello, Patricia P. McDougall, and Benjamin M. Oviatt, "The Emergence, Advance and Future of International Entrepreneurship Research—An Introduction to the Special Forum," *Journal of Business Venturing* 26, no. 6 (2011): 625–31; and Marian V. Jones, Nicole Coviello, and Yee Kwan Tang, "International Entrepreneurship Research (1988–2004): A Domain Ontology and Thematic Analysis," *Journal of Business Venturing* 26, no. 6 (2011): 632–59.

54. Nancy Upton, Elisabeth J. Teal, and Joe T. Felan, "Strategic and Business Planning Practices of Fast-Growing Family Firms," *Journal of Small Business Management* 39, no. 4 (2001): 60–72; Zhenyu Wu, Jess H. Chua, and James J. Chrisman, "Effects of Family Ownership and Management on Small Business Equity Financing," *Journal of Business Venturing* 22, no. 6 (2007): 875–95; Michael H. Morris, Jeffrey A. Allen, Donald F. Kuratko, and David Brannon, "Experiencing Family Business Creation: Differences Between Founders, Nonfamily Managers, and Founders of Nonfamily Firms," *Entrepreneurship Theory and Practice* 34, no. 6 (2010): 1057–84; and James J. Chrisman, Jess H. Chua, and Lloyd P. Steier, "Resilience of Family Firms: An Introduction," *Entrepreneurship Theory and Practice* 35, no. 6 (2011): 1107–19.

55. Kuratko, "The Emergence of Entrepreneurship Education"; Heidi M. Neck and Patricia G. Greene, "Entrepreneurship Education: Known Worlds and New Frontiers," *Journal of Small Business Management* 49, no. 1 (2011): 55–70; Michael H. Morris, Donald F. Kuratko, and Pryor, Christopher G. "Building Blocks for the Development of University-Wide Entrepreneurship," *Entrepreneurship Research Journal*, 4 no. 1 (2014): 45–68; Michael H. Morris, Donald F. Kuratko, and Jefrey R. Cornwall, *Entrepreneurship Programs and the Modern University* (Cheltenham, UK: Edward Elgar, 2013); and Michael H. Morris and Donald F. Kuratko, "Building University 21st Century Entrepreneurship Programs that Empower and Transform," *Advances in the Study of Entrepreneurship, Innovation, and Economic Growth* 24 (2014): 1–24 (edited by Sherry Hoskinson and Donald F. Kuratko).

56. Peter F. Drucker, *Innovation and Entrepreneurship* (New York: Harper & Row, 1985), 143; see also Howard H. Stevenson and J. Carlos Jarillo, "A Paradigm of Entrepreneurship: Entrepreneurial Management," *Strategic Management Journal* 11, Special Issue (Summer 1990): 17–27.

57. Donald F. Kuratko and Michael H. Morris, *Entrepreneurial Leadership* (The International Library of Entrepreneurship; Cheltenham, UK: Edward Elgar, 2013.)

CHAPTER 2

The Entrepreneurial Mind-Set in Individuals: Cognition and Ethics

LEARNING OBJECTIVES

1 To describe the entrepreneurial mind-set and entrepreneurial cognition

2 To identify and discuss the most commonly cited characteristics found in successful entrepreneurs

3 To discuss the "dark side" of entrepreneurship

4 To identify and describe the different types of risk entrepreneurs face as well as the major causes of stress for these individuals and the ways they can handle stress

5 To discuss the ethical dilemmas confronting entrepreneurs

6 To study ethics in a conceptual framework for a dynamic environment

7 To present strategies for establishing ethical responsibility and leadership

8 To examine entrepreneurial motivation

Entrepreneurial Thought

For all we know about balance sheets, income statements, and cash flow accounting; for all of our understanding about marketing strategies, tactics, and techniques; and for everything we have learned about management principles and practices, there remains something essential, yet mysterious, at the core of entrepreneurship. It is so mysterious that we cannot see it or touch it; yet we feel it and know it exists. It cannot be mined, manufactured, or bought; yet it can be discovered. Its source is invisible; yet its results are tangible and measurable. This mysterious core is so powerful that it can make the remarkable appear ordinary, so contagious that it can spread like wildfire from one to another and so persuasive that it can transform doubt and uncertainty into conviction. This mysterious core is PASSION!

— **Ray Smilor, PH.D.** *Daring Visionaries*

2-1 THE ENTREPRENEURIAL MIND-SET

LO1 Describe the entrepreneurial mind-set and entrepreneurial cognition

If past generations dreamed of the prestige and perks that come with the executive suite of a major corporation, the dream of the millennial generation (also known as Generation Y) appears quite different. They believe that career success will require them to be more nimble, independent, and entrepreneurial than past generations. In a recent study only 13 percent of millennials said their career goal involves climbing the corporate ladder to become a CEO or president. By contrast, almost two-thirds (67%) said their goal involves starting their own business. Millions of individuals younger than 35 are actively trying to start businesses, one-third of new entrepreneurs are younger than 30, and large numbers of 18- to 30-year-olds study entrepreneurship in business schools. Major universities are devoting more resources to entrepreneurship, and the success stories of young entrepreneurs are increasing.[1]

Every person has the potential and free choice to pursue a career as an entrepreneur, but exactly what motivates people to make this choice is not fully understood. As we demonstrated in Chapter 1, researchers are attempting better to understand the driving forces within entrepreneurs, but have not yet identified one single event, characteristic, or trait that pushes an individual into the domain.[2]

The chapters in this book focus on learning the discipline of entrepreneurship. This chapter, however, is devoted to a more psychological look at entrepreneurs: It describes entrepreneurial cognition, the most common characteristics associated with successful entrepreneurs, the elements associated with the "dark side" of entrepreneurship, as well as the ethical challenges that entrepreneurs confront. In this manner, we can gain a more complete perspective on the entrepreneurial behavior that a person with an entrepreneurial mind-set exhibits. Although it certainly is not an exact science, examining this mind-set provides interesting insights into the entrepreneurial potential within every individual.[3] Let's examine the cognition of entrepreneurs as a doorway to understanding the entrepreneurial mind-set.

2-2 ENTREPRENEURIAL COGNITION

In science, cognition refers to mental processes. These processes include attention, remembering, producing and understanding language, solving problems, and making decisions. The term comes from the Latin *cognoscere*, which means "to know," "to conceptualize," or "to recognize," and refers to a faculty for the processing of information, applying knowledge, and changing preferences. Cognition is used to refer to the mental functions, mental processes (thoughts), and mental states of intelligent humans. Social cognition theory introduces the idea of knowledge structures—mental models (cognitions) that are ordered in such a way as to optimize personal effectiveness within given situations—to the study of entrepreneurship. Concepts from cognitive psychology are increasingly being found to be useful tools to help probe entrepreneurial-related phenomena, and, increasingly, the applicability of the cognitive sciences to the entrepreneurial experience are cited in the research literature.

Researchers Ronald K. Mitchell, Lowell Busenitz, Theresa Lant, Patricia P. McDougall, Eric A. Morse, and J. Brock Smith define entrepreneurial cognition as *the knowledge structures that people use to make assessments, judgments, or decisions involving opportunity evaluation, venture creation, and growth*.[4] In other words, entrepreneurial cognition is about understanding how entrepreneurs use simplifying mental models to piece together previously unconnected information that helps them to identify and invent new products or services, and to assemble the necessary resources to start and grow businesses. Specifically, then, the entrepreneurial cognitions view offers an understanding as to how entrepreneurs think and "why" they do some of the things they do.

2-2a Metacognitive Perspective

While the research has focused on entrepreneurial cognitions, a new stream of thinking links the foundation of the entrepreneurial mind-set to cognitive adaptability, which can be defined as the ability to be dynamic, flexible, and self-regulating in one's cognitions given dynamic and uncertain task environments. Adaptable cognitions are important in achieving desirable outcomes from entrepreneurial actions.

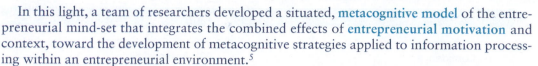

In this light, a team of researchers developed a situated, metacognitive model of the entrepreneurial mind-set that integrates the combined effects of entrepreneurial motivation and context, toward the development of metacognitive strategies applied to information processing within an entrepreneurial environment.[5]

Consider an entrepreneur faced with the entrepreneurial task of developing a sound explanation for a new venture in preparation for an important meeting with a venture capitalist. Before the entrepreneur is prepared to evaluate alternative strategies, the entrepreneur must first formulate a strategy to frame how he or she will "think" about this task. This process is metacognitive. The process responsible for ultimately selecting a response (i.e., a particular venture strategy) is cognitive—the process responsible for ultimately selecting how the entrepreneur will frame the entrepreneurial task is metacognitive. Thus, metacognition is not to study why the entrepreneur selected a particular strategy for a set of alternative strategies (cognition), but instead to study the higher-order cognitive process that resulted in the entrepreneur framing the task effectually, and thus why and how the particular strategy was included in a set of alternative responses to the decision task (metacognition).

Although it has become a significant area of study, entrepreneurial cognitive research presents future conceptual challenges that will have to be examined in order to be an effective contribution to the entrepreneurial world. For instance, many works are built on the premise that founders and entrepreneurs "think" differently than other individuals or business executives. But it is far less clear whether this "cognitive difference" originates from idiosyncratic factors and events that *predate* entrepreneurs' efforts and actions, or from the very experience of entrepreneurship by these individuals. Similarly, it is not clear whether the "cognitive difference" of entrepreneurs results from tasks and environmental conditions that "reward" individuals with particular "thinking," or from conditions that encourage the expression and/or development of such thinking. Those questions introduce the notion of the entrepreneurial experience, which we examine next.[6]

2-2b Who Are Entrepreneurs?

Frank Carney, one of the founders of Pizza Hut, Inc., once described entrepreneurs as the cornerstone of the American enterprise system and the self-renewing agents for our economic environment. Entrepreneurs—normally defined as "risk takers" in new-venture creations—are uniquely optimistic, hard-driving, committed individuals who derive great satisfaction from being independent. Starting a new business requires more than just an idea; it requires a special person, an entrepreneur, who combines sound judgment and planning with risk taking to ensure the success of his or her own business.

Entrepreneurs, driven by an intense commitment and determined perseverance, work very hard. They are optimists who see the cup as half full rather than half empty. They strive for integrity. They burn with the competitive desire to excel. They use failure as a tool for learning. They have enough confidence in themselves to believe that they personally can make a major difference in the final outcome of their ventures.[7]

The substantial failure rate of new ventures attests to the difficulty of entrepreneurship. Inexperience and incompetent management are the main reasons for failure. But what are the factors for success? Do they apply to all components of entrepreneurship? These are some of the issues we shall explore in this chapter.

2-2c Characteristics Associated with the Entrepreneurial Mind-Set

LO2 Identify and discuss the most commonly cited characteristics found in successful entrepreneurs

A review of the literature related to entrepreneurial characteristics reveals the existence of a large number of factors that can be consolidated into a much smaller set of profile dimensions.

Howard H. Stevenson and David E. Gumpert have presented an outline of the entrepreneurial organization that reveals such characteristics as imagination, flexibility, and willingness to accept risks.[8] William B. Gartner examined the literature and found a diversity of reported characteristics.[9] John Hornaday examined various research sources and formulated a list of 42 characteristics often attributed to entrepreneurs (see Table 2.1).

TABLE 2.1 CHARACTERISTICS OFTEN ATTRIBUTED TO ENTREPRENEURS

1. Confidence	22. Responsibility
2. Perseverance, determination	23. Foresight
3. Energy, diligence	24. Accuracy, thoroughness
4. Resourcefulness	25. Cooperativeness
5. Ability to take calculated risks	26. Profit orientation
6. Dynamism, leadership	27. Ability to learn from mistakes
7. Optimism	28. Sense of power
8. Need to achieve	29. Pleasant personality
9. Versatility; knowledge of product, market, machinery, technology	30. Egotism
	31. Courage
10. Creativity	32. Imagination
11. Ability to influence others	33. Perceptiveness
12. Ability to get along well with people	34. Toleration for ambiguity
13. Initiative	35. Aggressiveness
14. Flexibility	36. Capacity for enjoyment
15. Intelligence	37. Efficacy
16. Orientation to clear goals	38. Commitment
17. Positive response to challenges	39. Ability to trust workers
18. Independence	40. Sensitivity to others
19. Responsiveness to suggestions and criticism	41. Honesty, integrity
20. Time competence, efficiency	42. Maturity, balance
21. Ability to make decisions quickly	

Source: John A. Hornaday, "Research about Living Entrepreneurs," in *Encyclopedia of Entrepreneurship*, ed. Calvin Kent, Donald Sexton, and Karl Vesper (Englewood Cliffs, NJ: Prentice Hall, 1982), 26–27. Adapted by permission of Prentice Hall, Englewood Cliffs, NJ.

In the simplest of theoretical forms for studying entrepreneurship, entrepreneurs cause entrepreneurship. $E = f(e)$; that is, entrepreneurship is a function of the entrepreneur. Thus, the continuous examination of entrepreneurial characteristics aids the evolving understanding of the entrepreneurial mind-set. One author provides the following description:

> Would-be entrepreneurs live in a sea of dreams. Their destinations are private islands—places to build, create, and transform their particular dreams into reality. Being an entrepreneur entails envisioning your island, and even more important, it means getting in the boat and rowing to your island. All dreamers may one day be entrepreneurs if they can marshal the resources—external and internal—needed to transform their dreams into reality.[10]

Entrepreneurs also have been characterized as the interaction of the following skills: inner control, planning and goal setting, risk taking, innovation, reality perception, use of feedback, decision-making, human relations, and independence. In addition, many people believe that successful entrepreneurs are individuals who are not afraid to fail.

As we showed earlier in the chapter, research continues to expand our understanding of the cognitions of entrepreneurs.[11] New characteristics are continually being added to this ever-growing list. At this point, however, let us examine some of the most often cited entrepreneurial characteristics. Although this list admittedly is incomplete, it does provide important insights into the entrepreneurial mind-set.

DETERMINATION AND PERSEVERANCE

More than any other factor, total dedication to success as an entrepreneur can overcome obstacles and setbacks. Sheer determination and an unwavering commitment to succeed often win out against odds that many people would consider insurmountable. They also can compensate for personal shortcomings. Often, entrepreneurs with a high-potential venture and a plan that includes venture capital financing can expect investors to measure their commitment in several ways. Examples include a willingness to mortgage a home, take a cut in pay, sacrifice family time, and reduce standards of living.

DRIVE TO ACHIEVE

Entrepreneurs are self-starters who appear to others to be internally driven by a strong desire to compete, to excel against self-imposed standards, and to pursue and attain challenging goals. This drive to achieve is well documented in the entrepreneurial literature, beginning with David McClelland's pioneering work on motivation in the 1950s and 1960s.[12] High achievers tend to be moderate risk takers. They examine a situation, determine how to increase the odds of winning, and then push ahead. As a result, high-risk decisions for the average businessperson often are moderate risks for the well-prepared high achiever.

OPPORTUNITY ORIENTATION

One clear pattern among successful, growth-minded entrepreneurs is their focus on opportunity rather than on resources, structure, or strategy. Opportunity orientation is the constant awareness of opportunities that exist in everyday life. Successful entrepreneurs start with the opportunity and let their understanding of it guide other important decisions. They are goal oriented in their pursuit of opportunities. Setting high but attainable goals enables them to focus their energies, to selectively sort out opportunities, and to know when to say "no." Their goal orientation also helps them to define priorities and provides them with measures of how well they are performing.

PERSISTENT PROBLEM SOLVING

Entrepreneurs are not intimidated by difficult situations. In fact, their self-confidence and general optimism seem to translate into a view that the impossible just takes a little longer. Yet they are neither aimless nor foolhardy in their relentless attack on a problem or an obstacle that is impeding business operations. If the task is extremely easy or perceived to be unsolvable, entrepreneurs often will give up sooner than others—simple problems bore them; unsolvable ones do not warrant their time. Moreover, although entrepreneurs are extremely persistent, they are realistic in recognizing what they can and cannot do and where they can get help to solve difficult but unavoidable tasks.

SEEKING FEEDBACK

Effective entrepreneurs often are described as quick learners. Unlike many people, however, they also have a strong desire to know how well they are doing and how they might improve their performance. In attempting to make these determinations, they actively seek out and use feedback. Feedback is also central to their learning from mistakes and setbacks.

INTERNAL LOCUS OF CONTROL

Successful entrepreneurs believe in themselves. They do not believe that the success or failure of their venture will be governed by fate, luck, or similar forces. They believe that their accomplishments and setbacks are within their own control and influence, and that they can affect the outcome of their actions. This attribute is consistent with a high-achievement motivational drive, the desire to take personal responsibility, and self-confidence.

TOLERANCE FOR AMBIGUITY

Start-up entrepreneurs face uncertainty compounded by constant changes that introduce ambiguity and stress into every aspect of the enterprise. Setbacks and surprises are inevitable; lack of organization, structure, and order is a way of life. A tolerance for ambiguity exists when the entrepreneur can deal with the various setbacks and changes that constantly

THE ENTREPRENEURIAL PROCESS

Global Breakthrough Innovators

Over the past few decades we have witnessed the emergence of breakthrough innovators who, driven by goals beyond personal achievement and venture success, have changed the world with their ideas. Here are a few of the most notable breakthrough innovators.

Steve Jobs, of Apple

He was cofounder, chairman, and chief executive officer of Apple, Inc. An entrepreneur who is widely recognized as a charismatic pioneer of the personal computer revolution started his company in a garage in 1976. By 2011, Apple had over 50,000 employees worldwide with annual sales exceeding $65 billion. It was the largest publicly traded company in the world by market capitalization and the largest technology company in the world by revenue and profit. Steve Jobs passed away in 2011 at the age of 56.

Bill Gates, of Microsoft

One of the best-known entrepreneurs of the personal computer revolution, Gates was the chief software architect of Microsoft Corporation, the worldwide leader in software, services, and solutions. Microsoft would also come to dominate the office suite market with Microsoft Office. In 2011, Microsoft Corporation acquired Skype Communications for $8.5 billion. Microsoft revenues exceed $36 billion, employing more than 55,000 people in 85 countries and regions.

Larry Page and Sergey Brin, of Google

Together they founded Google, Inc. in 1998. Today, Google is one of the most financially successful and most innovative companies in the world, expanding its reach into many industries from Google maps to Google cell phones. With revenue at $30 billion, Google has been estimated to run over one million servers in data centers around the world to process over one billion search requests and about 24 petabytes of user-generated data every day.

Oprah Winfrey, of Harpo, Inc.

Oprah Winfrey is the first woman in history to own and produce her own talk show. Winfrey is best known for her award-winning talk show (nationally syndicated from 1986 to 2011), which became the highest-rated program of its kind in history. She has been ranked the richest African American of the twentieth century and the greatest black philanthropist in American history. According to some experts, she is one of the most influential women ever.

Sam Walton, of Walmart

He is best known for starting Walmart in 1962. His philosophy was to help bring a large variety of products and low prices to his consumers throughout his career. Today, Walmart is the world's 18th largest public corporation with over $400 billion in revenue and over 600,000 employees. Walmart has 8,500 stores in 15 countries, under 55 different names. As a result of his accomplishments, Sam Walton reached the ranks of the richest man in the United States from 1985 until 1988.

Gordon Moore, of Intel

Moore cofounded Intel in 1968, the world's largest semiconductor chip maker. In 2011, Intel's market capitalization was $122.41 billion. Moore is widely known for "Moore's Law," in which, in 1965, he predicted that the number of transistors the industry would be able to place on a computer chip would double once every two years. It has become the guiding principle for the industry.

Paul Orfalea, of Kinko's

Paul Orfalea founded Kinko's as a copy center. The name comes from how other kids joked about his "kinky" hair. In February, 2004, Kinko's was bought by FedEx for $2.4 billion, and then became known as FedEx Kinko's Office and Print Centers. Today Kinko's is a worldwide printing center offering a variety of services bringing in millions of dollars per year in revenue.

confront him or her. Successful entrepreneurs thrive on the fluidity and excitement of such an ambiguous existence. Job security and retirement generally are of no concern to them.

CALCULATED RISK TAKING

Successful entrepreneurs are not gamblers—they are *calculated risk takers*. When they decide to participate in a venture, they do so in a very calculated, carefully thought-out manner. They do everything possible to get the odds in their favor, and they often avoid taking unnecessary risks. These strategies include getting others to share inherent financial and business risks with them—for example, by persuading partners and investors to put up money, creditors to offer special terms, and suppliers to advance merchandise.

HIGH ENERGY LEVEL

The extraordinary workloads and stressful demands placed on entrepreneurs put a premium on their energy. Many entrepreneurs fine-tune their energy levels by carefully monitoring what they eat and drink, establishing exercise routines, and knowing when to get away for relaxation.

CREATIVITY AND INNOVATIVENESS

Creativity was once regarded as an exclusively inherited trait. Judging by the level of creativity and innovation in the United States compared with that of equally sophisticated but less creative and innovative cultures, it appears unlikely that this trait is solely genetic. An expanding school of thought believes that creativity can be learned (Chapter 5 provides a comprehensive examination of this critical characteristic). New ventures often possess a collective creativity that emerges from the joint efforts of the founders and personnel and produces unique goods and services.

VISION

Entrepreneurs know where they want to go. They have a vision or concept of what their firms can be. For example, Steve Jobs of Apple Computer fame wanted his firm to provide microcomputers that could be used by everyone, from schoolchildren to businesspeople. The computer would be more than a machine. It would be an integral part of the person's life in terms of learning and communicating. This vision helped make Apple a major competitor in the microcomputer industry. Not all entrepreneurs have predetermined visions for their firms, however. In many cases, this vision develops over time as the individual begins to realize what the firm is and what it can become.

THE ENTREPRENEURIAL PROCESS

Persistence Pays Off for Entrepreneurs

"If at first you don't succeed, try and try again." "If you fall off the horse, you have to get back on." "What doesn't kill you only makes you stronger." Whatever adage you choose, it seems they really do apply to entrepreneurs. Perhaps it is the constant optimism of entrepreneurs that forms this perception. Always keeping an eye open for opportunity and positive change is the earmark of successful entrepreneurs. Persistently asking why deviations occur and how they can be prevented or exploited, may be a key element for successful entrepreneurs.

There are certain principles that seasoned entrepreneurs understand more than first time entrepreneurs. For example, experienced entrepreneurs devour information within their industries. They keep abreast of new and prevailing trends and technologies in their current and related industries. Experienced entrepreneurs also see problems as opportunities for improvements and potential new ventures. So, these entrepreneurs are able to study and recognize patterns. More significantly they have certain targets in mind as they grow their ventures but their goals are always moving forward. Thus it may be that experience and persistence teaches lessons to entrepreneurs that are used to vault them into future successes.

One study from the Harvard Business School demonstrated that experienced entrepreneurs with some history of success are much more likely to succeed in new ventures than first-timers or those who failed previously. While this may not be shocking news, this is one of the first studies to establish that performance persistence does benefit the entrepreneur quite significantly. In the study experienced entrepreneurs were 34 percent more likely to succeed in their next venture-backed firm, compared with 23 percent for those who previously failed and 22 percent for first-timers. Essentially, the study showed that entrepreneurs who start successful venture-backed ventures were far more likely to be successful in their next venture-backed firm.

It should also be recognized that some component of performance persistence could stem from "success breeding success." In other words, entrepreneurs whose first venture succeeded at least in part due to good timing seem to also do well in subsequent ventures. Timing such as the internet boom of the late 1990s or the Apps popularity on I-Phones in 2012 could cause greater successes for those entrepreneurs who work within those domains. However they gain certain success, it is still an experience factor that benefits their next entrepreneurial effort.

One consideration that emerges from this study is for inexperienced entrepreneurs to find an experienced and previously successful partner. During stagnant economic times investors will be hesitant to place money on a huge risk. Therefore they will always consider the experience factor of the founding team. Persistence in entrepreneurship may be today's best asset!

Source: Adapted from: Lesson #1: "Persistence is the single most important thing for success" Evan Carmichael Blog on Famous Entrepreneurs; **http://www.evancarmichael.com/Famous-Entrepreneurs/4955/Lesson-1-Persistence-is-thesingle-most-important-thing-for-success.html**; Sarah Jane Gilbert, "The Success of Persistent Entrepreneurs" *HBS Newsletter*, February, 2009 **http://hbswk.hbs.edu/item/5941.html**; and Persistence: The only way for the entrepreneurs; Future StartUp April 14, 2012, **http://futurestartup.com/2012/04/14/persistence-the-only-way-for-the-entrepreneurs/**(accessed June 6, 2012).

PASSION

Entrepreneurial passion is a fundamental emotional experience for entrepreneurs. Researcher Melissa S. Cardon has devoted much of her efforts on examining this element of the entrepreneurial mind-set.[13] She has found that entrepreneurial passion is an expression constructed by the entrepreneur to provide a coherent understanding to an emotional experience of intense arousal and energy mobilization involving an entrepreneur and his or her venture. Moreover, entrepreneurial passion is characterized by a discrete emotion that is quite intense being described as an underlying force that fuels our strongest emotions, or the intensity felt when engaging in activities that are of deep interest, or the energy that enables entrepreneurs to achieve peak performance. Thus, entrepreneurial passion is recognized as a fundamental component of the entrepreneurial mind-set.

TEAM BUILDING

The desire for independence and autonomy does not preclude the entrepreneur's desire to build a strong entrepreneurial team. Most successful entrepreneurs have highly qualified, well-motivated teams that help handle the venture's growth and development. In fact, although the entrepreneur may have the clearest vision of where the firm is (or should be) headed, the personnel often are more qualified to handle the day-to-day implementation challenges.[14]

2-3 DEALING WITH FAILURE

Entrepreneurs use failure as a learning experience; hence, they have a *tolerance for failure*. The iterative, trial-and-error nature of becoming a successful entrepreneur makes serious setbacks and disappointments an integral part of the learning process. Keep in mind that entrepreneurial ventures that are created to pursue new and unique opportunities often fail due to the uncertain environment within which they develop. Although failure can be an important source of information for learning, this learning is not automatic or instantaneous. The emotions generated by failure (i.e., grief) can interfere with the learning process. While we espouse the importance of failure and the learning that must take place once failure has occurred, seldom do we recognize the importance of grief in the failure experience. Grief is a negative emotional response to the loss of something important triggering behavioral, psychological, and physiological symptoms.

2-3a The Grief Recovery Process

The traditional process of recovering from grief involves focusing on the particular loss to construct an account that explains why the loss occurred. As a plausible account for the failure is constructed, the individual is able to begin to break the emotional bonds to the project lost. However, empirical research has found that this *loss orientation* toward **grief recovery** can sometimes exacerbate the negative emotional reaction.[15] By focusing on the failure, the entrepreneur's thoughts can shift from the events leading up to the failure to the emotions surrounding the failure event. That is, by continually focusing on the failure, negative thoughts and memories become more salient and can lead to ruminations that escalate grief.[16]

A *restoration orientation* is an alternate approach and is based on both distracting oneself from thinking about the failure event and being proactive toward secondary causes of stress. Distraction takes the individual's thoughts away from the source of his or her negative emotions, and addressing secondary causes of stress (brought on by the failure) can diminish the primary stressor—the entrepreneurial failure. However, avoiding negative emotions is unlikely to be successful in the long-run—suppressing emotions leads to physical and psychological problems and these suppressed emotions are likely to reemerge and do so at an inopportune time.[17]

Researcher Dean A. Shepherd[18] proposed a dual process model of recovering from the grief over entrepreneurial failure. Based on this dual process model, an entrepreneur recovers more quickly from a failure if he or she oscillates between a loss and a restoration orientation. This oscillation means that the entrepreneur can gain the benefits of both orientations while minimizing the costs of maintaining either for an extended period. By oscillating (switching back and forth) between these orientations, entrepreneurs can learn more from their failure experiences.

The most effective entrepreneurs are realistic enough to expect difficulties and failures. If they can deal effectively with any grief that emanates from the failure, then they will not become disappointed, discouraged, or depressed by a setback or failure. In adverse and difficult times, they will continue to look for opportunity. In this way, entrepreneurs will believe that they learn more from their early failures to form the foundation of later successes.

2-4 THE ENTREPRENEURIAL EXPERIENCE

As we discussed in Chapter 1, the prevalent view in the literature is that entrepreneurs create ventures. Although that is a true statement, its narrow framing neglects the complete process of entrepreneurship and much of the reality regarding how ventures and entrepreneurs come into being. Researchers Michael H. Morris, Donald F. Kuratko, and Minet Schindehutte point out that—similar to a painting that emerges based on the individual interacting with, feeling, and agonizing over his or her creation—a venture is not simply produced by an entrepreneur. Entrepreneurs do not preexist; they emerge as a function of the novel, idiosyncratic, and experiential nature of the venture creation process. Venture creation is a lived experience that, as it unfolds, forms the entrepreneur. In fact, the creation of a sustainable enterprise involves three parallel, interactive phenomena: emergence of the opportunity, emergence of the venture, and emergence of the entrepreneur. None are predetermined or fixed—they define and are defined by one another.[19] Thus, this perspective on the entrepreneur has gained new momentum in the entrepreneurship research of the twenty-first century.

This experiential view of the entrepreneur captures the emergent and temporal nature of entrepreneurship. It moves us past a more static "snapshot" approach and encourages consideration of a dynamic, socially situated process that involves numerous actors and events. It allows for the fact that the many activities addressed as a venture unfolds are experienced by different actors in different ways.[20] Moreover, it acknowledges that venture creation transcends rational thought processes to include emotions, impulses, and physiological responses as individuals react to a diverse, multifaceted, and imposing array of activities, events, and developments. This perspective is consistent with recent research interest in a situated view of entrepreneurial action.[21] However, we must be aware that this psychological aspect of entrepreneurship presents a dark side as well.

2-5 THE DARK SIDE OF ENTREPRENEURSHIP

LO3 Discuss the "dark side" of entrepreneurship

A great deal of literature is devoted to extolling the rewards, successes, and achievements of entrepreneurs. However, a dark side of entrepreneurship also exists, and its destructive source can be found within the energetic drive of successful entrepreneurs. In examining this dual-edged approach to the entrepreneurial personality, researcher Manfred F. R. Kets de Vries has acknowledged the existence of certain negative factors that may envelop entrepreneurs and dominate their behavior.[22] Although each of these factors has a positive aspect, it is important for entrepreneurs to understand their potential destructive side as well.

2-5a The Entrepreneur's Confrontation with Risk

LO4 Identify and describe the different types of risk entrepreneurs face as well as the major causes of stress for these individuals and the ways they can handle stress

Starting or buying a new business involves risk. The higher the rewards, the greater the risks entrepreneurs usually face. This is why entrepreneurs tend to evaluate risk very carefully.

In an attempt to describe the risk-taking activity of entrepreneurs, researchers developed a typology of entrepreneurial styles.[23] Figure 2.1 illustrates these classifications in terms of the financial risk endured when a new venture is undertaken. In this model, the financial risk is measured against the level of *profit motive* (the desire for monetary gain or return from the venture), coupled with the type of activity. Profit-seeking activity is associated with the strong desire to maximize profit, and activity seeking refers to other activities associated with entrepreneurship, such as independence or the work of the venture itself. The thrust of

FIGURE 2.1 TYPOLOGY OF ENTREPRENEURIAL STYLES

		Level of Personal Financial Risk	
		Low	**High**
	Low	Risk avoiding Activity seeking	Risk accepting Activity seeking
Level of Profit Motive			
	High	Risk avoiding Profit seeking	Risk accepting Profit seeking

Source: Thomas Monroy and Robert Folger, "A Typology of Entrepreneurial Styles: Beyond Economic Rationality," *Journal of Private Enterprise* 9, no. 2 (1993): 71.

this theory argues that entrepreneurs vary with regard to the relationship between risk and financial return. This typology highlights the need to explore within economic theory the styles or entrepreneurial motivations that deviate from the styles most characteristic of the rational person.

"If different entrepreneurial styles exist, then not every person who founds a new business enterprise does so by seeking to minimize financial risk and maximize financial return. Models of organization formation would thus have to be adjusted for differences among those who form organizations."[24] Thus, not all entrepreneurs are driven solely by monetary gain, and the level of financial risk cannot be completely explained by profit opportunity. Entrepreneurial risk is a complex issue that requires far more than a simple economic risk-versus-return explanation.

It should be noted that "people who successfully innovate and start businesses come in all shapes and sizes. But they do have a few things others do not. In the deepest sense, they are willing to accept risk for what they believe in. They have the ability to cope with a professional life riddled by ambiguity, a consistent lack of clarity. Most have a drive to put their imprint on whatever they are creating. And while unbridled ego can be a destructive thing, try to find an entrepreneur whose ego isn't wrapped up in the enterprise."[25]

Entrepreneurs face a number of different types of risk. These can be grouped into four basic areas: (1) financial risk, (2) career risk, (3) family and social risk, and (4) psychic risk.[26]

FINANCIAL RISK

In most new ventures, the individual puts a significant portion of his or her savings or other resources at stake, which creates a serious financial risk. This money or these resources will, in all likelihood, be lost if the venture fails. The entrepreneur also may be required to sign personally on company obligations that far exceed his or her personal net worth. The entrepreneur is thus exposed to personal bankruptcy. Many people are unwilling to risk their savings, house, property, and salary to start a new business.

CAREER RISK

A question frequently raised by would-be entrepreneurs is whether they will be able to find a job or go back to their old job, should their venture fail. This career risk is a major concern to managers who have a secure organizational job with a high salary and a good benefit package.

FAMILY AND SOCIAL RISK

Starting a new venture requires much of the entrepreneur's energy and time, which can in turn create a family and social risk. Consequently, his or her other commitments may suffer. Entrepreneurs who are married, and especially those with children, expose their families to the risks of an incomplete family experience and the possibility of permanent emotional scars. In addition, old friends may vanish eventually because of missed get-togethers.

PSYCHIC RISK

The psychic risk may be the greatest risk to the well-being of the entrepreneur. Money can be replaced; a new house can be built; spouses, children, and friends usually can adapt. But some entrepreneurs who have suffered financial catastrophes have been unable to bounce back, at least not immediately. The psychological impact has proven to be too severe for them.

2-5b Stress and the Entrepreneur

Some of the most common entrepreneurial goals are independence, wealth, and work satisfaction. Research studies of entrepreneurs show that those who achieve these goals often pay a high price.[27] A majority of entrepreneurs surveyed had back problems, indigestion, insomnia, or headaches. To achieve their goals, however, these entrepreneurs were willing to tolerate these effects of stress. The rewards justified the costs.

WHAT IS ENTREPRENEURIAL STRESS?

In general, stress can be viewed as a function of discrepancies between a person's expectations and ability to meet demands, as well as discrepancies between the individual's expectations and personality. If a person is unable to fulfill role demands, stress occurs. When entrepreneurs' work demands and expectations exceed their abilities to perform as venture initiators, they are likely to experience stress. One researcher has pointed out how entrepreneurial roles and operating environments can lead to stress. Initiating and managing a business requires taking significant risk. As previously mentioned, these risks may be described as financial, career, family, social, or psychic. Entrepreneurs also must engage in constant communication activities—interacting with relevant external constituencies such as customers, suppliers, regulators, lawyers, and accountants—which can be stressful.

Lacking the depth of resources, entrepreneurs must bear the cost of their mistakes while playing a multitude of roles, such as salesperson, recruiter, spokesperson, and negotiator. These simultaneous demands can lead to role overload. Owning and operating a business requires a large commitment of time and energy, as noted previously, often at the expense of family and social activities. Finally, entrepreneurs often work alone or with a small number of employees and therefore lack the support from colleagues that may be available to managers in a large corporation.[28]

In addition to the roles and environment experienced by entrepreneurs, stress can result from a basic personality structure. Referred to as *type A* behavior, this personality structure describes people who are impatient, demanding, and overstrung. These individuals gravitate toward heavy workloads and find themselves completely immersed in their business demands. Some of the distinguishing characteristics associated with type A personalities are as follows:

- *Chronic and severe sense of time urgency*. For instance, type A people become particularly frustrated in traffic jams.
- *Constant involvement in multiple projects subject to deadlines*. Type A people take delight in the feeling of being swamped with work.
- *Neglect of all aspects of life except work*. These workaholics live to work rather than work to live.
- *A tendency to take on excessive responsibility*. Often combined with the feeling that "only I am capable of taking care of this matter."
- *Explosiveness of speech and a tendency to speak faster than most people*. Type A people are prone to ranting and swearing when upset.

A widespread belief in the stress literature is that type A behavior is related to coronary heart disease and that stress is a contributor to heart disease.[29]

Thus, to better understand stress, entrepreneurs need to be aware of their particular personality as well as the roles and operating environments that differentiate their business pursuits.[30]

SOURCES OF STRESS

Researchers David P. Boyd and David E. Gumpert have identified four causes of entrepreneurial stress: (1) loneliness, (2) immersion in business, (3) people problems, and (4) the need to achieve.[31]

Loneliness Although entrepreneurs usually are surrounded by others—employees, customers, accountants, and lawyers—they often are isolated from people in whom they can confide. Long hours at work prevent them from seeking the comfort and counsel of friends and family members. Moreover, they tend not to participate in social activities unless they provide a business benefit. A sense of *loneliness* can set in because of the inner feelings of isolation.

Immersion in Business One of the ironies of entrepreneurship is that successful entrepreneurs make enough money to partake of a variety of leisure activities, but they cannot take that exotic cruise, fishing trip, or skiing vacation because their business will not allow their absence. Most entrepreneurs are married to their business—*immersion in business* can mean they work long hours and have little time for civic organizations, recreation, or further education.

People Problems Entrepreneurs must depend on and work with partners, employees, customers, bankers, and professionals. Many experience frustration, disappointment, and aggravation in their experiences with these people. Successful entrepreneurs are to some extent perfectionists and know how they want things done; often they spend a lot of time trying to get lackadaisical employees to meet their strict performance standards. Frequently, because of irreconcilable conflict, partnerships are dissolved.

Need to Achieve Achievement brings satisfaction. During the Boyd and Gumpert study, however, it became clear that a fine line exists between attempting to achieve too much and failing to achieve enough. More often than not, the entrepreneur was trying to accomplish too much. Many are never satisfied with their work, no matter how well it is done. They seem to recognize the dangers (e.g., to their health) of unbridled ambition, but they have a difficult time tempering their achievement need. They appear to believe that if they stop or slow down, some competitor is going to come from behind and destroy everything they have worked so hard to build.

DEALING WITH STRESS

It is important to point out that not all stress is bad. Certainly, if stress becomes overbearing and unrelenting in a person's life, it wears down the body's physical abilities. However, if stress can be kept within constructive bounds, it can increase a person's efficiency and improve performance.

Researchers Boyd and Gumpert made a significant contribution to defining the causes of entrepreneurial stress, but what makes their study particularly noteworthy is the presentation of stress-reduction techniques—ways entrepreneurs can improve the quality of their business and personal lives.[32] Although classic stress-reduction techniques such as meditation, biofeedback, muscle relaxation, and regular exercise help reduce stress, they suggest that another important step entrepreneurs can take is to clarify the causes of their stress. Having identified these causes, entrepreneurs then can combat excessive stress by (1) acknowledging its existence, (2) developing coping mechanisms, and (3) probing unacknowledged personal needs.

Following are six specific ways entrepreneurs can cope with stress.

Networking   One way to relieve the loneliness of running a business is to share experiences by *networking* with other business owners. The objectivity gained from hearing about the triumphs and errors of others is itself therapeutic.

Getting Away from It All   The best antidote to immersion in business, report many entrepreneurs, is a holiday. If vacation days or weeks are limited by valid business constraints, short breaks still may be possible. Such interludes allow a measure of self-renewal.

Communicating with Employees   Entrepreneurs are in close contact with employees and can readily assess the concerns of their staffs. The personal touches often unavailable in large corporations—such as company-wide outings, flexible hours, and small loans to tide workers over until payday—are possible here. In such settings, employees often are more productive than their counterparts in large organizations and may experience less stress due to the personal touches that are applied.

Finding Satisfaction Outside the Company   Countering the obsessive need to achieve can be difficult, because the entrepreneur's personality is inextricably woven into the company fabric. Entrepreneurs need to get away from the business occasionally and become more passionate about life itself; they need to gain some new perspectives.

Delegating   Implementation of coping mechanisms requires implementation time. To gain this time, the entrepreneur has to *delegate* tasks. Entrepreneurs find delegation difficult, because they think they have to be at the business all of the time and be involved in every aspect of the operation. But if time is to be used for alleviation of stress, appropriate delegatees must be found and trained.

Exercising Rigorously   Researchers Michael G. Goldsby, Donald F. Kuratko, and James W. Bishop examined the relationship between exercise and the attainment of personal and professional goals for entrepreneurs.[33] The study addressed the issue by examining the exercise regimens of 366 entrepreneurs and the relationship of exercise frequency with both the company's sales and the entrepreneur's personal goals. Specifically, the study examined the relationship that two types of exercise—running and weightlifting—had with sales volume, extrinsic rewards, and intrinsic rewards. The results indicated that running is positively related to all three outcome variables, and weightlifting is positively related to extrinsic and intrinsic rewards. This study demonstrates the value of exercise regimens on relieving the stress associated with entrepreneurs.

2-5c   The Entrepreneurial Ego

In addition to the challenges of risk and stress, the entrepreneur also may experience the negative effects of an inflated ego. In other words, certain characteristics that usually propel entrepreneurs into success also can be exhibited to their extreme. We examine four of these characteristics that may hold destructive implications for entrepreneurs.[34]

OVERBEARING NEED FOR CONTROL

Entrepreneurs are driven by a strong *need to control* both their venture and their destiny. This internal focus of control spills over into a preoccupation with controlling everything. An obsession with autonomy and control may cause entrepreneurs to work in structured situations *only* when they have created the structure on *their* terms. This, of course, has serious implications for networking in an entrepreneurial team, because entrepreneurs can visualize external control by others as a threat of subjection or infringement on their will. Thus, the same characteristic that entrepreneurs need for successful venture creation also contains a destructive side.

SENSE OF DISTRUST

To remain alert to competition, customers, and government regulations, entrepreneurs must continually scan the environment. They try to anticipate and act on developments that others might recognize too late. This distrustful state can result in their focusing on trivial things and cause them to lose sight of reality, distort reasoning and logic, and take destructive actions. Again, distrust is a dual-edged characteristic.

OVERRIDING DESIRE FOR SUCCESS

The entrepreneur's ego is involved in the desire for success. Although many of today's entrepreneurs believe they are living on the edge of existence, constantly stirring within them is a strong desire to succeed in spite of the odds. Thus, the entrepreneur rises up as a defiant person who creatively acts to deny any feelings of insignificance. The individual is driven to succeed and takes pride in demonstrating that success. Therein lie the seeds of possible destructiveness. If the entrepreneur seeks to demonstrate achievement through the erection of a monument—such as a huge office building, an imposing factory, or a plush office—the danger exists that the individual will become more important than the venture itself. A loss of perspective like this can, of course, be the destructive side of the desire to succeed.

THE ENTREPRENEURIAL PROCESS

Entrepreneurial Fear 101

The fear an entrepreneur experiences has its own taste, its own smell, and its own gut wrenching pain—and it does not go away as long as the person remains an entrepreneur. It becomes an education: Entrepreneurial Fear 101. Although the course is very exclusive, admission is automatic; permission is neither needed nor sought, and tenure is indefinite. The fear that entrepreneurs experience cannot be anticipated, cannot be escaped, and cannot be prepared for. Because most entrepreneurs do not admit that they have experienced this entrepreneurial fear, it remains a deep, dark secret. Because it is not talked about, most entrepreneurs believe that they are the only ones who have ever experienced it.

According to Wilson Harrell, an entrepreneur from Jacksonville, Florida, entrepreneurial fear is much different from simple fear. Fear is usually accidental, unexpected, and short lived—such as the sudden rush of adrenaline experienced when you almost get hit by a bus, he explains. Entrepreneurial fear, on the other hand, is self-inflicted. It is a private world in which no sleep occurs, where nightmares filled with monsters constantly try to destroy every morsel of the entrepreneur's being.

What causes this fear? It is not the money—any entrepreneur will explain that money is simply a bonus of the accomplishment, and losing money is one of the risks taken. Fear of failure has a lot to do with it. Entrepreneurs do not want to become just another businessperson and pass into oblivion without leaving their mark. What induces this complex fear has yet to be determined.

For Harrell, the fear came when he started his own food brokerage business to sell products on military bases in Europe. Harrell was appointed a representative of Kraft Food Company and did so well increasing its sales that he sold himself out of a job. Because he had made his job look so easy, it was suggested to Kraft's management team that its own salespeople could do the work better and cheaper. So what did Harrell do? Because losing the Kraft account would put him out of business, he placed everything on the line and proposed that if Kraft kept brokering through his company and not take over the brokering in Germany, Harrell would help it take over the food industry everywhere. While Harrell experienced 30 days of immeasurable terror, Kraft made the decision to trust Harrell and to continue brokering through his company.

What is the secret to entrepreneurship, given such fear? Reward. No matter what pain is experienced because of the fear, the elation of success surmounts it. That high, along with fear, is an emotion reserved for entrepreneurs and becomes food for the spirit. It is like a roller-coaster ride: In the beginning, imagine pulling yourself up the incline very slowly, making any tough decisions with a growing sense of excitement and foreboding. Then, when you hit the top, for a brief moment it is frightening, and the anticipation accelerates before you lose all feelings of control. As you go screaming into the unknown, fear takes over. At first, all you feel is fear; then, suddenly, the ride is over and the fear is gone, but the exhilaration remains. What is next for the entrepreneur? He or she buys another ticket.

So, what is the key ingredient for entrepreneurial success? According to Wilson Harrell, it is the ability to handle fear. He believes that the lonely entrepreneur, living with his or her personal fear, breathes life and excitement into an otherwise dull and mundane world.

Source: Adapted from Wilson Harrell, "Entrepreneurial Terror," *Inc.* (February 1987): 74–76.

UNREALISTIC OPTIMISM

The ceaseless optimism that emanates from entrepreneurs (even through the bleak times) is a key factor in the drive toward success. Entrepreneurs maintain a high enthusiasm level that becomes an *external optimism*—which allows others to believe in them during rough periods. However, when taken to its extreme, this optimistic attitude can lead to a fantasy approach to the business. A self-deceptive state may arise in which entrepreneurs ignore trends, facts, and reports and delude themselves into thinking everything will turn out fine. This type of behavior can lead to an inability to handle the reality of the business world.

These examples do not imply that *all* entrepreneurs fall prey to these scenarios, nor that each of the characteristics presented always gives way to the "destructive" side. Nevertheless, all potential entrepreneurs need to know that the dark side of entrepreneurship exists.

2-6 ENTREPRENEURIAL ETHICS

LO6 Study ethics in a conceptual framework for a dynamic environment

Ethical issues in business are of great importance today, and with good reason. The prevalence of scandals, fraud, and various forms of executive misconduct in corporations has spurred the watchful eye of the public.[35]

Ethics is not a new topic, however. It has figured prominently in philosophical thought since the time of Socrates, Plato, and Aristotle. Derived from the Greek word *ethos*, meaning custom or mode of conduct, ethics has challenged philosophers for centuries to determine what exactly represents right or wrong conduct. For example, business executive Vernon R. Loucks, Jr., notes that "it was about 560 B.C. . . . when the Greek thinker Chilon registered the opinion that a merchant does better to take a loss than to make a dishonest profit. His reasoning was that a loss may be painful for a while, but dishonesty hurts forever—and it's still timely."[36]

Today's entrepreneurs are faced with many ethical decisions, especially during the early stages of their new ventures. And, as Sir Adrian Cadbury observed, "There is no simple universal formula for solving ethical problems. We have to choose from our own codes of conduct whichever rules are appropriate to the case in hand; the outcome of these choices makes us who we are."[37]

In the following sections, we examine some of the ethical dilemmas confronting entrepreneurs. It is our hope that aspiring entrepreneurs will realize the powerful impact that integrity and ethical conduct have on creating a successful venture.

2-7 ETHICAL DILEMMAS

LO5 Discuss the ethical dilemmas confronting entrepreneurs

In the broadest sense, ethics provides the basic rules or parameters for conducting any activity in an "acceptable" manner. More specifically, ethics represents a set of principles prescribing a behavioral code that explains what is good and right or bad and wrong; ethics may, in addition, outline moral duty and obligations.[38] The problem with most definitions of the term is not the description itself but its implications for implementation. The definition is a static description implying that society agrees on certain universal principles. Because society operates in a dynamic and ever-changing environment, however, such a consensus does not exist.[39] In fact, continual conflict over the ethical nature of decisions is quite prevalent.

This conflict arises for a number of reasons. First, business enterprises are confronted by many interests, both inside and outside the organization—for example, stockholders, customers, managers, the community, the government, employees, private interest groups, unions, peers, and so on. Second, society is undergoing dramatic change. Values, mores, and societal norms have gone through a drastic evolution in the past few decades. A definition of ethics in such a rapidly changing environment must be based more on a process than on a static code. Figure 2.2 illustrates a conceptual framework for viewing this process. As one ethicist states, "Deciding what is good or right or bad and wrong in such a dynamic environment is necessarily 'situational.' Therefore, instead of relying on a set of fixed ethical principles, we must now develop an ethical process."[40]

The quadrants depicted in Figure 2.2 demonstrate the age-old dilemma between law and ethics. Moving from the ideal ethical and legal position (Quadrant I) to an unethical and

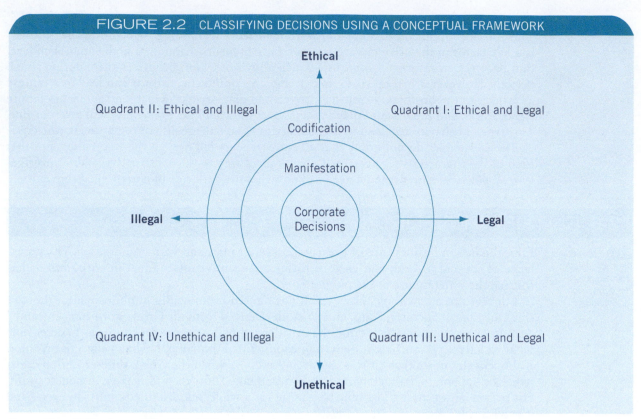

FIGURE 2.2 CLASSIFYING DECISIONS USING A CONCEPTUAL FRAMEWORK

Ethical

Quadrant II: Ethical and Illegal   Quadrant I: Ethical and Legal

Codification

Manifestation

Illegal   Corporate Decisions   Legal

Quadrant IV: Unethical and Illegal   Quadrant III: Unethical and Legal

Unethical

Source: Verne E. Henderson, "The Ethical Side of Enterprise," *Sloan Management Review* (Spring 1982): 42.

illegal position (Quadrant IV), one can see the continuum of activities within an ethical process. Yet legality provides societal standards but not definitive answers to ethical questions.

For the entrepreneur, the legal versus ethical dilemma is a vital one. Just how far can an entrepreneur go to establish his or her venture? Survival of the venture is a strong motivation for entrepreneurs, and, although the law provides the boundaries for what is illegal (even though the laws are subject to constant interpretation), it does not supply answers for ethical considerations.

2-7a Ethical Rationalizations

One researcher suggests that legal behavior represents one of four **rationalizations** managers use to justify questionable conduct. The four rationalizations are believing (1) that the activity is not "really" illegal or immoral; (2) that it is in the individual's or the corporation's best interest; (3) that it will never be found out; and (4) that, because it helps the company, the company will condone it.[41]

These rationalizations appear realistic, given the behavior of many business enterprises today. However, the legal aspect can be the most dubious. This is because the business world (and society) relies heavily on the law to qualify the actions of various situations. The law interprets the situations within the prescribed framework. Unfortunately, this framework does not always include ethical or moral behavior. This is left up to the individual, which is the precise reason for the dilemma.

In any examination of the realm of managerial rationalizations, the idea of morally questionable acts becomes a major concern for understanding ethical conduct. One research study developed a typology of morally questionable acts (Table 2.2 summarizes the distinctions made in this typology).[42] Morally questionable acts are either "against the firm" or "on behalf of the firm." In addition, the managerial role differs for various acts. Nonrole acts are those the person takes outside of his or her role as manager, yet they go against the firm; examples include expense account cheating and embezzlement. **Role failure** acts also go against the firm, but they involve a person failing to perform his or her managerial

TABLE 2.2   TYPES OF MORALLY QUESTIONABLE ACTS

Type	Direct Effect	Examples
Nonrole	Against the firm	Expense account cheating Embezzlement Stealing supplies
Role failure	Against the firm	Superficial performance appraisal Not confronting expense account cheating Palming off a poor performer with inflated praise
Role distortion	For the firm	Bribery Price fixing Manipulating suppliers
Role assertion	For the firm	Investing in unethically governed countries Using nuclear technology for energy generation Not withdrawing product line in face of initial allegations of inadequate safety

Source: James A. Waters and Frederick Bird, "Attending to Ethics in Management," *Journal of Business Ethics* 5 (1989): 494.

role, including superficial performance appraisals (not totally honest) and not confronting someone who is cheating on expense accounts. Role distortion acts and role assertion acts are rationalized as being "for the firm." These acts involve managers/entrepreneurs who rationalize that the long-run interests of the firm are foremost. Examples include bribery, price fixing, manipulating suppliers, and failing to withdraw a potentially dangerous product from the market. Role distortion is the behavior of individuals who think they are acting in the best interests of the firm, so their roles are "distorted." Role assertion is the behavior of individuals who assert their roles beyond what they should be, thinking (falsely) that they are helping the firm.

All four of the roles involved in the morally questionable acts—whether "for" or "against" the firm—illustrate the types of rationalizations that can occur. In addition, this typology presents an interesting insight into the distinctions involved with managerial rationalization.

2-7b The Matter of Morality

Ethical conduct may reach beyond the limits of the law.[43] As one group of noted legal writers has pointed out, morals and law are not synonymous but may be viewed as two circles partially superimposed on each other (see Figure 2.3). The area covered by both the moral standards circle and the legal requirements circle represents the body of ideas that is both moral and legal. Yet the largest expanse of area is outside this overlapping portion, indicating the vast difference that sometimes exists between morality (ethics) and law.[44]

Ethics researcher LaRue T. Hosmer has reached three conclusions regarding the relationship between legal requirements and moral judgment. First, as noted earlier, the requirements of law may overlap at times but do not duplicate the moral standards of society. Some laws have no moral content whatsoever (e.g., driving on the right side of the road), some laws are morally unjust (e.g., racial segregation laws, which were in effect in the United States into the 1960s and 1970s), and some moral standards have no legal basis (e.g., telling a lie). Second, legal requirements tend to be negative (forbidding acts), whereas morality tends to be positive (encouraging acts). Third, legal requirements usually lag behind the acceptable moral standards of society.[45]

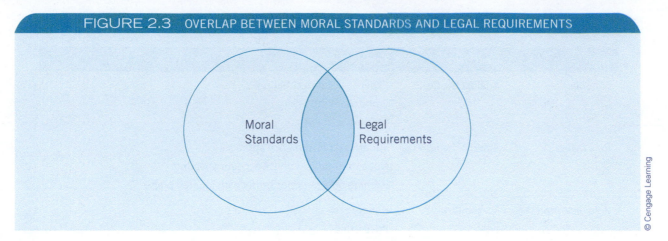

FIGURE 2.3 OVERLAP BETWEEN MORAL STANDARDS AND LEGAL REQUIREMENTS

Moral Standards

Legal Requirements

© Cengage Learning

In addition, even if the argument were made that laws are supposed to be the collective moral judgment of society, inherent problems arise when people believe that laws represent morality. Whether it is because of a lack of information on issues, misrepresentation of values or laws, or an imprecise judicial system, the legal environment has difficulty encompassing all ethical and moral expectations. Thus, the issue of law and ethics will continue to be a dilemma for entrepreneurs.

But it is clear that unethical behavior does take place in business. Why? A few possible explanations include (1) greed, (2) distinctions between activities at work and activities at home, (3) a lack of a foundation in ethics, (4) survival (bottom-line thinking), and (5) a reliance on other social institutions to convey and reinforce ethics. Whatever the reasons, ethical decision-making is a challenge that confronts every entrepreneur.[46]

2-7c Complexity of Decisions

Entrepreneurs are challenged by the need to make business decisions each day. Many of these decisions are complex and raise ethical considerations. The business decisions of entrepreneurs are highly complex for five reasons. First, ethical decisions have extended consequences. They often have a ripple effect in that the consequences are felt by others outside the venture. For example, the decision to use inexpensive but unsafe products in operations will affect both workers and consumers of the final good.

Second, business decisions that involve ethical questions have multiple alternatives—the choices are not always "do" or "don't do." Many decisions have a wide range of alternatives that may involve several less important decisions. With regard to the first example about the use of unsafe products, the entrepreneur may have the alternative of using still less expensive but nevertheless safe products.

Third, ethical business decisions often have mixed outcomes. Social benefits as well as costs are involved with every major business decision, as are financial revenues and expenses.

Fourth, most business decisions have uncertain ethical consequences. It is never absolutely certain what actual consequence(s) a decision will have, even when it appears logical; in other words, a decision is never without ethical risk.

Finally, most ethical business decisions have personal implications. It is difficult for an entrepreneur to divorce him- or herself from a decision and its potential outcome. Venture success, financial opportunity, and new-product development are all areas that may be affected by decisions with ethical consequences. The entrepreneur often will find it impossible to make a purely impersonal decision.[47]

These five statements about business decisions need to be considered when an entrepreneur is developing a new venture. They indicate the need to grasp as much information as possible about each major decision. One ethicist, who believes that this implies understanding the characteristic features of a venture's activities (which in turn allows for a stronger sensitivity to the outcomes), has noted that "someone in business needs to know its general tendencies—the special tracks it leaves—to anticipate points of crisis, and of special concern to us, to increase the possibility of intelligent moral actions."[48]

2-7d Online Ethical Dilemmas in E-Commerce

It is clear that e-commerce and online purchases have grown in popularity possibly redefining the social norms inherent in commerce. With the slow demise of face-to-face interactions, the question of how entrepreneurs can establish trust becomes a priority. Contributing to consumers' concerns is the fact that unethical behavior is more likely to take place through online transactions than through offline ones due to the ease in which businesses can deceive consumers online. So, we see consumers now relying on the opinions of fellow consumers posted through online consumer reviews to inform their own purchasing decisions.[49] These online consumer reviews are posted to *reputation management systems* which now play an integral role in e-commerce as they are commonly used on popular sites such as Amazon and Yelp.[50] However, a new ethical concern has arisen in regard to the use and sometimes abuse of these new systems.

Even though researchers have documented the importance of consumer trust in e-commerce,[51] the pressures faced by businesses to protect their online reputation has resulted in some businesses resorting to tactics that betray that trust, specifically posting online consumer reviews in order to strategically manipulate the reputation management systems.[52] One study revealed how young professionals have been conditioned by the anonymity of web-based interactions and the degree to which they rationalize the misrepresentation of information by business professionals for the purpose of manipulating consumers' purchasing decisions in order to drive sales.[53]

These questions concerning the ethical challenges that now confront entrepreneurs in the social media age strike at the potential venture success which is at stake in the hands of the social media reputation management sites. How should entrepreneurs proceed? Rather than using the *rationalizations* already discussed to justify questionable conduct, it would be far greater in the long run to exhibit strong ethical responsibility in their actions. In the next section we examine how to establish an ethical strategy.

2-8 ESTABLISHING A STRATEGY FOR AN ETHICAL VENTURE

Because the free enterprise system in which the entrepreneur flourishes is fraught with myriad conflicts, entrepreneurs need to commit to an established strategy for an ethical venture.

2-8a Ethical Codes of Conduct

A **code of conduct** is a statement of ethical practices or guidelines to which an enterprise adheres. Many such codes exist—some related to industry at large and others related directly to corporate conduct. These codes cover a multitude of subjects, ranging from misuse of corporate assets, conflict of interest, and use of inside information to equal employment practices, falsification of books or records, and antitrust violations. Based on the results of recent research, two important conclusions can be reached. First, codes of conduct are becoming more prevalent in industry. Management is not just giving lip service to ethics and moral behavior; it is putting its ideas into writing and distributing these guidelines for everyone in the organization to read and follow. Second, in contrast to earlier codes, the more recent ones are proving to be more meaningful in terms of external legal and social development, more comprehensive in terms of their coverage, and easier to implement in terms of the administrative procedures used to enforce them.[54]

Of course, the most important question remains to be answered: Will management really adhere to a high moral code? Many managers would respond to this question by answering "yes." Why? The main reason is that it is good business. One top executive put the idea this way: "Singly or in combination, unethical practices have a corrosive effect on free markets and free trade, which are fundamental to the survival of the free enterprise system. They subvert the laws of supply and demand, and they short-circuit competition based on classical ideas of product quality, service, and price. Free markets become replaced by contrived markets. The need for constant improvement in products or services is thus removed."[55]

A second, related reason is that by improving the moral climate of the enterprise, the corporation can eventually win back the public's confidence. This would mark a turnaround, because many people today question the moral and ethical integrity of companies and believe that businesspeople try to get away with everything they can. Only time will tell whether codes of conduct will improve business practices. Current trends indicate, however, that the business community is working hard to achieve this objective.[56]

Mark Twain once said, "Always do the right thing. This will surprise some people and astonish the rest." It will also motivate them to do the right thing. Indeed, without a good example from the top, ethical problems (and all the costs that go with them) are probably inevitable within your organization.

2-8b Ethical Responsibility

LO7 Present strategies for establishing ethical responsibility and leadership

Establishing a strategy for ethical responsibility is not an easy task for entrepreneurs. No single, ideal approach to organizational ethics exists. Entrepreneurs need to analyze the ethical consciousness of their organization, the process and structure devised to enhance ethical activity, and, finally, their own commitment to institutionalize ethical objectives within the company.[57] Keeping these points in mind, entrepreneurs eventually can begin to establish a strategy for ethical responsibility. This strategy should encompass three major elements: ethical consciousness, ethical process and structure, and institutionalization:

- *Ethical Consciousness* The development of ethical consciousness is the responsibility of the entrepreneur, because his or her vision created the venture. The key figure to set the tone for ethical decision-making and behavior is the entrepreneur. An open exchange of issues and processes within the venture, established codes of ethics for the company, and the setting of examples by the entrepreneur are all illustrations of how this is done. For example, when the CEO of a large corporation discovered bookkeeping discrepancies in

THE ENTREPRENEURIAL PROCESS

Shaping an Ethical Strategy

The development of an organizational climate for responsible and ethically sound behavior requires continuing effort and investment of time and resources. A code of conduct, ethics officers, training programs, and annual ethics audits do not necessarily add up to a responsible, ethical organization. A formal ethics program can serve as a catalyst and a support system, but organizational integrity depends on the integration of the company's values into its driving systems.

Following are a few key elements that entrepreneurs should keep in mind when developing an ethical strategy.

- *The entrepreneur's guiding values and commitments must make sense and be clearly communicated.* They should reflect important organizational obligations and widely shared aspirations that appeal to the organization's members. Employees at all levels must take them seriously, feel comfortable discussing them, and have a concrete understanding of their practical importance.

- *Entrepreneurs must be personally committed, credible, and willing to take action on the values they espouse.* They are not mere mouthpieces.

- They must be willing to scrutinize their own decisions. Consistency on the part of leadership is key. Entrepreneurs must assume responsibility for making tough calls when ethical obligations conflict.

- *The espoused values must be integrated into the normal channels of the organization's critical activities*: planning innovation, resource allocation, information communication, and personnel promotion and advancement.

- *The venture's systems and structures must support and reinforce its values.* Information systems, for example, must be designed to provide timely and accurate information. Reporting relationships must be structured to build in checks and balances to promote objective judgment.

- *Employees throughout the company must have the decision-making skills, knowledge, and competencies needed to make ethically sound decisions every day.* Ethical thinking and awareness must be part of every employee's skills.

Source: Adapted from Lynn Sharp Paine, "Managing for Organizational Integrity," *Harvard Business Review* (March/April 1994): 106–17.

one of the departments, he directed the 20 implicated employees to make retribution by donating \$8,500 to charity.[58] This action commanded positive ethical action and set the tone for ethical expectations.

- *Ethical Process and Structure* Ethical process and structure refer to the procedures, position statements (codes), and announced ethical goals designed to avoid ambiguity. Having all key personnel read the venture's specific ethical goals and sign affidavits affirming their willingness to follow those policies is a good practice for ventures.

- *Institutionalization* Institutionalization is a deliberate step to incorporate the entrepreneur's ethical objectives with the economic objectives of the venture. At times, an entrepreneur may have to modify policies or operations that become too intense and infringe on the ethics of the situation. This is where the entrepreneur's commitment to ethics and values is tested. Constant review of procedures and feedback in operations are vital to institutionalizing ethical responsibility.[59]

2-9 ETHICAL CONSIDERATIONS OF CORPORATE ENTREPRENEURS

Corporate entrepreneurs—described in the academic literature as those managers or employees who do not follow the status quo of their coworkers—are depicted as visionaries who dream of taking the company in new directions. As a result, in overcoming internal obstacles to reaching their professional goals, they often walk a fine line between clever resourcefulness and outright rule-breaking. Researchers Donald F. Kuratko and Michael G. Goldsby developed a framework as a guideline for managers and organizations seeking to impede unethical behaviors in the pursuit of entrepreneurial activity (see Figure 2.4).[60]

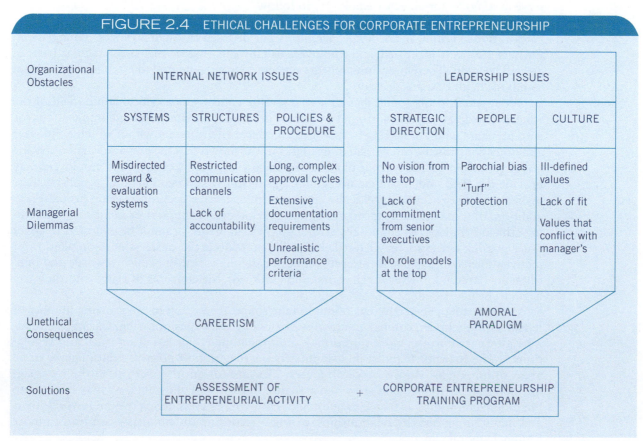

FIGURE 2.4   ETHICAL CHALLENGES FOR CORPORATE ENTREPRENEURSHIP

	INTERNAL NETWORK ISSUES			LEADERSHIP ISSUES		
Organizational Obstacles	SYSTEMS	STRUCTURES	POLICIES & PROCEDURE	STRATEGIC DIRECTION	PEOPLE	CULTURE
Managerial Dilemmas	Misdirected reward & evaluation systems	Restricted communication channels Lack of accountability	Long, complex approval cycles Extensive documentation requirements Unrealistic performance criteria	No vision from the top Lack of commitment from senior executives No role models at the top	Parochial bias "Turf" protection	Ill-defined values Lack of fit Values that conflict with manager's
Unethical Consequences		CAREERISM			AMORAL PARADIGM	
Solutions		ASSESSMENT OF ENTREPRENEURIAL ACTIVITY		+	CORPORATE ENTREPRENEURSHIP TRAINING PROGRAM	

Source: Donald F. Kuratko and Michael G. Goldsby, "Corporate Entrepreneurs or Rogue Middle Managers? A Framework for Ethical Corporate Entrepreneurship," *Journal of Business Ethics* 55 (2004): 18.

They examined the barriers that middle managers face in trying to be entrepreneurial in less supportive environments, the unethical consequences that can result, and a suggested assessment and training program to avert such dilemmas.

The barriers include organizational obstacles in two major categories: internal network issues and leadership issues. The specific barriers to innovative actions include systems, structures, policies and procedures, culture, strategic direction, and people. Based on these barriers and the managerial dilemmas that can be caused, the researchers advise companies that embrace corporate entrepreneurship to: (1) establish the needed flexibility, innovation, and support of employee initiative and risk taking; (2) remove the barriers that the entrepreneurial middle manager may face to more closely align personal and organizational initiatives and reduce the need to behave unethically; and (3) include an ethical component to corporate training that will provide guidelines for instituting compliance and values components into state-of-the-art corporate entrepreneurship programs. However, even if corporate entrepreneurship is supported, some managers still may pose ethical risks to the company. Rarely will everyone in an organization do the right thing. For this reason, it would be wise to include an ethical component in corporate training programs to ensure that everyone is aware of the expectations and vision of senior management. A more complete training program and approach to corporate entrepreneurship should make for a better future—for both the organization and its members—and prevent future ethical crises.

2-10 ETHICAL LEADERSHIP BY ENTREPRENEURS

Although ethics present complex challenges for entrepreneurs, the value system of an owner/entrepreneur is the key to establishing an ethical organization.[61] An owner has the unique opportunity to display honesty, integrity, and ethics in all key decisions. The owner's actions serve as a model for all other employees to follow.

In smaller ventures, the ethical influence of the owner is more powerful than in larger corporations because his or her leadership is not diffused through layers of management. Owners are easily identified, and employees usually can observe them on a regular basis in a small business. Therefore, entrepreneurs possess a strong potential to establish high ethical standards in all business decisions.

One research study found that an owner's value system was a critical component of the ethical considerations that surround a business decision. This study also had implications for entrepreneurs who are seeking to establish an ethical environment within which employees and other constituents can work. For example, it was shown that the preparation of a specific policy statement on ethics (code of ethics) by the owner and his or her other employees may provide the clear understanding needed for administrative decision-making. Small-business owners also may need to specifically address administrative decision-making processes. In addition, they may need to spend some time developing benchmarks or guidelines concerning ethical behaviors of employees. Although these guidelines cannot be expected to cover every possible scenario, they nevertheless will help address the business development/profit motive dimension. Finally, if entrepreneurs can carefully establish explicit rewards and punishments based upon ethical behaviors (and enforced), the concerns of crime and theft can begin to be addressed.[62]

An interesting perspective has begun to take shape. As a result of the growing number of female entrepreneurs, companies are now examining the ethics of caring. Caring is a feminine alternative to the more traditional and masculine ethics based on rules and regulations.[63] The focus of feminist philosophies is the fostering of positive relationships in all areas of life, or, as Milton Mayeroff states, "To care for another person, in the most significant sense, is to help him grow and actualize himself."[64] Following laws may not lead to building relationships as strong as one could. However, by considering the interests of others and maintaining healthy relationships, caring—according to feminists—can lead to more genuinely moral climates.

It is clear that entrepreneurial ethics will always be extremely difficult to define, codify, and implement because of the personal values and morality issues it surfaces. Yet the importance of ethics when initiating new enterprises must be stressed. As one writer has noted, "The singular importance of enterprises to our daily lives and our collective future demands our careful attention and finest efforts."[65]

Overall, entrepreneurs must realize that their personal integrity and ethical example will be the key to their employees' ethical performance. Their values can permeate and characterize the organization. This unique advantage creates a position of ethical leadership for entrepreneurs.[66]

2-11 ENTREPRENEURIAL MOTIVATION

LO8 Examine entrepreneurial motivation

Examining why people start businesses and how they differ from those who do not (or from those who start unsuccessful businesses) may help explain how the motivation that entrepreneurs exhibit during start-up is linked to the sustaining behavior exhibited later. Lanny Herron and Harry J. Sapienza have stated, "Because motivation plays an important part in the creation of new organizations, theories of organization creation that fail to address this notion are incomplete."[67] One researcher—in his review of achievement motivation and the entrepreneur—said, "It remains worthwhile to carefully study the role of the individual, including his or her psychological profile. Individuals are, after all, the energizers of the entrepreneurial process."[68]

Thus, although research on the psychological characteristics of entrepreneurs has not provided an agreed-on "profile" of an entrepreneur, it is still important to recognize the contribution of psychological factors to the entrepreneurial process.[69] In fact, the quest for new-venture creation as well as the willingness to *sustain* that venture is directly related to an *entrepreneur's motivation.*[70]

One research study examined the importance of satisfaction to an entrepreneur's willingness to remain with the venture. Particular goals, attitudes, and backgrounds were all important determinants of an entrepreneur's eventual satisfaction.[71] In that vein, another research approach examined the motivational process an entrepreneur experiences, concluding that the decision to behave entrepreneurially is the result of the interaction of several factors.[72] One set of factors includes the individual's personal characteristics, the individual's personal environment, the relevant business environment, the individual's personal goal set, and the existence of a viable business idea.[73] In addition, the individual compares his or her perception of the probable outcomes with the personal expectations he or she has in mind. Next, an individual looks at the relationship between the entrepreneurial behavior he or she would implement and the expected outcomes.

According to this approach, the entrepreneur's expectations finally are compared with the actual or perceived firm outcomes. Future entrepreneurial behavior is based on the results of all of these comparisons. When outcomes meet or exceed expectations, the entrepreneurial behavior is positively reinforced, and the individual is motivated to continue to behave entrepreneurially—either within the current venture or possibly through the initiation of additional ventures, depending on the existing entrepreneurial goal. When outcomes fail to meet expectations, the entrepreneur's motivation will be lower and will have a corresponding impact on the decision to continue to act entrepreneurially. These perceptions also affect succeeding strategies, strategy implementation, and management of the firm.[74]

Another line of new research examined the specific motivations as to how and why entrepreneurs persist with a venture, defining entrepreneurial persistence as an entrepreneur's choice to continue with an entrepreneurial opportunity regardless of counterinfluences or other enticing alternatives.[75] Researchers Daniel V. Holland and Dean A. Shepherd found that the decision to persist was influenced by personal characteristics as well as by feedback from the environment relative to certain thresholds of adversity. Their findings demonstrate that the decision policies of entrepreneurs regarding persistence differed based on their level of experience with adversity and individual values held.

SUMMARY

In attempting to explain the entrepreneurial mind-set within individuals, this chapter presented the concepts of entrepreneurial cognition and metacognition in examining the ways in which entrepreneurs view opportunities and make decisions. Several studies have been conducted to determine the personal qualities and traits of successful entrepreneurs. Some of these characteristics were examined in the chapter: determination and perseverance; drive to achieve; opportunity orientation; internal locus of control; tolerance for ambiguity; calculated risk taking; high energy level; creativity and innovativeness; vision; and passion.

An examination of failure and the grief recovery process was then introduced and the idea of the entrepreneurial experience was discussed to explore the links between entrepreneur, venture, and process. The next part of the chapter focused on the dark side of entrepreneurship, including the confrontation with risk, the problems of stress, and the particular traits that may permeate the entrepreneurial ego. Entrepreneurs have unique opportunities to exert personal influence on their ventures, thereby creating unique challenges of ethical leadership for all entrepreneurs.

The chapter then examined ethics as a set of principles prescribing a behavioral code that explains right and wrong; ethics also may outline moral duty and obligations. Because it is so difficult to define the term *ethics*, it is helpful to look at ethics more as a process than as a static code. Entrepreneurs face many ethical decisions, especially during the early stages of their new ventures.

When entrepreneurs make decisions that border on the unethical, they commonly rationalize their choices. These rationalizations may be based on morally questionable acts committed "against the firm" or "on behalf of the firm" by the managers involved. Within this framework are four distinct types of managerial roles: nonrole, role failure, role distortion, and role assertion. To establish ethical strategies, some entrepreneurs create codes of conduct. A code of conduct is a statement of ethical practices or guidelines to which an enterprise adheres. Codes are becoming more prevalent in organizations today, and they are proving to be more meaningful in their implementation. Despite the ever-present lack of clarity and direction in ethics, however, ethics will continue to be a major issue for entrepreneurs during the new century.

The chapter concluded with a discussion of entrepreneurial motivation. A research framework that recognizes the contribution of psychological factors to the process of entrepreneurship and demonstrates the importance of entrepreneurs' perceived expectations and actual outcomes in the motivation to start and sustain a venture was considered. Finally, some of the latest research on "entrepreneurial persistence" was introduced in order to acknowledge the growing interest in this concept.

KEY TERMS

career risk	entrepreneurial motivation	rationalizations
code of conduct	entrepreneurial persistence	risk
cognition	ethics	role assertion
cognitive adaptability	failure	role distortion
dark side of entrepreneurship	family and social risk	role failure
entrepreneurial behavior	financial risk	social cognition theory
entrepreneurial cognition	grief recovery	stress
entrepreneurial experience	metacognitive model	
entrepreneurial mind-set	psychic risk	

REVIEW AND DISCUSSION QUESTIONS

1. What is "entrepreneurial cognition" and how does it impact the mind-set of entrepreneurs? How does "metacognition" come into play here?

2. Entrepreneurs have a tolerance for ambiguity, are calculated risk takers, and exude passion. What do these characteristics mean for any potential entrepreneur?

3. Is it true that most successful entrepreneurs have failed at some point in their business careers? Explain.

4. How should failure be dealt with by entrepreneurs? How does "grief" play a role in this process?

5. Entrepreneurship has a "dark side." What is meant by this statement? Be complete in your answer.

6. What are the four specific areas of risk that entrepreneurs face? Describe each.

7. What are four causes of stress among entrepreneurs? How can an entrepreneur deal with each of them?

8. Describe factors associated with the entrepreneurial ego.

9. *Ethics must be based more on a process than on a static code.* What does this statement mean? Do you agree? Why or why not?

10. A small pharmaceutical firm has just received permission from the Food and Drug Administration (FDA) to market its new anticholesterol drug. Although the product has been tested for five years, management believes that serious side effects may still result from its use, and a warning to this effect is being printed on the label. If the company markets this FDA-approved drug, how would you describe its actions from an ethical and legal standpoint? Use Figure 2.2 to help you.

11. Explain the four distinct roles that managers may take in rationalizing morally questionable acts "against the firm" or "on behalf of the firm." Be complete in your answer.

12. Why do complex decisions often raise ethical considerations for the entrepreneur?

13. Cal Whiting believes that entrepreneurs need to address the importance of ethics in their organizations. However, he is unsure of where to begin in his own company because the entire area is unclear to him. What would you suggest? Where can he begin? What should he do? Be as practical as you can in your suggestions.

14. What is the concept of entrepreneurial motivation and how has it been depicted?

15. Explain the concept of entrepreneurial persistence and how it is being examined.

NOTES

1. Rob Asghar, "Study: Millennials Are the True Entrepreneur Generation," *Forbes*, November 11, 2014. Accessed online, January 2, 2015. http://www.forbes.com/sites/robasghar/2014/11/11/study-millennials-are-the-true-entrepreneur-generation/; Brian Dumaine and Elaine Pofeldt, "The Best Bolleges for Aspiring Entrepreneurs," *Fortune Small Business* (September, 2007): 61–75.

2. See, for example, William D. Bygrave and Charles W. Hofer, "Theorizing about Entrepreneurship," *Entrepreneurship Theory and Practice* 16, no. 2 (1991): 12–22; Ivan Bull and Gary E. Willard, "Towards a Theory of Entrepreneurship," *Journal of Business Venturing* 8, no. 3 (1993): 183–196; William B. Gartner, "Is There an Elephant in Entrepreneurship? Blind Assumptions in Theory Development," *Entrepreneurship Theory and Practice* 25, no. 4 (2001): 27–39; and Jeffery S. McMullen and Dean A. Shepherd, "Entrepreneurial Action and the Role of Uncertainty in the Theory of the Entrepreneur," *Academy of Management Review* 31, no. 1 (2006): 132–52.

3. See Robert A. Baron, "Cognitive Mechanisms in Entrepreneurship: Why and When Entrepreneurs Think Differently than Other People," *Journal of Business Venturing* 13, no. 4 (1998): 275–94; and Norris F. Krueger, "What Lies Beneath: The Experiential Essence of Entrepreneurial Thinking," *Entrepreneurship Theory and Practice* 31, no. 1 (2007): 123–38.

4. Ronald K. Mitchell, Lowell Busenitz, Theresa Lant, Patricia P. McDougall, Eric A. Morse, and J. Brock Smith, "Toward a Theory of Entrepreneurial Cognition: Rethinking the People Side of Entrepreneurship Research," *Entrepreneurship Theory and Practice* 27, no. 2 (2002): 93–105; see also R. W. Hafer and Garett Jones, "Are Entrepreneurship and Cognitive Skills Related? Some International Evidence," *Small Business Economics* 44, no. 2 (2015): 283–98.

5. J. Michael Haynie, Dean A. Shepherd, Elaine Mosakowski, and P. Christopher Earley, "A Situated Metacognitive Model of the Entrepreneurial Mindset," *Journal of Business Venturing* 25, no. 2 (2010): 217–29; and J. Michael Haynie, Dean A. Shepherd, and Holger

Patzelt, "Cognitive Adaptability and an Entrepreneurial Task: The Role of Metacognitive Ability and Feedback," *Entrepreneurship Theory and Practice* 36, no. 2 (2012): 237–65.

6. Denis A. Grégoire, Andrew C. Corbett, and Jeffery S. McMullen, "The Cognitive Perspective in Entrepreneurship: An Agenda for Future Research," *Journal of Management Studies*, 48, no. 6 (2011):1443–77; Chia-Huei Wu, Sharon K. Parker, and Jeroen P. J. de Jong, "Need for Cognition as an Antecedent of Individual Innovation Behavior," *Journal of Management* 40, No. 6 (2014): 1511–34; and Robert P. Garrett, Jr. and Daniel V. Holland, "Environmental Effects on the Cognitions of Corporate and Independent Entrepreneurs," *Small Business Economics* 45, no. 2 (2015): 369–81.

7. Melissa S. Cardon, Charlene Zietsma, Patrick Saparito, Brett P. Matherne, and Carolyn Davis, "A Tale of Passion, New Insights into Entrepreneurship from a Parenthood Metaphor," *Journal of Business Venturing* 20, no. 1 (January 2005): 23–45; and Simon C. Parker, "Who Become Serial and Portfolio Entrepreneurs?" *Small Business Economics* 43, no. 4 (2014): 887–98.

8. Howard H. Stevenson and David E. Gumpert, "The Heart of Entrepreneurship," *Harvard Business Review* 63, no. 2 (March/April 1985): 85–94.

9. See William B. Gartner, "Some Suggestions for Research on Entrepreneurial Traits and Characteristics," *Entrepreneurship Theory and Practice* 14, no. 1 (1989): 27–38.

10. Lloyd E. Shefsky, *Entrepreneurs Are Made Not Born* (New York: McGraw-Hill, Inc., 1994).

11. Robert A. Baron, "The Cognitive Perspective: A Valuable Tool for Answering Entrepreneurship's Basic 'Why' Questions," *Journal of Business Venturing* 19, no. 2 (March 2004): 221–39; Robert A. Baron and Thomas B. Ward, "Expanding Entrepreneurial Cognition's Toolbox: Potential Contributions from the Field of Cognitive Science," *Entrepreneurship Theory and Practice* 28, no. 6 (Winter 2004): 553–74; Robert M. Gemmell, Richard J. Boland, and David A. Kolb, "The Socio-Cognitive Dynamics of Entrepreneurial Ideation," *Entrepreneurship Theory and Practice* 36, no. 5 (2012): 1053–73.

12. David C. McClelland, *The Achieving Society* (New York: Van Nostrand, 1961); and David C. McClelland, "Business Drive and National Achievement," *Harvard Business Review* 40, no. 4 (July/August 1962): 99–112.

13. Melissa S. Cardon, Joakim Wincent, Jagdip Singh, and Mateja Drnovsek, "The Nature and Experience of Entrepreneurial Passion," *Academy of Management Review* 34, no.3 (2009): 511–32; Mellissa S. Cardon, "Is passion contagious? The Transference of Entrepreneurial Emotion to Employees," *Human Resource Management Review* 18 vol. 2 (2008): 77–86; and Melissa S. Cardon and Colleen P. Kirk, "Entrepreneurial Passion as Mediator of the Self-Efficacy to Persistence Relationship," *Entrepreneurship Theory & Practice* (2015): in press.

14. For some articles on entrepreneurial characteristics, see Rita Gunther McGrath, Ian C. MacMillan, and Sari Scheinberg, "Elitists, Risk Takers, and Rugged Individualists? An Exploratory Analysis of Cultural Differences Between Entrepreneurs and Non-Entrepreneurs," *Journal of Business Venturing* 7, no. 2 (1992): 115–36; Jill Kickul and Lisa K. Gundry, "Prospecting for Strategic Advantage: The Proactive Entrepreneurial Personality and Small Firm Innovation," *Journal of Small Business Management* 40, no. 2 (2002): 85–97; Moren Levesque and Maria Minniti, "The Effect of Aging on Entrepreneurial Behavior," *Journal of Business Venturing* 21, no. 2 (2006): 177–94; and Keith H. Brigham, Julio O. DeCastro, and Dean A. Shepherd, "A Person-Organization Fit Model of Owners-Managers' Cognitive Style and Organization Demands," *Entrepreneurship Theory and Practice* 31, no. 1 (2007): 29–51.

15. C. B. Wortman and R. C. Silver, "Coping with Irrevocable Loss" in G. R. Van de Bos and B. K. Bryant (eds.), *Cataclysms, Crises and Catastrophes: Psychology in Action* (Washington D.C.: American Psychological Association, 1987), 189–235.

16. S. Nolen-Hoeksema, A. McBride, and J. Larson (1997), "Rumination and Psychological Distress Among Bereaved Partners," *Journal of Personality and Social Psychology* 72, 855–62; Smita Singh, Patricia Doyle Corner, and Kathryn Pavlovich, "Failed, Not Finished: A Narrative Approach to Understanding Venture Failure Stigmatization," *Journal of Business Venturing* 30, no. 1 (2015): 150–66; and Anna S. Jenkins, Johan Wiklund, and Ethel Brundin, "Individual Responses to Firm Failure: Appraisals, Grief, and the Influence of Prior Failure Experience," *Journal of Business Venturing* 29, no. 1 (2014): 17–33.

17. J. Archer, *The Nature of Grief: The Evolution and Psychology of Reactions to Loss*. (New York: Routledge, 1999); Yasuhiro Yamakawa, Mike W. Peng and David L. Deeds, "Rising from the Ashes: Cognitive Determinants of Venture Growth After Entrepreneurial Failure," *Entrepreneurship Theory & Practice* 39, no. 2 (2015): 209–36.

18. Dean A. Shepherd, "Learning from Business Failure: Propositions About the Grief Recovery Process for the Self-Employed," *Academy of Management Review* 28 (2003), 318–29; Brandon A. Mueller and Dean A. Shepherd, "Making the Most of Failure Experiences: Exploring the Relationship Between Business Failure and the Identification of Business Opportunities," *Entrepreneurship Theory & Practice* (2015): in press; Marcus T. Wolfe and Dean A. Shepherd, "Bouncing Back from a Loss: Entrepreneurial Orientation, Emotions, and Failure Narratives," *Entrepreneurship Theory & Practice* 39, no. 3 (2015): 675–700; and Orla Byrne and Dean A. Shepherd, "Different Strokes for Different Folks: Entrepreneurial Narratives of Emotion, Cognition, and Making Sense of Business Failure," *Entrepreneurship Theory & Practice* 39, no. 2 (2015): 375–405.

19. Michael H. Morris, Donald F. Kuratko, and Minet Schindehutte, "Framing Entrepreneurial Experience," *Entrepreneurship Theory and Practice* 36 no. 1 (2012): 11–40.

20. Diamanto Politis, "The Process of Entrepreneurial Learning: A Conceptual Framework," *Entrepreneurship Theory and Practice* 29, no. 4 (2005): 399–424; John C. Dencker and Marc Gruber, "The Effects of Opportunities and Founder Experience on New Firm Performance," *Strategic Management Journal* 36, no. 7 (2015): 1035–52.

21. Per Davidsson, "A General Theory of Entrepreneurship: The Individual-Opportunity Nexus," *International Small Business Journal* 22, no. 2 (2004): 206–19; Henrik Berglund, "Entrepreneurship and Phenomenology: Researching Entrepreneurship as Lived Experience," in *Handbook of Qualitative Research Methods in Entrepreneurship*, ed. John Ulhoi and Helle Neergaard (London: Edward Elgar, 2007), 75–96; and Amanda Bullough, Maija Renko and Tamara Myatt, "Danger Zone Entrepreneurs: The Importance of Resilience and Self-Efficacy for Entrepreneurial Intentions," *Entrepreneurship Theory & Practice*, 38, no. 3 (2014): 473–99.

22. Manfred F. R. Kets de Vries, "The Dark Side of Entrepreneurship," *Harvard Business Review* 63, no. 6 (November/December 1985): 160–67; see also Shaker A. Zahra, R. Isil Yavuz, and Deniz Ucbascaran, "How Much Do You Trust Me? The Dark Side of Relational Trust in New Business Creation in Established Companies," *Entrepreneurship Theory and Practice* 30, no. 2 (2006): 541–59.

23. Thomas Monroy and Robert Folger, "A Typology of Entrepreneurial Styles: Beyond Economic Rationality," *Journal of Private Enterprise* 9, no. 2 (1993): 64–79.

24. Ibid., 75–76.

25. Michael O'Neal, "Just What Is an Entrepreneur?" special enterprise issue, *Business Week* (1993): 104–12.

26. Patrick R. Liles, *New Business Ventures and the Entrepreneur* (Homewood, IL: Irwin, 1974), 14–15; see also Jay J. Janney and Gregory G. Dess, "The Risk Concept for Entrepreneurs Reconsidered: New Challenges to the Conventional Wisdom," *Journal of Business Venturing* 21, no. 3 (2006): 385–400.

27. Adebowale Akande, "Coping with Entrepreneurial Stress," *Leadership & Organization Development Journal* 13, no. 2 (1992): 27–32; E. Holly Buttner, "Entrepreneurial Stress: Is It Hazardous to Your Health?" *Journal of Managerial Issues* 4, no. 2 (1992): 223–40; and Danny Miller, "A Downside to the Entrepreneurial Personality?" *Entrepreneurship Theory & Practice* 39, no. 1 (2015): 1–8.

28. Buttner, "Entrepreneurial Stress"; see also M. Afzalur Rabin, "Stress, Strain, and Their Moderators: An Empirical Comparison of Entrepreneurs and Managers," *Journal of Small Business Management* 34, no. 1 (1996): 46–58.

29. See K. A. Mathews and S. C. Haynes, "Type A Behavior Pattern and Coronary Disease Risk," *American Journal of Epistemology* 123 (1986): 923–60.

30. Akande, "Coping with Entrepreneurial Stress."

31. David P. Boyd and David E. Gumpert, "Coping with Entrepreneurial Stress," *Harvard Business Review* 61, no. 2 (March/April 1983): 46–56.

32. Ibid., 46–56 and Danny Miller and Cyrille Sardais, "Bifurcating Time: How Entrepreneurs Reconcile the Paradoxical Demands of the Job," *Entrepreneurship Theory & Practice* 39, no. 3 (2015): 489–512.

33. Michael G. Goldsby, Donald F. Kuratko, and James W. Bishop, "Entrepreneurship and Fitness: An Examination of Rigorous Exercise and Goal Attainment among Small Business Owners," *Journal of Small Business Management* 43, no. 1 (January 2005): 78–92; see also Levesque and Minniti, "The Effect of Aging on Entrepreneurial Behavior."

34. Kets de Vries, "The Dark Side of Entrepreneurship." See also, April J. Spivack, Alexander McKelvie, and J. Michael Haynie, "Habitual Entrepreneurs: Possible Cases of Entrepreneurship Addiction?" *Journal of Business Venturing*, 29, no. 5 (2014): 651–67.

35. Bruce Horovitz, "Scandals Shake Public Trust," *USA Today* (July 16, 2002): 1A–2A; John A. Byrne, Michael Arndt, Wendy Zellner, and Mike McNamee, "Restoring Trust in Corporate America: Business Must Lead the Way to Reform," *Business Week* (June 24, 2002): 31–39; and Amey Stone, "Putting Teeth in Corporate Ethics," *Business Week* (February 19, 2004). http://www.businessweek.com/bwdaily/dnflash/feb2004/nf20040219_5613_db035.htm, accessed on May 23, 2008.

36. Vernon R. Loucks, Jr., "A CEO Looks at Ethics," *Business Horizons* 30, no. 2 (March/April 1987): 2.

37. Sir Adrian Cadbury, "Ethical Managers Make Their Own Rules," *Harvard Business Review* 65, no. 5 (September/October 1987): 64.

38. Verne E. Henderson, "The Ethical Side of Enterprise," *Sloan Management Review* (Spring 1982): 38.

39. Richard Evans, "Business Ethics and Changes in Society," *Journal of Business Ethics* 10 (1991): 871–76; and Goran Svensson and Greg Wood, "A Model of Business Ethics," *Journal of Business Ethics* 77 (2008): 303–23.

40. Henderson, "The Ethical Side," 40.

41. Saul W. Gellerman, "Why Good Managers Make Bad Ethical Choices," *Harvard Business Review* 64, no. 4 (July/August 1986): 85.

42. James A. Waters and Frederick Bird, "Attending to Ethics in Management," *Journal of Business Ethics* 5 (1989): 493–97.

43. Christopher D. Stone, *Where the Law Ends: The Social Control of Corporate Behavior* (New York: Harper & Row, 1975).

44. Al H. Ringlab, Roger E. Meiners, and Frances L. Edwards, *Managing in the Legal Environment*, 3rd ed. (St. Paul, MN: West, 1996), 12–14; see also Roger LeRoy Miller and Frank B. Cross, *The Legal Environment Today: Business in Its Ethical, Regulatory, E-Commerce, and Global Setting*, 7th ed. (Mason, OH: South-Western /Cengage, 2013).

45. LaRue T. Hosmer, *The Ethics of Management*, 2nd ed. (Homewood, IL: Richard D. Irwin, 1991), 81–83.

46. Susan J. Harrington, "What Corporate America Is Teaching About Ethics," *Academy of Management Executive* 5, no. 1 (1991): 21–30.

47. LaRue T. Hosmer, *The Ethics of Management* (Homewood, IL: Richard D. Irwin, 1987), 13–15.

48. Wade L. Robison, "Management and Ethical Decision-Making," *Journal of Business Ethics* 3, no. 4 (1984): 287.

49. Xiao B and Benbasat I, "Product-Related Deception in e-Commerce: A Theoretical Perspective," *MIS Quarterly* 35, no. 1(2011): 169–96; Zhu F. and Zhang X, "Impact of Online Consumer Reviews on Sales: The Moderating role of Product and Consumer Characteristics," *Journal of Marketing*, 74, no. 2 (2010): 133–48.

50. Malaga, R. A, "Web-Based Reputation Management Systems: Problems and Suggested Solutions," *Electronic Commerce Research* 1, no. 4 (2001): 403–17; Jøsang, A., Ismail R and Boyd C, "A survey of Trust and Reputation Management Systems for Online Service Provision," *Decision support systems* 43, no. 2 (2007): 618–44.

51. Grabner-Kraeuter S, "The Role of Consumers' Trust in Online-Shopping," *Journal of Business Ethics* 39 no. 1–2 (2002): 43–50; Hemphill T. A, "Electronic Commerce and Consumer Privacy: Establishing Online Trust in the US Digital Economy," *Business and Society Review* 107 no. 2 (2002): 221–39; and Porter C. E and Donthu N, "Cultivating Trust and Harvesting Value in Virtual Communities," *Management Science* 54 no. 1 (2008): 113–28.

52. Dellarocas, C. "Strategic Manipulation of Internet Opinion Forums: Implications for Consumers and Firms," *Management Science* 52, no. 10 (2006): 1577–93; Dina Mayzlin, Yoniv Dover and Judith A. Chevalier J. A, "Promotional Reviews: An Empirical Investigation of Online Review Manipulation," *American Economic Review*, 104, no. 8 (2014): 2421–55.

53. Donald F. Kuratko, Travis J. Brown, and Marcus Wadell, "The Entrepreneur's Dilemma of Ethics vs. Professional Acceptability with Online Reputation Management Systems," in *Advances in the Study of Entrepreneurship, Innovation and Economic Growth Volume 25: The Challenges of Ethics and Entrepreneurship in the Global Environment* (Bradford, U.K., Emerald Group Publishing, 2015).

54. For more on this topic, see Donald R. Cressey and Charles A. Moore, "Managerial Values and Corporate Codes of Conduct," *California Management Review* (Summer 1983): 121–27; Steven Weller, "The Effectiveness of Corporate Codes of Ethics," *Journal of Business Ethics* (July 1988): 389–95; and Diane E. Kirrane, "Managing Values: A Systematic Approach to Business Ethics," *Training & Development Journal* (November 1990): 53–60.

55. Reported in Darrell J. Fashing, "A Case of Corporate and Management Ethics," *California Management Review* (Spring 1981): 84.

56. Amitai Etzioni, "Do Good Ethics Ensure Good Profits?" *Business and Society Review* (Summer 1989): 4–10; L. J. Brooks, "Corporate Ethical Performance: Trends, Forecasts, and Outlooks," *Journal of Business Ethics* 8 (1989): 31–38; Harrington, "What Corporate America Is Teaching about Ethics"; and Simcha B. Werner, "The Movement for Reforming American Business Ethics: A Twenty Year Perspective," *Journal of Business Ethics* 11 (1992): 61–70.

57. Patrick E. Murphy, "Creating Ethical Corporate Structures," *Sloan Management Review* (Winter 1989): 81–87.

58. Joseph A. Raelin, "The Professional as the Executive's Ethical Aide-de-Camp," *The Academy of Management Executive* 1, no. 3 (1987): 176.

59. Ibid., 177.

60. Donald F. Kuratko and Michael G. Goldsby, "Corporate Entrepreneurs or Rogue Middle Managers? A Framework for Ethical Corporate Entrepreneurship," *Journal of Business Ethics* 55 (2004): 13–30.

61. Elisabeth J. Teal and Archie B. Carroll, "Moral Reasoning Skills: Are Entrepreneurs Different?" *Journal of Business Ethics* (March 1999): 229–40; Dinah Payne and Brenda E. Joyner, "Successful U.S. Entrepreneurs: Identifying Ethical Decision–Making and Social Responsibility Behaviors," *Journal of Business Ethics* 65 (2006): 203–17.

62. Donald F. Kuratko, Michael G. Goldsby, and Jeffrey S. Hornsby, "The Ethical Perspectives of Entrepreneurs: An Examination of Stakeholder Salience," *Journal of Applied Management and Entrepreneurship* 9, no. 4 (October 2004): 19–42.

63. Nel Noddings, *Caring: A Feminine Approach to Ethics and Moral Education* (Berkeley: University of California Press, 1984).

64. Milton Mayeroff, *On Caring* (New York: Harper & Row, 1971), 1.

65. Henderson, "The Ethical Side," 46.

66. Justin G. Longenecker, Joseph A. McKinney, and Carlos W. Moore, "Do Smaller Firms Have Higher Ethics?" *Business and Society Review* (Fall 1989): 19–21; Paul J. Serwinek, "Demographic and Related Differences in Ethical Views among Small Businesses," *Journal of Business Ethics* (July 1992): 555–66; Donald F. Kuratko, "The Ethical Challenge for Entrepreneurs," *Entrepreneurship, Innovation, and Change* 4, no. 4 (1995): 291–94; and Kuratko, Goldsby, and Hornsby, "The Ethical Perspectives of Entrepreneurs: An Examination of Stakeholder Salience," *Journal of Applied Management and Entrepreneurship* 9, no. 4 (October 2004), 19–42.

67. Lanny Herron and Harry J. Sapienza, "The Entrepreneur and the Initiation of New Venture Launch Activities," *Entrepreneurship Theory and Practice* 17, no. 1 (1992): 49–55.

68. Bradley R. Johnson, "Toward a Multidimensional Model of Entrepreneurship: The Case of Achievement Motivation and the Entrepreneur," *Entrepreneurship Theory and Practice* 14, no. 3 (1990): 39–54; see also Wayne H. Stewart and Philip L. Roth, "A Meta-Analysis of Achievement Motivation Differences between Entrepreneurs and Managers," *Journal of Small Business Management* 45, no. 4 (2007): 401–21.

69. See Kelly G. Shaver and Linda R. Scott, "Person, Process, Choice: The Psychology of New Venture Creation," *Entrepreneurship Theory and Practice* 16, no. 2 (1991): 23–45.

70. Don E. Bradley and James A. Roberts, "Self-Employment and Job Satisfaction: Investigating and Role of Self-Efficacy, Depression, and Seniority," *Journal of Small Business Management* 42, no. 1 (January 2004): 37–58; see also J. Robert Baum, and Edwin A. Locke, "The Relationship of Entrepreneurial Traits, Skill, and Motivation to Subsequent Venture Growth," *Journal of Applied Psychology* 89, no. 4 (2004): 587–98.

71. Arnold C. Cooper and Kendall W. Artz, "Determinants of Satisfaction for Entrepreneurs," *Journal of Business Venturing* 10, no. 6 (1995): 439–58.

72. Douglas W. Naffziger, Jeffrey S. Hornsby, and Donald F. Kuratko, "A Proposed Research Model of Entrepreneurial Motivation," *Entrepreneurship Theory and Practice* 18, no. 3 (1994): 29–42.

73. A. Rebecca Reuber and Eileen Fischer, "Understanding the Consequences of Founders' Experience," *Journal of Small Business Management* 37, no. 2 (1999): 30–45.

74. Donald F. Kuratko, Jeffrey S. Hornsby, and Douglas W. Naffziger, "An Examination of Owner's Goals in Sustaining Entrepreneurship," *Journal of Small Business Management* 35, no. 1 (1997): 24–33.

75. Daniel V. Holland and Dean A. Shepherd, "Deciding to Persist: Adversity, Values, and Entrepreneurs' Decision Policies," *Entrepreneurship Theory and Practice* 37, no. 2 (2013): 331–58.

CHAPTER 3

The Entrepreneurial Mind-Set in Organizations: Corporate Entrepreneurship

LEARNING OBJECTIVES

1 To understand the entrepreneurial mind-set in organizations

2 To illustrate the need for entrepreneurial thinking in organizations

3 To define the term corporate entrepreneurship

4 To describe obstacles that prevent innovation within corporations

5 To highlight the considerations involved in reengineering corporate thinking

6 To describe the specific elements of a corporate entrepreneurial strategy

7 To examine the methods of developing managers for corporate entrepreneurship

8 To illustrate the interactive process of corporate entrepreneurship

Entrepreneurial Thought

There is nothing more difficult to take in hand, more perilous to conduct, than to take a lead in the introduction of a new order of things, because the innovation has for enemies all those who have done well under the old conditions and lukewarm defenders in those who may do well under the new.

—Machiavelli *The Prince*

3-1 THE ENTREPRENEURIAL MIND-SET IN ORGANIZATIONS

LO1 Understand the entrepreneurial mind-set in organizations

The global economy is profoundly and substantively changing organizations and industries throughout the world, making it necessary for businesses to reexamine their purposes and to select and follow strategies that have high probabilities of satisfying multiple stakeholders. In response to rapid, discontinuous, and significant changes in their external and internal environments, many companies have restructured their operations in fundamental and meaningful ways. In fact, after years of such restructuring, some companies bear little resemblance to their ancestors in scope, culture, or competitive approach.[1]

LO2 Illustrate the need for entrepreneurial thinking in organizations

The contemporary thrust of entrepreneurship as the major force in global business has led to a desire for this type of activity *inside* enterprises. Although some earlier researchers concluded that entrepreneurship and bureaucracies were mutually exclusive and could not coexist,[2] today we find many researchers examining entrepreneurial ventures within the enterprise framework.[3] Successful corporate venturing is present in many different companies, including 3M, AT&T, GE, Procter & Gamble, and Abbott Laboratories.[4] A wealth of popular business literature describes a new "corporate revolution" taking place, thanks to the infusion of entrepreneurial thinking into large bureaucratic structures.[5] This infusion is referred to as corporate entrepreneurship,[6] corporate innovation,[7] or intrapreneurship.[8] Why has corporate entrepreneurship become so popular? One reason is that it allows corporations to tap the innovative talents of their own workers and managers. Steven Brandt puts it this way:

> The challenge is relatively straightforward. The United States must upgrade its innovative prowess. To do so, U.S. companies must tap into the creative power of their members. Ideas come from people. Innovation is a capability of the many. That capability is utilized when people give commitment to the mission and life of the enterprise and have the power to do something with their capabilities.[9]

Corporate entrepreneurship (CE) has evolved over the last forty years to become a strategy that can facilitate firms' efforts to create innovation and cope effectively with the competitive realities in today's world markets. All organizations are facing a new global reality requiring innovation, courage, risk taking, and entrepreneurial leadership. As researcher Donald F. Kuratko pointed out, organizations must realize "the entrepreneurial imperative of the 21st Century" is now at hand.[10] Firms that exhibit corporate entrepreneurship are typically viewed as dynamic, flexible entities prepared to take advantage of new business opportunities when they arise. An "entrepreneurial orientation" of innovation, risk taking, and proactiveness is needed for today's organizations to implement the needed strategies for corporate entrepreneurship to develop[11].

Continuous innovation (in terms of products, processes, and administrative routines and structures) and an ability to compete effectively in global markets are among the skills that are increasingly expected to influence corporate performance in the twenty-first century. Today's executives agree that innovation is the most important pathway for companies to accelerate their pace of change in the global environment. Corporate entrepreneurship is a process that can facilitate efforts to innovate and can help firms cope with the competitive realities of world markets. Leading strategic thinkers are moving beyond traditional product and service innovations and are pioneering innovation in processes, value chains, business models, and all functions of management. Entrepreneurial attitudes and behaviors, it seems clear, are necessary for firms of all sizes to prosper and flourish in competitive environments.[12]

3-2 CORPORATE INNOVATION PHILOSOPHY

LO4 Describe obstacles that prevent innovation within corporations

Despite the fact that entrepreneurship and innovation are highly touted as a most viable strategy for successful results in today's corporations, the fact remains that successful implementation of corporate innovation has been quite elusive for most companies.[13] Corporate innovation succeeds in organizations that provide employees with the freedom and encouragement to develop their ideas, but top managers, if they do not believe that entrepreneurial ideas can be nurtured, have been known to hamper innovation. They may find it difficult, for example, to implement policies that endorse unstructured activity. If innovative people are to reach their potential, however, new types of thinking must overcome managerial hesitations. Five important practices for establishing innovation-driven organizations follow:

1. Set *explicit innovation goals*. These goals need to be mutually agreed on by the employee and management so that specific steps can be achieved.

2. Create a system of *feedback* and *positive reinforcement*. This is necessary for potential innovators or creators of ideas to realize that acceptance and reward exist.

3. Emphasize *individual responsibility*. Confidence, trust, and accountability are key features in the success of any innovative program.

4. Provide *rewards* for innovative ideas. Reward systems should enhance and encourage others to risk and to achieve.

5. *Do not punish failures*. Real learning takes place when failed projects are examined closely for what can be learned by individuals. In addition, individuals must feel free to experiment without fear of punishment.

Although each enterprise must develop its own philosophy of corporate innovation, the answers to these questions can inform the process:

- *Does our company encourage entrepreneurial thinking?* Will individuals receive the corporation's blessing for their self-appointed idea creations? Some corporations foolishly try to appoint people to carry out an innovation when, in fact, the ideas must surface on their own.

- *Does our company provide ways for innovators to stay with their ideas?* When the innovation process involves switching the people working on an idea—that is, handing off a developing business or product from a committed innovator to whoever is next in line—that person often is not as committed as the originator of the project.

- *Are people in our company permitted to do the job in their own way, or are they constantly stopping to explain their actions and ask for permission?* Some organizations push decisions up through a multilevel approval process so that the doers and the deciders never even meet.

- *Has our company evolved quick and informal ways to access the resources to try new ideas?* Innovators usually need discretionary resources to explore and develop new ideas. Some companies give employees the freedom to use a percentage of their time on projects of their own choosing and set aside funds to explore new ideas when they occur. Others control resources so tightly that nothing is available for the new and unexpected—the result is nothing new.

- *Has our company developed ways to manage many small and experimental innovations?* Today's corporate cultures favor a few well-studied, well-planned attempts to hit a home run. In fact, nobody bats a thousand; it is better to make more frequent attempts, with less careful and expensive preparation for each.

- *Is our system set up to encourage risk taking and to tolerate mistakes?* Innovation cannot be achieved without risk and mistakes. Even successful innovation generally begins with blunders and false starts.

- *Are people in our company more concerned with new ideas or with defending their turf?* Because new ideas almost always cross the boundaries of existing patterns of organization, a jealous tendency toward "turf protection" blocks innovation.

- *How easy is it to form functionally complete, autonomous teams in our corporate environment?* Small teams with full responsibility for developing an innovation solve many of the basic problems, yet some companies resist their formation.[14]

Another way to create an innovative corporate atmosphere is to apply rules for innovation. The rules in Table 3.1 can provide hands-on guidelines for developing the necessary innovative philosophy.

TABLE 3.1   RULES FOR AN INNOVATIVE ENVIRONMENT

1. Encourage action.
2. Use informal meetings whenever possible.
3. Tolerate failure, and use it as a learning experience.
4. Persist in getting an idea to market.
5. Reward innovation for innovation's sake.
6. Plan the physical layout of the enterprise to encourage informal communication.
7. Expect clever **bootlegging** of ideas—secretly working on new ideas on company time as well as on personal time.
8. Put people on small teams for future-oriented projects.
9. Encourage personnel to circumvent rigid procedures and bureaucratic red tape.
10. Reward and promote innovative personnel.

© Cengage Learning

When these rules are followed, they create an environment conducive to and supportive of potential entrepreneurial thinking. The result is a corporate philosophy that supports innovative behavior.

What can a corporation do to reengineer its thinking to foster the entrepreneurial process? The organization needs to examine and revise its management philosophy. Many enterprises have obsolete ideas about cooperative cultures, management techniques, and the values of managers and employees. Unfortunately, doing old tasks more efficiently is not the answer to new challenges; a new culture with new values has to be developed.[15] Bureaucrats and controllers must learn to coexist with—or give way to—the designer and innovator. Unfortunately, this is easier said than done. Organizations can, however, use the following methods to help restructure corporate thinking and encourage an entrepreneurial environment: (1) early identification of potential innovators, (2) top-management sponsorship of innovative projects, (3) creation of innovation goals in strategic activities, (4) promotion of entrepreneurial thinking through experimentation, and (5) development of collaboration between innovators and the organization at large.[16]

Developing a corporate entrepreneurial philosophy provides a number of advantages. One is that this type of atmosphere often leads to the development of new products and services, helping the organization expand and grow. Second, it creates a workforce that can help the enterprise maintain its competitive posture. A third advantage is that it promotes a climate conducive to high achievers and helps the enterprise motivate and keep its best people.

3-3 CORPORATE ENTREPRENEURSHIP AND INNOVATION

In recent years, the subject of corporate entrepreneurship/corporate innovation has become quite popular, though very few people thoroughly understand the concept. Most researchers agree that the term refers to entrepreneurial activities that receive organizational sanction and resource commitments for the purpose of innovative results.[17] The major thrust of corporate innovation is to develop the entrepreneurial spirit within organizational boundaries, thus allowing an atmosphere of innovation to prosper.

3-3a Defining the Concept of Corporate Entrepreneurship and Innovation

LO3 Define the term corporate entrepreneurship

Operational definitions of corporate entrepreneurship/corporate innovation have evolved over the last 35 years through scholars' work. For example, one researcher noted that corporate innovation is a very broad concept that includes the generation, development, and implementation of new ideas or behaviors. An innovation can be a new product or service, an administrative system, or a new plan or program that pertains to organizational members.[18] In this context, corporate entrepreneurship centers on reenergizing and enhancing the firm's ability to acquire innovative skills and capabilities.

Researcher Shaker A. Zahra observed that "corporate entrepreneurship may be formal or informal activities aimed at creating new businesses in established companies through product and process innovations and market developments. These activities may take place at the corporate, division (business), functional, or project levels, with the unifying objective of improving a company's competitive position and financial performance."[19] William D. Guth and Ari Ginsberg have stressed that corporate entrepreneurship encompasses two major phenomena: new venture creation within existing organizations and the transformation of organizations through strategic renewal.[20]

Researchers Michael H. Morris, Donald F. Kuratko, and Jeffrey G. Covin have cited two empirical phenomena as constituting the domain of corporate entrepreneurship—namely, corporate venturing and strategic entrepreneurship. Corporate venturing approaches have as their commonality the adding of new businesses (or portions of new businesses via equity investments) to the corporation. This can be accomplished through three implementation modes: internal corporate venturing, cooperative corporate venturing, and external corporate venturing. By contrast, strategic entrepreneurship approaches have as their commonality the exhibition of large-scale or otherwise highly consequential innovations that are adopted in the firm's pursuit of competitive advantage. These innovations may or may not result in new businesses for the corporation. With strategic entrepreneurship approaches, innovation can be in any of five areas: the firm's strategy, product offerings, served markets, internal organization (i.e., structure, processes, and capabilities), or business model.[21] Each of these categories of corporate entrepreneurship is outlined in Figure 3.1.

After a thorough analysis of the entrepreneurship construct and its dimensions, recent research has defined corporate entrepreneurship as a process whereby an individual (or a group of individuals), in association with an existing organization, creates a new organization or instigates renewal or innovation within the organization. Under this definition, strategic renewal (which is concerned with organizational renewal involving major strategic and/or structural changes), innovation (which is concerned with introducing something new to the marketplace), and corporate venturing (corporate entrepreneurial efforts that lead to the creation of new business organizations within the corporate organization) are all important and legitimate parts of the corporate entrepreneurship process.[22]

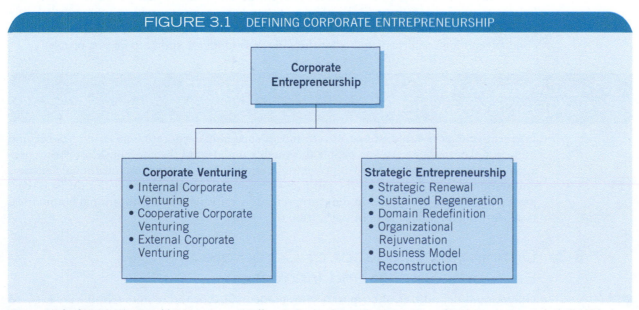

FIGURE 3.1   DEFINING CORPORATE ENTREPRENEURSHIP

Corporate Entrepreneurship

Corporate Venturing
- Internal Corporate Venturing
- Cooperative Corporate Venturing
- External Corporate Venturing

Strategic Entrepreneurship
- Strategic Renewal
- Sustained Regeneration
- Domain Redefinition
- Organizational Rejuvenation
- Business Model Reconstruction

Source: Michael H. Morris, Donald F. Kuratko, and Jeffrey G. Covin, *Corporate Entrepreneurship & Innovation*, 3rd ed. © 2011 South-Western, a part of Cengage Learning, Inc. Reproduced by permission. www.cengage.com/permissions.

As the field has further evolved, the concept of a corporate entrepreneurship strategy has developed. Researchers R. Duane Ireland, Jeffrey G. Covin, and Donald F. Kuratko define a corporate entrepreneurial strategy as "a vision-directed, organization-wide reliance on entrepreneurial behavior that purposefully and continuously rejuvenates the organization and shapes the scope of its operations through the recognition and exploitation of entrepreneurial opportunity."[23]

3-3b The Need for Corporate Entrepreneurship and Innovation

Many companies today are recognizing the need for corporate entrepreneurship. Articles in popular business magazines (*Business Week, Fortune, U.S. News & World Report*) report the infusion of entrepreneurial thinking into large bureaucratic structures. In fact, in many of today's popular business books, entire sections are devoted to innovation within the corporation.[24] Quite obviously, both business firms and consultants/authors are recognizing the need for in-house entrepreneurship.

This need has arisen in response to a number of pressing problems, including rapid growth in the number of new and sophisticated competitors, a sense of distrust in the traditional methods of corporate management, an exodus of some of the best and brightest people from corporations to become small-business entrepreneurs, international competition, downsizing of major corporations, and an overall desire to improve efficiency and productivity.[25]

The first of these issues, the problem of competition, has always plagued businesses. However, today's high-tech economy supports a far greater number of competitors than ever before. In contrast to previous decades, changes, innovations, and improvements are now very common in the marketplace. Thus, corporations must either innovate or become obsolete.

Another of these problems, losing the brightest people to independent entrepreneurship, is escalating as a result of two major developments. First, entrepreneurship is on the rise in terms of status, publicity, and economic development. This enhancement of entrepreneurship has made the choice more appealing to both young and seasoned employees. Second, in recent years venture capital has grown into a large industry capable of financing more new ventures than ever before. More significantly, as we will see in greater detail in Chapter 8, "angel investors" have emerged in unprecedented strength, which has created a new opportunity for capital funding. Healthy capital funding markets have enabled new entrepreneurs to launch their ideas. As a result, people with innovative ideas are more likely to leave large corporations and strike out on their own.

The modern organization, then, is forced into seeking avenues to develop in-house entrepreneuring. To do otherwise is to wait for stagnation, loss of personnel, and decline. This new "corporate revolution" represents an appreciation for and a desire to develop innovators within the corporate structure.

3-3c Obstacles to Corporate Entrepreneurship and Innovation

It should be noted that many obstacles exist for the corporate entrepreneurship process. The obstacles to corporate entrepreneurship usually reflect the ineffectiveness of traditional management techniques as applied to innovation development. Although it is unintentional, the adverse impact of a particular traditional management technique can be so destructive that the individuals within an enterprise will tend to avoid corporate entrepreneurial behavior. Table 3.2 provides a list of traditional management techniques, their adverse effects (when the technique is rigidly enforced), and the recommended actions to change or adjust the practice.

Understanding these obstacles is critical to fostering corporate entrepreneurship, because they are the foundation points for all other motivational efforts. To gain support and foster excitement for innovation development, managers must remove the perceived obstacles and seek alternative management actions.[26]

TABLE 3.2 SOURCES OF AND SOLUTIONS TO OBSTACLES IN CORPORATE INNOVATION

Traditional Management Practices	Adverse Effects	Recommended Actions
Enforce standard procedures to avoid mistakes	Innovative solutions blocked, funds misspent	Make ground rules specific to each situation
Manage resources for efficiency and ROI	Competitive lead lost, low market penetration	Focus effort on critical issues (e.g., market share)
Control against plan	Facts ignored that should replace assumptions	Change plan to reflect new learning
Plan for the long term	Nonviable goals locked in, high failure costs	Envision a goal, then set interim milestones, reassess after each
Manage functionally	Entrepreneur failure and/or venture failure	Support entrepreneur with managerial and multidiscipline skills
Avoid moves that risk the base business	Missed opportunities	Take small steps, build out from strengths
Protect the base business at all costs	Venturing dumped when base business is threatened	Make venturing mainstream, take affordable risks
Judge new steps from prior experience	Wrong decisions about competition and markets	Use learning strategies, test assumptions
Compensate uniformly	Low motivation and inefficient operations	Balance risk and reward, employ special compensation
Promote compatible individuals	Loss of innovators	Accommodate "boat rockers" and "doers"

Source: Reprinted by permission of the publisher from Hollister B. Sykes and Zenas Block, "Corporate Venturing Obstacles: Sources and Solutions," *Journal of Business Venturing* 4, no. 3 (Winter 1989): 161. Copyright © 1989 by Elsevier Science Publishing Co., Inc.

After recognizing the obstacles, managers need to adapt to the principles of successful innovative companies. James Brian Quinn, an expert in the innovation field, found the following factors in large corporations that have exhibited successful innovations:

- *Atmosphere and vision.* Innovative companies have a clear-cut vision of—and the recognized support for—an innovative atmosphere.
- *Orientation to the market.* Innovative companies tie their visions to the realities of the marketplace.
- *Small, flat organizations.* Most innovative companies keep the total organization flat and project teams small.
- *Multiple approaches.* Innovative managers encourage several projects to proceed in parallel development.
- *Interactive learning.* Within an innovative environment, interactive learning and investigation of ideas cut across traditional functional lines in the organization.
- *Skunk Works.* ("Skunk Works" is a nickname given to small groups that work on their ideas outside of normal organizational time and structure.) Every highly innovative enterprise uses groups that function outside traditional lines of authority. This eliminates bureaucracy, permits rapid turnaround, and instills a high level of group identity and loyalty.[27]

THE ENTREPRENEURIAL PROCESS

FutureWorks: Procter & Gamble's "Entrepreneurial Engine"

When you think about Procter & Gamble you think of a consumer product giant. They have 300 brands that produce $80 billion in revenue in 80 countries with 130,000 employees. But even at that size, Procter & Gamble is serious about corporate innovation. It spends nearly $2 billion every year on R&D with another $400 million invested in consumer research. It conducts over 20,000 studies in 100 countries. Why this emphasis on internal innovation? Because the CEO of P&G, Bob McDonald, recognizes that sales promotions may move a company through a season but true innovation can vault a company into future decades.

However, P&G learned after years of investment and experiments that corporate innovation is sometimes best executed through decentralized innovation units or departments. In this type of structure, senior-level managers worry only about major milestones that need to be achieved in the innovation process. The rest is left to the members of the innovation unit with complete dedication of their time in order to get the innovations to market as quickly as possible.

Procter & Gamble created one of the most successful innovation units that exists today which is named, "FutureWorks." It is a Corporate New Business Creation unit within Procter & Gamble reporting to the Corporate Innovation Fund board consisting of the top officers of the company. That unit is charged with creating, incubating, and scaling transformational new business models, new categories, or service experiences that capitalize on disruptive market innovations. The P&G FutureWorks team is experienced and diverse with close connections to the P&G leadership team and their strategic goals.

Using a technique of "open innovation" where external ideas and solutions are sought out by the organization, P&G has established a "Connect & Develop" division of FutureWorks for an effective external interface. The mission of that unit is to seek out partners and realize the innovation potential in those external networks. Innovations which in the past could have taken there years or more to get to market could be accelerated within 18 months. By connecting with external partners, P&G has expanded its strategic core businesses into new channels and domains. Some of those new domains of interest include services via franchising, health and well-being, information-based services, breakthrough platform technologies, and emerging markets.

Of particular interest to FutureWorks are models that leverage the power of a P&G's brand or a strong external brand (just think of the powerful brand names owned by P&G such as Crest, Duracell, Tide, Pampers, Charmin, Gillette, and Pringles, to name a few). Some examples of business models that have been developed leveraging some of P&G's brands include: Mr. Clean Car Wash and Tide Dry Cleaners. Also, any platform technologies are especially viable if they can bring disruptive cost, capability, and/or speed advantage to any current business models, retail partners, or even the industry; finally, information based ideas that serve the consumer or the retailer and provide unique information.

In order to better finance innovation projects P&G has established the P&G Corporate Innovation Fund (CIF) which provides financing for the development of disruptive innovations and of new businesses (P&G's innovative Crest Whitestrips were funded in this manner).

Vice President and Chief Innovation Czar at P&G, Nathan Estruth, claims that the "magic" is in his team and the culture they have created. He points out that they are characterized by humility, passionate about their work, thrive in ambiguity, and consistently challenge the status quo. The value in all of what FutureWorks is accomplishing is best summed up in the realization of the new businesses, greater efficiencies, and new capabilities that characterize P&G today. P&G is creating their future by seeking breakthrough innovations through a breakthrough development of their own: FutureWorks!

Sources: Adapted from numerous sources including: P&G website for FutureWorks, http://futureworks.pg.com, accessed February 1, 2012; Bruce Brown and Scott D. Anthony, "How P&G Tripled Its Innovation Success Rate," *Harvard Business Review* 89, no. 6 June 2011: 64–72; and personal visit to FutureWorks with interview with Nathan Estruth, July 2011.

3-4 CORPORATE ENTREPRENEURSHIP STRATEGY

LO6 Describe the specific elements of a corporate entrepreneurial strategy

As mentioned earlier, we define a corporate entrepreneurship strategy as a vision-directed, organization-wide reliance on entrepreneurial behavior that purposefully and continuously rejuvenates the organization and shapes the scope of its operations through the recognition and exploitation of entrepreneurial opportunity. As is true for all strategies, a corporate entrepreneurship strategy should be thought of in continuous, rather than dichotomous, terms. Stated more directly, corporate entrepreneurship strategies vary in their degree of entrepreneurial intensity.

Developed by researchers Jeffrey G. Covin, R. Duane Ireland, and Donald F. Kuratko, Figure 3.2 presents a model that illustrates how a corporate entrepreneurship strategy is

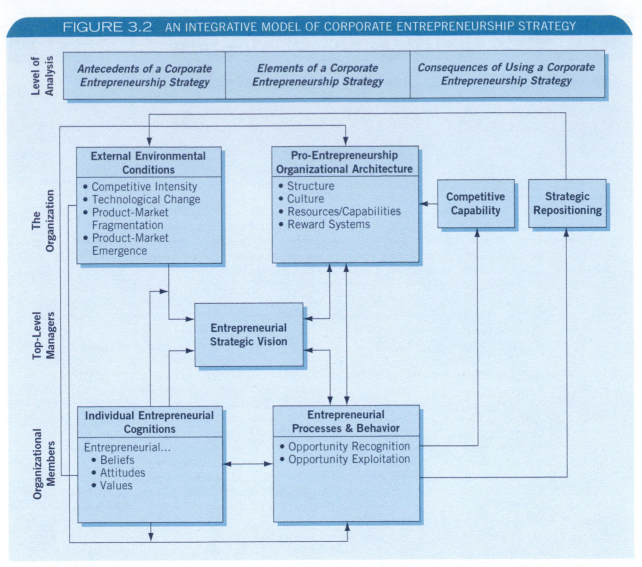

FIGURE 3.2 AN INTEGRATIVE MODEL OF CORPORATE ENTREPRENEURSHIP STRATEGY

Source: R. Duane Ireland, Jeffery G. Covin, and Donald F. Kuratko, "Conceptualizing Corporate Entrepreneurship Strategy," *Entrepreneurship Theory and Practice* 33, no. 1 (2009): 24.

manifested through the presence of three elements: an entrepreneurial strategic vision, a pro-entrepreneurship organizational architecture, and entrepreneurial processes and behavior as exhibited across the organizational hierarchy.[28] This model has several linkages, which include: (1) individual entrepreneurial cognitions of the organization's members, (2) external environmental conditions that invite entrepreneurial activity, (3) top management's entrepreneurial strategic vision for the firm, (4) organizational architectures that encourage entrepreneurial processes and behavior, (5) the entrepreneurial processes that are reflected in entrepreneurial behavior, and (6) organizational outcomes that result from entrepreneurial actions.

The model suggests that individual entrepreneurial cognitions and external environmental conditions are the initial impetus for adopting a corporate entrepreneurship strategy, and outcomes are assessed to provide justification for the strategy's continuance, modification, or rejection. The corporate entrepreneurship strategy itself is reflected in the three elements cited previously: an entrepreneurial strategic vision, a pro-entrepreneurship organizational architecture, and entrepreneurial processes and behavior as exhibited throughout the organization. A corporate entrepreneurship strategy cannot be consciously chosen and quickly enacted the way some strategies, such as acquisition, can be—it requires more than just a decision, act, or event. It requires the creation of congruence between the entrepreneurial vision of the organization's leaders and the entrepreneurial actions of those throughout the organization, as facilitated through the existence of a pro-entrepreneurship organizational architecture. Corporate entrepreneurship strategy is about creating self-renewing organizations through the unleashing and focusing of the entrepreneurial potential that exists throughout those organizations. It is also about consistency in approach and regularity in behavior. Firms that engage in corporate entrepreneurship strategies must encourage entrepreneurial behavior on a relatively regular or continuous basis. Obviously, how extensively firms must engage in entrepreneurial behavior before the presence of a corporate entrepreneurship strategy can be claimed is a matter of degree. At one end of the continuum is stability, or the absence of innovation; at the other end is chaos, or overwhelming innovation. Researchers Charles Baden-Fuller and Henk Volberda rightfully assert that

> Resolving the paradox of change and preservation means recognizing that continuous renewal inside a complex firm is misleading. Too much change will lead to chaos, loss of cultural glue, fatigue, and organizational breakdown. While in the short-term, organizations that are chaotic can survive, in the longer term they are likely to collapse.[29]

Researchers Kathleen Eisenhardt, Shona Brown, and Heidi Neck perhaps best captured where firms with corporate entrepreneurship strategies lie along the innovation continuum in their observations concerning "competing on the entrepreneurial edge." Firms with corporate entrepreneurship strategies remain close to the "edge of time," judiciously balancing the exploitation of current entrepreneurial opportunities with the search for future entrepreneurial opportunities. Such firms are always near chaos, both strategically and structurally, but they have the wisdom and discipline to recognize the possibility of (and avoid) the extreme collapse referred to earlier.[30]

LO5 Highlight the considerations involved in reengineering corporate thinking

Thus, for corporate entrepreneurship to operate as a strategy, it must "run deep" within organizations. Top managers are increasingly recognizing the need to respond to the entrepreneurial imperatives created by their competitive landscapes. Minimal responses to these entrepreneurial imperatives—reflecting superficial commitments to CE strategy—are bound to fail. Moreover, although top management can instigate the strategy, top management cannot dictate it. Those at the middle and lower ranks of an organization have a tremendous effect on and significant roles within entrepreneurial and strategic processes.[31] Without sustained and strong commitment from these lower levels of the organization, entrepreneurial behavior will never be a defining characteristic of the organization, as is required by CE strategy.

CE strategy will be hard to create and, perhaps, even harder to perpetuate in organizations. The presence of certain external environmental conditions may be sufficient to prompt an organization's leaders to explore the possibility of adopting a CE strategy. However, the commitment of individuals throughout the organization to making such a strategy work, and the realization of personal and organizational entrepreneurial outcomes that reinforce this commitment, will be necessary to assure that entrepreneurial behavior becomes a defining aspect of the organization. Thus, breakdowns in any of the three elements of CE strategy, or in linkages between or among these elements, would undermine the viability of such strategy. Moreover, alignments must be created in evaluation and reward systems such that congruence is achieved in the entrepreneurial behaviors induced at the individual and organizational levels. Although external conditions may be increasingly conducive to the adoption of CE strategies, managers should harbor no illusions that the effective implementation of these strategies will be easily accomplished.

Corporations that create an entrepreneurial strategy find that the ethos of the original enterprise often changes dramatically.[32] Traditions are set aside in favor of new processes and procedures. Some people, unaccustomed to operating in this environment, will leave; others will discover a new motivational system that encourages creativity, ingenuity, risk taking, teamwork, and informal networking, all designed to increase productivity and make the organization more viable. Some people thrive in an entrepreneurial environment; others dislike it intensely.

The five critical steps of a corporate entrepreneurship strategy are: (1) developing the vision, (2) encouraging innovation, (3) structuring for an entrepreneurial climate, (4) preparing individual managers for corporate innovation, and (5) developing venture teams. Each of these is now discussed in greater detail.

3-4a Developing the Vision

The first step in planning a corporate entrepreneurship strategy for the enterprise is to share the vision of innovation that the corporate leaders wish to achieve.[33] The vision must be clearly articulated by the organization's leaders; however, the specific objectives are then developed by the managers and employees of the organization. Because it is suggested that corporate entrepreneuring results from the creative talents of people within the organization, employees need to know about and understand this vision. Shared vision is a critical element for a strategy that seeks high achievement (see Figure 3.3). This shared vision requires identification of specific objectives for corporate entrepreneuring strategies and of the programs needed to achieve those objectives. Author and researcher Rosabeth Moss Kanter has described three major objectives and their respective programs designed for venture development within companies. These are outlined in Table 3.3.

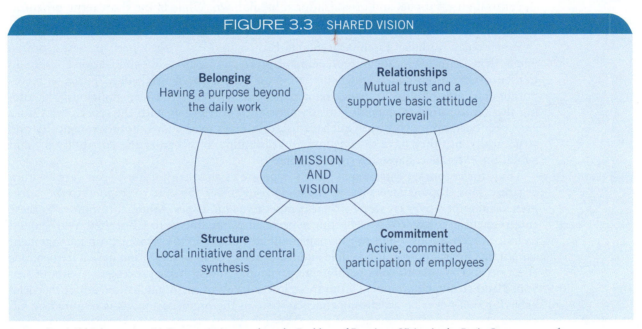

FIGURE 3.3 SHARED VISION

Source: Jon Arild Johannessen, "A Systematic Approach to the Problem of Rooting a Vision in the Basic Components of an Organization," in *Entrepreneurship, Innovation, and Change* 3, no. 1 (March 1994): 47. Reprinted with permission from Plenum Publishing Corporation, New York.

TABLE 3.3 OBJECTIVES AND PROGRAMS FOR VENTURE DEVELOPMENT

Objectives	Programs
Make sure that current systems, structures, and practices do not present insurmountable roadblocks to the flexibility and fast action needed for innovation.	Reduce unnecessary bureaucracy, and encourage communication across departments and functions.
Provide the incentives and tools for intrapreneurial projects.	Use internal "venture capital" and special project budgets. (This money has been termed *intracapital* to signify a special fund for intrapreneurial projects.) Allow discretionary time for projects (bootlegging time).
Seek synergies across business areas so new opportunities are discovered in new combinations.	Encourage joint projects and ventures among divisions, departments, and companies. Allow and encourage employees to discuss and brainstorm new ideas.

Source: Adapted by permission of the publisher from Rosabeth Moss Kanter, "Supporting Innovation and Venture Development in Established Companies," *Journal of Business Venturing* 1, no. 1 (Winter 1985): 56–59. Copyright © 1985 by Elsevier Science Publishing Co., Inc.

3-4b Encouraging Innovation

As will be discussed in Chapter 5, innovation is the specific tool of the entrepreneur. Therefore, corporations must understand and develop innovation as the key element in their strategy. Numerous researchers have examined the importance of innovation within the corporate environment.[34]

Innovation is described as chaotic and unplanned by some authors,[35] while other researchers insist it is a systematic discipline.[36] Both of these positions can be true, depending on the nature of the innovation. One way to understand this concept is to focus on two different types of innovation: radical and incremental.[37]

Radical innovation is the launching of inaugural breakthroughs such as social networking, mobile computing, cloud storage, online dating, and green technologies. These innovations take experimentation and determined vision, which are not necessarily managed but *must* be recognized and nurtured.

Incremental innovation refers to the systematic evolution of a product or service into newer or larger markets. Examples include microwave popcorn, popcorn used for packaging (to replace Styrofoam), frozen yogurt, and so forth. Many times, the incremental innovation will take over after a radical innovation introduces a breakthrough. The structure, marketing, financing, and formal systems of a corporation can help implement incremental innovation. It has been said that an organization, through its people, can do a thousand things 1 percent better rather than waiting to do one thing 1,000 percent better.

Both types of innovation require vision and support. This support takes different steps for effective development (see Table 3.4). In addition, they both need a **champion**—a person with a vision and the ability to share it.[38] Finally, both types of innovation require an effort by the top management of the corporation to develop and educate employees concerning innovation and intrapreneurship, a concept known as **top management support**.[39]

Encouraging innovation requires a willingness not only to tolerate failure but also to learn from it. For example, one of the founders of 3M, Francis G. Oakie, had an idea to replace razor blades with sandpaper. He believed that men could rub sandpaper on their face rather than use a sharp razor. He was wrong, and the idea failed, but his ideas evolved until he developed a waterproof sandpaper for the auto industry, which was a blockbuster success!

TABLE 3.4 DEVELOPING AND SUPPORTING RADICAL AND INCREMENTAL INNOVATION

Radical	Incremental
Stimulate through challenges and puzzles.	Set systematic goals and deadlines.
Remove budgetary and deadline constraints when possible.	Stimulate through competitive pressures.
Encourage technical education and exposure to customers.	Encourage technical education and exposure to customers.
Allow technical sharing and brainstorming sessions.	Hold weekly meetings that include key management and marketing staff.
Give personal attention—develop relationships of trust.	Delegate more responsibility.
Encourage praise from outside parties.	Set clear financial rewards for meeting goals and deadlines.
Have flexible funds for opportunities that arise.	
Reward with freedom and capital for new projects and interests.	

Source: Adapted from Harry S. Dent, Jr., "Growth through New Product Development," *Small Business Reports* (November 1990): 36.

Thus, 3M's philosophy was born. Innovation is a numbers game: The more ideas, the better the chances for a successful innovation. In other words, to master innovation, companies must have a tolerance for failure. This philosophy has paid off for 3M. Antistatic videotape, translucent dental braces, synthetic ligaments for knee surgery, heavy-duty reflective sheeting for construction signs, and, of course, Post-it notes are just some of the great innovations developed by the organization. Overall, the company has a catalog of 60,000 products.[40]

Today, 3M follows a set of innovative rules that encourages employees to foster ideas. The key rules include the following:

- *Don't kill a project.* If an idea can't find a home in one of 3M's divisions, a staffer can devote 15 percent of his or her time to prove it is workable. For those who need seed money, as many as 90 Genesis grants of $50,000 are awarded each year.

- *Tolerate failure.* Encouraging plenty of experimentation and risk taking allows more chances for a new product hit. The goal: Divisions must derive 25 percent of sales from products introduced in the past five years. The target may be boosted to 30 percent in some cases.

- *Keep divisions small.* Division managers must know each staffer's first name. When a division gets too big, perhaps reaching $250 million to $300 million in sales, it is split up.

- *Motivate the champions.* When a 3M employee has a product idea, he or she recruits an action team to develop it. Salaries and promotions are tied into the product's progress. The champion has a chance to someday run his or her own product group or division.

- *Stay close to the customer.* Researchers, marketers, and managers visit with customers and routinely invite them to help brainstorm product ideas.

- *Share the wealth.* Technology, wherever it is developed, belongs to everyone.[41]

3-4c Structuring the Work Environment

When establishing the drive to innovate in today's corporations, one of the most critical steps is to invest heavily in an innovative environment. A top-level manager's job is to create a work environment that is highly conducive to innovation and entrepreneurial behaviors. Within such an environment, each employee has the opportunity to "step up to the plate." The willingness and ability to act upon one's innate entrepreneurial potential is based on a calculated assessment. Conditions in the internal work environment dictate the perceived costs and benefits associated with taking personal risks, challenging current practices, devoting time to unproven approaches, persevering in the face of organizational resistance, and enduring the ambiguity and stress that entrepreneurial behavior can create. Therefore, credible innovation is more likely in companies where all individuals' entrepreneurial potential is sought and nurtured and where organizational knowledge is widely shared. The managerial challenge becomes that of using workplace design elements to develop an "innovation friendly" internal environment.

This concept, when coupled with the other elements of an innovation strategy, can enhance the potential for employees to become venture developers. To develop employees as a source of innovations, companies need to provide more nurturing and information-sharing activities.[42] In addition, they need to develop an environment that will help innovative-minded people reach their full potential. Employee perception of an innovative environment is critical for stressing the importance of management's commitment not only to the organization's people but also to the innovative projects.

A firm's internal entrepreneurial climate should be assessed to evaluate in what manner it is supportive for entrepreneurial behavior to exist and how that is perceived by the managers. When attempting to inventory the firm's current situation regarding the readiness for innovation, managers need to identify parts of the firm's structure, control systems, human resource management systems, and culture that inhibit and parts that facilitate entrepreneurial behavior as the foundation for successfully implementing corporate innovation.

One example of an assessment instrument that can be used is the **Corporate Entrepreneurship Assessment Instrument (CEAI)**, which was developed by researchers Donald F. Kuratko and Jeffrey S. Hornsby to provide for a psychometrically sound measurement of key entrepreneurial climate factors.[43] The responses to the CEAI were statistically analyzed and resulted in five identified factors. These five factors are critical to the internal environment of an organization seeking to have its managers pursue innovative activity. It is important to understand these factors in order to assess the organization's readiness for corporate entrepreneurial activity. Each of the factors discussed next are aspects of the organization over which management has some control. Each is briefly defined and includes illustrations of specific elements of a firm's environment relative to each dimension.

MANAGEMENT SUPPORT

LO7 Examine the methods of developing managers for corporate entrepreneurship

This is the extent to which the management structure itself encourages employees to believe that innovation is, in fact, part of the role set for all organization members. Some of the specific conditions that reflect management support include quick adoption of employee ideas, recognition of people who bring ideas forward, support for small experimental projects, and seed money to get projects off the ground.

AUTONOMY/WORK DISCRETION

Workers have discretion to the extent that they are able to make decisions about performing their own work in the way they believe is most effective. Organizations should allow employees to make decisions about their work process and should avoid criticizing them for making mistakes when innovating.

REWARDS/REINFORCEMENT

Rewards and reinforcement enhance the motivation of individuals to engage in innovative behavior. Organizations must be characterized by providing rewards contingent on performance, providing challenges, increasing responsibilities, and making the ideas of innovative people known to others in the organizational hierarchy.

TIME AVAILABILITY

The fostering of new and innovative ideas requires that individuals have time to incubate ideas. Organizations must moderate the workload of people, avoid putting time constraints on all aspects of a person's job, and allow people to work with others on long-term problem solving.

ORGANIZATIONAL BOUNDARIES

These boundaries, real and imagined, prevent people from looking at problems outside their own jobs. People must be encouraged to look at the organization from a broad perspective. Organizations should avoid having standard operating procedures for all major parts of jobs, and should reduce dependence on narrow job descriptions and rigid performance standards.[44]

The statistical results from the CEAI demonstrated support for this underlying set of internal environmental factors that organizations need to focus on when seeking to introduce an innovative strategy.[45] These factors, as well as the previous research mentioned, are the foundation for the critical steps involved in introducing a corporate entrepreneurial climate.

An instrument like the CEAI can be used to develop a profile of a firm across the five internal climate dimensions mentioned above. Low scores in one specific dimension of the CEAI suggest the need to focus on that particular dimension for improvement in order to enhance the firm's readiness for entrepreneurial behavior and eventually successful corporate innovation. This can significantly benefit organizations as it provides an indication of a firm's likelihood of being able to successfully use a corporate innovation process. It highlights the specific dimensions of the internal work environment that should be the focus of ongoing design and development efforts. Further, the CEAI can be used as an assessment tool for evaluating corporate training needs with respect to entrepreneurship and innovation. Determining these training needs sets the stage for improving managers' skills and increasing their sensitivity to the challenges of eliciting and then supporting entrepreneurial behavior.

Another researcher, Vijay Sathe, has suggested a number of areas on which corporations must focus if they are going to facilitate corporate entrepreneurial behavior. The first is to encourage—not mandate—innovative activity. Managers should use financial rewards and strong company recognition rather than rules or strict procedures to encourage corporate entrepreneurship. This is actually a stronger internal control and direction method than traditional parameters.

Another area of focus is the proper control of human resource policies. Managers need to remain in positions long enough to allow them to learn an industry and a particular division. Rather than move managers around in positions, as is the case in many companies, Sathe suggests "selected rotation," in which managers are exposed to different but related territories. This helps managers gain sufficient knowledge for innovation development.

A third factor is for management to sustain a commitment to innovative projects long enough for momentum to occur. Failures will inevitably occur, and learning must be the key aftermath of those failures. Thus, sustained commitment is an important element in managing corporate entrepreneurship.

A final element suggested by Sathe is to bet on people, not on analysis. Although analysis is always important to judge a project's progression, it should be done in a supportive rather than an imposed style. The supportive challenge can help innovators realize errors, test their convictions, and accomplish a self-analysis.[46]

It should be mentioned that the exact rewards for corporate entrepreneuring are not yet agreed on by most researchers.[47] Some believe that allowing the inventor to take charge of the new venture is the best reward. Others say it is allowing the corporate entrepreneur more discretionary time to work on future projects. Still others insist that special capital, called intracapital, should be set aside for the corporate entrepreneur to use whenever investment money is needed for further research ideas.

In light of these climate elements, it is clear that change in the corporate structure is inevitable if innovative activity is going to exist and prosper. The change process consists of a series of emerging constructions of people, corporate goals, and existing needs. In short, the organization can encourage innovation by relinquishing controls and changing the traditional bureaucratic structure. (See Table 3.5 for the Corporate Innovator's Commandments.)

Managers and employees across a firm are most likely to engage in entrepreneurial behavior when the organizational dimensions to that behavior are well-perceived, widely known, and universally accepted. Individuals assess their entrepreneurial capacities in reference to what they perceive to be is a set of organizational resources, opportunities, and obstacles related to entrepreneurial activity. Once it is determined that the value of an environment encouraging entrepreneurial behavior exceeds that of all other organizational behaviors, then managers will continuously champion, facilitate, and nurture that innovation-friendly environment.

TABLE 3.5 THE CORPORATE INNOVATOR'S COMMANDMENTS

1. Come to work each day willing to give up your job for the innovation.

2. Circumvent any bureaucratic orders aimed at stopping your innovation.

3. Ignore your job description—do any job needed to make your innovation work.

4. Build a spirited innovation team that has the "fire" to make it happen.

5. Keep your innovation "underground" until it is prepared for demonstration to the corporate management.

6. Find a key upper-level manager who believes in you and your ideas and who will serve as a sponsor to your innovation.

7. Permission is rarely granted in organizations; thus, always seek forgiveness for the "ignorance" of the rules that you will display.

8. Always be realistic about the ways to achieve the innovation goals.

9. Share the glory of the accomplishments with everyone on the team.

© Cengage Learning

3-4d Control versus Autonomy

As we have shown, employees engaging in entrepreneurial behavior are the foundation for organizational innovation, so in order to develop "corporate innovation," organizations must establish a process through which individuals in an established firm pursue entrepreneurial opportunities to innovate without regard to the level and nature of currently available resources. However, keep in mind that, in the absence of proper control mechanisms, firms that manifest corporate innovative activity may "tend to generate an incoherent mass of interesting but unrelated opportunities that may have profit potential, but that don't move [those] firms toward a desirable future."[48] Therefore, those factors that drives corporate entrepreneurial activity to produce high levels of innovation performance are likely contingent upon a firm's ability to judiciously use control mechanisms for the proper selection and effective guidance on entrepreneurial actions and initiatives.[49]

Although some consultants emphasize the need to "unleash the entrepreneurial hostages" in organizations simply by removing constraints on behavior, it is clear that, in doing so, they may be ignoring opportunities better to align innovations with organizational interests, which results from encouraging, directing, restricting, and prohibiting behaviors and initiatives. Not all corporate entrepreneurial behavior is good for the organization. Yet the literature in the corporate innovation area tends to implicitly regard such behavior as inherently virtuous. This is an unfortunate and potentially dangerous bias. As noted by researchers Donald F. Kuratko and Michael G. Goldsby,[50] the encouragement of corporate entrepreneurship can and often does result in counterproductive, rogue behavior by organizational members. Thus, the deliberate design and development of organizational systems reflecting the organizational dimensions for an environment conducive to corporate innovation is critical. As such, the senior manager's task is not simply to build an organization whose core qualities are conducive to innovation but rather to design and develop innovation-facilitating and control-facilitating mechanisms that complement one another such that the innovative potential that resides within the organization is leveraged for the highest and best organizational purposes.

The exhibition of certain controls is not antithetical to the interests of corporate innovation but rather inherent to those interests. As such, observations to the effect that control is the enemy of successful innovation are naïve. Managers should understand that innovation is a process amenable to the application of structured, disciplined oversight. The successful pursuit of innovation demands that managers approach innovation challenges with the understanding that the means by which potentially desirable outcomes might be generated can be well understood and deliberately constructed. There are rules, methods, and general process knowledge that can be brought to bear in facilitation of successful innovation efforts. As such, it's often not the absence of rules and well-understood procedures that results in successful innovation, it's their presence. Managers are well advised to recognize this reality.

3-4e Preparation for Failure

The idea of "learning from failure" is axiomatic in the corporate entrepreneurial community. However, dealing with failure on a personal level is something that has not been, until recently, fully examined. Researchers Dean A. Shepherd, Jeffrey G. Covin, and Donald F. Kuratko have written about the importance of managing grief that results from project failure. Grief, which triggers behavioral, psychological, and physiological symptoms, is a negative emotional response to the loss of something important. Managing grief, therefore, represents a particularly salient task in the context of corporate entrepreneurship practice, because the amount of commitment essential to project success is often matched by corresponding levels of grief when projects fail.

Organizational routines and rituals are likely to influence the grief recovery of those involved in failed projects. To the extent that an organization's social support systems can effectively channel negative emotions, greater learning and motivational outcomes from project failures are certainly possible. The inevitability of project failure tests social support mechanisms and failure-related coping skills of corporate managers, giving dedicated innovation units with adequate social supports for dealing with grief an operational edge that also strengthens coping self-efficacy of individuals.[51]

3-4f Preparing Management

Executive leaders must create an understanding of the innovation process for their employees. Having assessed the firm's internal work environment supports innovative activity, senior managers should also determine if corporate innovation and entrepreneurial behavior are understood by the firms' employees. Key decision makers must find ways to explain the purpose of using a corporate innovation process to those from whom entrepreneurial behaviors are expected.

Understanding and supporting a corporate innovation process should not be left to chance. Experience demonstrates that executives need to develop a program with the purpose of helping all parties who will be affected by corporate innovation to understand the value of the entrepreneurial behavior that the firm is requesting of them as the foundation for a successful innovation.

As a way for organizations to develop that understanding for innovation and entrepreneurial activity, a corporate entrepreneurship/innovation training program often induces the change needed in the work atmosphere. It is not our intent to elaborate completely on the content of a training program here, but a brief summary of an actual program is presented to provide a general understanding of how such a program is designed to introduce an entrepreneurial environment in a company. This award-winning training program is intended to create an awareness of entrepreneurial opportunities in organizations. The Corporate Innovation Training Program consists of six modules, each designed to train participants to support corporate innovations in their own work area.[52] The modules and a brief summary of their contents are as follows:

1. **The Entrepreneurial Experience.** An enthusiastic overview of the Entrepreneurial Experience, in which participants are introduced to the entrepreneurial revolution that has taken place throughout the world over the last three decades. Participants are challenged to think innovatively and recognize the need for breaking out of the old paradigms in today's organizations.

2. **Innovative Thinking.** The process of thinking innovatively is foreign to most traditional organizations. The misconceptions about thinking innovatively are reviewed, and a discussion of the most common inhibitors is presented. After completing an innovation inventory, managers engage in several exercises designed to facilitate their own innovative thinking.

3. **Idea Acceleration Process.** Managers generate a set of specific ideas on which they would like to work. The process includes examining a number of aspects of the corporation, including structural barriers and facilitators. Additionally, managers determine resources needed to accomplish their projects.

4. **Barriers and Facilitators to Innovative Thinking.** The most common barriers to innovative behavior are reviewed and discussed. Managers complete several exercises that will help them deal with barriers in the workplace. In addition, video case histories are shown that depict actual corporate innovators that have been successful in dealing with corporate barriers.

5. **Sustaining Innovation Teams (I-Teams).** The concept of forming I-Teams to focus on specific innovations is examined. Managers work together to form teams based on the ideas that have been circulating among the entire group. Team dynamics is reviewed for each group to understand.

6. **The Innovation Action Plan.** After managers examine several aspects of facilitators and barriers to behaving innovatively in their organization, teams are asked to begin the process of completing an action plan. The plan includes setting goals, establishing an I-Team, assessing current conditions, developing a step-by-step timetable for project completion, and project evaluation.

This type of program should be ongoing in nature. As new innovative opportunities surface in a firm's external environment, as the internal work environment changes, and as new employees join the organization, it is appropriate for those from whom entrepreneurial behavior is expected to work together to find the best ways to proceed to implement a corporate innovation process. In this sense, efforts to successfully engage in corporate innovation must themselves be innovative—changing in response to ever-changing conditions in the firm's internal and external environments.

3-4g Developing I-Teams

I-Teams and the potential they hold for producing innovative results are recognized as a twenty-first century productivity breakthrough. Certainly, no one doubts that their popularity is on the rise. Companies that have committed to an I-Team approach often label the change they have undergone a "transformation" or "revolution." This modern breed of work team is a new strategy for many firms. It is referred to as self-directing, self-managing, or high performing, although in reality an I-Team fits all of those descriptions.[53]

In examining the entrepreneurial development of corporations, Robert Reich found that entrepreneurial thinking is not the sole province of the company's founder or its top managers. Rather, it is diffused throughout the company, where experimentation and development occur all the time as the company searches for new ways to build on knowledge already accumulated by its workers. Reich defines collective entrepreneurship as follows:

> In collective entrepreneurship, individual skills are integrated into a group; this collective capacity to innovate becomes something greater than the sum of its parts. Over time, as group members work through various problems and approaches, they learn about each other's abilities. They learn how they can help one another perform better, what each can contribute to a particular project, how they can best take advantage of one another's experience. Each participant is constantly on the lookout for small adjustments that will speed and smooth the evolution of the whole. The net result of many such small-scale adaptations, effected throughout the organization, is to propel the enterprise forward.[54]

In keeping with Reich's focus on collective entrepreneurship, I-Teams offer corporations the opportunity to use the talents of individuals without losing a sense of teamwork.

An innovation team, or I-Team, is composed of two or more people who formally create and share ownership of a new organization.[55] The unit is semiautonomous in the sense that it has its own budget as well as a leader with the freedom to make decisions within broad guidelines. Sometimes the leader is called an "innovation champion" or a "corporate entrepreneur." The unit often is separated from other parts of the firm—in particular, from parts involved with daily activities. This prevents the unit from engaging in procedures that can stifle innovative activities. If the innovation proves successful, however, it eventually is treated the same as other outputs the organization produces. It is then integrated into the larger organization.[56]

In many ways, an I-Team is a small business operating within a large business, and its strength is its focus on design issues (i.e., on structure and process) for innovative activities. One organization that operated successfully with the I-Team concept was the Signode Corporation (see "Entrepreneurship in Practice").

Specific entrepreneurial strategies vary from firm to firm. However, they all follow similar patterns of seeking a proactive change of the status quo and a new, flexible approach to operations management.

3-5 SUSTAINING A CORPORATE ENTREPRENEURSHIP STRATEGY

While entrepreneurial actions are a phenomenon that have captivated the interest of executives in many corporate boardrooms, there is a danger that managers can get too caught up in the excitement of the concept of innovation or inspiring stories of individual corporate innovators. It is easy to become enamored with the idea of innovation, but the true value of innovation lies in the extent to which executive leaders are committed to making it a part of the overall corporate strategy to create sustainable competitive advantage.

It is well documented in the conceptual literature that managers at all structural levels have critical strategic roles to fulfill for the organization to be successful. Senior-, middle-, and first-level managers possess distinct responsibilities with respect to each subprocess. *Senior-level managers* have ratifying, recognizing, and directing roles that in turn are associated with particular managerial actions.[57] Researchers Donald F. Kuratko, R. Duane Ireland, Jeffrey G. Covin, and Jeffrey S. Hornsby contend that *middle-level managers* endorse, refine, and shepherd entrepreneurial opportunities, and identify, acquire, and deploy resources needed to pursue those opportunities. *First-level managers* have experimenting roles that correspond to the competence definition subprocess, adjusting roles that correspond to the competence modification subprocess, and conforming roles that correspond to the competence deployment subprocess.

Thus, organizations that pursue corporate entrepreneurship strategies likely exhibit a cascading yet integrated set of entrepreneurial actions at the senior, middle, and first levels of management.

At the senior level, managers act in concert with others throughout the firm to identify effective means through which new businesses can be created or existing ones reconfigured. Corporate entrepreneurship is pursued in light of environmental opportunities and threats, with the purpose of creating a more effective alignment between the company and conditions in its external environment. The entrepreneurial actions expected of middle-level managers are framed around the need for this group to propose and interpret entrepreneurial opportunities that might create new business for the firm or increase the firm's competitiveness in current business domains. First-line managers exhibit the "experimenting" role as they unearth the operational ideas for innovative improvements. An important interpretation of previous research has been the belief that managers would surface ideas for entrepreneurial actions from every level of management, particularly the first-line and middle levels. Therefore, managers across levels are jointly responsible for their organization's entrepreneurial actions.[58]

LO8 Illustrate the interactive process of corporate entrepreneurship

An organization's sustained effort in corporate entrepreneurship is contingent upon individual members continuing to undertake innovative activities and upon positive perceptions of the activity by the organization's executive management, which will in turn support the further allocation of necessary organizational antecedents. Figure 3.4 illustrates the importance of perceived implementation/output relationships at the organizational and individual levels for sustaining corporate entrepreneurship.[59]

The first part of the model is based on theoretical foundations from previous strategy and entrepreneurship research. The second part of the model considers the comparisons made at

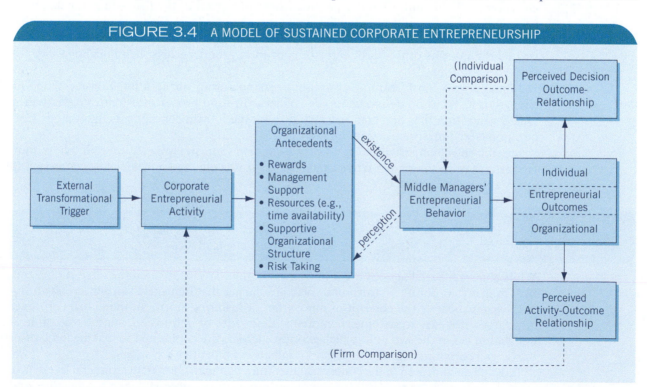

FIGURE 3.4 A MODEL OF SUSTAINED CORPORATE ENTREPRENEURSHIP

Source: Donald F. Kuratko, Jeffrey S. Hornsby, and Michael G. Goldsby, "Sustaining Corporate Entrepreneurship: Modeling Perceived Implementation and Outcome Comparisons at Organizational and Individual Levels," *International Journal of Entrepreneurship and Innovation* 5, no. 2 (May 2004): 79.

the individual and organizational level on organizational outcomes, both perceived and real, that influence the continuation of the entrepreneurial activity.

The model demonstrates that a transformational trigger (something external or internal to the company that causes a change to take place) initiates the need for strategic adaptation or change. One such change that can be chosen is corporate entrepreneurial activity. Based on this choice of strategic direction, the proposed model centers around the individual's decision to behave entrepreneurially. Sustained entrepreneurial activity is the result of the perception of the existence of several organizational antecedents, such as top management support, autonomy, rewards, resources, and flexible organizational boundaries. The outcomes realized from this entrepreneurial activity are then compared at both the individual and organizational level to previous expectations. Thus, corporate entrepreneurial activities are a result of an equity perception by both the individual and the organization. Both must be satisfied with the outcomes for the entrepreneurial activities to continue from the organizational perspective as well as the individual perspective. Satisfaction with performance outcomes serves as a feedback mechanism for either sustaining the current strategy or selecting an alternative one. Individuals, as agents of the strategic change, must also be satisfied with the intrinsic and extrinsic outcomes they receive for their entrepreneurial behavior. While it may be a "chicken-and-egg" question as to whether individual behavior or organizational strategy should change first, the model suggests that—for a major strategic change—both are instrumental in making the change successful.

THE ENTREPRENEURIAL PROCESS

Internal Innovators

Emphasizing that the success of corporate innovators is due to their dedication to pursuing a new, outside the box idea that benefit their employers, we look at a few young managers who adopted an entrepreneurial attitude and creative problem-solving to rise through their organization's hierarchy.

Matthew Zubiller: A corporate strategist at pharmaceutical company McKesson Corporation who started a high-tech healthcare business in an atmosphere unused to internal start-ups. Using the company's healthcare information technology unit as a starting point, Zubiller developed Advanced Diagnostics Management, a unit centered on a high-tech tool for physicians related to genetic testing. He likely had to overcome a number of traditional management practices in this large bureaucratic company that was unaccustomed to internal innovation, such as "It's not in our budget" or "That's a weird idea" response. To achieve internal support, he created a "shadow board" of company executives who advised the venture creation and helped secure $5 million in support. As a result of his efforts, Zubiller was promoted to vice president.

Kori Reed: A public relations manager at ConAgra and an expert in child hunger, Reed recognized that ConAgra could benefit by linking its products to initiatives to fight child hunger. She used her existing knowledge of antihunger campaigns and interest in combating childhood hunger to identify an opportunity. She noted the incongruity between working for a food products company, overflowing with food abundance, and starving and undernourished children. She brought executives into an advisory committee and made antihunger language a cornerstone of the company's

marketing campaign. Reed convinced senior executives that the organization needed a vice president of this cause, to which she was then promoted.

Pam Rogers Klyn: A product development manager at Whirlpool Corporation who focused on cost control efforts. Rather than having a "special committee" team dedicated to cutting costs, she advocated for a company-wide emphasis on cost savings, stressing small efforts like turning off lights and tying annual bonuses to cost goals. In developing and implementing this idea, she worked closely with her CEO and gave him a lot of credit. By linking cost savings requirements to yearly bonuses, Whirlpool's North American division was able to save over $850 million in one year.

One clear commonality among these individuals is their effort to gain senior leadership buy-in and involvement. In each case, they worked with a select few, picking individuals who could see the bigger picture while being excited about a small, focused effort. A successful corporate entrepreneurship program needs the executive support that can help build the new venture from the inside. Corporate bureaucracies usually require a champion for any change. Getting permission is always the most challenging part of any new idea but having a champion means having some help in moving the process along. It always takes individuals who are self-starters with a strong drive to achieve and an opportunity orientation.

Source: Adapted from Joann S. Lublin "Finding Their Way to the Fast Track," *Wall Street Journal,* January 19, 2012; and Donald F. Kuratko, Michael G. Goldsby, and Jeffrey S. Hornsby, *Innovation Acceleration: Transforming Organizational Thinking* (Upper Saddle River, NJ: Pearson/Prentice Hall, 2012).

SUMMARY

Corporate entrepreneurship is the process of profitably creating innovation within an organizational setting. Most companies are realizing the need for corporate entrepreneurship as a response to (1) the rapidly growing number of new, sophisticated competitors; (2) a sense of distrust in the traditional methods of corporate management; and (3) an exodus of some of the best and brightest people from corporations to become small-business entrepreneurs.

To create the right climate for in-house entrepreneurship, companies must develop the following four characteristics: (1) explicit goals, (2) a system of feedback and positive reinforcement, (3) an emphasis on individual responsibility, (4) rewards based on results, and (5) do not punish failures. Organizations create corporate entrepreneurship in a number of ways. The first step is to understand the obstacles to corporate venturing; these usually are based on the adverse impact of traditional management techniques. The next step is to adopt innovative principles that include atmosphere and vision, multiple approaches, interactive learning, and Skunk Works.

Specific strategies for corporate entrepreneurship entail the development of both vision and innovation. Two types of innovation exist: radical and incremental. To facilitate the development of innovation, corporations need to focus on the key factors of top management support, time, resources, and rewards. Thus, commitment to and support of innovative activity are critical.

I-Teams are the semiautonomous units that have the collective capacity to develop new ideas. Sometimes referred to as self-managing or high-performance teams, I-Teams are emerging as the new breed of work teams formed to strengthen innovative developments.

At the end of this chapter, we discussed the process of corporate entrepreneurship by examining the role of middle managers in corporate entrepreneurial activity and the concept of sustained corporate entrepreneurship.

KEY TERMS

bootlegging

champion

collective entrepreneurship

corporate entrepreneurship

Corporate Entrepreneurship
    Assessment Instrument (CEAI)

corporate venturing

incremental innovation

innovation team (I-Team)

interactive learning

intracapital

intrapreneurship

radical innovation

Skunk Works

strategic entrepreneurship

top management support

REVIEW AND DISCUSSION QUESTIONS

1. In your own words, what is corporate entrepreneurship?

2. What are two reasons that such a strong desire to develop corporate entrepreneurs has arisen in recent years?

3. What are some of the corporate obstacles that must be overcome to establish a corporate entrepreneurial environment?

4. What are some of the innovative principles identified by James Brian Quinn that companies need to establish?

5. A number of corporations today are working to reengineer corporate thinking and encourage an innovative environment. What types of steps would you recommend? Offer at least three and explain each.

6. What are five useful rules for innovation?

7. What are three advantages of developing a corporate entrepreneurial philosophy?

8. Identify the four key elements on which managers should concentrate to develop a corporate entrepreneurship strategy.

9. Explain the differences between radical and incremental innovation.

10. Identify the five specific entrepreneurial climate factors that organizations need to address in structuring their environment.

11. Why are innovation teams emerging as part of a new strategy for many corporations?

12. What are the roles of middle managers in corporate entrepreneurship? Be specific.

13. Describe the elements that are involved in sustaining corporate entrepreneurship.

NOTES

1. Shaker A. Zahra, Donald F. Kuratko, and Daniel F. Jennings, "Entrepreneurship and the Acquisition of Dynamic Organizational Capabilities," *Entrepreneurship Theory and Practice* 23, no. 3 (1999): 5–10.

2. See, for example, C. Wesley Morse, "The Delusion of Intrapreneurship," *Long Range Planning* 19 (1986): 92–95; W. Jack Duncan et al., "Intrapreneurship and the Reinvention of the Corporation," *Business Horizons* 30, no. 3 (May/June 1988): 16–21; and Neal Thornberry, "Corporate Entrepreneurship: Antidote or Oxymoron?" *European Management Journal* 19, no. 5 (2001): 526–33.

3. Donald F. Kuratko, R. Duane Ireland, and Jeffrey S. Hornsby, "Improving Firm Performance Through Entrepreneurial Actions: Acordia's Corporate Entrepreneurship Strategy," *Academy of Management Executive* 15, no. 4 (2001): 60–71; Jeffrey G. Covin and Morgan P. Miles, "Strategic Use of Corporate Venturing," *Entrepreneurship Theory and Practice* 31, no. 2 (2007): 183–207; and Matthew R. Marvel, Abbie Griffin, John Hebda, and Bruce Vojak, "Examining the Technical Corporate Entrepreneurs' Motivation: Voices from the Field," *Entrepreneurship Theory and Practice* 31, no. 5 (2007): 753–68.

4. For example, see Michael H. Morris and J. Don Trotter, "Institutionalizing Entrepreneurship in a Large Company: A Case Study at AT&T," *Industrial Marketing Management* 19 (1990): 131–34; Brian McWilliams, "Strength from Within—How Today's Companies Nurture Entrepreneurs," *Enterprise* (April 1993): 43–44; Donald F. Kuratko, Michael D. Houk, and Richard M. Hodgetts, "Acordia, Inc. Leadership Through the Transformation of Growing Small," *Journal of Leadership Studies* 5, no. 2 (1998): 152–64; and Michael H. Morris, Donald F. Kuratko, and Jeffrey G. Covin, *Corporate Entrepreneurship and Innovation*, 3rd ed. (Mason, OH: Cengage/South-Western, 2011).

5. See, for example, Gary Hamel, *Leading the Revolution* (Boston: Harvard Business School Press, 2000); Keith McFarland, *The Breakthrough Company* (New York: Crown, 2008); Carmine Gallo, *The Innovation Secrets of Steve Jobs* (New York: McGraw Hill, 2011; and Walter Isaacson, *The Innovators* (New York: Simon & Schuster, 2014)

6. Shaker A. Zahra, Daniel F. Jennings, and Donald F. Kuratko, "The Antecedents and Consequences of Firm-Level Entrepreneurship: The State of the Field," *Entrepreneurship Theory and Practice* 24, no. 2 (1999): 45–65; Donald F. Kuratko, "Corporate Entrepreneurship," in *Foundations and Trends in Entrepreneurship* (Boston: Now Publishers, 2007); Morris, Kuratko, and Covin, *Corporate Entrepreneurship and Innovation*.; and also, Donald F. Kuratko and Sarah Nagelvoort, "Corporate Entrepreneurship" in *Oxford Bibliographies* (Oxford University Press USA, 2015).

7. Donald F. Kuratko, Michael G. Goldsby, and Jeffrey S. Hornsby, *Innovation Acceleration: Transforming Organizational Thinking* (Upper Saddle River, NJ: Pearson/Prentice Hall, 2012).

8. Gifford Pinchot III, *Intrapreneuring* (New York: Harper & Row, 1985).

9. Steven C. Brandt, *Entrepreneuring in Established Companies* (Homewood, IL: Dow Jones-Irwin, 1986), 54.

10. Donald F. Kuratko, "The Entrepreneurial Imperative of the 21st Century," *Business Horizons* 52 no. 5 (2009): 421–28.

11. Jeffrey G. Covin and G. T. Lumpkin, "Entrepreneurial Orientation Theory and Research: Reflections on a Needed Construct," *Entrepreneurship Theory and Practice* 35 (2011): 855–72; Patrick M. Kreiser, Louis D. Marino, Donald F. Kuratko, and K. Mark Weaver, "Disaggregating entrepreneurial orientation: the non-linear impact of innovativeness, proactiveness and risk-taking on SME performance," *Small Business Economics* 40, no. 2 (2013): 273–91; and Brian S. Anderson, Patrick M. Kreiser, Donald F. Kuratko, Jeffrey S. Hornsby, and Yoshihiro Eshima, "Reconceptualizing Entrepreneurial Orientation," *Strategic Management Journal,* 2015. (in press).

12. Jeffrey G. Covin and Morgan P. Miles, "Corporate Entrepreneurship and the Pursuit of Competitive Advantage," *Entrepreneurship Theory and Practice* 23, no. 3 (1999): 47–64; Joanna Barsh, Marla M. Capozzi, and Jonathan Davidson, "Leadership and Innovation," *The McKinsey Quarterly* 1 (2008): 37–47; and Donald F. Kuratko, Jeffrey S. Hornsby, and James Hayton, "Corporate Entrepreneurship: The Innovative Challenge for a New Global Economic Reality," *Small Business Economics* 45, no. 2 (2015): 245–53.

13. Donald F. Kuratko, Jeffrey G. Covin, & Jeffrey S. Hornsby, "Why Implementing Corporate Innovation is so Difficult," *Business Horizons,* 57 No. 5 (2014): 647–655.

14. Adapted from: Pinchot III, *Intrapreneuring*, 198–99.

15. Robert Simons, "How Risky Is Your Company?" *Harvard Business Review* 77, no. 3 (May/June 1999): 85–94.

16. Deborah Dougherty, "Managing Your Core Incompetencies for Corporate Venturing," *Entrepreneurship Theory and Practice* (Spring 1995): 113–35.

17. See Robert A. Burgelman and L. Valikangas, "Managing Internal Corporate Venturing Cycles," *MIT Sloan Management Review* 45, no. 4 (2004): 47–55; Donald F. Kuratko, "Corporate Entrepreneurship"; and Michael Bierwerth, Christian Schwens, Rodrigo Isidor, and Rüdiger Kabst, "Corporate Entrepreneurship and Performance: A Meta-Analysis," *Small Business Economics* 45, no. 2 (2015): 255–78.

18. Fariborz Damanpour, "Organizational Innovation: A Meta-Analysis of Determinant and Moderators," *Academy of Management Journal* 34, no. 3 (1991): 355–90.

19. Shaker A. Zahra, "Predictors and Financial Outcomes of Corporate Entrepreneurship: An Exploratory Study," *Journal of Business Venturing* 6, no. 4 (1991): 259–86.

20. William D. Guth and Ari Ginsberg, "Corporate Entrepreneurship," Special Issue, *Strategic Management Journal* 11 (1990): 5–15.

21. Morris, Kuratko, and Covin, *Corporate Entrepreneurship and Innovation*; see also Donald F. Kuratko and David B. Audretsch, "Clarifying the Domains of Corporate Entrepreneurship," *International Entrepreneurship & Management Journal* 9, no. 3 (2013): 323–35.

22. Pramodita Sharma and James J. Chrisman, "Toward a Reconciliation of the Definitional Issues in the Field of Corporate Entrepreneurship," *Entrepreneurship Theory and Practice* 23, no. 3 (1999): 11–28; Robert P. Garrett Jr. and Jeffrey G. Covin, "Internal Corporate Venture Operations Independence and Performance: A Knowledge-Based Perspective," *Entrepreneurship Theory & Practice* (2015): in press; and Jeffrey G. Covin, Robert P. Garrett, Donald F. Kuratko, and Dean A. Shepherd, "Value Proposition Evolution and the Performance of Internal Corporate Ventures," *Journal of Business Venturing* 30, no. 5 (2015): 749–74.

23. R. Duane Ireland, Donald F. Kuratko, and Jeffrey G. Covin, "Antecedents, Elements, and Consequences of Corporate Entrepreneurship," *Best Paper Proceedings: National Academy of Management* (August 2003), CD-ROM: L1–L6; and R. Duane Ireland, Jeffrey G. Covin, and Donald F. Kuratko, "Conceptualizing Corporate Entrepreneurship Strategy," *Entrepreneurship Theory and Practice* 33, no. 1 (2009): 19–46.

24. Tom Peters, *Liberation Management* (New York: Alfred A. Knopf, 1992); Tom Peters, *The Circle of Innovation* (New York: Alfred A. Knopf, 1997); and Tom Peters, *Re-Imagine! Business Excellence in a Disruptive Age* (New York: DK Ltd., 2003).

25. Morgan P. Miles and Jeffrey G. Covin, "Exploring the Practice of Corporate Venturing: Some Common Forms and Their Organizational Implications," *Entrepreneurship Theory and Practice* 26, no. 3 (2002): 21–40; and Robert S. Nason, Alexander McKelvie, and G. Thomas Lumpkin, "The Role of Organizational Size in the Heterogeneous Nature of Corporate Entrepreneurship," *Small Business Economics* 45, no. 2 (2015): 279–304.

26. Hollister B. Sykes and Zenas Block, "Corporate Venturing Obstacles: Sources and Solutions," *Journal of Business Venturing* 4, no. 3 (1989): 159–67; Ian C. MacMillan, Zenas Block, and P. M. Subba Narasimha, "Corporate Venturing: Alternatives, Obstacles Encountered, and Experience Effects," *Journal of Business Venturing* 2, no. 2 (1986): 177–91; Ari Ginsberg and Michael Hay, "Confronting the Challenges of Corporate Entrepreneurship: Guidelines for Venture Managers," *European Management Journal* 12 (1994): 382–89; G. T. Lumpkin and Gregory G. Dess, "Linking Two Dimensions of Entrepreneurial Orientation to Firm Performance: The Moderating Role of Environment and Industry Life Cycle," *Journal of Business Venturing* 16, no. 5 (2001): 429–52; and Marina

G. Biniari, "The Emotional Embeddedness of Corporate Entrepreneurship: The Case of Envy," *Entrepreneurship Theory and Practice* 36, no. 1 (2012): 141–70.

27. James Brian Quinn, "Managing Innovation: Controlled Chaos," *Harvard Business Review* 63, no. 3 (May/June 1985): 73–84; see also James Brian Quinn, Jordan J. Baruch, and Karen Anne Zien, *Innovation Explosion* (New York: The Free Press, 1997).

28. Ireland, Covin, and Kuratko, "Conceptualizing Corporate Entrepreneurship Strategy; see also: G. Christopher Crawford and Patrick M. Kreiser, "Corporate Entrepreneurship Strategy: Extending the Integrative Framework through the Lens of Complexity Science," *Small Business Economics* 45, no. 2 (2015): 403–23.

29. Charles Baden-Fuller and Henk W. Volberda, "Strategic Renewal: How Large Complex Organizations Prepare for the Future," *International Studies of Management & Organization* 27, no. 2 (1997): 95–120.

30. Kathleen M. Eisenhardt, Shona L. Brown, and Heidi M. Neck, "Competing on the Entrepreneurial Edge," in *Entrepreneurship as Strategy*, ed. G. D. Meyer and K. A. Heppard (Thousand Oaks, CA: Sage Publications, 2000): 49–62.

31. See Donald F. Kuratko, R. Duane Ireland, Jeffrey G. Covin, and Jeffrey S. Hornsby, "A Model of Middle-Level Managers Corporate Entrepreneurial Behavior," *Entrepreneurship Theory and Practice* 29, no. 6 (2005): 699–716; Andrew C. Corbett and Keith M. Hmieleski, "The Conflicting Cognitions of Corporate Entrepreneurs," *Entrepreneurship Theory and Practice* 31, no. 1 (2007): 103–21; and Jeffrey S. Hornsby, Donald F. Kuratko, Dean A. Shepherd, and Jennifer P. Bott, "Managers' Corporate Entrepreneurial Actions: Examining Perception and Position," *Journal of Business Venturing* 24, no. 3 (2009): 236–47.

32. See Gregory G. Dess, G. T. Lumpkin, and Jeffrey E. McGee, "Linking Corporate Entrepreneurship to Strategy, Structure, and Process: Suggested Research Directions," *Entrepreneurship Theory and Practice* 23, no. 3 (1999): 85–102; and Shu-Jou Lin, Ji-Ren Lee, "Configuring a Corporate Venturing Portfolio to Create Growth Value: Within-Portfolio Diversity and Strategic Linkage," *Journal of Business Venturing* 26, no. 4 (2011): 489–503.

33. James C. Collins and Jerry I. Porras, "Building Your Company's Vision," *Harvard Business Review* 74, no. 5 (September/October 1996): 65–77.

34. See, for example, Dean M. Schroeder, "A Dynamic Perspective on the Impact of Process Innovation upon Competitive Strategies," *Strategic Management Journal* 2 (1990): 25–41; C. Marlene Fiol, "Thought Worlds Colliding: The Role of Contradiction in Corporate Innovation Processes," *Entrepreneurship Theory and Practice* 19, no. 3 (1995): 71–90.

35. Thomas J. Peters, *Thriving on Chaos* (New York: Harper & Row, 1987).

36. Peter F. Drucker, "The Discipline of Innovation," *Harvard Business Review* 63, no. 3 (May/June 1985):

67–72; Kuratko, Goldsby, and Hornsby, *Innovation Acceleration: Transforming Organizational Thinking.*

37. Harry S. Dent, Jr., "Reinventing Corporate Innovation," *Small Business Reports* (June 1990): 31–42; see also: Kuratko, Goldsby, and Hornsby, *Innovation Acceleration: Transforming Organizational Thinking.*

38. Jane M. Howell and Christopher A. Higgins, "Champions of Change: Identifying, Understanding, and Supporting Champions of Technology Innovations," *Organizational Dynamics* 19, no. 1 (Summer 1990): 40–55; Patricia G. Greene, Candida G. Brush, and Myra M. Hart, "The Corporate Venture Champion: A Resource-based Approach to Role and Process," *Entrepreneurship Theory and Practice* 23, no. 3 (1999): 103–122.

39. John A. Pearce II, Tracy Robertson Kramer, and D. Keith Robbins, "Effects of Managers' Entrepreneurial Behavior on Subordinates," *Journal of Business Venturing* 12 (1997): 147–60.

40. See Russell Mitchell, "Masters of Innovation," *Business Week* (April 1989): 58–63; *3M Annual Report,* 1995; and Rosabeth M. Kanter, John Kao, and Fred Wiersema, *Innovation: Breakthrough Ideas at 3M, DuPont, Pfizer, and Rubbermaid GE* (New York: HarperCollins, 1997).

41. Eric Von Hipple, Stefan Thomke, and Mary Sonnack, "Creating Breakthroughs at 3M," *Harvard Business Review* 77, no. 5 (September/October 1999): 47–57.

42. David Krackhardt, "Entrepreneurial Opportunities in an Entrepreneurial Firm: A Structural Approach," *Entrepreneurship Theory and Practice* 19, no. 3 (1995): 53–70; Miles and Covin, Exploring the Practice of Corporate Venturing.

43. Donald F. Kuratko, Ray V. Montagno, and Jeffrey S. Hornsby, "Developing an Entrepreneurial Assessment Instrument for an Effective Corporate Entrepreneurial Environment," *Strategic Management Journal* 11 (1990): 49–58; Jeffrey S. Hornsby, Donald F. Kuratko, and Shaker A. Zahra, "Middle Managers' Perception of the Internal Environment for Corporate Entrepreneurship: Assessing a Measurement Scale," *Journal of Business Venturing* 17, no. 3 (2002): 253–73; and Donald F. Kuratko, Jeffrey S. Hornsby, and Jeffrey G. Covin, "Diagnosing a Firm's Internal Environment for Corporate Entrepreneurship," *Business Horizons,* 57 no. 1 (2014): 37–47.

44. Hornsby, Kuratko, Shepherd, and Bott, Managers' Corporate Entrepreneurial Actions: Examining Perception and Position; Jeroen P.J. de Jong, Sharon K. Parker, Sander Wennekers and Chia-Huei Wu, "Entrepreneurial Behavior in Organizations: Does Job Design Matter?" *Entrepreneurship Theory & Practice* 39, no. 4 (2015): 981–95.

45. Jeffrey S. Hornsby, Daniel T. Holt, and Donald F. Kuratko, "The Dynamic Nature of Corporate Entrepreneurship Constructs: Assessing the CEAI," *National Academy of Management Best Paper Proceedings,* August 2008. CD ROM; Jeffrey S.

Hornsby, Donald F. Kuratko, Daniel T. Holt, and William J. Wales, "Assessing a Measurement of Organizational Preparedness for Corporate Entrepreneurship," *Journal of Product Innovation Management* 30, no. 5 (2013): 937–55.

46. Vijay Sathe, "From Surface to Deep Corporate Entrepreneurship," *Human Resource Management* 27, no. 4 (1988): 389–411.

47. Rosabeth M. Kanter, *Innovative Reward Systems for the Changing Workplace* (New York: McGraw-Hill, 1994); see also Drew Gannon, "How to Reward Great Ideas," *Inc.* July 19, 2011.

48. G. Getz and E. G. Tuttle, "A Comprehensive Approach to Corporate Venturing," *Handbook of Business Strategy* 2, no. 1 (2001): 277–79.

49. John C. Goodale, Donald F. Kuratko, Jeffrey S. Hornsby, and Jeffrey G. Covin, "Operations Management and Corporate Entrepreneurship: The Moderating Effect of Operations Control on the Antecedents of Corporate Entrepreneurial Activity in Relation to Innovation Performance," *Journal of Operations Management* 29, no. 2 (2011): 116–27.

50. Donald F. Kuratko and Michael G. Goldsby, "Corporate Entrepreneurs or Rogue Middle Managers? A Framework for Ethical Corporate Entrepreneurship," *Journal of Business Ethics* 55, no. 1 (2004): 13–30.

51. Dean A. Shepherd, Jeffrey G. Covin, and Donald F. Kuratko, "Project Failure from Corporate Entrepreneurship: Managing the Grief Process," *Journal of Business Venturing* 24, no. 6 (2009): 588–600; see also Dean A. Shepherd, "Learning from Business Failure: Propositions About the Grief Recovery Process for the Self-Employed," *Academy of Management Review* 28 (2003): 318–29.

52. Donald F. Kuratko and Jeffrey S. Hornsby, "Developing Entrepreneurial Leadership in Contemporary Organizations," *Journal of Management Systems* 8 (1997): 17–24.

53. Chris Lee, "Beyond Teamwork," *Training* (June 1990): 25–32; Michael F. Wolff, "Building Teams—What Works," *Research Technology Management* (November/December 1989): 9–10; Deborah H. Francis and William R. Sandberg, "Friendship within Entrepreneurial Teams and Its Association with Team and Venture Performance," *Entrepreneurship Theory and Practice* 25, no. 2 (2002): 5–25.

54. Robert B. Reich, "The Team as Hero," *Harvard Business Review* 65, no. 3 (May/June 1987): 81.

55. Judith B. Kamm and Aaron J. Nurick, "The Stages of Team Venture Formulation: A Decision-Making Model," *Entrepreneurship Theory and Practice* 18, no. 2 (1993): 17–27; Michael A. Hitt, Robert D. Nixon, Robert E. Hoskisson, and Rahul Kochhar, "Corporate Entrepreneurship and Cross-functional Fertilization: Activation, Process, and Disintegration of a New Product Design Team," *Entrepreneurship Theory and Practice* 23, no. 3 (1999): 145–68.

56. R. Duane Ireland, Donald F. Kuratko, and Michael H. Morris, "A Health Audit for Corporate Entrepreneurship: Innovation at All Levels," *Journal of Business Strategy* 27, no. 1 (2006): 10–17; Ireland, Kuratko, and Morris, A Health Audit for Corporate Entrepreneurship.

57. Steven W. Floyd and P. J. Lane, "Strategizing Throughout the Organization: Managing Role Conflict in Strategic Renewal," *Academy of Management Review* 25 (2000): 154–77.

58. Kuratko, Ireland, Covin, and Hornsby, A Model of Middle-Level Managers Corporate Entrepreneurial Behavior; see also Ethel Brundin, Holger Pazelt, and Dean A. Shepherd, "Managers' Emotional Displays and Employees' Willingness to Act Entrepreneurially," *Journal of Business Venturing* 23, no. 2 (2008): 221–43; Stewart Thornhill and Raphael Amit, "A Dynamic Perspective of Internal Fit in Corporate Venturing," *Journal of Business Venturing* 16, no. 1 (2001): 25–50; and Charlotte R. Ren and Chao Guo, "Middle Managers' Strategic Role in the Corporate Entrepreneurial Process: Attention-Based Effects," *Journal of Management* 37, no. 6 (2011): 1586–1610.

59. Donald F. Kuratko, Jeffrey S. Hornsby, and Michael G. Goldsby, "Sustaining Corporate Entrepreneurship: Modeling Perceived Implementation and Outcome Comparisons at Organizational and Individual Levels," *International Journal of Entrepreneurship and Innovation* 5, no. 2 (May 2004): 77–89.

CHAPTER 4

Social Entrepreneurship and the Global Environment for Entrepreneurship

LEARNING OBJECTIVES

1 To introduce the social entrepreneurship movement

2 To examine who would be a social entrepreneur

3 To delve into the concept of *shared value*

4 To discuss the challenges of social enterprise

5 To introduce the global opportunities and challenges for social entrepreneurs

6 To present the newest developments that have expanded the global marketplace

7 To examine the methods of entering the international arena

8 To set forth the key steps for entrepreneurs seeking global markets

Entrepreneurial Thought

No generation has had the opportunity, as we have now, to build a global economy that leaves no one behind. It is a wonderful opportunity, but also a profound responsibility.

—Bill Clinton 42nd President of the United States

4-1 SOCIAL ENTREPRENEURSHIP

LO1 Introduce the social entrepreneurship movement

Social entrepreneurship is a form of entrepreneurship that exhibits characteristics of nonprofits, governments, and businesses, combining private-sector focus on innovation, risk taking, and large-scale transformation with social problem solving. The social entrepreneurship process begins with a perceived social opportunity translated into an enterprise concept; resources are then ascertained and acquired to execute the enterprise's goals.[1] In recent years, public recognition of social entrepreneurship has taken many forms:

- In 2006, TEACHFORAMERICA founder Wendy Kopp and City Year cofounders Michael Brown and Alan Khazei were profiled in *U.S. News & World Report* as three of America's Top 25 Leaders.

- Muhammad Yunus and his organization, the Grameen Bank, were awarded the Nobel Peace Prize.

- Victoria Hale of the Institute for OneWorld Health and Jim Fruchterman of Benetech received "genius grants" from the MacArthur Foundation. They identify themselves as social entrepreneurs.

- In 2005, the Public Broadcasting Service (PBS) and the Skoll Foundation created and aired a two-part miniseries profiling "The New Heroes," 14 social entrepreneurs from around the globe. They followed the series with a three-year grant program encouraging filmmakers, documentary filmmakers, and journalists to "produce work that promotes large-scale public awareness of social entrepreneurship." In addition, the Skoll Foundation's website hosts a number of films entitled "Uncommon Heroes" and conducts an annual world forum on social entrepreneurship.[2]

- For the past decade, the World Economic Forum, which annually brings together business, government, and national leaders who are "committed to improving the state of the world," has hosted a Social Entrepreneurs' Summit. In partnership with the Schwab Foundation, the forum convenes social entrepreneurs as one of its special-interest communities, placing social entrepreneurship on par with only nine other interest groups, including global growth companies, international media, and labor leaders.[3]

- Founded in 1980 by Bill Drayton, Ashoka is leading a profound transformation in society.

- Beginning with the first Ashoka Fellows elected in India in 1981, Ashoka has grown to an association of more than 2,000 Fellows in more than 60 countries on the world's five main continents. Along with the global network of Fellows, business entrepreneurs, policy makers, investors, academics, and journalists, Ashoka is now working collectively to ensure that social entrepreneurs and their innovations continue to inspire a new generation of local change makers to create positive social change.[4]

- Dr. Mark Albion wrote *More Than Money: Questions Every MBA Needs to Answer* and then developed the More Than Money Careers with Dr. Mrim Boutla in 2010 to find career opportunities in corporate social responsibility, values-based businesses, and nonprofit management. The More Than Money Careers is a six-week course distilling Albion's 30+ years of work with MBAs and values-based businesses and Boutla's strategic and tactical career coaching strategies to build the responsible careers.[5]

Definitions of social entrepreneurship, likewise, have taken many forms,[6] but one that resonates with many scholars and practitioners was developed by researchers Johanna Mair and Ignasi Marti. Mair and Marti "view social entrepreneurship as a process of creating value by combining resources in new ways…. These resource combinations are intended primarily to explore and exploit opportunities to create social value by stimulating social change or meeting social needs…. When viewed as a process, social entrepreneurship involves the offering of services and products but can also refer to the creation of new organizations. Importantly, social entrepreneurship…can occur equally well in a new organization or in an established organization, where it may be labeled 'social intrapreneurship.' Like intrapreneurship in the business sector, social entrepreneurship can refer to either new venture creation or entrepreneurial process innovation."[7] Social entrepreneurship can also be considered a vehicle for sustainable development, which G. H. Brundtland succinctly defined as "meeting the needs of the present without compromising the ability of future generations to meet their needs."[8]

4-1a Defining the Social Entrepreneur

LO2 Examine who would be a social entrepreneur

The term *social entrepreneur* has come to mean a person (or small group of individuals) who founds and/or leads an organization or initiative engaged in social entrepreneurship. Social entrepreneurs are sometimes referred to as "public entrepreneurs," "civic entrepreneurs," or "social innovators." Noted expert Arthur C. Brooks outlines the following activities that characterize the social entrepreneur:

- Adoption of a mission to create and sustain social value (beyond personal value)
- Recognition and relentless pursuit of opportunities for social value
- Engagement in continuous innovation and learning
- Action beyond the limited resources at hand
- Heightened sense of accountability[9]

Numerous publications have brought the term *social entrepreneurship* into wider recognition. For example, in recent years the *New York Times*, the *Economist, Forbes,* and the *Harvard Business Review* have all published stories that focus on social entrepreneurship.[10]

As social entrepreneurship rapidly finds its way into the vocabulary of policy makers, journalists, academics, and the general public, the world faces incredible societal challenges. The social entrepreneurship boom, and its promise as a means to address daunting social problems across the globe, are of particular importance for every entrepreneur.

By adopting some of the same principles that have been so effective in successful entrepreneurship, all leaders have a similar opportunity to support social entrepreneurship—and thereby generate transformative, financially sustainable solutions to social problems that face the nation. As stated in a recent article for the *Stanford Social Innovation Review*, "Social entrepreneurship, we believe, is as vital to the progress of societies as is entrepreneurship to the progress of economies, and it merits more rigorous, serious attention than it has attracted so far."[11]

Ashoka founder Bill Drayton has famously commented that "social entrepreneurs are not content just to give a fish or teach how to fish. They will not rest until they have revolutionized the fishing industry."[12] Like other entrepreneurs, social entrepreneurs are creative thinkers continuously striving for innovation, which can involve new technologies, supply sources, distribution outlets, or methods of production. Innovation may also mean starting new organizations or offering new products or services. Innovative ideas can be completely new inventions or creative adaptations of existing ones.[13]

Social entrepreneurs are change agents; they create large-scale change using pattern-breaking ideas, they address the root causes of social problems, and they possess the ambition to create systemic change by introducing a new idea and persuading others to adopt it.[14] These types of transformative changes can be national or global. They also can be highly localized—but no less powerful—in their impact. Most often, social entrepreneurs who create transformative changes combine innovative practices, a deep knowledge of their social issue area, and cutting-edge research to achieve their goals. For entrepreneurs working in the social realm, innovation is not a one-time event—rather, it is a lifetime pursuit.

4-1b Defining the Social Enterprise

With the huge growth and interest in social entrepreneurship that we have mentioned comes the challenges to the boundaries of what is and what isn't a social enterprise. Because social causes can be so different and many times very personal, it can be very tough to decipher.[15]

There is general agreement that social entrepreneurs and their ventures are driven by social goals; that is, the desire to benefit society in some way. In other words, the social entrepreneur aims to increase social value, that is, to contribute to the welfare or well-being in a given community. However, arguments begin over the location of the social goals and with the purposes of the social goals.

LO4 Discuss the challenges of social enterprise

Researcher J. Gregory Dees believes that the social mission is the most important criterion, *not* wealth creation. He sees wealth as a means to an end for social entrepreneurs. The claim that any wealth generated is just a means to the social end suggests that financial benefit to the entrepreneur has no place among the goals of the undertaking.[16]

Thus, many critics argue that the location of any social enterprise should be in the world of not-for-profit organizations. For instance, one research article asked the question of whether earned income is essential to social entrepreneurship. The answer was an emphatic "no" as the researchers claimed that social entrepreneurship is about finding new and better ways to create and sustain social value.[17] There are, in fact, social entrepreneurs inventing ways to alleviate poverty, create sources of water, or provide health solutions, without necessarily looking for any income from their beneficiaries.

However, for-profit enterprises have made a significant contribution to the world of social entrepreneurship. Whether you point to Ben & Jerry's or the majority of *Forbes*'s list of the Top 30 Social Entrepreneurs,[18] it is evident that for-profit social entrepreneurs are establishing themselves and providing social value with their enterprises. Thus it would appear pointless to disqualify for-profit social entrepreneurs if in fact social goals are being accomplished.

It seems that the best way to alleviate the arguments is to accept social entrepreneurship activity along a continuum. One team of researchers offered an explanation of having one extreme being those social entrepreneurs who are driven exclusively by producing social benefits, while at the other extreme are social entrepreneurs who are motivated by profitability with social benefits being the means. In between these extremes, many nuances can exist.[19]

THE ENTREPRENEURIAL PROCESS

Hot Dogs, Ex-Convicts, and Social Enterprise

There are numerous ways to use an entrepreneurial means to solve a societal issue. However, some of those entrepreneurial means can be called into question as "pushing the boundaries" when the cause itself causes an issue.

In Chicago, Illinois, a hot-dog stand opened with a unique twist: hire ex-convicts, who need a chance to be rehabilitated into society, as employees. Felony Franks, where "the food is so good, it's criminal," began with a social purpose. By providing employment to a population that might otherwise have no options for work, entrepreneur James Andrews was hoping to alleviate the homeless problem.

This all sounds like a perfect application of entrepreneurial principles to solve a societal problem. However, not everyone buys into that mantra. The neighborhood rose up against Mr. Andrews and his clever concept. They see it as exploitation of these ex-convicts and the real drug problems that do plague the neighborhood. Over 70 people came to a town meeting to voice their displeasure. Some even felt that this business would harm the efforts to clean up the neighborhood such as the drug rehabilitation centers by making crime seem glamorous rather than trying to deter crime. Most significantly, the people complained that other local businesses were hiring ex-convicts but they kept it low key in order to not bring attention to these individuals as they try and reinsert themselves into society.

Whereas they believe that Felony Franks is exploiting these ex-convicts for profit.

Mr. Andrews has invested over $160,000 into this venture and he believes in his concept claiming no "ulterior" motive. But the neighbors see it differently. They see an entrepreneur capitalizing on a neighborhood problem and using a serious issue for the benefit of sales. San Francisco and New Jersey are two cities known to have businesses step up and hire ex-convicts with no backlash or questions. However, they, unlike Felony Franks did not employ clever slogans about the criminal issues to boost sales.

In 2012, due to a slow economy and a sluggish business, Mr. Andrews was forced to finally close his operation. However, the courage and creativity displayed by Mr. Andrews in establishing such a unique venture leads to a more significant underlying issue. In the future, what perception will society have when entrepreneurs use their creativity to seemingly blur the boundaries of social venture and capitalistic profit.

Source: Adapted from: Julie Jargon, "Slaw and Order: Hot-Dog Stand in Chicago Triggers a Frank Debate," *Wall Street Journal* (October 13, 2009); and "Owner: Crime-Themed Hot Dog in Chicago Is Slated to Close Citing Slow Business," *Chicago Tribune* (June 3, 2012), http://www.chicagotribune.com/news/local/sns-ap-il--felonyfranks,0,6979309.story?obref=obnetwork (accessed June 14, 2012).

4-2 SOCIAL ENTERPRISE AND SUSTAINABILITY

It is obvious from the preceding section that, in the twenty-first century, social enterprise has emerged as a major issue among entrepreneurial thinkers.[20] Although it takes various forms in different industries and companies, the basic challenge of social enterprise—addressing the obligations of a business to society—is the same for all. These obligations can extend into many different areas, as presented in Table 4.1, but questions concerning the *extent* to which corporations should be involved in these areas is open to debate.

4-2a Sustainable Entrepreneurship

Researchers Dean A. Shepherd and Holger Patzelt define **sustainable entrepreneurship** as being "focused on the preservation of nature, life support, and community in the pursuit of perceived opportunities to bring into existence future products, processes, and services for gain, where gain is broadly construed to include economic and noneconomic gains to individuals, the economy, and society."[21]

TABLE 4.1   EXAMPLES OF SOCIAL ENTERPRISE OBLIGATIONS

Environment	Pollution control
	Restoration or protection of environment Conservation of natural resources Recycling efforts
Energy	Conservation of energy in production and marketing operations
	Efforts to increase the energy efficiency of products
	Other energy-saving programs (e.g., company-sponsored carpools)
Fair Business Practices	Employment and advancement of women and minorities
	Employment and advancement of disadvantaged individuals (disabled, Vietnam veterans, ex-offenders, former drug addicts, mentally retarded, and hard-core unemployed)
	Support for minority-owned businesses
Human Resources	Promotion of employee health and safety
	Employee training and development
	Remedial education programs for disadvantaged employees; alcohol and drug counseling programs
	Career counseling
	Child day-care facilities for working parents
	Employee physical fitness and stress management programs
Community Involvement	Donations of cash, products, services, or employee time
	Sponsorship of public health projects
	Support of education and the arts
	Support of community recreation programs
	Cooperation in community projects (recycling centers, disaster assistance, and urban renewal)
Products	Enhancement of product safety
	Sponsorship of product safety education programs; reduction of polluting potential of products; improvement in nutritional value of products; improvement in packaging and labeling

Source: Richard M. Hodgetts and Donald F. Kuratko, *Management*, 3rd ed. (San Diego, CA: Harcourt Brace Jovanovich, 1991), 670.

Sustainable development is perhaps the most prominent topic of our time. Commonplace are reports of ozone depletion, climate change, and destruction of biodiversity that demonstrate the negative and potentially deadly consequences these processes hold for living species. However, scholars have claimed that entrepreneurial action can preserve ecosystems, counteract climate change, reduce environmental degradation and deforestation, improve agricultural practices and freshwater supply, and maintain biodiversity.[22]

Sustainable entrepreneurship includes

- **Ecopreneurship** (i.e., environmental entrepreneurship with entrepreneurial actions contributing to preserving the natural environment, including the Earth, biodiversity, and ecosystems);
- *Social entrepreneurship*, which encompasses the activities and processes undertaken to discover, define, and exploit opportunities in order to enhance social wealth by creating new ventures or managing existing organizations in an innovative manner;
- *Corporate social responsibility*, which refers to actions that appear to further some social good, beyond the interests of the firm and that which is required by law and often denotes societal engagement of organizations.[23]

Since many innovative initiatives carried out by social entrepreneurs have experienced challenges in becoming sustainable and effective, there are questions as to whether individuals possess the talent and skills of entrepreneurs in conjunction with socially-motivated goals. Yet there have been a number of examples of entrepreneurs who have carried out the social mission utilizing the entrepreneurial process. One certain asset has been the Internet for disseminating information across the globe. Social ideas are shared with broader audiences and networks can be developed at a much faster rate. In addition, social venture capitalists are increasing in greater numbers raising funds for socially motivated causes. In fact, what is now referred to as "**social impact investing**" has started to bring opportunities to harness entrepreneurial ideas and capital markets to finance social initiatives.[24] Increasing the funding capability of social entrepreneurship will increase the likelihood of more efficient, sustainable, and effective social initiatives.

4-2b Ecopreneurship

The twenty-first century is one of greater environmental concern. The reawakening of the need to preserve and protect our natural resources has motivated businesses toward a stronger *environmental awareness*. As illustrated in Table 4.1, the environment stands out as one of the major challenges of social enterprise. *Green capitalism* has emerged as a powerful new force in examining the manner in which business is conducted in relation to the environment. This term refers to a concept of *ecologically* sustainable development being transformed into *economically* sustainable development. Our recent "throwaway" culture has endangered our natural resources, from soil to water to air. Researchers Paul Hawken (coauthor of *Natural Capitalism: Creating the Next Industrial Revolution*) and William McDonough state: "Industry is being told that if it puts its hamburgers in coated-paper wrappers, eliminates emissions, and plants two trees for every car sold, we will be on the way to an environmentally sound world. Nothing could be further from the truth. The danger lies not in the half measures but in the illusions they foster, the belief that subtle course corrections can guide us to a good life that will include a 'conserved' natural world and cozy shopping malls."[25]

This quote illustrates the enormous challenges entrepreneurs confront as they attempt to build socially responsible organizations for the future. Of the 100 million enterprises worldwide, a growing number are attempting to redefine their social responsibilities because they no longer accept the notion that the business of business is business. Because of an international ability to communicate information widely and quickly, many entrepreneurs are beginning to recognize their responsibility to the world around them. Entrepreneurial organizations, the dominant inspiration for change throughout the world, are beginning the arduous task of addressing social-environmental problems.

Entrepreneurs need to take the lead in designing a new approach to business in which everyday acts of work and life accumulate—as a matter of course—into a better world.

One theorist has developed the term **ecovision** to describe a possible leadership style for innovative organizations.[26] Ecovision encourages open and flexible structures that encompass the employees, the organization, and the environment, with attention to evolving social demands.

The environmental movement consists of many initiatives connected primarily by values rather than by design. A plan to create a sustainable future should realize its objectives through a practical, clearly stated strategy. Some of the key steps recommended by Hawken and McDonough are as follows:

1. **Eliminate the concept of waste.** Seek newer methods of production and recycling.

2. **Restore accountability.** Encourage consumer involvement in making companies accountable.

3. **Make prices reflect costs.** Reconstruct the system to incorporate a "green fee" where taxes are added to energy, raw materials, and services to encourage conservation.

4. **Promote diversity.** Continue researching the needed compatibility of our ever-evolving products and inventions.

5. **Make conservation profitable.** Rather than demanding "low prices" to encourage production shortcuts, allow new costs for environmental stewardship.

6. **Insist on accountability of nations.** Develop a plan for every trading nation of sustainable development enforced by tariffs.[27]

4-3 SHARED VALUE AND THE TRIPLE BOTTOM LINE

LO3 Delve into the concept of *shared value*

Companies have traditionally viewed value creation with a narrow scope. They have tended to optimize short-term financial performance while ignoring the elements that determine their long-term success. These elements could include the viability of key suppliers or the economic distress of the communities in which they exist. Researchers Michael E. Porter and Mark R. Kramer believe that companies must take the lead in bringing business and society back together. The solution lies in a concept they refer to as **shared value**. It is an approach to creating economic value that also creates value for society by addressing its needs and challenges. It connects company success with social progress. Shared value is more than social responsibility or sustainability. It is a transformation of business thinking recognizing societal weaknesses that create internal costs for firms (e.g., wasted energy, accidents, inadequacies in education). By addressing those issues through using innovations and methods, productivity can be increased and newer markets can be expanded.[28]

The **triple bottom line** (sometimes referred to as **TBL**) is an accounting framework that goes beyond the traditional measures of profit, return on investment, and shareholder value to include environmental and social dimensions. By focusing on comprehensive investment results—that is, with respect to performance along the interrelated dimensions of *profits, people,* and the *planet*—TBL reporting can be an important tool to support sustainability goals.[29] It measures three dimensions of performance: economic, environmental, and social. Let's examine each measure.

4-3a Bottom-Line Measures of Economic Performance

Economic measures deal with the bottom line and income flows such as income, expenditures, taxes, business climate factors, employment, and business diversity factors. Examples include:

- Personal income
- Cost of underemployment
- Establishment sizes
- Job growth
- Employment distribution by sector

- Percentage of firms in each sector
- Revenue by sector contributing to gross state product

4-3b Bottom-Line Measures of Environmental Performance

Environmental measures are related to natural resources and reflect potential influences to its viability. Air and water quality, energy consumption, natural resources, solid and toxic waste, and land use are examples. Long-range trends for environmental variables help organizations identify the impacts a project or policy would have on the area. Specific examples include:

- Hazardous chemical concentrations
- Selected priority pollutants
- Electricity consumption
- Fossil fuel consumption
- Solid waste management
- Hazardous waste management
- Change in land use/land cover

4-3c Bottom-Line Measures of Social Performance

Social measures refer to social dimensions of a community or region such as education, social resources, health and well-being, and quality of life. Examples include:

- Unemployment rate
- Median household income
- Relative poverty
- Percentage of population with a post-secondary degree or certificate
- Average commute time
- Violent crimes per capita
- Health-adjusted life expectancy

4-4 BENEFIT CORPORATIONS: PROMOTING SUSTAINABLE ENTERPRISES

A new form of corporation introduced in the United States—the **benefit corporation**—has been enacted in 14 states, and bills are moving forward in several others. Benefit corporations are exactly the same as traditional corporations except for a few specific elements that make them more socially sustainable enterprises:

1. **Purpose:** to create a material positive impact on society and the environment
2. **Accountability:** to have a fiduciary duty to consider the interests of workers, the community, and the environment
3. **Transparency:** to report annually to the public on overall social and environmental performance with a credible and transparent third-party standard

Benefit corporations and certified **B corporations** are terms that are often used interchangeably. However, while they share similar features, they also have a few important differences. A certified B corporation is a certification conferred by the nonprofit B Lab. Benefit

THE ENTREPRENEURIAL PROCESS

L3C: A New Legal Form for Social Enterprises

A new legal form of business entity in the United States has been created to bridge the gap between nonprofit and for-profit investing. The new form, known as the low-profit, limited liability company, or L3C, provides a structure that facilitates investments in socially beneficial, for-profit ventures. L3Cs have been touted as "for profits with nonprofit souls."

The L3C is a new type of limited liability company (LLC) designed to attract private investment and philanthropic capital in ventures designed to provide a social benefit. Unlike a standard LLC, the L3C has an explicit primary charitable mission and only a secondary profit concern. But unlike a charity, the L3C is free to distribute profits, after taxes, to owners or investors.

A principal advantage of the L3C is its qualification as a program-related investment (PRI). That means it is an investment with a socially beneficial purpose that is consistent with a foundation's mission. Because foundations can only directly invest in for-profit ventures qualified as PRIs, many foundations refrain from investing in for-profit ventures due to the uncertainty of whether they would qualify as PRIs or use costly time and resources to acquire a Private Letter Ruling from the IRS to verify that the venture is a valid PRI. An L3C's operating agreement minimizes this problem by specifically outlining its respective PRI-qualified purpose in being formed, making it easier for foundations to identify social-purpose businesses as well as helping to ensure that their tax-exemptions remain secure. Thus, L3Cs could attract a greater amount of private capital from various sources in order to serve their charitable or education goals. It is the perfect vehicle for economic development, medical research, operation of social service agencies, museums, concert venues, housing, and any other activity with both a charitable purpose and a revenue stream.

The L3C was created by Robert Lang, CEO of the Mary Elizabeth & Gordon B. Mannweiler Foundation. In 2008, Vermont became the first state to recognize the L3C as an official legal structure. Similar legislation has since been pushed in other states such as Georgia, Michigan, Montana, and North Carolina. Although Vermont currently remains the only state to authorize the L3C, it has national applicability because L3Cs formed in Vermont can be used in any state or territory so it is legal in all 50 states. The L3C is a brand which signifies to the world that it puts mission before profit yet is self-sustaining. As a brand it makes these concepts easy to grasp and thereby will be frequently used.

© Cengage Learning

corporation is a legal status administered by the state. Benefit corporations do *not* need to be certified. Certified B corporations have been certified as having met a high standard of overall social and environmental performance and, as a result, have access to a portfolio of services and support from B Lab that benefit corporations do not. See also the Entrepreneurial Process box concerning the new legal form of organization known as L3C corporations, which also relate to social enterprises. We will discuss more on these new legal forms of organization in Chapter 9.

4-5 THE GLOBAL MARKETPLACE

LO5 Introduce the global opportunities and challenges for social entrepreneurs

Capitalism is the world's dominant economic system, having, over recent decades, replaced many socialistic and centrally planned systems worldwide. Like capitalism, entrepreneurship has expanded its reach across the globe and is now an engine for economic growth not only in America but elsewhere in the world. The last decade, in particular, has witnessed the emergence of a new breed of global entrepreneur, who relies on global networks for resources, design, and distribution. The trend has escalated the global economy, allowing it to reach new heights. By all accounts, the pace and magnitude of this global economy are likely to continue to accelerate. Adept at recognizing opportunities, the new breed of global entrepreneur recognizes that success in the global marketplace requires agility, certainty, ingenuity, and a global perspective. These global entrepreneurs and social entrepreneurs are the true vanguard in the second decade of the twenty-first century.[30]

In the sections that follow, we discuss new developments in the global marketplace that directly affect entrepreneurial opportunities. We also examine the various methods of international participation. Finally, we focus on researching the foreign market with the threats and risks to be considered.

4-5a Global Entrepreneurs

LO6 Resent the newest developments that have expanded the global marketplace

Global entrepreneurs are opportunity-minded and open-minded, able to see different points of view and weld them into a unified focus. They rise above nationalistic differences to see the big picture of global competition without abdicating their own nationalities. They have a core language plus working knowledge of others. They confront the learning difficulties of language barriers head-on, recognizing the barriers such ignorance can generate. The global entrepreneur is required to wear many hats, taking on various assignments, gaining experience in various countries, and seizing the opportunity to interact with people of different nationalities and cultural heritages.

4-5b Global Thinking

"Global thinking" is important because today's consumers can select products, ideas, and services from many nations and cultures. Entrepreneurs who expand into foreign markets must be global thinkers in order to design and adopt strategies for different countries. Therefore, one of the most exciting and promising avenues for entrepreneurs to expand their businesses is by participating in the global market. Each year thousands of smaller enterprises are actively engaged in the international arena. Two of the primary reasons for this emerging opportunity are the decline in trade barriers, especially among major trading nations, and the emergence of major trading blocs that have been brought about by the North American Free Trade Agreement and the European Union. In addition, over the past decade, Asia-Pacific region has become a hotbed for entrepreneurial opportunity.[31]

4-5c Diaspora Networks

Diaspora networks are relationships among ethnic groups that share cultural and social norms. While they are not new, as diasporas have been a part of the world for thousands of years, the new global economy has made them more powerful as vehicles for communication and trust. There has been a 40 percent increase in first generation migrants since 1990 with over 200 million worldwide.

Through easy communications technology (Internet and Skype) and the social media sites (Facebook, LinkedIn, Twitter, etc.), diasporas are linking together stronger than ever before offering potential linkages for global entrepreneurs.

Remember, in most emerging markets, laws can be uncertain and courts cannot be trusted to enforce contracts. Thus it is hard to conduct business with strangers and preferable to deal with someone you trust. Personal connections through a diaspora network make this feasible. These networks of kinship and language make it easier for an entrepreneur to do business across borders.

Diaspora networks have three powerful advantages for global entrepreneurs. First, they speed the flow of information across borders; second, they create a bond of trust; and third, they create connections that help entrepreneurs collaborate within a country and across ethnicities.

This new type of "hyper connectivity" enables global entrepreneurs to collaborate instantaneously and intimately to their communities of ethnic origin.[32]

4-5d Global Organizations and Agreements

Throughout the world today, significant developments have occurred which facilitate the expansion of the global marketplace. Organizations, unifications, and trade agreements are some of the vehicles that have developed to enhance global business. In this section, we examine the most significant international developments.

THE WORLD TRADE ORGANIZATION

The **World Trade Organization (WTO)** was established on January 1, 1995. The WTO is the umbrella organization governing the international trading system. Its job is to oversee international trade arrangements, but, contrary to popular belief, the WTO does not replace the General Agreement on Tariffs and Trade (GATT). An amended GATT remains one of the legal pillars of the world's trade system and, to a lesser extent, the world investment system.[33]

Located in Geneva, Switzerland, the WTO employs over 600 staff, and its experts—lawyers, economists, statisticians and communications experts—assist WTO members on a daily basis to ensure, among other things, that negotiations progress smoothly, and that the rules of international trade are correctly applied and enforced. The budget for the WTO is over US$205 million, and its functions include: administering WTO trade agreements; handling trade negotiations or trade disputes; monitoring national trade policies; and technical assistance and training for developing countries.

Membership in the WTO has increased from the 76 nations that founded the organization in 1995 to 157 members representing more than 97 percent of the world's population, and 26 observers, most seeking membership. Thus, the WTO includes virtually all of the developed world, and most of the developing countries; these nations collectively account for more than 90 percent of the world's trade and virtually all of its investment.[34]

THE NORTH AMERICAN FREE TRADE AGREEMENT

The North American Free Trade Agreement (NAFTA) is an international agreement among Canada, Mexico, and the United States that eliminates trade barriers among the three nations.[35] It created the world's largest free trade area, linking 444 million people and producing $17 trillion in goods and services annually. Estimates are that NAFTA increases U.S. GDP by as much as 0.5 percent a year because it eliminates tariffs and creates agreements on international rights for business investors. This reduces the cost of trade, which spurs investment and growth especially for entrepreneurial businesses. Eliminating tariffs also reduces inflation by decreasing the costs of imports.

Thus, new opportunities have arisen for entrepreneurs in North America. The importance of the agreement can be clearly seen when exports and imports among the three partners are examined. Table 4.2 shows the importance of Canadian and Mexican trade for the United States with these two countries ranked in the top two exporters (accounting for over $400 billion) and the top three importers (accounting for over $500 billion). As NAFTA has developed and trade barriers have been reduced, the amount of trade among the three partners continues to increase. Perhaps even more important, the competition that has been

TABLE 4.2 TOP TEN COUNTRIES WITH WHICH THE U.S. TRADES

The largest U.S. partners with their total trade (sum of imports and exports) in billions of U.S. dollars as of 2015:				
Rank	Country	Exports	Imports	Total Trade
1	Canada	261.8	290.6	552.5
2	China	99.6	384.0	483.6
3	Mexico	201.7	246.1	447.8
4	Japan	56.1	111.9	168.0
5	Germany	41.7	102.5	144.2
6	Korea, South	37.2	57.3	94.5
7	United Kingdom	45.0	44.9	89.9
8	France	26.4	39.2	65.6
9	Brazil	36.1	25.1	61.2
10	Taiwan	22.3	34.2	56.4

Source: U.S. Census Bureau, Washington, DC, 2015.

created by the removal of trade barriers has forced more entrepreneurial firms to increase their quality and overall competitiveness. In turn, this has made firms more competitive when doing business in Asia, South America, Europe, and other international markets.

Of particular importance to entrepreneurs is the fact that markets have increased for both exports and imports. The most efficient firms find themselves able to provide higher quality and lower prices than their competitors, and no tariffs or quotas will keep out their goods. At the same time, entrepreneurs in all three countries will find themselves protected from foreign competition because of local content laws. For example, NAFTA has created a trade surplus in services for the United States.

More than 40 percent of U.S. GDP is services, such as financial services and health care. These aren't easily transported, so being able to export them to nearby countries is important. NAFTA boosted U.S. service exports to Canada and Mexico from $25 billion in 1993 to $106.8 billion in 2012. NAFTA eliminated trade barriers in nearly all service sectors, which are often highly regulated. NAFTA requires governments to publish all regulations, lowering hidden costs of doing business.

In addition, NAFTA offers strong protection for patents, copyrights, industrial design rights, trade secret rights, and other forms of intellectual property. Many entrepreneurs could find that their success in this market bloc will prepare them to do business elsewhere, including the European Union.

THE EUROPEAN UNION

The **European Union (EU)** was founded in 1957 as the European Economic Community and in 1992 became a full-fledged economic union. The EU is an economic and political union of 27 member states which are located primarily in Europe. The objectives of the EU include (1) the elimination of custom duties among all member states, (2) the free flow of goods and services among all members, (3) the creation of common trade policies toward all countries outside the EU, (4) the free movement of capital and personnel within the bloc, (5) the encouragement of economic development throughout the bloc, and (6) monetary and fiscal coordination among all members.[36]

The EU remains one of the major markets for American goods and services as well as for foreign direct investment. Like the North American trading bloc, the goal of many entrepreneurs is to gain admission into this market so that the benefits that accrue to insiders can be realized. With a combined population of over 500 million inhabitants, or 7.3 percent of the world population, the EU generated a nominal GDP of US$16,242 billion in 2011, which represents an estimated 20 percent of global GDP when measured in terms of purchasing power parity. Another potential strategy is to work with EU partners in the American market by helping them extend their worldwide coverage. This reason is best explained in terms of global trade. Research reveals that a huge amount of international trade is conducted by three groups: the United States, EU countries, and the Asia-Pacific region.[37] This helps explain why entrepreneurs now are looking for emerging opportunities in the EU and EU-based firms.

4-5e Venturing Abroad

As global opportunities expand, entrepreneurs are becoming more open-minded about internationalizing. In past years, U.S. entrepreneurs shuddered at the thought of "going international" because it was just too big a step, too risky, and too uncertain. However, the twenty-first century has witnessed the global marketplace become a reality and entrepreneurs have rushed enthusiastically to capture a share of this global marketplace with prime targets, including China, India, Asia-Pacific nations, Latin America, Africa, and Eastern Europe.

GRADUAL INTERNATIONALIZATION

LO7 Examine the methods of entering the international arena

Whether their motives are for pure economic gain or to share knowledge and resources, entrepreneurs tend to act in rational ways. They acquire raw material and capital where they are most abundant, manufacture products where wages and other costs are lowest, and sell in the most profitable markets. If everyone does their assigned tasks, the economic law of comparative advantage will benefit everyone.[38]

Countries vary with respect to the quantity and proportion of resources they possess, which forms the basis for a competitive advantage of nations. **Resource-rich countries** (those having extractive assets) include the OPEC nations and many parts of Africa; labor-rich, rapidly developing countries include Brazil, India, the Philippines, and select countries in South and Central America. **Market-rich countries**, such as the countries of Europe, Brazil, Mexico, India, China, and the United States, have purchasing power. Each country has something that others need, thus forming the basis of an interdependent international trade system.

Internationalization can be viewed as the outcome of a sequential process of incremental adjustments to changing conditions of the firm and its environment. This process progresses step-by-step as risk and commitment increase and entrepreneurs acquire more knowledge through experience. The entrepreneur's impression of the risks and rewards of internationalizing can be determined by feasibility studies of the potential gains to be won.

As noted above, the principal advantage of trading internationally is enhanced prospects for growth through market expansion. Other advantages include utilizing idle capacity; minimizing cyclical or seasonal slumps; getting acquainted with manufacturing technology used in other countries; learning about products not sold domestically; learning about other cultures; acquiring growth capital more easily in other countries; and having the opportunity to travel for business and pleasure.[39]

INTERNATIONAL AT INCEPTION

Some entrepreneurial businesses internationalize immediately. They are "born global." Multinational from inception, these companies break the traditional expectation that a business must enter the international arena incrementally, becoming global only as it grows older and wiser. According to Researchers Ben Oviatt and Patricia P. McDougall, seven characteristics of successful global start-ups are: (1) global vision from inception; (2) internationally experienced management; (3) a strong international business network; (4) preemptive technology or marketing; (5) a unique intangible asset; (6) a linked product or service; and (7) tight organizational coordination worldwide.[40]

4-5f Methods of Going International

The entrepreneur can actively engage in the international market in a number of ways, including: importing, exporting, international alliances and joint ventures, direct foreign investment, and licensing.[41] Each of these methods involves increasing levels of risk.

IMPORTING

Importing is buying and shipping foreign-produced goods for domestic consumption. Each year the United States imports an increasing amount of goods. How does an entrepreneur become aware of import opportunities? One way is to attend trade shows and fairs where firms gather to display their products and services. Some of these shows are international in flavor, with firms from different countries exhibiting their products and services. Basically, the trade show gives the prospective customer the opportunity to window-shop. Another way is to monitor trade publications. Often, firms will advertise in trade publications to make themselves known to potential customers.

EXPORTING

When an entrepreneurial firm decides to participate actively in the international arena as a seller, rather than a buyer, it becomes an exporter. **Exporting** is the shipping of a domestically produced good to a foreign destination for consumption. Exporting is important for entrepreneurs because it often means increased market potential. Instead of limiting its market to the United States, the firm now has a broader sales sphere. According to the **learning curve concept**, increased sales will lead to greater efficiencies along the cost curve, which in turn will lead to increased profits. (The learning curve essentially states that as more and more units are produced, the firm becomes more efficient at production of the units, thereby lowering the cost per unit. The lower unit cost thus enables the firm to compete more effectively in the marketplace.) It should be pointed out, however, that exporting normally will take three to five years to become profitable. Even if the firm is producing more units efficiently, it will take time to learn the intricacies and efficiencies of international business. Exporting has been increasing as a method for venture growth and increased profitability among entrepreneurial firms.

INTERNATIONAL ALLIANCES AND JOINT VENTURES

Another alternative available to the entrepreneur in the international arena are international alliances. There are three main types of these strategic alliances: informal international cooperative alliances; formal international cooperative alliances (ICAs); and international joint ventures. (Table 4.3 provides a summary of these alliances.)

In general, informal alliances are agreements between companies from two or more countries, and they are not legally binding. Because the contract offers no legal protection, most entrepreneurs would either limit their involvement or avoid it altogether. The formal alliance usually requires a formal contract with specifics about what each company must contribute. The agreement then usually involves greater commitment by each company with transfer of proprietary information. These forms have become more popular in the high-tech industry because of the higher costs with internal research and development.

The joint venture is the more traditional self-standing legal entity. A joint venture occurs when two or more firms analyze the benefits of creating a relationship, pool their resources, and create a new entity to undertake productive economic activity. A joint venture thus implies the sharing of assets, profits, risks, and venture ownership with more than one firm.[42] A joint venture can take one of several different forms. In some countries, for example, it is not uncommon for a company to form a joint venture with the state or with a state-owned firm.

Advantages of Joint Ventures

A firm may decide to participate in a joint venture for several reasons.[43] One is that the firm would be able to gain an intimate knowledge of the local conditions and government where the facility is located. Another is that each participant would be able to use the resources of the other firms involved in the venture. This allows participating firms a chance to compensate for weaknesses they may possess. Finally, both the initial capital outlay and the overall risk would be lower than if the firm were setting up the operation alone.

Additional advantages of a joint venture relate to the strategic fit of the domestic firm with the foreign firm. One study examined the strategic fit of domestic firms (D-type) with Third World firms (TW-type) in a joint venture. The dimensions of corporate-level advantages, operational-level advantages, and environmental advantages were all compared to the strategic fit of the partners in the joint venture.[44]

TABLE 4.3   TYPES OF INTERNATIONAL ALLIANCES

Alliance Type	Degree of Involvement	Ease of Dissolution	Legal Entity
Informal international cooperative alliance	Limited in scope and time	Easy and convenient for either side	None
Formal international cooperative alliance	Deeper involvement; exchange of proprietary knowledge	More difficult to dissolve due to legal obligations and commitment	None
Internal joint venture	Deep involvement; requires exchange of financial information, proprietary knowledge, and resources	Most difficult to dissolve due to the significant investment of both companies and the existence of a legal entity	Separate company

Source: Adapted from John B. Cullen and K. Praveen Parboteeah, *Multinational Management: A Strategic Approach*, 5th ed. (Mason, OH: Cengage/South-Western, 2011), p. 352.

Disadvantages of Joint Ventures   One of the disadvantages associated with joint ventures is the problem of fragmented control.[45] For example, a carefully planned logistics flow may be hampered if one of the firms decides to block the acquisition of new equipment. This type of problem can be avoided or diminished in a number of ways: (1) One party can control more than 50 percent of the voting rights. This will normally give formal control; however, even a minority opposing view can carry considerable influence. This can be particularly true if the differences of opinion reflect different nationalities. (2) Only one of the parties is made responsible for the actual management of the venture. This may be complemented by a buyout clause. In case of a disagreement among the owners, one party can purchase the equity of the other. (3) One of the parties can control either the input or the output, exerting significant control over the venture decisions, despite voting and ownership rights.

The joint venture can be a powerful tool for growth in the international market. If used properly, it will effectively combine the strengths of the partners involved and thereby increase its competitive position.[46]

DIRECT FOREIGN INVESTMENT

A *direct foreign investment* is a domestically controlled foreign production facility. This does not mean the firm owns a majority of the operation. In some cases, less than 50 percent ownership can constitute effective control because the stock ownership is widely dispersed. On the other hand, the entrepreneur may own 100 percent of the stock and not have control over the company. In some instances, the government may dictate whom a firm may hire, what pricing structure the firm must use, and how earnings will be distributed. This causes some concern as to exactly who is in control of the organization. Because of the difficulty of identifying direct investments, governmental agencies have had to establish arbitrary definitions of the term. A direct foreign investment typically involves ownership of 10 to 25 percent of the voting stock in a foreign enterprise.[47]

A firm can make a direct foreign investment by several methods. One is to acquire an interest in an ongoing foreign operation. This initially may be a minority interest in the firm but enough to exert influence on the management of the operation. A second method is to obtain a majority interest in a foreign company. In this case, the company becomes a subsidiary of the acquiring firm. Third, the acquiring firm may simply purchase part of the assets of a foreign concern in order to establish a direct investment. An additional alternative is to build a facility in a foreign country.

Direct investment can be an exciting venture for entrepreneurial firms making efforts to increase their sales and their competitive positions in the marketplace. However, it is sometimes not practical for a firm to make a direct investment in a foreign location. If the firm has a unique or proprietary product or manufacturing process, it may want to consider the concept of licensing.

LICENSING

Licensing is a business arrangement in which the manufacturer of a product (or a firm with proprietary rights over certain technology or trademarks) grants permission to some other group or individual to manufacture that product in return for specified royalties or other payments. Foreign licensing covers myriad contractual arrangements in which the business (licenser) provides patents, trademarks, manufacturing expertise, or technical services to a foreign business (licensee). Under such an arrangement, the entrepreneur need not make an extensive capital outlay to participate in the international market. Nor does the licenser have to be concerned with the daily production, marketing, technical, or management requirements; the licensee will handle all of this. The foreign firm merely looks to the domestic firm for expertise and, perhaps, an additional opportunity to sell a product owned by the licenser.

For developing an international licensing program, three basic types of programs are available:

1. **Patents.** If the entrepreneur decides to use the patent approach, he or she should begin with a valid U.S. patent. Within one year, the entrepreneur should then file for patents in

the countries where business will be transacted. Although this step can be expensive, it is essential because this action will give the entrepreneur a stronger bargaining position. With the passage of the America Invents Act of 2011, the United States adjusted its patent system from "first to invent" to the international system of "first to file." It's being referred to as "patent harmonization" in order to be compatible with the international marketplace. The new system includes safeguards for small inventors, such as an inexpensive system for provisional patents. The goals are to make the patent process more efficient and to offer better foreign protection for inventors.[48] Currently, a single patent filing can cost tens of thousands of dollars, if you include all the attorney fees. The entrepreneur must file multiple applications as a defense against competitors—particularly in a global economy. A rule of thumb is that gaining sufficient protection for a patent internationally can cost about $100,000. Filing ten related patents to create a protective "picket fence" around his or her invention could cost the entrepreneur $1 million. Self-defense has increased the cost of international patent protection.[49]

2. **Trademarks.** Due to the difficulties that can occur in direct translations, it may be advisable for the entrepreneur to have more than one trademark licensed for the same product. The entrepreneur should keep in mind, however, that if the product is not well recognized in the international market, he or she will not be able to use it as a major incentive in the bargaining phase. Sometimes, licensees will want the patent rights but prefer to use their own trademarks. This can be particularly true if the foreign firm is well established.

3. **Technical know-how.** This type of licensing is often the hardest to enforce since it depends on the security of secrecy agreements. (The licenser should sign an agreement to prevent the licensee from legally revealing trade secrets.) In some localities, governments have strict regulations governing the use of technical know-how licensing. Frequently, one may protect the technical capabilities for only five years before the licensee is free to use this know-how without paying royalties. However, keep in mind that this may differ from country to country, depending on the particular regulations. Because this is a complex process, the entrepreneur must continue to develop his or her technical capabilities to ensure an ongoing international need for the company's services.[50]

To be competitive with larger firms, entrepreneurial businesses have to be on the cutting edge of bringing in new and innovative technology. Moreover, some entrepreneurial firms may not have the financial resources available to participate in the international marketplace by exporting, joint venture, or direct investment. For many of these firms, international licensing is a viable and exciting method of expanding operations.[51]

4-5g Researching Foreign Markets

LO8 Set forth the key steps for entrepreneurs seeking global markets

Before entering a foreign market, it is important to study the *unique culture* of potential customers. Different concepts of how the product is used, demographics, psychographics, and legal and political norms are usually different from those in the United States. Therefore, it is necessary to conduct market research to identify these important parameters.

- **Government regulations:** Must you conform to import regulations or patent, copyright, or trademark laws that would affect your product?
- **Political climate:** Will the relationship between government and business or political events and public attitudes in a given country affect foreign business transactions, particularly with the United States?
- **Infrastructure:** How will the packaging, shipping, and distribution system of your export product be affected by the local transportation system, for example, air, land, or water?
- **Distribution channels:** What are the generally accepted trade terms at both wholesale and retail levels? What are the normal commissions and service agency charges? What laws pertain to and distribution agreements?
- **Competition:** How many competitors do you have and in what countries are they located? On a country-by-country basis, how much market share does each of your competitors

have, and what prices do they charge? How do they promote their products? What distribution systems do they use?

- **Market size:** How big is the market for your product? Is it stable? What is its size individually, country by country? In what countries are markets opening, expanding, maturing, or declining?

- **Local customs and culture:** Is your product in violation of cultural taboos? How can entrepreneurial businesses learn about international cultures and thus know what is acceptable and what is not? A number of approaches can be employed. One of the most helpful is international business travel. This provides the individual with firsthand information regarding cultural dos and don'ts. Other useful methods include training programs, formal educational programs, and reading the current literature.[52]

INTERNATIONAL THREATS AND RISKS

Foreign markets may present dangers that must be monitored carefully. For example, *ignorance* and *uncertainty*, combined with *lack of experience* in problem solving in a foreign country, present a major issue. *Lack of information* about resources to help solve problems contributes to the unfamiliarity. *Restrictions* imposed by the host country often contribute to the risk. Many host countries demand development of their exports and insist on training and development of their nationals. They can also demand that certain positions in management and technological areas be held by nationals. Many seek technologically based industry rather than extractive industry. In other instances, the host country may require that it own controlling interest and/or limit the amount of profits or fees entrepreneurs are allowed to take out of the country.

Political risks include unstable governments, disruptions caused by territorial conflicts, wars, regionalism, illegal occupation, and political ideological differences. *Economic risks* that need to be monitored include changes in tax laws, rapid rises in costs, strikes, sudden increases in raw materials, and cyclical/dramatic shifts in GNP. Social risks include antagonism among classes, religious conflict, unequal income distribution, union militancy, civil war, and riots. *Financial risks* incorporate fluctuating exchange rates, repatriation of profits and capital, and seasonal cash flows.[53]

Foreign government import regulations can affect a company's ability to export successfully. These regulations represent an attempt by foreign governments to control their markets, to protect a domestic industry from excessive foreign competition, to limit health and environmental damage, or to restrict what they consider excessive or inappropriate cultural influence.

Most countries have import regulations that are potential barriers to exported products. Exporters need to be aware of import tariffs and consider them when pricing their products. While most countries have reduced their tariffs on imported goods, there are still major restrictions on global trading, such as nontariff barriers. Nontariff barriers include prohibitions, restrictions, conditions, or specific requirements that can make exporting products difficult and sometimes costly.

Many entrepreneurs have avoided international trade because they believe it is too complicated and fraught with bureaucratic red tape. They also believe that international trade is profitable only for large companies that have more resources than smaller businesses. Other perceived drawbacks to international trade include becoming too dependent on foreign markets; foreign government instability that could cause problems for domestic companies; tariffs and import duties that make it too expensive to trade in other countries; products manufactured in the United States that may need significant modification before they are accepted by people in other countries; and foreign cultures, customs, and languages that make it difficult for Americans.[54]

In pursuing international trade, entrepreneurs face the risks of confiscation, expropriation, domestication, and other government interference. Entrepreneurs may take out insurance to cover some political and economic risks. The Overseas Private Investment Corporation (OPIC) can cover three types of risk: currency inconvertibility insurance, expropriation insurance, and political environment insurance.

KEY QUESTIONS AND RESOURCES

International marketing research is critical to the success of entrepreneurial businesses in overseas markets. Entrepreneurial enterprise owners can tap a host of sources to obtain needed information directed toward answering the following three questions:

1. **Why is the company interested in going international?** The answer to this question will help the firm set its international objectives and direct the marketing-research effort. For example, if the entrepreneurial business owner wants to establish and cultivate an overseas market, then the firm will be interested in pinpointing geographic areas where future market potential is likely to be high. If the business owner wants to use the market to handle current overproduction, then the company will be interested in identifying markets that are most likely to want to make immediate purchases. Regardless, the firm will have established a focus for its marketing-research efforts.

THE ENTREPRENEURIAL PROCESS

Incentivizing Entrepreneurs in Chile

Start-Up Chile is a program created by the Chilean government, executed by Corfo via InnovaChile, that seeks to attract early stage, high-potential entrepreneurs to bootstrap their startups in Chile, using it as a platform to go global. The end goal of the accelerator program is to convert Chile into the definitive innovation and entrepreneurial hub of Latin America; this is a mission shared by the government of Chile and is a primary focus of the Ministry of Economy.

The government provides qualifying entrepreneurs with US$40,000 of equity-free seed capital and a temporary one-year visa to develop their projects for six months, along with access to the most potent social and capital networks in the country. With such a light requirement, it seems that Chile is very confident in the business environment that it possesses. And why not? Look at some of these facts:

The average temperature in January: 85 degrees Fahrenheit.

The average temperature in July: 57 degrees Fahrenheit.

Population in Chile: 17 million

Flight time from Miami, Florida, to Santiago, Chile: 8 hours

Amount of uncommitted venture capital: $200 million

Government Match Money: 3 to 1 ratio

Nicolas Shea, who founded the Start-Up Chile program with the Chilean Ministry of Economy, claims that long-term retention of these companies actually isn't the most important thing. He contends that the opportunity that Chile is giving these businesses, with its $40 million government investment in the program and a target of 300 companies, to grow beyond where they would have been able to previously will be instrumental in the country's global network.

In 2010, the program brought 22 startups from 14 countries to Chile. These selected entrepreneurs were approved by an admission process conducted by Silicon Valley experts and a Chilean Innovation board that focuses ardently on global mind-sets and worldwide potential. The goal is 300 startups in Chile with the end hope of having 1,000 bootstrappers participate in the program by the end of 2014. Of all required criteria, it is essential that the chosen entrepreneurs work with a global mind-set, believing that the route to success is via expansion not isolation. From the perspective of the Chilean government, it is very important to make sure that this money is being invested within Chile, and they know that in order for that to happen they need to bring in worthy companies.

There are a couple of problems that are going to inhibit this program. The first is the language barrier. The primary language spoken in Chile is Spanish, and this could create issues with the new companies, especially with regard to innovation, which may occur simply from having meetings of entrepreneurial minds. If you are unable to have these conversations, it could stunt your group. The second issue is the consequence of failure. In Chile, bankruptcy proceedings for a failed company can take years, compared with only a couple of months in the United States. Add to that the cultural shame associated with failing, which is much more difficult to remedy, and Chile could be an intimidating atmosphere in which to start a business.

However, in spite of these potential challenges, the $40,000 of funding from the Start-Up Chile program gives their entrepreneurs the opportunity to focus their passion toward developing their business, or "bootstrapping," and take the pressure off of the potential need to sell their company to a larger organization as funding begins to run thin, and risk the possible effect of the business losing its passion.

Former Minister of Economy Juan Andrés Fontaine stated: "Instead of changing the world through revolution, we can change the world through innovation." This has become the tagline for Start-Up Chile.

Source: Adapted from: Ryan Underwood, "The Silicon Valley of South America?" *Inc.*, April 2011; Start-Up Chile, http://www.startupchile.org (accessed February 7, 2012).

2. **What does the foreign-market assessment reveal about the nature and functioning of the markets under investigation?** The answer to this question, which often is comprehensive in scope, helps identify market opportunities and provide insights regarding the specific activities of these individual markets. For example, if the firm identifies potential markets in Brazil, Africa, and China, the next step is to evaluate these opportunities. This can be done by gathering information related to the size of the markets, competition that exists in each, the respective government's attitude to foreign businesses, and steps that will have to be taken to do business in each location. Based on this information, a cost/benefit analysis can be conducted and a decision made regarding the market(s) to be pursued.

3. **What specific market strategy is needed to tap the potential of this market?** The answer to this question involves a careful consideration of the marketing mix: product, price, place, and promotion. What product should the firm offer? What specific features should it contain? Does it need to be adapted for the overseas market, or can the firm sell the same product it sells domestically? At what stage in the product life cycle will this product be? How much should the firm charge? Can the market be segmented so that a variety of prices can be set? How will the product move through the marketing channel? What type of promotional efforts—advertising, sales promotion, personal selling, or a combination of these—will be needed?

Once these questions have been answered, the entrepreneurial business owner will be in a position to begin implementing the international phase of the firm's strategy.

SUMMARY

The challenge of social enterprise has emerged in this century as a major issue for entrepreneurs. Social enterprise consists of obligations that a business has to society. The boom in social entrepreneurship and its promise of ending daunting social problems across the globe are of particular importance. Studies reveal that entrepreneurs recognize social enterprise as part of their role and that the structure of smaller firms allows entrepreneurs to influence their organizations more personally. Social entrepreneurs are change agents: they create large-scale change with pattern-breaking ideas, they address the root causes of social problems, and they possess the ambition to create systemic change.

With the huge growth and interest in social entrepreneurship that we mention in the chapter comes the challenges to the boundaries of what is and what isn't a social enterprise. Because social causes can be so different and, at times, so oddly personal, enterprises that embrace them can be very tough to decipher. It seems that the best way to end the confusion is to accept social entrepreneurship activity as a continuum, with one extreme being social entrepreneurs driven exclusively by producing social benefits, and at the other extreme, social entrepreneurs motivated primarily by profitability with social benefits being the means.

Sustainable development is perhaps the most prominent topic of our time. Scholars suggest that entrepreneurial action can preserve ecosystems, counteract climate change, reduce environmental degradation and deforestation, improve agricultural practices and freshwater supply, and maintain biodiversity. Sustainable entrepreneurship includes *ecopreneurship* (i.e., environmental entrepreneurship), with entrepreneurial actions contributing to preserving the natural environment.

The chapter includes coverage of a concept referred to as "shared value." It is an approach to creating economic value that also creates value for society by addressing its needs and challenges. It connects company success with social progress. This concept coupled with "triple bottom line" thinking (*profits, people,* and the *planet*) will shape the transformation of organizations in the twenty-first century.

Doing business globally is rapidly becoming a profitable and popular strategy for many entrepreneurial ventures. The NAFTA, the EU, and the WTO are examples of the powerful economic forces creating opportunities for global entrepreneurs.

This chapter examined why entrepreneurs seek to internationalize and discussed five ways to actively engage in the international markets: importing, exporting, joint ventures, direct foreign investment, and licensing. Researching the foreign market was described as well as the threats and risks to be avoided.

The last part of the chapter examined the five steps for entering the international marketplace: (1) conduct research, (2) prepare a feasibility study, (3) secure adequate financing, (4) file the proper documents, and (5) draw up and implement the plan.

KEY TERMS

B corporation	international alliances	shared value
benefit corporation	joint venture	social entrepreneurship
diaspora networks	learning curve concept	social impact investing
ecopreneurship	licensing	social value
ecovision	market-rich countries	sustainable entrepreneurship
European Union (EU)	North American Free Trade	triple bottom line (TBL)
exporting	Agreement (NAFTA)	World Trade Organization
global entrepreneurs	political risks	(WTO)
importing	resource-rich countries	

REVIEW AND DISCUSSION QUESTIONS

1. Outline a few of the current trends that illustrate the social entrepreneurship movement.

2. Define a *social entrepreneur.*

3. Describe the challenging boundaries involved with social enterprise.

4. Social enterprise can be classified into distinct categories. List some of the categories.

5. How would you describe *sustainable entrepreneurship*?

6. What is *ecopreneurship* and how does *ecovision* play a role? Outline some specific recommendations for entrepreneurs to consider that promote environmental awareness.

7. Explain the concepts of *shared vision* and *triple bottom line.*

8. Describe some of the powerful economic forces that are creating global expansion of entrepreneurship.

9. What are diaspora networks and why are they important for global entrepreneurs?

10. How do the following organizations impact international entrepreneurship: NAFTA; WTO; and the EU?

11. Identify the various methods available to entrepreneurs to "go international."

12. What are the forms of international alliances?

13. How does a joint venture work? What are the advantages of this arrangement? What are the disadvantages?

14. How does a licensing arrangement work? What are the advantages and disadvantages of such an arrangement?

15. When entering the international marketplace, entrepreneurs should follow what five specific steps?

NOTES

1. David Bornstein, *How to Change the World: Social Entrepreneurs and the Power of New Ideas* (Oxford: Oxford University Press, 2004); Johanna Mair and Ignasi Marti, "Social Entrepreneurship Research: A Source of Explanation, Prediction, and Delight," *Journal of World Business* 41 (2006): 36–44; James Austin, Howard Stevenson, and Jane Wei-Skillern, "Social and Commercial Entrepreneurship: Same, Different, or Both?" *Entrepreneurship Theory and Practice* 30, no. 1 (2006): 1–22; Patricia Doyle Corner and Marcus Ho, "How Opportunities Develop in Social Entrepreneurship," *Entrepreneurship Theory and Practice* 34, no. 4 (2010): 635–59; Michael H. Morris, Justin W. Webb, and Rebecca J. Franklin, "Understanding the Manifestation of Entrepreneurial Orientation in the Nonprofit Context," *Entrepreneurship Theory and Practice* 35, no. 5 (2011): 947–71.

2. Skoll Foundation, "PBS Foundation and Skoll Foundation Establish Fund to Produce Unique Programming About Social Entrepreneurship," September 19, 2006, http://www.skollfoundation.org/media/press_releases /internal/092006.asp (accessed April 21, 2008); "The New Heroes," http://www.pbs.org/opb/thenewheroes /whatis/ (accessed January 29, 2012); and http://www .skollfoundation.org (accessed January 29, 2012).

3. Schwab Foundation for Social Entrepreneurship, Social Entrepreneurs' Summit, Davos-Klosters, Switzerland, January 25–29, 2012, http://www.schwabfound.org/sf/Events/WorldEconomicForumEvents/index.htm (accessed January 29, 2012).

4. Moriah Meyskens, Colleen Robb-Post, Jeffrey A. Stamp, Alan L. Carsrud, and Paul D. Reynolds, "Social Ventures from a Resource-Based Perspective: An Exploratory Study Assessing Global Ashoka Fellows," *Entrepreneurship Theory and Practice* 34, no. 4 (2010): 661–80; http://www.ashoka.org/about (accessed January 29, 2012);

5. See *More Than Money Careers* (accessed July 1, 2015). http://www.mtmc.co/aboutus/

6. Jeremy C. Short, Todd W. Moss, and G. T. Lumpkin, "Research in Social Entrepreneurship: Past Contributions and Future Opportunities," *Strategic Entrepreneurship Journal* 3, no. 2 (2009): 161–94.

7. Mair and Marti, "Social Entrepreneurship Research."

8. Gro Harlem Brundtland, *Our Common Future, World Commission on Environment and Development* (Oxford, UK: Oxford University Press, 1987).

9. Arthur C. Brooks, *Social Entrepreneurship: A Modern Approach to Social Value Creation* (Upper Saddle River, NJ: Pearson/Prentice Hall, 2008).

10. Alan Finder, "A Subject for Those Who Want to Make a Difference," *New York Times*, August 17, 2005, education section; Matthew Bishop, "The Rise of the Social Entrepreneur," *Economist*, February 25, 2006, 11–13; Timothy Ogden, "Lessons for Social Entrepreneurs from the Microfinance Crisis," *Harvard Business Review*, April 22, 2011, http://blogs.hbr.org/cs/2011/04/microfinance.html (accessed February 1, 2012); "Faces of Social Entrepreneurship," *New York Times*, March 9, 2008, http://www.nytimes.com/slideshow/2008/03/09/magazine/0309-FACES_index.html (accessed February 1, 2012); and "Forbes' List of the Top 30 Social Entrepreneurs," *Forbes*, November 30, 2011, http://www.forbes.com/sites/helencoster/2011/11/30/forbes-list-of-the-top-30-social-entrepreneurs/ (accessed February 1, 2012).

11. Roger L. Martin and Sally Osberg, "Social Entrepreneurship: The Case for Definition," *Stanford Social Innovation Review* 18 (Spring 2007): 29–39; see also Christine A. Hemingway, "Personal Values as a Catalyst for Corporate Social Entrepreneurship," *Journal of Business Ethics* 60 (2005): 233–49; Geoffrey M. Kistruck and Paul W. Beamish, "The Interplay of Form, Structure, and Embeddedness in Social Intrapreneurship," *Entrepreneurship Theory and Practice* 34, no. 4 (2010): 735–61; Susan M. T. Coombes, Michael H. Morris, Jeffrey A. Allen, and Justin W. Webb, "Behavioral Orientations of Non-Profit Boards as a Factor in Entrepreneurial Performance: Does Governance Matter?" *Journal of Management Studies* 48, no. 4 (2011): 829–56; and Nia Choi and Satyajit Majumdar, "Social Entrepreneurship as an Essentially Contested Concept: Opening a New Avenue for Systematic Future Research," *Journal of Business Venturing* 29 no. 3 (2014): 363–76.

12. "What Is a Social Entrepreneur?" Ashoka, http://ashoka.org/social_entrepreneur (accessed March 24, 2008).

13. Sarah H. Alvord, David L. Brown, and Christine W. Letts, "Social Entrepreneurship and Societal Transformation: An Exploratory Study," *Journal of Applied Behavioral Science* 40, no. 3 (2004): 260–82; Toyah L. Miller and Curtis L. Wesley II, "Assessing Mission and Resources for Social Change: An Organizational Identity Perspective on Social Venture Capitalists' Decision Criteria," *Entrepreneurship Theory and Practice* 34, no. 4 (2010): 705–33; Geoffrey Desa, "Resource Mobilization in International Social Entrepreneurship: Bricolage as a Mechanism of Institutional Transformation," *Entrepreneurship Theory and Practice* 36, no. 4 (2012): 727–51.

14. Jeffery S. McMullen, "Delineating the Domain of Development Entrepreneurship: A Market-Based Approach to Facilitating Inclusive Economic Growth," *Entrepreneurship Theory and Practice* 35, no. 1 (2011): 185–93; Robin Stevens, Nathalie Moray and Johan Bruneel, "The Social and Economic Mission of Social Enterprises: Dimensions, Measurement, Validation, and Relation," *Entrepreneurship Theory and Practice* (2015): in press.

15. Trish Ruebottom, "The Microstructures of Rhetorical Strategy in Social Entrepreneurship: Building Legitimacy Through Heroes and Villains," *Journal of Business Venturing* 28, no. 1 (2013): 98–116.

16. J. Gregory Dees, "Enterprising Nonprofits," *Harvard Business Review* 76, no. 1 (1998): 54–67.

17. B. B. Anderson and J. G. Dees, "Developing Viable Earned Income Strategies," in J. G. Dees, J. Emerson, P. Economy (eds.), *Strategic Tools for Social Entrepreneurs: Enhancing the Performance of Your Enterprising Nonprofit* (New York: John Wiley & Sons, Inc., 2002).

18. "Forbes' List of the Top 30 Social Entrepreneurs," *Forbes*, November 30, 2011, http://www.forbes.com/sites/helencoster/2011/11/30/forbes-list-of-the-top-30-social-entrepreneurs (accessed February 1, 2012).

19. Ana Maria Peredo and Murdith McLean, "Social Entrepreneurship: A Critical Review of the Concept," *Journal of World Business* 41, no. 1 (2006): 56–65; Felipe M. Santos, "A Positive Theory of Social Entrepreneurship," *Journal of Business Ethics* 111, no. 3 (2012): 335–51.

20. Ana Maria Peredo and James J. Chrisman, "Toward a Theory of Community-Based Enterprise," *Academy of Management Review* 31, no. 2 (2006): 309–28; see also, MariaLaura Di Domenico, Helen Haugh, and Paul Tracey, "Social Bricolage: Theorizing Social Value Creation in Social Enterprises," *Entrepreneurship Theory and Practice* 34, no. 4 (2010): 681–703.

21. Dean A. Shepherd and Holger Patzelt, "The New Field of Sustainable Entrepreneurship: Studying Entrepreneurial Action Linking 'What Is to Be Sustained' with 'What Is to Be Developed'," *Entrepreneurship Theory and Practice* 35, no. 1 (2011): 137–63.

22. Thomas J. Dean and Jeffery S. McMullen, "Toward a Theory of Sustainable Entrepreneurship: Reducing Environmental Degradation through Entrepreneurial Action," *Journal of Business Venturing* 22, no. 1 (2007): 50–76; Desirée F. Pacheco, Thomas J. Dean, and David S. Payne, "Escaping the Green Prison: Entrepreneurship and the Creation of Opportunities for Sustainable Development," *Journal of Business Venturing* 25, no. 5 (2010): 464–80; Kai Hockerts and Rolf Wüstenhagen, "Greening Goliaths versus Emerging Davids—Theorizing About the Role of Incumbents and New Entrants in Sustainable Entrepreneurship," *Journal of Business Venturing* 25, no. 5 (2010): 481–92; Bradley D. Parrish, "Sustainability-Driven Entrepreneurship: Principles of Organization Design," *Journal of Business Venturing* 25, no. 5 (2010): 510–23.

23. Shepherd and Patzelt, "The New Field of Sustainable Entrepreneurship."

24. Ronald Cohen and William A. Sahlman, "Social Impact Investing Will Be the New Venture Capital," *Harvard Business Review*, January 17, 2013. https://hbr.org/2013/01/social-impact-investing-will-b/ accessed on line January 3, 2015; Ronald Cohen & Matt Bannick, "Is Social Impact Investing the Next Venture Capital?" *Forbes,* September 20, 2014. http://www.forbes.com/sites/realspin/2014/09/20/is-social-impact-investing-the-next-venture-capital/ (accessed online January 3, 2015).

25. Paul Hawken and William McDonough, "Seven Steps to Doing Good Business," *Inc.* (November 1993): 79–92.

26. Reginald Shareef, "Ecovision: A Leadership Theory for Innovative Organizations," *Organizational Dynamics* 20 (Summer 1991): 50–63; Dean and McMullen, "Toward a Theory of Sustainable Entrepreneurship"; William R. Meek, Desirée F. Pacheco, and Jeffrey G. York, "The Impact of Social Norms on Entrepreneurial Action: Evidence from the Environmental Entrepreneurship Context," *Journal of Business Venturing* 25, no. 5 (2010): 493–509; and Andreas Kuckertz and Marcus Wagner, "The Influence of Sustainability Orientation on Entrepreneurial Intentions—Investigating the Role of Business Experience," *Journal of Business Venturing* 25, no. 5 (2010): 524–539.

27. Hawken and McDonough, "Seven Steps," 81–88.

28. Michael E. Porter and Mark R. Kramer, "Creating Shared Value," *Harvard Business Review*, http://hbr.org/2011/01/the-big-idea-creating-shared-value, 2011.

29. See Andrew W. Savitz, *The Triple Bottom Line* (San Francisco, CA: Jossy Bass, 2006); Laura Quinn and Jessica Baltes, *Leadership and the Triple Bottom Line* (Greensboro, NC: Center for Creative Leadership, 2007).

30. Rosabeth Moss Kanter, "Change is Everyone's Job: Managing the Extended Enterprise in a Globally Connected World," *Organizational Dynamics* 28, no. 1 (1999): 7–23; Mike W. Peng, "How Entrepreneurs Create Wealth in Transition Economies," *Academy of Management Executive* 15, no. 1 (2001): 95–110; Erkko Autio, Gerard George, and Oliver Alexy, "International Entrepreneurship and Capability Development—Qualitative Evidence and Future Research Direction," *Entrepreneurship Theory and Practice* 35, no. 1 (2011): 11–37.

31. Shaker Zahra, James Hayton, Jeremy Marcel, and Hugh O'Neill, "Fostering Entrepreneurship During International Expansion: Managing Key Challenges," *European Management Journal* 19, no. 4 (2001): 359–69; Sheila M. Puffer, Daniel J. McCarthy, and Max Boisot, "Entrepreneurship in Russia and China: The Impact of Formal Institutional Voids," *Entrepreneurship Theory and Practice* 34, no. 3 (2010): 441–67; and Andrea N. Kiss, Wade M. Danis, and S. Tamer Cavusgil, "International Entrepreneurship Research in Emerging Economies: A Critical Review and Research Agenda," *Journal of Business Venturing* 27, no. 2 (2012): 266–90.

32. Daniel J. Isenberg, "The Global Entrepreneur," *Harvard Business Review*, HBR Blog, December 2008; "The Magic of Diasporas," *The Economist*, November 19, 2011; and "Weaving the World Together," *The Economist*, November 19, 2011.

33. John B. Cullen and K. Praveen Parboteeah, *Multinational Management: A Strategic Approach*, 5th ed. (Mason, OH: Cengage/South-Western, 2011); see also Fred Luthans and Jonathan P. Doh, *International Management: Culture, Strategy, and Behavior*, 8th ed. (Whitby, ON: McGraw Hill-Ryerson, 2012).

34. World Trade Organization website: http://www.wto.org (accessed February 6, 2012).

35. North American Free Trade Agreement, Office of the United States Trade Representative, http://www.ustr.gov/trade-agreements/free-trade-agreements/northamerican-free-trade-agreement-nafta (accessed February 6, 2012).

36. Europa: Gateway to the European Union, official website: http://europa.eu/index_en.htm (accessed February 6, 2012); see also Luthans and Doh, *International Management.*

37. A. Rebecca Reuber and Eileen Fischer, "International Entrepreneurship in Internet-enabled Markets," *Journal of Business Venturing* 26, no. 6 (2011): 660–79; Pekka Stenholm, Zoltan J. Acs, and Robert Wuebker, "Exploring Country-Level Institutional Arrangements on the Rate and Type of Entrepreneurial Activity," *Journal of Business Venturing,* 28, no. 1 (2013): 176–93.

38. Cullen and Parboteeah, *Multinational Management*; see also Luthans and Doh, *International Management.*

39. Patrick M. Kreiser, Louis D. Marino, Pat Dickson, and K. Mark Weaver, "Cultural Influences on Entrepreneurial Orientation: The Impact of National Culture on Risk Taking and Proactiveness in SMEs," *Entrepreneurship Theory and Practice* 34, no. 5 (2010): 959–83; Shameen Prashantham and Charles Dhanaraj, "The Dynamic Influence of Social Capital on the International Growth of New Ventures," *Journal of Management Studies* 47, no. 6 (2010): 967–94;

and Lucia Naldi and Per Davidsson, "Entrepreneurial Growth: The Role of International Knowledge Acquisition as Moderated by Firm Age," *Journal of Business Venturing* 29, no. 5 (2014): 687–703.

40. Benjamin M. Oviatt and Patricia P. McDougall, "Global Start-ups," *Inc.*, June 1993: 23; see also: Nicole E. Coviello, Patricia P. McDougall, and Benjamin M. Oviatt, "The Emergence, Advance and Future of International Entrepreneurship Research—An Introduction to the Special Forum," *Journal of Business Venturing* 26, no. 6 (2011): 625–31.

41. Richard M. Hodgetts and Donald F. Kuratko (with Margaret Burlingame and Don Gulbrandsen), *Small Business Management: Essential Tools and Skills for Entrepreneurial Success*, Wiley Pathways Series (Hoboken, NJ: Wiley, 2008).

42. David A. Kirby and Stefan Kaiser, "Joint Ventures as an Internationalisation Strategy for SMEs," *Small Business Economics* 21, no. 3 (2003): 229–42; Hana Milanov and Stephanie A. Fernhaber, "When Do Domestic Alliances Help Ventures Abroad? Direct and Moderating Effects from a Learning Perspective," *Journal of Business Venturing* 29, no. 3 (2014): 377–91.

43. Deepak K. Datta, Martina Musteen, and Pol Herrmann, "Board Characteristics, Managerial Incentives, and the Choice Between Foreign Acquisitions and International Joint Ventures," *Journal of Management* 35, no. 4 (2009): 928–53.

44. Derrick E. D'Souza and Patricia P. McDougall, "Third World Joint Venturing: A Strategic Option for the Smaller Firm," *Entrepreneurship Theory and Practice* 13, no. 4 (1989): 20.

45. Jane W. Lu and Dean Xu, "Growth and Survival of International Joint Ventures: An External-Internal Legitimacy Perspective," *Journal of Management* 32, no. 3 (2006): 426–48.

46. Hong Ren, Barbara Gray and Kwangho Kim, "Performance of International Joint Ventures: What Factors Really Make a Difference and How?" *Journal of Management* 35, no. 3 (2009): 805–32.

47. Fred Luthans and Jonathan P. Doh, *International Management: Culture, Strategy, and Behavior*, 8th ed. (Whitby, ON: McGraw Hill-Ryerson, 2012); Lee Li, Gongming Qian, and Zhengming Qian, "Should Small, Young Technology-Based Firms Internalize

Transactions in Their Internationalization?" *Entrepreneurship Theory and Practice,* 39, no. 4 (2015): 839–62.

48. America Invents Act of 2011, Committee on the Judiciary, website: http://judiciary.house.gov/issues/issues_patentreformact2011.html (accessed February 7, 2012).

49. Michael S. Malone, "The Smother of Invention," *Forbes* (July 24, 2002): 33–40.

50. Anne Parmigiani and Miguel Rivera-Santos, "Clearing a Path Through the Forest: A Meta-Review of Interorganizational Relationships," *Journal of Management* 37, no. 4 (2011): 1108–36.

51. Gaétan de Rassenfosse, "How SMEs Exploit Their Intellectual Property Assets: Evidence from Survey Data," *Small Business Economics* 39, no. 2 (2012): 437–52.

52. Tomasz Obloj, Krzysztof Obloj, and Michael G. Pratt, "Dominant Logic and Entrepreneurial Firms' Performance in a Transition Economy," *Entrepreneurship Theory and Practice* 34, no. 1 (2010): 151–70; Stephanie A. Fernhaber and Dan Li, "The Impact of Interorganizational Imitation on New Venture International Entry and Performance," *Entrepreneurship Theory and Practice* 34, no. 1 (2010): 1–30; see also: Cullen and Parboteeah, *Multinational Management*; and Li Dai, Vladislav Maksimov, Brett Anitra Gilbert, and Stephanie A. Fernhaber, "Entrepreneurial Orientation and International Scope: The Differential Roles of Innovativeness, Proactiveness, and Risk-Taking," *Journal of Business Venturing* 29, no. 4 (2014): 511–524.

53. See Luthans and Doh, *International Management: Culture, Strategy, and Behavior*, 8th ed. (Whitby, ON: McGraw Hill-Ryerson, 2012).

54. Dirk De Clercq, Harry J. Sapienza, R. Isil Yavuz, and Lianxi Zhou, "Learning and Knowledge in Early Internationalization Research: Past Accomplishments and Future Directions," *Journal of Business Venturing* 27, no. 1 (2012): 143–65; Seok-Woo Kwon and Pia Arenius, "Nations of Entrepreneurs: A Social Capital Perspective," *Journal of Business Venturing* 25, no. 5 (2010): 315–30; and Leo Sleuwaegen and Jonas Onkelinx, "International Commitment, Post-Entry Growth and Survival of International New Ventures," *Journal of Business Venturing* 29, no. 1 (2014): 106–20.

PART 2

Initiating Entrepreneurial Ventures

CHAPTER 5

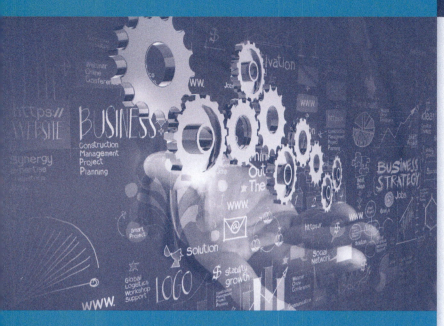

Innovation: The Creative Pursuit of Ideas

LEARNING OBJECTIVES

1 To explore the opportunity identification process

2 To define and illustrate the sources of innovative ideas for entrepreneurs

3 To examine the role of creativity and to review the major components of the creative process: knowledge accumulation, incubation process, idea experience, evaluation, and implementation

4 To present ways of developing personal creativity: recognize relationships, develop a functional perspective, use your "brains," and eliminate muddling mind-sets

5 To introduce the four major types of innovation: invention, extension, duplication, and synthesis

6 To review some of the major myths associated with innovation and to define the ten principles of innovation

Entrepreneurial Thought

The era of the intelligent man/woman is almost over and a new one is emerging— the era of the creative man/woman.

—Pinchas Noy

5-1 OPPORTUNITY IDENTIFICATION: THE SEARCH FOR NEW IDEAS

LO1 Explore the opportunity identification process

Opportunity identification is central to the domain of entrepreneurship. "At its core entrepreneurship revolves around the questions of why, when, and how opportunities for the creation of goods and services in the future arise in an economy. Thus, opportunity recognition is the progenitor of both personal and societal wealth."[1] It has been argued that understanding the opportunity identification process is one of the primary challenges of entrepreneurship research.[2]

This chapter is a study of the creative pursuit of new ideas and the innovation process: two major topics that are keys to understanding entrepreneurial opportunities. It examines the sources that can be useful in searching out innovative ideas and the avenues that lead to their discovery. First, let's examine some productive sources of innovative ideas.

5-1a Sources of Innovative Ideas

LO2 Define and illustrate the sources of innovative ideas for entrepreneurs

Entrepreneurs, ever alert to opportunities that inhabit the external and internal environments around them, often spot potential opportunities that others simply cannot recognize. Where do they find inspiration? All of the following places:

TRENDS

Trends signal shifts in the current paradigm (or thinking) of the major population. The close observation of trends—whether societal, technological, economic, or governmental—and the valuable insights that emanate therefrom constitute an abundant source of potential entrepreneurial ideas.

Societal Trends: aging demographics, health and fitness growth, senior living

Technology Trends: mobile (cell phone) technology, e-commerce, Internet advances

Economic Trends: higher disposable incomes, dual wage-earner families, performance pressures

Government Trends: increased regulations, petroleum prices, terrorism

UNEXPECTED OCCURRENCES

Successes or failures that, because they were unanticipated or unplanned, often prove to be major sources of innovation. The infamous 9/11 terrorist attack on the United States is a good example of an unexpected occurrence; it produced an influx of innovative solutions to new homeland security challenges. (See "Entrepreneurship in Practice: Terrorism Ignites Creativity" on page 120.)

INCONGRUITIES

Incongruities exist in the gap between expectations and reality. For example, when Fred Smith proposed overnight mail delivery, he was told, "If it were that profitable, the U.S. Post Office would be doing it." It turned out Smith was right. An incongruity existed between the assumption that a new, faster level of mail service would never make economic sense, given that mail delivery was, at the time, a three-day affair. So Smith started FedEx.

PROCESS NEEDS

Venture capitalists often refer to process needs in the marketplace as "pain" and to innovative solutions to these needs as "painkillers." When the need is to do something better, innovative new medical devices, healthier foods, more effective pharmaceuticals, and time-saving devices can be the result.

INDUSTRY AND MARKET CHANGES

Continual shifts in the marketplace caused by changes in consumer attitudes, advancements in technology, and growth in the structure, design, or definition of markets or industries are sources of emerging opportunity. An example can be found in the health care industry, where in-patient care has undergone radical changes, and at-home health care and preventive medicine have replaced hospitalization and surgery as primary focus areas.

TABLE 5.1 SOURCES OF INNOVATIVE IDEAS	
Source	**Examples**
Unexpected occurrences	Unexpected success: Apple Computer (microcomputers) Unexpected tragedy: 9/11 terrorist attack
Incongruities	Overnight package delivery
Process needs	Sugar-free products, caffeine-free coffee, microwave ovens
Industry and market changes	Health care industry: changing to home health care
Demographic changes	Retirement communities for older people
Perceptual changes	Exercise (aerobics) and the growing concern for fitness
Knowledge-based concepts	Mobile (cell phone) technology, pharmaceutical industry, robotics

DEMOGRAPHIC CHANGES

Changes in population size, age, education, occupation, geographic locality, and similar demographic variables often catalyze new entrepreneurial opportunities. For example, as the average population age in Florida and Arizona has increased (due largely to the influx of retirees), land development, recreation, and health care industries all have profited.

PERCEPTUAL CHANGES

Perceptual changes in people's interpretation of facts and concepts may be intangible but meaningful. The perceived need to be healthy and physically fit has created a demand for both health foods and health facilities throughout the country. People's desire to better use their personal time has been a boon to the travel industry which, capitalizing on consumers' desires to "see the world" while they are young and healthy, has led to increasing interest in time-share condominiums and travel clubs.

KNOWLEDGE-BASED CONCEPTS

Inventions, which are the product of new thinking, new methods, and new knowledge, often require the longest time period between initiation and market implementation because of the need for testing and modification. For example, cell phone technology has advanced to include not just phone service but cameras, Internet access, and music. This has revolutionized the way we use cell phones today. These concepts were not thought possible just five years ago; some examples of these innovation sources are presented in Table 5.1.

5-1b   The Knowledge and Learning Process

Once sources of ideas are recognized, entrepreneurs must use their existing knowledge base, acquired through work, experience, and education, to hone ideas into actual opportunities. General industry knowledge, prior market knowledge, prior customer understanding, specific interest knowledge, or any previous knowledge helps entrepreneurs to distill unusual sources of innovative ideas into potential opportunities.[3]

In addition to simply having a particular experience in their knowledge base, entrepreneurs must be able to learn from their experiences as well. Researcher Andrew C. Corbett has identified the importance of acquiring and transforming information, knowledge, and experience through the learning process. His research lends credence to theories about the cognitive ability of individuals to transform information into recognizable opportunities.[4] How an individual entrepreneur acquires, processes, and learns from prior knowledge is critical to the opportunity identification process. With that in mind, we next examine the imagination and creativity needed to transform experiences into entrepreneurial insight and know-how.

5-2 ENTREPRENEURIAL IMAGINATION AND CREATIVITY

Entrepreneurs blend imaginative and creative thinking with a systematic, logical process ability. This combination is a key to successful innovation. In addition, potential entrepreneurs are always looking for unique opportunities to fill needs or wants. They sense economic potential in business problems by continually asking "What if...?" or "Why not...?" They develop an ability to see, recognize, and create opportunity where others find only problems. It has been said that the first rule for developing entrepreneurial vision is to recognize that problems are to solutions what demand is to supply. Analysis that blends creative thinking with systematic inquiry such that problems are looked at from every possible angle is a hallmark of the entrepreneurial imagination.[5] What is the problem? Whom does it affect? How does it affect them? What costs are involved? Can it be solved? Would the marketplace pay for a solution? Entrepreneurs continually and imaginatively cycle through these types of questions.

5-2a The Role of Creative Thinking

LO3 Examine the role of creativity and to review the major components of the creative process: knowledge accumulation, incubation process, idea experience, evaluation, and implementation

It is important to recognize the role of creative thinking in the innovative process. Creativity is the generation of ideas that results in the improved efficiency or effectiveness of a system.[6]

Two important components of creative problem solving are process and people. Process is goal oriented; it is designed to attain a solution to a problem. People are the resources that determine the solution. The process remains the same, but the approach that people take toward problem solving varies: sometimes they will adapt a solution, and, at other times, they will formulate a highly innovative solution.[7] Table 5.2 compares the approaches of adaptors versus innovators.

One study examined the validity of these two approaches for distinguishing innovative entrepreneurs from adaptive entrepreneurs and found their application very effective.[8] Thus, understanding the problem-solving orientation of individuals helps develop their creative abilities.

5-2b The Nature of the Creative Process

Creativity is a process that can be developed and improved.[9] Everyone is creative to some degree. However, as is the case with many abilities and talents (athletic, artistic, etc.), some individuals have a greater aptitude for creativity than others. Also, some people have been raised and educated in an environment that encouraged them to develop their creativity. They have been taught to think and act creatively. For others, the process is more difficult because they have not been positively reinforced; if they are to be creative, they must learn how to implement the creative process.[10]

TABLE 5.2   TWO APPROACHES TO CREATIVE PROBLEM SOLVING

Adaptor	Innovator
Employs a disciplined, precise, methodical approach	Approaches tasks from unusual angles
Is concerned with solving, rather than finding, problems	Discovers problems and avenues of solutions
Attempts to refine current practices	Questions basic assumptions related to current practices
Tends to be means oriented	Has little regard for means; is more interested in ends
Is capable of extended detail work	Has little tolerance for routine work
Is sensitive to group cohesion and cooperation	Has little or no need for consensus; often is insensitive to others

Source: Michael Kirton, "Adaptors and Innovators: A Description and Measure," *Journal of Applied Psychology* (October 1976): 623. Copyright © 1976 by The American Psychological Association.

Many people incorrectly believe that only geniuses can be creative.[11] Most people also wrongly assume that some people are born creative whereas others are not and that only the gifted or highly intelligent person is capable of generating creative ideas and insights. The real barriers to creative thinking are sometimes the inadvertent "killer phrases" that we all routinely use in our communications. Table 5.3 lists ten key idea "killers" we hear every day. People may not intentionally seek to kill creative ideas, but their negative expressions often quash creative ideas from further development.[12]

Creativity is not some mysterious and rare talent reserved for a select few. It is a distinct way of looking at the world that is often illogical. The creative process involves seeing relationships among things that others have not seen (e.g., the use of USB flash drives, known as thumb drives, to store or transfer data).[13]

The creative process has four commonly agreed-on phases or steps. Most experts agree on the general nature and relationships among these phases, although they refer to them by a variety of names.[14] Experts also agree that these phases do not always occur in the same order for every creative activity. For creativity to occur, chaos is necessary—but a structured and focused chaos. We shall examine this four-step process using the most typical structural development.

PHASE 1: BACKGROUND OR KNOWLEDGE ACCUMULATION

Successful creations are generally preceded by investigation and information gathering. This usually involves extensive reading, conversations with others working in the field, attendance at professional meetings and workshops, and a general absorption of information relative to the problem or issue under study. Additional investigation in both related and unrelated fields is sometimes involved. This exploration provides the individual with a variety of perspectives on the problem, and it is particularly important to the entrepreneur, who needs a basic understanding of all aspects of the development of a new product, service, or business venture.

People practice the creative search for background knowledge in a number of ways. Some of the most helpful are to: (1) read in a variety of fields; (2) join professional groups and associations; (3) attend professional meetings and seminars; (4) travel to new places; (5) talk to anyone and everyone about your subject; (6) scan magazines, newspapers, and journals for articles related to the subject; (7) develop a subject library for future reference; (8) carry a small notebook and record useful information; and (9) devote time to pursue natural curiosities.[15]

PHASE 2: THE INCUBATION PROCESS

Creative individuals allow their subconscious to mull over tremendous amounts of information gathered during the preparation phase. This incubation process often occurs while they are engaged in activities totally unrelated to the subject or problem. It happens

---

TABLE 5.3   THE MOST COMMON IDEA KILLERS

1. "Naah."
2. "Can't" (said with a shake of the head and an air of finality).
3. "That's the dumbest thing I've ever heard."
4. "Yeah, but if you did that..." (poses an extreme or unlikely disaster case).
5. "We already tried that—years ago."
6. "I don't see anything wrong with the way we're doing it now."
7. "We've never done anything like that before."
8. "We've got deadlines to meet—we don't have time to consider that."
9. "It's not in the budget."
10. "Where do you get these weird ideas?"

Source: Kuratko and Hodgetts, *Entrepreneurship*, 8th ed. © 2009 Cengage Learning.

even when they are sleeping. This accounts for the advice frequently given to a person who is frustrated by what appears to be an unsolvable problem: "Why don't you sleep on it?"[16] Getting away from a problem and letting the subconscious mind work on it allows creativity to spring forth. Some of the most helpful steps to induce incubation are to: (1) engage in routine, "mindless" activities (cutting the grass, painting the house); (2) exercise regularly; (3) play (sports, board games, puzzles); (4) think about the project or problem before falling asleep; (5) meditate or practice self-hypnosis; and (6) sit back and relax on a regular basis.[17]

PHASE 3: THE IDEA EXPERIENCE

This phase of the creative process is often the most exciting, because it is when the idea or solution the individual is seeking is discovered. Sometimes referred to as the "eureka factor," this phase is also the one the average person incorrectly perceives as the only component of creativity.[18]

As with the incubation process, new and innovative ideas often emerge while the person is busy doing something unrelated to the enterprise, venture, or investigation (e.g., taking a shower, driving on an interstate highway, or leafing through a newspaper).[19] Sometimes the idea appears as a bolt out of the blue. In most cases, however, the answer comes to the individual incrementally. Slowly but surely, the person begins to formulate the solution. Because it is often difficult to determine when the incubation process ends and the idea experience phase begins, many people are unaware of moving from Phase 2 to Phase 3.

Following are ways to speed up the idea experience: (1) daydream and fantasize about your project, (2) practice your hobbies, (3) work in a leisurely environment (e.g., at home instead of at the office), (4) put the problem on the back burner, (5) keep a notebook at bedside to record late-night or early-morning ideas, and (6) take breaks while working.[20]

PHASE 4: EVALUATION AND IMPLEMENTATION

This is the most difficult step of a creative endeavor and requires a great deal of courage, self-discipline, and perseverance. Successful entrepreneurs can identify ideas that are workable and that they have the skills to implement. More important, they do not give up when they run into temporary obstacles.[21] Often they will fail several times before they successfully develop their best ideas. In some cases, entrepreneurs will take the idea in an entirely different direction or will discover a new and more workable idea while struggling to implement the original one.

Another important part of this phase is the reworking of ideas to put them into final form. Frequently an idea emerges from Phase 3 in rough form, so it needs to be modified or tested to achieve its final shape. Some of the most useful suggestions for carrying out this phase are to: (1) increase your energy level with proper exercise, diet, and rest; (2) educate yourself in the business-planning process and all facets of business; (3) test your ideas with knowledgeable people; (4) take notice of your intuitive hunches and feelings; (5) educate yourself in the selling process; (6) learn about organizational policies and practices; (7) seek advice from others (friends, experts, etc.); and (8) view the problems you encounter while implementing your ideas as challenges.[22]

Figure 5.1 illustrates the four phases of the creative thinking process. If a person encounters a major problem while moving through the process, it is sometimes helpful to go back to a previous phase and try again. For example, if an individual is unable to formulate an idea or solution (Phase 3), a return to Phase 1 often helps. By immersing him- or herself in the data, the individual allows the unconscious mind to begin anew processing the data, establishing cause–effect relationships, and formulating potential solutions.

5-2c Developing Your Creativity

You can do a number of things to improve your own creative talents; one of the most helpful is to become aware of some of the habits and mental blocks that stifle creativity.[23] Of course, as with most processes, your development will be more effective if you regularly practice exercises designed to increase your creative abilities. The following section is designed to

FIGURE 5.1 THE CRITICAL THINKING PROCESS

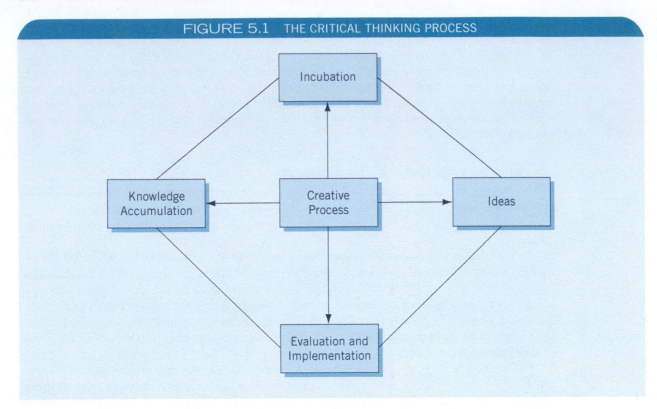

LO4 Present ways of developing personal creativity: recognize relationships, develop a functional perspective, use your "brains," and eliminate muddling mind-sets

improve your awareness of some of the thought habits that limit your creativity and to assist you in developing a personalized creativity improvement program.

RECOGNIZING RELATIONSHIPS

Many inventions and innovations are a result of the inventor's ability to see new and different relationships among objects, processes, materials, technologies, and people.[24] Examples range widely and include (1) adding fruit juice to soft drinks to create Slice, (2) combining combustion engine technology with the wheel to create the automobile, and (3) using a 330-pound defensive football player as a running back and pass receiver.

If you wish to improve your creativity, it helps to look for different or unorthodox relationships among the elements and people around you. This activity involves *perceiving in a relational mode.* You can develop this talent by viewing things and people as existing in a complementary or appositional relationship with other things and people. Simply stated, things and people exist in the world in relation to other things and people. Creative people seem to be intuitively aware of this phenomenon and have developed a talent for recognizing new and different relationships. These relationships often lead to visions that result in new ideas, products, and services.[25] In order to develop the ability to recognize new relationships, you must practice perceiving in a relational mode. The following exercise helps with this development.

5-3 A CREATIVE EXERCISE

Analyze and elaborate on how the following pairs relate to each other in a complementary way: nut and bolt, husband and wife, chocolate cake and vanilla ice cream, grass clippings and tomato plants, peanut butter and jelly, athlete and coach, humanity and water, winning and losing, television and overhead projectors, and managers and production workers.

DEVELOPING A FUNCTIONAL PERSPECTIVE

If expanded, the principle of perceiving in a relational mode helps develop a functional perspective toward things and people. A creative person tends to view things and people in terms of how they can satisfy his or her needs and help complete a project. For example, a homemaker who cannot find a screwdriver often will use a butter knife to tighten a loose screw, or a cereal manufacturer will add fruit to its product to create a new product line that appeals to a health-conscious market.

If you wish to become more innovative and creative, you need to visualize yourself in complementary relationships to the things and people of the world. You must learn to look at them in terms of how they complement attempts to satisfy your own needs and to complete your projects. You must begin to look at things and people in nonconventional ways and from a different perspective.[26] The following exercise is designed to help you develop a functional perspective.

5-4 A CREATIVE EXERCISE

Think of and write down all of the functions you can imagine for the following items (spend five minutes on each item):

- An egotistical staff member
- A large pebble
- A fallen tree branch
- A chair
- A computer "whiz kid"
- An obsessively organized employee
- The office "gossip"
- An old hubcap
- A new secretary
- An empty roll of masking tape
- A yardstick
- An old coat hanger
- The office "tightwad"
- This exercise

USING YOUR BRAINS

Ever since split-brain studies were conducted in the 1950s and 1960s, experts on creativity, innovation, and self-development have emphasized the importance of developing the skills associated with both hemispheres of the brain.[27]

The right brain hemisphere helps an individual understand analogies, imagine things, and synthesize information. The left brain hemisphere helps the person analyze, verbalize, and use rational approaches to problem solving. Although these two brain hemispheres process information differently and are responsible for different brain activities and skills (see Table 5.4), they are integrated through a group of connecting nerve fibers called the corpus callosum. Because of this connection and the nature of the relationship between the activities of each hemisphere, each hemisphere should be viewed as existing and functioning in a complementary relationship with the other hemisphere.[28]

The creative process involves logical and analytical thinking in the knowledge accumulation, evaluation, and implementation stages. In addition, it calls for imagination, intuition, analogy conceptualization, and synthesizing in the incubation and idea creation stages. So, to become more creative, it is necessary to practice and develop both right- and left-hemisphere skills. The following problem-solving exercise is designed to demonstrate the effectiveness of combining the skills of both hemispheres when solving problems.

TABLE 5.4 PROCESSES ASSOCIATED WITH THE TWO HEMISPHERES OF THE BRAIN	
Left Hemisphere	**Right Hemisphere**
Verbal	Nonverbal
Analytical	Synthesizing
Abstract	Seeing analogies
Rational	Nonrational
Logical	Spatial
Linear	Intuitive
	Imaginative

Sources: Tasneem Sayeed, "Left vs. Right Brain: Which Hemisphere Dominates You?" *Hub Pages*, http://tasneemsayeed .hubpages.com/hub/Left_Right_Brain (Accessed February 10, 2012); Kendra Cherry, "Left Brain vs. Right Brain: Understanding the Myth and Reality of Left Brain and Right Brain Dominance," *About.com*, http://psychology.about.com/od /cognitivepsychology/a/left-brain-right-brain.htm (Accessed February 10, 2012).

5-5 A CREATIVE EXERCISE

Assume you have an idea that will save your organization time and money in processing customer complaints. Your supervisor has been extremely busy and has been unwilling to stop and listen to your idea.

1. Write down all of the left-hemisphere-type solutions to this problem you can think of in five minutes.
2. Write down all of the right-hemisphere-type solutions to this problem you can think of in five minutes.
3. Compare these lists and combine two or more solutions from each list that will result in a unique and innovative way to solve this problem.
4. Repeat steps 1, 2, and 3 using a current problem you are facing at work or at home.

Our society and its educational institutions reward individuals who have been successful at developing their logical, analytical, and rational left-brain skills. Little emphasis, however, has been placed on practicing and using right-brain skills. Table 5.5 represents some ways you can practice developing both left- and right-hemisphere skills. [29]

ELIMINATING MUDDLING MIND-SETS

A number of mental habits block or impede creative thinking. It has been estimated that adults use only 2 to 10 percent of their creative potential.[30] For example, many individuals tend to make quick judgments about new things, people, and ideas. Another inclination is to point out the negative components of a new or different idea because of the psychological discomfort associated with change. Some common mental habits that inhibit creativity and innovation are "either/or" thinking, security hunting, stereotyping, and probability thinking. These habits, or **muddling mind-sets**, tend to hinder creative thought processes, and different thought processes must be used to enhance creative thinking.[31]

- **Either/or thinking** Because of the speed of change in the modern world, personal lives are filled with a great deal of uncertainty and ambiguity. People often get bogged down with striving for an unreasonable amount of certainty in their lives. But the creative person learns to accept a reasonable amount of ambiguity in his or her work and life. In fact, many exceptionally creative people thrive in an uncertain environment and find it exhilarating.[32]

THE ENTREPRENEURIAL PROCESS

Developing Creativity

What color is the sky when you dream? Do you consider yourself to be creative? *Creativity* has been defined as having the quality or power of creating. People are innately creative. Really. Let your creativity out of the playpen! Millions of dollars are made from truly simple creative endeavors. You can cash in too if you use some of these methods to boost your creativity.

1. **Brainstorm!** This is the old-school way to drum up creative ideas and solve problems, but it's still by far the best. The corporate world was woken up when Alex Osborn introduced this concept in the 1950s. Established rules were easy to follow:

   - Shout out or write down every solution that comes to mind.
   - Off-the-wall ideas are welcome.
   - Criticize nothing.
   - Organize later.

2. **Opposites attract.** Here's an interesting concept: synectics. Similar to the word itself, synectics involves putting two "nonsensical" things together to see what happens. Examples include: "Imagine a restaurant with no waiters, tables, or silverware" (McDonald's); "Imagine a bookstore with no books—and no store" (Amazon .com); "Imagine moving trucks with no movers" (U-Haul). Don't hesitate to explore that which is strange!

3. **THINKubate.** Gerald Haman created (there's that word again) the "THINKubator"—a playground where businesspeople, entrepreneurs, and the like can go to escape the humdrum environment of offices and "can't doers." The playground houses comfortable seating, toys, and fun pictures, and it offers an environment that favors brain stimulation and idea creation. It must work, because Haman has developed numerous products for Procter & Gamble and Arthur Andersen.

4. **Trigger great ideas.** Triggers are everyday items that can be used to stimulate the brain: abstract photos, inspiring quotes, uncompleted ideas, tips, and so on. Place trigger items in various places you look or visit often—for example, the refrigerator door, your dashboard, or your phone. You never know when a connection will be made.

5. **Connect.** Every person you meet or place you visit might be an opportunity waiting to happen. The key is to be prepared for that opportunity when it arises. Creativity consultant Jordan Ayan suggests building up your CORE: curiosity, openness, risk, and energy. These traits can be enhanced by reading up on trends, attending trade shows, browsing, and trying new things. Spotting open windows isn't necessarily easy, but increasing the number of windows can be.

6. **Always celebrate failure.** Try and try again. What doesn't kill you only makes you stronger. Dare to be great! Get the idea? Don't suffer from insanity! Enjoy every minute of it!

7. **Make 'em laugh.** Humor is a great way to relieve stress. Use it in your creative endeavors. Can you imagine Dennis the Menace helping you build your prototype? How about letting the Disney World characters coauthor your business plan? Let your youngest relative in on your invention. Humor and laughter certainly encourage creativity.

8. **Sweat it.** Yes! Sweat it out! Exercise gets the creative juices—endorphins—flowing. Let the mind wander while you're jogging, or ride the exercise bike while reading the year-end reports. Just be sure to keep a notepad handy to jot down all of your great ideas!

9. **Remember your wildest dreams.** Has anyone ever replied to you with this statement? "In your dreams!" Well, go figure. Dreams are a great place to start when it comes to unleashing creativity. Elias Howe once had a dream in which cannibals were piercing his flesh with spears. Thus, the sewing machine was invented. Don't ignore daydreams or spur-of-the-moment ideas, either. Your subconscious could be trying to tell you something.

Source: Adapted from Nick D'Alto, "Think Big," *Business Start Ups* (January 2000): 61–65.

- **Security hunting** Many people try to make the right decision or take the correct action every time. In doing so, they rely on averages, stereotypes, and probability theory to minimize their risks. Although this strategy often is appropriate, at times a creator or innovator must take some calculated risks.[33] Sometimes these risks result in the innovator being wrong and making mistakes. Yet by recognizing this as part of the innovation game, the creative person learns from his or her mistakes and moves on to create bigger and better things. We all know that Thomas Edison failed numerous times when searching for the correct materials to use inside the incandescent lightbulb.

- **Stereotyping** It is ironic that, although averages and stereotypes are fabricated abstractions, people act and make decisions based on them as if these were data entities that exist

TABLE 5.5 WAYS TO DEVELOP LEFT- AND RIGHT-HEMISPHERE SKILLS	
Left-Hemisphere Skills	**Right-Hemisphere Skills**
1. Step-by-step planning of your work and life activities	1. Using metaphors and analogies to describe things and people in your conversations and writing
2. Reading ancient, medieval, and scholastic philosophy, legal cases, and books on logic	2. Taking off your watch when you are not working
3. Establishing timetables for all of your activities	3. Suspending your initial judgment of ideas, new acquaintances, movies, TV programs, and so on
4. Using and working with a computer program	4. Recording your hunches, feelings, and intuitions and calculating their accuracy
5. Detailed fantasizing and visualizing of things and situations in the future	
6. Drawing faces, caricatures, and landscapes	

in the real world. For example, one could hypothesize that the average homemaker is female, 38 years old, and 5' 4" tall; weighs 120 pounds; and has two children, a part-time job, and 14.5 years of formal education. If one tried to find a person who fits this description, however, the chances of success would be small. In short, the more descriptive the abstraction or *stereotype*, the less real it becomes. Predicating actions from stereotypes and averages can cause an individual to act on the basis of a distorted picture of reality. More important, relying on these abstractions can limit a person's perception of the real entities and possibilities in the world. Creativity expert Edward deBono argues that people must alter their thinking to enhance their creativity; only new patterns of thinking will lead to new ideas and innovations.[34]

- **Probability thinking** In their struggle to achieve security, many people also tend to rely on the theory of **probability thinking** to make decisions. An overreliance on this decision-making method, however, can distort reality and prohibit one from taking calculated risks that may lead to creative endeavors.

Probability experts report that the predictive power of probability theory increases in proportion to the number of times an event is repeated. If a person wishes to predict the probability of tossing the number 3 when rolling dice a certain number of times, probability theory is extremely useful. However, if the person wishes to know the likelihood of rolling a 4 with one roll of the dice, the predictive ability of probability theory is much less valuable.

In the creative game, often an individual is looking at an opportunity or situation that may occur only once in a lifetime. In a single-event situation, intuition and educated guesses are just as useful, if not more useful, than logic and probability.[35] One way of increasing your creative capacities is to practice looking at some of the situations in your life as a 50/50 game, and then begin to take some risks. Additionally, the following problem-solving exercises are designed to help eliminate muddling mind-sets:

- Practice taking small risks in your personal life and at work, relying on your intuition and hunches. Keep a log of these risks, and chart their accuracy and consequences. For example, try to draw an inside straight in your next family poker game.

- Go out of your way to talk to people who you think conform to a commonly accepted stereotype.

- Take on a number of complex projects at work and at home that do not lend themselves to guaranteed and predictable results. Allow yourself to live with a manageable amount of ambiguity. Notice how you react to this ambiguity.

- When an idea is presented to you, first think of all the positive aspects of the idea, then of all the negative aspects, and finally of all the interesting aspects.

- When listening to people, suspend initial judgment of them, their ideas, and their information, and simply listen.
- Try making some decisions in the present. That is, do not let your personal history or your estimates about the future dominate your decision-making process.[36]

5-5a Arenas of Creativity

Remember, people are inherently creative. Some act on that creativity all of the time while others stifle it, and most of us fall somewhere in between the two. The reality is that people often do not recognize when or how they are being creative. Furthermore, they fail to recognize the many opportunities for creativity that arise within their jobs on a daily basis. Creativity researcher William Miller argues that people often do not recognize when they are being creative, and they frequently overlook opportunities to be creative. He suggests that the path to creativity begins by first recognizing all of the ways in which we are or can be creative. People in organizations can channel their creativity into seven different arenas:

- **Idea creativity:** thinking up a new idea or concept, such as an idea for a new product or service or a way to solve a problem.
- **Material creativity:** inventing and building a tangible object such as a product, an advertisement, a report, or a photograph.
- **Organization creativity:** organizing people or projects and coming up with a new organizational form or approach to structuring things. Examples could include organizing a project, starting a new type of venture, putting together or reorganizing a work group, and changing the policies and rules of a group.
- **Relationship creativity:** an innovative approach to achieving collaboration, cooperation, and win–win relationships with others. The person who handles a difficult situation well or deals with a particular person in an especially effective manner is being creative in a relationship or one-on-one context.
- **Event creativity:** producing an event such as an awards ceremony, team outing, or annual meeting. The creativity here also encompasses décor, ways in which people are involved, sequence of happenings, setting, and so forth.
- **Inner creativity:** changing one's inner self; being open to new approaches to how one does things and thinking about oneself in different ways; achieving a change of heart or finding a new perspective or way to look at things that is a significant departure from how one has traditionally looked at them.
- **Spontaneous creativity:** acting in a spontaneous or spur-of-the-moment manner, such as coming up with a witty response in a meeting, an off-the-cuff speech, a quick and simple way to settle a dispute, or an innovative appeal when trying to close a sale.[37]

5-5b The Creative Climate

Creativity is most likely to occur when the business climate is right. No enterprise will have creative owners and managers for long if the right climate is not established and nurtured. Following are some important characteristics of this climate:

- A trustful management that does not overcontrol employees
- Open channels of communication among all business members
- Considerable contact and communication with outsiders
- A large variety of personality types
- A willingness to accept change
- An enjoyment in experimenting with new ideas
- Little fear of negative consequences for making a mistake
- The selection and promotion of employees on the basis of merit

- The use of techniques that encourage ideas, including suggestion systems and brainstorming

- Sufficient financial, managerial, human, and time resources for accomplishing goals[38]

5-6 INNOVATION AND THE ENTREPRENEUR

Innovation is a key function in the entrepreneurial process. Researchers and authors in the field of entrepreneurship agree, for the most part, with renowned consultant and author Peter F. Drucker about the concept of innovation: "Innovation is the specific function of entrepreneurship.... It is the means by which the entrepreneur either creates new wealth-producing resources or endows existing resources with enhanced potential for creating wealth."[39]

Innovation is the process by which entrepreneurs convert opportunities (ideas) into marketable solutions. It is the means by which they become catalysts for change.[40] We demonstrated in the earlier parts of this chapter that the innovation process starts with a good idea. The origin of an idea is important, and the role of creative thinking may be vital to that development.[41] A major difference exists between an idea that arises from mere speculation and one that is the product of extended thinking, research, experience, and work. More important, a prospective entrepreneur must have the desire to bring a good idea through the development stages. Thus, innovation is a combination of the vision to create a good idea and the perseverance and dedication to remain with the concept through implementation.

5-6a The Innovation Process

Most innovations result from a conscious, purposeful search for new opportunities.[42] This process begins with the analysis of the sources of new opportunities. Drucker has noted that, because innovation is both conceptual and perceptual, would-be innovators must go out and look, ask, and listen. Successful innovators use both the right and left sides of their brains. They look at figures. They look at people. They analytically work out what the innovation has to be to satisfy the opportunity. Then they go out and look at potential product users to study their expectations, values, and needs.[43]

Most successful innovations are simple and focused. They are directed toward a specific, clear, and carefully designed application. In the process, they create new customers and markets. Today's mobile technology (cell phones) is a good example. Although this technology is highly sophisticated, it has become easy to use and it appeals to a specific market niche: people who want their technology all in one and on the go.

Above all, innovation often involves more work than genius. As Thomas Edison once said, "Genius is 1 percent inspiration and 99 percent perspiration." Moreover, innovators rarely work in more than one area. For all his systematic innovative accomplishments, Edison worked only in the electricity field.

5-6b Types of Innovation

LO5 Introduce the four major types of innovation: invention, extension, duplication, and synthesis

Four basic types of innovation exist (see Table 5.6). These extend from the totally new to modifications of existing products or services. Following are the four types, in order of originality:

- **Invention**: the creation of a new product, service, or process—often one that is novel or untried. Such concepts tend to be "revolutionary."

- **Extension**: the expansion of a product, service, or process already in existence. Such concepts make a different application of a current idea.

- **Duplication**: the replication of an already existing product, service, or process. The duplication effort, however, is not simply copying but adding the entrepreneur's own creative touch to enhance or improve the concept and beat the competition.

- **Synthesis**: the combination of existing concepts and factors into a new formulation. This involves taking a number of ideas or items already invented and finding a way that they can form a new application. [44]

TABLE 5.6	INNOVATION IN ACTION	
Type	**Description**	**Examples**
Invention	Totally new product, service, or process	Wright brothers—airplane Thomas Edison—lightbulb Alexander Graham Bell—telephone
Extension	New use or different application of an already existing product, service, or process	Ray Kroc—McDonald's Mark Zuckerberg—Facebook Barry Sternlicht—Starwood Hotels & Resorts
Duplication	Creative replication of an existing concept	Wal-Mart—department stores Gateway—personal computers Pizza Hut—pizza parlor
Synthesis	Combination of existing concepts and factors into a new formulation or use	Fred Smith—FedEx Howard Schultz—Starbucks

5-6c The Major Misconceptions of Innovation

LO6 Review some of the major myths associated with innovation and to define the ten principles of innovation

The entire concept of innovation conjures up many thoughts and misconceptions; it seems that everyone has an opinion as to what innovation entails. In this section, we outline some of the commonly accepted innovation misconceptions and provide reasons why these are misconceptions and not facts. [45]

- *Innovation is planned and predictable.* This statement is based on the old concept that innovation should be left to the research and development (R&D) department under a planned format. In truth, innovation is unpredictable and may be introduced by anyone.

- *Technical specifications must be thoroughly prepared.* This statement comes from the engineering arena, which drafts complete plans before moving on. Thorough preparation is good, but it sometimes takes too long. Quite often, it is more important to use a try/test/revise approach.

- *Innovation relies on dreams and blue-sky ideas.* As we have demonstrated in this chapter, the creative process is extremely important to recognizing innovative ideas. However, accomplished innovators are very practical people and create from opportunities grounded in reality—not daydreams.

- *Big projects will develop better innovations than smaller ones.* This statement has been proven false time and time again. Larger firms are now encouraging their people to work in smaller groups, where it often is easier to generate creative ideas. In Chapter 3, we discussed the importance of I-teams as a method of getting smaller teams to work on innovative projects.

- *Technology is the driving force of innovation success.* Technology is certainly one source for innovation, but it is not the only one. As we outlined earlier in this chapter, numerous sources exist for innovative ideas; technology is certainly a driving factor in many innovations, but it is not the only success factor. Moreover, the customer or market is the driving force behind any innovation. Market-driven or customer-based innovations have the highest probability of success.

5-6d Principles of Innovation

Potential entrepreneurs need to realize that innovation principles exist. These principles can be learned and—when combined with opportunity—can enable individuals to innovate. The major motivation principles are as follows:

- *Be action oriented.* Innovators always must be active and searching for new ideas, opportunities, or sources of innovation.

- *Make the product, process, or service simple and understandable.* People must readily understand how the innovation works.

- *Make the product, process, or service customer-based.* Innovators always must keep the customer in mind. The more an innovator has the end user in mind, the greater the chance the concept will be accepted and used.

- *Start small.* Innovators should not attempt a project or development on a grandiose scale. They should begin small and then build and develop, allowing for planned growth and proper expansion in the right manner and at the right time.

- *Aim high.* Innovators should aim high for success by seeking a niche in the marketplace.

- *Try/test/revise.* Innovators always should follow the rule of *try, test, and revise.* This helps work out any flaws in the product, process, or service.

- *Learn from failures.* Innovation does not guarantee success. More important, failures often give rise to innovations.[46]

- *Follow a milestone schedule.* Every innovator should follow a schedule that indicates milestone accomplishments. Although the project may run ahead or behind schedule, it still is important to have a schedule in order to plan and evaluate the project.

- *Reward heroic activity.* This principle applies more to those involved in seeking and motivating others to innovate. Innovative activity should be rewarded and given the proper amount of respect. This also means tolerating and, to a limited degree, accepting failures as a means of accomplishing innovation. Innovative work must be viewed as a heroic activity that will reveal new horizons for the enterprise.

- *Work, work, work.* This is a simple but accurate exhortation with which to conclude the innovation principles. It takes work—not genius or mystery—to innovate successfully.[47]

ENTREPRENEURSHIP IN PRACTICE

Terrorism Ignites Innovation

Ask not how America can innovate; ask what you can do to innovate America—this might as well have been the slogan on a war poster with Uncle Sam pointing his finger at us. Only days after September 11, 2001, the still-smoldering Pentagon advertised for the help of American citizens, asking them to send new ideas to combat the threat of terrorism. The Pentagon's Technical Support Working Group (TSWG) usually receives around 900 proposals a year for new technology and ideas to aid the world's most powerful military force; that October, they received 12,500. The TSWG agencies range from the Energy Department to the Federal Bureau of Investigation (FBI), Central Intelligence Agency (CIA), and Federal Aviation Administration, as well as local police and fire departments. The group sends out an annual list of problems it is interested in solving and then evaluates the proposals it receives. They will then choose only 100 to 200 proposals for research each year and fund $50 to $100 million for the projects.

One company that proposes their products to TSWG is Equator Technologies, Inc. Equator makes superfast digital signal processors used in video cameras and is creating an automated baggage inspection system that would use a database of weapons images rotated on all possible planes of vision. It has been shown that a gun—laid on end—can be mistaken for a shaving-cream can when traditional baggage scanners are used. Another company envisions the use of surveillance cameras equipped with software to identify terrorists whose facial measurements match those found in police files, photos of known terrorists, and possibly FBI records.

Many of the TSWG's projects end up in local firehouses, police stations, airports, and border crossings. Some projects, such as handheld radiation detectors and bomb-resistant building plans, proved successful during the 2002 Olympics and at the Pentagon.

However, the group isn't without failure. They once funded a special radio antenna that picked up signals no better than a chain-link fence. The unofficial motto at TSWG is "If you fail, fail right...don't just fail because you didn't try everything or you stopped short."

Source: Paul Magnusson, "Small Biz vs. the Terrorists," *BusinessWeek Online*, March 4, 2002, http://www.businessweek.com/magazine/content/02_09/b3772087.htm (accessed March 18, 2008).

SUMMARY

This chapter examined the importance of creative thinking and innovation to the entrepreneur. Opportunity identification was discussed in relation to the knowledge and learning needed to recognize good ideas. The sources of innovative ideas were outlined and examined. The creativity process was then described, and ways to develop creativity were presented. Exercises and suggestions were included to help the reader increase the development of his or her creativity. The nature of the creative climate also was presented.

The four basic types of innovation—invention, extension, duplication, and synthesis—were explained. The last part of the chapter reviewed the misconceptions commonly associated with innovation and presented the major innovation principles.

KEY TERMS

appositional relationship	functional perspective	opportunity identification
creative process	incongruities	probability thinking
creativity	innovation	right brain
duplication	invention	security hunting
either/or thinking	left brain	stereotyping
extension	muddling mind-sets	synthesis

REVIEW AND DISCUSSION QUESTIONS

1. Describe opportunity identification for the entrepreneur.
2. How are prior knowledge and learning important to the recognition of opportunities?
3. What are the major sources of innovative ideas? Explain and give an example of each.
4. What is the difference between an adaptor and an innovator?
5. What are four major components in the creative process?
6. What are the four steps involved in developing personal creativity?
7. In your own words, state what is meant by the term *innovation*.
8. What are four major types of innovation?
9. Briefly describe the five major misconceptions commonly associated with innovation.
10. Identify and describe five of the innovation principles.

NOTES

1. S Venkataraman, "The Distinctive Domain of Entrepreneurship Research," in *Advances in Entrepreneurship, Firm Emergence, and Growth*, vol. 3, ed. J. A. Katz (Greenwich, CT: JAI Press, 1997): 119–38; see also, Matthew S. Wood, Alexander McKelvie, and J. Michael Haynie, "Making it personal: Opportunity individuation and the shaping of opportunity beliefs," *Journal of Business Venturing* 29, no. 2 (2014): 252–72; Stratos Ramoglou and Stelios C. Zyglidopoulos, The Constructivist View of Entrepreneurial Opportunities: A Critical Analysis," *Small Business Economics* 44, no. 1 (2015): 71–78.

2. Ivan P. Vaghely and Pierre-André Julien, "Are Opportunities Recognized or Constructed? An Information Perspective on Entrepreneurial Opportunity Identification," *Journal of Business Venturing* 25, no. 1 (2010): 73–86; Jintong Tang, K. Michele (Micki) Kacmar and Lowell Busenitz, "Entrepreneurial Alertness in the Pursuit of New Opportunities," *Journal of Business Venturing* 27, no. 1 (2012): 77–94; Dave Valliere, "Towards a Schematic Theory of Entrepreneurial Alertness," *Journal of Business Venturing* 28, no. 3 (2013): 430–42; Vishal K. Gupta, A. Banu Goktan, and Gonca Gunay, "Gender Differences in Evaluation of New BusinessOpportunity: A Stereotype Threat Perspective," *Journal of Business Venturing* 29, no. 2 (2014): 273–88; and Maw-Der Foo, Marilyn A. Uy, and Charles Murnieks, "Beyond Affective Valence: Untangling Valence and Activation Influences on Opportunity Identification," *Entrepreneurship Theory and Practice*, 39, no. 2 (2015): 407–31.

3. A Ardichvili, R. Cardozo, and S. Ray, "A Theory of Entrepreneurial Opportunity Identification and Development," *Journal of Business Venturing* 18, no. 1 (2003): 105–23; Andranik Tumasjan and Reiner Braun, "In the Eye of the Beholder: How Regulatory Focus and Self-Efficacy Interact in Influencing Opportunity Recognition," *Journal of Business Venturing* 27, no. 6 (2012): 622–36; and Dean A. Shepherd, J. Michael Haynie, and Jeffery S. McMullen,

"Confirmatory Search as a Useful Heuristic? Testing the Veracity of Entrepreneurial Conjectures," *Journal of Business Venturing* 27, no. 6 (2012): 637–51.

4. Andrew C. Corbett, "Experiential Learning within the Process of Opportunity Identification and Exploitation," *Entrepreneurship Theory and Practice* 29, no. 4 (2005): 473–91; Andrew C. Corbett, "Learning Asymmetries and the Discovery of Entrepreneurial Opportunities," *Journal of Business Venturing* 22, no. 1 (2007): 97–118.

5. Lloyd W. Fernald, Jr., "The Underlying Relationship Between Creativity, Innovation, and Entrepreneurship," *Journal of Creative Behavior* 22, no. 3 (1988): 196–202; Thomas B. Ward, "Cognition, Creativity, and Entrepreneurship," *Journal of Business Venturing* 19, no. 2 (March 2004): 173–88; and Michael M. Gielnik, Michael Frese, Johanna M. Graf, and Anna Kampschulte, "Creativity in the Opportunity Identification Process and the Moderating Effect of Diversity of Information," *Journal of Business Venturing* 27, no. 5 (2012): 559–76.

6. Timothy A. Matherly and Ronald E. Goldsmith, "The Two Faces of Creativity," *Business Horizons* 28, no. 5 (September/October 1985): 8; see also Bruce G. Whiting, "Creativity and Entrepreneurship: How Do They Relate?" *Journal of Creative Behavior* 22, no. 3 (1988): 178–83.

7. Michael Kirton, "Adaptors and Innovators: A Description and Measure," *Journal of Applied Psychology* 61, no. 5 (October 1976): 622–29.

8. E. Holly Buttner and Nur Gryskiewicz, "Entrepreneurs' Problem-Solving Styles: An Empirical Study Using the Kirton Adaption/Innovation Theory," *Journal of Small Business Management* 31, no. 1 (1993): 22–31.

9. See Edward deBono, *Serious Creativity: Using the Power of Creativity to Create New Ideas* (New York: HarperBusiness, 1992).

10. Eleni Mellow, "The Two Conditions View of Creativity," *Journal of Creative Behavior* 30, no. 2 (1996): 126–43; Alice H.Y. Hon, Matt Bloom, and J. Michael Crant, "Overcoming Resistance to Change and Enhancing Creative Performance," *Journal of Management* 40, no. 3 (2014): 919–41.

11. H. J. Eysenck, *Genius: The Nature of Creativity* (New York: Cambridge University Press, 1995); B. Taylor, *Into the Open: Reflections on Genius and Modernity* (New York: New York University Press, 1995).

12. Teresa Amabile, "How to Kill Creativity," *Harvard Business Review* 76 (September/October 1998): 77–87.

13. See Dale Dauten, *Taking Chances: Lessons in Putting Passion and Creativity in Your Work Life* (New York: New Market Press, 1986); Dimo Dimov, "Grappling with the Unbearable Elusiveness of Entrepreneurial Opportunities," *Entrepreneurship Theory and Practice* 35, no. 1 (2011): 57–81.

14. Edward deBono, *Six Thinking Hats* (Boston: Little, Brown, 1985); Edward deBono, "Serious Creativity,"

The Journal for Quality and Participation 18, no. 5 (1995): 12.

15. For a discussion of the development of creativity, see Eugene Raudsepp, *How Creative Are You?* (New York: Perigee Books, 1981); Arthur B. Van Gundy, *108 Ways to Get a Bright Idea and Increase Your Creative Potential* (Englewood Cliffs, NJ: Prentice Hall, 1983); Roger L. Firestien, *Why Didn't I Think of That?* (Buffalo, NY: United Education Services, 1989).

16. T. A. Nosanchuk, J. A. Ogrodnik, and Tom Henigan, "A Preliminary Investigation of Incubation in Short Story Writing," *Journal of Creative Behavior* 22, no. 4 (1988): 279–80.

17. W. W. Harman and H. Rheingold, *Higher Creativity: Liberating the Unconscious for Breakthrough Insights* (Los Angeles: Tarcher, 1984); Daniel Goleman, Paul Kaufman, and Michael Ray, *The Creative Spirit* (New York: Penguin Books, 1993).

18. See J. Conrath, "Developing More Powerful Ideas," *Supervisory Management* (March 1985): 2–9; Denise Shekerjian, *Uncommon Genius: How Great Ideas Are Born* (New York: Viking Press, 1990); and Keng L. Siau, "Group Creativity and Technology," *Journal of Creative Behavior* 29, no. 3 (1995): 201–16.

19. Deborah Funk, "I Was Showering When …," *Baltimore Business Journal* 12, no. 46 (March 1995): 13–14.

20. For more on idea development, see A. F. Osborn, *Applied Imagination*, 3rd ed. (New York: Scribner's, 1963); William J. Gordon, *Synectics* (New York: Harper & Row, 1961); and Ted Pollock, "A Personal File of Stimulating Ideas, Little-Known Facts and Daily Problem-Solvers," *Supervision* 4 (April 1995): 24.

21. Martin F. Rosenman, "Serendipity and Scientific Discovery," *Journal of Creative Behavior* 22, no. 2 (1988): 132–38.

22. For more on implementation, see John M. Keil, *The Creative Mystique: How to Manage It, Nurture It, and Make It Pay* (New York: Wiley, 1985); James F. Brandowski, *Corporate Imagination Plus: Five Steps to Translating Innovative Strategies into Action* (New York: The Free Press, 1990).

23. J Wajec, *Five Star Minds: Recipes to Stimulate Your Creativity and Imagination* (New York: Doubleday, 1995); Frank Barron, *No Rootless Flower: An Ecology of Creativity* (Cresskill, New Jersey: Hampton Press, 1995).

24. See Dale Dauten, *Taking Chances*; and Gary A. Davis, *Creativity Is Forever* (Dubuque, IA: Kendall/Hunt, 1986).

25. Sidney J. Parnes, *Visionizing: State-of-the-Art Processes for Encouraging Innovative Excellence* (East Aurora, NY: D.O.K., 1988).

26. See E. Paul Torrance, *The Search for Sartori and Creativity* (Buffalo, NY: Creative Education Foundations, 1979); Erik K. Winslow and George T. Solomon,

"Further Development of a Descriptive Profile of Entrepreneurs," *Journal of Creative Behavior* 23, no. 3 (1989): 149–61; and Roger von Oech, *A Whack on the Side of the Head* (New York: Warner Books, 1998).

27. Tony Buzan, *Make the Most of Your Mind* (New York: Simon & Schuster, 1984).

28. Weston H. Agor, *Intuitive Management: Integrating Left and Right Brain Management Skills* (Englewood Cliffs, NJ: Prentice Hall, 1984); Tony Buzan, *Using Both Sides of Your Brain* (New York: Dutton, 1976); and D. Hall, *Jump Start Your Brain* (New York: Warner Books, 1995).

29. For more on this topic, see Jacquelyn Wonder and Priscilla Donovan, *Whole-Brain Thinking* (New York: Morrow, 1984), 60–61; see also: Maw-Der Foo, "Emotions and Entrepreneurial Opportunity Evaluation," *Entrepreneurship Theory and Practice*, 35, no. 2 (2011): 375–93; and Isabell M. Welpe, Matthias Spörrle, Dietmar Grichnik, Theresa Michl, and David B. Audretsch, "Emotions and Opportunities: The Interplay of Opportunity Evaluation, Fear, Joy, and Anger as Antecedent of Entrepreneurial Exploitation," *Entrepreneurship Theory and Practice*, 36, no. 1 (2012): 69–96.

30. Doris Shallcross and Anthony M. Gawienowski, "Top Experts Address Issues on Creativity Gap in Higher Education," *Journal of Creative Behavior* 23, no. 2 (1989): 75.

31. Vincent Ryan Ruggiero, *The Art of Thinking: A Guide to Critical and Creative Thought* (New York: HarperCollins, 1995).

32. David Campbell, *Take the Road to Creativity and Get Off Your Dead End* (Greensboro, NC: Center for Creative Leadership, 1985).

33. James O'Toole, *Vanguard Management: Redesigning the Corporate Future* (New York: Berkley Books, 1987).

34. Edward deBono, *Lateral Thinking: Creativity Step by Step* (New York: Harper & Row, 1970).

35. Zoa Rockenstein, "Intuitive Processes in Executive Decision Making," *Journal of Creative Behavior* 22, no. 2 (1988): 77–84.

36. Adapted from deBono, *Lateral Thinking*; and Eugene Raudsepp, *How to Create New Ideas: For Corporate Profit and Personal Success* (Englewood Cliffs, NJ: Prentice Hall, 1982).

37. William C. Miller, *Flash of Brilliance* (Reading, PA: Perseus Books, 1999).

38. Karl Albrecht, *The Creative Corporation* (Homewood, IL: Dow Jones-Irwin, 1987); see also William C. Miller, *The Creative Edge: Fostering Innovation Where You Work* (New York: Addison-Wesley, 1987); K. Mark Weaver, "Developing and Implementing Entrepreneurial Cultures," *Journal of Creative Behavior* 22, no. 3 (1988): 184–95; American Management Association, *Creative Edge: How Corporations Support Creativity and Innovation* (New York: AMA, 1995); D. Leonard and S. Straus, "Putting the Company's Whole Brain to Work," *Harvard Business Review* 75 (July/August 1997): 111–21; and J. Hirshberg, *The Creative Priority* (New York: Harper & Row, 1998).

39. Peter F. Drucker, *Innovation and Entrepreneurship* (New York: Harper & Row, 1985), 20.

40. Nina Rosenbusch, Jan Brinckmann, and Andreas Bausch, "Is Innovation Always Beneficial? A Meta-Analysis of the Relationship Between Innovation and Performance in SMEs," *Journal of Business Venturing*, 26, no. 4 (2011): 441–57; Robert A. Baron and Jintong Tan, "The Role of Entrepreneurs in Firm-Level Innovation: Joint Effects of Positive Affect, Creativity, and Environmental Dynamism," *Journal of Business Venturing* 26, no. 1 (2011): 49–60; Jeroen P. J. de Jong, "The Decision to Exploit Opportunities for Innovation: A Study of High-Tech Small-Business Owners," *Entrepreneurship Theory and Practice* 37, no. 2 (2013): 281–301.

41. Peter F. Drucker, "The Discipline of Innovation," *Harvard Business Review* 63, no. 3 (May/June 1985): 67–72.

42. See Peter L. Josty, "A Tentative Model of the Innovation Process," *R & D Management* 20, no. 1 (January 1990): 35–44.

43. Drucker, "The Discipline of Innovation," 67.

44. Adapted from Richard M. Hodgetts and Donald F. Kuratko, *Effective Small Business Management*, 7th ed. (Fort Worth, TX: Harcourt College Publishers, 2001), 21–23.

45. Adapted from Drucker, *Innovation and Entrepreneurship*; and Thomas J. Peters and Nancy J. Austin, *A Passion for Excellence* (New York: Random House, 1985).

46. For a good example, see Ronald A. Mitsch, "Three Roads to Innovation," *Journal of Business Strategy* 11, no. 5 (September/October 1990): 18–21.

47. William Taylor, "The Business of Innovation," *Harvard Business Review* 68, no. 2 (March/April 1990): 97–106.

CHAPTER 6

Assessment of Entrepreneurial Opportunities

LEARNING OBJECTIVES

1 To explain the challenge of new-venture start-ups

2 To review common pitfalls in the selection of new-venture ideas

3 To present critical factors involved in new-venture development

4 To examine why new ventures fail

5 To study certain factors that underlie venture success

6 To analyze the traditional venture evaluation process methods: profile analysis, feasibility criteria approach, and comprehensive feasibility method

7 To highlight the contemporary venture evaluation methods: design methodology and the lean start-up methodology

Entrepreneurial Thought

To avoid all mistakes in the conduct of a great enterprise is beyond man's powers.... But, when a mistake has once been made, to use his reverses as lessons for the future is the part of a brave and sensible man.

—Minucius (A.D. 209)

6.1 THE CHALLENGE OF NEW-VENTURE START-UPS

LO1 Explain the challenge of new-venture start-ups

During the past two decades, the number of new-venture start-ups has been consistently high. It is reported that more than 400,000 new firms have emerged in the United States every year since 2010; that works out to approximately 1,100 business start-ups per day. In addition, the ideas for potential new businesses are also surfacing in record numbers; the U.S. Patent Office currently receives approximately 500,000 patent applications per year.[1]

The reasons that entrepreneurs start new ventures are numerous. One study reported seven components of new-venture motivation: (1) the need for approval, (2) the need for independence, (3) the need for personal development, (4) welfare (philanthropic) considerations, (5) perception of wealth, (6) tax reduction and indirect benefits, and (7) following role models.[2] These motivations are similar to the characteristics discussed in Chapter 3 on the entrepreneurial mind-set. Although researchers agree that many reasons exist for starting a venture, the entrepreneurial motivations of individuals usually relate to the *personal characteristics* of the entrepreneur, the *environment*, and the *venture* itself. The complexity of these factors makes the assessment of new ventures extremely difficult. One recent study examined the importance of start-up activities to potential entrepreneurs (those attempting to start a venture). Entrepreneurs who successfully started a business "were more aggressive in making their business real; that is, they undertook activities that made their businesses tangible to others: they looked for facilities and equipment, sought and got financial support, formed a legal entity, organized a team, bought facilities and equipment, and devoted full time to the business. Individuals who started businesses seemed to act with a greater level of intensity. They undertook more activities than those individuals who did not start their businesses. The pattern of activities seems to indicate that individuals who started firms put themselves into the day-to-day process of running an ongoing business as quickly as they could and that these activities resulted in starting firms that generated sales (94 percent of the entrepreneurs) and positive cash flow (50 percent of the entrepreneurs)."[3] Another study examined the quantitative and qualitative managerial factors that contribute to the success or failure of a young firm, and the results showed that firms do not have equal resources starting out. More important, the successful firms made greater use of professional advice and developed more detailed business plans.[4] Yet another recent study examined the importance of obtaining legitimacy with the early stakeholders as a prerequisite to venture survival.[5] As researcher Arnold C. Cooper points out, the challenges to predicting new-firm performance include environmental effects (the risk of new products or services, narrow markets, and scarce resources), the entrepreneur's personal goals and founding processes (reasons for start-up), and the diversity of the ventures themselves (differing scales and potential).[6] (See Figure 6.1 for illustration.) Some of the latest research studies are emphasizing the importance of "fit" for the entrepreneur with the organization—the idea that an individual's cognitive abilities must match with the organization or venture that he or she is attempting to develop.[7]

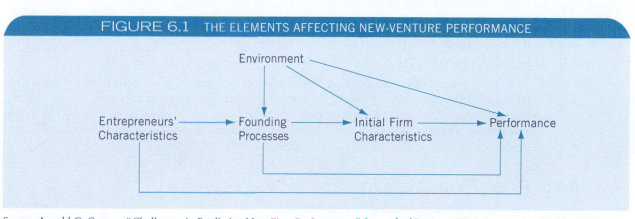

FIGURE 6.1   THE ELEMENTS AFFECTING NEW-VENTURE PERFORMANCE

Source: Arnold C. Cooper, "Challenges in Predicting New Firm Performance," *Journal of Business Venturing* 8, no. 3(1993): 243.

In addition to the problems presented by the complexity of the factors in new-venture performance, it is difficult to obtain reliable data concerning start-up, performance, and failure. Surveys by phone and mail have been used with owners, employees, and competitors to obtain measures of sales, profit, technology, market share, and so forth.[8] The results are not completely comparable to all ventures or all industries. It is from this pioneering work, however, that more and better data are being gathered for the evaluation of new ventures.

It should be understood that new-venture assessment begins with the idea and venture selection stage. However, most studies of new-venture development deal with established start-up businesses. A "fully developed new firm" has been described as one that requires the full-time commitment of one or more individuals, is selling a product or service, has formal financial support, and has hired one or more individuals.[9]

Therefore, as ideas develop into new-venture start-ups, the real challenge is for those firms to survive and grow. In order to do this, they need to have a clear understanding of the critical factors for selecting ventures, the known reasons for venture failure, and an effective evaluation process.

6-2 PITFALLS IN SELECTING NEW VENTURES

LO2 Review common pitfalls in the selection of new-venture ideas

The first key area of analysis is the selection of a new venture. This stage of transition—from an idea to a potential venture—can be the most critical for understanding new-venture development. Following are six of the most important pitfalls commonly encountered in the process of selecting a new venture.

6-2a Lack of Objective Evaluation

Many entrepreneurs lack objectivity. Engineers and technically trained people are particularly prone to falling in love with an idea for a product or service. They seem unaware of the need for the scrutiny they would give to a design or project in the ordinary course of their professional work. The way to avoid this pitfall is to subject all ideas to rigorous study and investigation.[10]

6-2b No Real Insight into the Market

Many entrepreneurs do not realize the importance of developing a marketing approach in laying the foundation for a new venture. They show a managerial shortsightedness.[11] Also, they do not understand the life cycle that must be considered when introducing a new product or service.

No product is instantaneously profitable, nor does its success endure indefinitely. Entrepreneurs must not only project the life cycle of the new product, they must also recognize that introducing the product at the right time is important to its success. Timing is critical. Action taken too soon or too late will often result in failure.

6-2c Inadequate Understanding of Technical Requirements

The development of a new product often involves new techniques. Failure to anticipate the technical difficulties related to developing or producing a product can sink a new venture. Entrepreneurs cannot be too thorough when studying the project before initiating it. Encountering unexpected technical difficulties frequently poses time-consuming and costly problems.

6-2d Poor Financial Understanding

A common difficulty with the development of a new product is an overly optimistic estimate of the funds required to carry the project to completion. Sometimes entrepreneurs are ignorant of costs or are victims of inadequate research and planning. Quite often they tend to underestimate development costs by wide margins. It is not unusual for estimates to be less than half of what is eventually required.

6-2e Lack of Venture Uniqueness

A new venture should be unique. Uniqueness refers to the special characteristics and design concepts that draw the customer to the venture, which should provide performance or service that is superior to that of competitive offerings. The best way to ensure customer awareness of differences between the company's product and competitors' products is through product differentiation. Pricing becomes less of a problem when the customer sees the product as superior to its competitors. A product that is unique in a significant way can gain the advantage of differentiation.

6-2f Ignorance of Legal Issues

Business is subject to many legal requirements. One is the need to make the workplace safe for employees. A second is to provide reliable and safe products and services. A third is the necessity for patents, trademarks, and copyrights to protect one's inventions and products. When these legal issues are overlooked, major problems can result.

6-3 CRITICAL FACTORS FOR NEW-VENTURE DEVELOPMENT

LO3 Present critical factors involved in new-venture development

LO5 Study certain factors that underlie venture success

A number of critical factors are important for new-venture assessment. One way to identify and evaluate them is with a checklist (see Table 6.1). In most cases, however, such a questionnaire approach is too general. The assessment must be tailor-made for the specific venture.

A new venture goes through three specific phases: prestart-up, start-up, and poststart-up. The prestart-up phase begins with an idea for the venture and ends when the doors are opened for business. The start-up phase commences with the initiation of sales activity and the delivery of products and services, and ends when the business is firmly established and beyond short-term threats to survival. The poststart-up phase lasts until the venture is terminated or the surviving organizational entity is no longer controlled by an entrepreneur.

The major focus in this chapter is on the prestart-up and start-up phases, because these are the critical segments for entrepreneurs. During these two phases, five factors are critical: (1) the relative uniqueness of the venture, (2) the relative investment size at start-up, (3) the expected growth of sales and/or profits as the venture moves through its start-up phase, (4) the availability of products during the prestart-up and start-up phases, and (5) the availability of customers during the prestart-up and start-up phases.

6-3a Uniqueness

A new venture's range of uniqueness can be considerable, extending from fairly routine to highly nonroutine. What separates the routine from the nonroutine venture is the amount of innovation required during prestart-up. This distinction is based on the need for new process technology to produce services or products and on the need to service new market segments. Venture uniqueness is further characterized by the length of time a nonroutine venture will remain nonroutine. For instance, will new products, new technology, and new markets be required on a continuing basis? Or will the venture be able to "settle down" after the start-up period and use existing products, technologies, and markets?

6-3b Investment

The capital investment required to start a new venture can vary considerably. In some industries less than $100,000 may be required, whereas in other industries millions of dollars are necessary. Moreover, in some industries only large-scale start-ups are feasible. For example, in the publishing industry one can start a small venture that can remain small or grow into a

TABLE 6.1 A NEW-VENTURE IDEA CHECKLIST

Basic Feasibility of the Venture
1. Can the product or service work?
2. Is it legal?

Competitive Advantages of the Venture
1. What specific competitive advantages will the product or service offer?
2. What are the competitive advantages of the companies already in business?
3. How are the competitors likely to respond?
4. How will the initial competitive advantage be maintained?

Buyer Decisions in the Venture
1. Who are the customers likely to be?
2. How much will each customer buy, and how many customers are there?
3. Where are these customers located, and how will they be serviced?

Marketing of the Goods and Services
1. How much will be spent on advertising and selling?
2. What share of market will the company capture? By when?
3. Who will perform the selling functions?
4. How will prices be set? How will they compare with the competition's prices?
5. How important is location, and how will it be determined?
6. What distribution channels will be used—wholesale, retail, agents, direct mail?
7. What are the sales targets? By when should they be met?
8. Can any orders be obtained before starting the business? How many? For what total amount?

Production of the Goods and Services
1. Will the company make or buy what it sells? Or will it use a combination of these two strategies?
2. Are sources of supplies available at reasonable prices?
3. How long will delivery take?
4. Have adequate lease arrangements for premises been made?
5. Will the needed equipment be available on time?
6. Do any special problems with plant setup, clearances, or insurance exist? How will they be resolved?
7. How will quality be controlled?
8. How will returns and servicing be handled?
9. How will pilferage, waste, spoilage, and scrap be controlled?

Staffing Decisions in the Venture
1. How will competence in each area of the business be ensured?
2. Who will have to be hired? By when? How will they be found and recruited?
3. Will a banker, lawyer, accountant, or other advisers be needed?
4. How will replacements be obtained if key people leave?
5. Will special benefit plans have to be arranged?

Control of the Venture
1. What records will be needed? When?
2. Will any special controls be required? What are they? Who will be responsible for them?

Financing the Venture
1. How much will be needed for development of the product or service?
2. How much will be needed for setting up operations?
3. How much will be needed for working capital?
4. Where will the money come from? What if more is needed?
5. Which assumptions in the financial forecasts are most uncertain?
6. What will be the return on equity, or sales, and how does it compare with the rest of the industry?
7. When and how will investors get their money back?
8. What will be needed from the bank, and what is the bank's response?

Source: Karl H. Vesper, *New Venture Strategies*, (Revised Edition), 1st Edition, © 1990. Reprinted by permission of Pearson Education, Inc., Upper Saddle River, NJ.

larger venture. By contrast, an entrepreneur attempting to break into the airline industry will need a considerable upfront investment.

Another finance-related critical issue is the extent and timing of funds needed to move through the venture process. To determine the amount of needed investment, entrepreneurs must answer questions such as these: Will industry growth be sufficient to maintain break-even sales to cover a high fixed-cost structure during the start-up period? Do the principal entrepreneurs have access to substantial financial reserves to protect a large initial investment? Do the entrepreneurs have the appropriate contacts to take advantage of various environmental opportunities? Do the entrepreneurs have both industry and entrepreneurial track records that justify the financial risk of a large-scale start-up?[12]

6-3c Growth of Sales

The **growth of sales** through the start-up phase is another critical factor. Key questions are as follows: What is the growth pattern anticipated for new-venture sales and profits? Are sales and profits expected to grow slowly or level off shortly after start-up? Are large profits expected at some point, with only small or moderate sales growth? Or are both high sales growth and high profit growth likely? Or will initial profits be limited, with eventual high profit growth over a multiyear period? In answering these questions, it is important to remember that most ventures fit into one of the three following classifications.

- **Lifestyle ventures** appear to have independence, autonomy, and control as their primary driving forces. Neither large sales nor profits are deemed important beyond providing a sufficient and comfortable living for the entrepreneur.

- In **small profitable ventures**, financial considerations play a major role. Autonomy and control also are important in the sense that the entrepreneur does not want venture sales (and employment) to become so large that he or she must relinquish equity or an ownership position and thus give up control over cash flow and profits—which, it is hoped, will be substantial.

- In **high-growth ventures**, significant sales and profit growth are expected to the extent that it may be possible to attract venture capital money and funds raised through public or private placements.[13]

6-3d Product Availability

Essential to the success of any venture is **product availability**, the availability of a salable good or service at the time the venture opens its doors. Some ventures have problems in this regard because the product or service is still in development and needs further modification or testing. Other ventures find that, because they bring their product to market too soon, it must be recalled for further work. A typical example is the software firm that rushes the development of its product and is then besieged by customers who find "bugs" in the program. Lack of product availability in finished form can affect the company's image and its bottom line.

6-3e Customer Availability

If the product is available before the venture is started, the likelihood of venture success is considerably better than it would be otherwise. Similarly, venture risk is affected by **customer availability** for start-up. At one end of the risk continuum is the situation where customers are willing to pay cash for products or services before delivery. At the other end of the continuum is the enterprise that gets started without knowing exactly who will buy its product. A critical consideration is how long it will take to determine who the customers are, as well as their buying habits. As one researcher noted:

> The decision to ignore the market is an extremely risky one. There are, after all, two fundamental criteria for entrepreneurial success. The first is having a customer who is willing to pay you a profitable price for a product or a service. The second is that you must

actually produce and deliver the product or service. The farther a venture removes itself from certainty about these two rules, the greater the risk and the greater the time required to offset this risk as the venture moves through the prestart-up and start-up periods.[14]

6-4 WHY NEW VENTURES FAIL

LO4 Examine why new ventures fail

Every year, many millions of dollars are spent on starting new enterprises. Many of these newly established businesses vanish within a year or two; only a small percentage succeeds. Most studies have found that the factors underlying the failure of new ventures are, in most cases, within the control of the entrepreneur. Some of the major reasons for the failure of new ventures follow.

One research study examined 250 high-tech firms and found three major categories of causes for failure: product/market problems, financial difficulties, and managerial problems.[15] Product/market problems involved the following factors:

- *Poor timing.* A premature entry into the marketplace contributed to failure in 40 percent of the cases studied.

- *Product design problems.* Although these may be related to timing, product design and development became key factors at earlier stages of the venture; when the essential makeup of the product or service changed, failure resulted.

- *Inappropriate distribution strategy.* Whether it was based on commissioned sales, representatives, or direct sales at trade shows, the distribution strategy had to be geared toward the product and customer.

- *Unclear business definition.* Uncertainty about the "exact" business they were in caused these firms to undergo constant change and to lack stabilization.

- *Overreliance on one customer.* This resulted in a failure to diversify and brought about the eventual demise of some of the firms.

The financial difficulties category involved the following factors:

- *Initial undercapitalization.* Undercapitalization contributed to failure in 30 percent of the case studies.

- *Assuming debt too early.* Some of the firms attempted to obtain debt financing too soon and in too large an amount. This led to debt service problems.

- *Venture capital relationship problems.* Differing goals, visions, and motivations of the entrepreneur and the venture capitalist resulted in problems for the enterprise.

Managerial problems involved two important factors:

- *Concept of a team approach.* The following problems associated with the managerial team were found: (1) hirings and promotions on the basis of nepotism rather than qualifications, (2) poor relationships with parent companies and venture capitalists, (3) founders who focused on their weaknesses rather than on their strengths (though weakening the company, they supposedly were building their skills), and (4) incompetent support professionals (e.g., attorneys who were unable to read contracts or collect on court judgments that already had been made).

- *Human resource problems.* Inflated owner ego, employee-related concerns, and control factors were all problems that led to business failure. The study also revealed such interpersonal problems as (1) kickbacks and subsequent firings that resulted in an almost total loss of customers, (2) deceit on the part of a venture capitalist in one case and on the part of a company president in another, (3) verbal agreements between the entrepreneur and the venture capitalists that were not honored, and (4) protracted lawsuits around the time of discontinuance.

In a study of successful ventures (firms listed in the Inc. 500 group of fastest-growing privately held companies), the most significant problems encountered at start-up were researched in order to systematically sort them into a schematic. Table 6.2 lists the types and

TABLE 6.2   TYPES AND CLASSES OF FIRST-YEAR PROBLEMS

1. *Obtaining external financing*

   Obtaining financing for growth

   Other or general financing problems

2. *Internal financial management*

   Inadequate working capital

   Cash-flow problems

   Other or general financial management problems

3. *Sales/marketing*

   Low sales

   Dependence on one or few clients/customers

   Marketing or distribution channels

   Promotion/public relations/advertising

   Other or general marketing problems

4. *Product development*

   Developing products/services

   Other or general product development problems

5. *Production/operations management*

   Establishing or maintaining quality control

   Raw materials/resources/supplies

   Other or general production/operations management problems

6. *General management*

   Lack of management experience

   Only one person/no time

   Managing/controlling growth

   Administrative problems

   Other or general management problems

7. *Human resource management*

   Recruitment/selection

   Turnover/retention

   Satisfaction/morale

   Employee development

   Other or general human resource management problems

8. *Economic environment*

   Poor economy/recession

   Other or general economic environment problems

9. *Regulatory environment*

   Insurance

Source: David E. Terpstra and Philip D. Olson, "Entrepreneurial Start-Up and Growth: A Classification of Problems," *Entrepreneurship Theory and Practice* 17, no. 3 (Spring 1993): 19.

classes of problems identified during the first year of operation. The researcher also surveyed the current problems the owners of these successful firms encountered in order to explore the possible changes in problem patterns of new firms. It was found that dominant problems at start-up related to sales/marketing (38 percent), obtaining external financing (17 percent), and internal financial management (16 percent). General management problems were also frequently cited in the start-up stage (11 percent). Sales/marketing remained the most dominant problem (22 percent) in the **growth stage**, but it was less important than in the start-up stage. Internal financial management (21 percent) continued to be a dominant problem, as were human resource management (17 percent) and general management (14 percent). Additionally, more regulatory environment problems occurred in the growth stage (8 percent) than were mentioned in the start-up stage (1 percent). Finally, organizational structure/design (6 percent) emerged as a problem in the growth stage.[16] It is important for entrepreneurs to recognize these problem areas at the outset because they remain challenges to the venture as it grows.

Another study of 645 entrepreneurs focused on the classification of start-up and growth problems experienced internally versus externally.[17] The percentages were calculated for each of the problems. **Internal problems** involved adequate capital (15.9 percent), cash flow (14.9 percent), facilities/equipment (12.6 percent), inventory control (12.3 percent), human resources (12.0 percent), leadership (11.1 percent), organizational structure (10.8 percent), and accounting systems (10.4 percent). **External problems** were related to customer contact (27.3 percent), market knowledge (19.3 percent), marketing planning (14.4 percent), location (11.1 percent), pricing (8.4 percent), product considerations (7.6 percent), competitors (6.3 percent), and expansion (5.5 percent). The researchers found that the "intensity of competition" rather than life cycle stages was crucial in changing the relative importance of the problem areas. Thus, entrepreneurs need to recognize not only that **start-up problems** remain with the venture but also that the increasing competition will adjust the relative importance of the problems.

The differing perceptions of new-venture failure were examined in another study conducted by researchers Andrew Zacharakis, G. Dale Meyer, and Julio DeCastro. Internal and external factors were identified and ranked by a sample of venture capitalists as well as a sample of entrepreneurs. Entrepreneurs, who attributed new-venture failure, in general, to *internal* factors 89 percent of the time, ranked the highest contributing internal factors as lack of management skill, poor management strategy, lack of capitalization, and lack of vision. Venture capitalists overwhelmingly attributed the failure of most new ventures to *internal* causes as well (84 percent), similarly attributing failure most often to these three internal factors: lack of management skill, poor management strategy, and lack of capitalization. An external factor, poor external market conditions, ranked fourth on the venture capitalists' list.[18]

A fourth "failure" or problem study dealt with a proposed **failure prediction model** based on financial data from newly founded ventures. The study assumed that the financial failure process was characterized by too much initial indebtedness and too little revenue financing. As shown by the failure process schematic in Table 6.3, the risk of failure can be reduced by using less debt as initial financing and by generating enough revenue in the initial stages. Furthermore, the study recognized the risk associated with the initial size of the venture being developed. Specific applications of the model included the following:[19]

1. **Role of profitability and cash flows.** The entrepreneur and manager should ensure that the products are able to yield positive profitability and cash flows in the first years.

2. **Role of debt.** The entrepreneur and manager should ensure that enough stockholders' capital is in the initial balance sheet to buffer future losses.

3. **Combination of both.** The entrepreneur and manager should not start a business if the share of stockholders' capital in the initial balance sheet is low and if negative cash flows in the first years are probable.

4. **Role of initial size.** The entrepreneur and manager should understand that the more probable the negative cash flows and the larger the debt share in the initial balance sheet, the smaller the initial size of the business should be.

TABLE 6.3   THE FAILURE PROCESS OF A NEWLY FOUNDED FIRM

1. Extremely high indebtedness (poor static solidity) and small size

2. Too slow velocity of capital, too fast growth, too poor profitability (as compared to the budget), or some combination of these

3. Unexpected lack of revenue financing (poor dynamic liquidity)

4. Poor static liquidity and debt service ability (dynamic solidity)

A. Profitability

1. Return on investment ratio defined on end-of-the-year basis $= \dfrac{\text{Net Profit} + \text{Interest Expenses}}{\text{Total Capital at the End of the Year}} \times 100$

B. Liquidity

Dynamic

2. Cash flow to net sales $= \dfrac{\text{Net Profit} + \text{Depreciations}}{\text{Net Sales}} \times 100$

Static

3. Quick ratio $= \dfrac{\text{Financial Assets}}{\text{Current Debt}}$

C. Solidity

Static

4. Stockholders' capital to total capital $= \dfrac{\text{Total Capital} - \text{Debt Capital}}{\text{Total Capital}} \times 100$

Dynamic

5. Cash flow to total debt $= \dfrac{\text{Net Profit} + \text{Depreciations}}{\text{Total Debt}} \times 100$

D. Other Factors

Growth or Dynamic Size

6. Rate of annual growth in net sales $= \dfrac{\text{Net Sales in Year } t}{\text{Net Sales in Year } t - 1} \times 100$

Size

7. Logarithmic net sales $= \text{In (Net Sales)}$

Velocity of Capital

8. Net sales to total capital $= \dfrac{\text{Net Sales}}{\text{Total Capital at the End of the year}} \times 100$

Source: Erkki K. Laitinen, "Prediction of Failure of a Newly Founded Firm," *Journal of Business Venturing* 7, no. 4(1992): 326–28.

5. **Role of velocity of capital.** The entrepreneur and manager should not budget for fast velocity of capital in the initial years if the risk of negative cash flows is high. More sales in comparison to capital results in more negative cash flows and poorer profitability.

6. **Role of control.** The entrepreneur and manager should monitor financial ratios from the first year, especially the cash-flow-to-total-debt ratio. Risky combinations of ratios—especially negative cash flows, a low stockholders' capital-to-total-capital ratio, and a

high velocity of capital—should be monitored and compared with industrial standards. The entrepreneur should try to identify the reasons for poor ratios and pay special attention to keeping profitability at the planned level (with control ratios).

6-5 THE TRADITIONAL VENTURE EVALUATION PROCESSES

A critical task in starting a new business is conducting a solid analysis of the feasibility of the product/service in getting off the ground. Entrepreneurs must put ideas through feasibility analyses to discover if their proposals contain any fatal flaws. The following sections provide an explanation of the more traditional approaches to venture assessment.

6-5a Profile Analysis Approach

LO6 Analyze the traditional venture evaluation process methods: profile analysis, feasibility criteria approach, and comprehensive feasibility method

A *profile analysis* is a tool that enables entrepreneurs to judge a business venture's potential by sizing up the venture's strengths and weaknesses along a number of key dimensions or variables. A single strategic variable seldom shapes the ultimate success or failure of a new venture. In most situations, a combination of variables influences the outcome. It is important, therefore, to identify and investigate these variables before committing resources to launch a new venture.

The internal profile analysis in the experiential exercise found at the end of this chapter presents a framework, in checklist format, for determining the relative strengths and weaknesses of the financial, marketing, organizational, and human resources available to a new venture. Through careful profile analysis, entrepreneurs can mitigate for possible weaknesses that may inhibit the growth of their ventures, avoiding many of the mistakes cited earlier in this chapter that can lead to venture failures.

6-5b Feasibility Criteria Approach

Another evaluation method, the **feasibility criteria approach**, is a criteria selection list, based on the following questions, from which entrepreneurs can gain insights into the viability of their venture:

- *Is it proprietary?* The product does not have to be patented, but it should be sufficiently proprietary to permit a long head start against competitors and a period of extraordinary profits early in the venture to offset start-up costs.

- *Are initial production costs realistic?* Most estimates are too low. A careful, detailed analysis should be made so that no large unexpected expenses arise.

- *Are the initial marketing costs realistic?* This answer requires the venture to identify target markets, market channels, and promotional strategy.

- *Does the product have potential for very high margins?* This is almost a necessity for a fledgling company. Gross margins are one thing the financial community understands. Without them, funding can be difficult.

- *Is the time required to get to market and to reach the break-even point realistic?* In most cases, the faster the better. In all cases, the venture plan will be tied to this answer, and an error here can spell trouble later on.

- *Is the potential market large?* In determining the potential market, entrepreneurs must look three to five years into the future, because some markets take this long to emerge. The cellular telephone, for example, had an annual demand of approximately 400,000 units in 1982; today, the number of smartphones sold in any given quarter is many times higher than that.

- *Is the product the first of a growing family?* If it is, the venture is more attractive to investors. If they do not realize a large return on the first product, they might on the second, third, or fourth.

- *Does an initial customer exist?* It is certainly impressive to financial backers when a venture can list its first ten customers by name. Pent-up demand signals that the first quarter's results are likely to be good, and the focus of attention can be directed to later quarters.

- *Are the development costs and calendar times realistic?* Preferably, they are zero. A ready-to-go product gives the venture a big advantage over competitors. If costs exist, they should be complete, detailed, and tied to a month-by-month schedule.

- *Is this a growing industry?* Industry growth is not absolutely essential if profits and company growth can be substantiated, but it means less room for mistakes. In a growing industry, good companies do even better.

- *Can the product—and the need for it—be understood by the financial community?* If financiers can grasp the concept and its value, the chances for funding will increase. For example, a portable heart-monitoring system for postcoronary monitoring is a product many can understand. Undoubtedly, some of those hearing a presentation for such a device will already have had coronaries or heart problems of some sort.[20]

The criteria selection approach provides a means of analyzing the internal strengths and weaknesses that exist in a new venture by focusing on the marketing and industry potential critical to assessment. If the new venture meets fewer than six of these criteria, it typically lacks feasibility for funding. If the new venture meets seven or more of the criteria, it may stand a good chance of being funded.

6-5c Comprehensive Feasibility Approach

A more comprehensive and systematic feasibility analysis, a **comprehensive feasibility approach**, incorporates external factors in addition to those included in the criteria questions cited above. Figure 6.2 presents a breakdown of the factors involved in a comprehensive feasibility study of a new venture: technical, market, financial, organizational, and competitive. Although all five of the areas presented in Figure 6.2 are important, two merit special attention: technical and market.

TECHNICAL FEASIBILITY
The evaluation of a new-venture idea should start with identifying the technical requirements—the **technical feasibility**—for producing a product or service that will satisfy the expectations of potential customers. The most important of these are:

- Functional design of the product and attractiveness in appearance

- Flexibility, permitting ready modification of the external features of the product to meet customer demands or technological and competitive changes

- Durability of the materials from which the product is made

- Reliability, ensuring performance as expected under normal operating conditions

- Product safety, posing no potential dangers under normal operating conditions

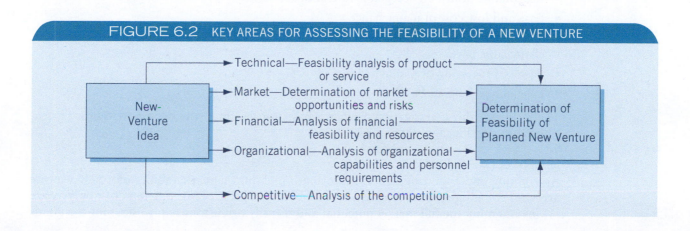

FIGURE 6.2   KEY AREAS FOR ASSESSING THE FEASIBILITY OF A NEW VENTURE

THE ENTREPRENEURIAL PROCESS

Facing Your Fears!

The inner journey to the creation of an entrepreneurial venture can be even more fearful than the external process of developing a business plan and searching for capital. Building up the courage to quit a job and start a new venture can sound easy and yet pose enormous emotional challenges when the actual events are about to unfold. One consultant, Suzanne Mulvehill—author of *Employee to Entrepreneur* and host of her own radio talk show—suggests particular strategies to follow when confronting the emotional challenges of entrepreneurial start-ups. She coined the term *Emotional Endurance* to signify the inner strength that is needed to make the jump from job to venture. Following are a few of the more significant strategies that may help entrepreneurs move through the emotional journey.

1. **Say yes to your yearning.** In other words acknowledge the desire you are experiencing to venture out on your own. It all begins with accepting the possibility that it could happen.

2. **Visualize your success.** Creating a vision of what *could* be may be a powerful motivator to what *will* be. It is important to write down this vision so it has tangible reality in this early stage.

3. **Evaluate your beliefs.** On a sheet of paper, list all of your beliefs about money, business, and yourself. Then, in a similar column, write down how you would *like* to view money, business, and yourself. Compare these beliefs and decide how far apart they are and why.

4. **Do what you love.** There is no replacement for passion. What you love is what will drive you to succeed, even in the tough times. Develop your business ideas around the types of things that you absolutely love to do.

5. **Get educated.** Avoid the myth that education saps out any desire to be an entrepreneur. That may have been true 20 years ago, but we have come a long way

in our approaches to business education. Entrepreneurship education is the hottest subject in universities worldwide. Remember, knowledge is power.

6. **Eliminate excuses.** Whenever you hear yourself make an excuse for not doing something, write it down and examine it later. Become aware of common excuses you may be using that have no real foundation. Turn your "I can'ts" into open-ended questions that allow you to explore the possibilities rather than shut the door.

7. **Know that there is no "right time."** Waiting for the proverbial perfect time is a trap that many people fall into, only to find later that time passed them by. The only guarantee we have about time is that it continues on, with or without us. Rather than wait, you need to proactively move on your idea.

8. **Start small.** It is always better to be realistic and reach for what you can accomplish in the near future. The longer-term future may hold greater things for the venture, but at the beginning you need to avoid being overwhelmed.

9. **Answer the "what ifs."** Stop for a moment and write down all of the "what ifs" that you question yourself with. See if you can begin to logically answer the questions. It's amazing how much courage will be gained by analyzing these contingencies.

10. **Ask for help.** Reach out and find help. The maverick entrepreneur is a myth of the past. Today, there is so much assistance available if you are willing to seek it out. Ignorance is not asking questions; rather, ignorance is being arrogant enough to think you have all the answers.

Source: Adapted from Suzanne Mulvehill, "Fear Factor," *Entrepreneur* (April 2005): 104–11.

- Reasonable utility, an acceptable rate of obsolescence
- Ease and low cost of maintenance
- Standardization through elimination of unnecessary variety among potentially interchangeable parts
- Ease of processing or manufacture
- Ease in handling and use[21]

The results of this investigation provide a basis for deciding whether a new venture is feasible from a technical point of view.

MARKETABILITY

Assembling and analyzing relevant information about the marketability of a new venture are vital for judging its potential success. Three major areas in this type of analysis are (1) investigating the full market potential and identifying customers (or users) for the goods or service, (2) analyzing the extent to which the enterprise might exploit this potential market, and (3) using market analysis to determine the opportunities and risks associated with the venture. To address these areas, a variety of informational sources must be found and used. For a market feasibility analysis, general sources would include the following:

- *General economic trends.* various economic indicators such as new orders, housing starts, inventories, and consumer spending
- *Market data.* customers, customer demand patterns (e.g., seasonal variations in demand, governmental regulations affecting demand)
- *Pricing data.* range of prices for the same, complementary, and substitute products; base prices; and discount structures
- *Competitive data.* major competitors and their competitive strength

More attention is given to marketing issues in Chapter 10. At this point, it is important to note the value of marketing research in the overall assessment and evaluation of a new venture.[22]

The comprehensive feasibility analysis approach is closely related to the preparation of a thorough business plan (covered in detail in Chapter 12). The approach clearly illustrates the need to evaluate each segment of the venture *before* initiating the business or presenting it to capital sources.

To assist in understanding feasibility analysis, Appendix 6A includes a template used for a complete feasibility plan. This template has a question-and-answer format that allows entrepreneurs to consider important segments before moving forward with an idea. Venture capitalists generally agree that the risks in any entrepreneurial venture are you, your management team, and any apparent fundamental flaws in your venture idea. Therefore, you need to make a reasonable evaluation of these risks.

6-6 THE CONTEMPORARY METHODOLOGIES FOR VENTURE EVALUATION

LO7 Highlight the contemporary venture evaluation methods: design methodology and the lean start-up methodology

With newer movements taking shape in the everchanging entrepreneurial world, the following sections highlight some of the more contemporary methodologies being utilized for concept assessment and new venture evaluation. From design methods to lean start-up procedures, the fast paced entrepreneurial environment is demonstrating newer methods to enhance venture concepts though development.

6-6a The Design Methodology

Design is now a hot topic in the business world. The demand is becoming so great that universities are now building programs that take a general approach to design rather than concentrating it in just technical schools like architecture and engineering. Mirroring the general design approach of companies like IDEO that tackle problems in industries ranging from medicine to consumer products, Stanford University has founded an Institute of Design (also known as the d school) and the Rotman School of Management at the University of Toronto has built a curriculum based on the power of design in business. The goal of such programs is to train future business leaders to incorporate design thinking into their general practices much like P&G and Microsoft, who have embraced design methods. This methodology can be a vital source of assessment for entrepreneurs and their early stage venture concepts.

DESIGN AND LEARN
Design is a learning process that shapes and converts ideas into form, whether that is a plan of action, an experience, or a physical thing.[23] Designers often begin the search for viable solutions through the iterative process of learning the language, issues, critical success factors, and constraints inherent in the domains of interest. Mistakes and failures along the way are to be seen as opportunities to learn and adapt. As a result, knowledge of and credibility within the venture's domain are increased. Researchers Michael G. Goldsby, Donald

F. Kuratko, and Thomas Nelson believe that design methodology provides specific learning mechanisms important for converting ideas into form. For example:

- *Learning from qualitative research*—including impartial observations of stakeholders related to the problem, participatory involvement with said stakeholders regarding the problem, and immersion in available secondary research.

- *Learning from prototyping*—a prototype (physical representation of the venture) captures the essence of an idea in a form that can be shared with others for communication and feedback that closes the gap between concept and reality.

- *Learning from feedback*—this feedback is on the efficacy of the venture idea and need not be complicated. First impressions and instincts provide honest observations that can be used in shaping future versions of the venture concept.[24]

DESIGN DEVELOPMENT

The design development methodology utilizes skills we all possess but are generally ignored due to more conventional problem solving practices. Traditional methods have relied on rational and analytical techniques while design relies on intuition, recognition, and emotion. While most businesses tend to focus on traditional dimensions of product, performance, or price, latent needs are where the design methodology focuses. Latent needs are often found in the areas of safety, reuse, sustainability, personalization, or convenience.

Design methodology takes an initial concept idea and develops a proof of concept that elicits feedback from relevant stakeholders. To accomplish this, several criteria must be met including concept feasibility, concept desirability, and concept viability.[25] The design method converts ideas into form by integrating what is desirable from a user's point of view with what is technically and economically viable.

- *Proof of Concept Feasibility*—focuses on whether a potential venture concept can be produced or is functionally possible.

- *Proof of Concept Desirability*—focuses on whether a potential venture concept is desirable to customers—form, function, aesthetics, and user behavior are considered.

- *Proof of Concept Viability*—focuses on whether the venture concept can produce viable financial outcomes.[26]

Simply put, a successful design process is made evident by a proof of concept that provides evidence that a product or solution can be made, that it is desirable to customers, and that it makes financial sense. It is largely up to the discretion of designers as to what feedback, learning, and suggestions they choose to use in iterative versions of solutions. Consequently, designers make judgment calls as to when good, better, or best solutions are reached. Gestalt moments of insight and understanding affect the process and indicate when a concept is ready for implementation[27]

6-6b Design-Centered Entrepreneurship

Researchers Michael G. Goldsby, Donald F. Kuratko, Matthew R. Marvel, and Thomas Nelson, have introduced the concept of design-centered entrepreneurship with a conceptual model. In essence, the entrepreneur applies design methods in four action stages of developing an opportunity. Ideation involves taking action and learning that culminates in a venture concept for further development. The prototyping stage addresses the technical issues of the concept, and ensures that a feasible product or service can be made and delivered. The market engagement action stage refines the concept for the customer, as well as contributing to the acquisition of knowledge, or learning, from early users. The business model action stage completes the development of the opportunity by identifying the varying components of the model that will need to be in place for the concept to be financially viable. Once the entrepreneur has developed a business concept that appears feasible, desirable, and viable, start-up activities bring about the fulfillment of the opportunity.[28]

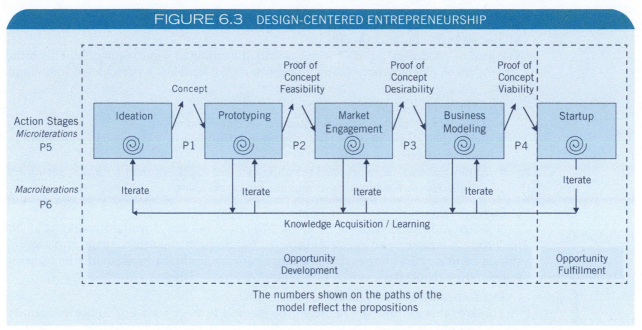

FIGURE 6.3   DESIGN-CENTERED ENTREPRENEURSHIP

The numbers shown on the paths of the model reflect the propositions

Source: Michael G. Goldsby, Thomas Nelson, & Donald F. Kuratko, "Design-Centered Entrepreneurship: A Process for Developing Opportunities," *Annals of Entrepreneurship Education & Pedagogy* (edited by Michael H. Morris; Edward Elgar Publishing, 2014: 200-217).

Utilizing design methodology within each action stage aids in creating a distinctive proof of concept that assists in developing their venture idea. Design-centered entrepreneurship includes two types: **microiterations** (within each action stage to improve the outcome) and **macroiterations** (moving from one particular action stage back to a previous stage for further development). Both microiterations and macroiterations involve taking action, learning, and refinement, all of which are beneficial to the process.

6-6c   The Lean Start-Up Methodology

Similar to design methodology, the **Lean Start-Up methodology** provides a scientific approach to creating early venture concepts and delivers a desired product to customers' hands faster. Its philosophy originates from the Japanese concept of *lean manufacturing*, which seeks to increase value-creating practices and eliminate wasteful practices. The Lean Start-Up methodology begins with the premise that every new venture is a grand experiment that attempts to answer questions such as: "Should this venture be created?" and "Will it be a sustainable business?"[29]

The Lean Start-Up methodology was first developed in 2011 by Eric Ries, founder of IMVU Inc. as a way to prevent waste in start-ups and ensure that the business plan remains a living document. The hard truth is that no matter how much research is conducted, how many surveys are developed, and how great you create your financial predictions, your new venture concept will still be based on certain assumptions. It is critical that these assumptions either be validated or discarded as soon as possible. Reducing waste, in the Lean Start-Up methodology, is minimizing the time and effort that goes into an incorrect hypothesis by putting a lean-focused process on the development of your product or service. As Ries states in his bestselling book, "work smarter, not harder."[30] Today, Steve Blank, who is recognized for developing the Customer Development methodology, which launched the Lean Start-up movement, along with Jerry Engel at the University of California Berkeley, have created an entire course for educators known as the *Lean Launchpad*.[31]

The Lean Start-Up methodology is hypothesis-driven and entrepreneurs must work to gather and *incorporate* customer feedback early and often. While it is impossible to condense the entire book and methodology, here are a few key points and concepts through which you can understand the basics of the Lean Start-Up methodology.

KEY LEAN START-UP KEY TERMINOLOGY

Minimum Viable Product (MVP):
The goal of producing an MVP is to get started learning as soon as possible. This is the version of the product that enables a full turn on the feedback loop with a minimum of effort.

The Three A's of Metrics:
- Actionable. report must demonstrate clear cause and effect.
- Accessible. report must be clear to entrepreneurs who are supposed to use them to guide their decision-making.
- Auditable. entrepreneurs need the ability to spot check the data with real customers and the report mechanisms should not be too complex.

Pivot:
A structured course correction designed to test a new fundamental hypothesis about the product, strategy, and engine of growth. The decision whether to **pivot** or persevere should be evaluated after each build-measure-learn feedback loop for the hypotheses tested during that cycle.

Build-Measure-Learn Feedback Loop:
Think of this as applying the scientific method to your start-up. To begin, identify which hypotheses to test (the value hypothesis and the growth hypothesis are always a good place to start). The build stage consists of developing the MVP for this cycle. The most critical section of the loop is ensuring you are measuring the correct thing. Do the development efforts lead to *real* progress? This is where the three A's of metrics come in handy. The final stage in the cycle, learn, requires the entrepreneur to take a hard look at their results and determine whether a pivot is required. (See Figure 6.4.)

Validated Learning:
Validated learning is defined as a process in which one learns by trying out an initial idea and then measuring it to *validate* the effect. Each test of an idea is a single *iteration* in a larger process of many iterations whereby something is learnt and then applied to succeeding tests.

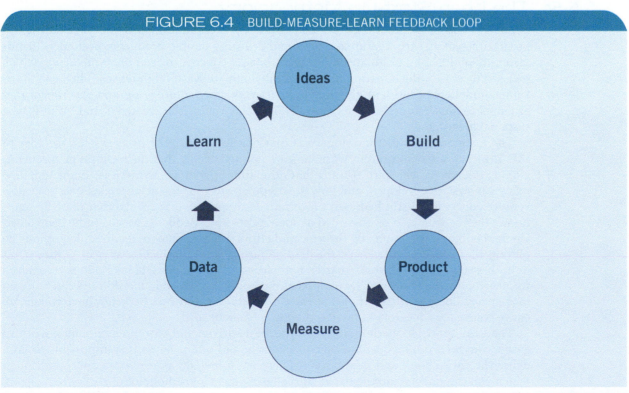

FIGURE 6.4 BUILD-MEASURE-LEARN FEEDBACK LOOP

Source: Eric Ries, *The Lean Startup: How Today's Entrepreneurs Use Continuous Innovation to Create Radically Successful Businesses* New York: Crown Business, 2011.

SUMMARY

The complexity of factors involved in new-venture start-up (as shown in Figure 6.1) makes it difficult to clearly assess and evaluate each one. In addition, the difficulty of obtaining reliable data on failed firms adds to this dilemma. Improvements are being made, however, and new-venture assessment is becoming a stronger process.

A number of pitfalls may occur in the selection of a new venture: lack of an objective evaluation of the venture, lack of insight into the market, inadequate understanding of technical requirements, poor financial understanding, lack of venture uniqueness, and failure to be aware of legal issues.

When assessing a new venture, an entrepreneur needs to consider several critical factors: the uniqueness of the good or service, the amount of capital investment required to start the venture, the growth of sales, and the availability of the product.

Some major reasons for new ventures, failure are inadequate knowledge of the market, faulty product performance, ineffective marketing and sales effort, inadequate awareness of competitive pressures, rapid product obsolescence, poor timing, and undercapitalization. In drawing together these and other reasons, recent research reveals three major categories of causes for failure: product/market problems, financial difficulties, and managerial problems. In addition, entrepreneurs face internal and external problems.

The feasibility of the entrepreneur's product or service can be assessed by asking the right questions, by making a profile analysis of the venture, and by carrying out a comprehensive feasibility study.

KEY TERMS

comprehensive feasibility approach	growth of sales	minimum viable product (MVP)
critical factors	growth stage	pivot
customer availability	high-growth venture	product availability
external problems	internal problems	prototyping
design-centered entrepreneurship	lean start-up methodology	small profitable venture
design methodology	lifestyle venture	start-up problems
failure prediction model	macroiteration	technical feasibility
feasibility criteria approach	marketability	uniqueness
	microiteration	validated learning

REVIEW AND DISCUSSION QUESTIONS

1. Explain the challenges involved in new-venture development.

2. Describe some of the key factors involved in new-venture performance (use Figure 6.1).

3. Many entrepreneurs lack objectivity and have no real insight into the market. Why are these characteristics considered pitfalls of selecting new ventures?

4. Many entrepreneurs have a poor understanding of the finances associated with their new venture and/or have a venture that lacks uniqueness. Why are these characteristics considered pitfalls of selecting new ventures?

5. Describe each of the five critical factors involved in the prestart-up and start-up phases of a new venture.

6. Identify and discuss three examples of product/market problems that can cause a venture to fail.

7. Identify and discuss two examples of financial difficulties that can cause a venture to fail.

8. Identify and discuss two examples of managerial problems that can cause a venture to fail.

9. List four major types of problems that new ventures confront.

10. How can asking the right questions help an entrepreneur evaluate a new venture? What types of questions are involved?

11. Explain the traditional methods of new venture evaluation: profile analysis, feasibility criteria approach, and comprehensive feasibility method.

12. Describe the contemporary methods of new venture evaluation: design methodology and the lean start-up methodology.

NOTES

1. Michael S. Malone, "The 200-Year-Old U.S. Patent Office Is Beginning to Show Its Age," *Forbes* (June 24, 2002): 33–40; "Patent Applications Filed," http://www.inventionstatistics.com/Number_of_Patent_Applications_Filed_Annually_Year.html (accessed February 13, 2012).

2. Sue Birley and Paul Westhead, "A Taxonomy of Business Start-Up Reasons and Their Impact on Firm Growth and Size," *Journal of Business Venturing* 9, no. 1 (1994): 7–32.

3. Nancy M. Carter, William B. Gartner, and Paul D. Reynolds, "Exploring Start-Up Event Sequences," *Journal of Business Venturing* 11, no. 3 (1996): 151–66; see also Benyamin B. Lichtenstein, Kevin J. Dooley, and G. T. Lumpkin, "Measuring Emergence in the Dynamics of New Venture Creation," *Journal of Business Venturing* 21, no. 2 (2006): 153–75.

4. Robert N. Lussier, "A Nonfinancial Business Success versus Failure Prediction Model for Young Firms," *Journal of Small Business Management* 33, no. 1 (1995): 8–20.

5. Frédéric Delmar and Scott Shane, "Legitimating First: Organizing Activities and the Survival of New Ventures," *Journal of Business Venturing* 19, no. 3 (2004): 385–410.

6. Arnold C. Cooper, "Challenges in Predicting New Firm Performance," *Journal of Business Venturing* 8, no. 3 (1993): 241–53.

7. Keith H. Brigham, Julio O. De Castro, and Dean A. Shepherd, "A Person-Organization Fit Model of Owner-Managers' Cognitive Style and Organizational Demands," *Entrepreneurship Theory and Practice* 31, no. 1 (2007): 29–51; Dimo Dimov, "From Opportunity Insight to Opportunity Intention: The Importance of Person-Situation Learning Match," *Entrepreneurship Theory and Practice* 31, no. 4 (2007): 561–84; and Nils Plambeck, "The Development of New Products: The Role of Firm Context and Managerial Cognition," *Journal of Business Venturing* 27, no. 6 (2012): 607–21.

8. Candida G. Brush and Pieter A. Vanderwerf, "A Comparison of Methods and Sources for Obtaining Estimates of New Venture Performance," *Journal of Business Venturing* 7, no. 2 (1992): 157–70; see also Gaylen N. Chandler and Steven H. Hanks, "Measuring the Performance of Emerging Businesses: A Validation Study," *Journal of Business Venturing* 8, no. 5 (1993): 391–408; and Scott L. Newbert, "New Firm Formation: A Dynamic Capability," *Journal of Small Business Management* 43, no. 1 (2005): 55–77.

9. Paul Reynolds and Brenda Miller, "New Firm Gestation: Conception, Birth, and Implications for Research," *Journal of Business Venturing* 7, no. 5 (1992): 405–17.

10. Bhaskar Chakravorti, "The New Rules for Bringing Innovations to the Market," *Harvard Business Review* 82, no. 2 (March 2004): 58–67; see also Eric A. Morse, Sally B. Fowler, and Thomas B. Lawrence, "The Impact of Virtual Embeddedness on New Venture Survival: Overcoming the Liabilities of Newness," *Entrepreneurship Theory and Practice* 31, no. 2 (2007): 139–60; and Mark Simon, Rodney C. Shrader, "Entrepreneurial Actions and Optimistic Overconfidence: The Role of Motivated Reasoning in New Product Introductions," *Journal of Business Venturing* 27, no. 3 (2012): 291–309.

11. Theodore Levitt, "Marketing Myopia," *Harvard Business Review* 38, no. 3 (July/August 1960): 45–56; see also Eileen Fischer and Rebecca Reuber, "The Good, the Bad, and the Unfamiliar: The Challenges of Reputation Formation Facing New Firms," *Entrepreneurship Theory and Practice* 31, no. 1 (2007): 53–76.

12. Robert C. Ronstadt, *Entrepreneurship* (Dover, MA: Lord Publishing, 1984), 74.

13. Adapted from Ronstadt, *Entrepreneurship*, 75.

14. Ibid., 79.

15. Timothy Bates, "Analysis of Young, Small Firms That Have Closed: Delineating Successful from Unsuccessful Closures," *Journal of Business Venturing* 20, no. 3 (2005): 343–58; Steven C. Michael and James G. Combs, "Entrepreneurial Failure: The Case of Franchisees," *Journal of Small Business Management* 46, no. 1 (2008): 75–90; and Daniel P. Forbes and David A. Kirsch, "The Study of Emerging Industries: Recognizing and Responding to Some Central Problems," *Journal of Business Venturing* 26, no. 5 (2011): 589–602.

16. David E. Terpstra and Philip D. Olson, "Entrepreneurial Start-Up and Growth: A Classification of Problems," *Entrepreneurship Theory and Practice* 17, no. 3 (1993): 5–20.

17. H. Robert Dodge, Sam Fullerton, and John E. Robbins, "Stage of the Organizational Life Cycle and Competition as Mediators of Problem Perception for Small Businesses," *Strategic Management Journal* 15 (1994): 121–34.

18. Andrew L. Zacharakis, G. Dale Meyer, and Julio DeCastro, "Differing Perceptions of New Venture Failure: A Matched Exploratory Study of Venture Capitalists and Entrepreneurs," *Journal of Small Business Management* 37, no. 3 (1999): 1–14.

19. Erkki K. Laitinen, "Prediction of Failure of a Newly Founded Firm," *Journal of Business Venturing* 7, no. 4 (1992): 323–40; Jan Brinckman, Soeren Salomo and Hans Georg Gemuenden, "Financial Management Competence of Founding Teams and Growth of New Technology-Based Firms," *Entrepreneurship Theory and Practice* 35, no. 2 (2011): 217–43.

20. Gordon B. Baty, *Entrepreneurship: Playing to Win* (Reston, VA: Reston Publishing, 1974), 33–34.

21. Hans Schollhammer and Arthur H. Kuriloff, *Entrepreneurship and Small Business Management* (New York: John Wiley & Sons, 1979), 58; see also Kwaku Atuahene-Gima and Haiyang Li, "Strategic Decision

Comprehensiveness and New Product Development Outcomes in New Technology Ventures," *Academy of Management Journal* 47, no. 4 (2004): 583–97; and Andreas Rauch and Serge A. Rijsdijk, "The Effects of General and Specific Human Capital on Long-Term Growth and Failure of Newly Founded Businesses," *Entrepreneurship Theory and Practice* 37, no. 4 (2013): 923–41.

22. Frans J. H. M. Verhees and Matthew T. G. Meulenberg, "Market Orientation, Innovativeness, Product Innovation, and Performance in Small Firms," *Journal of Small Business Management* 42, no. 2 (2004): 134–54; Minet Schindehutte, Michael H. Morris, and Akin Kocak, "Understanding Market-Driven Behavior: The Role of Entrepreneurship" *Journal of Small Business Management* 46, no. 1 (2008): 4–26; and Gerald E. Hills, Claes M. Hultman, and Morgan P. Miles, "The Evolution and Development of Entrepreneurial Marketing," *Journal of Small Business Management* 46, no. 1 (2008): 99–112.

23. Herbert A. Simon, *The Sciences of the Artificial* (Cambridge, MA: M.I.T. Press, 1996).

24. Michael G. Goldsby, Thomas Nelson, and Donald F. Kuratko, "Design-Centered Entrepreneurship: A Process for Developing Opportunities," in *Annals of Entrepreneurship Education & Pedagogy* ed. Michael H. Morris (Cheltenham, UK: Edward Elgar Publishing, 2014), 200–17.

25. Tim Brown, *Change by design: How design thinking transforms organizations and inspires innovation.* (New York: HarperCollins, 2009).

26. Donald F. Kuratko, Michael G. Goldsby, and Jeffrey S. Hornsby, *Innovation Acceleration: Transforming Organizational Thinking.* (Upper Saddle River: New Jersey Pearson, 2012).

27. Annette Aboulafia, and Liam J. Bannon "Understanding Affect in Design: An Outline Conceptual Framework," *Theoretical Issues in Ergonomics Science* 5, no. 1 (2004): 4–15; Violina Rindova, Walter J. Ferrier, and Robert Wiltbank, "Value from Gestalt: How Sequences of Competitive Actions Create Advantage for Firms in Nascent Markets," *Strategic Management Journal* 31 (2010): 1474–97.

28. Michael G. Goldsby, Thomas Nelson, & Donald F. Kuratko, "Design-Centered Entrepreneurship: A Process for Developing Opportunities," *Annals of Entrepreneurship Education & Pedagogy* (edited by Michael H. Morris; Edward Elgar Publishing, 2014: 200-217).

29. Eric Ries, *The Lean Startup Movement*, http://theleanstartup.com/ (accessed January 4, 2015).

30. Eric Ries, *The Lean Startup: How Today's Entrepreneurs Use Continuous Innovation to Create Radically Successful Businesses.* (New York: Crown Business, 2011).

31. Steve Blank and Jerry Engel, *The Lean LaunchPad Educators Teaching Handbook* (Hadley, MA: VentureWell – formerly the National Collegiate Inventors and Innovators Alliance, 2013); Steve Blank, "The Lean LaunchPad Educators Course," *Forbes*, June 18, 2013. http://www.forbes.com/sites/steveblank/2013/06/18/the-lean-launchpad-educators-course/ (accessed January 4, 2015); see also: Steve Blank, "Why the Lean Start-Up Changes Everything," *Harvard Business Review* 91, no. 5 (2013): 63–72.

APPENDIX 6A: Feasibility Plan Outline

This outline provides a framework to help entrepreneurs recognize the actual feasibility of proposed ventures and clarify their thinking before considering potential funding. It focuses on the viability of the idea, asking whether there is a market for the concept and if the concept can be produced and sold at a profit.

TITLE PAGE

Name of proposed company: _____

Names and titles of the founding team members:

_____

_____

_____

_____

Relevant contact information (name, title, address, phone, e-mail):

_____

_____

_____

_____

_____

TABLE OF CONTENTS

Make sure that all of the contents in the feasibility plan have page numbers and are listed carefully in the table of contents.

6A-1 THE SECTIONS OF A FEASIBILITY PLAN

6A-1a Executive Summary

Explanation: Include the most important highlights from each section of the feasibility study. Be sure to include a clear and concise description of the venture, whatever proprietary aspects it may possess, the target market, the amount of financing needed, and the type of financing that is being requested.

_____

_____

_____

_____

6A-1b The Business Concept

Explanation: Using the following directions, articulate a compelling story that explains why this is an excellent concept. This section allows the reader to understand what concept is being proposed and why it has true potential in the marketplace. It also provides an opportunity for the entrepreneur to prove that he or she can articulate this concept in clear and comprehensible terms to people outside their circle of friends and close associates.

KEY CONCEPTS

Describe whether the proposed concept is a retail, wholesale, manufacturing, or service business. Identify the current stage of development for the venture (concept stage, start-up, initial operations, or expansion).

_____

_____

_____

Include a clear description of the targeted customer, the value proposition (in terms of benefits gained) for that customer, and the potential growth opportunities.

_____

_____

_____

_____

Summarize any proprietary rights associated with this concept, whether that be patents, copyrights, licenses, royalties, distribution rights, or franchise agreements.

_____

_____

_____

6A-1c Industry/Market Analysis

Explanation: The industry/market analysis is critical. Is there a market for the product or service resulting from the venture? What are the current trends in this industry? What are the predicted trends for this industry? Can any of this be substantiated? The market for the product/service may be obvious, yet the feasibility analysis must validate its existence. In the venture feasibility analysis, it may be enough to prove that a sufficient market exists for the venture and that no further in-depth research is warranted. However, entrepreneurs should always study their competitors in the marketplace. Lessons learned from competitors provide opportunities for entrepreneurs to find the unique distinctions in their own concept.

KEY CONCEPTS

Explain the industry that this concept focuses on, as well as whatever trends may exist in that particular industry today.

_____

_____

_____

_____

Discuss the target market analysis that has been used and what specific market niche that has produced. In addition, identify the market size, its growth potential, and your plan for market penetration based on research.

_____

_____

_____

_____

Explain the customer profile in terms of who the specific customer is and—again—what value proposition (in terms of benefits) is being offered the customer.

_____

_____

_____

_____

Finally, be sure to include a competitor analysis that describes thoroughly the competition existing today and how specifically your concept will match up or exceed the competition and why.

_____

_____

_____

_____

6A-1d Management Team

Explanation: Keep in mind that all new ventures must stand the scrutiny of whether the founding team can really move this idea to market. The experience of the management team may end up being one of the most critical factors to outside investors. Many times, venture capitalists have expressed their belief that they prefer a "B" idea with an "A" team as opposed to an "A" idea with a "B" team. In other words, there is a real concern about the implementation phase of a proposed concept. Does this founding team have the background, experience, skills, and networks to make the concept operationally successful?

KEY CONCEPTS

Identify the founding team members and the key personnel in place to guide the proposed company.

_____

_____

_____

_____

Explain the team's qualifications and how the critical tasks are being assigned. Also include any board of directors/advisors that are in place.

_____

_____

_____

_____

Finally, outline any "gaps" in the management team (in terms of skills and abilities) and explain how those will be addressed.

_____

_____

_____

_____

6A-1e Product/Service Development Analysis

Explanation: Before going any further with a conceptual idea, the entrepreneur must determine whether the concept has any practical feasibility. One of the most important questions in this section of the feasibility analysis would be: "What unique features distinguish your product/service?" The more unique the features of a product or service, the better chance the business concept has of being successful.

KEY CONCEPTS

Provide a detailed description of the proposed concept, including any unique features that make it distinctive.

_____

_____

_____

_____

Explain the current status of the project and include a clear timeline of the key tasks to complete.

_____

_____

_____

_____

Identify any intellectual property involved with this potential venture, and discuss the proprietary protection that exists. Any proposed or completed prototype testing should be described here as well.

_____

_____

_____

_____

Finally, identify any anticipated critical risks in terms of potential product liability, governmental regulations, or raw material issues that may hinder this project at any stage.

_____

_____

_____

_____

6A-1f Financial Analysis

Explanation: Summarize the critical assumptions upon which the financial information is based; in other words, show how the numbers have been derived. A pro forma income statement and a statement of cash flows are the two most critical financial documents to add here—even though they may include preliminary outside sources needed to get some idea of the generation of revenue and the cash position of the venture during the first three years. If possible, provide a break-even analysis to demonstrate where the venture moves from survival to growth.

KEY CONCEPTS

Assumptions:

_____

_____

_____

Pro Forma Income Statement:

_____

_____

_____

Pro Forma Cash-Flow Statement:

_____

_____

_____

Break-Even Analysis:

_____

_____

_____

_____

6A-1g Timeline

Explanation: Use a graphic representation of the dates and the related tasks in order of their completion until actual concept launch.

_____

_____

_____

_____

6A-1h Bibliography

Explanation: Provide any key endnotes, footnotes, sources, or extra information that would be critical for a funding source to see in relation to the work you performed in creating this feasibility study.

_____

_____

_____

CHAPTER 7

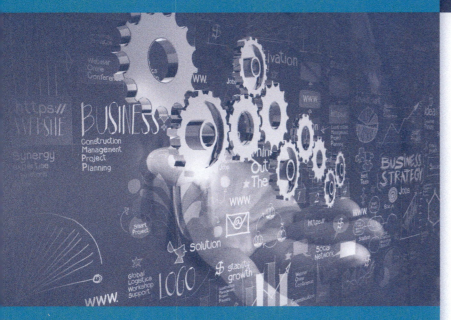

Pathways to Entrepreneurial Ventures

LEARNING OBJECTIVES

1 To describe the major pathways and structures for entrepreneurial ventures

2 To present the factors involved in creating a new venture

3 To identify and discuss the elements involved in acquiring an established venture

4 To outline ten key questions to ask when buying an ongoing venture

5 To examine the underlying issues involved in the acquisition process

6 To define a franchise and outline its structure

7 To examine the benefits and drawbacks of franchising

8 To present the franchise disclosure document (FDD) as a key item in franchises

Entrepreneurial Thought

Every large and successful company was once a start-up struggling to survive. Some of these successful companies were conceived in a flash of inspiration and planned on the back of a napkin in a coffee shop. Others took shape painstakingly over time in a basement or a garage. Some start-ups were created and then flourished overnight, while others achieved success only through a long series of painful fits and starts. The point is, every company that exists today began rather small.

—Joel Kurtzman *Start-Ups That Work*

LO1 Describe the major pathways and structures for entrepreneurial ventures

Every prospective entrepreneur wants to know the best methods for getting a business started. They ask themselves, what are the ideal pathways to starting a venture? In this chapter, we examine the three most common methods: creating a new venture, acquiring an existing venture, or obtaining a franchise. Each pathway represents a particular form of entry and has its own particular advantages and disadvantages.[1] This chapter outlines some of the particular issues associated with each form.

7-1 CREATING NEW VENTURES

LO2 Present the factors involved in creating a new venture

The most effective way to start a new business is to create a new and unique product or service. The next-best way is to adapt an existing product or service or to extend an offering into an area wherein it is not presently available. The first approach is often referred to as *new-new*; the second, as *new-old*.

7-1a New-New Approach to Creating New Ventures

New products or services frequently enter the market. Typical examples include smartphones, MP3 players, plasma televisions, and global positioning systems (GPS). All of these products and more were introduced as the result of research and development (R&D) efforts by major corporations (see Table 7.1 for a list of emerging ideas). What we must realize, however, is that unique ideas are not the sole province of large companies. Individuals create, too.

How does one discover or invent new products? As discussed earlier in Chapter 5, one of the ways to uncover new-product concepts is through close observation of the world around you. Making lists of annoying everyday experiences or of problems in using known products or services has led to innovative business ventures. Objects that fall out of one's hand, household chores that are difficult to do, and items that are hard to store are examples of everyday annoyances that have led to new venture creations. An engineer once observed the mechanism for recording the revolutions of a ship's propeller. As he watched the device tally the propeller's cycles, he realized that the idea could be adapted to the recording of sales transactions—a problem he had been trying to solve for some time. The result led eventually to the development, in 1879, of the mechanical cash register.

Most business ideas tend to come from people's experiences. Figure 7.1 illustrates the sources of new business ideas from a study conducted by the National Federation of Independent Business. In general, the main sources for both men and women are prior jobs, hobbies or interests, and personally identified problems. The **new-new approach** indicates the importance of people's awareness of their daily lives (work and free time) for developing new business ideas.

Facebook was founded in February 2004 by Harvard University student Mark Zuckerberg, who was frustrated by the lack of networking facilities on campus—a simple annoyance that has led to a spectacularly successful technological juggernaut. Now one of the most trafficked sites on the Internet, Facebook has, only 12 years after its inception, over 1.3 billion users and revenues exceeding $7 billion.[2] In addition, Facebook's initial public offering in 2012 rivaled the largest ever accomplished.[3]

7-1b New-Old Approach to Creating New Ventures

Most small ventures do not start with a totally unique idea. Instead, an individual "piggybacks" on someone else's idea by either improving a product or offering a service in an area in which it is not currently available—hence the term **new-old approach**. Some of the most common examples are setting up restaurants, clothing stores, or similar outlets in sprawling suburban areas that do not have an abundance of these stores. Of course, these kinds of operations can be risky because competitors can move in easily. Potential owners considering this kind of enterprise should try to offer a product or service that is difficult to copy. For example, a computerized billing and accounting service for medical doctors can be successful if the business serves a sufficient number of doctors to cover the cost of computer operators

TABLE 7.1 TRENDS IN CREATING BUSINESS OPPORTUNITIES

Emerging Opportunities	Emerging Internet Opportunities
Green Products	*Mobile Advertising*
Organic foods	Cell phones
Organic fibers/textiles	PDAs
Alternative Energy	*Concierge Services*
Solar	*Niche Social Networks*
Biofuel	Seniors
Fuel cells	Music fans
Energy conservation	Groups of local users
Health Care	Pet owners
Healthy food	Dating groups
School and govt-sponsored programs	*Virtual Economies*
Exercise	"Online auctions"
Yoga	*Educational Tutoring*
Niche gyms	*Human Resources Services*
Children	"Matchmaking"
Nonmedical	"Virtual HR"
Pre-assisted living	"Online Staffing"
Assisted living transition services	*Nanotechnology*
Niche Consumables	*Wireless Technology*
Wine	
Chocolate	
Burgers	
Coffeehouses	
Exotic salads	
Home Automation and Media Storage	
Lighting control	
Security systems	
Energy management	
Comfort management	
Entertainment systems	
Networked kitchen appliances	

Source: adapted from Steve Cooper, Amanda C. Kooser, Kristin Ohlson, Karen E. Spaeder, Nichole L. Torres, and Sara Wilson, "2007 Hot List," *Entrepreneur* (December 2006): 80–93; and "The World's 50 Most Innovative Companies," *Fast Company*, (March, 2015).

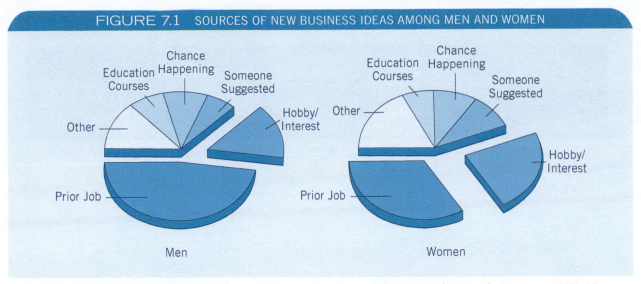

FIGURE 7.1 SOURCES OF NEW BUSINESS IDEAS AMONG MEN AND WOMEN

Source: William J. Dennis, *A Small Business Primer* (Washington, D.C.: National Federation of Independent Business, 1993), 27.

and administrative expenses in order to turn an adequate profit. Or perhaps another type of enterprise is likely to be overlooked by other would-be entrepreneurs.

Regardless of whether the business is based on a new-new or a new-old idea, the prospective owner cannot rely exclusively on gut feeling or intuition to get started. As we demonstrate in Part III of this book, proper planning and analysis are the keys to any successful venture.

7-1c Examining the Financial Picture When Creating New Ventures

If, through a thorough feasibility analysis and business plan (covered in detail in Chapter 12), a prospective entrepreneur decides that creating a new venture is a wise option, it is imperative to remember that the plan may not work perfectly. Some modification may be necessary, and flexibility is key. A contingency or backup plan should be available because the worst thing an entrepreneur can do is adopt an all-or-nothing strategy.

As we know, prospective entrepreneurs of new ventures must evaluate an enterprise's financial picture. How much will it cost to stay in business for the first year? How much revenue will the firm generate during this time period? If the outflow of cash is greater than the inflow, how long will it take before the business turns the corner? It is time to look at these questions in more detail.

Answering these questions requires consideration of two kinds of expenses: start-up and monthly. Table 7.2 illustrates a typical worksheet for making the necessary calculations of start-up expenses. Notice that this worksheet is based on the assumption that no money will flow in for about three months. Also, all start-up costs are totally covered. If the firm is in the manufacturing business, however, it will be three to four months before any goods are produced and sold, so the factors in Column 3 have to be doubled, and the amount of cash needed for start-up will be greater. Much of the information needed to fill in this worksheet already should have been gathered and at least partially analyzed. Now, however, it can be put into a format that allows the owner to look at the overall financial picture.

At this point, the individual should be concerned with what is called **upside gain and downside loss**. This term refers to the profits the business can make and the losses it can suffer. How much money will the enterprise take in if everything goes well? How much will it gross if operations run as expected? How much will it lose if operations do not work out well? Answers to these questions provide a composite picture of the most optimistic, the most likely, and the most pessimistic results. The owner has to keep in mind that the upside gain may be minimal, whereas the downside loss may be great.

TABLE 7.2   CHECKLIST FOR ESTIMATING START-UP EXPENSES

Monthly Item	Expenses Estimate based on sales of $____ per year	Cash Needed to Start The Business (see Column 3)	What to Put in Column 2 (These figures are estimates. The owner/manager decides how many months to allow, depending on the type of business)
	Column 1	Column 2	Column 3
Salary of owner/manager	$	$	3 times Column 1
Other salaries and wages			3 times Column 1
Rent			3 times Column 1
Advertising			3 times Column 1
Delivery expense			3 times Column 1
Supplies			3 times Column 1
Telephone and telegraph			3 times Column 1
Other utilities			3 times Column 1
Insurance			6 times Column 1
Taxes, Social Security			4 times Column 1
Interest			3 times Column 1
Maintenance			3 times Column 1
Legal and other professional assistance			3 times Column 1
Miscellaneous			3 times Column 1

Start-Up Costs		
Item	**Estimate**	**To Arrive at Esttimate**
Fixtures and equipment	$	Determine what is typical for this kind of business; talk to suppliers.
Decorating and remodeling		Talk to a contractor.
Installation of fixtures, equipment	t	Talk to suppliers.
Starting inventory		Talk to suppliers.
Deposits with public utilities		Talk to utility companies.
Legal and other professional fees		Talk to a lawyer, accountant, or other professional.
Licenses and permits		Contact appropriate city offices.
Advertising and promotion		Decide what will be used; talk to media.
Accounts receivable		Estimate how much will be tied up in receivables by credit customers and for how long.
Cash		Allow for unexpected expenses and losses, special purchases, and other expenditures.
Other Expenses		List them and estimate costs.
TOTAL CASH NEEDED TO START	$_____	Add all estimated amounts.

Source: U.S. Small Business Administration, "Management Aids," MA. 2.025 (Washington, D.C.: U.S. Government Printing Office).

It is necessary to examine overall gains and losses. This kind of analysis is referred to as **risk versus reward** analysis and points out the importance of getting an adequate return on the amount of money risked.

7-2 ACQUIRING AN ESTABLISHED ENTREPRENEURIAL VENTURE

LO3 Identify and discuss the elements involved in acquiring an established venture

A prospective entrepreneur may seek to purchase a business venture rather than start an enterprise. This can be a successful method of getting into business, but numerous factors need to be analyzed. Purchasing a business venture is a complex transaction, and the advice of professionals always should be sought. However, a few basic steps that can be easily understood are presented here, including the entrepreneur's personal preferences, examination of opportunities, evaluation of the selected venture, and key questions to ask.

7-2a Personal Preferences

Entrepreneurs need to recognize certain personal factors and to limit their choices of ventures accordingly. An entrepreneur's background, skills, interests, and experience are all important factors in selecting the type of business to buy. In addition, personal preferences for location and size of a business should guide the selection process. If an entrepreneur always has desired to own a business in the South or West, then that is exactly where the search should begin.

7-2b Examination of Opportunities

Entrepreneurs in search of a possible venture to buy need to examine the available opportunities through various sources:

- *Business brokers*. Professionals specializing in business opportunities often can provide leads and assistance in finding a venture for sale. However, the buyer should evaluate the broker's reputation, services, and contacts. The entrepreneur also should remember that the broker usually represents—and gets a commission on the sale from—the seller.
- *Newspaper ads*. "Business Opportunity" classified ads are another source. Because an ad often will appear in one paper and not another, it may be necessary to check the classified sections of all the papers in the area.
- *Trade sources*. Suppliers, distributors, manufacturers, trade publications, trade associations, and trade schools may have information about businesses for sale.
- *Professional sources*. Professionals such as management consultants, attorneys, and accountants often know of businesses available for purchase.

7-2c Advantages of Acquiring an Ongoing Venture

Of the numerous advantages to buying an ongoing venture, three of the most important are as follows:

1. Because the enterprise is already in operation, its successful future operation is likely.
2. The time and effort associated with starting a new enterprise are eliminated.
3. It sometimes is possible to buy an ongoing business at a bargain price.
4. Each of these three advantages is discussed next.

LESS FEAR ABOUT SUCCESSFUL FUTURE OPERATION
A new business faces two great dangers: the possibility that it will not find a market for its goods or services, and the chance that it will not be able to control its costs. If either event occurs, the new business will go bankrupt.

Buying an existing concern, however, alleviates most of these fears. A successful business already has demonstrated the ability to attract customers, control costs, and make a profit. Additionally, many of the problems a newly formed firm faces are sidestepped. For example: Where should the company be located? How should it advertise? What type of plant or merchandise layout will be the most effective? How much should be reordered every three months? What types of customers will this business attract? What pricing strategy should the firm use? Questions such as these already have been asked and answered. Thus, when a new owner buys an ongoing operation, he or she is often purchasing a known quantity. Of course, it is important to check whether hidden problems exist in the operation. Barring something of this nature, however, the purchase of an existing successful operating venture can be a wise investment.

REDUCED TIME AND EFFORT

An ongoing enterprise already has assembled the inventory, equipment, personnel, and facilities necessary to run it. In many cases, this has taken the owners a long time to do. They have spent countless hours "working out the bugs" so that the business is as efficient as possible. Likewise, they probably have gone through a fair number of employees before getting the right type of personnel. Except for the top management in an operating venture, the personnel usually stay with the sale. Therefore, if the new owners treat the workers fairly, they should not have to worry about hiring, placing, and training personnel.

In addition, the previous owners undoubtedly have established relations with suppliers, bankers, and other businesspeople. These individuals often can be relied on to provide assistance to the new owners. The suppliers know the type of merchandise the business orders and how often it needs to be replenished. They can be a source of advice about managing the operation, as can the bankers with whom the enterprise has been doing business. These individuals know the enterprise's capital needs and often provide new owners with the same credit line and assistance they gave the previous owners. The same holds true for the accountant, the lawyer, and any other professionals who served the business in an advisory capacity. Naturally, the new owners may have their own bankers, accountant, or lawyer, but these old relationships are there if the new owners need them.

A GOOD PRICE

Sometimes it is possible to buy an ongoing operating venture at a very good price. The owner may want to sell quickly because of a retirement decision or illness. Or the owner may be forced to sell the business to raise money for some emergency that has occurred. Or the owner may seek a greater opportunity in another type of business and therefore be willing to sell at a low price in order to take advantage of the new opportunity.

Ideally, when one is looking to buy an ongoing, successful operating venture, one of these three advantages (especially the last one) is present. However, seldom does someone in business sell a successful firm at an extraordinarily low price. The owner of a successful small venture built the enterprise through skillful business practices, knows how to deal with people, and has a good idea of the operation's fair market value. That person will rarely sell for much below the fair market value. Therefore, the prospective owner must avoid bidding high on a poor investment or walking away from a good bargain because "it smells fishy." The way to prevent making the wrong decision is to evaluate the existing operation in a logical manner.

7-2d Evaluation of the Selected Venture

After the entrepreneur considers personal preferences and examines information sources, the next step is to evaluate specific factors of the venture being offered for sale:

- *The business environment.* The local environment for business should be analyzed to establish the potential of the venture in its present location.
- *Profits, sales, and operating ratios.* The business's profit potential is a key factor in evaluating the venture's attractiveness and in later determining a reasonable price for it. To estimate the potential earning power of the business, the buyer should review past profits, sales, and operating ratios, and project sales and profits for the next one to two years. Valuation will be further discussed later in the chapter.

- *The business assets*. The tangible (physical) and intangible (e.g., reputation) assets of the business need to be assessed. The following assets should be examined:
  - Inventory (age, quality, salability, condition)
  - Furniture, equipment, fixtures (value, condition, leased or owned)
  - Accounts receivable (age of outstanding debts, past collection periods, credit standing of customers)
  - Trademarks, patents, copyrights, business name (value, role in the business's success, degree of competitive edge)
  - Goodwill (reputation, established clientele, trusted name)

A lot of headaches can be avoided by taking the approach of purchasing an existing venture. For example, start-up problems will have been taken care of by previous owners. Additionally, the business has a track record the buyer can examine to determine the types of products to sell, the prices to charge, and so on. But buying an existing business also has potential pitfalls. Examples include buying a company whose success has been due to the personality and charisma of the owner/manager, buying a company when the market for its product has peaked, and paying too much for a company.

7-2e Key Questions to Ask

LO4 Outline ten key questions to ask when buying an ongoing venture

When deciding whether to buy, the astute prospective owner needs to ask and answer a series of "right questions."[4] The following section discusses questions and provides insights into the types of actions to take for each response.

LO5 Examine the underlying issues involved in the acquisition process

WHY IS THE BUSINESS BEING SOLD?

One of the first questions that should be asked is *why* the owner is selling the business.[5] Quite often, a difference exists between the reason given to prospective buyers and the real reason. Typical responses include "I'm thinking about retiring," "I've proven to myself that I can be successful in this line of business, so now I'm moving to another operation that will provide me with new challenges," and "I want to move to California and go into business with my brother-in-law there."

Any of these statements may be accurate, and—if they can be substantiated—the buyer may find that the business is indeed worth purchasing. However, because it is difficult to substantiate this sort of personal information, the next best thing to do is to check around and gather business-related information. Is the owner in trouble with the suppliers? Is the lease on the building due for renewal and the landlord planning to triple the rent? Worse yet, is the building about to be torn down? Other site-location problems may relate to competition in the nearby area or zoning changes. Is a new shopping mall about to be built nearby that will take much of the business away from this location? Has the city council passed a new ordinance that calls for the closing of business on Sunday, the day of the week when this store does 25 percent of its business?

Financially, what is the owner going to do after selling the business? Is the seller planning to stay in town? What employment opportunities does he or she have? The reason for asking these questions is that the new owner's worst nightmare is to find that the previous owner has set up a similar business a block away and is drawing back all of the customers. One way to prevent this from happening is to have an attorney write into the contract an agreement that the previous owner will refrain from conducting the same business within a reasonable distance for a period of at least five years. This is known as a **legal restraint of trade**—covenant not to compete or "**non-compete agreement**." Doing this helps the new owner retain the business's customers.

WHAT IS THE CURRENT PHYSICAL CONDITION OF THE BUSINESS?

Even if the asking price for the operation appears to be fair, it is necessary to examine the *physical condition of the assets*. Does the company own the building? If it does, how much repair work needs to be done? If the building is leased, does the lease provide for the kinds of repairs that will enhance the successful operation of the business? For example, if a flower shop has a somewhat large refrigerator for keeping flowers cool, who has to pay to expand the size of the refrigerator? If the landlord agrees to do so and to recover the investment through an increase in the lease price, the total cost of the additional refrigerated space must be compared to the expected increase in business. Meanwhile, if the landlord does not want to make this type of investment, the new owners must realize that any *permanent additions to the property remain with the property*. This means that if something simply cannot be carried out of the building, it stays. Pictures on the walls, chairs, and desks the previous business owner purchased can be removed. However, new bookshelves nailed to the wall, carpeting attached to the floor, a new acoustic ceiling installed to cut down on noise in the shop, and the new refrigerated area all become permanent property of the building owner. Therefore, the overriding question while examining the physical facilities is, "How much will it cost to get things in order?"

WHAT IS THE CONDITION OF THE INVENTORY?

How much inventory does the current owner show on the books? Does a physical check show that inventory actually exists? Additionally, is inventory salable, or is it out-of-date or badly deteriorated?

WHAT IS THE STATE OF THE COMPANY'S OTHER ASSETS?

Most operating ventures have assets in addition to the physical facilities and the inventory. A machine shop, for example, may have various types of presses and other machinery. An office may have computers, copiers, and other technology that belong to the business. The question to ask about all of this equipment is, "Is it still useful, or has it been replaced by more modern technology?" In short, are these assets obsolete?

Another often overlooked asset is the firm's records. If the business has kept careful records, it may be possible to determine who is a good credit risk and who is not. Additionally, these records make it easy for a new owner to decide how much credit to extend to the prior customers. Likewise, sales records can be very important because they show seasonal demands and peak periods. This can provide the new owner with information for inventory-control purposes and can greatly reduce the risks of over- or under-stocking.

Still another commonly overlooked asset is past contracts. What type of lease does the current owner have on the building? If the lease was signed three years ago and is a seven year lease with a fixed rent, it may have been somewhat high when it came into effect but could be somewhat on the low side for comparable facilities today. Furthermore, over the next four years, the rent should prove to be quite low considering what competitors will be paying. Of course, if the lease is about to expire, this is a different story. Then the prospective owner has to talk to the landlord to find out what the terms of the lease will be. Additionally, a prospective owner's lawyer should look at the old lease to determine if it can be passed on to a new owner and, regardless of the rent, how difficult it is to break the lease if the business should start to fail.

Finally, the prospective buyer must look at an intangible asset called goodwill. Goodwill is often defined as the value of the company beyond what is shown on the books. For example, if a software company has a reputation for quick and accurate service, the company has built up goodwill among its customers. If the owners were to sell the business, the buyer would have to pay not only for the physical assets in the software company (office furniture, computers, etc.) but also for the goodwill the firm has accumulated over the years. The reputation of the business has a value.[6]

HOW MANY OF THE EMPLOYEES WILL REMAIN?

It is often difficult to give customers the good service they have come to expect if seasoned employees decide they do not want to remain with the new owner. The owner is certainly an important asset of the firm, but so are the employees; they play a role in making the business a success. Therefore, one question the prospective buyer must ask is, "If some people will be leaving, will enough be left to maintain the type of service the customer is used to getting?" In particular, the new owner must be concerned about key people who are not staying. Key employees are part of the value of the business. If it is evident that these people will not be staying, the prospective buyer must subtract something from the purchase price by making some allowance for the decline in sales and the accompanying expense associated with replacing key personnel.

When purchasing an existing business, the prospective owner should conduct an assessment of the current group of employees. He or she should review existing performance evaluations and talk with the current owners about the quality of each employee and his or her value to the business. It may be easier to retain valuable employees by seeking them out before the purchase to ensure their feelings of security. The incoming owner should interview all of the current employees and make decisions about who to keep and who to let go before actually taking over the enterprise.

WHAT TYPE OF COMPETITION DOES THE BUSINESS FACE?

No matter what goods or service the business provides, the number of people who will want it and the total amount of money they will spend for it is limited. Thus, the greater the competition, the less the business's chance of earning large profits. As the number of competitors increases, the cost of fighting them usually goes up. More money must be spent on advertising. Price competition must be met with accompanying reductions in overall revenue. Simply too many companies are pursuing the same market.

Additionally, the quality of competition must be considered. If nine competitors exist, a new owner could estimate a market share of 10 percent. However, some of these competitors undoubtedly will be more effective than others. One or two may have very good advertising and know how to use it to capture 25 percent of the market. A few others may offer outstanding service and use this advantage to capture 20 percent of the market. Meanwhile, the remaining six fight for what is left.

Then the location of the competition must be considered. In many instances, a new venture does not offer anything unique, so people buy on the basis of convenience. A service located on the corner may get most of the business of local residents. One located across town will get virtually none. Because the product is the same at each location, no one is going to drive across town for it. This analogy holds true for groceries, notions, drugs, and hardware. If competitors are located near one another, each will take some of the business the others could have expected, but none is going to maximize its income. But if the merchandise is an item that people shop for very carefully—furniture, for example—a competitor in the immediate area can be a distinct advantage. For example, two furniture stores located near each other tend to draw a greater number of customers than they would if located ten blocks apart. When people shop for furniture, they go where a large selection is available. With adjacent stores, customers will reason that if the furniture they are looking for is not in one, it might be in the other. Additionally, since they can step from one store to the next, they can easily compare prices and the sale terms.

Finally, any analysis of competition should look for **unscrupulous practices**. How cutthroat are the competitors? If they are very cutthroat, the prospective buyer will have to be continually alert for practices such as price fixing and kickbacks to suppliers for special services. Usually, if the company has been around for a couple of years, it has been successful dealing with these types of practices. However, if some competitors are getting bad reputations, the new owner will want to know this. After all, over time the customers are likely to form a stereotyped impression of enterprises in a given geographic area and will simply refuse to do business with any of them. In this case, the customers retaliate against unethical business practices by boycotting the entire area in which these firms are located. In short, an unethical business competitor can drag down other firms as well.

WHAT DOES THE FIRM'S FINANCIAL PICTURE LOOK LIKE?

It may be necessary for a prospective buyer to hire an accountant to look over the company's books. It is important to get an idea of how well the firm is doing financially. One of the primary areas of interest should be the **company's profitability**.[7] Is the business doing anything wrong that can be spotted from the statements? If so, can the prospective buyer eliminate these problems?

Individuals who are skilled in buying companies that are in trouble, straightening them out, and reselling them at a profit know what to look for when examining the books. So do good accountants. Both also know that the seller's books alone should not be taken as proof of sales or profits. One should insist on seeing records of bank deposits for the past two to three years. If the current owner has held the firm for only a short time, the records of the previous owner also should be examined. In fact, it is not out of line to ask for the owner's income tax return. The astute buyer knows that the firm's records reflect its condition.

Another area of interest is the firm's **profit trend**. Is it making more money year after year? More important, are profits going up as fast as sales, or is more and more revenue necessary to attain the same profit? If the latter is true, this means the business may have to increase sales 5 to 10 percent annually to net as much as it did the previous year. This spells trouble and is often a sign that the owner is selling because "there are easier ways to make a living."

Finally, even if the company is making money, the prospective buyer should compare the firm's performance to that of similar companies. For example, if a small retail shop is making a 22 percent return in investment this year in contrast to 16 percent two years ago, is this good or bad? It certainly appears to be good, but what if competing stores are making a 32 percent return on investment? Given this information, the firm is not doing as well.

One way to compare a company to the competition is to obtain comparative information put out by firms such as Dun & Bradstreet that gather data on retail and wholesale firms in various fields and provide businesspeople with an overall view of many key financial ratios. For example, one of the most important is the comparison of current assets (cash, or items that can be turned into cash in the short run) to current liabilities (debts that will come due in the short run). This key ratio reflects a business's ability to meet its current obligations. A second key ratio is the comparison of net profits to net sales (net profit margin). How much profit is the owner making for every dollar in sales? A third key ratio is net profit to net worth (return on net worth). How much profit is the individual making for every dollar invested in the firm?

By comparing the accounting information obtained from a business's books to external financial comparison data (industry ratios, industry multiples used for valuation, etc.), it is possible to determine how well the business is doing. If the facts look good, then the prospective buyer can turn to the question of how much to offer the seller.

7-2f Negotiating the Deal

The potential buyer must negotiate the final deal.[8] This negotiation process, however, involves a number of factors. Four critical elements should be recognized: information, time, pressure, and alternatives.

Information may be the most critical element during negotiations. The performance of the company, the nature of its competition, the condition of the market, and clear answers to all of the key questions presented earlier are all vital components in the determination of the business's real potential. Without reliable information, the buyer is at a costly disadvantage. The seller never should be relied on as the sole information source. Although the seller may not falsify any information, he or she is likely to make available only the information that presents the business in the most favorable light. Therefore, the buyer should develop as many sources as possible. The rule should be to investigate every possible source.

Time is also a critical element. If the seller already has purchased another business and a potential buyer is the only prospect to buy the existing firm, then that buyer has the power to win some important concessions from the seller. If, however, the owner has no such deadline but simply is headed to retirement, or if the buyer's financial sources wish to invest in the project quickly, then the buyer is at a serious disadvantage. In short, having more time than the other party can be very beneficial.

Pressure from others also will affect the negotiation process. If the company is owned by several partners, then the individual who is selling the company may not have complete autonomy. If one of the owners is in favor of accepting an offer, the negotiator for the company must decide whether to accept the bid on behalf of all owners or attempt to hold out for more money. This causes a distraction during the negotiation process.

Finally, the alternatives available to each party become important factors. The party with no other alternatives has a great deal of interest in concluding negotiations quickly.

Additional considerations that a person should keep in mind when purchasing a business include the following:

1. Request that the seller retain a minority interest in the business or establish the final purchase price dependent on the performance of the business over a three-to-five-year span, to keep the seller concerned about the immediate future performance of the business.

2. Buyers should be wary of any promises made without written corroboration.

3. Spend time with the seller's books, reconstructing financial statements to determine how much cash is actually available, is an absolute.

4. And, it goes without saying, investigations should be thorough and wide-ranging, encompassing interviews not only with the owner but with vendors, competitors, customers, and employees as well.[9]

For the seller, alternatives include finding another buyer in the near future or not selling at all. He or she may continue to run the business, hire a manager to do so, or sell off parts of the company. Likewise, the buyer may choose not to purchase the business or may have alternative investment opportunities available. In any event, the negotiating parties' alternatives should be recognized because they impact the ability to reach an agreement.

7-3 FRANCHISING: THE HYBRID

LO6 Define a franchise and outline its structure

One form of business that incorporates some of the independence of an entrepreneur with the larger umbrella of a corporation is the franchise. Thus, it is a "hybrid" form of entering business. Today, more than a third of all retail sales and an increasing part of the gross domestic product are generated by private franchises. A **franchise** is any arrangement in which the owner of a trademark, trade name, or copyright has licensed others to use it in selling goods or services. A **franchisee** (a purchaser of a franchise) generally is legally independent but economically dependent on the integrated business system of the **franchisor** (the seller of the franchise). In other words, a franchisee can operate as an independent businessperson but still realize the advantages of a regional or national organization.[10]

7-3a How Franchising Works

Business franchise systems for goods and services generally work the same way. The franchisee, an independent businessperson, contracts for a complete business package. This usually requires the individual to do one or more of the following:

1. Make a financial investment in the operation

2. Obtain and maintain a standardized inventory and/or equipment package usually purchased from the franchisor

3. Maintain a specified quality of performance

4. Follow a **franchise fee** as well as a percentage of the gross revenues

5. Engage in a continuing business relationship

In turn, the franchisor provides the following types of benefits and assistance:

1. The company name. For example, if someone bought a Burger King franchise, this would provide the business with drawing power. A well-known name, such as Burger King, ensures higher sales than an unknown name, such as Ralph's Big Burgers.

2. Identifying symbols, logos, designs, and facilities. For example, all McDonald's units have the same identifying golden arches on the premises. Likewise, the facilities are similar inside.

3. Professional management training for each independent unit's staff.

4. Sale of specific merchandise necessary for the unit's operation at wholesale prices. Usually provided is all of the equipment to run the operation and the food or materials needed for the final product.

5. Financial assistance, if needed, to help the unit in any way possible.

6. Continuing aid and guidance to ensure that everything is done in accordance with the contract.[11]

7-3b Advantages of Franchising

LO7 Examine the benefits and drawbacks of franchising

A number of advantages are associated with franchising. In the following section, we describe four of the most well-known advantages: training and guidance, brand-name appeal, a proven track record, and financial assistance.

TRAINING AND GUIDANCE

Perhaps the greatest advantage of buying a franchise, as compared to starting a new business or buying an existing one, is that the franchisor usually will provide both training and guidance to the franchisee. As a result, the likelihood of success is much greater for national franchisees who receive this assistance than for small-business owners in general. For example, it has been reported that the ratio of failure for small enterprises in general to franchised businesses may be as high as 4:1 or 5:1.

BRAND-NAME APPEAL

An individual who buys a well-known national franchise, especially a big-name one, has a good chance to succeed. The franchisor's name is a drawing card for the establishment. People are often more aware of the product or service offered by a national franchise and prefer it to those offered by lesser-known outlets. See Table 7.3 for some examples of well known franchise names.

A PROVEN TRACK RECORD

Another benefit of buying a franchise is that the franchisor has already proved that the operation can be successful. Of course, if someone is the first individual to buy a franchise, this is not the case. However, if the organization has been around for 5 to 10 years and has 50 or more units, it should not be difficult to see how successful the operations have been. If all of the units are still in operation and the owners report they are doing well financially, one can be certain the franchisor has proved that the layout and location of the store, the pricing policy, the quality of the goods or service, and the overall management system are successful.

FINANCIAL ASSISTANCE

Another reason a franchise can be a good investment is that the franchisor may be able to help the new owner secure the financial assistance needed to run the operation. In fact, some

TABLE 7.3   SOME OF THE MOST RECOGNIZED FRANCHISES

- Burger King
- Dairy Queen
- Days Inn
- Denny's
- Dunkin' Donuts
- H&R Block (Tax Preparation)
- McDonald's
- Meineke Car Care Centers
- Papa John's Pizza
- 7-Eleven
- Snap-on Tools
- Sports Clips (Hair Salons)
- Subway
- UPS Store (Mail Boxes Etc.)

franchisors have personally helped the franchisee get started by lending money and not requiring any repayment until the operation is running smoothly. In short, buying a franchise is often an ideal way to ensure assistance from the financial community.

7-3c Disadvantages of Franchising

The prospective franchisee must weigh the advantages of franchising against the accompanying disadvantages. Some of the most important drawbacks are franchise fees, the control exercised by the franchisor, and unfulfilled promises by some franchisors. The following sections examine each of these disadvantages.

FRANCHISE FEES

In business, no one gets something for nothing. The larger and more successful the franchisor, the greater the franchise fee. For a franchise from a national chain, it is not uncommon for a buyer to be faced with a fee that could range from $50,000 to $1,000,000. Smaller franchisors or those who have not had great success charge less. Nevertheless, entrepreneurs deciding whether or not to take the franchise route into small business should weigh the fee against the return they could get putting the money into another type of business. Also, remember that this fee covers only the benefits discussed in the previous section. The prospective franchisee also must pay to build the unit and stock it, although the franchisor may provide assistance in securing a bank loan. Additionally, a fee is usually tied to gross sales. The franchise buyer typically pays an initial franchise fee, spends his or her own money to build a store, buys the equipment and inventory, and then pays a continuing royalty based on sales (usually between 5 and 12 percent). Most franchisors require buyers to have 25 to 50 percent of the initial costs in cash. The rest can be borrowed—in some cases, from the franchising organization itself.[12] Table 7.4 presents a list of the costs involved in buying a franchise.

TABLE 7.4   THE COST OF FRANCHISING

Don't let the advantages of franchising cloud the significant costs involved. Although the franchise fee may be $75,000, the actual cost of "opening your doors for business" can be more than $200,000! Depending on the type of franchise, the following expenditures are possible:

1. *The basic franchising fee.* For this, you may receive a wide range of services: personnel training, licenses, operations manuals, training materials, site selection and location preparation assistance, and more. Or you may receive none of these.

2. *Insurance.* You will need coverage for a variety of items, such as plate glass, office contents, vehicles, and others. You also should obtain so-called "umbrella" insurance. It is inexpensive and is meant to help out in the event of crippling million- or multimillion-dollar lawsuits.

3. *Opening product inventory.* If initial inventory is not included in your franchise fee, you will have to obtain enough to open your franchise.

4. *Remodeling and leasehold improvements.* Under most commercial leases, you are responsible for these costs.

5. *Utility charges.* Deposits to cover the first month or two are usually required for electricity, gas, oil, telephone, and water.

6. *Payroll.* This should include the costs of training employees before the store opens. You should include a reasonable salary for yourself.

7. *Debt service.* This includes principal and interest payments.

8. *Bookkeeping and accounting fees.* In addition to the services the franchisor may supply in this area, it is always wise to use your own accountant.

9. *Legal and professional fees.* The cost of hiring an attorney to review the franchise contract, to file for and obtain any necessary zoning or planning ordinances, and to handle any unforeseen conflicts must be factored into your opening costs projections.

10. *State and local licenses, permits, and certificates.* These run the gamut from liquor licenses to building permits for renovations.

Source: Donald F. Kuratko, "Achieving the American Dream as a Franchise," *Small Business Network* 3 (July 1987): 2 (updated by author April 2012).

THE ENTREPRENEURIAL PROCESS

To Franchise or Not to Franchise: That Is the Question

Franchises area vehicle for those individuals with entrepreneurial tendencies but without the desire to base a business on their own idea. Given this fact, franchising would seem a logical fit for young entrepreneurs fresh from college. Experts differ on the merits of such an approach. Following are reasons for and against becoming a franchisee straight out of college:

For

- *Students learn best in structured learning environments, as provided by franchising.* The support structure provided by franchisors makes franchising an ideal option for students looking to experience entrepreneurship with a proven formula. The educational materials provided to new franchisees extend the classroom environment to a real-world application.

- *Students are experienced customers and, in many cases, employees of franchises.* Because fewer families have stay-at-home parents, today's students have experienced an active childhood, which often involved relying on "fast" food between appointments. Many students also have taken part-time positions with these franchises, which has given them a behind-the-scenes look at how they are run.

- *So-called "helicopter parents" often continue to provide support beyond college.* The support that students require when starting their first business extends beyond financial needs. Having parents who are actively involved can give students the boost they need to venture out on their own, knowing that there is a safety net in the event that they fail. Although some would argue that the limited financial contribution of the students inevitably leads to a lack of accountability, others argue that having the investments from family and friends on the line further motivates the students to succeed.

- *Students are accustomed to being visionary, which fuels innovation.* The Internet has given students a venue for self-expression on a grand scale. The immediacy of results from the digitization of society has taught students how to generate an idea, implement it, and assess the results. This enthusiasm often translates to ambition that franchisors look for in their franchisees.

Against

- *Few college students have the financial wherewithal to start a franchise.* Although the costs associated with starting a franchise in the long run can be less than those for developing a new concept, the upfront franchising fees can cost several hundred thousand dollars, making the financial requirements a significant hurdle for individuals without the credit history to acquire a bank loan without a cosigner.

- *Students usually find staying motivated difficult when the business struggles.* Business concepts that initially were exciting can quickly lose their luster when they lose momentum. Given that most students will have had financial assistance from family or friends, they have little to no financial commitment to the business, which can lead to a lack of ownership when problems arise.

- *Lack of management experience makes dealing with employees a challenge.* Franchisors will provide marketing materials, supplier connections, and operational plans, but the responsibility for managing employees falls squarely on the shoulders of the franchisees. The recruitment, management, and retention of employees can be stressful for even the most seasoned manager, so students with no experience in management find it difficult to keep employees motivated and committed. Gaining experience through trial and error as a manager in a large corporation is unlikely to lead to the collapse of the entire organization, whereas franchises are far more susceptible to management mistakes.

In the end, students have to determine what makes the most sense for their career aspirations as well as for their management style. Although there is more risk inherent with a new concept, franchising is not for everyone. Some entrepreneurs have concluded that franchisor agreements are too restrictive, relegating them to what they consider to be mere employees; however, all franchisors stipulate different policies and procedures. Deciding whether to purchase a franchise is only the beginning of the process. The real work begins when an entrepreneur decides what franchise to purchase.

Source: Adapted from Jeff Elgin and Jennifer Kushell, "He Said, She Said," *Entrepreneur*, January 2008, http://www.entrepreneur.com/magazine /entrepreneur/2008/January/187674.html (accessed March 16, 2008).

FRANCHISOR CONTROL

In a large corporation, the company controls the employee's activities. If an individual has a personal business, he or she controls his or her own activities. A franchise operator is somewhere between these extremes. The franchisor generally exercises a fair amount of control over the operation in order to achieve a degree of uniformity. If entrepreneurs do not follow franchisor directions, they may not have their franchise license renewed when the contract expires.

UNFULFILLED PROMISES

In some cases, especially among less-known franchisors, the franchisees have not received all they were promised.[13] For example, many franchisees have found themselves with trade names that have no drawing power. Also, many franchisees have found that the promised assistance from the franchisor has not been forthcoming. For example, instead of being able to purchase supplies more cheaply through the franchisor, many operators have found themselves paying exorbitant prices for supplies. If franchisees complain, they risk having their agreement with the franchisor terminated or not renewed.

7-3d Franchise Law

The growth in franchise operations has outdistanced laws about franchising. A solid body of appellate decisions under federal or state laws that relate to franchises has yet to be developed.[14] In the absence of case law that precisely addresses franchising, the courts tend to apply general common-law principles and appropriate federal or state statutory definitions and rules. Characteristics associated with a franchising relationship are similar in some respects to those of principal/agent, employer/employee, and employer/independent contractor relationships, yet a franchising relationship does not truly fit into any of these traditional classifications. So, the Federal Trade Commission (FTC) enacted The Franchise Rule in an attempt to provide disclosure requirements from franchisors. (See "Entrepreneurship in Practice: The Franchise Disclosure Document.") However, that is most valuable in the purchase of a franchise rather than any ongoing legal issues that arise. Much franchise litigation has arisen over termination provisions. Because the franchise agreement is normally a form contract the franchisor draws and prepares, and because the bargaining power of the franchisee is rarely equal to that of the franchisor, the termination provisions of contracts are generally more favorable to the franchisor. This means that the franchisee, who normally invests a substantial amount of time and money in the franchise operation to make it successful, may receive little or nothing for the business upon termination. The franchisor owns the trademark and hence the business.[15]

7-3e Evaluating Franchising Opportunities

How can the average entrepreneur evaluate a franchise operation and decide if it is a good deal? Unfortunately, no mathematical formula exists (although the best valuation methods are presented in Chapter 14). Nor is it possible simply to ask a friend, because the most popular franchises, which are probably the only ones the individual is familiar with, do not give franchises to people seeking to enter the field. This leaves only the smaller, lesser-known, and more risky franchise operations.[16]

One research study examined the relationship between the base fees and royalties paid to the franchise's overall value. The findings indicated that the age of a franchise, number of retail units, concentration in the state, and national representation are all reflected in the size of base fees and royalties. However, the key to examining the value of a prospective franchise is a proper information search.[17] In addition, to ensure an adequately protected investment, an evaluation of all franchise opportunities must be undertaken. Figure 7.2 illustrates a complete process model for analyzing the purchase of a franchise.

LEARNING OF FRANCHISING OPPORTUNITIES

One of the first things a prospective franchisee must do is to find a reliable source of information about franchising opportunities. Some of the most readily available sources are newspapers, trade publications, and the Internet (see Table 7.5 for a list of useful websites). *Entrepreneur* magazine carries advertisements of franchise opportunities, and exhibitions and trade shows are held by franchisors from time to time in various cities. Entrepreneur .com annually lists the top franchises and the fastest-growing franchises.

Finally, franchisors themselves offer information on specific opportunities—although, in this case, one needs to beware of promises that exceed what may be delivered.

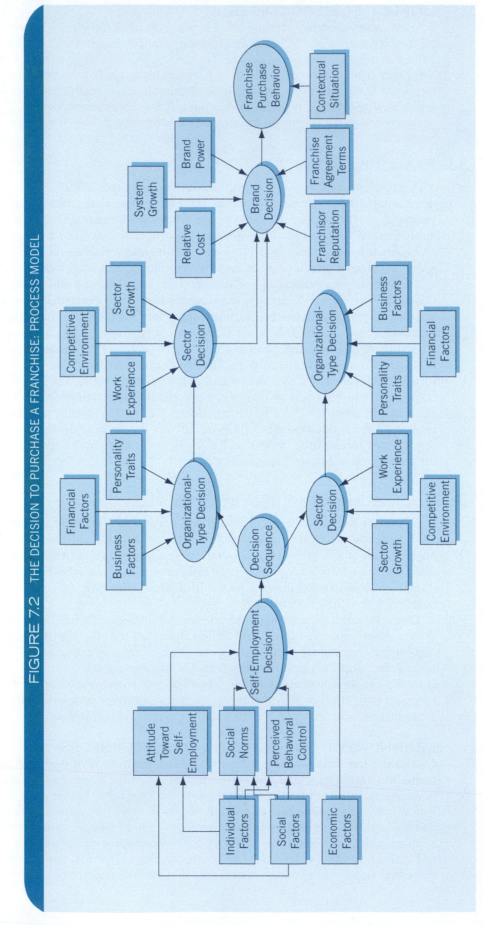

FIGURE 7.2 THE DECISION TO PURCHASE A FRANCHISE: PROCESS MODEL

Source: Patrick J. Kaufmann, "Franchising and the Choice of Self Employment," *Journal of Business Venturing* 14, no. 4 (1999): 348.

TABLE 7.5   WORLD WIDE WEB FRANCHISE SITES

The Internet has become the foremost source of information for people of all ages, trades, and interests. Short of handing over the funds, the prospective franchisee can find everything he or she needs to ensure the successful research, selecting, and planning of a franchise business in the comfort of his or her own home.

You can search for the perfect match by location, category, investment, and actual franchise at http://www.franchiseexpo.com. This site allows you to obtain pertinent information about certain franchises via "showcases" that provide histories, business summaries, frequently asked questions, and investment requirements. Basic franchise information, including interactive financial worksheets, ways to select the right franchise, expo information, and links to other valuable Web resources are also available.

The Franchise Handbook, http://www.franchise1.com, offers the serious person serious answers to his or her questions. Directories, associations, a message board, and industry news are just a few of the resources available on the Web's most popular franchise site.

Franchise Works can be found at http://www.franchiseworks.com. Here you will find different franchises listed by category, as well as other available business opportunities. Also on the site are resources that can be used to cover all aspects of the start of a business.

The International Franchise Association is a premier source for industry data. Browse http://www.franchise.org to stay on top of the latest government developments and hot topics that affect franchisees and franchisors worldwide.

Other Valuable Sites:

American Bar Association Forum on Franchising	www.americanbar.org/groups/franchising.html
U.S. Small Business Administration	www.sba.gov
Entrepreneur Magazine	www.entrepreneur.com/franchises/
Minority Business Entrepreneur Magazine	www.mbemag.com
Franchise Times	www.franchisetimes.com
Franchise Update	www.franchising.com
National Restaurant Association	www.restaurant.org/tools/
Source Book Publications	www.franchisordatabase.com
Federal Trade Commission	www.ftc.gov/bcp/franchise/
Franchise.com	www.franchise.com
World Franchising	www.worldfranchising.com
Franchise Solutions	www.franchisesolutions.com
Franchise Opportunities	www.franchiseopportunities.com
Franchise Know How	http://www.franchiseknowhow.com/
The Franchise Magazine	www.thefranchisemagazine.net
Franchise Mall	http://www.thefranchisemall.com/
Franchise Advantage	www.franchiseadvantage.com
U.S. Franchise News	www.usfranchisenews.com

THE ENTREPRENEURIAL PROCESS

The Franchise Disclosure Document

In 1979, the Federal Trade Commission (FTC) established a Franchise Disclosure Rule that required franchisors to make full presale disclosure nationwide. This was amended in 2007 by the FTC to enact greater disclosure requirements from franchisors. From that amendment, a legal disclosure document entitled the **Franchise Disclosure Document (FDD)** must now be presented to prospective buyers of franchises in the presale disclosure process in the United States. It was originally known as the Uniform Franchise Offering Circular (UFOC).

The FDD underlies the franchise agreement (the formal sales contract) between the parties at the time the contract is formally signed. This franchise sales contract governs the long-term relationship and contains the *only* promises and obligations of the parties to each other that will remain in effect over the stated time term of the contracts—the terms of which generally range from 5 to 20 years. The contracts cannot be changed unless there is agreement of both parties.

Under the Franchise Rule, which is enforced by the Federal Trade Commission (FTC), a prospective franchisee must receive the franchisor's FDD franchise disclosure document at least 10 days before they are asked to sign any contract or pay any money to the franchisor or an affiliate of the franchisor. The prospective franchisee has the right to ask for (and get) a copy of the sample franchise disclosure document once the franchisor has received the prospective franchisee's application and agreed to consider it. The franchisor may provide a copy of its franchise disclosure documents on paper, via e-mail, over the Web, or on a disc.

There are 23 categories of information that must be provided by the franchisor to the prospective franchisee prior to the execution of the franchise agreement. These categories include:

1. The franchisor, its predecessors, and affiliates
2. Business experience of key persons
3. Litigation history
4. Bankruptcy
5. Initial franchise fee
6. Other fees
7. Initial investment
8. Restrictions on sources of products
9. Franchisee's obligations
10. Financing arrangements
11. Franchisor's obligations
12. Territory
13. Trademarks
14. Patents, copyrights, and proprietary information
15. Obligation to participate in the actual operation of the franchised business
16. Restrictions on what the franchisee may sell
17. Renewal, termination, transfer, and dispute resolution
18. Public figures
19. Financial performance representations: Sales, profits, earnings claims
20. List of franchise outlets
21. Financial statements
22. Contracts
23. Acknowledgment of receipt

Source: Adapted from the Federal Trade Commission, 2015.

INVESTIGATING THE FRANCHISOR

The prospective investor should get as much information as possible on the franchisor. So many people have lost their life savings in franchise schemes that, except when dealing with a long-established franchisor, one is best advised to enter the investigation prepared for the worst. In particular, if the franchisor seems too eager to sell dealerships or units, it is cause for alarm. Likewise, if the franchisor does not make a vigorous effort to check out prospective investors, it is usually a sign that the seller does not think the operation will last long and probably is interested in just taking the franchise fees and absconding with them.

LO8 Present the franchise disclosure document (FDD) as a key item in franchises

Remember: No reputable franchisor will sell a franchise without ensuring that the buyer is capable of operating it successfully. McDonald's—one of the most cautious of all franchisors—carefully screens all applicants, and it claims it has never had a unit go bankrupt.

SEEKING PROFESSIONAL HELP

If the franchisor passes the initial investigation and offers a franchise contract, the prospective franchisee should first take it to a qualified attorney. The attorney will understand the terms of the agreement and can explain any penalties or restrictive clauses that limit what the franchisee can do.

Of major importance are contract provisions related to cancellation and renewal of the franchise. Can the franchisor take away the franchise for some minor rule infraction? More important, if the agreement is canceled, how much of the initial franchise fee will be refunded to the individual? If the franchise can be purchased back by the franchisor at 20 percent of the initial fee, the lawyer will need to examine carefully how easily the franchisor can terminate the agreement.

Other consideration include the franchise fee, the percentage of gross revenues to be paid to the franchisor, the type and extent of training to be provided, the territorial limits of the franchise, and the provisions for supplying materials to the unit. In addition, the lawyer needs to examine the degree of control the franchisor will have over operations, including price requirements, performance standards, and the required days and hours of operation. The individual also should seek financial counsel. A good banker should be able to look over the franchisor's prospectus and give an opinion regarding its feasibility. Is the projected revenue too high for a new unit? Is the return on investment overly optimistic? Would the bank be prepared to advance to advance a loan on this type of business undertaking?

Finally, the investor should talk to a certified public accountant (CPA), who can review the data and construct a projected income statement for the first few years. Does the investment look promising? What might go wrong and jeopardize the investment? How likely are those developments? Is this the type of investment that constitutes an acceptable risk for the prospective buyer, or should the individual walk away from the deal?

Legal and financial professionals will help the prospective franchisee answer some very important questions. In particular, they will force the individual to face the risks inherent in a franchise and answer the question, "Am I willing to take this type of risk?"

MAKING THE DECISION: IT'S UP TO THE ENTREPRENEUR

After the prospective entrepreneur has gathered all of the necessary information, it is up to him or her to make the final decision on the matter. As with buying an ongoing business, however, the series of "right questions" outlined previously can help.

SUMMARY

The easiest and best way to approach a new business venture is to design a unique product or service. Sometimes this involves what is called a new-new approach—that is, the development of an entirely new idea for a product or service (as was the case with Zynga and Google). In most instances, however, the prospective owner/manager must be content to use a new-old approach by "piggybacking" on someone else's ideas. This involves either expanding on what the competition is doing or offering a product or service in an area in which it is not presently available.

On the financial side, the prospective owner/manager needs to examine the enterprise's financial picture and to determine the costs of setting up the operation and the amount of revenue that will be generated during the initial period. Finally, the prospective owner/ manager must review a series of other operational considerations ranging from the building, merchandise, and equipment needed for operations to record keeping, insurance, legal, marketing, and personal matters.

Another opportunity is the purchase of an existing successful firm, which has a number of advantages. Three of the most important are that its successful future operation is likely, the time and effort associated with starting a new enterprise are eliminated, and a bargain price may be possible.

Before deciding whether to buy, however, the prospective owner needs to ask and answer a series of "right questions." These include: Why is the business being sold? What is the physical condition of the business? What is the condition of the inventory? What is the state of the company's other assets? How many of the employees will remain? What competition does the business face? What is the firm's financial picture?

After all questions have been answered satisfactorily, the prospective buyer must negotiate for the business. In the final analysis, however, the prospective owner should be concerned with buying the company's assets at *market value* and then paying something for *goodwill* if it is deemed an asset. Valuation is discussed further in Chapter 14.

KEY TERMS

business broker	franchise fee	new-old approach
company's profitability	franchisor	non-compete agreement
franchise	franchisor control	profit trend
Franchise Disclosure Document (FDD)	goodwill	risk versus reward
	legal restraint of trade	unscrupulous practices
franchisee	new-new approach	upside gain and downside loss

REVIEW AND DISCUSSION QUESTIONS

1. Identify the three main pathways to entering business for a prospective entrepreneur.

2. What is the new-new approach to starting a new venture? How does this approach differ from a new-old approach?

3. How can an individual who is thinking of going into business evaluate the financial picture of the enterprise? Use the methodology of Table 7.2 to prepare your answer.

4. In addition to personal and financial issues, what other factors should the prospective owner be concerned with? Describe at least four.

5. What are the advantages of buying an ongoing business? Explain them.

6. What "right questions" need to be answered when deciding whether to buy a business?

7. How should a prospective buyer examine the assets of a company? Explain.

8. What is meant by the term *franchise*?

9. In a franchising agreement, what is the franchisee often called on to do? What responsibility does the franchisor assume?

10. What are some of the major advantages of franchising? Cite and explain three.

11. What are some of the major disadvantages of franchising? Cite and explain at least two.

12. How can a prospective franchisee evaluate a franchise opportunity? Explain.

13. In evaluating whether or not to buy a franchise operation, the potential investor should ask a series of questions. What questions should the potential investor ask about the franchisor, the franchise, the market, and the potential investor (himself or herself)?

14. Where can a prospective franchisee seek professional help to evaluate a franchise?

15. Identify the Franchise Disclosure Document. Explain why it is important in franchising.

NOTES

1. Simon C. Parker and C. Mirjam van Praag, "The Entrepreneur's Mode of Entry: Business Takeover or New Venture Start?," *Journal of Business Venturing* 27, no. 1 (2012): 31–46; Magnus Lofstrom, Timothy Bates, and Simon C. Parker, "Why Are Some People More Likely to Become Small-Businesses Owners than Others: Entrepreneurship Entry and Industry-Specific Barriers," *Journal of Business Venturing* 29, no. 2 (2014): 232–51; and Gerhard Speckbacher, Kerstin Neumann and Werner H. Hoffmann, "Resource Relatedness and the Mode of Entry into New Businesses: Internal Resource Accumulation vs. Access by Collaborative Arrangement, *Strategic Management Journal*, 2015. (in press).

2. Brian Womack, "Facebook Revenue Will Reach $4.27 Billion," *Bloomberg*, September 20, 2011.

3. Shayndi Raice, "Facebook Sets Historic IPO: Potential $10 Billion Offering Would Dwarf Google's," *Wall Street Journal*, February 2, 2012.

4. Donald F. Kuratko and Jeffrey S. Hornsby, *New Venture Management* (Upper Saddle River, NJ: Pearson/ Prentice Hall, 2009), 33–38.

5. Fred Steingold and Emily Dostow, *The Complete Guide to Buying a Business* (Berkeley, CA: Nolo Press, 2005).

6. Jay B. Abrams, *How to Value Your Business and Increase Its Potential* (New York: McGraw-Hill Publishing, 2005); see also Roberto Ragozzino and

Jeffrey J. Reuer, "Contingent Earnouts in Acquisitions of Privately Held Targets," *Journal of Management* 35, no. 4 (2009): 857–79.

7. For a good discussion of buying or selling a small business, see Rene V. Richards, *How to Buy and/or Sell a Small Business for Maximum Profit* (Charleston, SC: Atlantic Publishing Group, 2006).

8. See Roy J. Lewicki, David M. Saunders, and John W. Minton, *Negotiation*, 3rd ed. (New York: McGraw-Hill/Irwin, 2002). This paperback gives practical examples and advice about negotiating. See also Michael Watkins, *Negotiation: Harvard Business Essentials* (Boston, MA: Harvard Business School Press, 2003).

9. Bruce J. Blechman, "Good Buy," *Entrepreneur* (February 1994): 22–25.

10. For an excellent overview of franchises, see Rupert Barkoff, *Fundamentals of Business Franchising*, 2nd ed. (Chicago: American Bar Association, 2005); Roger LeRoy Miller and Frank B. Cross, *The Legal Environment Today: Business in Its Ethical, Regulatory, E-Commerce, and Global Setting*, 7th ed. (Mason, OH: South-Western/Cengage, 2013), and Kenneth W. Clarkson, Roger LeRoy Miller, and Frank B. Cross, *West's Business Law*, 12th ed. (Mason, OH: South-Western/Cengage, 2012), 708–16.

11. Patrick J. Kaufmann, "Franchising and the Choice of Self-Employment," *Journal of Business Venturing* 14, no. 4 (1999): 345–62; David J. Ketchen, Jr., Jeremy C. Short, and James G. Combs, "Is Franchising Entrepreneurship? Yes, No, and Maybe So," *Entrepreneurship Theory and Practice* 35, no. 3 (2011): 583–93; Nada Mumdžiev and Josef Windsperger, "The Structure of Decision Rights in Franchising Networks: A Property Rights Perspective," *Entrepreneurship Theory and Practice* 35, no. 3 (2011): 449–65; and Roland E. Kidwell and Arne Nygaard, "A Strategic Deviance Perspective on the Franchise Form of Organizing," *Entrepreneurship Theory and Practice* 35, no. 3 (2011): 467–82.

12. Robert T. Justis and Richard J. Judd, *Franchising*, 3rd ed. (Mason, OH: Thomson, 2004); Joe Mathews, Don DeBolt, and Deb Percival, *Street Smart Franchising* (Irvine, CA: Entrepreneur Press, 2006).

13. Darrell L. Williams, "Why Do Entrepreneurs Become Franchisees? An Empirical Analysis of Organizational Choice," *Journal of Business Venturing* 14, no. 1 (1999): 103–24; Jérôme Barthélemy, "Agency and Institutional Influences on Franchising Decisions," *Journal of Business Venturing* 26, no. 1 (2011): 93–103; and Mark A. P. Davies, Walfried Lassar, Chris Manolis, Melvin Prince, and Robert D. Winsor, "A Model of Trust and Compliance in Franchise Relationships," *Journal of Business Venturing* 26, no. 3 (2011): 321–40.

14. See Roger LeRoy Miller and Frank B. Cross, *The Legal Environment Today: Business in Its Ethical, Regulatory, E-Commerce, and Global Setting*, 8th ed. (Mason, OH: South-Western/Cengage, 2016); William R. Meek, Beth Davis-Sramek, Melissa S. Baucus, and Richard N. Germain, "Commitment in Franchising: The Role of Collaborative Communication and a Franchisee's Propensity to Leave," *Entrepreneurship Theory and Practice* 35, no. 3 (2011): 559–81.

15. See Steven C. Michael, "To Franchise or Not to Franchise: An Analysis of Decision Rights and Organizational Form Shares," *Journal of Business Venturing* 11, no. 1 (1996): 59–71; see also Nerilee Hing, "Franchisee Satisfaction: Contributors and Consequences," *Journal of Small Business Management* 33, no. 2 (1995): 12–25; and Marko Grunhagen and Robert A. Mittelstaedt, "Entrepreneurs or Investors: Do Multi-Unit Franchisees Have Different Philosophical Orientations?," *Journal of Small Business Management* 43, no. 3 (2005): 207–25.

16. Thani Jambulingam and John R. Nevin, "Influence of Franchisee Selection Criteria of Outcomes Desired by the Franchisor," *Journal of Business Venturing* 14, no. 4 (1999): 363–96; see also Gary J. Castrogiovanni, James G. Combs, and Robert T. Justis, "Shifting Imperatives: An Integrative View of Resource Scarcity and Agency Reasons for Franchising," *Entrepreneurship Theory and Practice* 30, no. 1 (January 2006): 23–40; Roland E. Kidwell, Arne Nygaard, and Ragnhild Silkoset, "Antecedents and Effects of Free Riding in the Franchisor–Franchisee Relationship," *Journal of Business Venturing* 22, no. 4 (2007): 522–44; Steven C. Michael and James G. Combs, "Entrepreneurial Failure: The Case of Franchisees," *Journal of Small Business Management* 46, no. 1 (2008): 73–90; and Karim Mignonac, Christian Vandenberghe, Rozenn Perrigot, Assâad El Akremi, and Olivier Herrbach, "A Multi-Study Investigation of Outcomes of Franchisees' Affective Commitment to Their Franchise Organization," *Entrepreneurship Theory and Practice* 39, no. 3 (2015): 461–88.

17. Andrew J. Sherman, *Franchising & Licensing: Two Powerful Ways to Grow Your Business in Any Economy*, 3rd ed. (New York: AMACOM Books, 2004); Dhruv Grewal, Gopalkrishnan R. Iyer, Rajshekhar (Raj) G. Javalgi, and Lori Radulovich, "Franchise Partnership and International Expansion: A Conceptual Framework and Research Propositions," *Entrepreneurship Theory and Practice* 35, no. 3 (2011): 533–57; James G. Combs, David J. Ketchen, Jr., and Jeremy C. Short, "Franchising Research: Major Milestones, New Directions, and Its Future Within Entrepreneurship," *Entrepreneurship Theory and Practice* 35, no. 3 (2011): 413–25; and Steven C. Michael, "Can Franchising Be an Economic Development Strategy? An Empirical Investigation," *Small Business Economics* 42, no. 3 (2014): 611–20.

CHAPTER 8

Sources of Capital for Entrepreneurs

LEARNING OBJECTIVES

1 To differentiate between debt and equity as methods of financing

2 To examine commercial loans and social lending as sources of capital

3 To review initial public offerings (IPOs) as a source of capital

4 To discuss private placements as an opportunity for equity capital

5 To study the market for venture capital and to review venture capitalists' evaluation criteria for new ventures

6 To discuss the importance of evaluating venture capitalists for a proper selection

7 To examine the existing informal risk-capital market ("angel capital")

Entrepreneurial Thought

Money is like a sixth sense without which you cannot make a complete use of the other five.

—William Somerset Maugham *Of Human Bondage*

8-1 THE SEARCH FOR CAPITAL

Every entrepreneur planning a new venture confronts the same dilemma: where to find start-up capital. But every entrepreneur may not be aware that numerous possibilities for funding exist nor that combinations of financial packages, rather than a single source, may be appropriate. It is important, therefore, to understand not only various sources of capital but also the expectations and requirements of each.

Commercial loans, public offerings, private placements, convertible debentures, venture capital, and informal risk capital are some of the major types of financing encountered in the search for capital. But what exactly are they, and what is expected of an entrepreneur applying for these funds?

Studies have investigated the various sources of capital preferred by entrepreneurs.[1] These sources range from debt to equity, depending on the type of financing that is arranged. As illustrated in Figure 8.1, entrepreneurs have a number of sources of capital as their ventures develop. Notice that the level of risk and the stage of the firm's development impact the appropriate source financing for the entrepreneurial ventures.

In this chapter, we examine the various sources of capital available to new ventures, along with some insights into the processes expected of the entrepreneur. We begin with an examination of the differences between debt and equity financing.

8-2 DEBT VERSUS EQUITY FINANCING

LO1 Differentiate between debt and equity as methods of financing

The use of *debt* to finance a new venture involves a payback of the funds plus a fee (interest) for the use of the money. *Equity* financing involves the sale of some of the ownership in the venture. Debt places a burden on the entrepreneur of loan repayment with interest, whereas equity financing forces the entrepreneur to relinquish some degree of control. In short, the choice is this: (1) take on debt without giving up ownership in the venture or (2) relinquish a percentage of ownership in order to avoid having to borrow. In most cases, a combination of debt and equity proves most appropriate.

FIGURE 8.1   WHO IS FUNDING ENTREPRENEURIAL START-UP COMPANIES?

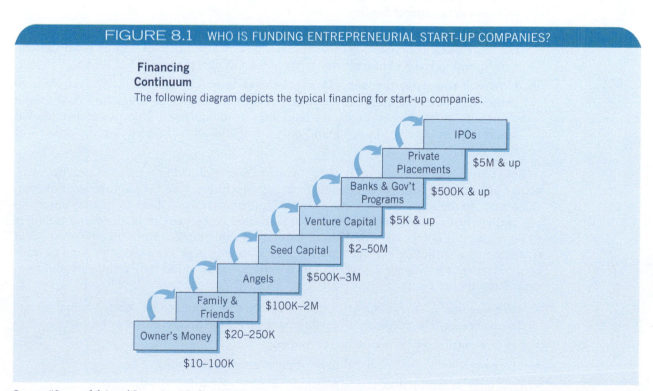

Financing Continuum

The following diagram depicts the typical financing for start-up companies.

- IPOs
- Private Placements — $5M & up
- Banks & Gov't Programs — $500K & up
- Venture Capital — $5K & up
- Seed Capital — $2–50M
- Angels — $500K–3M
- Family & Friends — $100K–2M
- Owner's Money — $20–250K
- $10–100K

Source: "Successful Angel Investing," Indiana Venture Center, March 2008.

8-2a Debt Financing

LO2 Examine commercial loans and social lending as sources of capital

Many new ventures find that **debt financing** is not a choice but a necessity. Short-term borrowing (one year or less) often is required to obtain working capital and is repaid out of proceeds from sales. Long-term debt (term loans of one to five years or long-term loans maturing in more than five years) is used to finance the purchase of property or equipment, with the purchased asset serving as collateral for the loans. The most common sources of debt financing are commercial banks.[2]

COMMERCIAL BANKS

About 5,600 commercial banks operate in the United States today, although that number, since the 2008 economic downturn, keeps decreasing. It has been predicted that by the end of the decade, only 4,000 commercial banks will have survived the tough times.[3] Although some banks make unsecured short-term loans, most bank loans are secured by receivables, inventories, or other assets. Commercial banks also make a large number of intermediate term loans with maturities of one to five years. In about 90 percent of these cases, the banks require collateral, which generally consists of stocks, machinery, equipment, and real estate, and systematic repayment over the life of the loan are required. Apart from real estate mortgages and loans guaranteed by the Small Business Administration (SBA) or a similar organization, commercial banks make few loans with maturities greater than five years. Banks also may offer a number of services to a new venture, including computerized payroll preparation, letters of credit, international services, lease financing, and money market accounts.

To secure a bank loan, entrepreneurs typically have to answer a number of questions. Five of the most common questions, together with descriptive commentaries, follow:

1. **What do you plan to do with the money?** Do not plan on using bank loans for high-risk ventures. Banks typically lend only to the surest of all possible ventures.

2. **How much do you need?** Some entrepreneurs go to their bank with no clear idea of how much money they need. All they know is that they need cash. The more precisely an entrepreneur can answer this question, the more likely the loan will be granted.

3. **When do you need it?** Never rush to a bank with immediate requests for money. Poor planners never attract lenders.

4. **How long will you need it?** The shorter the period of time entrepreneurs need the money, the more likely they are to get loans. The time at which the loan will be repaid should correspond to some important milestone in the business plan.

5. **How will you repay the loan?** This is the most important question. What if plans go awry? Can other income be diverted to pay off the loan? Does collateral exist? Even if a quantity of fixed assets exists, the bank may be unimpressed. Experience dictates that assets sold at liquidation command only a fraction—5 to 10 cents on the dollar—of their value.[4]

Banks are not the only source of debt financing. Sometimes long-term financing for a particular piece of equipment is obtainable from manufacturers, who take a portion of the purchase price in the form of a long-term note. Manufacturers are willing to finance purchases especially when an active market exists for their used equipment, thus allowing machinery to be resold if it is repossessed. Also, new ventures sometimes can obtain short-term debt financing by negotiating extended credit terms with suppliers. However, this kind of trade credit restricts the venture's flexibility in selecting suppliers and may reduce its ability to negotiate supplier prices.

- *Advantages of Debt Financing*. Not surprisingly, debt financing has both advantages and disadvantages. The advantages of debt financing can be characterized as follows:
- No relinquishment of ownership is required.
- More borrowing, potentially, allows for greater return on equity.
- Low interest rates reduce the opportunity cost of borrowing.

- *Disadvantages of Debt Financing.* Financing with debt has its downside:
- Regular (monthly) interest payments are required.
- Cash-flow problems can intensify because of payback responsibilities.
- Heavy use of debt can inhibit growth and development.

PEER-TO-PEER LENDING (P2P)

Peer-to-peer lending commonly abbreviated as P2P lending is the practice of lending money to unrelated individuals, or "peers," without going through a bank or other traditional financial institution. Also known as "debt-based crowdfunding" this lending takes place online on peer-to-peer lending companies' websites using various different lending platforms. This form of financing is a twenty-first century phenomenon.

Peer-to-peer lenders are Internet-based sites that pool money from investors willing to lend capital at agreed-upon rates. P2P lenders charge fees for brokering and servicing loans and collect penalties for late payments as well. The average size of social loans is around $17,000, with maximums predicted to increase to a potential of $250,000. Peer-to-peer lending is one of the fastest growing areas of finance with 100 percent increases each year. The interest rates range from 5.6 to 35.8 percent, depending on the loan term and borrower rating. The default rates vary from about 1.5 to 10 percent for the more risky borrowers. Lending Club, a well-known social-lending company, has the largest loan volume among social-lending sites in the United States, matching borrowers and lenders based on loan size, risk tolerance, and social familiarity (e.g., coworkers, fellow alumni, hometown residents, etc.).

Once thought of as an alternative funding option only for entrepreneurs unable to qualify for commercial loans, P2P lending is beginning to attract borrowers among established entrepreneurs seeking quick capital without the administrative overhead of traditional lenders. The first P2P lending sites appeared in 2005, bringing scale to the age-old idea of borrowing from friends. They multiplied in the latest economic downturn as traditional pools of credit dried up. When word got out in 2008 that some lenders were getting burned by defaulters, the U.S. Securities and Exchange Commission (SEC) stepped in to regulate the industry. The two largest players—Lending Club and Prosper—have collectively serviced over 180,000 loans with $2 billion in total.

Social lending sites are different from so-called microlending sites like Kiva.org, a nonprofit organization that allows donors to make zero-interest loans to specific causes around the globe. Kiva collects the money and gives it to a microfinance institution that disburses the funds and hounds borrowers for repayment.

Some analysts attribute the success of social lending to the weakening economy. Commercial lenders have been forced to be more conservative in their lending practices, which has led to a depleted pool of capital for entrepreneurs. Most of the businesses that utilize social lending sites are start-ups, largely due to the fact that the most popular sites set the maximum loan amount at $25,000. The relatively small loan amounts and the ease with which people can submit their ideas has led many individuals—who otherwise would have avoided pursuing their business venture due to a lack of confidence in their ability to obtain a commercial loan—to view social lending as a low-risk mechanism for getting started.

P2P lending is very similar to other social networking phenomena in that it is largely dependent on the site providers' ability to provide a forum in which an open, trusting community can be built. As the P2P lending movement continues, entrepreneurs will have an effective weapon in their arsenal to combat the cash-flow issues inherent in running a business. As with all lenders, entrepreneurs need to carefully review the policies and procedures as well as the reputation for any peer-to-peer lender they are considering taking a loan through. For those individuals who have been putting their entrepreneurial aspirations on hold due to financial fears, P2P lending could provide the peace of mind needed for them to dust off their ideas and put them into action. Recently there have been signs of the P2P becoming more mainstream as executives from traditional financial institutions are joining peer-to-peer companies as board members, lenders and investors. While the use of P2P lending provides many immediate advantages for entrepreneurs in start-up mode, potential dangers include:

- *Funding success rate.* Most loans are difficult to complete; so the funding success rate could be questionable.
- *Business plan disclosure.* The entrepreneur's business plan is now released to the public domain.
- *No ongoing counseling relationship.* The entrepreneur does not receive any advice or gain experience from the lender, and there are no future rounds of lending or investment.
- *Potential tax liability.* There are tax implications for the borrower and the lender.
- *Uncertain regulatory environment.* The SEC continues to review these sites for potential regulatory policies.[5]

OTHER DEBT-FINANCING SOURCES

In addition to commercial banks and social lenders, other debt-financing sources include trade credit, accounts receivable factoring, finance companies, leasing companies, mutual savings banks, savings and loan associations, and insurance companies. Table 8.1 provides a summary of these sources, the business types they often finance, and their financing terms.

Trade credit is credit given by suppliers who sell goods on account. This credit is reflected on the entrepreneur's balance sheet as accounts payable, and in most cases, it must be paid in 30 to 90 days. Many small, new businesses obtain this credit when no other form of financing is available to them. Suppliers typically offer this credit as a way to attract new customers.

Accounts receivable financing is short-term financing that involves either the pledge of receivables as collateral for a loan or the sale of receivables (factoring). Accounts receivable loans are made by commercial banks, whereas factoring is done primarily by commercial finance companies and factoring concerns.

Accounts receivable bank loans are made on a discounted value of the receivables pledged. A bank may make receivable loans on a notification or nonnotification plan. Under the notification plan, purchasers of goods are informed that their accounts have been assigned to the bank. They then make payments directly to the bank, which credits them to the borrower's

TABLE 8.1   COMMON DEBT SOURCES

Source	Business Type Financed			Financing Term	
	Start-Up Firm	**Existing Firm**	**Short Term**	**Intermediate Term**	**Long Term**
Trade credit	Yes	Yes	Yes	No	No
Commercial banks	Sometimes, but only if strong capital or collateral exists	Yes	Frequently	Sometimes	Seldom
Peer-to-peer (P2P)	Yes	Yes	Yes	Sometimes	No
Finance companies	Seldom	Yes	Most frequent	Yes	Seldom
Factors	Seldom	Yes	Most frequent	Seldom	No
Leasing companies	Seldom	Yes	No	Most frequent	Occasionally
Mutual savings banks and savings-and-loan associations	Seldom	Real estate ventures only	No	No	Real estate ventures only
Insurance companies	Rarely	Yes	No	No	Yes

account. Under the nonnotification plan, borrowers collect their accounts as usual and then pay off the bank loan.

Factoring is the sale of accounts receivable. Under this arrangement, the receivables are sold, at a discounted value, to a factoring company. Some commercial finance companies also do factoring. Under a standard arrangement, the factor will buy the client's receivables outright, without recourse, as soon as the client creates them by its shipment of goods to customers. Factoring fits some businesses better than others, and it has become almost traditional in industries such as textiles, furniture manufacturing, clothing manufacturing, toys, shoes, and plastics.

Finance companies are asset-based lenders that lend money against assets such as receivables, inventory, and equipment. The advantage of dealing with a commercial finance company is that it often will make loans that banks will not. The interest rate varies from two to six percent over that charged by a bank. New ventures that are unable to raise money from banks and factors often turn to finance companies.

8-2b Equity Financing

Equity financing is money invested in the venture with no legal obligation for entrepreneurs to repay the principal amount or pay interest on it. The use of equity funding thus requires no repayment in the form of debt. It does, however, require sharing the ownership and profits with the funding source. Because no repayment is required, equity capital can be much safer for new ventures than debt financing. However, the entrepreneur must consciously decide to give up part of the ownership in return for this funding.[6] Financial equity instruments, which give investors a share of the ownership, may include:

- *Loan with warrants* provides the investor with the right to buy stock at a fixed price at some future date. Terms on the warrants are negotiable. The warrant customarily provides for the purchase of additional stock, such as up to 10 percent of the total issue at 130 percent of the original offering price within a five-year period following the offering date.

- *Convertible debentures* are unsecured loans that can be converted into stock. The conversion price, the interest rate, and the provisions of the loan agreement are all areas for negotiation.

- *Preferred stock* is equity that gives investors a preferred place among the creditors in the event the venture is dissolved. The stock also pays a dividend and can increase in price, thus giving investors an even greater return. Some preferred stock issues are convertible to common stock, a feature that can make them even more attractive.

- *Common stock* is the most basic form of ownership. This stock usually carries the right to vote for the board of directors. If a new venture does well, common-stock investors often make a large return on their investment. These stock issues often are sold through public or private offerings.

During the past 40 years, a tremendous boom has taken place in the private equity industry. The pool of U.S. private equity funds—partnerships that specialize in venture capital, leveraged buyouts, mezzanine investments, build-ups, distressed debt, and related investments—grew from $5 billion in 1980 to more than an estimated $900 billion today.[7]

Equity capital can be raised through two major sources: public stock offerings and private placements. In both cases, entrepreneurs must follow the state laws pertaining to the raising of such funds and must meet the requirements set forth by the SEC. This entire process can be difficult, expensive, and time consuming. The laws and regulations are complex and often vary from state to state. On the other hand, successful stock offerings can help a fledgling enterprise raise a great deal of money.

PUBLIC OFFERINGS

Going public is a term used to refer to a corporation's raising capital through the sale of securities on the public markets. Following are some of the advantages to this approach.

- *Size of capital amount.* Selling securities is one of the fastest ways to raise large sums of capital in a short period of time.

- *Liquidity.* The public market provides liquidity for owners since they can readily sell their stock.
- *Value.* The marketplace puts a value on the company's stock, which in turn allows value to be placed on the corporation.
- *Image.* The image of a publicly traded corporation often is stronger in the eyes of suppliers, financiers, and customers.[8]

LO3 Review initial public offerings (IPOs) as a source of capital

During the last two decades, many new ventures have sought capital through the public markets. The term **initial public offering (IPO)** is used to represent the registered public offering of a company's securities for the first time. Many times, the number of companies "going public" does not vary much, but the amount of financing raised certainly does. In addition, the economy has a major effect on the IPO markets—as evidenced by the huge upswing in IPOs from 1995 to 1999, when 2,994 companies went public during an economic period of continual growth and prosperity. The year 2000 introduced a correction on the economy, and everything began to constrict, including the IPO market. In 2001, only 91 firms went public, raising $37.1 billion—quite a slump from the all-time high of 868 IPOs in 1996. From 2003 to 2007 there was much more stable and conservative activity among the IPO markets, as evidenced by an approximate average of 220 IPOs. Then 2008 brought the economic downturn globally, and IPOs fell to an all time low of 37 with only $27 billion raised. However since that time the markets have slowly crept back, with 2010 and 2011 demonstrating significant increase with averages of about 180 IPOs with the amounts approaching $45 billion. By 2015 the IPO markets gained their greatest amounts since 2000 with numbers reaching 288 IPOs raising $94 billion. Some of that growth was fueled by the recent IPOs that included some of the largest in history, including Alibaba ($25 billion), Visa ($19.7 billion) and Facebook ($16 billion).[9]

These figures reflect the tremendous *volatility* that exists within the stock market over the years, and thus, entrepreneurs should be aware of the concerns that confront them when they pursue the IPO market. In addition, many new ventures have begun to recognize some other disadvantages of going public. Several of these follow.

- *Costs.* The expenses involved with a public offering are significantly higher than for other sources of capital. Accounting fees, legal fees, and prospectus printing and distribution, as well as the cost of underwriting the stock, can result in high costs.
- *Disclosure.* Detailed disclosures of the company's affairs must be made public. New-venture firms often prefer to keep such information private.
- *Requirements.* The paperwork involved with SEC regulations, as well as continuing performance information, drains large amounts of time, energy, and money from management. Many new ventures consider these elements better invested in helping the company grow.
- *Shareholder pressure.* Management decisions are sometimes short term in nature to maintain a good performance record for earnings and dividends to the shareholders. This pressure can lead to a failure to give adequate consideration to the company's long-term growth and improvement.[10]

The advantages and disadvantages of going public must be weighed carefully. If the decision is to undertake a public offering, it is important that the entrepreneur understand the process involved. Chapter 15 presents some of the complex requirements involved in the IPO process. Here, we summarize by saying that entrepreneurs who pursue the public securities route should be prepared for reporting requirements, disclosure statements, and the shared control and ownership with outside shareholders.

PRIVATE PLACEMENTS

LO4 Discuss private placements as an opportunity for equity capital

Another method of raising capital is through the **private placement** of securities. Small ventures often use this approach.

The SEC provides **Regulation D**, which allows smaller firms to sell stock through what is referred to as **direct public offerings (DPOs)**. It eases the regulations for the reports and statements required for selling stock to private parties—friends, employees, customers, relatives, and local professionals. The most common type of DPO is the Small Corporate Offering Registration, or SCOR (which is included in Rule 504), which provides an exemption to private companies that raise no more than $1 million in any 12-month period through the sale of stock. There are no restrictions on the number or types of investors, and the stock may be freely traded. The SCOR process is easy enough for a small business owner to complete with the assistance of a knowledgeable accountant and attorney. Regulation D defines four separate exemptions, which are based on the amount of money being raised. Along with their accompanying rule, these exemptions follow.

1. **Rule 504—placements up to $1 million.** No specific disclosure/information requirements and no limits on the kind or type of purchasers exist. This makes marketing offerings of this size easier than it was heretofore.

2. **Rule 505—placements of up to $5 million.** The criteria for a public offering exemption are somewhat more difficult to meet than those for smaller offerings. Sales of securities can be made to not more than 35 nonaccredited purchasers and to an unlimited number of accredited purchasers. If purchasers are nonaccredited as well as accredited, then the company must follow specified information disclosure requirements. Investors must have the opportunity to obtain additional information about the company and its management.

3. **Rule 506—placements in excess of $5 million.** Sales can be made to no more than 35 nonaccredited purchasers and an unlimited number of accredited purchasers. However, the nonaccredited purchasers must be "sophisticated" in investment matters. Also, the specific disclosure requirements are more detailed than those for offerings between $500,000 and $5 million. Investors must have the opportunity to obtain additional information about the company and its management.[11]

As noted in Rules 505 and 506, Regulation D uses the term **accredited purchaser**. Included in this category are institutional investors such as banks, insurance companies, venture capital firms, registered investment companies, and small-business investment companies (SBICs), wealthy individuals, and certain tax-exempt organizations with more than $5 million in assets. Everyone not covered in these descriptions is regarded as a nonaccredited purchaser.

THE ENTREPRENEURIAL PROCESS

Bootstrapping: The Art of Doing More with Less

Entrepreneurs continually start up ventures with no investment funds or major bank loans. The National Federation of Independent Business (NFIB) estimates that more than 25 percent of all small ventures were started with less than $500. Now that is making it on a "shoestring." Yet, year after year, we see thousands of new ventures persist through the tough times relying for survival on nothing more than the entrepreneur's grit. Some key aspects to bootstrapping: control costs, remember that cash is king, live frugally, find ways to borrow or leverage rather than buy, and always remain resourceful and creative.

Here are some proven bootstrapping techniques to keep in mind:

1. Make the most of what you have.
2. Be frugal.
3. Search rummage (or garage) sales.
4. Leverage the resources of others.
5. Wear multiple hats in the venture.
6. Share office space.
7. Hire student interns to assist in your business.
8. Find used furniture and equipment to purchase.
9. Encourage customers to pay early.
10. Trade equity for services (not too much though).

In the end, the key is survival; so persistence is the entrepreneur's true asset. As Winston Churchill once said, "Never, never, never give up!!"

Source: Adapted from Laurie Lumenti Garty, "Portrait of a Modern Day Bootstrapper," *SVB Accelerator* (Silicon Valley Bank, 2012); and Andrew J. Sherman, *Raising Capital*, (AMACOM Books, 2012).

"Sophisticated" investors are wealthy individuals who invest more or less regularly in new and early- and late-stage ventures. They are knowledgeable about the technical and commercial opportunities and risks of the businesses in which they invest. They know the kind of information they want about their prospective investment, and they have the experience and ability needed to obtain and analyze the data provided.

The objective of Regulation D is to make it easier and less expensive for small ventures to sell stock. However, many states have not kept pace with these rules. Consequently, many new ventures still find it costly and time consuming to try to clear their offerings in some states. In addition, many are discouraged by the disclosure requirements for offerings of $1,000,000 and over, which are cited under Rules 505 and 506. Despite these difficulties, Regulation D does a lot to simplify small-company financing.[12]

Crowdfunding   A recent financial phenomenon of the twenty-first century is the creation of a funding vehicle for ventures through the use of the general public. Known as crowdfunding, this practice seeks funding for a venture by raising monetary contributions from a large number of people, typically via the internet. In the United States, legislation that is mentioned in the 2012 Jobs Act will allow for a wider pool of small investors with fewer restrictions following the implementation of the act. The crowdfunding model has three principal parts: the entrepreneur who proposes the idea and/or venture to be funded; individuals or groups who support the idea; and a moderating organization (the "platform") that brings the parties together to launch the idea.[13]

There are two distinct forms of crowdfunding. In one form, known as rewards crowdfunding, the entrepreneur will seek a target amount of funding to launch a business concept without incurring debt or sacrificing equity. In return for a donation from those interested in the venture, the entrepreneur provides some type of gift or incentive for participating (e.g., t-shirt, gift card). The other form (and now growing in popularity) is equity crowdfunding where the entrepreneur will share equity in the venture, usually in its early stages, in exchange for the money pledged.[14]

In 2014, there were over 450 crowdfunding platforms (Kickstarter and Indiegogo are the most well-known) as the industry grew to be over $5.1 billion worldwide. It is now estimated that crowdfunding now raises over $2 million per day with some predictions of 100 percent growth each year.

In spite of these promising numbers and predictions, there are numerous critics of crowdfunding. One skeptic warns that equity crowdfunding may be just hype and that it will fail to significantly improve the supply of investment capital or improve the investment return of investors. The fear of future regulations is still a reality to some. In comparing to SEC's Regulation D, crowdfunding appears to be a much tougher approach because Regulation D's disclosure requirement is relatively easier and it lets a venture raise an unlimited amount of capital from an unlimited number of investors, provided those investors are "accredited." So the types of ventures seeking nonaccredited investors through crowdfunding may be only the desperate ones.[15] Therefore, it is wise for any entrepreneur to be aware of the potential concerns that still exist with crowdfunding such as:

- Reputation. reaching financial goals and successfully gathering substantial public support but being unable to deliver on the venture could have a negative impact.
- IP protection. concerns about idea theft and protecting intellectual property.
- Donor dilution. if the same network of supporters is reached out to multiple times, they will eventually tire of the necessary support.
- Public fear. without a proper regulatory framework, the likelihood of a scam or an abuse of funds is high.[16]

In any event, this new form of equity financing is here to stay and with predictions of huge growth, crowdfunding may serve as a viable vehicle for raising those early seed-stage dollars. As with any potential funding mechanism, entrepreneurs must be diligent in their pursuit of complete understanding of the regulations and drawbacks involved with the investments.

8-3 THE VENTURE CAPITAL MARKET

LO5 Study the market for venture capital and to review venture capitalists' evaluation criteria for new ventures

Venture capitalists are professional investors who invest in business ventures, providing capital for start-up, early stage, or expansion. Venture capitalists are looking for a higher rate of return than would be given by more traditional investments. They are a valuable and powerful source of equity funding for new ventures. These experienced professionals provide a full range of financial services for new or growing ventures, including the following.

- Capital for start-ups and expansion
- Market research and strategy for businesses that do not have their own marketing departments
- Management-consulting functions and management audit and evaluation
- Contacts with prospective customers, suppliers, and other important businesspeople
- Assistance in negotiating technical agreements
- Help in establishing management and accounting controls
- Help in employee recruitment and development of employee agreements
- Help in risk management and the establishment of an effective insurance program
- Counseling and guidance in complying with a myriad of government regulations

8-3a Recent Developments in Venture Capital

Following a five-year upward trend from 2004 to 2008, where venture capital grew from investing $22.4 billion in 3,178 deals to investing $30.6 billion in 4,111 deals, the global economic downturn in 2008 caused a major constriction in activity. Venture capitalists (VCs) invested only $19 billion in 3,065 deals in 2009. However, a slow climb back was witnessed in the following years with 3,526 deals drawing $23.2 billion in 2010 and $28.5 billion into 3,673 deals in 2011. By 2015 venture capital deals grew to well over 4,300 with an excess of $48 billion invested.[17] However, it should be understood that the VCs normally raise their investments in later-stage companies and not start-ups. Recently, however, VCs have increased investments in early stage funding from due to number of reasons including:

- The ease and efficiency to launch a venture, get the product to market, and reach larger markets than ever before.
- Sharp reductions in infrastructure costs because of cloud-based computing.
- Shorter product cycles and iterative development processes.
- Selling to global consumers has become feasible for start-up entrepreneurs who can access much larger markets through the Internet.
- College graduates have more sophisticated knowledge about some of the most important technological developments such as mobile, social, and cloud.[18]

Even with this recent surge in early stage funding, it must be understood that today's VCs are far less inclined to finance a start-up firm as opposed to a firm in its more mature stages of early development.

In addition to these developments, a number of major trends have occurred in venture capital over the last few years.

First, the predominant investor class is changing from individuals, foundations, and families to pension institutions. Therefore, sources of capital commitments will continue to shift away from the less-experienced venture capital firm (less than three years) to the more-experienced firm (greater than three years).

Second, innovation has become more global and is no longer the exclusive domain of Silicon Valley and Route 128 in Boston. Therefore, many VCs have opened offices in China, India, Israel, and Vietnam.[19]

Third, funds are becoming more specialized and less homogeneous. The industry has become more diverse, more specialized, and less uniform than is generally thought. Sharp differences are apparent in terms of investing objectives and criteria, strategy, and focusing on particular stages, sizes, and market technology niches. Some of the tech sectors that have funds focused exclusively on them are life sciences, biotech, cleantech, and digital media.[20]

Fourth, syndicated deals are emerging. Accompanying this specialization is a new "farm team" system. Large, established venture capital firms have crafted both formal and informal relationships with new funds as feeder funds. Often, one general partner of the established fund will provide time and know-how to the new fund. The team may share deal flow and coinvest in a syndicated deal. More often than not, these new funds focus on seed-stage or start-up deals that can feed later deals to the more conventional, mainstream venture capital firm with which they are associated.[21]

Fifth, small start-up investments have weakened over the last decade. Many venture capital firms have experienced challenges with some of the high-risk ventures in today's technological environment in their portfolios. As a result, general partners—who are often the most experienced and skillful at finding and nurturing innovative technological ventures—are allocating premium time to salvaging or turning around problem ventures. In addition, because start-up and first-stage investing demands the greatest intensity of involvement by venture capital investors, this type of venture has felt the greatest effects. Finally, other venture capital funds lack professionals who have experience with start-ups and first-stage ventures. Consequently, the level of seed and start-up financing is much lower in comparison to the financing available for early stages, expansion, and acquisition.[22]

Sixth, the industry has become more efficient and more responsive to the needs of the entrepreneur as a result of greater professionalism and greater competition. Now most VCs view themselves as service providers whose job is to provide advice and counsel, which adds more value to the enterprise than just cash. Many VCs today were successful entrepreneurs themselves and can therefore relate to the challenges faced by entrepreneurs and can help with strategies to finance and build a successful enterprise. Entrepreneurs should look for a VC that not only is a source of capital but also has deep industry knowledge and a broad network.[23]

Seventh, the trend is toward a stronger legal environment. The heated competition for venture capital in recent years has resulted in a more sophisticated legal and contractual environment. The frequency and extent of litigation are rising. As an example, the final document governing the investor/entrepreneur relationship—called the investment agreement—can be a few inches thick and can comprise two volumes. In this regard, legal experts recommend that the following provisions be carefully considered in the investment agreement: choice of securities (preferred stock, common stock, convertible debt, etc.), control issues (who maintains voting power), evaluation issues and financial covenants (ability to proceed with mergers and acquisitions), and remedies for breach of contract (rescission of the contract or monetary damages).[24]

8-3b Dispelling Venture Capital Myths

Because many people have mistaken ideas about the role and function of VCs, a number of myths have sprung up about them. Some of these, along with their rebuttals, follow.

MYTH 1: VENTURE CAPITAL FIRMS WANT TO OWN CONTROL OF YOUR COMPANY AND TELL YOU HOW TO RUN THE BUSINESS

No venture capital firm intentionally sets out to own control of a small business. VCs have no desire to run the business. They do not want to tell entrepreneurs how to make day-to-day decisions and have the owner report to them daily. They want the entrepreneur and the management team to run the company profitably. They do want to be consulted on any major decision, but they want no say in daily business operations.[25]

MYTH 2: VENTURE CAPITALISTS ARE SATISFIED WITH A REASONABLE RETURN ON INVESTMENTS

VCs expect very high, exorbitant, unreasonable returns. They can obtain reasonable returns from hundreds of publicly traded companies. They can obtain reasonable returns from many types of investments that do not have the degree of risk involved in financing a small business. Because every venture capital investment involves a high degree of risk, it must have a correspondingly high return on investment.[26]

MYTH 3: VENTURE CAPITALISTS ARE QUICK TO INVEST

It takes a long time to raise venture capital. On the average, it will take six to eight weeks from the initial contact to raise venture capital. If the entrepreneur has a well-prepared business plan, the investor will be able to raise money in that time frame. A VC will see from 50 to 100 proposals a month; of that number, 10 will be of some interest. Of those, two or three will receive a fair amount of analysis, negotiation, and investigation. Of the two or three, just one may be funded. This funneling process of selecting 1 out of a 100 takes a great deal of time. Once the venture capitalist has found that one, he or she will spend a significant amount of time investigating possible outcomes before funding it.

MYTH 4: VENTURE CAPITALISTS ARE INTERESTED IN BACKING NEW IDEAS OR HIGH-TECHNOLOGY INVENTIONS— MANAGEMENT IS A SECONDARY CONSIDERATION

"Execution" is the operative word in the VC world. So, VCs back only good management. If an entrepreneur has a bright idea but a poor managerial background and no experience in the industry, the individual should try to find someone in the industry to bring onto the team. The VC will have a hard time believing that an entrepreneur with no experience in that industry and no managerial ability in his or her background can follow through on a business plan. A good idea is important, but a good management team is even more important.[27]

MYTH 5: VENTURE CAPITALISTS NEED ONLY BASIC SUMMARY INFORMATION BEFORE THEY MAKE AN INVESTMENT

A detailed and well-organized business plan is the only way to gain a venture capital investor's attention and obtain funding. Every VC, before becoming involved, wants the entrepreneur to have thought out the entire business plan and to have written it down in detail.[28]

THE ENTREPRENEURIAL PROCESS

Venture Capitalists' Due Diligence "Deal Killers"

When venture capitalists examine a business plan and then conduct their own due diligence on a proposed venture, certain areas stand out immediately as negative. These are referred to as "deal killers," because it is sometime impossible to get a deal done if any one of these items is identified.

An arrogant management team. This is a team that will not listen, or one that has displayed a lack of integrity or is preoccupied with complete control.

No defendable market position. This occurs when there is no identified intellectual property to defend or any specific market niche to occupy.

Excessive founder salaries. If the focus seems to be on the founders' distributing the proceeds to themselves quickly (or bonuses), then there is a problem of commitment to the venture.

Vulnerability of the founder. Whenever there is overdependence on one person (a particular founder) for his or her skills or persona, there could be a major issue.

Yesterday's news. If a business plan is perceived as "overshopped" or simply presented too much over a short period of time, then it may be perceived as an "old idea."

Ignorance of the competitive landscape. Whenever the team lacks the understanding of the real strengths and weaknesses of the competition, a major red flag goes up for the VC.

Unrealistic expectations. A typical problem of entrepreneurs is their lack of understanding of the valuation of their venture and the deal terms involved in the VC investment proposal. Usually the entrepreneurs think that their venture is worth far more than the VC does.

Source: Adapted from: Andrew J. Sherman, *Raising Capital*, 3rd ed. (New York: AMACOM Books, 2012), 196.

8-3c Venture Capitalists' Objectives

VCs have different objectives from most others who provide capital to new ventures. Lenders, for example, are interested in security and payback. As partial owners of the companies they invest in, VCs, however, are most concerned with return on investment. As a result, they put a great deal of time into weighing the risk of a venture against the potential return. They carefully measure both the product/service and the management. Figure 8.2 illustrates an evaluation system for measuring these two critical factors—status of product/service and status of management—on four levels. The figure demonstrates that ideas as well as entrepreneurs are evaluated when the viability of a venture proposal is determined.

VCs are particularly interested in making a large return on investment (ROI). Table 8.2 provides some commonly sought targets. Of course, these targets are flexible. They would be reduced, for example, in cases where a company has a strong market potential, is able to generate good cash flow, or the management has invested a sizable portion of its own funds in the venture. However, an annual goal of 20 to 30 percent ROI would not be considered too high, regardless of the risks involved.

FIGURE 8.2   VENTURE CAPITALIST SYSTEM OF EVALUATING PRODUCT/SERVICE AND MANAGEMENT

Status of Product/Service

Level 4 Fully developed product/service Established market Satisfied users	4/1	4/2	4/3	4/4
Level 3 Fully developed product/service Few users as of yet Market assumed	3/1	3/2	3/3	3/4
Level 2 Operable pilot or prototype Not yet developed for production Market assumed	2/1	2/2	2/3	2/4
Level 1 Product/service idea Not yet operable Market assumed	1/1	1/2	1/3	1/4

Riskiest (for Status of Product/Service)

Level 1	**Level 2**	**Level 3**	**Level 4**
Individual founder/ entrepreneur	Two founders Other personnel not yet identified	Partial management team Members identified to join company when funding is received	Fully staffed, experienced management team

◄— Riskiest —►

Status of Management

Source: Stanley Rich and David Gumpert, *Business Plans That Win $$$* (New York: Harper & Row, 1985), 169.

TABLE 8.2 RETURNS ON INVESTMENT TYPICALLY SOUGHT BY VENTURE CAPITALISTS		
Stage of Business	**Expected Annual Return on Investment**	**Expected Increase on Initial Investment**
Start-up business (idea stage)	60% +	10–15 × investment
First-stage financing (new business)	40%–60%	6–12 × investment
Second-stage financing (development stage)	30%–50%	4–8 × investment
Third-stage financing (expansion stage)	25%–40%	3–6 × investment
Turnaround situation	50% +	8–15 × investment

Source: Adapted from W. Keith Schilit, "How to Obtain Venture Capital," *Business Horizons* (May/June 1987): 78. Copyright © 1987 by the Foundation for the School of Business at Indiana University.

8-3d Criteria for Evaluating New-Venture Proposals

In addition to the evaluation of product ideas and management strength, numerous criteria are used to evaluate new-venture proposals. Researcher Dean A. Shepherd developed a list of eight critical factors that VCs use in the evaluation of new ventures, as follows:

1. Timing of entry
2. Key success factor stability
3. Educational capability
4. Lead time
5. Competitive rivalry
6. Entry wedge imitation
7. Scope
8. Industry-related competence[29]

Each factor was defined from the high/low perspective (see Table 8.3 for definitions).

Another set of researchers developed 28 of these criteria, grouped into six major categories:

1. Entrepreneur's personality
2. Entrepreneur's experience
3. Product or service characteristics
4. Market characteristics
5. Financial considerations
6. Nature of the venture team[30]

Other researchers have uncovered similar results. For example, one study examined the criteria venture capitalists use during a proposal screening and evaluation. Table 8.4 outlines the factors used in the study.[31] Their results showed that venture capitalists reached a "go/no go" decision in an average of six minutes on the initial screening and in less than 21 minutes on the overall proposal evaluation. They found that the venture capital firm's requirements and the long-term growth and profitability of the proposed venture's industry were the critical factors for initial screening. In the more-detailed evaluation, the background of the entrepreneurs as well as the characteristics of the proposal itself were important.

In a study that examined the "demand side" of venture capital, researchers surveyed 318 private entrepreneurs who sought out venture capital in amounts of $100,000 or more. The study found that entrepreneurs' success with acquiring funding is related to four general,

TABLE 8.3 FACTORS IN VENTURE CAPITALISTS' EVALUATION PROCESS

Attribute	Level	Definition
Timing of entry	Pioneer	Enters a new industry first
	Late follower	Enters an industry late in the industry's stage of development
Key success factor stability	High	Requirements necessary for success will not change radically during industry development
	Low	Requirements necessary for success will change radically during industry development
Educational capability	High	Considerable resources and skills available to overcome market ignorance through education
	Low	Few resources or skills available to overcome market ignorance through education
Lead time	Long	An extended period of monopoly for the first entrant prior to competitors entering the industry
	Short	A minimal period of monopoly for the first entrant prior to competitors entering this industry
Competitive rivalry	High	Intense competition among industry members during industry development
	Low	Little competition among industry members during industry development
Entry wedge mimicry	High	Considerable imitation of the mechanisms used by other firms to enter this, or any other, industry—e.g., a franchisee
	Low	Minimal imitation of the mechanisms used by other firms to enter this, or any other, industry—e.g., introducing a new product
Scope	Broad	A firm that spreads its resources across a wide spectrum of the market—e.g., many segments of the market
	Narrow	A firm that concentrates on intensively exploiting a small segment of the market—e.g., targeting a niche
Industry-related competence	High	Venturer has considerable experience and knowledge with the industry being entered or a related industry
	Low	Venturer has minimal experience and knowledge with the industry being entered or a related industry

Source: Dean A. Shepherd, "Venture Capitalists' Introspection: A Comparison of 'In Use' and 'Espoused' Decision Policies," *Journal of Small Business Management* (April 1999): 76–87; and "Venture Capitalists' Assessment of New Venture Survival," *Management Science* (May 1999): 621–32. Reprinted by permission. Copyright © 1999, the Institute for Operation Research and the Management Sciences (INFORMS), 7240 Parkway Drive, Suite 310, Hanover, MD 21076 USA.

variable categories: (1) characteristics of the entrepreneurs, including education, experience, and age; (2) characteristics of the enterprise, including stage, industry type, and location (e.g., rural or urban); (3) characteristics of the request, including amount, business plan, and prospective capital source; and (4) sources of advice, including technology, preparation of the business plan, and places to seek funding.[32]

TABLE 8.4   VENTURE CAPITALISTS' SCREENING CRITERIA

Venture Capital Firm Requirements

Must fit within lending guidelines of venture firm for stage and size of investment

Proposed business must be within geographic area of interest

Prefer proposals recommended by someone known to venture capitalist

Proposed industry must be kind of industry invested in by venture firm

Nature of the Proposed Business

Projected growth should be relatively large within five years of investment

Economic Environment of Proposed Industry

Industry must be capable of long-term growth and profitability

Economic environment should be favorable to a new entrant

Proposed Business Strategy

Selection of distribution channel(s) must be feasible

Product must demonstrate defendable competitive position

Financial Information on the Proposed Business

Financial projections should be realistic

Proposal Characteristics

Must have full information

Should be a reasonable length, be easy to scan, have an executive summary, and be professionally presented

Must contain a balanced presentation

Use graphics and large print to emphasize key points

Entrepreneur/Team Characteristics

Must have relevant experience

Should have a balanced management team in place

Management must be willing to work with venture partners

Entrepreneur who has successfully started previous business given special consideration

Source: John Hall and Charles W. Hofer, "Venture Capitalists' Decision Criteria in New Venture Evaluation," *Journal of Business Venturing* (January 1993): 37.

The business plan is a critical element in a new-venture proposal and should be complete, clear, and well presented. VCs generally will analyze five major aspects of the plan: (1) the proposal size, (2) financial projections, (3) investment recovery, (4) competitive advantage, and (5) company management.

The evaluation process typically takes place in stages. The four most common stages follow.

STAGE 1: INITIAL SCREENING

This is a quick review of the basic venture to see if it meets the VC's particular interests.

TABLE 8.5 ESSENTIAL ELEMENTS FOR A SUCCESSFUL PRESENTATION TO A VENTURE CAPITALIST

Team Must:

- Be able to adapt
- Know the competition
- Be able to manage rapid growth
- Be able to manage an industry leader
- Have relevant background and industry experience
- Show financial commitment to company, not just sweat equity
- Be strong with a proven track record in the industry unless the company is a start-up or seed investment

Product Must:

- Be real and work
- Be unique
- Be proprietary
- Meet a well-defined need in the marketplace
- Demonstrate potential for product expansion, to avoid being a one-product company Emphasize usability
- Solve a problem or improve a process significantly
- Be for mass production with potential for cost reduction

Market Must:

- Have current customers and the potential for many more
- Grow rapidly (25% to 45% per year)
- Have a potential for market size in excess of $250 million
- Show where and how you are competing in the marketplace
- Have potential to become a market leader
- Outline any barriers to entry

Business Plan Must:

- Tell the full story, not just one chapter
- Promote a company, not just a product
- Be compelling
- Show the potential for rapid growth and knowledge of your industry, especially competition and market vision Include milestones for measuring performance
- Show how you plan to beat or exceed those milestones
- Address all of the key areas
- Detail projections and assumptions; be realistic
- Serve as a sales document
- Include a strong and well-written executive summary
- Show excitement and color
- Show superior rate of return (a minimum of 30% to 40% per year) with a clear exit strategy

Source: Andrew J. Sherman, *Raising Capital*, 3rd ed. (New York: AMACOM Books, 2012), 190.

STAGE 2: EVALUATION OF THE BUSINESS PLAN

A detailed reading of the plan is done to evaluate the factors mentioned earlier.

STAGE 3: ORAL PRESENTATION

The entrepreneur verbally presents the plan to the VC. See Table 8.5 for a thorough understanding of the key elements necessary in presenting to a VC.

STAGE 4: FINAL EVALUATION

After analyzing the plan and visiting with suppliers, customers, consultants, and others, the VC makes a final decision.

This four-step process screens out approximately 98 percent of all venture plans. The rest receive some degree of financial backing.

8-3e Evaluating the Venture Capitalist

The VC will evaluate the entrepreneur's proposal carefully, and the entrepreneur should not hesitate to evaluate the venture capitalist. Does the VC understand the proposal? Is the individual familiar with the business? Is the person someone with whom the entrepreneur can work? If the answers reveal a poor fit, it is best for the entrepreneur to look for a different VC.

One researcher found that VCs do add value to an entrepreneurial firm beyond the money they supply, especially in high-innovation ventures. Because of this finding, entrepreneurs need to choose the appropriate VC at the outset, and, most important, they must keep the communication channels open as the firm grows.[33]

LO6 Discuss the importance of evaluating venture capitalists for a proper selection

On the other hand, it is important to realize that the choice of a VC can be limited. Although funds are available today, they tend to be controlled by fewer groups, and the quality of the venture must be promising. Even though two-and-one-half times more money is available today for seed financing than was available 10 years ago, the number of venture capital firms is not increasing. In addition, the trend toward concentration of venture capital under the control of a few firms is increasing.[34]

Nevertheless, the entrepreneur should not be deterred from evaluating prospective VCs.

There are a number of important questions that entrepreneurs should ask of venture capitalists. Following are seven of the most important, along with their rationales.

Key Questions or Evaluating a VC Firm

1. Does the venture capital firm in fact invest in your industry? How many deals has the firm actually done in your field?

2. What is it like to work with this venture capital firm? Get references. (An unscreened list of referrals, including CEOs of companies that the firm has been successful with—as well as those it has not—can be very helpful.)

3. What experience does the partner doing your deal have, and what is his or her clout within the firm? Check out the experiences of other entrepreneurs.

4. How much time will the partner spend with your company if you run into trouble? A seed-stage company should ask, "You guys are a big fund, and you say you can seed me a quarter of a million dollars. How often will you be able to see me?" The answer should be at least once a week.

5. How healthy is the venture capital fund, and how much has been invested? A venture firm with a lot of troubled investments will not have much time to spare. If most of the fund is invested, there may not be much money available for your follow-on rounds.

6. Are the investment goals of the venture capitalists consistent with your own?

7. Have the venture firm and the partner championing your deal been through any economic downturns? A good venture capitalist won't panic when things get bad.[35]

Evaluating and even negotiating with the VC are critical to establishing the best equity funding. You may worry that if you rock the boat by demanding too much, the venture capital firm will lose interest. That's an understandable attitude; venture capital is hard to get and if you've gotten as far as the negotiating process, you're already among the lucky few.

But that doesn't mean you have to roll over and play dead. A venture capital investment is a business deal that you may have to live with for a long time. Although you'll have to give ground on many issues when you come to the bargaining table, there is always a point beyond which the deal no longer makes sense for you. You must draw a line and fight for the points that really count.[36]

8-4 INFORMAL RISK CAPITAL: ANGEL FINANCING

LO7 Examine the existing informal risk-capital market ("angel capital")

Not all venture capital is raised through formal sources such as public and private placements. Many wealthy people in the United States are looking for investment opportunities; they are referred to as **business angels** or **informal risk capitalists**. These individuals constitute a huge potential investment pool, as the following calculations show. Using the recent Forbes richest 400 list,[37] a few interesting and creative assumptions could be made to demonstrate the power of individuals' ability to finance new ventures.

- The aggregate net worth of the *Forbes* richest 400 Americans was $2.29 trillion ($5.73 billion per person)

- 11 members of the list are under 40 years old

- Ten of the top 15 are entrepreneurs including: Bill Gates (Microsoft); Warren Buffett (Berkshire Hathaway); Larry Ellison (Oracle); Charles and David Koch (Koch Industries); Michael Bloomberg (Bloomberg); Mark Zuckerberg (Facebook); Larry Page & Sergey Brin (Google); Jeff Bezos (Amazon). Their total worth is $444 billion.

- If 1 percent of those entrepreneurs' wealth were available for venture financing, the pool of funds would amount to $4.4 billion.

- 113 billionaires did not even make the list. If 1 percent of their funds were available for venture financing, the pool of funds would be at least $1.1 billion

- If both amounts could be available for venture deals, there would be a total of $5.5 billion.

- If the typical venture deal took $200,000 there would be the potential of 27,500 deals!

William E. Wetzel, Jr., considered to be the pioneer researcher in the field of informal risk capital, defined this type of investor as someone who has already made his or her money and now seeks out promising young ventures to support financially. "Angels are typically entrepreneurs, retired corporate executives, or professionals who have a net worth of more than $1 million and an income of more than $100,000 a year. They're self-starters. And they're trying to perpetuate the system that made them successful."[38] If entrepreneurs are looking for such an angel, Wetzel would advise, "Don't look very far away—within 50 miles or within a day's drive at most. And that's because this is not a full-time profession for them."[39]

Why would individuals be interested in investing in a new venture from which professional VCs see no powerful payoff? It may be, of course, that the reduced investment amount reduces the total risk involved in the investment. However, informal investors seek other, nonfinancial returns—among them the creation of jobs in areas of high unemployment, development of technology for social needs (e.g., medical or energy), urban revitalization, minority or disadvantaged assistance, and personal satisfaction from assisting entrepreneurs.[40]

How do informal investors find projects? Research studies indicate that they use a network of friends. Additionally, many states are formulating venture capital networks, which attempt to link informal investors with entrepreneurs and their new or growing ventures.

8-4a Types of Angel Investors

Angel investors can be classified into five basic groups:

- **Corporate angels.** Typically, so-called "corporate angels" are senior managers at *Fortune* 1000 corporations who have been laid off with generous severances or have taken early retirement. In addition to receiving the cash, an entrepreneur may persuade the corporate angel to occupy a senior management position.

- **Entrepreneurial angels.** The most prevalent type of investors, most of these individuals own and operate highly successful businesses. Because these investors have other sources of income, and perhaps significant wealth from IPOs or partial buyouts, they will take bigger risks and invest more capital. The best way to market your deal to these angels, therefore, is as a synergistic opportunity. Reflecting this orientation, entrepreneurial angels seldom look at companies outside of their own area of expertise and will participate in no more than a handful of investments at any one time. These investors almost always take a seat on the board of directors but rarely assume management duties. They will make fair-sized investments—typically $200,000 to $500,000—and invest more as the company progresses.

- **Enthusiast angels.** Whereas entrepreneurial angels tend to be somewhat calculating, enthusiasts simply like to be involved in deals. Most enthusiast angels are age 65 or older, independently wealthy from success in a business they started, and have abbreviated work schedules. For them, investing is a hobby. As a result, they typically play no role in management and rarely seek to be placed on a board. Because they spread themselves across so many companies, the size of their investments tends to be small—ranging from as little as $10,000 to perhaps a few hundred thousand dollars.

- **Micromanagement angels.** Micromanagers are very serious investors. Some of them were born wealthy, but the vast majority attained wealth through their own efforts. Unfortunately, this heritage makes them dangerous. Because most have successfully built a company, micromanagers attempt to impose the tactics that worked for them on their portfolio companies. Although they do not seek an active management role, micromanagers usually demand a seat on the board of directors. If business is not going well, they will try to bring in new managers.

- **Professional angels.** The term *professional* in this context refers to the investor's occupation, such as doctor, lawyer, and, in some very rare instances, accountant. Professional angels like to invest in companies that offer a product or service with which they have some experience. They rarely seek a board seat, but they can be unpleasant to deal with when the going gets rough and may believe that a company is in trouble before it actually is. Professional angels will invest in several companies at one time, and their capital contributions range from $25,000 to $200,000.[41]

The importance of understanding the role of informal risk capital is illustrated by the fact that the pool of today's angel capital is five times the amount in the institutional venture capital market, providing money to 20 to 30 times as many companies. Angels invest more than $25 billion a year in 60,000 to 70,000 companies nationwide, twice the amount of money and twice the number of companies as 10 years ago.[42]

Recent research by Jeffrey Sohl, who worked with William E. Wetzel, Jr. on angel capital and who is now the director of the Center for Venture Research at the University of New Hampshire, shows a marked increase in angel investing activity over the past few years. In 2013 there were a total of $24.8 billion invested in 70,730 entrepreneurial ventures. This accounted for 298,800 active angel investors with an average of $83,050 per investment. Software remained the top sector position with 23 percent of total angel investments, followed by media (16 percent), healthcare services/medical devices and equipment (14 percent), and biotech (11 percent). Angels increased their investments in the seed and start-up stage (45 percent) as well as increased interest in early stage investing (41 percent). Angel investments continue to be a significant contributor to job growth with the creation of 290,020 new jobs in the United States in 2013, or 4.1 jobs per angel investment.

Another important consideration for *angel capital* is that a larger percentage of informal investment is devoted to seed a start-up business as opposed to venture capital. The median size of an informal investment is $350,000, which indicates the importance of informal risk capital to entrepreneurs seeking smaller amounts of start-up financing.[43] (See Table 8.6 for some "angel stats.") Obviously, informal networks are a major potential capital source for entrepreneurs. However, every entrepreneur should be careful and thorough in his or her approach to business angels—there are advantages and disadvantages associated with angel financing. Table 8.7 outlines some of the critical pros and cons of dealing with business angels. Only through recognition of these issues will entrepreneurs be able to establish the best relationship with a business angel.

TABLE 8.6 "ANGEL STATS"	
Typical deal size	$250,000–$600,000
Typical recipient	Start-up firms
Cash-out time frame	5 to 7 years
Expected return	35% to 50% a year
Ownership stake	Less than 50%

Source: Jeffrey Sohl, University of New Hampshire's Center for Venture Research, 2011; and the Halo Report, 2011.

TABLE 8.7 PROS AND CONS OF DEALING WITH ANGEL INVESTORS

Pros:

1. Angels engage in smaller financial deals.

2. Angels prefer seed stage or start-up stage.

3. Angels invest in various industry sectors.

4. Angels are located in local geographic areas.

5. Angels are genuinely interested in the entrepreneur.

Cons:

1. Angels offer no additional investment money.

2. Angels cannot offer any national image.

3. Angels lack important contacts for future leverage.

4. Angels may want some decision making with the entrepreneur.

5. Angels are getting more sophisticated in their investment decisions.

SUMMARY

This chapter has examined the various forms of capital formation for entrepreneurs. Initial consideration was given to debt and equity financing in the form of commercial banks, trade credit, accounts receivable financing, factoring and finance companies, and various forms of equity instruments.

Public stock offerings have advantages and disadvantages as a source of equity capital. Although large amounts of money can be raised in short periods of time, the entrepreneur must sacrifice a degree of control and ownership. In addition, the SEC has myriad requirements and regulations that must be followed.

Private placements are an alternative means of raising equity capital for new ventures. This source is often available to entrepreneurs who seek venture capital in amounts of less than $500,000, although it is possible that up to $5 million could be raised with no more than 35 nonaccredited purchasers. The SEC's Regulation D clearly outlines the exemptions and requirements involved in a private placement. This placement's greatest advantage to the entrepreneur is limited company disclosure and only a small number of shareholders.

In recent years, the venture capital market has grown dramatically. Billions of dollars are now invested annually to seed new ventures or help fledgling enterprises grow. The individuals who invest these funds are known as VCs. A number of myths that have sprung up about these capitalists were discussed and refuted.

VCs use a number of different criteria when evaluating new-venture proposals. In the main, these criteria focus on two areas: the entrepreneur and the investment potential of the venture. The evaluation process typically involves four stages: initial screening, business plan evaluation, oral presentation, and final evaluation.

In recent years, informal risk capital has begun to play an important role in new-venture financing. Everyone with money to invest in new ventures can be considered a source for this type of capital. Some estimates put the informal risk capital pool at more than $25 billion. Entrepreneurs who are unable to secure financing through banks or through public or private stock offerings typically will turn to the informal risk capital market by seeking out friends, associates, and other contacts who may have (or know of someone who has) money to invest in a new venture.

KEY TERMS

accounts receivable financing	direct public offering (DPO)	Peer-to-peer lending (P2P)
accredited purchaser	equity financing	private placement
angel capital	factoring	Regulation D
business angel	finance companies	sophisticated investor
crowdfunding	informal risk capitalist	trade credit
debt financing	initial public offering (IPO)	venture capitalist

REVIEW AND DISCUSSION QUESTIONS

1. Using Figure 8.1, describe some of the sources of capital available to entrepreneurs, and discuss how they correlate to the varying levels of risk involved with each stage of the venture.

2. What are the benefits and drawbacks of equity and of debt financing? Briefly discuss both.

3. If a new venture has its choice between long-term debt and equity financing, which would you recommend? Why?

4. Why would a venture capitalist be more interested in buying a convertible debenture for $500,000 than in lending the new business $500,000 at a 4 percent interest rate?

5. What are some of the advantages of going public? What are some of the disadvantages?

6. What is the objective of Regulation D?

7. If a person inherited $100,000 and decided to buy stock in a new venture through a private placement, how would Regulation D affect this investor?

8. Is it easier or more difficult to get new-venture financing today? Why?

9. Some entrepreneurs do not like to seek new-venture financing because they feel that venture capitalists are greedy. In your opinion, is this true? Do these capitalists want too much?

10. Identify and describe three objectives of venture capitalists.

11. How would a venture capitalist use Figure 8.2 to evaluate an investment? Use an illustration in your answer.

12. Identify and describe four of the most common criteria venture capitalists use to evaluate a proposal.

13. In a new-venture evaluation, what are the four stages through which a proposal typically goes? Describe each in detail.

14. An entrepreneur is in the process of contacting three different venture capitalists and asking each to evaluate her new business proposal. What questions should she be able to answer about each of the three?

15. An entrepreneur of a new venture has had no success in getting financing from formal venture capitalists. He now has decided to turn to the informal risk capital market. Who is in this market? How would you recommend that the entrepreneur contact these individuals?

NOTES

1. Gavin Cassar, "The Financing of Business Start-Ups," *Journal of Business Venturing* 19, no. 2 (2004): 261–83; Brian T. Gregory, Matthew W. Rutherford, Sharon Oswald, and Lorraine Gardiner, "An Empirical Investigation of the Growth Cycle Theory of Small Firm Financing," *Journal of Small Business Management* 43, no. 4 (2005): 382–92; Jay Ebben and Alec Johnson, "Bootstrapping in Small Firms: An Empirical Analysis of Change over Time," *Journal of Business Venturing* 21, no. 6 (2006): 851–65; Armin Schweinbacher, "A Theoretical Analysis of Optimal Financing Strategies for Different Types of Capital Constrained Entrepreneurs," *Journal of Business Venturing* 22, no. 6 (2007): 753–81; Arnout Seghers, Sophie Manigart, and Tom Vanacker, "The Impact of Human and Social Capital on Entrepreneurs' Knowledge of Finance Alternatives," *Journal of Small Business Management* 50, no. 1 (2012): 63–86; and Sara Jonsson and Jessica Lindbergh, "The Development of Social Capital and Financing of Entrepreneurial Firms: From Financial Bootstrapping to Bank Funding," *Entrepreneurship Theory and Practice* 37, no. 4 (2013): 661–86.

2. *The State of Small Business: A Report of the President,* 2007 (Washington, DC: Government Printing Office, 2007), 25–48; Jean-Etienne de Bettignies and James A. Brander, "Financing Entrepreneurship: Bank Finance versus Venture Capital, *Journal of Business Venturing* 22, no. 6 (2007): 808–32; see also http://www.sba.gov(Services-Financial Assistance), 2008.

3. John M. Mason, "The Number of Commercial Banks in the U.S Banking System Continues to Decline," *Seeking Alpha*, August 23, 2011. Data updated for 2015.

4. A complete explanation can be found in Ralph Alterowitz and Jon Zonderman, *Financing Your New*

or *Growing Business* (Irvine, CA: Entrepreneur Press, 2002); see also Elijah Brewer III, "On Lending to Small Firms," *Journal of Small Business Management* 45, no. 1 (2007): 42–46; and Jess H. Chua, James J. Chrisman, Franz Kellermanns, and Zhenyu Wu, "Family Involvement and New Venture Debt Financing," *Journal of Business Venturing* 26, no. 4 (2011): 472–88.

5. Angus Loten, "Peer-to-Peer Loans Grow," *Wall Street Journal,* June 17, 2011; http://online.wsj.com /article/SB100014240527487034212045763311 41779953526.html (accessed February 21, 2012); Garry Bruton, Susanna Khavul, Donald Siegel and Mike Wright, "New Financial Alternatives in Seeding Entrepreneurship: Microfinance, Crowdfunding, and Peer-to-Peer Innovations," *Entrepreneurship Theory and Practice* 39, no. 1 (2015): 9–26; and Emanuele Brancati, "Innovation Financing and the Role of Relationship Lending for SMEs," *Small Business Economics* 44, no. 2 (2015): 449–73.

6. Truls Erikson, "Entrepreneurial Capital: The Emerging Venture's Most Important Asset and Competitive Advantage," *Journal of Business Venturing* 17, no. 3 (2002): 275–90; see also Larry D. Wall, "On Investing in the Equity of Small Firms," *Journal of Small Business Management* 45, no. 1 (2007): 89–93.

7. PriceWaterhouseCoopers, MoneyTree™ Survey 2014, https://www.pwcmoneytree.com/

8. See "Going Public," *NASDAQ Stock Market,* 2005, http://www.nasdaq.com/about/GP2005_cover_toc.pdf (accessed April 11, 2008).

9. Jean-Sébastien Michel, "Return on Recent VC Investment and Long-Run IPO Returns," *Entrepreneurship Theory and Practice* 38, no. 3 (2014): 527–49; J. J. McGrath, "2014 Biggest Year for US IPO Market Since 2000, with Alibaba Leading the Way," *International Business Times,* January 5, 2015 (accessed January 6, 2015).

10. See "Going Public," *NASDAQ Stock Market*, 2005, http://www.nasdaq.com/about/GP2005_cover_toc.pdf (accessed April 11, 2008).

11. A summary can be found in business law texts such as Jane P. Mallor, A. James Barnes, Thomas Bowers, and Arlen W. Langvardt, *Business Law: The Ethical, Global, and E-Commerce Environment,* 15th ed. (New York: McGraw-Hill Irwin, 2013), 1150–55.

12. For more on private placements, see T. B. Folta and J. J. Janney, "Strategic Benefits to Firms Issuing Private Equity Placements," *Strategic Management Journal* 25, no. 3 (March 2004): 223–42; Thomas J. Morgan, "Raising Capital—What You Don't Know Could Hurt You," *The National Law Review*, March 6, 2013 (accessed January 7, 2015).

13. Paul Belleflamme, Thomas Lambert and Armin Schwienbacher, "Crowdfunding: Tapping the Right Crowd," *Journal of Business Venturing* 29, no. 5 (2014): 585–609; Ethan Mollick, "The Dynamics of Crowdfunding: An Exploratory Study," *Journal of Business Venturing* 29 no. 1 (2014): 1–16; and John Prpić, Prashant P. Shukla, Jan H. Kietzmann, and Ian

P. McCarthy, "How to Work a Crowd: Developing Crowd Capital Through Crowdsourcing," *Business Horizons* 58, no. 1 (2015): 77–85.

14. Carol Tice, "The Myth of Magical Crowdfunding— And What Actually Works," Forbes, October 10, 2014 (accessed January 6, 2015); Massimo G. Colombo, Chiara Franzoni, and Cristina Rossi-Lamastra, "Internal Social Capital and the Attraction of Early Contributions in Crowdfunding," *Entrepreneurship Theory and Practice* 39, no. 1 (2015): 75–100; and Magdalena Cholakova and Bart Clarysse, "Does the Possibility to Make Equity Investments in Crowdfunding Projects Crowd Out Reward-Based Investments?" *Entrepreneurship Theory and Practice* 39, no. 1 (2015): 145–72.

15. Jim Saksa, "Equity Crowdfunding is a Disaster Waiting to Happen," *Slate,* June 23, 2014 (accessed January 6, 2015).

16. Daniel Isenberg, "The Road to Crowdfunding Hell," *Harvard Business Review*, April 23, 2012 (accessed January 6, 2015).

17. PricewaterhouseCoopers/National Venture Capital Association, MoneyTree™ Report, 2014; Bryan Pearce, "Adapting and Evolving: Global Venture Capital Insights and Trends 2014," E&Y Venture Capital Center of Excellence, Ernst & Young, 2014.

18. David Blumberg, "The Ascent of Early-Stage Venture Capital," *Tech Crunch*, June 7, 2014 (accessed January 5, 2015).

19. Douglas Cumming, Daniel Schmidt, and Uwe Walz, "Legality and Venture Capital Governance Around the World," *Journal of Business Venturing* 25, no. 1 (2010): 54–72; Joseph A. LiPuma and Sarah Park, "Venture Capitalists' Risk Mitigation of Portfolio Company Internationalization," *Entrepreneurship Theory and Practice* 38, no. 5 (2014): 1183–205.

20. Edgar Norton and Bernard H. Tenenbaum, "Specialization versus Diversification as a Venture Capital Investment Strategy," *Journal of Business Venturing* 8, no. 5 (1993): 431–42; Jens Burchardt, Ulrich Hommel, Dzidziso Samuel Kamuriwo, and Carolina Billitteri, "Venture Capital Contracting in Theory and Practice: Implications for Entrepreneurship Research," *Entrepreneurship Theory and Practice* (2015), in press.

21. Dirk De Clercq, Vance H. Fried, Oskari Lehtonen, and Harry J. Sapienza, "An Entrepreneur's Guide to the Venture Capital Galaxy," *Academy of Management Perspectives* 20 (August 2006): 90–112; Dimo Dimov and Hana Milanov, "The Interplay of Need and Opportunity in Venture Capital Investment Syndication," *Journal of Business Venturing* 25, no. 4 (2010): 331–48; and Michel Ferrary, "Syndication of Venture Capital Investment: The Art of Resource Pooling," *Entrepreneurship Theory and Practice* 34, no. 5 (2010): 885–907.

22. Douglas Cumming and Sofia Johan, "Venture Capital Investment Duration," *Journal of Small Business Management* 48, no. 2 (2010): 228–57; Sandip Basu, Corey Phelps, and Suresh Kotha, "Towards Understanding

Who Makes Corporate Venture Capital Investments and Why," *Journal of Business Venturing* 26, no. 2 (2011): 153–71; and Jeffrey S. Petty and Marc Gruber, "In Pursuit of the Real Deal": A Longitudinal Study of VC Decision Making," *Journal of Business Venturing* 26, no. 2 (2011): 172–88.

23. Interview with Sanjay Subhedar, founding partner of Storm Ventures, Menlo Park, CA, May 2014; Haemen Dennis Park and H. Kevin Steensma, "When Does Corporate Venture Capital Add Value for New Ventures," *Strategic Management Journal* 33, no. 1 (2012): 1–22; Violetta Gerasymenko and Jonathan D. Arthurs, "New Insights into Venture Capitalists' Activity: IPO and Time-to-Exit Forecast as Antecedents of Their Post-Investment Involvement," *Journal of Business Venturing* 29, no. 3 (2014): 405–20.

24. Ghislaine Bouillet-Cordonnier, "Legal Aspects of Start-Up Evaluation and Adjustment Methods," *Journal of Business Venturing* 7, no. 2 (1992): 91–102; PriceWaterhouseCoopers, MoneyTree™ Report, 2011; and Cumming, Schmidt, and Walz, "Legality and Venture Capital Governance Around the World."

25. Sharon Gifford, "Limited Attention and the Role of the Venture Capitalist," *Journal of Business Venturing* 12, no. 6 (1997): 459–82; Dimo Dimov, Dean A. Shepherd, and Kathleen M. Sutcliffe, "Requisite Expertise, Firm Reputation, and Status in Venture Capital Investment Allocation Decisions," *Journal of Business Venturing* 22, no. 4 (2007): 481–502; and Will Drover, Matthew S. Wood, and G. Tyge Payne, "The Effects of Perceived Control on Venture Capitalist Investment Decisions: A Configurational Perspective," *Entrepreneurship Theory and Practice* 38, no. 4 (2014): 833–61.

26. Jonathan D. Arthurs and Lowell W. Busenitz, "Dynamic Capabilities and Venture Performance: The Effects of Venture Capitalists," *Journal of Business Venturing* 21, no. 2 (2006): 195–216; and Dirk De Lercq and Harry J. Sapienza, "Effects of Relational Capital and Commitment on Venture Capitalists' Perception of Portfolio Company Performance," *Journal of Business Venturing* 21, no. 3 (2006): 326–47. See also Charles Baden-Fuller, Alison Dean, Peter McNamara, and Bill Hilliard, "Raising the Returns to Venture Finance," *Journal of Business Venturing* 21, no. 3 (2006): 265–85; Yixi Ning, Wei Wang and Bo Yu, "The driving forces of venture capital investments," *Small Business Economics* 44, no. 2 (2015): 315–44.

27. Howard E. Van Auken, "Financing Small Technology-Based Companies: The Relationship Between Familiarity with Capital and Ability to Price and Negotiate Investment," *Journal of Small Business Management* 39, no. 3 (2001): 240–58; Joris J. Ebbers and Nachoem M. Wijnberg, "Nascent Ventures Competing for Start-up Capital: Matching Reputations and Investors," *Journal of Business Venturing* 27, no. 3 (2012): 372–84; and Andrew L. Maxwell and Moren Lévesque, "Trustworthiness: A Critical gredient for Entrepreneurs Seeking Investors," *Entrepreneurship Theory and Practice* 38, no. 5 (2014): 1057–80.

28. Andrew J. Sherman, *Raising Capital,* 3rd ed. (New York: AMACOM Books, 2012); Yong Li and Joseph T. Mahoney, "When Are Venture Capital Projects Initiated?" *Journal of Business Venturing* 26, no. 2 (2011): 239–54; Spyros Arvanitis and Tobias Stucki, "The Impact of Venture Capital on the Persistence of Innovation Activities of Start-ups," *Small Business Economics* 42, no. 4 (2014): 849–70; and Kimberly A. Eddleston, Jamie J. Ladge, Cheryl Mitteness and Lakshmi Balachandra, "Do You See What I See? Signaling Effects of Gender and Firm Characteristics on Financing Entrepreneurial Ventures," *Entrepreneurship Theory and Practice* (2015), in press.

29. Dean A. Shepherd, "Venture Capitalists' Introspection: A Comparison of 'In Use' and 'Espoused' Decision Policies," *Journal of Small Business Management* 37, no. 2 (1999): 76–87; and Dean A. Shepherd, "Venture Capitalists' Assessment of New Venture Survival," *Management Science* 45, no. 5 (1999): 621–32.

30. Ian C. MacMillan, Robin Siegel, and P. N. Subba Narasimha, "Criteria Used by Venture Capitalists to Evaluate New Venture Proposals," *Journal of Business Venturing* 1, no. 1 (Winter 1985): 119–28.

31. John Hall and Charles W. Hofer, "Venture Capitalist's Decision Criteria in New Venture Evaluation," *Journal of Business Venturing* 8, no. 1 (1993): 25–42; see also Nikolaus Franke, Marc Gruber, Dietmar Harhoff, and Joachim Henkel, "What You Are Is What You Like—Similarity Biases in Venture Capitalists' Evaluations of Start-Up Teams," *Journal of Business Venturing* 21, no. 6 (2006): 802–26.

32. Ronald J. Hustedde and Glen C. Pulver, "Factors Affecting Equity Capital Acquisition: The Demand Side," *Journal of Business Venturing* 7, no. 5 (1992): 363–74; Petty and Gruber, "In Pursuit of the 'Real Deal': A Longitudinal Study of VC Decision Making," *Journal of Business Venturing* 26, no. 2 (2011): 172–88.

33. Harry J. Sapienza, "When Do Venture Capitalists Add Value?," *Journal of Business Venturing* 7, no. 1 (1992): 9–28; see also Juan Florin, "Is Venture Capital Worth It? Effects on Firm Performance and Founder Returns," *Journal of Business Venturing* 20, no. 1 (2005): 113–35; and Lowell W. Busenitz, James O. Fiet, and Douglas D. Moesel, "Reconsidering the Venture Capitalists' 'Value Added' Proposition: An Interorganizational Learning Perspective," *Journal of Business Venturing* 19, no. 6 (2004): 787–807.

34. B. Elango, Vance H. Fried, Robert D. Hisrich, and Amy Polonchek, "How Venture Capital Firms Differ," *Journal of Business Venturing* 10, no. 2 (1995): 157–79; Dean A. Shepherd and Andrew L. Zacharakis, "Venture Capitalists' Expertise: A Call for Research into Decision Aids and Cognitive Feedback," *Journal of Business Venturing* 17, no. 1 (2002): 1–20; and Dick De Clercq and Harry J. Sapienza, "When Do Venture Capitalists Learn from Their Portfolio Companies?," *Entrepreneurship Theory and Practice* 29, no. 4 (2005): 517–35; and Richard Fairchild, "An Entrepreneur's Choice of Venture Capitalist or Angel-Financing: A Behavioral

Game-Theoretic Approach," *Journal of Business Venturing* 26, no. 3 (2011): 359–74.

35. Marie-Jeanne Juilland, "What Do You Want from a Venture Capitalist?" August 1987 issue of *Venture, For Entrepreneurial Business Owners & Investors*, by special permission. Copyright © 1987 Venture Magazine, Inc., 521 Fifth Ave., New York, NY 10175-0028; Will Drover, Matthew S. Wood, and Yves Fassin, "Take the Money or Run? Investors' Ethical Reputation and Entrepreneurs' Willingness to Partner," *Journal of Business Venturing* 29, no. 6 (2014): 723–40.

36. Harold M. Hoffman and James Blakey, "You Can Negotiate with Venture Capitalists," *Harvard Business Review* 65, no. 2 (March/April 1987): 16; Andrew L. Zacharakis and Dean A. Shepherd, "The Nature of Information and Overconfidence on Venture Capitalist's Decision Making," *Journal of Business Venturing* 16, no. 4 (July 2001): 311–32; Lowell W. Busenitz, James O. Fiet, and Douglas D. Moesel, "Signaling in Venture Capitalist—New Venture Team Funding Decisions: Does It Indicate Long-Term Venture Outcomes?," *Entrepreneurship Theory and Practice* 29, no. 1 (2005): 1–12; and Ebbers and Wijnberg, "Nascent Ventures Competing for Start-up Capital."

37. The Richest People in America, 2014. The Forbes 400. http://www.forbes.com/forbes-400/ (accessed January 7, 2015).

38. William E. Wetzel, Jr., as quoted by Dale D. Buss, "Heaven Help Us," *Nation's Business* (November 1993): 29; also John R. Becker-Blease and Jeffrey E. Sohl, "The Effect of Gender Diversity on Angel Group Investment," *Entrepreneurship Theory and Practice* 35, no. 4 (2011): 709–33.

39. William E. Wetzel, Jr., "Angel Money," *In-Business* (November/December 1989): 44.

40. William E. Wetzel, Jr., "Angels and Informal Risk Capital," *Sloan Management Review* 24, no. 4 (Summer 1983); see also John Freear, Jeffrey E. Sohl, and William E. Wetzel, Jr., "Angels and Non-angels: Are There Differences?" *Journal of Business Venturing* 19, no. 2 (1994): 109–23; Andrew L. Maxwell, Scott A. Jeffrey and Moren Lévesque, "Business Angel Early Stage Decision Making," *Journal of Business Venturing* 26, no. 2 (2011): 212–25; Cheryl Mitteness, Richard Sudek, and Melissa S. Cardon, "Angel Investor Characteristics That Determine Whether Perceived Passion Leads to Higher Evaluations of Funding Potential," *Journal of Business Venturing* 27, no. 5 (2012): 592–606; Annaleena Parhankangas and Michael Ehrlich, "How Entrepreneurs Seduce business Angels: An Impression Management Approach," *Journal of Business Venturing* 29, no. 4 (2014): 543–64; Veroniek Collewaert and Harry J. Sapienza, "How Does Angel Investor–Entrepreneur Conflict Affect Venture Innovation? It Depends," *Entrepreneurship Theory and Practice* (2015). In press.

41. Mark Van Osnabrugge and Robert J. Robinson, *Angel Investing: Matching Startup Funds with Startup Companies* (San Francisco, CA: Jossy-Bass, 2000); Cheryl R. Mitteness, Rich DeJordy, Manju K. Ahuja, and Richard Sudek, "Extending the Role of Similarity Attraction in Friendship and Advice Networks in Angel Groups," *Entrepreneurship Theory and Practice* (2015): in press; Douglas J. Cumming, J. Ari Pandes, and Michael J. Robinson, "The Role of Agents in Private Entrepreneurial Finance," *Entrepreneurship Theory and Practice* 39, no. 2 (2015): 345–74; and John R. Becker-Bleaseand Jeffrey E. Sohl, New Venture Legitimacy: The Conditions for Angel Investors, *Small Business Economics* (2015), in press.

42. Buss, "Heaven Help Us," 29–30; see also John Freear, Jeffrey E. Sohl, and William E. Wetzel, Jr., "Angels: Personal Investors in the Venture Capital Market," *Entrepreneurship & Regional Development* 7, no. 1 (1995): 85–94; Jeffrey Sohl, "The Angel Investor Market in 2011," Center for Venture Research, University of New Hampshire, May 2012; and SVB Financial Group, "2011 Halo Report: Angel Group Year In Review," March 2012.

43. Wetzel, "Angel Money," 42–44; and Colin M. Mason and Richard T. Harrison, "Is It Worth It? The Rates of Return from Informal Venture Capital Investments," *Journal of Business Venturing* 17, no. 3 (2002): 211–36.

PART 3

Developing the Entrepreneurial Plan

CHAPTER 9

Legal Challenges for Entrepreneurial Ventures

LEARNING OBJECTIVES

1 To introduce the importance of legal issues to entrepreneurs

2 To examine patent protection, including definitions and preparation

3 To review copyrights and their relevance to entrepreneurs

4 To study trademarks and their impact on new ventures

5 To examine the legal forms of organization—sole proprietorship, partnership, and corporation

6 To illustrate the advantages and disadvantages of each of these three legal forms

7 To explain the nature of the limited partnership and limited liability partnerships (LLPs)

8 To examine how an S corporation works

9 To define the additional classifications of corporations, including limited liability companies (LLCs), B corporations, and low-profit, limited liability companies (L3Cs)

10 To present the major segments of the bankruptcy law that apply to entrepreneurs

Entrepreneurial Thought

A major difficulty for the inexperienced entrepreneur is the host of strange terms and phrases which are scattered throughout most legal documents. The novice in this kind of reading should have some understanding not only of what is contained in such documents, but also why these provisions have been included. If an entrepreneur cannot find the time or take the interest to read and understand the major contracts into which his company will enter, he should be very cautious about being an entrepreneur at all.

—Patrick R. Liles, *Harvard Business School*

LO1 Introduce
the importance
of legal issues to
entrepreneurs
Entrepreneurs cannot hope to have the legal expertise or background of an attorney, of course, but they should be sufficiently knowledgeable about certain legal concepts that have implications for the business venture.[1]

Table 9.1 sets forth some of the major legal concepts that can affect entrepreneurial ventures. These concepts can be divided into three groups: (1) those that relate to the inception of the venture, (2) those that relate to the ongoing venture, and (3) those that relate to the growth and continuity of the venture. The focus of this chapter will be on the legal concepts related to the first and third groups. Specifically, we shall examine intellectual property protection (patents, copyrights, trademarks), the legal forms of organization, and bankruptcy law.

TABLE 9.1   MAJOR LEGAL CONCEPTS AND ENTREPRENEURIAL VENTURES

I. Inception of an Entrepreneurial Venture

   A. Laws governing intellectual property

      1. Patents

      2. Copyrights

      3. Trademarks

   B. Forms of business organization

      1. Sole proprietorship

      2. Partnership

      3. Corporation

      4. Franchise

   C. Tax considerations

   D. Capital formation

   E. Liability questions

II. An Ongoing Venture: Business Development and Transactions

   A. Personnel law

      1. Hiring and firing policies

      2. Equal Employment Opportunity Commission

      3. Collective bargaining

   B. Contract law

      1. Legal contracts

      2. Sales contracts

      3. Leases

III. Growth and Continuity of a Successful Entrepreneurial Venture

   A. Tax considerations

      1. Federal, state, local

      2. Payroll

      3. Incentives

   B. Governmental regulations

      1. Zoning (property)

      2. Administrative agencies (regulatory)

      3. Consumer law

   C. Continuity of ownership rights

      1. Property laws and ownership

      2. Wills, trusts, estates

      3. Bankruptcy

9-1 INTELLECTUAL PROPERTY PROTECTION: PATENTS

LO2 Examine patent protection, including definitions and preparation

A **patent** provides the owner with exclusive rights to hold, transfer, and license the production and sale of the patented product or process. Design patents last for 14 years; all others last for 20 years. The objective of a patent is to provide the holder with a temporary monopoly on his or her innovation and thus to encourage the creation and disclosure of new ideas and innovations in the marketplace. Securing a patent, however, is not always an easy process.

A patent is an **intellectual property right**. It is the result of a unique discovery, and patent holders are provided protection against infringement by others. In general, a number of items can qualify for patent protection, among them processes, machines, products, plants, compositions of elements (chemical compounds), and improvements on already existing items.[2]

9-1a Securing a Patent: Basic Rules

Because quite often the patent process is complex (see Figure 9.1), careful planning is required. For pursuing a patent, the following basic rules are recommended by the experts:

Rule 1: Pursue patents that are broad, are commercially significant, and offer a strong position. This means that relevant patent law must be researched to obtain the widest coverage possible on the idea or concept. In addition, there must be something significantly novel or proprietary about the innovation. Record all steps or processes in a notebook and have them witnessed so that documentation secures a strong proprietary position.

Rule 2: Prepare a patent plan in detail. This plan should outline the costs to develop and market the innovation as well as analyze the competition and technological similarities to your idea. Attempt to detail the precise value of the innovation.

Rule 3: Have your actions relate to your original patent plan. This does not mean a plan cannot be changed. However, it is wise to remain close to the plan during the early stages of establishing the patent. Later, the path that is prepared may change—for example, licensing out the patent versus keeping it for yourself.

Rule 4: Establish an **infringement budget**. Patent rights are effective only if potential infringers fear legal damages. Thus, it is important to prepare a realistic budget for prosecuting violations of the patent.

Rule 5: Evaluate the patent plan strategically. The typical patent process takes three years. This should be compared to the actual life cycle of the proposed innovation or technology. Will the patent be worth defending in three years, or will enforcement cost more than the damages collected?[3]

These rules about proper definition, preparation, planning, and evaluation can help entrepreneurs establish effective patent protection. In addition, they can help the patent attorney conduct the search process.

9-1b Securing a Patent: The Application

Patent applications must include detailed specifications of the innovation that any skilled person in the specific area can understand. A patent application has two parts:

1. **Specification** is the text of a patent and may include any accompanying illustrations. Because its purpose is to teach those fluent in this area of technology all they need to understand, duplicate, and use the invention, it may be quite long. The specification typically includes:
   a. An introduction explaining why the invention will be useful.
   b. Description of all prior art that you are aware of and that could be considered similar to the invention. The specification usually lists other patents by number—with a brief description of each—but you can cite and describe unpatented technology as well.

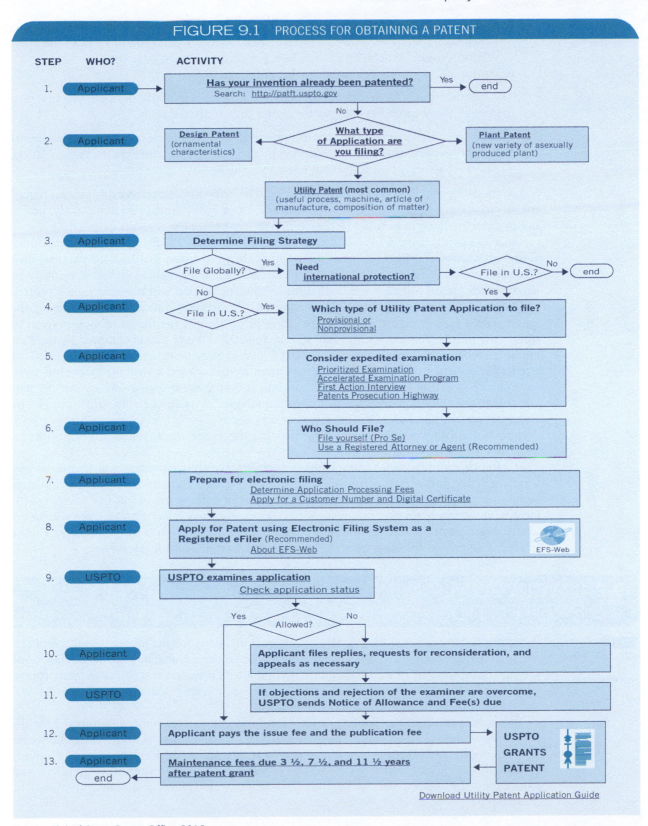

FIGURE 9.1   PROCESS FOR OBTAINING A PATENT

Source: United States Patent Office, 2015

    c. A summary of the invention that describes the essence of the new technology and emphasizes its difference from prior art, while including all its requisite features, whether novel or not.

    d. A detailed description of the invention, including anything that could be remotely relevant, reference to all reasonable variations, and number bounds. Take as much space as you like. Use as many numbers as necessary, including close or tight limits based on experience, as well as loose ones based on what might be possible. This section should be detailed enough to really teach a skilled practitioner.

e. Examples and/or experimental results, in full detail.

The specification is inherently broad because its intent is to teach and also, as a practical matter, to allow some flexibility in the claims that are based on it.

2. **Claims** are a series of short paragraphs, each of which identifies a particular feature or combination of features that is protected by the patent. The entire claims section, at the end of the patent, is typically about one page long or less.

Claims define and limit the patented invention. The invention can be broad (a process requiring an "inorganic, nonmetal solid" would cover a lot of possibilities, e.g.) but sharply limited not to cover anything in prior art (other existing processes that use organics or metals).[4]

Once the application is filed with the **Patent and Trademark Office** of the Department of Commerce, an examiner will determine whether the innovation qualifies for patentability. The examiner will do this by researching technical data in journals as well as previously issued patents. Based on the individual's findings, the application will be rejected or accepted.

Only a small percentage of issued patents are commercially valuable. Consequently, the entrepreneur must weigh the value of the innovation against the time and money spent to obtain the patent. Also, it is important to remember that many patents granted by the Patent and Trademark Office have been declared invalid after being challenged in court. This occurs for several reasons. One is that the patent holder waited an unreasonable length of time before asserting his or her rights. A second is that those bringing suit against the patent holder are able to prove that the individual misused the patent rights—for example, by requiring certain purchases of other goods or services as part of the patent-use arrangement. A third is that other parties are able to prove that the patent itself fails to meet tests of patentability and is therefore invalid.[5]

If, after careful review, an entrepreneur concludes that the innovation will withstand any legal challenge and is commercially worthwhile, a patent should be pursued. If a challenge is mounted, legal fees may be sizable, but a successful defense can result in damages sufficient to compensate for the infringement plus court costs and interest. In fact, the court may award damages of up to three times the actual amount. In addition, a patent infringer can be liable for all profits resulting from the infringement as well as for legal fees.[6]

9-2 INTELLECTUAL PROPERTY PROTECTION: COPYRIGHTS

LO3 Review copyrights and their relevance to entrepreneurs

A **copyright** provides exclusive rights to creative individuals for the protection of their literary or artistic productions. It is not possible to copyright an idea, but the particular mode for expression of that idea often can be copyrighted. This expression can take many forms, including books, periodicals, dramatic or musical compositions, art, motion pictures, lectures, sound recordings, and computer programs.

Any works created after January 1, 1978, and receiving a copyright are protected for the life of the author plus 70 years. The owner of this copyright may (1) reproduce the work, (2) prepare derivative works based on it (e.g., a condensation or movie version of a novel), (3) distribute copies of the work by sale or otherwise, (4) perform the work publicly, and (5) display the work publicly. Each of these rights, or a portion of each, also may be transferred.[7]

9-2a Understanding Copyright Protection

For the author of creative material to obtain copyright protection, the material must be in a tangible form so it can be communicated or reproduced. It also must be the author's own work and thus the product of his or her skill or judgment. Concepts, principles, processes, systems, or discoveries are not valid for copyright protection until they are put in tangible form—written or recorded.

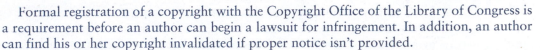

Formal registration of a copyright with the Copyright Office of the Library of Congress is a requirement before an author can begin a lawsuit for infringement. In addition, an author can find his or her copyright invalidated if proper notice isn't provided.

Anyone who violates an author's exclusive rights under a copyright is liable for infringement. However, because of the fair use doctrine, it is sometimes difficult to establish infringement. Fair use is described as the reproduction of a copyrighted work for purposes such as criticism, comment, news reporting, teaching (including multiple copies for classroom use), scholarship, or research. These uses may be good candidates for the fair use defense, as they may be deemed not an infringement of copyright. In determining whether the use made of a work in any particular case is a fair use, the factors to be considered include (1) the purpose and character of the use, including whether such use is of a commercial nature or is for nonprofit educational purposes; (2) the nature of the copyrighted work; (3) the amount and substantiality of the portion used in relation to the copyrighted work as a whole; and (4) the effect of the use upon the potential market for a value of the copyrighted work.[8]

If, however, an author substantiates a copyright infringement, the normal remedy is recovery of actual damages plus any profits the violator receives. Keep in mind that there is absolutely no cost or risk involved in protecting material that you generate by copyright. Therefore, as a matter of course, any writing that you prepare and spend a lot of time on should be copyrighted by putting the copyright notice (©) on it. Also, it is not necessary to register copyrights with the Copyright Office unless and until you want to sue somebody for infringement. In the overwhelming majority of cases—assuming you are not in the publishing business—you can simply use the copyright notice and do not need to spend the time and effort necessary to register copyrights with the U.S. Copyright Office.

9-2b Protecting Ideas?

The Copyright Act specifically excludes copyright protection for any "idea, procedure, process, system, method of operation, concept, principle, or discovery, regardless of the form in which it is described, explained, illustrated, or embodied." Note that it is not possible to copyright an *idea*—the underlying ideas embodied in a work may be used freely by others. What is copyrightable is the particular way an idea is expressed. Whenever an idea and an expression are inseparable, the expression cannot be copyrighted.

Generally, anything that is not an original expression will not qualify for copyright protection. Facts widely known to the public are not copyrightable. Page numbers are not copyrightable because they follow a sequence known to everyone. Mathematical calculations are not copyrightable. Compilations of facts, however, are copyrightable. The Copyright Act defines a compilation as "a work formed by the collection and assembling of preexisting materials of data that are selected, coordinated, or arranged in such a way that the resulting work as a whole constitutes an original work of authorship."[9]

9-3 INTELLECTUAL PROPERTY PROTECTION: TRADEMARKS

LO4 Study trademarks and their impact on new ventures

A trademark is a distinctive name, mark, symbol, or motto identified with a company's product(s) and registered at the Patent and Trademark Office. Thanks to trademark law, no confusion should result from one venture's using the symbol or name of another.

Specific legal terms differentiate the exact types of marks. For example, trademarks identify and distinguish goods. Service marks identify and distinguish services. Certification marks denote the quality, materials, or other aspects of goods and services and are used by someone other than the mark's owner. Collective marks are trademarks or service marks that members of groups or organizations use to identify themselves as the source of goods or services.[10]

Usually, personal names or words that are considered generic or descriptive are not trademarked, unless the words are in some way suggestive or fanciful, or the personal name is accompanied by a specific design. For example, "English Leather" may not be trademarked to describe a leather processed in England; however, English Leather is trademarked as a name for aftershave lotion, because this constitutes a fanciful use of the words. Consider also that even the common name of an individual may be trademarked if that name is accompanied by a picture or some fanciful design that allows easy identification of the product, such as Smith Brothers Cough Drops.

In most cases, the Patent and Trademark Office will reject an application for marks, symbols, or names that are flags or insignias of governments, portraits or signatures of living persons, immoral or deceptive, or items likely to cause problems because of resemblance to a previously registered mark. Once issued, the trademark is listed in the Principal Register of the Patent and Trademark Office. This listing offers several advantages: (1) nationwide constructive notice of the owner's right to use the mark (thus eliminating the need to show that the defendant in an infringement suit had notice of the mark), (2) Bureau of Customs protection against importers using the mark, and (3) incontestability of the mark after five years.[11]

In 1995, Congress amended the Trademark Act by passing the Federal Trademark Dilution Act, which extended the protection available to trademark owners by creating a federal cause of action for trademark dilution. Until the passage of this amendment, federal trademark law prohibited only the unauthorized use of the same mark on competing—or on noncompeting but "related"—goods or services when such use would likely confuse consumers as to the origin of those goods and services. In 2006, Congress enacted a further amendment known as the Trademark Dilution Revision Act (TDRA) to protect "distinctive" or "famous" trademarks (such as McDonald's, Google, Nike, and Apple) from certain unauthorized uses of the marks *regardless* of a showing of competition or a likelihood of confusion.[12]

Historically, a trademark registration lasted 20 years; however, the current registrations are good for only 10 years, with the possibility for continuous renewal every 10 years. It is most important to understand that a trademark may be invalidated in four specific ways:

1. **Cancellation proceedings.** a third party's challenge to the mark's distinctiveness within five years of its issuance.

2. **Cleaning-out procedure.** the failure of a trademark owner to file an affidavit stating it is in use or justifying its lack of use within six years of registration.

3. **Abandonment.** the nonuse of a trademark for two consecutive years without justification or a statement regarding the trademark's abandonment.

4. **Generic meaning.** the allowance of a trademark to represent a general grouping of products or services. For example, cellophane has come to represent plastic wrap, and Scotch tape has come to represent adhesive tape. Xerox is currently seeking, through national advertising, to avoid having its name used to represent copier machines.

If a trademark is properly registered, used, and protected, the owner can obtain an injunction against any uses of the mark that are likely to cause confusion. Moreover, if infringement and damages can be proven in court, a monetary award may be given to the trademark holder.

9-3a Avoiding Trademark Pitfalls

Trademark registration and search can be costly, sometimes ranging into the thousands of dollars. Trademark infringement can be even more expensive. To avoid these pitfalls, one author has noted five basic rules that entrepreneurs should follow when selecting trademarks for their new ventures, as follows:

- Never select a corporate name or a mark without first doing a trademark search.
- If your attorney says you have a potential problem with a mark, trust his or her judgment.
- Seek a coined or fanciful name or mark before you settle for a descriptive or highly suggestive one.
- Whenever marketing or other considerations dictate the use of a name or mark that is highly suggestive of the product, select a distinctive logotype for the descriptive or suggestive words.
- Avoid abbreviations and acronyms wherever possible, and when no alternative is acceptable, select a distinctive logotype in which the abbreviation or acronym appears.[13]

THE ENTREPRENEURIAL PROCESS

Parody or Trademark Infringement?

Parody is sometimes used as a defense against trademark infringement. A parody must convey two simultaneous and contradictory messages: not only it is the original, but also that it is not the original and is instead a parody. According to the U.S. Trademark Office a true parody actually decreases the likelihood of confusion because the effect of the parody is to create a distinction in the viewer's mind between the actual product and the joke. The customer must be amused, not confused.

Haute Diggity Dog is a company that sells pet toys. They have made a number of parody products including Chewnel No. 5, Jimmy Chew, and Dog Perignon. However, their parody pet toy called *Chewy Vuiton* enraged the Louis Vuitton company and their brand with a stylized LV monogram that represented to consumers an image of quality and exclusivity with products retailing from $995 to $4500. *Chewy Vuiton* did mimic the shape, design, and color of Louis Vuitton's handbags, but instead of LV, the toy's pattern included a CV with a flower, cross, and diamond pattern that resembled but was not identical to the Vuitton pattern. The chew toy sold for less than $20 in pet stores.

The court ruled this to be a parody. The *Chewy Vuiton* toy was found to be similar, indicating that the toy is an imitation, but also was found to be different from the original handbags, being a small dog toy not an expensive, luxury handbag. After finding that the *Chewy Vuiton* toy was a parody, the Court still had to examine for infringement (i.e., whether or not the use created a likelihood of confusion).

To assess whether a trademark infringement has occurred, the courts consider seven factors: (1) the degree of similarity between the trademarks, (2) the similarity of the products for which the name is used, (3) the area and manner of concurrent use, (4) the degree of care likely to be exercised by consumers, (5) the strength of the complainant's trademark, (6) whether actual product confusion exists among buyers, and (7) an intent on the part of the alleged infringer to palm off his or her products as those of another.

The *Chewy Vuiton* parody was sufficiently similar to invoke the famous trademark in the mind of consumers yet still distinguish the products. The dissimilarity of the products was in Haute Diggity Dog's favor as one product is a chew toy and the other is a designer purse. Haute Diggity Dog's products generally were sold at pet stores with other pet products, including other parody products, while Louis Vuitton handbags generally are sold in Louis Vuitton boutiques or department stores.

Having found no trademark infringement, the court turned to the issue of dilution (Trademark Dilution Revision Act of 2006): whether or not Haute Diggity Dog's use of *Chewy Vuiton* was likely to impair the distinctiveness or harm the reputation of the Louis Vuitton marks. In doing this courts examine a number of factors including: (1) the degree of similarity between the mark or trade name and the famous mark; (2) the degree of inherent or acquired distinctiveness of the famous mark; (3) the extent to which the owner of the famous mark is engaging in substantially exclusive use of the mark; (4) the degree of recognition of the famous mark; (5) whether the user of the mark or trade name

intended to create an association with the famous mark; and (6) any actual association between the mark or trade name and the famous mark. Because the product was a parody, the Court supported Haute Diggity Dog and found no violation against Louis Vuitton.

The *Chewy Vuiton* case brings to mind several questions that every entrepreneurial company should consider whenever attempting parody:

Is the parody humorous? If it doesn't make you laugh, be concerned. In order to be an effective parody, it must communicate the necessary element of satire, ridicule, joking, or amusement.

Is the proposed trademark similar enough and different enough from the mark being parodied? Haute Diggity Dog escaped liability as a trademark parody because each element of its mark and design were similar but not identical to the Louis Vuitton marks and design.

Is the proposed parody mark in a product line that is too close to those offered by the target? In Chewy Vuiton, the products were dissimilar and the court found it unlikely that Louis Vuitton would sell pet chew toys. Beware that courts have been very strict where the mark is used on a competing product.

Are you prepared for legal action? Despite the fact that it was ultimately successful, Haute Diggity Dog spent several hundred thousands of dollars defending itself, lost distributors, and had merchandise sent back as a result of the lawsuit. Is it worth a legal battle with companies like Microsoft, Hard Rock cafe, McDonald's, Coca-Cola, or Nike? Companies are getting more aggressive about protecting their trademarks and an infringement suit filed by a well-funded company can mean years of legal issues and huge legal bills.

Examples of other court rulings include:

- Hard Rain Cafe was likely to confuse consumers regarding the Hard Rock Cafe.

- Enjoy Cocaine was not a valid parody of Enjoy Coca-Cola, where both used the familiar red-and-white logo.

- Lardash was considered a valid parody of Jordache.

- Mutant of Omaha and the subtitle Nuclear Holocaust Insurance was not a valid parody of Mutual of Omaha.

- Bagzilla was a permissible pun of Godzilla and would not confuse consumers.

- Spy Notes was a valid parody of CliffsNotes.

Source: Adapted from Maxine S. Lans, "Parody as a Marketing Strategy," *Marketing News* (January 3, 1994): 20; Diane E. Burke, "Trademark Parody: Taking a Bite Out of Owner's Rights," web post, 2009, http://www.steptoejohnson.com/publications/publicationstory/TrademarkParodyTakingaBiteOutof,249.aspx (accessed January 15, 2012); and Jane P. Mallor, A. James Barnes, Thomas Bowers, and Arlen W. Langvardt, *Business Law: The Ethical, Global, and E-Commerce Environment*, 15th ed. (New York: McGraw-Hill Irwin, 2013), 288–92.

THE ENTREPRENEURIAL PROCESS

Internet Intellectual Property Information Sources

http://www.uspto.gov

The U.S. Patent and Trademark Office website provides a wealth of valuable information for entrepreneurs. Users can locate patent and trademark information, such as registration forms, international patents, legal issues, and frequently asked questions (FAQs). Users can also check the status of a trademark or patent application on this site.

http://www.patents.com

This site provides basic patent information in a very organized manner. It also provides access to patents filed by each state as well as a patent lawyer directory. It is also updated frequently.

http://www.bustpatents.com

This site, sponsored by Source Translation and Optimization, offers assistance with Internet, biotech, and e-commerce patents. Users also can sign up for the free daily information e-mail, Internet Patent News Service, at this site.

http://www.copyright.gov/

The U.S. Copyright Office at the Library of Congress website provides information on copyright protecting works,

licensing, and legal issues. Users also can search copyright records on the site.

http://www.law.cornell.edu/

The website for the Legal Information Institute at the Cornell School of Law provides legal documentation and a history of copyright law. It also offers information on international copyrights and links to other copyright information resources.

http://www.findlaw.com

This site allows the user to search for any topic and yield returns of the actual written law, court precedence, and current cases and interpretations. The site also provides topical searches that aid the user in getting started as well as a business section to help put the laws into more practical applications.

http://www.cengage.com/search/showresults.do?N=4 294922453+4294922239+4294966221

Cengage Learning offers numerous business law textbooks. This website offers an overview of each book with updates that allows surfers to check contents before purchasing.

9-3b Trade Secrets

Certain business processes and information cannot be patented, copyrighted, or trademarked. Yet they may be protected as trade secrets. Customer lists, plans, research and development, pricing information, marketing techniques, and production techniques are examples of potential trade secrets. Generally, anything that makes an individual company unique and has value to a competitor could be a trade secret.[14]

Protection of trade secrets extends both to ideas and to their expression. For this reason, and because a trade secret involves no registration or filing requirements, trade-secret protection is ideal for software. Of course, the secret formula, method, or other information must be disclosed to key employees. Businesses generally attempt to protect their trade secrets by having all employees who use the process or information agree in their contracts never to divulge it. Theft of confidential business data by industrial espionage—such as stealing a competitor's documents—is a theft of trade secrets without any contractual violation and is actionable in itself.

The law clearly outlines the area of trade secrets: Information is a trade secret if (1) it is not known by the competition, (2) the business would lose its advantage if the competition were to obtain it, and (3) the owner has taken reasonable steps to protect the secret from disclosure.[15] Keep in mind that prosecution is still difficult in many of these cases.

9-3c Trademark Protection on the Internet

Because of the unique nature of the Internet, its use creates unique legal questions and issues—particularly with respect to intellectual property rights. The emerging body of law governing cyberspace is often referred to as *cyberlaw*.

One of the initial trademark issues involving intellectual property in cyberspace has been whether domain names (Internet addresses) should be treated as trademarks or simply as a means of access, similar to street addresses in the physical world. Increasingly, the courts are holding that the principles of trademark law should apply to domain names. One problem in applying trademark law to Internet domain names, however, is that trademark law allows multiple parties to use the same mark—as long as the mark is used for different goods or services and will not cause customer confusion. On the Internet as it is currently structured, only one party can use a particular domain name, regardless of the type of goods or services offered. In other words, although two or more businesses can own the trademark Entrevision, only one business can operate on the Internet with the domain name Entrevision.com. Because of this restrictive feature of domain names, a question has arisen as to whether domain names should function as trademarks. To date, the courts that have considered this question have held that the unauthorized use of another's mark in a domain name may constitute trademark infringement.[16]

Table 9.2 provides a comprehensive outline of the forms of intellectual property protection.

9-4 LEGAL STRUCTURES FOR ENTREPRENEURIAL VENTURES

LO5 Examine the legal forms of organization—sole proprietorship, partnership, and corporation

Prospective entrepreneurs need to identify the legal structure that will best suit the demands of the venture. The necessity for this derives from changing tax laws, liability situations, the availability of capital, and the complexity of business formation.[17] When examining these legal forms of organizations, entrepreneurs need to consider a few important factors:

- How easily the form of business organization can be implemented
- The amount of capital required to implement the form of business organization
- Legal considerations that might limit the options available to the entrepreneur
- The tax effects of the form of organization selected
- The potential liability to the owner of the form of organization selected

Three primary legal forms of organization are the sole proprietorship, the partnership, and the corporation. Because each form has specific advantages and disadvantages, it is impossible to recommend one form over the other. The entrepreneur's specific situation, concerns, and desires will dictate this choice.[18]

9-4a Sole Proprietorships

A **sole proprietorship** is a business that is owned and operated by one person. The enterprise has no existence apart from its owner. This individual has a right to all of the profits and bears all of the liability for the debts and obligations of the business. The individual also has **unlimited liability**, which means that his or her business and personal assets stand behind the operation. If the company cannot meet its financial obligations, the owner may be forced to sell the family car, house, and whatever assets would satisfy the creditors.

To establish a sole proprietorship, a person merely needs to obtain whatever local and state licenses are necessary to begin operations. If the proprietor chooses a fictitious or assumed name, he or she also must file a *certificate of assumed business name* with the county. Because of its ease of formation, the sole proprietorship is the most widely used legal form of organization.[19]

ADVANTAGES OF SOLE PROPRIETORSHIPS

LO6 Illustrate the advantages and disadvantages of each of the three legal forms

Some of the advantages associated with sole proprietorships are as follows:

- *Ease of formation.* Less formality and fewer restrictions are associated with establishing a sole proprietorship than with any other legal form. The proprietorship needs little or no governmental approval, and it usually is less expensive than a partnership or corporation.
- *Sole ownership of profits.* The proprietor is not required to share profits with anyone.

TABLE 9.2 FORMS OF INTELLECTUAL PROPERTY

	Patent	Copyright	Trademarks (Service Marks and Trade Dress)	Trade Secrets
Definition	A grant from the government that gives an inventor exclusive rights to an invention.	An intangible property right granted to authors and originators of a literary work or artistic production that falls within specified categories.	Any distinctive word, name, symbol, or device (image or appearance), or combination thereof, that an entity uses to identify and distinguish its goods or services from those of others.	Any information (including formulas, patterns, programs, devices, techniques, and processes) that a business possesses and that gives the business an advantage over competitors who do not know the information or process.
Requirements	An invention must be: 1. Novel. 2. Not obvious. 3. Useful.	Literary or artistic works must be: 1. Original. 2. Fixed in a durable medium that can be perceived, reproduced, or communicated. 3. Within a copyrightable category.	Trademarks, service marks, and trade dresses must be sufficiently distinctive (or must have acquired a secondary meaning) to enable consumers and others to distinguish the manufacturer's, seller's, or business user's products or services from those of competitors.	Information and processes that have commercial value, that are not known or easily ascertainable by the general public or others, and that are reasonably protected from disclosure.
Types or Categories	1. Utility (general). 2. Design. 3. Plant (flowers, vegetables, and so on).	1. Literary works (including computer programs). 2. Musical works. 3. Dramatic works. 4. Pantomime and choreographic works. 5. Pictorial, graphic, and sculptural works. 6. Films and audiovisual works. 7. Sound recordings.	1. Strong, distinctive marks (such as fanciful, arbitrary, or suggestive marks). 2. Marks that have acquired a secondary meaning by use. 3. Other types of marks, including certification marks and collective marks. 4. Trade dress (such as a distinctive decor, menu, style, or type of service).	1. Customer lists. 2. Research and development. 3. Plans and programs. 4. Pricing information. 5. Production techniques. 6. Marketing techniques. 7. Formulas. 8. Compilations.
How Acquired	By filing a patent application with the U.S. Patent and Trademark Office and receiving that office's approval.	Automatic (once in tangible form); to recover for infringement, the copyright must be registered with the U.S. Copyright Office.	1. At common law, ownership is created by use of mark. 2. Registration (either with the U.S. Patent and Trademark Office or with the appropriate state office) gives constructive notice of date of use. 3. Federal registration is permitted if the mark is currently in use or if the applicant intends use within six months (period can be extended to three years). 4. Federal registration can be renewed between the fifth and sixth years and, thereafter, every ten years.	Through the originality and development of information and processes that are unique to a business, that are unknown by others, and that would be valuable to competitors if they knew of the information and processes.

Rights	An inventor has the right to make, use, sell, assign, or license the invention during the duration of the patent's term. The first to invent has patent rights.	The author or originator has the exclusive right to reproduce, distribute, display, license, or transfer a copyrighted work.	The owner has the right to use the mark or trade dress and to exclude others from using it. The right of use can be licensed or sold (assigned) to another	The owner has the right to sole and exclusive use of the trade secrets and the right to use legal means to protect against misappropriation of the trade secrets by others. The owner can license or assign a trade secret.
Duration	20 years from the date of application; for design patents, 14 years.	1. For authors: the life of the author, plus 70 years. 2. For publishers: 95 years after the date of publication or 120 years after creation.	Unlimited, as long as it is in use. To continue notice by registration, the registration must be renewed by filing.	Unlimited, as long as not revealed to others.
Civil Remedies for Infringement	Monetary damages, which include reasonable royalties and lost profits, plus attorneys' fees. (Treble damages are available for intentional infringement.)	Actual damages, plus profits received by the infringer; or statutory damages of not less than $500 and not more than $20,000 ($100,000, if infringement is willful); plus costs and attorneys' fees.	1. Injunction prohibiting future use of mark. 2. Actual damages, plus profits received by the infringer (can be increased to three times the actual damages under the Lanham Act). 3. Impoundment and destruction of infringing articles. 4. Plus costs and attorneys' fees.	Monetary damages for misappropriation (the Uniform Trade Secrets Act permits punitive damages up to twice the amount of actual damages for wilful and malicious misappropriation); plus costs and attorneys' fees.

Source: Frank B. Cross and Roger LeRoy Miller, *West's Legal Environment of Business*, 4th ed. © 2001 Cengage Learning; see also: Roger LeRoy Miller and Frank B. Cross, *The Legal Environment Today: Business in Its Ethical, Regulatory, E-Commerce, and Global Setting*, 8th ed. (Mason, OH: South-Western/Cengage, 2016)

- *Decision making and control vested in one owner.* No co-owners or partners must be consulted in the running of the operation.
- *Flexibility.* Management is able to respond quickly to business needs in the form of day-to-day management decisions as governed by various laws and good sense.
- *Relative freedom from governmental control.* Except for requiring the necessary licenses, very little governmental interference occurs in the operation.
- *Freedom from corporate business taxes.* Proprietors are taxed as individual taxpayers and not as businesses.

DISADVANTAGES OF SOLE PROPRIETORSHIPS

Sole proprietorships also have disadvantages. Some of these are as follows:

- *Unlimited liability.* The individual proprietor is personally responsible for all business debts. This liability extends to **all** of the proprietor's assets.
- *Lack of continuity.* The enterprise may be crippled or terminated if the owner becomes ill or dies.
- *Less available capital.* Ordinarily, proprietorships have less available capital than other types of business organizations, such as partnerships and corporations.
- *Relative difficulty obtaining long-term financing.* Because the enterprise rests exclusively on one person, it often has difficulty raising long-term capital.
- *Relatively limited viewpoint and experience.* The operation depends on one person, and this individual's ability, training, and expertise will limit its direction and scope.

9-4b Partnerships

A **partnership**, as defined by the **Revised Uniform Partnership Act (RUPA),** is an association of two or more persons who act as co-owners of a business for profit. Each partner contributes money, property, labor, or skills, and each shares in the profits (as well as the losses) of the business.[20] Though not specifically required, written articles of partnership are usually executed and are always recommended. This is because, unless otherwise agreed to in writing, the courts assume equal partnership—that is, equal sharing of profits, losses, assets, management, and other aspects of the business.

The articles of partnership clearly outline the financial and managerial contributions of the partners and carefully delineate the roles in the partnership relationship, including such items as: duration of agreement; character of partners (general or limited, active or silent); division of profits and losses; salaries; death of a partner (dissolution and windup); authority (individual partner's authority on business conduct); settlement of disputes; and additions, alterations, or modifications of partnership.

In addition to the written articles, entrepreneurs must consider a number of different types of partnership arrangements. Depending on the needs of the enterprise, one or more of these may be used. Examples include the percentage of financial investment of each partner, the amount of managerial control of each partner, and the actual duties assigned to each partner. It is important to remember that, in a typical partnership arrangement, at least one partner must be a general partner who is responsible for the debts of the enterprise and who has unlimited liability.[21]

ADVANTAGES OF PARTNERSHIPS

The advantages associated with the partnership form of organization are as follows:

- *Ease of formation.* Legal formalities and expenses are few compared with those for creating a more complex enterprise, such as a corporation.
- *Direct rewards.* Partners are motivated to put forth their best efforts by direct sharing of the profits.

- *Growth and performance facilitated.* It often is possible to obtain more capital and a better range of skills in a partnership than in a sole proprietorship.
- *Flexibility.* A partnership often is able to respond quickly to business needs in the form of day-to-day decisions.
- *Relative freedom from governmental control and regulation.* Very little governmental interference occurs in the operation of a partnership.
- *Possible tax advantage.* Most partnerships pay taxes as individuals, thus escaping the higher rate assessed against corporations.

DISADVANTAGES OF PARTNERSHIPS

Partnerships also have disadvantages. Some of these are as follows:

- *Unlimited liability of at least one partner.* Although some partners can have limited liability, at least one must be a general partner who assumes unlimited liability.
- *Lack of continuity.* If any partner dies, is adjudged insane, or simply withdraws from the business, the partnership arrangement ceases. However, operation of the business can continue based on the right of survivorship and the possible creation of a new partnership by the remaining members or by the addition of new members.
- *Relative difficulty obtaining large sums of capital.* Most partnerships have some problems raising a great deal of capital, especially when long-term financing is involved. Usually the collective wealth of the partners dictates the amount of total capital the partnership can raise, especially when first starting out.
- *Bound by the acts of just one partner.* A general partner can commit the enterprise to contracts and obligations that may prove disastrous to the enterprise in general and to the other partners in particular.
- *Difficulty of disposing of partnership interest.* The buyout of a partner may be difficult unless specifically arranged for in the written agreement.

9-4c Corporations

According to Supreme Court Justice John Marshall (1819), a **corporation** is "an artificial being, invisible, intangible, and existing only in contemplation of the law." As such, a corporation is a separate legal entity apart from the individuals who own it. A corporation is created by the authority of state laws and usually is formed when a transfer of money or property by prospective shareholders (owners) takes place in exchange for capital stock (ownership certificates) in the corporation.[22] The procedures ordinarily required to form a corporation are (1) subscriptions for capital stock must be taken and a tentative organization created, and (2) approval must be obtained from the secretary of state in the state in which the corporation is to be formed. This approval is in the form of a charter for the corporation, which states the powers and limitations of the particular enterprise. Corporations that do business in more than one state must comply with federal laws regarding interstate commerce and with the varying state laws that cover foreign (out-of-state) corporations.

ADVANTAGES OF CORPORATIONS

Some of the advantages associated with corporations are as follows:

- *Limited liability.* The stockholder's liability is limited to the individual's investment. This is the most money the person can lose.
- *Transfer of ownership.* Ownership can be transferred through the sale of stock to interested buyers.

THE ENTREPRENEURIAL PROCESS

Incorporating on the Web

Today forming a corporation is easier than ever. Individuals who wish to form a corporation can simply access the services of one of the many companies that provide online incorporation services. Although one has always been able to incorporate in states outside of his or her residence, online incorporation service providers have made this process much more simple. Delaware has been the favorite of many out-of-state incorporations over the past several years. This is due, in large part, to the state's limited restrictions on the formation and operation of corporations.

Web Incorporation Firms

Hundreds of firms offer online incorporation services, and most of these firms offer a very simple process for incorporation in any state. Most of these sites also offer valuable information, such as the various forms of corporation and the positives and negatives of the different options, FAQs on incorporation, the cost of incorporation and maintenance of a corporation, and advantages and disadvantages of incorporation. Harvard Business Services (http://www.delawareinc.com), The Company Corporation (http://www.incorporate.com), and American Incorporators Ltd. (http://www.ailcorp.com) are a few examples of these online incorporation firms. Entrepreneurs also can simply search using a search engine by typing in the word "incorporation" to locate other online incorporation firms.

Considerations for the Entrepreneur

The entrepreneur must consider the future of the business that he or she wishes to incorporate. In most cases, online incorporation is fine for individuals who are interested in starting smaller businesses with limited growth potential, but other avenues are recommended for entrepreneurs who plan to start a business with higher growth potential. If high growth is possible and large amounts of funding is likely necessary, then entrepreneurs are recommended to seek legal counsel through the process of incorporation.

How to Incorporate on the Web

In most cases, filing for incorporation on the Web is as simple as filling out an online incorporation form on one of these firm's websites. The firms then take this information and file the necessary forms at the state office in which the entrepreneur wishes to incorporate. The given state will then issue a certificate of incorporation.

- *Unlimited life.* The company has a life separate and distinct from that of its owners and can continue for an indefinite period of time.
- *Relative ease of securing capital in large amounts.* Capital can be acquired through the issuance of bonds and shares of stock and through short-term loans made against the assets of the business or personal guarantees of the major stockholders.
- *Increased ability and expertise.* The corporation is able to draw on the expertise and skills of a number of individuals, ranging from the major stockholders to the professional managers who are brought on board.

DISADVANTAGES OF CORPORATIONS

Corporations also have disadvantages. Some of these are as follows:

- *Activity restrictions.* Corporate activities are limited by the charter and by various laws.
- *Lack of representation.* Minority stockholders are sometimes outvoted by the majority, who force their will on the others.
- *Regulation.* Extensive governmental regulations and reports required by local, state, and federal agencies often result in a great deal of paperwork and red tape.
- *Organizing expenses.* A multitude of expenses are involved in forming a corporation.
- *Double taxation.* Income taxes are levied both on corporate profits and on individual salaries and dividends.

Table 9.3 compares the characteristics of sole proprietorships, partnerships, and corporations.

TABLE 9.3   GENERAL CHARACTERISTICS OF FORMS OF BUSINESS

	Sole Proprietorship	Partnership	Limited Liability Partnership	Limited Partnership	Limited Liability Limited Partnership	Corporation S	Corporation	Limited Liability Company
Formation	When one person owns a business without forming a corporation or LLC	By agreement of owners or by default when two or more owners conduct business together without forming a limited partnership, an LLC, or a corporation	By agreement of owners; must comply with limited liability partnership statute	By agreement of owners; must comply with limited partnership statute	By agreement of owners; must comply with limited liability limited partnership statute	By agreement of owners; must comply with corporation statute	By agreement of owners; must comply with corporation state; must elect S Corporation status under Subchapter S of Internal Revenue Code	By agreement of owners; must comply with limited liability company statute
Duration	Terminates on death or withdrawal of sole proprietor	Usually unaffected by death or withdrawal of partner	Unaffected by death or withdrawal of partner	Unaffected by death or withdrawal of partner, unless sole general partner dissociates	Unaffected by death or withdrawal of partner, unless sole general partner dissociates	Unaffected by death or withdrawal of shareholder	Unaffected by death or withdrawal of shareholder	Usually unaffected by death or withdrawal of member
Management	By sole proprietor	By partners	By partners	By general partners	By general partners	By board of directors	By board of directors	By managers or members
Owner Liability	Unlimited	Unlimited	Mostly limited to capital contribution	Unlimited for general partners; limited to capital contribution for limited partners	Limited to capital contribution	Limited to capital contribution	Limited to capital contribution	Limited to capital contribution
Transferability of Owners' Interest	None	None	None	None, unless agreed otherwise	None, unless agreed otherwise	Freely transferable, although shareholders may agree otherwise	Freely transferable, although shareholders usually agree otherwise	None, unless agreed otherwise
Federal Income Taxation	Only sole proprietor taxed	Only partners taxed	Usually only partners taxed; may elect to be taxed like a corporation	Usually only partners taxed; may elect to be taxed like a corporation	Usually only partners taxed; may elect to be taxed like a corporation	Corporation taxed; shareholders taxed on dividends (double tax)	Only shareholders taxed	Usually only members taxed; may elect to be taxed like a corporation

Source: Jane P. Mallor, A. James Barnes, Thomas Bowers, and Arlen W. Langvardt, *Business Law: The Ethical, Global, and E-Commerce Environment,* 16th ed. (New York: McGraw-Hill Irwin, 2016), 995. © The McGraw-Hill Companies, Inc.

9-5 PARTNERSHIPS AND CORPORATIONS: SPECIFIC FORMS

A number of specific forms of partnerships and corporations warrant special attention. The following sections examine these.

9-5a Limited Partnerships

 LO7 Explain the nature of the limited partnership and limited liability partnerships (LLPs)

Limited partnerships are used in situations where a form of organization is needed that permits capital investment without responsibility for management *and* without liability for losses beyond the initial investment. Such an organization allows the right to share in the profits with limited liability for the losses.

Limited partnerships are governed by the **Revised Uniform Limited Partnership Act (RULPA)**.[23] The act contains 11 articles and 64 sections of guidelines covering areas such as (1) general provisions, (2) formation, (3) limited partners, (4) general partners, (5) finance, (6) distributions and withdrawals, (7) assignment of partnership interest, (8) dissolution, (9) foreign limited partnerships, (10) derivative actions, and (11) miscellaneous. If a limited partnership appears to be the desired legal form of organization, the prospective partners must examine these RULPA guidelines.

9-5b Limited Liability Partnerships

The **limited liability partnership (LLP)** is a relatively new form of partnership that allows professionals the tax benefits of a partnership while avoiding personal liability for the malpractice of other partners. If a professional group organizes as an LLP, innocent partners are not personally liable for the wrongdoing of the other partners.

The LLP is similar to the *limited liability company (LLC)* discussed later. The difference is that LLPs are designed more for professionals who normally do business as a partnership. As with LLCs, LLPs must be formed and operated in compliance with state statutes.

One of the reasons why LLPs are becoming so popular among professionals is that most statutes make it relatively easy to establish an LLP. This is particularly true for an already formal partnership.

Converting from a partnership to an LLP also is easy because the firm's basic organizational structure remains the same. Additionally, all of the statutory and common-law rules governing partnerships still apply (apart from those modified by the LLP statute). Normally, LLP statutes are simply amendments to a state's already existing partnership law.[24]

The **limited liability limited partnership (LLLP)** is a relatively new variant of the limited partnership. An LLLP has elected limited liability status for all of its partners, including general partners. Except for this liability status of general partners, limited partnerships and LLLPs are identical (see Table 9.4 for characteristics of limited partnerships and LLLPs).

9-5c S Corporations

LO8 Examine how an S corporation works

Formerly termed a Subchapter S corporation, the **S corporation** takes its name from Subchapter S of the Internal Revenue Code, under which a business can seek to avoid the imposition of income taxes at the corporate level, yet retain some of the benefits of a corporate form (especially the limited liability).

Commonly known as a "tax option corporation," an S corporation is taxed similarly to a partnership.[12] Only an information form is filed with the IRS to indicate the shareholders' income. In this manner, the double-taxation problem of corporations is avoided. Corporate income is not taxed but instead flows to the personal income of shareholders of businesses and is taxable at that point.

Although this is very useful for small businesses, strict guidelines must be followed:

1. The corporation must be a domestic corporation.
2. The corporation must not be a member of an affiliated group of corporations.

TABLE 9.4 PRINCIPAL CHARACTERISTICS OF LIMITED PARTNERSHIPS AND LLLPS

1. A limited partnership or LLLP may be *created only in accordance with a statute.*

2. A limited partnership or LLLP has two types of partners: *general partners* and *limited partners.* It must have one or more of each type.

3. All partners, limited and general, *share the profits* of the business.

4. Each limited partner has liability *limited to his capital contribution* to the business. Each general partner of a limited partnership has *unlimited liability* for the obligations of the business. A general partner in an LLLP, however, has liability *limited to his capital contribution.*

5. Each general partner has a *right to manage* the business, and he or she is an agent of the limited partnership or LLLP. A limited partner has *no right to manage* the business or to act as its agent, but he or she does have the right to vote on fundamental matters. A limited partner may manage the business, yet retain limited liability for partnership obligations.

6. General partners, as agents, are *fiduciaries* of the business. Limited partners are not fiduciaries.

7. A partner's rights in a limited partnership or LLLP *are not freely transferable.* A transferee of a general or limited partnership interest in not a partner, but is entitled only to the transferring partner's share of capital and profits.

8. The death or other withdrawal of a partner does not dissolve a limited partnership or LLLP, unless there is no surviving general partner.

9. Usually, a limited partnership or LLLP is taxed like a partnership.

Source: Adapted from Jane P. Mallor, A. James Barnes, Thomas Bowers, and Arlen W. Langvardt, *Business Law: The Ethical, Global, and E-Commerce Environment,* 16th ed. (New York: McGraw-Hill Irwin, 2016), 1056.

3. The shareholders of the corporation must be individuals, estates, or certain trusts. Corporations, partnerships, and nonqualifying trusts cannot be shareholders.

4. The corporation must have 100 or fewer shareholders.

5. The corporation must have only one class of stock, although not all shareholders need have the same voting rights.

6. No shareholder of the corporation may be a nonresident alien.

The S corporation offers a number of benefits. For example, when the corporation has losses, Subchapter S allows the shareholders to use these losses to offset taxable income. Also, when the stockholders are in a tax bracket lower than that of the corporation, Subchapter S causes the company's entire income to be taxed in the shareholders' bracket, whether or not it is distributed. This is particularly attractive when the corporation wants to accumulate earnings for future business purposes.

The taxable income of an S corporation is taxable only to those who are shareholders at the end of the corporate year when that income is distributed. The S corporation can choose a fiscal year that will permit it to defer some of its shareholders' taxes. This is important because undistributed earnings are not taxed to the shareholders until after the corporation's (not the shareholders') fiscal year. In addition, the shareholder in an S corporation can give some of his or her stock to other members of the family who are in a lower tax bracket. Additionally, up to six generations of one family may elect to be treated as one shareholder. Finally, an S corporation can offer some tax-free corporate benefits. These benefits typically mean federal tax savings to the shareholders.

9-5d Limited Liability Companies

Since 1977, an increasing number of states have authorized a new form of business organization called the **limited liability company (LLC).** The LLC is a hybrid form of business enterprise that offers the limited liability of a corporation but the tax advantages of a partnership.

A major advantage of the LLC is that it does not pay taxes on an entity; rather, profits are "passed through" the LLC and paid personally by company members. Another advantage is that the liability of members is limited to the amount of their investments. In an LLC, members are allowed to participate fully in management activities, and—under at least one state's statute—the firm's managers need not even be LLC members. Yet another advantage is that corporations and partnerships, as well as foreign investors, can be LLC members. Also, no limit exists on the number of LLC shareholder members.

The disadvantages of the LLC are relatively few. Perhaps the greatest disadvantage is that LLC statutes differ from state to state, and thus any firm engaged in multistate operations may face difficulties. In an attempt to promote some uniformity among the states in respect to LLC statutes, the National Conference of Commissioners on Uniform State Laws adopted the Revised Uniform Limited Liability Company Act in 2006. However, as of 2011 only nine states had adopted it. Until all of the states have adopted the uniform law, an LLC in one state will have to check the rules in the other states in which the firm does business to ensure that it retains its limited liability.[25]

9-5e B Corporations

As discussed in Chapter 4, there is a new legal form of a socially responsible corporation being introduced across the United States—the **B corporation**. Certified B corporations are a new way for businesses to solve social and environmental problems. B Lab, a nonprofit organization, certifies B corporations. B corporations address two critical problems:

1. Corporate laws make it difficult for businesses to consider employee, community, and environmental interests in their decision-making.
2. The lack of transparent standards makes it difficult to tell the difference between a socially proactive company and just good marketing

To address these issues, B corporations' legal structure expands corporate accountability so they are required to make decisions that are good for society, not just their shareholders. B corporations' performance standards enable consumers to support businesses that align with their values, investors to drive capital to higher impact investments, and governments and multinational corporations to implement sustainable procurement policies.

B corporations have specific requirements, including:

1. Comprehensive and transparent social and environmental performance standards.
2. Higher legal accountability standards.
3. Expected relations with constituencies established for public policies that support sustainable business.

There are over 500 Certified B corporations across 60 different industries (from food and apparel to attorneys and office supplies). B corporations may be quite diverse, but they share one unifying goal: *to redefine success in business.* Through a company's public B Impact Report, anyone can access performance data about the social and environmental practices that stand behind their products.[26]

9-5f L3C

A low-profit, limited liability company, known as the **L3C**, can provide a structure that facilitates investments in socially beneficial, for-profit ventures. In 2008, Vermont became the first state to recognize the L3C as a legal corporate structure; however similar legislation has been introduced in Georgia, Michigan, Montana, and North Carolina. Currently the L3C is legal for activity all across the United States because it is designed to attract private investments and philanthropic capital in ventures designed to provide a social benefit. Unlike a standard LLC, the L3C has an explicit primary charitable mission and only a secondary profit concern. But unlike a charity, the L3C is free to distribute the profits, after taxes, to owners or investors. A principal advantage of the L3C is its qualification as a "program related investment" (PRI). That means it is an investment with a socially beneficial purpose that is consistent with a foundation's mission. Because foundations can only directly invest in for-profit ventures qualified as PRIs, the L3C's operating agreement specifically outlines its respective PRI-qualified purpose in being formed, making it easier for foundations to identify social-purpose businesses as well as helping to ensure that their tax exemptions remain secure. L3Cs could attract a greater amount of private capital from various sources in order to serve their charitable or education goals.

Similar to the standard LLC, the L3C is able to form flexible partnerships where ownership rights are set to meet the requirements of each partner. This flexibility permits a tiered ownership structure. Because a foundation can invest through PRIs at less than the market rate while embracing higher risk levels, this lowers the risk to other investors and increases their potential rate of return. So the remaining L3C memberships can then be marketed at risk/return profiles necessary to attract market driven investors. The end result: the L3C is able to leverage PRIs to access a wide range of investment dollars. Like the standard LLC, profits and losses flow through the L3C to its members and are taxed according to each investor's particular tax situation.[27]

9-6 FINAL THOUGHTS ON LEGAL FORMS

As mentioned earlier, an entrepreneur always should seek professional legal advice to avoid misunderstandings, mistakes, and, of course, added expenses. The average entrepreneur encounters many diverse problems and stumbling blocks in venture formation. Because he or she does not have a thorough knowledge of law, accounting, real estate, taxes, and governmental regulations, an understanding of certain basic concepts in these areas is imperative.

The material in this chapter is a good start toward understanding the legal forms of organizations. It can provide entrepreneurs with guidelines for seeking further and more specific advice on the legal form that appears most applicable to their situation.

9-7 BANKRUPTCY

LO10 Present the major segments of the bankruptcy law that apply to entrepreneurs

Bankruptcy occurs when a venture's financial obligations are greater than its assets. No entrepreneur intentionally seeks bankruptcy. Although problems occasionally can arise out of the blue, following are several ways to foresee impending failure: (1) New competition enters the market, (2) other firms seem to be selling products that are a generation ahead, (3) the research and development budget is proportionately less than the competition's, and (4) retailers always seem to be overstocked.[28]

9-7a The Bankruptcy Act

The **Bankruptcy Act** is a federal law that provides for specific procedures to handle **insolvent debtors**—those who are unable to pay debts as they become due. The initial act of 1912 was completely revised in 1978; significant amendments were added in 1984, 1986, 1994, and the most substantial revision in 2005. The purposes of the Bankruptcy Act are (1) to ensure that the property of the debtor is distributed fairly to the creditors, (2) to protect creditors from having debtors unreasonably diminish their assets, and (3) to protect debtors from extreme demands by creditors. The law was set up to provide assistance to both debtors and creditors.

Each of the various types of bankruptcy proceedings has its own particular provisions. For purposes of business ventures, the three major sections are called straight bankruptcy (Chapter 7), reorganization (Chapter 11), and adjustment of debts (Chapter 13). Table 9.5 provides a comparison of these three types of bankruptcies. The following sections examine each type.

TABLE 9.5	BANKRUPTCY: A COMPARISON OF CHAPTERS 7, 11, AND 13		
	Chapter 7	**Chapter 11**	**Chapter 13**
Purpose	Liquidation	Reorganization	Adjustment
Who Can Petition	Debtor (voluntary) or creditors (involuntary)	Debtor (voluntary) or creditors (involuntary)	Debtor (voluntary) only
Who Can Be a Debtor	Any "person" (including partnerships and corporations) except railroads, insurance companies, banks, savings and loan institutions, and credit unions. Farmers and charitable institutions cannot be involuntarily petitioned.	Any debtor eligible for Chapter 7 relief.	Any individual (not partnerships or corporations) with regular income who owes fixed unsecured debt of less than $360,475 or secured debt of less than $1,081,400.
Basic Procedure	Nonexempt property is sold with proceeds to be distributed (in order) to priority groups. Dischargeable debts are terminated.	A plan is submitted and, if it is approved and followed, debts are discharged.	A plan is submitted in which unsecured creditors must receive at least liquidation value. If it is approved and followed, debts are discharged.
Advantages	On liquidation and distribution, most debts are discharged, and the debtor has an opportunity for a fresh start.	The debtor continues in business. The plan allows for a reorganization and liquidation of debts over the plan period.	The debtor continues in business or keeps possession of assets. If the plan is approved, most debts are discharged after a three-to five-year period.

Source: Adapted from Jane P. Mallor, A. James Barnes, Thomas Bowers, and Arlen W. Langvardt, *Business Law: The Ethical, Global, and E-Commerce Environment*, 16th ed. (New York: McGraw-Hill Irwin, 2016), 855; and also Kenneth W. Clarkson, Roger LeRoy Miller, and Frank B. Cross, *Business Law*, 13th ed. (Mason, OH: South-Western/Cengage, 2015), 601.

9-7b Chapter 7: Straight Bankruptcy

Chapter 7 bankruptcy, sometimes referred to as liquidation, requires the debtor to surrender all property to a trustee appointed by the court. The trustee then sells the assets and turns the proceeds over to the creditors. The remaining debts (with certain exceptions) are then discharged, and the debtor is relieved of his or her obligations.

A liquidation proceeding may be voluntary or involuntary. In a voluntary bankruptcy, the debtor files a petition with the bankruptcy court that provides a list of all creditors, a statement of financial affairs, a list of all owned property, and a list of current income and expenses. In an involuntary bankruptcy, the creditors force the debtor into bankruptcy. For this to occur, 12 or more creditors (of which at least three have a total of $14,425 of claims) must exist; if fewer than 12 exist, one or more creditors must have a claim of $14,425 against the debtor.[29]

9-7c Chapter 11: Reorganization

Reorganization is the most common form of bankruptcy. Under this format, a debtor attempts to formulate a plan to pay a portion of the debts, have the remaining sum discharged, and continue to stay in operation. The plan is essentially a contract between the debtor and creditors. In addition to being viewed as "fair and equitable," the plan must (1) divide the creditors into classes, (2) set forth how each creditor will be satisfied, (3) state which claims

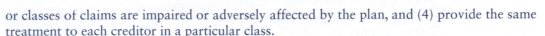

or classes of claims are impaired or adversely affected by the plan, and (4) provide the same treatment to each creditor in a particular class.

The same basic principles that govern Chapter 7 bankruptcy petitions also govern the Chapter 11 petitions. The proceedings may be either voluntary or involuntary, and the provisions for protection and discharge are similar to the Chapter 7 regulations.

Once an order for relief (the petition) is filed, the debtor in a Chapter 11 proceeding continues to operate the business as a debtor-in-possession, which means that the court appoints a trustee to oversee the management of the business. The plan is then submitted to the creditors for approval. Approval generally requires that creditors holding two-thirds of the amount and one-half of the number of each class of claims impaired by the plan must accept it. Once approved, the plan goes before the court for confirmation. If the plan is confirmed, the debtor is responsible for carrying it out.[30]

Once the plan is confirmed by the creditors, it is binding for the debtor. This type of bankruptcy provides an alternative to liquidating the entire business and thus extends to the creditors and debtor the benefits of keeping the enterprise in operation.

9-7d Chapter 13: Adjustment of Debts

Under this arrangement, individuals are allowed to (1) avoid a declaration of bankruptcy, (2) pay their debts in installments, and (3) be protected by the federal court. Individuals or sole proprietors with unsecured debts of less than $360,475 and secured debts of less than $1,081,400 are eligible to file under a Chapter 13 procedure. This petition must be voluntary only; creditors are not allowed to file a Chapter 13 proceeding. In the petition, the debtor declares an inability to pay his or her debts and requests some form of extension through future earnings (longer period of time to pay) or a composition of debt (reduction in the amount owed).

The individual debtor then files a plan providing the details for treatment of the debts. A Chapter 13 plan must provide for (1) the turnover of such future earnings or income of the debtor to the trustee as is necessary for execution of the plan, (2) full payment in deferred cash payments of all claims entitled to priority, and (3) the same treatment of each claim within a particular class.[31] The plan must provide for payment within three years unless the court specifically grants an extension to five years.

Once the debtor has completed all scheduled payments, the court will issue a discharge of all other debts provided for in the plan. As always, some exceptions to the discharge exist, such as child support and certain long-term debts. In addition, the debtor can be discharged even though he or she does not complete the payments within the three years if the court is satisfied that the failure is due to circumstances for which the debtor cannot justly be held accountable. During a Chapter 13 proceeding, no other bankruptcy petition (Chapter 7 or 11) may be filed against the debtor. Thus, an individual has an opportunity to relieve a debt situation without liquidation or the stigma of bankruptcy. In addition, the creditors may benefit by recovering a larger percentage than they would through a liquidation.

9-8 MINIMIZING LEGAL EXPENSES

Throughout any legal proceedings, the entrepreneur can run up large legal bills. Following are some suggestions for minimizing these expenses:

- Establish a clear fee structure with an attorney before any legal matters are handled. This structure may be based on an hourly charge, a flat fee (straight contract fee), or a contingent fee (percentage of negotiated settlement).

- Attorneys also operate in a competitive environment; thus, fee structures are negotiable.

- Establish clear written agreements on all critical matters that affect business operations, including agreements between principals, employment agreements, confidentiality agreements, and noncompete agreements.

- Always attempt to settle any dispute rather than litigate.

- Have your attorney share forms in electronic format that you can use in routine transactions.
- Use a less expensive attorney for smaller transactions.
- Suggest cost-saving methods to your attorney for ordinary business matters.
- Always check with your attorney during normal business hours.
- Client inefficiency rewards attorneys: Consult with your attorney on several matters at one time.
- Keep abreast of legal developments in your field.
- Handle matters within your "comfort zone" yourself.
- Involve attorneys early on when it is feasible: An ounce of prevention is worth a pound of cure.
- Shop around, but don't attorney-hop. Once you find a good attorney, stick with that person. An attorney who is familiar with your business can handle your affairs much more efficiently than a succession of attorneys, each of whom must research your case from scratch.[32]

SUMMARY

A patent is an intellectual property right that is a result of a unique discovery. Patent holders are provided protection against infringement by others. This protection lasts for 14 years in the case of design patents and for 20 years in all other cases.

Securing a patent can be a complex process, and careful planning is required. Some of the useful rules to follow in acquiring a patent were set forth in this chapter.

A patent may be declared invalid for several reasons: failure to assert the property right for an unreasonable length of time, misuse of the patent, and inability to prove that the patent meets patentability tests. On the other hand, if a patent is valid, the owner can prevent others from infringing on it; if they do infringe on it, the owner can bring legal action to prevent the infringement as well as, in some cases, obtain financial damages.

A copyright provides exclusive rights to creative individuals for the protection of their literary or artistic productions. This protection lasts for the life of the author plus 70 years. In case of infringement, the author (or whoever holds the copyright) can initiate a lawsuit for infringement. This action can result in an end to the infringement and, in some cases, the awarding of financial damages.

A trademark is a distinctive name, mark, symbol, or motto identified with a company's product(s). When an organization registers a trademark, it has the exclusive right to use that mark. Registration acquired before 1989 lasts for 20 years. However, after 1989, registration lasts for 10 years and is renewable every 10 years thereafter. In case of infringement, the trademark holder can seek legal action and damages.

This chapter examined the three major forms of legal organization: sole proprietorship, partnership, and corporation. The advantages and disadvantages of each form were highlighted and compared. In addition, the characteristics and tax considerations of partnerships were compared with those of corporations.

The specific forms of partnerships and corporations were examined. In particular, the requirements and benefits of limited partnerships, LLLPs, S corporations, LLCs, B corporations, and L3Cs were presented.

During the last two decades, numerous business failures have occurred. Three major sections of the Bankruptcy Act are of importance to entrepreneurs. Chapter 7 deals with straight bankruptcy and calls for a liquidation of all assets to satisfy outstanding debts. Chapter 11 deals with reorganization, a format wherein a business continues operating and attempts to formulate a plan to pay a portion of the debts, to have the remaining sum discharged, and to continue to pay the debt in installments. Chapter 13 deals with individual debtors who file a plan for adjustment of their debts. This would apply to sole proprietorships because they are individually owned. More business bankruptcies are handled under Chapter 11 than under the other two sections.

KEY TERMS

abandonment
bankruptcy
Bankruptcy Act
B corporation
cancellation proceedings
claims
cleaning-out procedure
copyright
corporation
debtor-in-possession
fair use doctrine
generic meaning

infringement budget
insolvent debtor
intellectual property right
L3C
limited liability company (LLC)
limited liability limited partnership (LLLP)
limited liability partnership (LLP)
limited partnership
liquidation
partnership
patent

patent and trademark office
Revised Uniform Limited Partnership Act (RULPA)
Revised Uniform Partnership Act
(RUPA)
S corporation
sole proprietorship
specification
trademark
trade secrets
unlimited liability

REVIEW AND DISCUSSION QUESTIONS

1. In your own words, what is a patent? Of what value is a patent to an entrepreneur? What benefits does it provide?

2. What are four basic rules entrepreneurs should remember about securing a patent?

3. When can a patent be declared invalid? Cite two examples.

4. In your own words, what is a copyright? What benefits does a copyright provide?

5. How much protection does a copyright afford the owner? Can any of the individual's work be copied without paying a fee? Explain in detail. If an infringement of the copyright occurs, what legal recourse does the owner have?

6. In your own words, what is a trademark? Why are generic or descriptive names or words not given trademarks?

7. When may a trademark be invalidated? Explain.

8. What are three of the pitfalls individuals should avoid when seeking a trademark?

9. Identify the legal forms available for entrepreneurs structuring their ventures: sole proprietorship, partnership, and corporation.

10. What are the specific advantages and disadvantages associated with each primary legal form of organization?

11. What is the ULPA? Describe it.

12. Explain the limited liability partnership.

13. What is the nature of an S corporation? List five requirements for such a corporation.

14. What is a limited liability company?

15. Explain the value of the B corporation and the L3C as new legal forms.

16. What type of protection does Chapter 7 offer to a bankrupt entrepreneur?

17. What type of protection does Chapter 11 offer to a bankrupt entrepreneur? Why do many people prefer Chapter 11 to Chapter 7?

18. What type of protection does Chapter 13 offer to a bankrupt entrepreneur? How does Chapter 13 differ from Chapter 7 or Chapter 11?

NOTES

1. Roger LeRoy Miller and Frank B. Cross, *The Legal Environment Today: Business in Its Ethical, Regulatory, E-Commerce, and Global Setting*, 8th ed. (Mason, OH: South-Western/Cengage, 2016); see also Constance E. Bagley and Craig E. Dauchy, *The Entrepreneur's Guide to Business Law*, 4th ed. (Mason, OH: Cengage/ South-Western, 2012); and Marianne M. Jennings, *Business: Its Legal, Ethical, and Global Environment*, 10th ed. (Mason, OH: Thomson/South-Western, 2015).

2. Gerald R. Ferrera, Margo E. K. Reder, Robert C. Bird, Jonathan J. Darrow, Jeffrey M. Aresty, Jacqueline Klosek, and Stephen D. Lichtenstein, *Cyberlaw*, 3rd ed. (Mason, OH: South-Western/Cengage, 2012); see also Daniel V. Davidson and Lynn M. Forsythe, *The Entrepreneur's Legal Companion* (Upper Saddle River, NJ: Pearson/Prentice Hall, 2011).

3. Reprinted by permission of the *Harvard Business Review*. An excerpt from "Making Patents Work for Small Companies," by Ronald D. Rothchild, July/ August 1987, 24–30. Copyright © 1987 by the President and Fellows of Harvard College; all rights reserved; See also David Pressman, *Patent It Yourself: Your Step-by-Step Guide to Filing at the U.S. Patent Office*, 15th ed. (Berkeley, CA: Nolo Press, 2011).

4. See Rothchild, 28; Pressman, 14.

5. Kenneth W. Clarkson, Roger LeRoy Miller, and Frank B. Cross, *Business Law*, 13th ed. (Mason, OH: Cengage/ South-Western, 2015), 158–62; see also H. Kevin Steensma, Mukund Chari and Ralph Heidl, "The Quest for Expansive Intellectual Property Rights and the Failure to Disclose Known Relevant Prior Art," *Strategic Management Journal* 36, no. 8 (2015): 1186–204.

6. See Jane P. Mallor, A. James Barnes, Thomas Bowers, Arlen W. Langvardt, Jamie Darin Prenkert and Martin A. McCrory, *Business Law: The Ethical, Global, and E-Commerce Environment*, 16th ed. (New York: McGraw-Hill Irwin, 2016), 257–71.

7. Ibid., 271–74.

8. Ibid., 275.

9. Ibid., 271–72.

10. Trademark Basics, The United States Patent and Trademark Office, 2015 (USPTO.Gov) http://www.uspto.gov/trademarks/basics/index.jsp# (accessed January 8, 2015).

11. "Trademark Portfolio Management Strategies," International Trademark Association, 2015. http://www.inta.org/TrademarkBasics/FactSheets/Pages/TrademarkPortfolioManagementStrategies.aspx (accessed online January 8, 2015).

12. Mallor, *Business Law,* 286–87.

13. Michael Finn, "Everything You Need to Know About Trademarks and Publishing," *Publishers Weekly* (January 6, 1992): 41–44; Joern H. Block, Geertjan De Vries, and Jan H. Schumann, Philipp Sandner, "Trademarks and Venture Capital Valuation, *Journal of Business Venturing* 29, no. 4 (2014): 525–42.

14. See Mallor, *Business Law,* 296–98.

15. Ibid., 297.

16. Ferrera, *Cyberlaw,* 103–29; see also Mallor, *Business Law,* 296.

17. Sandra Malach, Peter Robinson, and Tannis Radcliffe, "Differentiating Legal Issues by Business Type," *Journal of Small Business Management* 44, no. 4 (2006): 563–76; Mina Baliamoune-Lutz and Pierre Garello, "Tax Structure and Eentrepreneurship," *Small Business Economics* 42, no. 1 (2014): 165–90.

18. For a detailed discussion of each form, see Clarkson, *West's Business Law,* 706–854.

19. For further discussion on the legal aspects of proprietorships, see Clarkson, *West's Business Law,* 706–708; see also: Stephan F. Gohmann, Jose M. Fernandez, "Proprietorship and Unemployment in the United States, *Journal of Business Venturing* 29 no. 2 (2014): 289–309.

20. For a good analysis of partnerships, see Clarkson, *West's Business Law,* 719–36.

21. For the complete Revised Uniform Partnership Act and the Revised Uniform Limited Partnership Act, see Mallor, *Business Law,* 954–1029.

22. For a detailed discussion of corporate laws and regulations, see Mallor, *Business Law,* 1223–417.

23. For a good outline of the Revised Uniform Partnership Act and the Revised Uniform Limited Partnership Act, see Clarkson, *West's Business Law,* 732.

24. For more detail on limited partnerships, see Mallor, *Business Law,* 956–59.

25. See Bagley and Dauchy, *The Entrepreneur's Guide to Business Law.* See also "Limited Liability Company," U.S. Small Business Administration, 2015. https://www.sba.gov/content/limited-liability-company-llc (accessed online, Janary 9, 2015); "The Revised Uniform Limited Liability Company Act," National Conference of Commissioners on Uniform State Laws, 2006. http://www.uniformlaws.org/shared/docs/limited%20liability%20company/ullca_final_06rev.pdf (accessed online January 9, 2015). For further discussion on the legal aspects of LLPs, see Mallor, *Business Law,* 956–59.

26. Certified B corporation, http://www.bcorporation.net/ (accessed online January 9, 2015); Jamie Raskin, "The Rise of Benefit Corporations," *The Nation,* June 27, 2011; James Surowiecki, "Companies with Benefits" *The New Yorker,* August 4, 2014 http://www.newyorker.com/magazine/2014/08/04/companies-benefits accessed online January 9, 2015).

27. Gene Takagi, L3C—Low Profit Limited Liability Company, *Non Profit Law Blog*: http://www.nonprofitlawblog.com/home/2008/07/l3c.html (accessed online January 9, 2015).

28. Harlan D. Platt, *Why Companies Fail* (Lexington, MA: Lexington Books, 1985), 83; Howard Van Auken, Jeffrey Kaufmann and Pol Herrmann, "An Empirical Analysis of the Relationship Between Capital Acquisition and Bankruptcy Laws," *Journal of Small Business Management* 47, no. 1 (2009): 23–37; and Mike W. Peng, Yasuhiro Yamakawa and Seung-Hyun Lee, "Bankruptcy Laws and Entrepreneur-Friendliness," *Entrepreneurship Theory and Practice* 34, no. 3 (2010): 517–30.

29. For a detailed discussion of Chapter 7 bankruptcy, see Mallor, *Business Law,* 791–812; see also Clarkson, *West's Business Law,* 581–94.

30. For a detailed discussion of Chapter 11 bankruptcy, see Mallor, *Business Law,* 813–14; see also Clarkson, *West's Business Law,* 595–96.

31. For a detailed discussion of Chapter 13 bankruptcy, see Mallor, *Business Law,* 816–19; see also Clarkson, *West's Business Law,* 596–99.

32. Interview with Mark E. Need, JD/MBA, Director, Elmore Entrepreneurship Law Clinic, Indiana University, April 2015.

CHAPTER 10

Marketing Challenges for Entrepreneurial Ventures

LEARNING OBJECTIVES

1 To introduce the new marketing concept for entrepreneurs

2 To review the importance of marketing research for new ventures

3 To identify the key elements of an effective market survey

4 To present factors that inhibit the use of marketing

5 To present the emerging use of social media marketing and mobile marketing for entrepreneurial firms

6 To identify entrepreneurial tactics in marketing research

7 To examine the marketing concept: philosophy, segmentation, and consumer orientation

8 To establish the areas vital to a marketing plan

9 To discuss the key features of a pricing strategy

10 To discuss pricing in the social media age

Entrepreneurial Thought

The new marketing is dynamic and happening in real time. This requires the marketer to accept that the customer is in control, and therefore drives decisions. It also requires reconceptualization of the marketing mix from the perspective of the customer: beyond customer-centric to customer-made. This generation is connected, creative, collaborative, and contextual. The customer is at the center of marketing activity.

—Minet Schindehutte, Michael H. Morris, and Leyland

F. Pitt *Rethinking Marketing*

10-1 THE NEW MARKETING CONCEPT FOR ENTREPRENEURS

LO1 Introduce the new marketing concept for entrepreneurs

Marketing has been and always will be a major element of any entrepreneurial venture. The challenge today is to understand the fundamental shifts that have taken place in our world.

Researchers Minet Schindehutte, Michael H. Morris, and Leyland F. Pitt describe how the new marketing logic requires a fundamental rethinking of the old rules that applied in a world of stability and control. The speed of transactions is higher, dynamic, and happening in real time. In a demand-based economy, entrepreneurs must realize that the customer is in control, and therefore drives decisions. This fact requires a reconceptualization of the marketing mix from customer-centric to customer-made. To illustrate this major rethinking in marketing, we must shift from the 4Ps to the 4Cs:

From Product........*to Cocreated*

From Promotion....*to Communities*

From Price...........*to Customizable*

From Place...........*to Choice*

This is the era of Generation C where the C stands for CONTENT. This generation is connected, creative, collaborative, and contextual. Entrepreneurs must realize that the customer is now at the center of all effective marketing activity.[1]

The new *marketing concept* for entrepreneurs includes knowing what a market consists of, the understanding of marketing research, the development of a marketing plan, the proper understanding and application of social media marketing, and the proper approach to a pricing strategy. In this chapter, we examine each of these key components.

A **market** is a group of consumers (potential customers) who have purchasing power and unsatisfied needs.[2] A new venture will survive only if a market exists for its product or service.[3] This is so obvious that it would seem every entrepreneur would prepare thoroughly the market analysis needed to establish a target market. However, many entrepreneurs know very little about their market, and some even attempt to launch new ventures without identifying any market. (See Table 10.1 concerning the marketing skills of great entrepreneurs.)

A number of techniques and strategies can assist entrepreneurs to effectively analyze a potential market. By using them, entrepreneurs can gain in-depth knowledge about the specific market and can translate this knowledge into a well-formulated business plan. Effective marketing analysis also can help a new venture position itself and make changes that will result in increased sales.[4] The key to this process is marketing research.

10-2 MARKETING RESEARCH

LO2 Review the importance of marketing research for new ventures

Marketing research involves the gathering of information about a particular market, followed by analysis of that information.[5] A knowledge and understanding of the procedures involved in marketing research can be very helpful to the entrepreneur in gathering, processing, and interpreting market information.

10-2a Defining the Research Purpose and Objectives

The first step in marketing research is to define precisely the informational requirements of the decision to be made. Although this may seem too obvious to mention, the fact is that needs are too often identified without sufficient probing. If the problem is not defined clearly, the information gathered will be useless.

In addition, specific objectives should be established. For example, one study has suggested the following set of questions to establish objectives for general marketing research:

- Where do potential customers go to purchase the good or service in question?
- Why do they choose to go there?

TABLE 10.1   COMMON ELEMENTS IN THE MARKETING SKILLS OF GREAT ENTREPRENEURS

1. They possess unique environmental insight, which they use to spot opportunities that others overlook or view as problems.

2. They develop new marketing strategies that draw on their unique insights. They view the status quo and conventional wisdom as something to be challenged.

3. They take risks that others, lacking their vision, consider foolish.

4. They live in fear of being preempted in the market.

5. They are fiercely competitive.

6. They think through the implications of any proposed strategy, screening it against their knowledge of how the marketplace functions. They identify and solve problems that others do not even recognize.

7. They are meticulous about details and are always in search of new competitive advantages in quality and cost reduction, however small.

8. They lead from the front, executing their management strategies enthusiastically and autocratically. They maintain close information control when they delegate.

9. They drive themselves and their subordinates.

10. They are prepared to adapt their strategies quickly and to keep adapting them until they work. They persevere long after others have given up.

11. They have clear visions of what they want to achieve next. They can see further down the road than the average manager can see.

Source: Peter R. Dickson, *Marketing Management*, 1st ed. © 1994 Cengage Learning; see also Barry J. Babin and William G. Zikmund, *Essentials of Marketing Research*, 6th ed. (Mason, OH: Cengage/South-Western, 2016).

- What is the size of the market? How much of it can the business capture?
- How does the business compare with competitors?
- What impact does the business's promotion have on customers?
- What types of products or services are desired by potential customers?[6]

10-2b Gathering Secondary Data

Information that has already been compiled is known as **secondary data**. Generally speaking, secondary data are less expensive to gather than are new, or primary, data. The entrepreneur should exhaust all the available sources of secondary data before going further into the research process. Marketing decisions often can be made entirely with secondary data.

Secondary data may be internal or external. Internal secondary data consist of information that exists within the venture. The records of the business, for example, may contain useful information. External secondary data are available in numerous periodicals, trade association literature, and government publications.

Unfortunately, several problems accompany the use of secondary data. One is that such data may be outdated and, therefore, less useful. Another is that the units of measure in the secondary data may not fit the current problem. Finally, the question of validity is always present. Some sources of secondary data are less valid than others.

10-2c Gathering Primary Data

If secondary data are insufficient, a search for new information, or **primary data**, is the next step. Several techniques can be used to accumulate primary data; these are often classified as observational methods or questioning methods. Observational methods avoid contact with respondents, whereas questioning methods involve respondents in varying degrees. Observation is probably the oldest form of research in existence. Observational methods can be used very economically, and they avoid a potential bias that can result from a respondent's awareness of his or her participation in questioning methods. A major disadvantage of observational methods, however, is that they are limited to descriptive studies.

Surveys and experimentation are two questioning methods that involve contact with respondents. *Surveys* include contact by mail, contact by telephone, and personal interviews. Mail surveys are often used when respondents are widely dispersed; however, these are characterized by low response rates. Telephone surveys and personal interview surveys involve verbal communication with respondents and provide higher response rates. Personal interview surveys, however, are more expensive than mail and telephone surveys. Moreover, individuals often are reluctant to grant personal interviews, because they feel a sales pitch is forthcoming. (Table 10.2 describes the major survey research techniques.)

Experimentation is a form of research that concentrates on investigating cause-and-effect relationships. The goal is to establish the effect an experimental variable has on a dependent variable. For example, what effect will a price change have on sales? Here, the price is the experimental variable, and sales volume is the dependent variable. Measuring the relationship between these two variables would not be difficult were it not for the many other variables involved.[7]

DEVELOPING AN INFORMATION-GATHERING INSTRUMENT

LO3 Identify the key elements of an effective market survey

The questionnaire is the basic instrument for guiding the researcher and the respondent through a survey. The questionnaire should be developed carefully before it is used. Several major considerations for designing a questionnaire are as follows:

- Make sure each question pertains to a specific objective that is in line with the purpose of the study.
- Place simple questions first and difficult-to-answer questions later in the questionnaire.
- Avoid leading and biased questions.
- Ask yourself: "How could this question be misinterpreted?" Reword questions to reduce or eliminate the possibility that they will be misunderstood.
- Give concise but complete directions in the questionnaire. Succinctly explain the information desired, and route respondents around questions that may not relate to them.
- When possible, use scaled questions rather than simple yes/no questions to measure intensity of an attitude or frequency of an experience. For example, instead of asking: "Do we have friendly sales clerks?" (yes/no), ask: "How would you evaluate the friendliness of our sales clerks?" Have respondents choose a response on a five-point scale ranging from "Very unfriendly" (1) to "Very friendly" (5).[8]

10-2d Quantitative versus Qualitative Marketing Research

Quantitative research involves empirical assessments that work from numerical measurements and analytical approaches to compare the results in some way. The researcher is an uninvolved observer so that the results are "objective." However, larger samples are needed to be able to perform the statistical analyses effectively. **Qualitative research** needs far less sample size as it involves the researcher into the process and is able to delve deeper into the questions with the respondents. Since it relies less on analytical testing, and the researcher is engaged in the process, the results are thus considered "subjective."[9]

10-2e Interpreting and Reporting Information

After the necessary data have been accumulated, they should be developed into usable information. Large quantities of data are merely facts. To be useful, they must be organized and molded into meaningful information. The methods of summarizing and simplifying information for users include tables, charts, and other graphic methods. Descriptive statistics—such as the mean, mode, and median—are most helpful in this step of the research procedure.

TABLE 10.2   COMPARISON OF MAJOR SURVEY RESEARCH TECHNIQUES

	Door-to-Door Personal Interview	Mall Intercept Personal Interview	Telephone Interview	Mail Survey	Internet Survey
Speed of Date Collection	Moderate to fast	Fast	Very fast	Slow; researcher has no control over return of questionnaire	Instantaneous; 24/7
Geographic Flexibility	Limited to moderate	Confined; possible urban bias	High	High	High (worldwide)
Respondent Cooperation	Excellent	Moderate to low	Good	Moderate; poorly designed questionnaire will have low response rate	Varies depending on website; high from consumer panels
Versatility of Questioning	Quite versatile	Extremely versatile	Moderate	Not versatile; requires highly standardized format	Extremely versatile
Questionnaire Length	Long	Moderate to long	Moderate	Varies depending on incentive	Moderate; length customized based on answers
Item Nonresponse Rate	Low	Medium	Medium	High	Software can assure none
Possibility for Respondent Misunderstanding	Low	Low	Average	High; no interviewer present for clarification	High
Degree Of Interviewer Influence on Answer	High	High	Moderate	None; interviewer absent	None
Supervision of Interviewers	Moderate	Moderate to high	High; especially with central location interviewing	Not applicable	Not applicable
Anonymity of Respondent	Low	Low	Moderate	High	Respondent can be either anonymous or known
Ease Of Call-Back or Follow-Up	Difficult	Difficult	Easy	Easy, but takes time	Difficult, unless e-mail address is known
Cost	Highest	Moderate to high	Low to moderate	Lowest	Low
Special Features	Visual materials may be shown or demonstrated; extended probing possible	Taste tests, viewing of TV commercials possible	Fieldwork and supervision of data collection are simplified; quite adaptable to computer technology	Respondent may answer questions at own convenience; has time to reflect on answers	Streaming media software allows use of graphics and animation

Source: Peter R. Dickson, *Marketing Management*, 1st ed., © 1994 Cengage Learning; see also Barry J. Babin and William G. Zikmund, *Essentials of Marketing Research*, 6th ed. (Mason, OH: Cengage/South-Western, 2016).

10-2f Marketing Research Questions

The need for marketing research before and during a venture will depend on the type of venture. However, typical research questions might include the following, which are divided by subject:

Sales

1. Do you know all you need to know about your competitors' sales performance by type of product and territory?
2. Do you know which accounts are profitable and how to recognize a potentially profitable one?
3. Is your sales power deployed where it can do the most good and maximize your investment in selling costs?

Distribution

1. If you are considering introducing a new product or line of products, do you know all you should about distributors' and dealers' attitudes toward it?
2. Are your distributors' and dealers' salespeople saying the right things about your products or services?
3. Has your distribution pattern changed along with the geographic shifts of your markets?

Markets

1. Do you know all that would be useful about the differences in buying habits and tastes by territory and kind of product?
2. Do you have as much information as you need on brand or manufacturer loyalty and repeat purchasing in your product category?
3. Can you now plot, from period to period, your market share of sales by products?

Advertising

1. Is your advertising reaching the right people?
2. Do you know how effective your advertising is compared to that of your competitors?
3. Is your budget allocated appropriately for greater profit—according to products, territories, and market potentials?

Products

1. Do you have a reliable quantitative method for testing the market acceptability of new products and product changes?
2. Do you have a reliable method for testing the effect on sales of new or changed packaging?
3. Do you know whether adding higher or lower quality levels would make new profitable markets for your products?

10-3 INHIBITORS TO MARKETING RESEARCH

LO4 Present factors that inhibit the use of marketing

Despite the fact that most entrepreneurs would benefit from marketing research, many fail to do it. A number of reasons exist for this omission, among them cost, complexity, level of need for strategic decisions, and irrelevancy. Several articles have dealt with the lack of marketing research by entrepreneurs in the face of its obvious advantages and vital importance to the success of entrepreneurial businesses.[10]

10-3a Cost

Marketing research can be expensive, and some entrepreneurs believe that only major organizations can afford it. Indeed, some high-level marketing research is expensive, but smaller companies can also use very affordable marketing techniques.

10-3b Complexity

A number of marketing research techniques rely on sampling, surveying, and statistical analysis. This complexity—especially the quantitative aspects—is frightening to many entrepreneurs, and they shun it. The important point to remember is that the key concern is interpretation of the data, and an entrepreneur always can obtain the advice and counsel of those skilled in statistical design and evaluation by calling on the services of marketing research specialists or university professors trained in this area.

10-3c Strategic Decisions

Some entrepreneurs feel that only major strategic decisions need to be supported through marketing research. This idea is tied to the cost and complexity issues already mentioned. The contention is that, because of the cost and statistical complexity of marketing research, it should be conducted only when the decisions to be made are major. The problem lies not only in the misunderstanding of cost and complexity but also in the belief that marketing research's value is restricted to major decisions. Much of the entrepreneur's sales efforts could be enhanced through the results of such research.[11]

10-3d Irrelevancy

Many entrepreneurs believe that marketing research data will contain either information that merely supports what they already know or irrelevant information. Although it is true that marketing research does produce a variety of data, some of which may be irrelevant, it is also a fact that much of the information is useful. In addition, even if certain data merely confirm what the entrepreneur already knows, it is knowledge that has been tested and thus allows the individual to act on it with more confidence.

As indicated by these inhibitors, most of the reasons that entrepreneurs do not use marketing research center either on a misunderstanding of its value or on a fear of its cost. However, the approach to marketing does not have to be expensive and can prove extremely valuable.

10-4 SOCIAL MEDIA MARKETING

LO5 Present the emerging use of social media marketing and mobile marketing for entrepreneurial firms

"Mobile apps, social media, advertising networks, video streaming, broadband, Flash, optimization! These are only a few of the Internet-related terms that have entered the marketing vocabulary in recent years…suggesting how complex the marketing job has become in the Internet age."[12]

Today our world is dominated by social networks, online communities, blogs, wikis, and other online collaborative media. **Social media marketing** describes the use of these tools for marketing purposes. The most common social media marketing tools include Twitter, blogs, LinkedIn, Facebook, Pinterest, Instagram, and YouTube. There are three important aspects to consider with social media marketing:

1. *Create* something of value with an event, a video, a tweet, or a blog entry, that attracts attention and becomes viral in nature. This viral replication of a message through user to user contact is what makes social media marketing work.

2. *Enable* customers to promote a message themselves with multiple online social media venues. Fan pages in Twitter and Facebook are examples of this.

3. *Encourage* user participation and dialogue. A successful social media marketing program must fully engage and respect the customers with online conversations. Social media marketing is not controlled by the organization.[13]

As you can see in these three elements, the real goal of social media marketing is to create a conversation among customers in your market space—a type of word-of-mouth marketing that reaches a critical mass. And why is this so critical for entrepreneurs and their start-up ventures? Researchers focused on social media marketing have pointed to the following facts:

- Facebook now has over one billion users. (Larger than the populations of the United States, Canada, and Mexico combined.)
- According to a social media study, three-quarters of the online population is comprised of frequent social media users.
- Google processes over 3.5 billion online searches every day (or 1.2 trillion per year).
- Forrester Research estimates that online U.S. retail spending will reach $414 billion by 2018, or 11 percent of the entire retail market.[14]

10-4a Key Distinctions of Social Media Marketing

As we pointed out earlier in the chapter, it is a complete misconception to think that social media marketing is just using online social media sites to do traditional marketing. The traditional marketing approach, emphasizing the 4Ps (product, price, place, and promotion), still has some important lessons for marketing, but in the new terrain of social media, it has to be adapted or in some areas changed completely. That is why we presented the 4Cs based on the customer focused concept in this new age of marketing.

In addition, there are several other aspects that distinguish social media marketing from the traditional marketing. One distinction is referred to as *control versus contributions*. Traditional marketing seeks to control the content seen by the audience and attempts to dominate the territory by excluding their competitors' message. Social media marketing emphasizes audience contribution and relinquishes control over large parts of the content. Effective social media marketing can sometimes influence what participants say and think about a brand, but rarely can they control the conversation.

A second important distinction is *trust building*. Firms cannot fully control the content that users will create, so a venture must develop trusting relationships with the customer audience. Unlike traditional advertisements in which consumers have grown to expect some exaggeration to be applied to a product, on social media it is important to be completely honest. Any firm that bends the truth will be held accountable and have to explain those actions.

A third distinction is in how social media messages are consumed. Traditional marketing was "one-way" from the firm to the customers. Social media involves *two-way communication* to an audience that is interested in responding. If the message being delivered is boring, inaccurate, or irrelevant, the customer will look elsewhere. Social media creates an ongoing conversation between the new venture and the customer.[15] Table 10.3 provides an excellent outline of the differences in traditional marketing versus entrepreneurial marketing.

10-4b Developing a Social Media Marketing Plan

A social media marketing plan details an organization's social media goals and the actions necessary to achieve them. Key among these actions is the creation of solid marketing strategies without which there is little chance of successfully executing the plan. Here are some critical steps to keep in mind.

Listen What people are saying about a company enables the organization to determine its current social media presence, which in turn guides the setting of social media goals and strategies to achieve them.

Identify the target market (*niche*) so marketing strategies can be organized to efficiently reach those most receptive customers and eventually advocates.

Categorize social media platforms by target market relevancy. In other words, a company should focus its efforts on the social media sites where its target audience resides in the greatest numbers, resulting in a higher return on investment (ROI).

Appraise The location, behavior, tastes, and needs of the target audience, as well as the competition, need to be appraised to determine an organization's strengths and weaknesses and the opportunities and threats (SWOT Analysis covered in Chapter 13) in the environment.

	TABLE 10.3 TRADITIONAL VERSUS ENTREPRENEURIAL MARKETING	
	Conventional Marketing	**Entrepreneurial Marketing**
Basic Premise	Facilitation of transactions and market control	Sustainable competitive advantage through value-creating innovation
Orientation	Marketing as objective, dispassionate science	Central role of passion, zeal, persistence, and creativity in marketing
Context	Established, relatively stable markets	Envisioned, emerging, and fragmented markets with high levels of turbulence
Marketer's Role	Coordinator of marketing mix; builder of the brand	Internal and external change agent; creator of the category
Market Approach	Reactive and adaptive approach to current market situation with incremental innovation	Proactive approach, leading the customer with dynamic innovation
Customer Needs	Articulated, assumed, expressed by customers through survey research	Unarticulated, discovered, identified through lead users
Risk Perspective	Risk minimization in marketing actions	Marketing as vehicle for calculated risk-taking; emphasis on finding ways to mitigate, stage, or share risks
Resource Management	Efficient use of existing resources, scarcity mentality	Leveraging, creative use of the resources of others; doing more with less; actions are not constrained by resources currently controlled
New Product/ Service Development	Marketing supports new product/ service development activities of R&D and other technical departments	Marketing is the home of innovation; customer is coactive producer
Customer's Role	External source of intelligence and feedback	Active participant in firm's marketing decision process, defining product, price, distribution, and communications approaches.

Source: Minet Schindehutte, Michael H. Morris, and Leyland F. Pitt, *Rethinking Marketing* (Upper Saddle River, NJ. 2009), p. 30.

Implement Choosing the right tools is accomplished by finding the social media sites where the target audience resides and then focusing the company's social media efforts on those platforms.

Collaborate with platform members as a means of establishing a mutually beneficial relationship with the platform participants. Social media is a key way to build relationships. People who feel a personal connection with a company are apt to like and trust the associated brand or product. A faceless corporation is unlikely to inspire confidence, but seeing the people behind the brand can build customer loyalty and support.

Contribute content to build reputation and become a valued member, helping to improve the community. A brand or company can be positioned as thought leaders or experts in an industry by showcasing their unique knowledge. This positioning can develop positive equity for that brand or company; if a firm knows more about the subject area than anyone else, it signals that its product will most likely be of higher quality.

Convert strategy execution into desired outcomes such as brand building, increasing customer satisfaction, driving word-of-mouth recommendations, producing new product ideas, generating leads, handling crisis reputation management, integrating social media marketing with PR and advertising, and increasing search engine ranking and site traffic.

Monitor Evaluate the organization's social media marketing initiatives.[16]

These key steps for a social media marketing plan are just a beginning. It is most important to develop an approach that links the specific goals of the entrepreneur with the marketing strategies. The specifics will depend on information from listening to and observing the target market.

10-4c Mobile Marketing

Mobile computing is the use of portable wireless devices to connect to the Internet. It enables people to access data and to interact on the social web while on the move as long as they are in range of a cellular or WiFi (Wireless Fidelity) network. Common mobile computing devices include cell phones, PDAs, smartphones, tablet PCs, and netbooks. Cell phones provide wireless voice communications and short message service (SMS) for sending and receiving text messages. PDAs (portable digital assistants) are handheld computers that frequently fuse pen-based input to function as personal organizers, thus allowing users to synchronize files with larger computers. Smartphones combine the power of cell phones and PDAs; using mini keyboards for either mechanical or touchscreen input, they can receive and store text messages and e-mail, act as web browsers, run mobile applications to perform a growing variety of tasks, and take pictures with increasingly high-quality miniaturized digital cameras. Tablet PCs are similar to laptop computers, but they use touchscreens to replace bulky keywords, offering a more compact form with maximum screen size. Netbooks are basically laptop computers, but on a smaller scale, more lightweight, and about the size of a hardback book.

Mobile devices are now within everyone's reach, and thus people are connected with their social networks constantly. This means that participants in the social networks are always on and always connected. As a result, people tend to post and share content on social networks more often. Authors Melissa S. Barker, Donald I. Barker, Nicholas F. Bormann, and Krista E. Neher reported that nearly a third of Facebook's one billion active users are currently accessing Facebook through their mobile devices. Twitter shows similar statistics, with reports that 95 percent of Twitter users own a mobile phone, and half of the users access Twitter through their mobile device. It is the way of the future.[17]

Mobile social media marketing is a fast-paced and high-impact marketing tool that many companies have started to use very successfully as part of their overall marketing strategy. Many companies are now using mobile social media applications their standard communication strategy to connect with consumers. It can be defined as a group of mobile marketing applications that allow the creation and exchange of user-generated content. Mobile computing provides a plethora of marketing opportunities, such as text messaging, mobile applications, and mobile advertising.

Companies using mobile social media often obtain personal data about their consumers such as current geographical position in time or space. Mobile social media applications can be differentiated based on location-sensitivity (does the message take account of the specific location of the user?) as well as on time-sensitivity (is the message received and processed by the user instantaneously or with a time-delay?). The most sophisticated forms of mobile social media applications are those that account for both time and location simultaneously.

The overall mobile social media strategy can be complicated but researcher Andreas Kaplan recommends the following "Four Is" to help grasp the overall strategy: integrate, individualize, involve, and initiate.[18]

1. **Integrate.** the best way to integrate the application into the daily life of the user is to offer incentives, prizes, or discounts to the user of the application.

2. **Individualize.** mobile marketing allows for an even higher level of individualized company-to-consumer communication by directing customized messages to different users based on location, taste preferences, and shopping habits.

3. **Involve.** effective mobile campaigns involve the user interactively with a type of a story or game. Mobile social media games often involve prizes for the winners, often in the form of discounts, coupons, or gift cards. Even without prizes, users are still motivated to win one of these interactive games because their social media network "friends" will see if they have won.

4. **Initiate.** Companies sometimes need to initiate the creation of user-generated content in order to start a meaningful dialogue between different consumers as they communicate online. This initiation of consumer dialogue is not straightforward, and many companies may not achieve this no matter how much effort they put into it.

Overall, the future of mobile social media marketing is very promising, and firms should try to capitalize on this type of marketing as soon as possible. The future will bring continued technology enhancements, and the integration of virtual life and real life is inevitable. **Mobile marketing** using social media will be revolutionary and potentially more important than almost any other type of marketing.

10-5 ENTREPRENEURIAL TACTICS IN MARKET RESEARCH

LO6 Identify entrepreneurial tactics in marketing research

Since new start-up ventures are many times resource constrained, entrepreneurs need to sometimes become innovative with their market research. Researchers Minet Schindehutte, Michael H. Morris, and Leyland F. Pitt recommend a number of possible avenues for entrepreneurs to pursue in their marketing research process.[19] These tactics include:

Guerrilla Marketing The use of nonconventional tactics and unorthodox practices applied to marketing research. Realizing that there are an unlimited number of ways in which to collect information regarding a given question, the entrepreneur must thrive on tapping into unutilized sources of information and collecting information in very creative ways.

Insights in Ordinary Patterns The entrepreneur needs to understand that patterns emerge over time, so identifying and tracking them is invaluable. Here are a few of the identifiable trends:

    Potential customers buying at certain times of the year.

    Questions that customers ask employees at similar stores.

    Information sources customers rely on for different types of purchases.

    Patterns in the characteristics of repeat users of similar products.

    Methods that potential customers rely on to reduce risk when they are purchasing.

Technological Tools Today technology can be extremely valuable to entrepreneurs and their research efforts. Tracking software to see exactly how a visitor to the firm's website behaves, what features are examined, and how long they remain on the site, may be a viable tool. Technology that facilitates surveys, such as Survey Monkey, could prove helpful. The emergence of smartphones that allow customers to take pictures of things that interest them represents another research tool with rich potential. Tools to track response rates to advertisements or promotions placed in certain media, especially the Internet, are also valuable.

Customer Observation Insights can be gained from observing situations as they occur. Observational approaches can take many creative forms. They can be obtrusive, where the subject is aware that he or she is being observed, or unobtrusive, where he or she is not aware. An example of the obtrusive approach would be having potential customers use their smartphones to identify preferences and questions as they peruse their choices. An unobtrusive example would be when the entrepreneur counts cars or people that pass a given location at certain times of the day. Either method can be a systematic means of capturing market information.

Web-Based Surveys As we mentioned in the technological tools earlier, Survey Monkey is an example of the easy-to-use tools for creating online surveys. These services help an entrepreneur to design a survey, drop it into an established online questionnaire format, and post it on a secure website. These web-based services will format the data and provide the statistical analysis as well. Web-based surveys are inexpensive and can reach very large numbers of people in a short period of time.

Focus Groups Gathering small groups of potential customers (usually 6–10) for an in-depth discussion about the new venture the entrepreneur is proposing may be a valuable source of insights. Participants elaborate on their feelings, beliefs, perceptions, and experiences with this new venture. Because they are small and less representative of entire market segments, focus groups are valuable ways for getting preliminary insights that are relevant to a particular venture decision.

Lead User Research Find lead users in the marketplace or in particular industries—people who have needs for which no solution exists and who often have ideas for effective products that have not yet been developed. They sometimes are experimenting with prototype solutions that, with modification, have the potential for addressing the lead user's needs. Lead users are often experienced in a particular field of endeavor and are driven to seek a solution to a problem they recognize. These prototype experiments do not produce satisfactory solutions, which creates the opportunity for innovation. The lead user approach would allow the entrepreneur to take pieces of information from these experts about the future and combining them in novel ways.

Blog Monitoring Blog sites have produced a new source of market research insights. A blog is a website that includes user-generated content, typically on some focused topic where anyone can post opinions or information allowing for interactive discussions. Photos, videos, audio inputs, and links to other websites can also be posted. Simple content analysis can be applied to identify prominent terms or themes that appear in blog discussions. Today there are technologies that foster linguistic observation and social network analysis as well.

Archival Research Archives are a collection of records that have been created or accumulated over time. These records might be written documents, magazines, videos, computer files, online databases, patent records, and so forth. Access to most archives is free and the information is objective. They are a type of secondary information that can reveal important insights to the creative researcher. For example, the historical records of Country Business Patterns from the Bureau of the Census can reveal growth patterns for certain industries in different regions of the country. As we discussed in the section on secondary research, there are numerous files and data available if the entrepreneur is willing to search.

10-6 THE COMPONENTS OF EFFECTIVE MARKETING

LO7 Examine the marketing concept: philosophy, segmentation, and consumer orientation

Effective marketing is based on three key elements: marketing philosophy, market segmentation, and consumer behavior. A new venture must integrate all three elements when developing its marketing concept and its approach to the market. This approach helps set the stage for how the firm will seek to market its goods and services.

10-6a Marketing Philosophy

Three distinct types of marketing philosophies exist among new ventures: production driven, sales driven, and consumer driven.

The **production-driven philosophy** is based on the belief you must "produce efficiently and worry about sales later." Production is the main emphasis; sales follow in the wake of production. New ventures that produce high-tech, state-of-the-art output sometimes use a production-driven philosophy. A **sales-driven philosophy** focuses on personal selling and advertising to persuade customers to buy the company's output. This philosophy often surfaces when an overabundance of supply occurs in the market. New auto dealers, for example, rely heavily on a sales-driven philosophy. A **consumer-driven philosophy** relies on research to discover consumer preferences, desires, and needs *before* production actually begins. This philosophy stresses the need for marketing research to better understand where or who a market is and to develop a strategy targeted toward that group. Of the three philosophies, a consumer-driven orientation is often most effective, although many ventures do not adopt it.

Three major factors influence the choice of a marketing philosophy:

1. **Competitive pressure.** The intensity of the competition will many times dictate a new venture's philosophy. For example, strong competition will force many entrepreneurs to develop a consumer orientation in order to gain an edge over competitors. If, on the other hand, little competition exists, the entrepreneur may remain with a production orientation in the belief that what is produced will be sold.

2. **Entrepreneur's background.** The range of skills and abilities entrepreneurs possess varies greatly. Whereas some have a sales and marketing background, others possess production and operations experience. The entrepreneur's strengths will influence the choice of a market philosophy.

3. **Short-term focus.** Sometimes a sales-driven philosophy may be preferred due to a short-term focus on "moving the merchandise" and generating sales. Although this focus appears to increase sales (which is why many entrepreneurs pursue this philosophy), it also can develop into a hard-selling approach that soon ignores customer preferences and contributes to long-range dissatisfaction.

Any one of the three marketing philosophies can be successful for an entrepreneur's new venture. It is important to note, however, that over the long run, the consumer-driven philosophy is the most successful. This approach focuses on the needs, preferences, and satisfactions of the consumer and works to serve the end user of the product or service.

10-6b   Market Segmentation

Market segmentation is the process of identifying a specific set of characteristics that differentiates one group of consumers from the rest. For example, although many people eat ice cream, the market for ice cream can be segmented based on taste and price. Some individuals prefer high-quality ice cream made with real sugar and cream because of its taste; many others cannot tell the difference between high-quality and average-quality ingredients and, based solely on taste, are indifferent between the two types. The price is higher for high-quality ice cream such as Häagen-Dazs or Ben & Jerry's, so the market niche is smaller for these offerings than it is for lower-priced competitors. This process of segmenting the market can be critical for new ventures with very limited resources.

To identify specific market segments, entrepreneurs need to analyze a number of variables. As an example, two major variables that can be focused on are *demographic* and *benefit* variables. Demographic variables include age, marital status, sex, occupation, income, location, and the like. These characteristics are used to determine a geographic and demographic profile of the consumers and their purchasing potential. The benefit variables help to identify unsatisfied needs that exist within this market. Examples may include convenience, cost, style, trends, and the like, depending on the nature of the particular new venture. Whatever the product or service, it is extremely valuable to ascertain the benefits a market segment is seeking in order to further differentiate a particular target group.

10-6c   Consumer Behavior

Consumer behavior is defined by the many types and patterns of consumer characteristics. However, entrepreneurs can focus their attention on only two considerations: personal characteristics and psychological characteristics. Traditionally some marketing experts have tied these characteristics to the five types of consumers: (1) innovators, (2) early adopters, (3) early majority, (4) late majority, and (5) laggards.

The differences in social class, income, occupation, education, housing, family influence, and time orientation are all possible personal characteristics, while the psychological characteristics are needs, perceptions, self-concept, aspiration groups, and reference groups. This type of breakdown can provide an entrepreneur with a visual picture of the type of consumer to target for the sales effort.

The next step is to link the characteristic makeup of potential consumers with buying trends in the marketplace. Table 10.4 shows the changing priorities that have shaped buying decisions. Each of these factors relates to consumer attitudes and behaviors based on education, the economy, the environment, and/or societal changes. By using some of the common

THE ENTREPRENEURIAL PROCESS

Competitive Information

Following is a list of potential techniques to use to assess your competition and avoid paying a high-priced market research firm to collect information for you.

1. Networking. Speaking with people in the field will help you get a feel for what's going on in your industry. Vendors, customers, and anyone who does business with companies in your field may have information on emerging competition. Venture capitalists can be a great source of information because of the due diligence they must perform with pending venture loans. Much like what happens during the start-up phase of a business, a person can become so immersed in a project that he or she develops tunnel vision. Social networking also can provide a fresh view of the industry.

2. Related products. This market is the obvious place to look. Companies that can provide anything that complements your product or service are primed to become competition, because they also know what the customers' needs are and how to fulfill them. Large companies whose customers are businesses will assess this issue very differently compared to a small business with the average person as its primary consumer. A good example of a complementary relationship is the one that exists among cameras, film, photo disks, and so on. The number and type of photographic products available have increased substantially in recent years, and different fields have capitalized on this trend.

3. Value chain. Whereas related products fall on the horizontal axis of an industry, exploring the value chain forces a vertical assessment of potential entrants into your competitive pool. The value chain for a given product or service offers many opportunities for expansion, both for you and for the potential competition. In this situation, the potential competition is fully aware of, and understands, the business environment in which you operate. They already have easy access to suppliers, buyers, and services that you deal with on a daily basis.

4. Companies with related competencies. One of the more ignored avenues involves companies that can take their expertise and apply it to an indirectly related field. Competencies can be both technological and nontechnological. Just because one company has unparalleled customer service and sales in the cellular industry doesn't mean the company couldn't use the same spectacular service in the cable business. The perfect example of expanding on technological similarities is Motorola, whose original intent was to focus on the defense industry. Surely that was not an area cellular providers were examining when trying to anticipate potential competition!

5. Internet. It goes without saying that the Internet is one of the premiere sources of information available to anyone who knows how to use it. Using search engines to access millions of web pages allows a business to easily scope out anyone that offers similar products or services. Searches can be both broad and defined. Most important, they can be done cheaply and as often as desired. It is best to use words that customers might use and avoiding technological or industry jargon when surfing, but try and brainstorming all possible relations to ensure a thorough and effective search. Queries to search engines, such as Bing, Google, and Yahoo! are logged by those search engines, along with basic connectivity information such as IP address and browser version. In the past, analysts had to rely on external companies to provide search behavior data, but increasingly search engines are providing tools to directly mine their data. You can use search engine data with a greater degree of confidence, because it comes directly from the search engine. In Google AdWords, you can use Keyword Tool, the Search-based Keyword Tool, and Insights for Search.

6. Benchmarks from Web analytics vendors. Web analytics vendors have many customers and thus a great deal of data. Many vendors now aggregate this real customer data and present it in the form of benchmarks that you can use to index your own performance. Benchmarking data is currently available from Fireclick, Coremetrics, and Google Analytics. Often, as is the case with Google Analytics, customers have to explicitly opt in their data into this benchmarking service.

Once the sufficient information has been gathered, a plan to beat the current and emerging competition should be prepared. The plan created will be analogous to the business's strengths and resources. Issues such as losing sales to another company could be addressed, a SWOT (strengths, weaknesses, opportunities, threats) analysis could be executed, or the plan to offer a new product or change price points could be outlined.

Source: Adapted from Mark Henricks, "Friendly Competition?," *Entrepreneur* (December 1999): 114–17; "The Definitive Guide to Competitive Intelligence Data Sources," February 22, 2010, http://www.kaushik.net/avinash/competitive-intelligence-data-sources-best-practices/ (accessed April 30, 2012); and "Gathering Competitive Information," United Technologies Corporation, http://utc.com/StaticFiles/UTC/StaticFiles/info_englishlanguage.pdf (accessed April 30, 2012).

TABLE 10.4	CHANGING PRIORITIES AND PURCHASES IN THE FAMILY LIFE CYCLE

Stage	Priorities	Major Purchases
Fledgling: teens and early 20s	Self; socializing; education	Appearance products, clothing, automobiles, recreation, hobbies, travel
Courting: 20s	Self and other; pair bonding; career	Furniture and furnishings, entertainment and entertaining, savings
Nest building: 20s early 30s	Babies and career	Home, garden, do-it-yourself items, baby-care products, insurance
Full nest: 30–50s	Children and others; career; midlife crisis	Children's food, clothing, education, transportation, orthodontics, career and life counseling
Empty nest: 50–75	Self and others; relaxation	Furniture and furnishings, entertainment, travel, hobbies, luxury automobiles, boats, investments
Sole survivor: 70–90	Self; health; loneliness	Health care services, diet, security and comfort products, TV and books, long-distance telephone services

Source: Peter R. Dickson, *Marketing Management*, 1st ed., © 1994 Cengage Learning; see also William M. Pride and O. C. Ferrell, *Marketing* 18th ed. (Mason, OH: Cengage/South-Western, 2016).

consumer characteristics and combining them with Table 10.4, the entrepreneur can begin to examine consumer behavior more closely.

An analysis of the way consumers view the venture's product or service provides additional data. Entrepreneurs should be aware of five major consumer classifications:

1. **Convenience goods.** whether staple goods (foods), impulse goods (checkout counter items), or emergency goods and services, consumers will want these goods and services but will not be willing to spend time shopping for them.

2. **Shopping goods.** products consumers will take time to examine carefully and compare for quality and price.

3. **Specialty goods.** products or services consumers make a special effort to find and purchase.

4. **Unsought goods.** items consumers do not currently need or seek. Common examples are life insurance, encyclopedias, and cemetery plots. These products require explanation or demonstration.

5. **New products.** items that are unknown due to lack of advertising or are new products that take time to be understood. When microcomputers were first introduced, for example, they fell into this category.

10-7 DEVELOPING A MARKETING PLAN

LO8 Establish the areas vital to a marketing plan

A *marketing plan* is the process of determining a clear, comprehensive approach to the creation of customers. The following elements are critical for developing this plan:

• *Current marketing research*. determining who the customers are, what they want, and how they buy

• *Current sales analysis*. promoting and distributing products according to marketing research findings

- *Marketing information system.* collecting, screening, analyzing, storing, retrieving, and disseminating marketing information on which to base plans, decisions, and actions
- *Sales forecasting.* coordinating personal judgment with reliable market information *Evaluation*: identifying and assessing deviations from marketing plans[20]

10-7a   Current Marketing Research

The purpose of current marketing research is to identify customers—target markets—and to fulfill their desires. For current marketing research to be effective for the growing venture, the following areas warrant consideration:

- *The company's major strengths and weaknesses.* These factors offer insights into profitable opportunities and potential problems and provide the basis for effective decision making.
- *Market profile.* A market profile helps a company identify its current market and service needs: How profitable are existing company services? Which of these services offer the most potential? Which (if any) are inappropriate? Which will customers cease to need in the future?
- *Current and best customers.* Identifying the company's current clients allows management to determine where to allocate resources. Defining the best customers enables management to segment this market niche more directly.
- *Potential customers.* By identifying potential customers—either geographically or with an industry-wide analysis of its marketing area—a company increases its ability to target this group, thus turning potential customers into current customers.
- *Competition.* By identifying the competition, a company can determine which firms are most willing to pursue the same basic market niche.
- *Outside factors.* This analysis focuses on changing trends in demographics, economics, technology, cultural attitudes, and governmental policy. These factors may have substantial impact on customer needs and, consequently, expected services.
- *Legal changes.* Marketing research performs the important task of keeping management abreast of significant changes in governmental rates, standards, and tax laws.[21]

10-7b   Current Sales Analysis

An entrepreneur needs to continually review the methods employed for sales and distribution in relation to the market research that has been conducted. Matching the correct customer profile with sales priorities is a major goal in sales analysis. Following is a list of potential questions to be answered by this analysis:

- Do salespeople call on their most qualified prospects on a proper priority and time-allocation basis?
- Does the sales force contact decision makers?
- Are territories aligned according to sales potential and salespeople's abilities?
- Are sales calls coordinated with other selling efforts, such as trade publication advertising, trade shows, and direct mail?
- Do salespeople ask the right questions on sales calls? Do sales reports contain appropriate information? Does the sales force understand potential customers' needs?
- How does the growth or decline of a customer's or a prospect's business affect the company's own sales?

10-7c   Marketing Information System

A marketing information system compiles and organizes data relating to cost, revenue, and profit from the customer base. This information can be useful for monitoring the strategies, decisions, and programs concerned with marketing. As with all information systems designs,

THE ENTREPRENEURIAL PROCESS

The Guerrilla Marketing Plan

A business plan is essential for any entrepreneur planning to start an initiative; however, by the time you include your market research results, pro forma statements, and critical risks, your business plan will become a dense packet of information to be used when guiding your entire business—a document that few will read in its entirety. Given this fact, entrepreneurs should be able to quickly articulate the key aspects of their venture in a matter of a few minutes. One tool that can be used for this purpose is what is known as a *guerrilla marketing plan*.

A guerrilla marketing plan forces an entrepreneur to specify the seven most important marketing issues that face his or her company. Of course, there will most certainly be more than seven key areas to address; however, by going through the exercise of consolidating the marketing topics that require the most focus, an entrepreneur will be better prepared to get to the heart of his or her concept, both when presenting to potential investors and when managing the business.

The key is to address each area using no more than a sentence. Guerrilla marketing plans give people a quick understanding of exactly what is of the utmost concern to your business by eliminating much of the detail provided in your full business plan. Large companies make use of such plans by developing different ones for different products. For instance, Procter & Gamble develops a guerrilla marketing plan for each of its products.

Although some companies choose to attach several pages of documentation to their plans, the key is to get the seven sentences right. Following are guidelines for developing a guerrilla marketing plan:

- You should begin your guerrilla marketing plan with a sentence that describes the purpose of your marketing. This sentence should be very specific and should address what impact your marketing initiative should have on a potential customer. Goals such as "to be more successful than my competitors" or "to be more profitable" are not useful. This sentence should quantify your overarching goal so that it is measurable. The point is to envision exactly what you want your customer to ideally do, and then to establish a goal for ensuring that customers will act in that way.

- The next sentence is meant for you to address the competitive advantages of the enterprise; in other words, what are the characteristics of the business that make it uniquely positioned to offer value to the public? The objective with this sentence is to outline your business's strengths that are the most unique so that you can emphasize them in your marketing materials.

- You will address your target audience in the third sentence. By specifying exactly who will be exposed to a marketing campaign, you will find the process of engineering an effective plan to be much more straightforward. Companies often have more than one target audience, so guerrilla marketing plans should be written to address all potential customers in order to avoid losing sales to competitors.

- For the fourth point, a list is most appropriate. This topic addresses the marketing weapons that you will use. The important idea of this section is to include only those tools that the company can understand, afford, and use properly. Countless tools are now readily available to entrepreneurs, so filtering out those that do not meet these three criteria will help you avoid making poorly directed investments.

- You should discuss the company's market niche in the fifth sentence. Now that you have addressed the purpose, benefits, and target market, understanding your marketing niche is the next logical step. The market niche should capture what customers most readily associate with your company. It could be speed, value, variety, or any number of other characteristics. You will not be able to please everyone, so defining what your company is and what it is not will help to narrow your focus when promoting it to potential customers.

- The sixth sentence is where you will establish the identity of your company. Entrepreneurs should ensure that the marketing image they broadcast to the world is supported by the identity of their companies, which means that the companies' operating procedures need to reinforce whatever identity they establish.

- The final sentence in your guerrilla marketing plan needs to explicitly state what percentage of projected gross sales you are willing to earmark as your marketing budget. The quality of your marketing materials will clearly reflect on your business, so this step requires a significant amount of research to ensure that the amount you have allotted will be sufficient for supporting all previous steps.

When developing your guerrilla marketing plan, all subsequent steps should be framed by the first sentence you write, which is meant to define the purpose of your plan. Entrepreneurs should theoretically be able to write a plan of this nature within five minutes, given its brevity. The more practice you get at articulating your business objectives, the easier you will find using tools—such as the guerrilla marketing plan—to communicate your business goals.

Source: Adapted from Jay Conrad Levinson and Jeannie Levinson, "Here's the Plan," *Entrepreneur*, February 2008, http://www.entrepreneur.com/magazine/entrepreneur/2008/february/188842.html (accessed March 20, 2008).

the key factors that affect the value of such a system are (1) data reliability, (2) data usefulness or understandability, (3) reporting system timeliness, (4) data relevancy, and (5) system cost.

10-7d Sales Forecasting

Sales forecasting is the process of projecting future sales through historical sales figures and the application of statistical techniques. The process is limited in value due to its reliance on historical data, which many times fail to reflect current market conditions. As a segment of the comprehensive marketing-planning process, however, sales forecasting can be very valuable.

10-7e Evaluation

The final critical factor in the marketing planning process is evaluation. Because a number of variables can affect the outcome of marketing planning, it is important to evaluate performance. Most important, reports should be generated from a customer analysis: attraction or loss of customers, with reasons for the gain or loss, as well as established customer preferences and reactions. This analysis can be measured against performance in sales volume, gross sales dollars, or market share. It is only through this type of evaluation that flexibility and adjustment can be incorporated into marketing planning.

10-7f Final Considerations for Entrepreneurs

Marketing plans are part of a venture's overall strategic effort.[22] To be effective, these plans must be based on the venture's specific goals. Following is an example of a five-step program designed to help entrepreneurs create a structured approach to developing a market plan:

Step 1: Appraise marketing strengths and weaknesses, emphasizing factors that will contribute to the firm's "competitive edge." Consider product design, reliability, durability, price/quality ratios, production capacities and limitations, resources, and need for specialized expertise.

Step 2: Develop marketing objectives, along with the short- and intermediate-range sales goals necessary to meet those objectives. Next, develop specific sales plans for the current fiscal period. These goals should be clearly stated, measurable, and within the company's capabilities. To be realistic, these goals should require only reasonable efforts and affordable expenditures.

Step 3: Develop product/service strategies. The product strategy begins with identifying the end users, wholesalers, and retailers, as well as their needs and specifications. The product's design, features, performance, cost, and price then should be matched to these needs.

Step 4: Develop marketing strategies. Strategies are needed to achieve the company's intermediate- and long-range sales goals and long-term marketing objectives. These strategies should include advertising, sales promotion campaigns, trade shows, direct mail, and telemarketing. Strategies also may be necessary to increase the size of the sales force or market new products. Contingency plans will be needed in the event of technological changes, geographic market shifts, or inflation.

Step 5: Determine a pricing structure. A firm's pricing structure dictates which customers will be attracted, as well as the type or quality of products/services that will be provided. Many firms believe that the market dictates a "competitive" pricing structure. However, this is not always the case—many companies with a high price structure are very successful. Regardless of the strategies, customers must believe that the product's price is appropriate. The price of a product or service, therefore, should not be set until marketing strategies have been developed.[23]

10-8 PRICING STRATEGIES

One final marketing issue that needs to be addressed is that of pricing strategies. Many entrepreneurs are unsure of how to price their product or service, even after marketing research is conducted. A number of factors affect this decision: the degree of competitive pressure, the availability of sufficient supply, seasonal or cyclical changes in demand, distribution costs, the product's life-cycle stage, changes in production costs, prevailing economic conditions, customer services provided by the seller, the amount of promotion done, and the market's buying power. Obviously, the ultimate price decision will balance many of these factors and, usually, will not satisfy *all* conditions. However, awareness of the various factors is important.

Other considerations, sometimes overlooked, are psychological in nature:

- In some situations, the quality of a product is interpreted by customers according to the level of the item's price.

- Some customer groups shy away from purchasing a product when no printed price schedule is available.

- An emphasis on the monthly cost of purchasing an expensive item often results in greater sales than an emphasis on total selling price.

- Most buyers expect to pay even-numbered prices for prestigious items and odd-numbered prices for commonly available goods.

- The greater the number of meaningful customer benefits the seller can convey about a given product, the less the price resistance (generally).[24]

10-8a Views of Pricing

Pricing can be viewed as value, variable, variety, visible, and virtual. When seen as *value*, the amount a customer is willing to pay is, in the final analysis, a statement of the amount of value they perceive in the product or service. Pricing can be *variable*, such as varying the components of payment, what is actually being paid for, the time of payment, the form of payment, the terms of payment, and the person doing some or all of the paying. There is a *variety* of pricing because firms typically sell multiple products and services, and they may use the price of some items to influence the sales of others or price in a manner that pushes items with higher versus lower profit margins. The *visible* nature of pricing means that customers see and are aware of the prices of most things that they buy, which signals to the customer ideas about value, image, product availability, demand conditions, and exclusivity. Finally, pricing is *virtual* because it is the easiest and quickest to change in response to market conditions, especially in today's technological age.[25]

10-8b Product Life Cycle Pricing

Pricing procedures differ depending on the nature of the venture: retail, manufacturing, or service. Pricing for the product life cycle as presented in Table 10.5, however, might be applied to any type of business. The table demonstrates the basic steps of developing a pricing system and indicates how that system should relate to the desired pricing goals.

10-8c Pricing in the Social Media Age

Today's social media start-ups are finding unique ways of generating revenue from the very beginning. There are numerous variations of revenue models, including freemium, affiliate, subscription, virtual goods, and advertising. Let's briefly examine these.

Freemium Model Offers a basic service for free, while charging for a premium service with advanced features to paying members. Examples of companies that have used this method include Flickr and LinkedIn. The biggest challenge for businesses using the freemium model is figuring how much to give away for free so that users will still need and want to upgrade to a paying plan. If most users can get by with the basic free plan, they won't have a need to upgrade.

Affiliate Model The business makes money by driving traffic, leads, or sales to another, affiliated company's website. Businesses that sell a product, meanwhile, rely on affiliated sites to send them the traffic or leads they need to make sales. Like businesses that rely on advertising, high-traffic sites have an easier time making money using affiliate links than sites that are just starting out. The biggest challenge may be reader trust and proper

TABLE 10.5 PRICING FOR THE PRODUCT LIFE CYCLE

Customer demand and sales volume will vary with the development of a product. Thus, pricing for products needs to be adjusted at each stage of their life cycle. The following outline provides some suggested pricing methods that relate to the different stages in the product life cycle. With this general outline in mind, potential entrepreneurs can formulate the most appropriate pricing strategy.

Product Life-Cycle Stage	Pricing Strategy	Reasons/Effects
Introductory Stage		
Unique product	**Skimming**—deliberately setting a high price to maximize short-term profits	Initial price set high to establish a quality image, to provide capital to offset development costs, and to allow for future price reductions to handle competition
Nonunique product	**Penetration**—setting prices at such a low level that products are sold at a loss	Allows quick gains in market share by setting a price below competitors' prices
Growth Stage	**Consumer pricing**—combining penetration and competitive pricing to gain market share; depends on consumer's perceived value of product	Depends on the number of potential competitors, size of total market, and distribution of that market
Maturity Stage	**Demand-oriented pricing**—a flexible strategy that bases pricing decisions on the demand level for the product	Sales growth declines; customers are very price-sensitive
Decline Stage	**Loss leader pricing**—pricing the product below cost in an attempt to attract customers to other products	Product possesses little or no attraction to customers; the idea is to have low prices bring customers to newer product lines

Source: Adapted from Colleen Green, "Strategic Pricing," *Small Business Reports* (August 1989): 27–33; updated for accuracy February, 2015.

targeting. It's worth the time researching those in your market niche and initiate conversations with them.

Subscription Model This requires users to pay a fee (generally monthly or yearly) to access a product or service. If you are creating a long-term relationship with customers, then this model would be better in the long run. However, you need content and features every month that will be new and exciting. You should also recognize that monthly membership sites have a high attrition rate—after the first time they log in, they forget about it and never come back.

Virtual Goods Model Users pay for virtual goods, such as upgrades, points, or gifts, on a website or in a game. Virtual goods come in all shapes and sizes. The attraction of virtual goods is that margins are high, since goods essentially only cost as much as the bandwidth required to serve them, which is generally almost zero.

Advertising Model Advertisements are sold against the traffic of the site. Simply put, the more traffic you have on your site, the more you can charge for ads (additional demographics about your site's visitors, such as age, gender, location, or interests, also affects the amount you can charge advertisers to place ads on your site). However, it is never easy to monetize something that sits on top of a free service. Maintaining and increasing the value proposition is a daily challenge. Free trials may be the key as they demonstrate respect for the users, as well as confidence in the value that the service provides.[26]

SUMMARY

The new marketing logic requires a fundamental rethinking of the old rules and realizes that today's marketing is dynamic and happening in real time where the customer is in control. This new marketing for entrepreneurs includes knowing what a market consists of, the understanding of marketing research, the development of a marketing plan, the effective understanding and application of social media marketing, and the proper approach to a pricing strategy.

Marketing research involves the gathering of information about a particular market, followed by analysis of that information. The marketing research process has five steps: (1) Define the purpose and objectives of the research, (2) gather secondary data, (3) gather primary data, (4) develop an information-gathering instrument (if necessary), and (5) interpret and report the information.

Four major reasons that entrepreneurs may not carry out marketing research are: (1) cost, (2) complexity of the undertaking, (3) belief that only major strategic decisions need to be supported through marketing research, and (4) belief that the data will be irrelevant to company operations. Usually they misunderstand the value of marketing research or fear its cost.

Social media marketing describes the use of social networks, online communities, blogs, wikis, and other online collaborative media for marketing purposes. The most common social media marketing tools include Twitter, blogs, LinkedIn, Facebook, Flickr, and YouTube. A social media marketing plan should be developed that details the venture's social media goals and the actions necessary to achieve them. Mobile devices are now within everyone's reach, and thus people are connected with their social networks constantly. Mobile social media marketing is a fast-paced and high-impact marketing tool that many companies have started to use very successfully as part of their overall marketing strategy. Many companies are now using mobile social media applications as their standard communication strategy to connect with consumers.

Because new start-up ventures are resource constrained, the chapter covered some innovative methods for entrepreneurs to conduct market research. From there, we examined the development of a marketing concept which has three important parts. The first part is the formulation of a marketing philosophy. Some entrepreneurs are production driven, others are sales driven, and still others are consumer driven. The entrepreneur's values and the market conditions will help determine this philosophy. The second part is market segmentation, which is the process of identifying a specific set of characteristics that differentiates one group of consumers from the rest. Demographic and benefit variables often are used in this process. The third part is an understanding of consumer behavior. Because many types and patterns of consumer behavior exist, entrepreneurs need to focus on the personal and psychological characteristics of their customers. In this way, they can determine a tailor-made, consumer-oriented strategy. This customer analysis focuses on such important factors as general buying trends in the marketplace, specific buying trends of targeted consumers, and the types of goods and services being sold.

A marketing plan is the process of determining a clear, comprehensive approach to the creation of customers. The following elements are critical for developing this plan: current marketing research, current sales analysis, a marketing information system, sales forecasting, and evaluation.

Pricing strategies are a reflection of marketing research and must consider such factors as marketing competitiveness, consumer demand, life cycle of the goods or services being sold, costs, and prevailing economic conditions. Today's social media start-ups are finding unique ways of generating revenue from the very beginning. In the chapter, we presented five revenue models, including freemium, affiliate, subscription, virtual goods, and advertising.

KEY TERMS

advertising model
affiliate model
blog monitoring

consumer-driven philosophy
consumer pricing
demand-oriented pricing

freemium model
guerrilla marketing
individualize

initiate
integrate
involve
loss leader pricing
mobile marketing
market
marketing research

market segmentation
penetration
primary data
production-driven philosophy
qualitative research
quantitative research
sales-driven philosophy

secondary data
skimming
social media marketing
subscription model
virtual goods model

REVIEW AND DISCUSSION QUESTIONS

1. Describe the "new" marketing concept for entrepreneurs with the 4Cs.

2. In your own words, what is a market? How can marketing research help an entrepreneur identify a market?

3. What are the five steps in the marketing research process? Briefly describe each.

4. Which is of greater value to the entrepreneur, primary or secondary data? Why?

5. Identify and describe three of the primary obstacles to undertaking marketing research.

6. Describe social media marketing and mobile marketing. Be specific in your answer.

7. Discuss some of the entrepreneurial tactics in market research that are accomplished with limited resources.

8. How would an entrepreneur's new-venture strategy differ under each of the following marketing philosophies: production driven, sales driven, consumer driven? Be complete in your answer.

9. In your own words, what is market segmentation? What role do demographic and benefit variables play in the segmentation process?

10. Identify and discuss three of the psychological characteristics that help an entrepreneur identify and describe customers. Also, explain how the product life cycle will affect the purchasing behavior of these customers.

11. What are the five steps that are particularly helpful for developing a marketing plan? Identify and describe each.

12. What are some of the major environmental factors that affect pricing strategies? What are some of the major psychological factors that affect pricing? Identify and discuss three of each.

13. Explain how pricing is viewed in different ways. Be specific.

14. How do pricing strategies differ based on the product life cycle?

15. Identify the five revenue models for social media start-ups.

NOTES

1. Minet Schindehutte, Michael H. Morris, and Leyland F. Pitt, *Rethinking Marketing* (Upper Saddle River, NJ: Pearson Prentice Hall, 2009).

2. For a discussion of markets, see Louis E. Boone and David L. Kurtz, *Contemporary Marketing* 17th ed. (Mason, OH: Cengage/South-Western, 2016); Philip Kotler and Gary Armstrong, *Principles of Marketing* 16th ed. (Upper Saddle River, NJ: Pearson/Prentice Hall, 2016); and William M. Pride and O. C. Ferrell, *Marketing* 18th ed. (Mason, OH: Cengage/South-Western, 2016).

3. Minet Schindehutte, Michael H. Morris, and Akin Kocak, "Understanding Market-Driven Behavior: The Role of Entrepreneurship," *Journal of Small Business Management* 46, no. 1 (2008): 4–26; Jonas Dahlqvist and Johan Wiklund, "Measuring the Market Newness of New Ventures" *Journal of Business Venturing* 27, no. 2 (2012): 185–96.

4. Bret Golan, "Achieving Growth and Responsiveness: Process Management and Market Orientation in Small Firms," *Journal of Small Business Management* 44, no. 3 (2006): 369–85; Michael Song, Tang Wang, and Mark E. Parry, "Do Market Information

Processes Improve New Venture Performance?" *Journal of Business Venturing* 25, no. 6 (2010): 556–68.

5. For a thorough presentation, see R. Ganeshasundaram and N. Henley, "The Prevalence and Usefulness of Market Research: An Empirical Investigation into 'Background' versus 'Decision' Research," *International Journal of Market Research* 48, no. 5 (2006): 525–50; Malte Brettel, Andreas Engelen, Thomas Müller, and Oliver Schilke, "Distribution Channel Choice of New Entrepreneurial Ventures," *Entrepreneurship Theory and Practice* 35, no. 4 (2011): 683–708; and Barry J. Babin and William G. Zikmund, *Essentials of Marketing Research*, 6th ed. (Mason, OH: Cengage/South-Western, 2016).

6. Timothy M. Baye, "Relationship Marketing: A Six-Step Guide for the Business Start-Up," *Small Business Forum* (Spring 1995): 26–41; William G. Zikmund and Barry J. Babin, *Exploring Marketing Research*, 11th ed. (Mason, OH: Cengage/South-Western, 2016).

7. Thomas J. Callahan and Michael D. Cassar, "Small Business Owners' Assessments of Their Abilities to Perform and Interpret Formal Market Studies,"

Journal of Small Business Management 33, no. 4 (1995): 1–9.

8. Stephen W. McDaniel and A. Parasuraman, "Practical Guidelines for Small Business Marketing Research," *Journal of Small Business Management* 24, no. 1 (1986): 5.

9. Zikmund and Babin, *Essentials of Marketing Research*.

10. As an example, see Schindehutte, Morris, and Kocak, "Understanding Market-Driving Behavior: The Role of Entrepreneurship," *Journal of Small Business Management*, 46, No. 1 (2008): 4–26; Frank Hoy, "Organizational Learning at the Marketing/Entrepreneurship Interface," *Journal of Small Business Management* 46, no. 1 (2008): 152–58.

11. John A. Pearce II and Steven C. Michael, "Marketing Strategies That Make Entrepreneurial Firms Recession-Resistant," *Journal of Business Venturing* 12, no. 4 (1997): 301–14; Matthew Bumgardner, Urs Buehlmann, Albert Schuler, and Jeff Crissey, "Competitive Actions of Small Firms in a Declining Market," *Journal of Small Business Management* 49, no. 4 (2011): 578–98.

12. Melissa S. Barker, Donald I. Barker, Nicholas F. Borman, and Krista E. Neher, *Social Media Marketing: A Strategic Approach* (Mason, OH: South-Western/Cengage, 2013).

13. For a thorough review of Social Media and Mobile Marketing, see Barker, Barker, Borman, and Neher, *Social Media Marketing*; and Mary Lou Roberts and Debra Zahay, *Internet Marketing: Integrating Online and Offline Strategies* (Mason, OH: South-Western/Cengage 2013); see also: Maria Teresa Pinheiro Melo Borges Tiago, and José Manuel Cristóvão Veríssimo, "Digital marketing and social media: Why bother?" *Business Horizons* 57, no. 6 (2014): 703–708; Ana Margarida Gamboa and Helena Martins Gonçalves, "Customer Loyalty Through Social Networks: Lessons from Zara on Facebook," *Business Horizons* 57, no. 6 (2014): 709–717; and Paola Barbara Floreddu, Francesca Cabiddu, and Roberto Evaristo, "Inside Your Social Media Ring: How to Optimize Online Corporate Reputation," *Business Horizons* 57, no. 6 (2014): 737–45.

14. Barker, Barker, Borman, and Neher, *Social Media Marketing*; and Allison Enright, "U.S. Online Retail Sales Will Grow 57% by 2018," Internet Retailer, May 12, 2014 (accessed online January 9, 2015).

15. Schindehutte, Morris, and Pitt, *Rethinking Marketing*; see also: Hélia Gonçalves Pereira, Maria de Fátima Salgueiro, and Inês Mateus, "Say Yes to Facebook and Get your Customers Involved! Relationships in a World of Social Networks," *Business Horizons* 57, no. 6 (2014): 695–702.

16. Roberts and Zahay, *Internet Marketing*; Barker, Barker, Borman, and Neher, *Social Media Marketing*; see also: Jordi Paniagua and Juan Sapena, "Business Performance and Social Media: Love or Hate?" *Business Horizons* 57, no. 6 (2014): 719–28.

17. Barker, Barker, Borman, and Neher, *Social Media Marketing*; see also: Eileen Fischer and A. Rebecca Reuber, "Online Entrepreneurial Communication: Mitigating Uncertainty and Increasing Differentiation via Twitter, *Journal of Business Venturing* 29, no. 4 (2014): 565–83.

18. Andreas Kaplan, "If You Love Something, Let It Go Mobile: Mobile Marketing and Mobile Social Media 4×4," *Business Horizons* 55, no. 2 (2012): 129–39.

19. Schindehutte, Morris, and Pitt, *Rethinking Marketing*; see also Gerald E. Hills, Claes M. Hultman, and Morgan P. Miles, "The Evolution and Development of Entrepreneurial Marketing," *Journal of Small Business Management* 46, no. 1 (2008): 99–112; Rex Yuxing Du, Ye Hu, and Sina Damangir, "Leveraging Trends in Online Searches for Product Features in Market Response Modeling," *Journal of Marketing* 79 no. 1 (2015): 29–43; and William C. Moncrief, Greg W. Marshall, and John M. Rudd, "Social Media and Related Technology: Drivers of Change in Managing the Contemporary Sales Force," *Business Horizons* 58, no. 1 (2015): 45–55.

20. "Marketing Planning," *Small Business Reports* (April 1986): 68–72; and Philip Kotler and Kevin Lane Keller, *Marketing Management*, 15th ed. (Upper Saddle, NJ: Pearson Prentice Hall, 2016).

21. "Marketing Planning," 70; and Kotler and Keller, *Marketing Management*.

22. Boyd Cohen and Monika I. Winn, "Market Imperfections, Opportunity, and Sustainable Entrepreneurship," *Journal of Business Venturing* 22, no. 1 (January 2007): 29–49; Bumgardner, Buehlmann, Schuler, and Crissey, "Competitive Actions of Small Firms in a Declining Market."

23. "Marketing Planning," 71; see also Timothy Matanovich, Gary L. Lilien, and Arvind Rangaswamy, "Engineering the Price-Value Relationship," *Marketing Management* (Spring 1999): 48–53.

24. Babin and Zikmund, *Essentials of Marketing Research*; and Kotler and Keller, *Marketing Management*.

25. Schindehutte, Morris, and Pitt, *Rethinking Marketing*; see also Tessa Christina Flatten, Andreas Engelen, Timo Möller & Malte Brettel, "How Entrepreneurial Firms Profit from Pricing Capabilities: An Examination of Technology-Based Ventures," *Entrepreneurship Theory and Practice* (2015): in press.

26. Jun Loayza, "5 Business Models for Social Media Start-Ups," *Mashable Business*, July 14, 2009, http://mashable.com/2009/07/14/social-mediabusiness-models/ (accessed May 1, 2012); Aylin Aydinli, Marco Bertini, and Anja Lambrecht, "Price Promotion for Emotional Impact," *Journal of Marketing* 78 no. 4 (2014): 80–96.

CHAPTER 11

Financial Preparation for Entrepreneurial Ventures

LEARNING OBJECTIVES

1 To explain the principal financial statements needed for any entrepreneurial venture: the balance sheet, income statement, and cash-flow statement

2 To outline the process of preparing an operating budget

3 To discuss the nature of cash flow and to explain how to draw up such a document

4 To describe how pro forma statements are prepared

5 To explain how capital budgeting can be used in the decision-making process

6 To illustrate how to use break-even analysis

7 To describe ratio analysis and illustrate the use of some of the important measures and their meanings

Entrepreneurial Thought

Small company managers are too inclined to delegate to outside accountants every decision about their companies' financial statements. Indeed, it is most unfair to suppose that accountants can produce—without management's advice and counsel—the perfect statement for a company. Instead, I contend, top managers of growing small companies must work with their independent accountants in preparing company financial statements to ensure that the right message is being conveyed….

—James Mcneill Stancill *Growing Concerns*

11-1 THE IMPORTANCE OF FINANCIAL INFORMATION FOR ENTREPRENEURS

Today's entrepreneur operates in a competitive environment characterized by the constraining forces of governmental regulation, competition, and resources. In regard to the latter, no firm has access to an unlimited amount of resources. So, in order to compete effectively, the entrepreneur must allocate resources efficiently. Three kinds of resources are available to the entrepreneur: human, material, and financial. This chapter focuses on financial resources in the entrepreneurial environment, beginning with a discussion of financial statements as a managerial planning tool. How the budgeting process translates into the preparation of pro forma statements is presented, and attention is also given to break-even analysis and ratio analysis as profit-planning tools.

Financial information pulls together all of the information presented in the other segments of the business: marketing, distribution, manufacturing, and management. It also quantifies all of the assumptions and historical information concerning business operations.[1]

It should be remembered that entrepreneurs make assumptions to explain how numbers are derived, and they correlate these assumptions with information presented in other parts of the business operations. The set of assumptions on which projections are based should be clearly and precisely presented; without these assumptions, numbers will have little meaning. It is only after carefully considering such assumptions that the entrepreneur can assess the validity of financial projections. Because the rest of the financial plan is an outgrowth of these assumptions, they are the most integral part of any financial segment. (See Table 11.1 for a financial glossary for entrepreneurs.)

In order for entrepreneurs to develop the key components of a financial segment, they should follow a clear process, described in the next section.

TABLE 11.1   A FINANCIAL GLOSSARY FOR THE ENTREPRENEUR

Accrual system of accounting A method of recording and allocating income and costs for the period in which each is involved, regardless of the date of payment or collection. For example, if you were paid $100 in April for goods you sold in March, the $100 would be income for March under an accrual system. (Accrual is the opposite of the cash system of accounting.)

Asset Anything of value that is owned by you or your business.

Balance sheet An itemized statement listing the total assets and liabilities of your business at a given moment. It is also called a *statement of condition*.

Capital (1) The amount invested in a business by the proprietor(s) or stockholders. (2) The money available for investment or money invested.

Cash flow The schedule of your cash receipts and disbursements.

Cash system of accounting A method of accounting whereby revenue and expenses are recorded when received and paid, respectively, without regard for the period to which they apply.

Collateral Property you own that you pledge to the lender as security on a loan until the loan is repaid. Collateral can be a car, home, stocks, bonds, or equipment.

Cost of goods sold This is determined by subtracting the value of the ending inventory from the sum of the beginning inventory and purchases made during the period. Gross sales less cost of goods sold gives you gross profit.

Current assets Cash and assets that can be easily converted to cash, such as accounts receivable and inventory. Current assets should exceed current liabilities.

Current liabilities Debts you must pay within a year (also called short-term liabilities).

Depreciation Lost usefulness; expired utility; the diminution of service yield from a fixed asset or fixed asset group that cannot or will not be restored by repairs or by replacement of parts.

Equity An interest in property or in a business, subject to prior creditors. An owner's equity in his or her business is the difference between the value of the company's assets and the debt owed by the company. For example, if you borrow $30,000 to purchase assets for which you pay a total of $50,000, your equity is $20,000.

Expense An expired cost; any item or class of cost of (or loss from) carrying on an activity; a present or past expenditure defraying a present operating cost or representing an irrecoverable cost or loss; an item of capital expenditures written down or off; or a term often used with some qualifying expression denoting function, organization, or time, such as a selling expense, factory expense, or monthly expense.

(Continued)

TABLE 11.1 A FINANCIAL GLOSSARY FOR THE ENTREPRENEUR (*Continued*)

Financial statement A report summarizing the financial condition of a business. It normally includes a balance sheet and an income statement.

Gross profit Sales less the cost of goods sold. For example, if you sell $100,000 worth of merchandise for which you paid $80,000, your gross profit would be $20,000. To get net profit, however, you would have to deduct other expenses incurred during the period in which the sales were made, such as rent, insurance, and sales staff salaries.

Income statement Also called *profit and loss statement*. A statement summarizing the income of a business during a specific period.

Interest The cost of borrowing money. It is paid to the lender and is usually expressed as an annual percentage of the loan. That is, if you borrow $100 at 12 percent, you pay 1 percent (0.01 $100 $1) interest per month. Interest is an expense of doing business.

Liability Money you owe to your creditors. Liabilities can be in the form of a bank loan, accounts payable, and so on. They represent a claim against your assets.

Loss When a business's total expenses for the period are greater than the income.

Net profit Total income for the period less total expenses for the period. (See *Gross profit*.)

Net worth The same as *equity*.

Personal financial statement A report summarizing your personal financial condition. Normally it includes a listing of your assets, liabilities, large monthly expenses, and sources of income.

Profit (See *Net profit* and *Gross profit*.) "Profit" usually refers to net profit.

Profit and loss statement Same as *income statement*.

Variable cost Costs that vary with the level of production on sales, such as direct labor, material, and sales commissions.

Working capital The excess of current assets over current liabilities.

© Cengage Learning

11-2 UNDERSTANDING THE KEY FINANCIAL STATEMENTS

Financial statements are powerful tools that entrepreneurs can use to manage their ventures.[2] The basic financial statements an entrepreneur needs to be familiar with are the balance sheet, the income statement, and the cash-flow statement. The following sections examine each of these in depth, providing a foundation for understanding the books of record all ventures need.

11-2a The Balance Sheet

LO1 Explain the principal financial statements needed for any entrepreneurial venture: the balance sheet, income statement, and cash-flow statement

A balance sheet is a financial statement that reports a business's financial position at a specific time. Many accountants like to think of it as a picture taken at the close of business on a particular day, such as December 31. The closing date is usually the one that marks the end of the business year for the organization.

The balance sheet is divided into two parts: the financial resources owned by the firm and the claims against these resources. Traditionally, these claims against the resources come from two groups: creditors who have a claim to the firm's assets and can sue the company if these obligations are not paid, and owners who have rights to anything left over after the creditors' claims have been paid.

The financial resources the firm owns are called *assets*. The claims that creditors have against the company are called *liabilities*. The residual interest of the firm's owners is known as *owners' equity*. When all three are placed on the balance sheet, the assets are listed on the left, and the liabilities and owners' equity are listed on the right.

An asset is something of value the business owns. To determine the value of an asset, the owner/manager must do the following:

1. Identify the resource.
2. Provide a monetary measurement of that resource's value.
3. Establish the degree of ownership in the resource.

Most assets can be identified easily. They are tangible, such as cash, land, and equipment. However, *intangible assets* also exist. These are assets that cannot be seen; examples include copyrights and patents.

Liabilities are the debts of the business. These may be incurred either through normal operations or through the process of obtaining funds to finance operations. A common liability is a short-term account payable in which the business orders some merchandise, receives it, and has not yet paid for it. This often occurs when a company receives merchandise during the third week of the month and does not pay for it until it pays all of its bills on the first day of the next month. If the balance sheet was constructed as of the end of the month, the account still would be payable at that time.

Liabilities are divided into two categories: short term and long term. Short-term liabilities (also called current liabilities) are those that must be paid during the coming 12 months. Long-term liabilities are those that are not due and payable within the next 12 months, such as a mortgage on a building or a five-year bank loan.

Owners' equity is what remains after the firm's liabilities are subtracted from its assets—it is the claim the owners have against the firm's assets. If the business loses money, its owners' equity will decline. This concept will become clearer when we explain why a balance sheet always balances.[3]

UNDERSTANDING THE BALANCE SHEET

To fully explain the balance sheet, it is necessary to examine a typical one and determine what each entry means. Table 11.2 provides an illustration. Note that it has three sections: assets, liabilities, and owners' equity. Within each of these classifications are various types of accounts. The following sections examine each type of account presented in the table.

Current Assets
Current assets consist of cash and other assets that are reasonably expected to be turned into cash, sold, or used up during a normal operating cycle. The most common types of current assets are those shown in Table 11.2.

Cash refers to coins, currency, and checks on hand. It also includes money that the business has in its checking and savings accounts.

Accounts receivable are claims of the business against its customers for unpaid balances from the sale of merchandise or the performance of services. For example, many firms sell on credit and expect their customers to pay by the end of the month. Or, in many of these cases, they send customers a bill at the end of the month and ask for payment within 10 days.

The *allowance for uncollectible accounts* refers to accounts receivable judged to be uncollectible. How does a business know when receivables are not collectible? This question can be difficult to answer, and a definitive answer is not known. However, assume that the business asks all of its customers to pay within the first 10 days of the month following the purchase. Furthermore, an aging of the accounts receivable shows that the following amounts are due the firm:

Number of Days Outstanding	Amount of Receivables
1–11	$325,000
11–20	25,000
21–30	20,000
31–60	5,000
61–90	7,500
91+	17,500

In this case, the firm might believe that anything more than 60 days old will not be paid and will write it off as uncollectible. Note that, in Table 11.2, the allowance for uncollectible accounts is $25,000, the amount that has been outstanding more than 60 days.

TABLE 11.2 KENDON CORPORATION BALANCE SHEET FOR THE YEAR ENDED DECEMBER 31, 2018

Assets

Current Assets

Cash		$200,000
Accounts receivable	$375,000	
Less: allowance for uncollectible accounts	$25,000	350,000
Inventory		150,000
Prepaid expenses		35,000
Total current assets		$735,000

Fixed Assets

Land		$330,000
Building	$315,000	
Less: accumulated depreciation of building	80,000	
Equipment	410,000	
Less: accumulated depreciation of equipment	60,000	
Total fixed assets		915,000
Total assets		$1,650,000

Liabilities

Current Liabilities

Accounts payable	$150,000	
Notes payable	25,000	
Taxes payable	75,000	
Loan payable	50,000	
Total current liabilities		$300,000
Bank loan		200,000
Total liabilities		$500,000

Owners' Equity

Contributed Capital

Common stock, $10 par, 40,000 shares	$400,000	
Preferred stock, $100 par, 500 shares		
Authorized, none sold	————	
Retained Earnings	750,000	
Total owners' equity		1,150,000
Total liabilities and owners' equity		$1,650,000

Inventory is merchandise held by the company for resale to customers. Current inventory in our example is $150,000, but this is not all of the inventory the firm had on hand all year. Naturally, the company started the year with some inventory and purchased more as sales were made. This balance sheet figure is what was left at the end of the fiscal year.

Prepaid expenses are expenses the firm already has paid but that have not yet been used. For example, insurance paid on the company car every six months is a prepaid-expense entry because it will be six months before all of the premium has been used. As a result, the accountant would reduce this prepaid amount by one-sixth each month. Sometimes supplies, services, and rent are also prepaid, in which case the same approach is followed.

Fixed Assets consist of land, building, equipment, and other assets expected to remain with the firm for an extended period. They are not totally used up in the production of the firm's goods and services. Some of the most common types are shown in Table 11.2.

Land is property used in the operation of the firm. This is not land that has been purchased for expansion or speculation; that would be listed as an investment rather than a fixed asset. Land is listed on the balance sheet at cost, and its value usually is changed only periodically. For example, every five years, the value of the land might be recalculated so that its value on the balance sheet and its resale value are the same.

Building consists of the structures that house the business. If the firm has more than one building, the total cost of all the structures is listed.

Accumulated depreciation of building refers to the amount of the building that has been written off the books due to wear and tear. For example, referring to Table 11.2, the original cost of the building was $315,000, but accumulated depreciation is $80,000, leaving a net value of $235,000. The amount of depreciation charged each year is determined by the company accountant after checking with the Internal Revenue Service rules. A standard depreciation is 5 percent per year for new buildings, although an accelerated method sometimes is used. In any event, the amount written off is a tax-deductible expense. Depreciation therefore reduces the amount of taxable income to the firm and helps lower the tax liability. In this way, the business gets the opportunity to recover part of its investment.

Equipment is the machinery the business uses to produce goods. This is placed on the books at cost and then depreciated and listed as the *accumulated depreciation of equipment*. In our example, it is $60,000. The logic behind equipment depreciation and its effect on the firm's income taxes is the same as that for accumulated depreciation on the building.

Current Liabilities Current liabilities are obligations that will become due and payable during the next year or within the operating cycle. The most common current liabilities are listed in Table 11.2.

Accounts payable are liabilities incurred when goods or supplies are purchased on credit. For example, if the business buys on a basis of net 30 days, during that 30 days, the bill for the goods will constitute an account payable.

A **note payable** is a promissory note given as tangible recognition of a supplier's claim or a note given in connection with an acquisition of funds, such as for a bank loan. Some suppliers require that a note be given when a company buys merchandise and is unable to pay for it immediately.

Taxes payable are liabilities owed to the government—federal, state, and local. Most businesses pay their federal and state income taxes on a quarterly basis. Typically, payments are made on April 15, June 15, and September 15 of the current year and January 15 of the following year. Then the business closes its books, determines whether it still owes any taxes, and makes the required payments by April 15. Other taxes payable are sales taxes. For example, most states (and some cities) levy a sales tax. Each merchant must collect the taxes and remit them to the appropriate agency.

A **loan payable** is the current installment on a long-term debt that must be paid this year. As a result, it becomes a part of the current liabilities. The remainder is carried as a long-term debt. Note that, in Table 11.2, $50,000 of this debt was paid in 2018 by the Kendon Corporation.

Long-Term Liabilities As we have said, long-term liabilities consist of obligations that will not become due or payable for at least one year or not within the current operating cycle. The most common are bank loans.

A *bank loan* is a long-term liability due to a loan from a lending institution. Although it is unclear from the balance sheet in Table 11.2 how large the bank loan originally was, it is being paid down at the rate of $50,000 annually. Thus, it will take four more years to pay off the loan.

Contributed Capital
The Kendon Corporation is owned by individuals who have purchased stock in the business. Various kinds of stock can be sold by a corporation, the most typical being common stock and preferred stock. Only common stock has been sold by this company.

Common stock is the most basic form of corporate ownership. This ownership gives the individual the right to vote for the board of directors. Usually, for every share of common stock held, the individual is entitled to one vote. As shown in Table 11.2, the corporation has issued 40,000 shares of $10 par common stock, raising $400,000. Although the term *par value* may have little meaning to most stockholders, it has legal implications: It determines the legal capital of the corporation. This legal capital constitutes an amount that total stockholders' equity cannot be reduced below except under certain circumstances (the most common is a series of net losses). For legal reasons, the total par value of the stock is maintained in the accounting records. However, it has no effect on the *market value* of the stock.

Preferred stock differs from common stock in that its holders have preference to the assets of the firm in case of dissolution. This means that, after the creditors are paid, preferred stockholders have the next claim on whatever assets are left. The common stockholders' claims come last. Table 11.2 shows that 500 shares of preferred stock were issued, each worth a par value of $100, but none has been sold. Therefore, it is not shown as a number on the balance sheet.

Retained Earnings
Retained earnings are the accumulated net income over the life of the business to date. In Table 11.2, the retained earnings are shown as $750,000. Every year this amount increases by the profit the firm makes and keeps within the company. If dividends are declared on the stock, they, of course, are paid from the total net earnings. Retained earnings are what remain after that.

WHY THE BALANCE SHEET ALWAYS BALANCES
By definition, the balance sheet always balances.[4] If something happens on one side of the balance sheet, it is offset by something on the other side. Hence, the balance sheet remains in balance. Before examining some illustrations, let us restate the balance-sheet equation:

$$\text{Assets} = \text{Liabilities} + \text{Owners' Equity}$$

With this in mind, let us look at some typical examples of business transactions and their effect on the balance sheet.

A Credit Transaction
The Kendon Corporation calls one of its suppliers and asks for delivery of $11,000 in materials. The materials arrive the next day, and the company takes possession of them.

The bill is to be paid within 30 days. How is the balance sheet affected? *Inventory* goes up by $11,000, and *accounts payable* rise by $11,000. The increase in current assets is offset by an increase in current liabilities.

Continuing this illustration, what happens when the bill is paid? The company issues a check for $11,000, and *cash* declines by this amount. At the same time, *accounts payable* decrease by $11,000. Again, these are offsetting transactions, and the balance sheet remains in balance.

A Bank Loan
Table 11.2 shows that the Kendon Corporation had an outstanding bank loan of $200,000 in 2018. Assume that the company increases this loan by $110,000 in 2016. How is the balance sheet affected? *Cash* goes up by $110,000, and *bank loan* increases by the same amount; again, balance is achieved. However, what if the firm uses this $110,000 to buy new machinery? In this case, *cash* decreases by $110,000 and *equipment* increases by a like amount. Again, a balance exists. Finally, what if Kendon decides to pay

THE ENTREPRENEURIAL PROCESS

Watching Your Accounts Receivables

One of the primary issues that plagues start-up companies is poor cash flow, and one of the largest contributors to this problem is uncollected or extremely delayed accounts receivables. When the economy is in decline, the first tactic that most businesses will employ is to stretch out the payments on their accounts payables as long as they can, which presents an issue for their vendors. Most entrepreneurs offer credit to their customers to encourage business, but when those customers choose not to pay off that credit in a timely manner, businesses servicing them can face a cash deficit, making payments to their own vendors problematic. In some cases, entrepreneurs are left with no choice but to take on credit cards that charge excessive interest rates just to keep their business afloat.

Avoiding this situation takes significant forethought on the part of the management team. A good rule of thumb is to always secure funding before your company needs it. You will usually find cash when in dire straights, but the cost of that capital can be significant. Securing an operating line of credit and keeping tabs on your accounts receivable will help prevent expensive mistakes when the going gets tough.

Following are five tips for making sure that you are paid what is coming to you:

Track your accounts receivable with software. Given the abundance of free and inexpensive invoice creating and tracking software, the only reason not to use one is if you do not have a computer or a smartphone. One example is Quickbooks which is cost effective and user friendly. However there are a plethora of other choices as well.

Develop a process. Customers will stretch out their payments to you if they think they can get away with it; do not let them. Being consistent when dealing with your customers will let them know that you take collecting your receivables seriously. Establish a payment due date and enforce it. If you let your customers slide, you will be sending them the message that they can pay when they want to, which might work fine when your company is flush with cash but will be a significant burden if your business hits a lull.

Make some noise. Once you have provided a product or service, you are entitled to get paid. You should not feel guilty about contacting your customers about a delinquent payment. After all, you have upheld your end of the deal. Your customers are going to pay the vendors who are the most committed to getting paid. If you choose to sit idle, you may never get your money.

Get paid up front. When in doubt, there is no better way to ensure payment than by mandating that your customers pay up front; this is especially useful when working with new clients. You can always charge a percentage so that you and your customers are sharing the burden of responsibility. In the event that you choose to issue credit to a customer, make sure to perform a credit check first.

Find an advocate. The person paying your company is most likely not the entrepreneur. Find out who is responsible for issuing payments in each of your respective customers' businesses so that you get to know him or her. The order in which payments are submitted will usually be at the discretion of this individual, so you stand a greater chance of being at the top of that list if he or she knows you.

Discounts for early payment. Incentivize customers to pay as soon as possible by offering discounts. One of the more popular credit terms is 2%/10, Net 30 Days. This means that a customer receives a 2 percent discount if they pay within 10 days and the total balance is due within 30 days of the date of the invoice.

Know when to walk away. Despite what traditional thinking suggests, customers are not always right and they are not always profitable. The time spent collecting fees from a customer and the cost of carrying the credit for that customer might outweigh the margins that customer's business is generating. If that turns out to be the case, do not be afraid to discontinue the relationship. Often the costs far outweigh what appears on your financial statements, given that time spent on troublesome customers could be spent acquiring new business. To prevent such issues from burdening your company, conduct annual audits of your customers and consider eliminating those that cost you money.

Cash-flow management is a process that never ends for an entrepreneur. Liquidity is an important metric when considering the health of your business; if you are allowing your customers to postpone their payments, you risk them putting your company's life in jeopardy.

Sources: Adapted from C. J. Prince, "Time Bomb," *Entrepreneur*, January 2008, http://www.entrepreneur.com/magazine/entrepreneur/2008/january/187658.html (accessed May 12, 2012); and Ronika Khanna, "Tips on Managing Your Accounts Receivable," *Toolbox.com*, November 23, 2010, http://finance.toolbox.com/blogs/montreal-financial/tips-on-managing-your-accounts-receivable-42717 (accessed May 12, 2012).

off its bank loan? In this case, the first situation is reversed; *cash* and *bank loan* (long-term liabilities) decrease in equal amounts.

A Stock Sale   Suppose that the company issues and sells another 40,000 shares of $10 par *common* stock. How does this action affect the balance sheet? (This answer is rather simple.) *Common stock* increases by $400,000, and so does *cash*. Once more, a balance exists.

With these examples in mind, it should be obvious why the balance sheet always balances. Every entry has an equal and offsetting entry to maintain this equation:

$$\text{Assets} = \text{Liabilities} + \text{Owners' Equity}$$

Keep in mind that, in accounting language, the terms *debit* and *credit* denote increases and decreases in assets, liabilities, and owners' equity. The following chart relates debits and credits to increases and decreases.

Category	A Transaction Increasing the Amount	A Transaction Decreasing the Amount
Asset	Debit	Credit
Liability	Credit	Debit
Owners' equity	Credit	Debit

Applying this idea to the preceding examples results in the following:

	Debit	Credit
Credit Transaction		
Inventory	$11,000	
Accounts payable		$11,000
Bank Loan		
Cash	110,000	
Bank Loan		110,000
Stock Sale		
Cash	400,000	
Common Stock		400,000
	$511,000	$511,000

11-2b The Income Statement

The income statement is a financial statement that shows the change that has occurred in a firm's position as a result of its operations over a specific period. This is in contrast to the balance sheet, which reflects the company's position at a particular point in time.

The income statement, sometimes referred to as a "profit and loss statement" or "P&L," reports the success (or failure) of the business during the period. In essence, it shows whether revenues were greater than or less than expenses. These *revenues* are the monies the small business has received from the sale of its goods and services. The *expenses* are the costs of the resources used to obtain the revenues. These costs range from the cost of materials used in the products the firm makes to the salaries it pays its employees.

Most income statements cover a one-year interval, but it is not uncommon to find monthly, quarterly, or semiannual income statements. All of the revenues and expenses accumulated during this time are determined, and the net income for the period is identified. Many firms prepare quarterly income statements but construct a balance sheet only once a year. This is because they are interested far more in their profits and losses than in examining their asset, liability, and owners' equity positions. However, it should be noted that the income statement drawn up at the end of the year will coincide with the firm's fiscal year, just as the balance sheet does. As a result, at the end of the business year, the organization will have both a balance sheet and an income statement. In this way, they can be considered together and the interrelationship between them can be studied. A number of different types of income and expenses are reported on the income statement. However, for purposes of simplicity, the income statement can be reduced to three primary categories: (1) revenues, (2) expenses, and (3) net income.

Revenues are the gross sales the business made during the particular period under review. Revenue often consists of the money actually received from sales, but this need not be the case. For example, sales made on account still are recognized as revenue, as when a furniture store sells $500 of furniture to a customer today, delivers it tomorrow, and will receive payment two weeks from now. From the moment the goods are delivered, the company can claim an increase in revenue.

Expenses are the costs associated with producing goods or services. For the furniture store in the preceding paragraph, the expenses associated with the sale would include the costs of acquiring, selling, and delivering the merchandise. Sometimes these are expenses that will be paid later. For example, the people who deliver the furniture may be paid every two weeks, so the actual outflow of expense money in the form of salaries will not occur at the same time the work is performed. Nevertheless, it is treated as an expense.

Net income is the excess of revenue over expenses during the particular period under discussion. If revenues exceed expenses, the result is a *net profit*. If the reverse is true, the firm suffers a *net loss*. At the end of the accounting period, all of the revenues and expenses associated with all of the sales of goods and services are added together, and then the expenses are subtracted from the revenues. In this way, the firm knows whether it made an overall profit or suffered an overall loss.[5]

UNDERSTANDING THE INCOME STATEMENT

To explain the income statement fully, it is necessary to examine one and determine what each account is. Table 11.3 illustrates a typical income statement. It has five major sections: (1) sales revenue, (2) cost of goods sold, (3) operating expenses, (4) financial expense, and (5) income taxes estimated.

TABLE 11.3 KENDON CORPORATION INCOME STATEMENT FOR THE YEAR ENDED DECEMBER 31, 2018

Sales Revenue	$1,750,000	
Less: Sales returns and allowances	50,000	
Net sales	⎯⎯⎯	$1,700,000
Cost of Goods Sold		
Inventory, January, 2000	$150,000	
Purchases	1,050,000	
Goods available for sale	$1,200,000	
Less: Inventory, December, 2000	200,000	
Cost of goods sold		1,000,000
Gross margin		$700,000
Operating Expenses		
Selling expenses	$150,000	
Administrative expenses	100,000	
Total operating expenses		250,000
Operating income		$450,000
Financial Expenses		$20,000
Income before income taxes		$430,000
Estimated Income Taxes		172,000
Net profit		$258,000

© Cengage Learning

Revenue   Every time a business sells a product or performs a service, it obtains revenue. This often is referred to as *gross revenue* or *sales revenue*. However, it is usually an overstated figure, because the company finds that some of its goods are returned or some customers take advantage of prompt-payment discounts.

In Table 11.3, sales revenue is $1,750,000. However, the firm also has returns and allowances of $50,000. These returns are common for companies that operate on a "satisfaction or your money back" policy. In any event, a small business should keep tabs on these returns and allowances to see if the total is high in relation to the total sales revenue. If so, the firm will know that something is wrong with what it is selling, and it can take action to correct the situation.

Deducting the sales returns and allowances from the sales revenue, the company finds its *net sales*. This amount must be great enough to offset the accompanying expenses in order to ensure a profit.

Cost of Goods Sold   As the name implies, the cost of goods sold section reports the cost of merchandise sold during the accounting period. Simply put, the cost of goods for a given period equals the beginning inventory plus any purchases the firm makes minus the inventory on hand at the end of the period. Note that, in Table 11.3, the beginning inventory was $150,000 and the purchases totaled $1,050,000. This gave Kendon goods available for sale of $1,200,000. The ending inventory for the period was $200,000, so the cost of goods sold was $1,000,000. This is what it cost the company to buy the inventory it sold. When this cost of goods sold is subtracted from net sales, the result is the *gross margin*. The gross margin is the amount available to meet expenses and to provide some net income for the firm's owners.

Operating Expenses   The major expenses, exclusive of costs of goods sold, are classified as **operating expenses**. These represent the resources expended, except for inventory purchases, to generate the revenue for the period. Expenses often are divided into two broad subclassifications: selling expenses and administrative expenses.

Selling expenses result from activities such as displaying, selling, delivering, and installing a product or performing a service. Expenses for displaying a product include rent for storage space, depreciation on fixtures and furniture, property insurance, and utility and tax expenses. Sales expenses, salaries, commissions, and advertising also fall into this category. Costs associated with getting the product from the store to the customer also are considered selling expenses. Finally, if the firm installs the product for the customer, all costs—including the parts used in the job—are considered in this total. Taken as a whole, these are the selling expenses.

Administrative expenses is a catchall term for operating expenses not directly related to selling or borrowing. In broad terms, these expenses include the costs associated with running the firm. They include salaries of the managers, expenses associated with operating the office, general expenses that cannot be related directly to buying or selling activities, and expenses that arise from delinquent or uncollectible accounts.

When these selling and administrative expenses are added together, the result is *total operating expenses*. Subtracting them from gross margin gives the firm its *operating income*. Note that, in Table 11.3, selling expenses are $150,000, administrative expenses are $100,000, and total operating expenses are $250,000. When subtracted from the gross margin of $700,000, the operating income is $450,000.

Financial Expense   The **financial expense** is the interest expense on long-term loans. As seen in Table 11.3, this expense is $20,000. Additionally, many companies include their interest expense on short-term obligations as part of their financial expense.

Estimated Income Taxes   As noted earlier, corporations pay estimated income taxes; then, at some predetermined time (e.g., December 31), the books are closed, actual taxes are determined, and any additional payments are made (or refunds claimed). When these taxes are subtracted from the income before income taxes, the result is the *net profit*. In our example, the Kendon Corporation made $258,000.

11-2c The Cash-Flow Statement

The **cash-flow statement** (also known as *statement of cash flows*) shows the effects of a company's operating, investing, and financing activities on its cash balance. The principal purpose of the statement of cash flows is to provide relevant information about a company's cash receipts and cash payments during a particular accounting period. It is useful for answering such questions as:

- How much cash did the firm generate from operations? How did the firm finance fixed capital expenditures?
- How much new debt did the firm add?
- Was the cash from operations sufficient to finance fixed asset purchases?

The statement of cash flows is a supplement to the balance sheet and income statements. One of the limitations of the income and balance sheet statements is that they are based on accrual accounting. In accrual accounting, revenues and expenses are recorded when incurred—not when cash changes hands. For example, if a sale is made for credit, under accrual accounting the sale is recognized but cash has not been received. Similarly, a tax expense may be shown in the income statement, but it may not be paid until later. The statement of cash flows reconciles the accrual-based figures in the income and balance sheet statements to the actual cash balance reported in the balance sheet.

The statement of cash flows is broken down into *operating, investing*, and *financing* activities. Table 11.4 provides an outline of a statement of cash flows. *Operating cash flows* refer to cash generated from or used in the course of business operations of the firm. The net operating cash flows will be positive for most firms, because their operating inflows (primarily from revenue collections) will exceed operating cash outflows (e.g., payment for raw materials and wages).

Investing activities refer to cash-flow effects from long-term investing activities, such as purchase or sale of plant and equipment. The net cash flow from investing activities can be either positive or negative. A firm that is still in the growth phase would be building up fixed assets (installing new equipment or building new plants) and therefore would show negative cash flows from investing activities. On the other hand, a firm that is divesting unprofitable divisions may realize cash inflows from the sale of assets and therefore would show a positive cash flow from investing activities.

Financing activities refer to cash-flow effects of financing decisions of the firm, including sale of new securities (such as stocks and bonds), repurchase of securities, and payment of dividends. Note that payment of interest to lenders is *not* included under financing activities. Accounting convention in determining the statement of cash flows assumes that interest payments are part of operating cash flows. Once the cash flows from the three different sources—operating, investing, and financing—are identified, the beginning and ending cash balances are reconciled.

TABLE 11.4   FORMAT OF STATEMENT OF CASH FLOWS

Cash flows from operating activities	$50,000
Cash flows from investing activities	($10,000)
Cash flows from financing activities	$5,000
Net increase (decrease) in cash	$45,000
Cash at beginning of period	$400,000
Cash at end of period	$445,000

Because this statement is most frequently used by those analyzing the firm, the use of a cash budget may be the best approach for an entrepreneur starting up a venture. The cash budget procedure will be covered in the next section.

11-3 PREPARING FINANCIAL BUDGETS

One of the most powerful tools the entrepreneur can use in planning financial operations is a **budget**.[6] The *operating budget* is a statement of estimated income and expenses during a specified period of time. Another common type of budget is the *cash-flow budget*, which is a statement of estimated cash receipts and expenditures during a specified period of time. It is typical for a firm to prepare both types of budgets by first computing an operating budget and then constructing a cash budget based on the operating budget. A third common type of budget is the *capital budget*, which is used to plan expenditures on assets whose returns are expected to last beyond one year. This section examines all three of these budgets: operating, cash flow, and capital. Then the preparation of pro forma financial statements from these budgets is discussed.

11-3a   The Operating Budget

LO2 Outline the process of preparing an operating budget

Typically, the first step in creating an **operating budget** is the preparation of the **sales forecast**.[7] An entrepreneur can prepare the sales forecast in several ways. One way is to implement a statistical forecasting technique such as **simple linear regression**. Simple linear regression is a technique in which a linear equation states the relationship among three variables:

$$Y = a + bx$$

Y is a dependent variable (it is dependent on the values of a, b, and x), x is an independent variable (it is not dependent on any of the other variables), a is a constant (in regression analysis, Y is dependent on the variable x, all other things held constant), and b is the slope of the line (the change in Y divided by the change in x). For estimating sales, Y is the variable used to represent the expected sales, and x is the variable used to represent the factor on which sales are dependent. Some retail stores may believe that their sales are dependent on their advertising expenditures, whereas other stores may believe that their sales are dependent on some other variable, such as the amount of foot traffic past the store.

When using regression analysis, the entrepreneur will draw conclusions about the relationship between, for example, product sales and advertising expenditures. Presented next is an example of how Mary Tindle, owner of a clothing store, used regression analysis.

Mary began with two initial assumptions: (1) If no money is spent on advertising, total sales will be $200,000, and (2) for every dollar spent on advertising, sales will be increased by two times that amount. Relating these two observations yields the following simple linear regression formula:

$$S = \$200{,}000 + 2A$$

where

$$S = \text{Projected Sales}$$

$$A = \text{Advertising Expenditures}$$

(Note that it is often easier to substitute more meaningful letters into an equation. In this case, the letter S was substituted for the letter Y simply because the word *sales* starts with that letter. The same is true for the letter A, which was substituted for the letter x.) In order to determine the expected sales level, Mary must insert different advertising expenditures and complete the simple linear regression formula for each different expenditure. The following data and Figure 11.1 demonstrate the results.

Another commonly used technique for the preparation of a sales forecast is the estimation that current sales will increase a certain percentage over the prior period's sales. This

FIGURE 11.1   REGRESSION ANALYSIS

Simple Linear Regression ($000)		
A	2A	S = $200 × 2A
$50	$100	$300
100	200	400
150	300	500
200	400	600
250	500	700
300	600	800

TABLE 11.5   NORTH CENTRAL SCIENTIFIC: SALES FORECAST FOR 2018

	January	February	March	April	May	June
Sales	$300	$350	$400	$375	$500	$450
×1.05	315	368	420	394	525	473
	July	August	September	October	November	December
Sales	$475	$480	$440	$490	$510	$550
×1.05	499	504	462	515	536	578

percentage is based on a trend line analysis that covers the five preceding sales periods and assumes that the seasonal variations will continue to run in the same pattern. Obviously, because it needs five preceding sales periods, trend line analysis is used for more established ventures. It is nevertheless an important tool that entrepreneurs should be aware of as the venture grows and becomes more established. Following is an example of how John Wheatman, owner of North Central Scientific, used trend line analysis to forecast sales for his computer retail store:

After considerable analysis of his store's sales history, John Wheatman decided to use trend line analysis and estimated that sales would increase 5 percent during the next year, with the seasonal variations following roughly the same pattern. Because he has a personal computer with an electronic spreadsheet program, John chose to use the input of last year's sales figures in the spreadsheet and then to increase each month by 5 percent. The results are shown in Table 11.5.

After a firm has forecast its sales for the budget period, expenses must be estimated. The first type of expenses that should be estimated is the cost of goods sold, which follows sales on the income statement. For retail firms, this is a matter of projecting purchases and the corresponding desired beginning and ending inventories. Many firms prefer to have a certain percentage of the next month's sales on hand in inventory. Here is how John Wheatman determines his store's expected purchases and inventory requirements:

For determining his purchase requirements, John Wheatman believes that his gross profit will represent 20 percent of his sales dollar. This is based on analysis of the past five years' income statement. Consequently, cost of goods sold will represent 80 percent of the sales for the current month. In addition, John wants to have approximately one week's inventory on hand. Thus, the ending inventory is estimated to be 25 percent of next month's sales. The results are shown in Table 11.6.

TABLE 11.6 NORTH CENTRAL SCIENTIFIC: PURCHASE REQUIREMENTS BUDGET FOR 2018

	Jan.	Feb.	Mar.	Apr.	May	June	July	Aug.	Sept.	Oct.	Nov.	Dec.
Sales revenue	$315	$368	$420	$394	$525	$473	$499	$504	$462	$515	$536	$578
Cost of goods sold												
Beginning inventory	$63	$74	$84	$79	$105	$95	$100	$101	$92	$103	$107	$116
Purchases	263	305	331	341	410	383	400	395	380	416	437	413
Cost of goods available	$326	$379	$415	$420	$515	$478	$500	$496	$472	$519	$544	$529
Ending inventory	74	85	79	105	95	100	101	92	102	107	116	66
Cost of goods sold	$252	$294	$336	$315	$420	$378	$399	$403	$370	$412	$428	$462
Gross profit	$63	$74	$84	$79	$105	$95	$100	$101	$92	$103	$108	$116

Cost of goods sold = Current period sales × .80

Ending inventory = Next month's sales × (0.80)(0.25) (since inventory is carried at cost)

Cost of goods available = Cost of goods sold − Ending inventory

Beginning inventory = Prior month's ending inventory or current month's sales × (0.80)(0.25)

Purchases = Cost of goods available − Beginning inventory

Gross profit = Sales − Cost of goods sold

A manufacturing firm, on the other hand, will need to establish its production budget, a material purchases budget based on the production budget, and the corresponding direct labor budget. The production budget is management's estimate of the number of units that need to be produced in order to meet the sales forecast. This budget is prepared by working backward through the cost of goods sold section. First, the predicted number of units that will be sold during that month is determined. Then the desired ending-inventory-level balance is added to this figure. The sum of these two figures is the number of units that will be needed in inventory. Once the inventory requirements have been determined, the entrepreneur must determine how many of these units will be accounted for by the beginning inventory (which is the prior month's ending inventory) and how many units will have to be produced. The production requirement is calculated by subtracting the period's beginning inventory from the inventory needed for that period. For example:

Tom B. Good, president and founder of Dynamic Manufacturing, has decided to implement a budget to help plan for his company's growth. After Tom received the unit sales forecast from his sales manager, he examined last year's product movement reports and determined that he would like to have 11 percent of the next month's sales on hand as a buffer against possible fluctuations in demand. He also has received a report from his production manager that his ending inventory this year is expected to be 12,000 widgets, which also will be the beginning inventory for the budget period. Table 11.7 shows the results.

After the production budget has been calculated, the materials required for producing the specified number of units can be determined from an analysis of the bill of materials for the product being manufactured. In addition, by examining the amount of direct labor needed to produce each unit, management can determine the amount of direct labor that will be needed during the forthcoming budget period.

TABLE 11.7		DYNAMIC MANUFACTURING: PRODUCTION BUDGET WORKSHEET FOR 2018										
	Jan.	**Feb.**	**Mar.**	**Apr.**	**May**	**June**	**July**	**Aug.**	**Sept.**	**Oct.**	**Nov.**	**Dec.**
Projected sales (units)	125	136	123	143	154	234	212	267	236	345	367	498
Desired ending inventory	14	12	14	15	23	21	27	24	35	37	50	26
Available for sale	139	148	137	158	177	255	239	291	271	382	417	524
Less: Beginning inventory	12	14	12	14	15	23	21	27	24	35	37	50
Total production requirements	127	134	125	144	162	232	218	264	247	347	380	474

© Cengage Learning

The last step in preparing the operating budget is to estimate the operating expenses for the period. Three of the key concepts in developing an expense budget are fixed, variable, and mixed costs. A **fixed cost** is one that does not change in response to changes in activity for a given period of time; rent, depreciation, and certain salaries are examples. A variable cost is one that changes in the same direction as, and in direct proportion to, changes in operating activity; direct labor, direct materials, and sales commissions are examples. **Mixed costs** are a blend of fixed and variable costs. An example is utilities, because part of this expense would be responsive to change in activity, and the rest would be a fixed expense, remaining relatively stable during the budget period. Mixed costs can present a problem for management in that it is sometimes difficult to determine how much of the expense is variable and how much is fixed.

After the expenses have been budgeted, the sales, cost of goods, and expense budget are combined to form the operating budget. Table 11.8 outlines North Central Scientific's anticipated expenses for the budget year and the completed operating budget for the period. Each month represents the pro forma, or projected, income and expenses for that period.

11-3b   The Cash-Flow Budget

LO3 Discuss the nature of cash flow and to explain how to draw up such a document

After the operating budget has been prepared, the entrepreneur can proceed to the next phase of the budget process, the **cash-flow budget**. This budget, which often is prepared with the assistance of an accountant, provides an overview of the cash inflows and outflows during the period. By pinpointing cash problems in advance, management can make the necessary financing arrangements.[8]

The first step in the preparation of the cash-flow budget is the identification and timing of cash inflows. For the typical business, cash inflows will come from three sources: (1) cash sales, (2) cash payments received on account, and (3) loan proceeds. Not all of a firm's sales revenues are cash. In an effort to increase sales, most businesses will allow some customers to purchase goods on account. Consequently, part of the funds will arrive in later periods and will be identified as cash payments received on account. Loan proceeds represent another form of cash inflow that is not directly tied to the sales revenues. A firm may receive loan proceeds for several reasons—for example, the planned expansion of the firm (new building and equipment) or meeting cash-flow problems stemming from an inability to pay current bills.

Some businesses have a desired minimum balance of cash indicated on the cash-flow budget, highlighting the point at which it will be necessary to seek additional financing. Table 11.9 provides an example of how North Central Scientific prepared its cash-flow budget.

TABLE 11.8 NORTH CENTRAL SCIENTIFIC: EXPENSE AND OPERATING BUDGETS

In order to identify the behavior of the different expense accounts, John Wheatman decided to analyze the past five years' income statements. Following are the results of his analysis:

- Rent is a constant expense and is expected to remain the same during the next year.
- Payroll expense changes in proportion to sales, because the more sales the store has, the more people it must hire to meet increased consumer demands.
- Utilities are expected to remain relatively constant during the budget period.
- Taxes are based primarily on sales and payroll and are therefore considered a variable expense.
- Supplies will vary in proportion to sales. This is because most of the supplies will be used to support sales.
- Repairs are relatively stable and are a fixed expense. John has maintenance contracts on the equipment in the store, and the cost is not scheduled to rise during the budget period.

North Central Scientific: Expense Budget for 2018												
	Jan.	Feb.	Mar.	Apr.	May	June	July	Aug.	Sept.	Oct.	Nov.	Dec.
Anticipated operating expenses												
Rent	$2	$2	$2	$2	$2	$2	$2	$2	$2	$2	$2	$2
Payroll	32	37	42	39	53	47	50	50	46	51	54	58
Utilities	5	5	5	5	5	5	5	5	5	5	5	5
Taxes	3	4	4	4	5	5	5	5	5	5	5	6
Supplies	16	18	21	20	26	24	25	25	23	26	27	29
Repairs	2	2	2	2	2	2	2	2	2	2	2	2
Total expenses	$60	$68	$76	$72	$93	$85	$89	$89	$83	$91	$95	$102
Sales revenue	$315	$368	$420	$394	$525	$473	$499	$504	$462	$515	$536	$578
Cost of goods sold												
Beginning inventory	$63	$74	$84	$79	$105	$95	$100	$101	$92	$103	$107	$116
Purchases	263	305	331	341	410	383	400	395	380	416	437	413
Cost of goods available	$326	$379	$415	$420	$515	$478	$500	$496	$472	$519	$544	$529
Ending inventory	74	85	79	105	95	100	101	92	102	107	116	66
Cost of goods sold	$252	$294	$336	$315	$420	$378	$399	$403	$370	$412	$428	$462
Gross profit	$63	$74	$84	$79	$105	$95	$100	$101	$92	$103	$108	$116
Operating expenses												
Rent	$2	$2	$2	$2	$2	$2	$2	$2	$2	$2	$2	$2
Payroll	32	37	42	39	53	47	50	50	46	51	54	58
Utilities	5	5	5	5	5	5	5	5	5	5	5	5
Taxes	3	4	4	4	5	5	5	5	5	5	5	6
Supplies	16	18	21	20	26	24	25	25	23	26	27	29
Repairs	2	2	2	2	2	2	2	2	2	2	2	2
Total expenses	$60	$68	$76	$72	$93	$85	$89	$89	$83	$91	$95	$102
Net profit	$3	$6	$8	$7	$12	$10	$11	$12	$9	$12	$12	$14

TABLE 11.9 NORTH CENTRAL SCIENTIFIC: CASH-FLOW BUDGET

John Wheatman has successfully completed his operating budget and is now ready to prepare his cash-flow worksheet. After analyzing the sales figures and the cash receipts, John has determined that 80 percent of monthly sales are in cash. Of the remaining 20 percent, 15 percent is collected in the next month, and the final 5 percent is collected in the month following (see the cash receipts worksheet below). Wheatman's purchases are typically paid during the week following the purchase. Therefore, approximately one-fourth of the purchases are paid for in the following month. Rent expense is paid a month in advance. However, because it is not expected to go up during the budget period, the monthly cash outlay for rent remains the same. All the other expenses are paid in the month of consumption (see the cash disbursements worksheet below). Finally, the cash-flow worksheet is constructed by taking the beginning cash balance, adding the cash receipts for that month, and deducting the cash disbursements for the same month.

North Central Scientific: Cash Receipts Worksheet for 2018

	Jan.	Feb.	Mar.	Apr.	May	June	July	Aug.	Sept.	Oct.	Nov.	Dec.
Sales	$315	$388	$420	$394	$525	$473	$499	$504	$462	$515	$536	$578
Current month	$252	$294	$336	$315	$420	$378	$399	$403	$370	$412	$428	$462
Prior month	82	47	55	63	59	79	71	75	76	69	77	80
Two months back	26	28	16	18	21	19	26	24	24	25	24	26
Cash receipts	$360	$369	$407	$396	$500	$476	$496	$502	$470	$506	$529	$568

North Central Scientific: Cash Disbursements Worksheet for 2018

	Jan.	Feb.	Mar.	Apr.	May	June	July	Aug.	Sept.	Oct.	Nov.	Dec.
Purchases	$263	$305	$331	$341	$410	$383	$400	$395	$380	$416	$437	$413
Current month	$197	$228	$248	$256	$307	$287	$300	$296	$285	$312	$328	$309
Prior month	98	66	76	83	85	102	96	100	99	95	104	109
Purchase payments	$295	$294	$324	$339	$392	$396	$396	$396	$384	$407	$432	$419
Operating expenses	$60	$68	$76	$72	$93	$85	$89	$89	$83	$91	$95	$102
Cash payments	$355	$362	$400	$412	$485	$481	$485	$485	$467	$498	$527	$521

North Central Scientific: Cash-Flow Worksheet for 2018

	Jan.	Feb.	Mar.	Apr.	May	June	July	Aug.	Sept.	Oct.	Nov.	Dec.
Beginning cash	$122	$127	$134	$141	$127	$141	$143	$154	$170	$173	$181	$184
Add: Receipts	360	369	407	396	500	476	496	502	470	506	529	568
Cash available	$482	$496	$541	$537	$627	$617	$639	$656	$640	$679	$710	$752
Less: Payments	355	362	400	411	485	481	485	485	467	498	527	521
Ending cash	$127	$134	$141	$126	$142	$136	$154	$171	$173	$181	$183	$231

THE ENTREPRENEURIAL PROCESS

Characteristics of Credible Financials

Although every section of a business plan has its purpose, the financial section bears the most scrutiny. A business's financial statements are deserving of this attention for two reasons: (1) the management team has significant discretion in how the financials are constructed and (2) potential investors reviewing a business plan will be interested in the financial viability of the company's strategy. Following are characteristics that convincing financial statements have in common:

- **Holistic** An income statement tells only part of your business's financial story; the balance sheet and cash-flow statement are necessary to fill in the remaining details. Investors and lenders are interested in every detail of your company's financial health, so never exclude relevant information, such as the amount of and the timeline for the cash you will need.

- **Precise** Although investors will carefully analyze your financial statements, helping them to pinpoint the important details will ensure that they do not lose patience searching through your plan. To aid the readers of your plan, focus your sales and cost of goods sold numbers on major product lines. In addition, pay attention to how you label your line items to ensure that your readers will understand what you are trying to communicate. For instance, "costs" are what you pay for what you are selling while "expenses," like payroll and rent, are overhead charges you would have without sales.

- **Realistic** When you tailor your figures to achieve a predetermined revenue goal, you will have trouble justifying your numbers when questioned. Instead, build your financials by starting with your costs and sales in your local market to anchor your figures in reality. In addition, your projections beyond the first year should be annual or quarterly.

- **Simple** Significant volatility in your industry should be noted, such as your business being impacted by seasonality; however, bogging down your plan with lengthy explanations regarding the probability of your projections will only serve to confuse the reader. By including clarifying statements, such as "most likely," and supporting addendums, such as your break-even analysis, will be sufficient.

- **Accurate** Investors know that your plan will change repeatedly as you build your business; however, overlooking simple expenses, such as interest payments, can cast doubt on your attention to detail. Once you have your financial statements completed, verifying the finer points, such as the accuracy of the interest and tax rates, will show that you are able to take your business from plan to implementation.

Sources: Adapted from Tim Berry, "The Facts About Financial Projections," *Entrepreneur* (May 2007). Retrieved June 21, 2008, from https://www.entrepreneur.com/startingabusiness/businessplans/businessplancoachtimberry/article178210.html; Jim Casparie, "Realistic Projections That Attract Investors," *Entrepreneur* (April 2006). Retrieved June 21, 2008, from http://www.entrepreneur.com/money/financing/raisingmoneycoachjimcasparie/article159516.html; and "5 Tips for Coming Up with Financial Projections for Your Business Plan, *National Federation of Independent Business*, http://www.nfib.com/business-resources/business-resourcesitem?cmsid=55331; (accessed May 29, 2012).

11-4 PRO FORMA STATEMENTS

LO4 Describe how pro forma statements are prepared

The final step in the budget process is the preparation of **pro forma statements**, which are projections of a firm's financial position during a future period (pro forma income statement) or on a future date (pro forma balance sheet). In the normal accounting cycle, the income statement is prepared first, followed by the balance sheet. Similarly, in the preparation of pro forma statements, the pro forma income statement is followed by the pro forma balance sheet.

In the process of preparing the operating budget, the firm already will have prepared the pro forma income statements for each month in the budget period. Each month presents the anticipated income and expense for that particular period, which is what the monthly pro forma income statements do. To prepare an annual pro forma income statement, the firm combines all months of the year.

The process for preparing a pro forma balance sheet is more complex: The last balance sheet prepared before the budget period began, the operating budget, and the cash-flow budget are needed to prepare it. Starting with the beginning balance sheet balances, the projected changes as depicted on the budgets are added to create the projected balance sheet totals.

After preparing the pro forma balance sheet, the entrepreneur should verify the accuracy of his or her work with the application of the traditional accounting equation:

$$\text{Assets} = \text{Liabilities} + \text{Owner's Equity}$$

If the equation is not in balance, the work should be rechecked. Table 11.10 provides a brief account of the process of preparing pro forma financial statements for North Central Scientific.

TABLE 11.10 NORTH CENTRAL SCIENTIFIC: PRO FORMA STATEMENTS

At this point in the budget process, John Wheatman has the information necessary to prepare pro forma financial statements. The first set he has decided to prepare is the pro forma income statements. To do this, John simply copies the information from the operating budget (see the following comparative income statements and compare with the operating budget). The next set of pro forma statements is the pro forma balance sheets. In order to compile these, John uses the following information along with the operating budget and the cash-flow worksheet he has prepared:

Cash: the ending cash balance for each month from the cash-flow worksheet

Accounts receivable: 20 percent of the current month's sales plus 5 percent of the preceding month's sales

Inventory: the current month's ending inventory on the pro forma income statements

Prepaid rent: the $2,000 is expected to remain constant throughout the budget period and is always paid one month in advance

Building and equipment: no new acquisitions are expected in this area, so the amount will remain constant

Accumulated depreciation: because no new acquisitions are anticipated, this will stay the same; all buildings and equipment are fully depreciated

Accounts payable: 25 percent of current purchases

Capital: prior month's capital balance plus current month's net income

North Central Scientific: Comparative Pro Forma Income Statements												
	Jan.	Feb.	Mar.	Apr.	May	June	July	Aug.	Sept.	Oct.	Nov.	Dec.
Sales	$315	$388	$420	$394	$525	$473	$499	$504	$462	$515	$536	$578
Cost of goods sold												
Beginning inventory	$63	$74	$84	$79	$105	$95	$100	$101	$92	$103	$107	$116
Purchases	263	305	331	341	410	383	400	395	380	416	437	413
Cost of goods available	$326	$379	$415	$420	$515	$478	$500	$496	$472	$519	$544	$529
Ending inventory	74	85	79	105	95	100	101	92	102	107	116	66
Cost of goods sold	$252	$294	$336	$315	$420	$378	$399	$403	$370	$412	$428	$462
Gross profit	$63	$74	$84	$79	$105	$95	$100	$101	$92	$103	$108	$116
Operating expenses												
Rent	$2	$2	$2	$2	$2	$2	$2	$2	$2	$2	$2	$2
Payroll	32	37	42	39	53	47	50	50	46	51	54	58
Utilities	5	5	5	5	5	5	5	5	5	5	5	5
Taxes	3	4	4	4	5	5	5	5	5	5	5	6
Supplies	16	18	21	20	26	24	25	25	23	26	27	29
Repairs	2	2	2	2	2	2	2	2	2	2	2	2
Total expenses	$60	$68	$76	$72	$93	$85	$89	$89	$83	$91	$95	$102
Net profit	$3	$6	$8	$7	$12	$10	$11	$12	$9	$12	$12	$14

(Continued)

TABLE 11.10 NORTH CENTRAL SCIENTIFIC: PRO FORMA STATEMENTS (*Continued*)

North Central Scientific: Comparative Pro Forma Balance Sheet											
	Jan.	Feb.	Mar.	Apr.	May	June	July	Aug.	Sept.	Oct.	Nov.	Dec.
Assets												
Cash	$127	$134	$141	$126	$142	$136	$154	$171	$173	$181	$183	$231
Accounts receivable	91	89	102	100	125	121	123	126	117	126	133	142
Inventory	74	84	79	105	95	100	101	92	103	107	116	66
Prepaid rent	2	2	2	2	2	2	2	2	2	2	2	2
Building and equipment	350	350	350	350	350	350	350	350	350	350	350	350
Less: Accumulated depreciation	−350	−350	−350	−350	−350	−350	−350	−350	−350	−350	−350	−350
Total assets	$294	$309	$324	$333	$364	$359	$380	$391	$395	$416	$434	$441
Liabilities												
Accounts payable	$66	$76	$83	$85	$102	$96	$100	$99	$95	$104	$109	$103
Capital	228	234	242	249	261	270	280	292	300	312	326	339
Total liabilities and equity	$294	$310	$325	$334	$363	$366	$380	$391	$395	$416	$435	$442

© Cengage Learning

11-5 CAPITAL BUDGETING

LO5 Explain how capital budgeting can be used in the decision-making process

Entrepreneurs may be required to make several investment decisions in the process of managing their firms. The impact of some of these decisions will be felt primarily within one year. Returns on other investments, however, are expected to extend beyond one year. Investments that fit into this second category are commonly referred to as capital investments or capital expenditures. A technique the entrepreneur can use to help plan for capital expenditures is capital budgeting.[9]

The first step in capital budgeting is to identify the cash flows and their timing. The inflows—or returns, as they are commonly called—are equal to net operating income before deduction of payments to the financing sources but after the deduction of applicable taxes and with depreciation added back, as represented by the following formula:

$$\text{Expected Returns} = X(1 - 2T)1 \text{ Depreciation}$$

X is equal to the net operating income, and T is defined as the appropriate tax rate. An illustration follows.

John Wheatman is faced with a dilemma. He has two mutually exclusive projects, both of which require an outlay of $1,000. The problem is that he can afford only one of the projects. After discussing the problem with his accountant, John discovers that the first step he needs to take is to determine the expected return on each project. In order to gather this information, he has studied the probable effect on the store's operations and has developed the data shown in Table 11.11.

TABLE 11.11	NORTH CENTRAL SCIENTIFIC: EXPECTED RETURN WORKSHEET

Proposal A					
Year	**X**	**$(1-T)(T=.40)$**	**$X(1-T)$**	**Depreciation**	**$X(1-T)$ + Depreciation**
1	$500	$0.60	$300	$200	$500
2	333	0.60	200	200	400
3	167	0.60	100	200	300
4	−300	0.60	−180	200	20
5	−317	0.60	−190	200	10

Proposal B					
Year	**X**	**$(1-T)(T=.40)$**	**$X(1-T)$**	**Depreciation**	**$X(1-T)$ + Depreciation**
1	−$167	$0.60	−$100	$200	$100
2	0	0.60	100	200	200
3	167	0.60	100	200	300
4	333	0.60	200	200	400
5	500	0.60	300	200	500

X = Anticipated change in net income

T = Applicable tax rate (0.40)

Depreciation = Depreciation (computed on a straight-line basis) Cost/Life 1,000/5

Table 11.11 provides a good illustration of the expected returns for John Wheatman's two projects. At this point, however, the cash inflows of each year are shown without consideration of the time value of money. The cash outflow is used to refer to the initial cash outlay that must be made in the beginning (the purchase price). When gathering data to estimate the cash flows over the life of a project, it is imperative to obtain reliable estimates of the savings and expenses associated with the project.

The principal objective of capital budgeting is to maximize the value of the firm. It is designed to answer two basic questions:

1. Which of several mutually exclusive projects should be selected? (Mutually exclusive projects are alternative methods of doing the same job. If one method is chosen, the other methods will not be required.)

2. How many projects, in total, should be selected?[10]

The three most common methods used in capital budgeting are the payback method, the net present value (NPV) method, and the internal rate of return (IRR) method. Each has certain advantages and disadvantages. In this section, the same proposal will be used with each method to more clearly illustrate these three techniques.

11-5a Payback Method

One of the easiest capital-budgeting techniques to understand is the **payback method** or, as it is sometimes called, the *payback period*. In this method, the length of time required to "pay back" the original investment is the determining criterion. The entrepreneur will select a maximum time frame for the payback period. Any project that requires a longer period will be rejected, and projects that fall within the time frame will be accepted. Following is an example of the payback method used by North Central Scientific:

John Wheatman has a decision to make. He would like to purchase a new cash register for his store but is unsure about which of two proposals to accept. Each machine costs $1,000. An analysis of the projected returns reveals the following information:

Year	Proposal A	Proposal B
1	$500	$100
2	400	200
3	300	300
4	20	400
5	11	500

After careful consideration, John decides to use the payback method with a cutoff period of three years. In this case, he discovers that Proposal A would pay back his investment in 28 months; $900 of the original investment will be paid back in the first two years, and the last $100 in the third year. Proposal B, on the other hand, will require four years for its payback. Using this criterion, John chooses Proposal A and rejects Proposal B.

One of the problems with the payback method is that it ignores cash flows beyond the payback period. Thus, it is possible for the wrong decision to be made. Nevertheless, many companies, particularly entrepreneurial firms, continue to use this method for several reasons: (1) It is very simple to use in comparison to other methods, (2) projects with a faster payback period normally have more favorable short-term effects on earnings, and (3) if a firm is short on cash, it may prefer to use the payback method because it provides a faster return of funds.

11-5b Net Present Value

The **net present value (NPV) method** is a technique that helps to minimize some of the shortcomings of the payback method by recognizing the future cash flows beyond the payback period. The concept works on the premise that a dollar today is worth more than a dollar in the future—how much more depends on the applicable cost of capital for the firm. The cost of capital is the rate used to adjust future cash flows to determine their value in present period terms. This procedure is referred to as *discounting the future cash flows*, and the discounted cash value is determined by the present value of the cash flow.

To use this approach, the entrepreneur must find the present value of the expected net cash flows of the investment, discounted at the appropriate cost of capital, and subtract from it the initial cost outlay of the project. The result is the NPV of the proposed project. Many financial accounting and finance textbooks include tables (called present value tables) that list the appropriate discount factors to multiply by the future cash flow to determine the present value. In addition, financial calculators are available that will compute the present value given the cost of capital, future cash flow, and the year of the cash flow. Finally, given the appropriate data, electronic spreadsheet programs can be programmed to determine the present value. After the NPV has been calculated for all of the proposals, the entrepreneur can select the project with the highest NPV. Following is an example of the NPV method used by North Central Scientific:

John Wheatman is not very satisfied with the results he has obtained from the payback method, so he has decided to use the NPV method to see what result it would produce. After conferring with his accountant, John learns that the cost of capital for his firm is 11 percent. He then prepares the following tables:

Proposal A

Year	Cash Flow	Discount Factor	Present Value
1	$500	0.9091	$454.55
2	400	0.8264	330.56
3	300	0.7513	225.39
4	20	0.6830	13.66
5	11	0.6209	6.21
			$1,030.37
Less: Initial outlay			−1,000.00
Net present value			$30.37

Proposal B

Year	Cash Flow	Discount Factor	Present Value
1	$100	0.9091	$90.91
2	200	0.8264	165.28
3	300	0.7513	225.39
4	400	0.6830	273.20
5	500	0.6209	311.45
			$1,065.23
Less: Initial outlay			−1,000.00
Net present value			$65.23

Because Proposal B has the higher NPV, John selects Proposal B and rejects Proposal A.

11-5c Internal Rate of Return

The **internal rate of return (IRR) method** is similar to the NPV method in that the future cash flows are discounted. However, they are discounted at a rate that makes the NPV of the project equal to zero. This rate is referred to as the *internal rate of return* of the project. The project with the highest IRR is then selected. Thus, a project that would be selected under the NPV method also would be selected under the IRR method.

One of the major drawbacks to the use of the IRR method is the difficulty that can be encountered when using the technique. Using the NPV method, it is quite simple to look up the appropriate discount factors in the present value tables. When using the IRR concept, however, the entrepreneur must begin with a NPV of zero and work backward through the tables. What this means, essentially, is that the entrepreneur must estimate the approximate rate and eventually try to track the actual IRR for the project. Although this may not seem too difficult for projects with even cash flows (i.e., cash flows that are fairly equal over the business periods), projects with uneven cash flows (fluctuating periods of cash inflow and cash outflow) can be a nightmare. Unfortunately, reality dictates that most projects will probably have uneven cash flows. Fortunately, electronic calculators and spreadsheet programs are available that can determine the actual IRR given the cash flows, initial cash outlays, and appropriate cash-flow periods. Following is an example of the IRR method used by North Central Scientific:

Having obtained different results from the payback period and the NPV method, John Wheatman is confused about which alternative to select. To alleviate this confusion, he has chosen to use the IRR to evaluate the two proposals, and he has decided that the project with the higher IRR will be selected (after all, it would win two out of three times). Accordingly, he has prepared the following tables with the help of his calculator:

Proposal A (11.83% IRR)

Year	Cash Flow	Discount Factor	Present Value
1	$500	0.8942	$447.11
2	400	0.7996	319.84
3	300	0.7151	214.53
4	20	0.6394	12.80
5	11	0.5718	5.73
			$1,000.00
Less: Initial outlay			−1,000.00
Net present value			$0.00

Proposal B (12.01% IRR)

Year	Cash Flow	Discount Factor	Present Value
1	$100	0.8928	$89.27
2	200	0.7971	159.42
3	300	0.7117	213.51
4	400	0.6354	254.15
5	500	0.5673	283.65
			$1,000.00
Less: Initial outlay			−1,000.00
Net present value			$0.00

Proposal B is selected because it has the higher IRR. This conclusion supports the statement that the project with the higher NPV will also have the higher IRR.

The North Central Scientific examples illustrate the use of all three capital-budgeting methods. Although Proposal A was chosen by the first method (payback), Proposal B surfaced as the better proposal when the other two methods (NPV and IRR) were used. It is important for entrepreneurs to understand all three methods and to use the one that best fits their needs. If payback had been John Wheatman's only consideration, then Proposal A would have been selected. When future cash flows beyond payback are to be considered, the NPV and IRR methods will determine the best proposal.

The budgeting concepts discussed so far are extremely powerful planning tools. But how can entrepreneurs monitor their progress during the budget period? How can they use the information accumulated during the course of the business to help plan for future periods? Can this information be used for pricing decisions? The answer to the third question is "yes," and the other questions are answered in the following sections.

11-6 BREAK-EVEN ANALYSIS

LO6 Illustrate how to use break-even analysis

In today's competitive marketplace, entrepreneurs need relevant, timely, and accurate information that will enable them to price their products and services competitively and still be able to earn a fair profit. **Break-even analysis** supplies this information.

11-6a Break-Even Point Computation

Break-even analysis is a technique commonly used to assess expected product profitability. It helps determine how many units must be sold to break even at a particular selling price.

CONTRIBUTION MARGIN APPROACH

A common approach to break-even analysis is the **contribution margin approach**. Contribution margin is the difference between the selling price and the variable cost per unit. It is the amount per unit that is contributed to covering all other costs.[11] Because the break-even point occurs where income equals expenses, the contribution margin approach formula is

$$0 = (SP - VC)\ S - FC\ or\ FC = (SP - VC)S$$

where

SP = Unit selling price
VC = Variable costs per unit
S = Sales in units
FC = Fixed cost

This model also can be used for profit planning by including the desired profit as part of the fixed cost.

GRAPHIC APPROACH

Another approach to break-even analysis taken by entrepreneurial firms is the graphic approach. To use this approach, the entrepreneur needs to graph at least two numbers: total revenue and total costs. The intersection of these two lines (i.e., where total revenues are equal to the total costs) is the firm's break-even point. Two additional costs—variable costs and fixed costs—also may be plotted. Doing so enables the entrepreneur to visualize the various relationships in the firm's cost structure.

HANDLING QUESTIONABLE COSTS

Although the first two approaches are adequate for situations in which costs can be broken down into fixed and variable components, some firms have expenses that are difficult to assign. For example, are repairs and maintenance expenses fixed or variable expenses? Can firms that face this type of problem use break-even analysis for profit planning? The answer is "yes," thanks to a new technique designed specifically for entrepreneurial firms. This technique calculates break-even points under alternative assumptions of fixed or variable costs to see if a product's profitability is sensitive to cost behavior. The decision rules for this concept are as follows: If expected sales exceed the higher break-even point, then the product should be profitable, regardless of the other break-even point; if expected sales do not exceed the lower break-even point, then the product should be unprofitable. Only if expected sales are between the two break-even points is further investigation of the questionable cost's behavior needed.[12]

The concept works by substituting the cost in question (QC) first as a fixed cost and then as a variable cost. The break-even formulas presented earlier would have to be modified to determine the break-even levels under the two assumptions. For the fixed-cost assumption, the entrepreneur would use the following equation:

$$0 = (SP - VC)\ S - FC - QC$$

To calculate the break-even point assuming QC is variable, the following equation would be used:

$$0 = [SP - VC - (QC/U)]\ S - FC$$

U is the number of units for which the questionable cost normally would be appropriate. What the entrepreneur is determining is the appropriate unit cost that should be used if the cost is a variable cost. Following is an example of how an entrepreneur could use the technique:

> Tim Goodman, president of Dynamic Manufacturing—a small manufacturer of round widgets—has decided to use break-even analysis as a profit-planning tool for his company. He believes that using this technique will enable his firm to compete more effectively in the marketplace. From an analysis of the operating costs, Tim has determined that the variable cost per unit is $9, while fixed costs are estimated to be $1,200 per month. The anticipated selling price per unit is $15. He also has discovered that he is unable to classify one cost as either variable or fixed. It is a $200 repair and maintenance expense allocation. This $200 is appropriate for an activity level of 400 units; therefore, if the cost were variable, it would be $.50 per unit ($200/400). Finally, sales are projected to be 400 units during the next budget period.

The first step in this process is to determine the break-even point assuming the cost in question is fixed. Consequently, Tim would use the following equation:

$$
\begin{aligned}
0 &= (SC - VC)S - FC - QC \\
&= (15 - 9)S - 1,200 - 200 \\
&= 6S - 1,400 \\
1,400 &= 6S \\
234 &= S
\end{aligned}
$$

Figure 11.2 provides a graphic illustration of the results. The final quantity was rounded up to the next unit, because a business normally will not sell part of a unit.

The next step in the process is to calculate the break-even point assuming the cost in question is a variable cost. Tim would use the following equation to ascertain the second break-even point:

$$
\begin{aligned}
0 &= [SC - VC - (QC/U)]S - FC \\
&= [15 - 9 - (200/400)]S - 1,200 \\
&= (6 - .50)S - 1,200 \\
1,200 &= 5.50S \\
219 &= S
\end{aligned}
$$

Figure 11.3 presents a graphic illustration of the results.

Now that the two possible break-even points have been established, Tim must compare them to his projected sales. The variable-cost sales of 400 units are greater than the larger break-even point of 234 units. Therefore, the product is assumed to be profitable regardless of the cost behavior of the repair and maintenance expense. It does not matter whether the cost is variable or fixed; the firm still will be profitable.

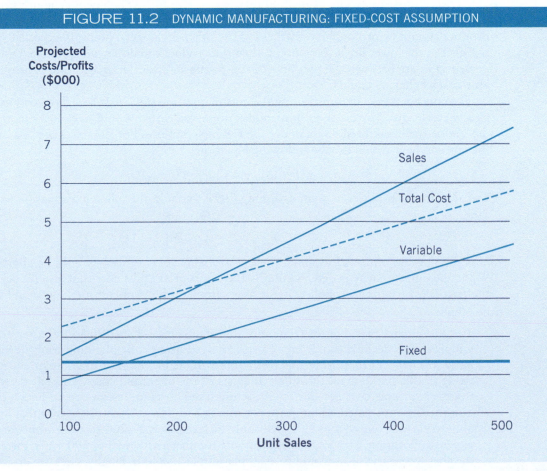

FIGURE 11.2 DYNAMIC MANUFACTURING: FIXED-COST ASSUMPTION

© Cengage Learning

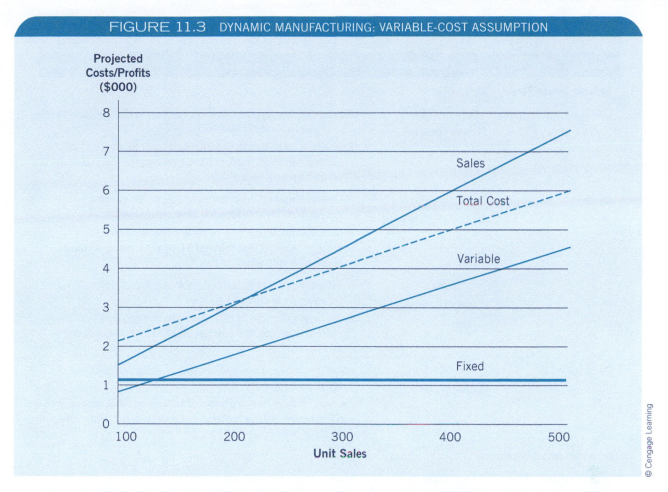

FIGURE 11.3   DYNAMIC MANUFACTURING: VARIABLE-COST ASSUMPTION

© Cengage Learning

11-7 RATIO ANALYSIS

LO7 Describe ratio analysis and illustrate the use of some of the important measures and their meanings

Financial statements report on both a firm's position at a point in time and its operations during some past period. However, the real value of financial statements lies in the fact that they can be used to help predict the firm's earnings and dividends. From an investor's standpoint, predicting the future is what financial statement analysis is all about; from an entrepreneur's standpoint, financial statement analysis is useful both as a way to anticipate conditions and, more important, as a starting point for planning actions that will influence the course of events.

An analysis of the firm's ratios is generally the key step in a financial analysis. The **ratios** are designed to show relationships among financial statement accounts. For example, Firm A might have a debt of $6,250,000 and interest charges of $520,000, whereas Firm B might have a debt of $62,800,000 and interest charges of $5,840,000. Which company is stronger? The true burden of these debts, and the companies' ability to repay them, can be ascertained (1) by comparing each firm's debt to its assets and (2) by comparing the interest each must pay to the income it has available for interest payment. Such comparisons are made by ratio analysis.[13]

Table 11.12 displays a series of financial ratios useful for understanding the relationships among financial statements. The formulas for calculating each ratio are given, along with explanations of what each ratio means for business decision-making using a dollars-and-cents approach. Different ratios are important to owners, managers, and creditors for different reasons. As the table demonstrates, entrepreneurs can use ratios to gauge the advisability of various business decisions so that they know, for example, when it makes sense to borrow and if they have the capacity to meet short-term debt obligations. Ratios can be focused on the balance sheet, where issues of liquidity (e.g., current, quick, or cash ratios) as well as

TABLE 11.12 FINANCIAL RATIOS

Ratio Name	How to Calculate	What It Means in Dollars and Cents
Balance Sheet Ratios		
Current	$\dfrac{Current\ Assets}{Current\ Liabilities}$	Measures solvency: the number of dollars in current assets for every $1 in current liabilities
		Example: A current ratio of 1.76 means that for every $1 of current liabilities, the firm has $1.76 in current assets with which to pay it.
Quick	$\dfrac{Cash\ +\ Accounts\ Receivable}{Current\ Liabilities}$	Measures liquidity: the number of dollars in cash and accounts receivable for each $1 in current liabilities
		Example: A quick ratio of 1.14 means that for every $1 of current liabilities, the firm has $1.14 in cash and accounts receivable with which to pay it.
Cash	$\dfrac{Cash}{Current\ Liabilities}$	Measures liquidity more strictly: the number of dollars in cash for every $1 in current liabilities
		Example: A cash ratio of 0.17 means that for every $1 of current liabilities, the firm has $0.17 in cash with which to pay it.
Debt-to-worth	$\dfrac{Total\ Liabilities}{Net\ Worth}$	Measures financial risk: the number of dollars of debt owed for every $1 in net worth
		Example: A debt-to-worth ratio of 1.05 means that for every $1 of net worth the owners have invested, the firm owes $1.05 of debt to its creditors.
Income Statement Ratios		
Gross margin	$\dfrac{Gross\ Margin}{Sales}$	Measures profitability at the gross profit level: the number of dollars of gross margin produced for every $1 of sales
		Example: A gross margin ratio of 34.4% means that for every $1 of sales, the firm produces 34.4¢ of gross margin.
Net margin	$\dfrac{Net\ Profit\ before\ Tax}{Sales}$	Measures profitability at the net profit level: the number of dollars of net profit produced for every $1 of sales
		Example: A net margin ratio of 2.9% means that for every $1 of sales, the firm produces 2.9¢ of net margin.
Overall Efficiency Ratios		
Sales-to-assets	$\dfrac{Sales}{Total\ Assets}$	Measures the efficiency of total assets in generating sales: the number of dollars in sales produced for every $1 invested in total assets
		Example: A sales-to-assets ratio of 2.35 means that for every $1 invested in total assets, the firm generates $2.35 in sales.
Return on assets	$\dfrac{Net\ Profit\ before\ Tax}{Total\ Assets}$	Measures the efficiency of total assets in generating net profit: the number of dollars in net profit produced for every $1 invested in total assets
		Example: A return on assets ratio of 7.1% means that for every $1 invested in assets, the firm is generating 7.1¢ in net profit before tax.
Return on investment	$\dfrac{Net\ Profit\ before\ Tax}{Net\ Worth}$	Measures the efficiency of net worth in generating net profit: the number of dollars in net profit produced for every $1 invested in net worth
		Example: A return on investment ratio of 16.1% means that for every $1 invested in net worth, the firm is generating 16.1¢ in net profit before tax.

TABLE 11.12   FINANCIAL RATIOS (*Continued*)

Ratio Name	How to Calculate	What It Means in Dollars and Cents
Specific Efficiency Ratios		
Inventory turnover	$\dfrac{Cost\ of\ Goods\ Sold}{Inventory}$	Measures the rate at which inventory is being used on an annual basis *Example:* An inventory turnover ratio of 9.81 means that the average dollar volume of inventory is used up almost ten times during the fiscal year.
Inventory turn-days	$\dfrac{360}{Inventory\ Turnover}$	Converts the inventory turnover ratio into an average "days inventory on hand" figure *Example:* An inventory turn-days ratio of 37 means that the firm keeps an average of 37 days of inventory on hand throughout the year.
Accounts receivable turnover	$\dfrac{Sales}{Accounts\ Receivable}$	Measures the rate at which accounts receivable are being collected on an annual basis *Example:* An accounts receivable turnover ratio of 8.00 means that the average dollar volume of accounts receivable is collected eight times during the year.
Average collection period	$\dfrac{360}{Accounts\ Receivable\ Turnover}$	Converts the accounts receivable turnover ratio into the average number of days the firm must wait for its accounts receivable to be paid *Example:* An average collection period ratio of 45 means that it takes the firm 45 days on average to collect its receivables.
Accounts payable turnover	$\dfrac{Cost\ of\ Goods\ Sold}{Accounts\ Payable}$	Measures the rate at which accounts payable are being paid on an annual basis *Example:* An accounts payable turnover ratio of 12.04 means that the average dollar volume of accounts payable is paid about 12 times during the year.
Average payment period	$\dfrac{360}{Accounts\ Payable\ Turnover}$	Converts the accounts payable turnover ratio into the average number of days a firm takes to pay its accounts payable *Example:* An accounts payable turnover ratio of 30 means that it takes the firm 30 days on average to pay its bills.

© Cengage Learning

issues of stability (e.g., debt to worth) can be measured, or on the income statement, where margins for profitability can be examined. There are also efficiency ratios that compute general returns on assets and on investments in addition to specific points, such as inventory or accounts receivable turnover. These ratios provide the most effective tools for monitoring a venture's performance over time; however, it should be kept in mind that effective ratio analysis must be done in comparison with firms within the same industry in order to gain the broadest possible insights.

Ratio analysis can be applied from two directions. Vertical analysis is the application of ratio analysis to one set of financial statements; an analysis "up and down" the statements is done to find signs of strengths and weaknesses. Horizontal analysis looks at financial statements and ratios over time. In horizontal analysis, the trends are critical: Are the numbers increasing or decreasing? Are particular components of the company's financial position getting better or worse?[14]

SUMMARY

Three principal financial statements are important to entrepreneurs: the balance sheet, the income statement, and the cash-flow statement. The budgeting process facilitates financial statement preparation. Some key budgets that entrepreneurs should prepare are the operating budget, the cash-flow budget, and the capital budget. The operating budget typically begins with a sales forecast, followed by an estimation of operating expenses. A cash-flow budget provides an overview of the inflows and outflows of cash during a specific period. Pro forma financial statements then are prepared as projections of the firm's financial position over a future period (pro forma income statement) or on a future date (pro forma balance sheet). The operating and cash-flow budgets often are used to prepare these pro forma statements. The capital budget is used to help entrepreneurs make investment decisions. The three most common methods of capital budgeting are the payback period, the NPV method, and the IRR method.

Another commonly used decision-making tool is break-even analysis, which tells how many units must be sold to break even at a particular selling price. It is possible to use this analysis even when fixed or variable costs can only be estimated. The last part of the chapter examined ratio analysis, which can be a helpful analytical tool for entrepreneurs. Ratios are designed to show relationships between financial statement accounts.

KEY TERMS

accounts payable
accounts receivable
administrative expenses
balance sheet
break-even analysis
budget
capital budgeting
cash
cash-flow budget
cash-flow statement
contribution margin approach
expenses
financial expense
fixed assets

fixed cost
horizontal analysis
income statement
internal rate of return (IRR)
inventory
liabilities
loan payable
long-term liabilities
mixed costs
net income
net present value (NPV) method
note payable
operating budget
operating expenses

owners' equity
payback method
prepaid expenses
pro forma statements
ratios
retained earnings
revenues
sales forecast
short-term liabilities (current liabilities)
simple linear regression
taxes payable
variable cost
vertical analysis

REVIEW AND DISCUSSION QUESTIONS

1. What is the importance of financial information for entrepreneurs? Briefly describe the key components.

2. What are the benefits of the budgeting process?

3. How is the statistical forecasting technique of simple linear regression used in making a sales forecast?

4. Describe how an operating budget is constructed.

5. Describe how a cash-flow budget is constructed.

6. What are pro forma statements? How are they constructed? Be complete in your answer.

7. Describe how a capital budget is constructed.

8. One of the most popular capital-budgeting techniques is the payback method. How does this method work? Give an example.

9. Describe the net present value method. When would an entrepreneur use this method? Why?

10. Describe the internal rate of return method. When would an entrepreneur use this method? Why?

11. When would an entrepreneur be interested in break-even analysis?

12. If an entrepreneur wants to use break-even analysis but has trouble assigning some costs as either fixed or variable, can break-even analysis still be used? Explain.

13. What is ratio analysis? How is horizontal analysis different from vertical analysis?

NOTES

1. See Richard G. P. McMahon and Leslie G. Davies, "Financial Reporting and Analysis Practices in Small Enterprises: Their Association with Growth Rate and Financial Performance," *Journal of Small Business Management* 32, no. 1 (January 1994): 9–17; and Jan Brinckmann, Soeren Salomo, and Hans Georg Gemuenden, "Financial Management Competence of Founding Teams and Growth of New Technology-Based Firms," *Entrepreneurship Theory and Practice* 35, no. 2 (2011): 217–43.

2. Kenneth M. Macur and Lyal Gustafson, "Financial Statements as a Management Tool," *Small Business Forum* (Fall 1992): 23–34; see also Robert Dove, "Financial Statements," *Accountancy* (January 2000): 7; and James M. Whalen, Stephen P. Baginski, and Mark Bradshaw, *Financial Reporting, Financial Statement Analysis, and Valuation: A Strategic Perspective*, 8th ed. (Mason, OH: South-Western/Cengage, 2015).

3. See Carl S. Warren, James M. Reeve, and Jonathan Duchac, *Accounting*, 26th ed. (Mason, OH: South-Western/Cengage, 2016).

4. See Jacqueline Emigh, "Balance Sheet," *Computer-World* (November 15, 1999): 86.

5. See John Capel, "Balancing the Books," *Supply Management* (November 1999): 94; and Eugene F. Brigham and Joel F. Houston, *Fundamentals of Financial Management*, 14th ed. (Mason, OH: South-Western/Cengage, 2016).

6. Neil C. Churchill, "Budget Choice: Planning vs. Control," *Harvard Business Review* (July/August 1984): 151; and James M. Whalen, Jefferson P. Jones, and Donald P. Pagach, *Intermediate Accounting: Reporting and Analysis*, 2nd ed. (Mason, OH: South-Western/Cengage, 2016).

7. Whalen, Baginski, and Bradshaw, *Financial Reporting, Financial Statement Analysis, and Valuation*.

8. Fred Waedt, "Understanding Cash Flow Statements, or What You Need to Know Before You Ask for a Loan,"

Small Business Forum (Spring 1995): 42–51; see also Ram Mudambi and Monica Zimmerman Treichel, "Cash Crisis in Newly Public Internet-Based Firms: An Empirical Analysis," *Journal of Business Venturing* 20, no. 4 (July 2005): 543–71; Pam Newman, "The Ins and Outs of Cash Flow Statements: Understanding Your Cash Flow-Statement Is Key to Tracking Your Business's Financial Health," *Entrepreneur*, May 14, 2007 (accessed January 10, 2015). Analyze Cash Flow the Easy Way, *Forbes*, November 28, 2012 (accessed January 10, 2015).

9. See J. Chris Leach and Ronald W. Melicher, *Entrepreneurial Finance*, 4th ed. (Mason, OH: South-Western/Cengage, 2012); and Brigham and Houston, *Fundamentals of Financial Management*.

10. Ibid.

11. Warren, Reeve, and Duchac, *Accounting*.

12. Kenneth P. Sinclair and James A. Talbott, Jr., "Using Break-Even Analysis When Cost Behavior Is Unknown," *Management Accounting* (July 1986): 53; see also Whalen, Baginski, and Bradshaw, *Financial Reporting, Financial Statement Analysis, and Valuation*.

13. See Brigham and Houston, *Fundamentals of Financial Management*.

14. Macur and Gustafson, "Financial Statements as a Management Tool"; see also Robert Hitchings, "Ratio Analysis as a Tool in Credit Assessment," *Commercial Lending Review* (Summer 1999): 45–49. For an interesting discussion, see Patricia Lee Huff, "Should You Consider Company Size When Making Ratio Comparisons?" *National Public Accountant* (February/March 2000): 8–12; Donna Marie Thompson, "3 Key Financial Ratios to Gauge the Health of Your Small Business," *Firepole Marketing*, November 26, 2013. Accessed online January 10, 2015; see also Whalen, Baginski, and Bradshaw, *Financial Reporting, Financial Statement Analysis, and Valuation*.

CHAPTER 12

Developing an Effective Business Plan

CHAPTER OBJECTIVES

1 To explore the planning pitfalls that plague many new ventures

2 To explain the business model canvas as an initial step in the planning process

3 To define a business plan and demonstrate its value

4 To describe the benefits of a business plan

5 To set forth the viewpoints of those who read a business plan

6 To emphasize the importance of coordinating the business plan segments

7 To review key recommendations by venture capital experts regarding a plan

8 To present a complete outline of an effective business plan

9 To present some helpful hints for writing an effective business plan

10 To highlight points to remember in the presentation of a business plan

Entrepreneurial Thought

It is well established that you can't raise money without a business plan... a business plan is a work of art in its own right. It's the document that personifies and expresses your company. Each plan, like every snowflake, must be different. Each is a separate piece of art. Each must be reflective of the individuality of the entrepreneur. Just as you wouldn't copy someone else's romancing techniques, so should you seek to distinguish your plan for its differences.

— Joseph R. Mancuso *How to Write a Winning Business Plan*

12-1 PITFALLS TO AVOID IN THE VENTURE PLANNING PROCESS

LO1 Explore the planning pitfalls that plague many new ventures

A number of pitfalls in the business plan process should be avoided. The five pitfalls presented in this section represent the most common errors committed by entrepreneurs. To make these danger areas more easily recognizable, certain indicators or warning signs are presented. We also include a possible solution to each pitfall that will help entrepreneurs avoid the particular trap that limits a new venture's opportunity to succeed.

12-1a Pitfall 1: No Realistic Goals

Although this pitfall may sound self-explanatory, the following indicators demonstrate how common and well disguised it can be: lack of any attainable goals, lack of a time frame to accomplish things, lack of priorities, and lack of action steps.

One way to avoid this pitfall is to set up a timetable of specific steps to be accomplished during a specific period.

12-1b Pitfall 2: Failure to Anticipate Roadblocks

One of the most common pitfalls occurs when the entrepreneur is so immersed in his or her idea that objectivity goes out the window. In other words, the person does not recognize the possible problems that may arise. Indicators are: no recognition of future problems, no admission of possible flaws or weaknesses in the plan, and no contingency or alternative plans.

The best way to avoid this pitfall is to list (1) the possible obstacles that may arise and (2) the alternatives that state what might have to be done to overcome the obstacles.

12-1c Pitfall 3: No Commitment or Dedication

Too many entrepreneurs appear to lack real commitment to their ventures. Although ventures may have started from a hobby or part-time endeavor, entrepreneurs must be careful to avoid the impression that they do not take their ventures seriously. Indicators are: copying the latest social media craze, no interest in researching the idea, no desire to invest personal money, and the appearance of making a "fast buck" from an "app" or a "whim."

The easiest way to avoid this pitfall is to act quickly and to be sure to follow up all professional appointments. Also, be ready and willing to demonstrate a financial commitment to the venture.

12-1d Pitfall 4: Lack of Demonstrated Experience (Business or Technical)

Many investors weigh very heavily the entrepreneur's actual experience in a venture, so it is important that entrepreneurs demonstrate what background they possess. Because too many beginners attempt to promote ideas they really have no true knowledge of, they are doomed to fail simply because they are perceived as ignorant of the specifics in the proposed business. Indicators are: no experience in business, no experience in the specific area of the venture, lack of understanding of the industry in which the venture fits, and failure to convey a clear picture of how and why the venture will work and who will accept it.

To avoid this pitfall, entrepreneurs need to give evidence of personal experience and background for the venture. If they lack specific knowledge or skills, they should obtain assistance from those who possess this knowledge or these skills. Demonstrating a team concept about those who help out also may be useful.

12-1e Pitfall 5: No Market Niche (Segment)

Many entrepreneurs propose an idea without establishing who the potential customers will be. Just because the entrepreneur likes the product or service does not mean that others will buy it. Numerous inventions at the U.S. Patent Office never reached the marketplace because no customers were targeted to buy them—no market was ever established. Indicators are: uncertainty about who will buy the basic idea(s) behind the venture, no proof of a need or desire for the good or product proposed, and an assumption that customers or clients will purchase just because the entrepreneur thinks so.

The best possible way to avoid this pitfall is to have a market segment specifically targeted and to demonstrate why and how the specific product or service will meet the needs or desires of this target group. (See Chapter 10 for specific information on market research.)

The five pitfalls detailed here represent the most common points of failure entrepreneurs experience *before* their business plans ever gets reviewed. In other words, these critical areas must be carefully addressed before a business plan is developed. If these pitfalls can be avoided, the entire business plan will be written more carefully and thus will be reviewed more thoroughly. This preparation helps entrepreneurs establish a solid foundation on which to develop an effective business plan.

12-2 BUSINESS MODEL CANVAS: INITIATING THE VENTURE FORMATION PROCESS

LO2 Explain the business model canvas as an initial step in the planning process

The **Business Model Canvas** is a structured brainstorming tool for entrepreneurs to use to define and understand the strategic focus and the questions that need to be answered for each of the nine business building blocks. The complete **Business Plan** provides a more specific and detailed exploration of the venture's goals and operations with a clear path on how the venture will succeed. Let's examine the *business model canvas* as a starting point.

A **business model** is a description of how a venture will create and deliver value. Since it is a strategic tool that was introduced decades ago, the sophistication levels have raised through the years. However, the *Business Model Canvas* was introduced as a way to simplify the process.[1] This entrepreneurial tool allows you to visually describe, design, challenge, invent, and pivot your business model. As shown in Figure 12.1 this design template helps the entrepreneur to systematically understand, design, and implement a game-changing business model. Along the way an entrepreneur can gain a deeper understanding of his or her customers, distribution channels, partners, revenue streams, costs, and core value proposition.

There are nine essential components:[2]

1. **Value Proposition.** The products and services that create value for a specific customer segment. A new venture's value proposition is what distinguishes it from potential competition. Value can be provided through various elements such as newness, performance, customization, design, brand, status, price, risk reduction, accessibility, and convenience or usability.

2. **Customer Segments.** The different groups of people or entities that the venture aims to reach and serve. As discussed in Chapter 10 on marketing, customers can be segmented (niche) based on the different needs and attributes to ensure appropriate implementation of corporate strategy meets the characteristics of selected group of clients.

3. **Channels.** Ways the venture communicates with and reaches its customer segments. A new venture can deliver its value proposition to its targeted customers through different channels such as opening a store, using major distributors, or a combination of both. Effective channels will distribute a venture's value proposition in ways that are fast, efficient, and cost effective.

4. **Customer Relationships.** The types of relationships a venture establishes with specific customer segments. To ensure the survival and success of any businesses, entrepreneurs must identify the type of relationship they want to create with their customer segments. Customer relationships can include personal assistance, self-service, automated services, or community platforms.

5. **Revenue Streams.** The cash a new venture proposes to generate from the particular customer niche. Several ways to generate a revenue stream include selling an item, service fees, subscription fees, lease or rental income, licensing fees, or advertising income.

6. **Key Activities.** These are the most important elements that a venture must do to make its business model work. For example, if lower prices are the unique value proposition then creating an efficient supply chain to drive down costs would be a key activity.

7. **Key Resources.** The most important assets required to make the business model work and create value for the customer. They are needed in order to sustain and support the business and could be human, financial, physical, or intellectual.

8. **Key Partners.** The network of suppliers and partners that optimize operations and reduce risks to make the business model work. Complementary alliances also can be considered through joint ventures or strategic alliances with other firms.

9. **Cost Structure.** The most significant costs incurred to operate the business model. Characteristics of cost structures include:
   - Fixed costs—Costs are unchanged across different applications, for example, salary, rent.
   - Variable costs—These costs vary depending on the amount of production of goods or services, for example, music festivals.
   - Economies of scale—Costs go down as the amount of good are ordered or produced.
   - Economies of scope—Costs go down due to incorporating other businesses which have a direct relation to the original product.

Once the nine elements of the business plan canvas are completed, the entrepreneur has a much greater understanding of the feasible value inherent in the proposed venture. If assessed as positive then the next step is to develop the complete *business plan* that will serve as the major descriptive document for the venture.

12-3 WHAT IS A BUSINESS PLAN?

LO3 Define a business plan and demonstrate its value

A **business plan** is the written document that details the proposed venture. It must describe current status, expected needs, and projected results of the new business. Every aspect of the venture needs to be covered: the project, marketing, research and development (R&D), management, critical risks, financial projections, and milestones or a timetable. A description of all of these facets of the proposed venture is necessary to demonstrate a clear picture of what that venture is, where it is projected to go, and how the entrepreneur proposes it will get there. The business plan is the entrepreneur's *road map* for a successful enterprise.[3]

In some professional areas, the business plan is referred to as a venture plan, a loan proposal, or an investment prospectus. Whatever the name, the business plan is the minimum document required by any financial source. The business plan allows the entrepreneur entrance into the investment process. Although it should be used as a working document once the venture is established, the major thrust of the business plan is to encapsulate the strategic development of the project in a comprehensive document for outside investors to read and understand.

The business plan describes to investors and financial sources all of the events that may affect the proposed venture. Details are needed for various projected actions of the venture, with associated revenues and costs outlined. It is vital to explicitly state the assumptions on which the plan is based. For example, increases/decreases in the market or upswings/downswings in the economy during the start-up period of the new venture should be stated.

The emphasis of the business plan always should be the final implementation of the venture. In other words, it's not just the writing of an effective plan that is important but also the translation of that plan into a successful enterprise.[4]

The comprehensive business plan, which should be the result of meetings and reflections on the direction of the new venture, is the major tool for determining the essential operation of a venture. It also is the primary document for managing the venture. One of the major benefits of this plan is that it helps the enterprise avoid common pitfalls that were mentioned which often undo all previous efforts.

12-4 BENEFITS OF A BUSINESS PLAN

LO4 Describe the benefits of a business plan

The entire business planning process forces the entrepreneur to analyze all aspects of the venture and to prepare an effective strategy to deal with the uncertainties that arise. Thus, a business plan may help an entrepreneur avoid a project doomed to failure. As one researcher states, "If your proposed venture is marginal at best, the business plan will show you why and may help you avoid paying the high tuition of business failure. It is far cheaper not to begin an ill-fated business than to learn by experience what your business plan could have taught you at a cost of several hours of concentrated work."[5]

It is important that entrepreneurs prepare their own business plan. If an entrepreneurial team is involved, then all of the key members should be part of writing the plan; in this case, it is important that the lead entrepreneur understand the contribution of each team member. If consultants are sought to help prepare a business plan, the entrepreneur must remain the driving force behind the plan. Seeking the advice and assistance of outside professionals is always wise, but entrepreneurs need to understand every aspect of the business plan, because they are the ones who come under the scrutiny of financial sources. Thus, the business plan stands as the entrepreneur's description and prediction for his or her venture, and it must be defended by the entrepreneur—simply put, it is the entrepreneur's responsibility.[6]

Other benefits are derived from a business plan, for both the entrepreneur and the financial sources that read it and evaluate the venture. For the entrepreneur, the following benefits are gained:

- The time, effort, research, and discipline needed to put together a formal business plan force the entrepreneur to view the venture critically and objectively.
- The competitive, economic, and financial analyses included in the business plan subject the entrepreneur to close scrutiny of his or her assumptions about the venture's success.
- Because all aspects of the business venture must be addressed in the plan, the entrepreneur develops and examines operating strategies and expected results for outside evaluators.
- The business plan quantifies objectives, providing measurable benchmarks for comparing forecasts with actual results.
- The completed business plan provides the entrepreneur with a communication tool for outside financial sources as well as an operational tool for guiding the venture toward success.[7]

The financial sources that read the plan derive the following benefits from the business plan:

- The business plan provides the details of the market potential and plans for securing a share of that market.
- Through prospective financial statements, the business plan illustrates the venture's ability to service debt or provide an adequate return on equity.
- The plan identifies critical risks and crucial events with a discussion of contingency plans that provide opportunity for the venture's success.
- By providing a comprehensive overview of the entire operation, the business plan gives financial sources a clear, concise document that contains the necessary information for a thorough business and financial evaluation.
- For a financial source with no prior knowledge of the entrepreneur or the venture, the business plan provides a useful guide for assessing the individual entrepreneur's planning and managerial ability.[8]

12-5 DEVELOPING A WELL-CONCEIVED BUSINESS PLAN

Most investors agree that only a well-conceived and well-developed business plan can gather the necessary support that will eventually lead to financing. The business plan must describe the new venture with excitement and yet with complete accuracy.

12-5a Who Reads the Plan?

LO5 Set forth the viewpoints of those who read a business plan

It is important to understand the audience for whom the business plan is written. Although numerous professionals may be involved with reading the business plan—such as venture capitalists, bankers, angel investors, potential large customers, lawyers, consultants, and suppliers—entrepreneurs need to clearly understand three main viewpoints when preparing the plan.[9]

The first viewpoint is, of course, the entrepreneur's, because he or she is the one developing the venture and clearly has the most in-depth knowledge of the technology or creativity involved. This is the most common viewpoint in business plans, and it is essential. However, too many plans emphasize this viewpoint and neglect the viewpoints of potential customers and investors.

More important than high technology or creative flair is the marketability of a new venture. This type of enterprise, referred to as "market-driven," convincingly demonstrates the benefits to users (the particular group of customers it is aiming for) and the existence of a substantial market. This viewpoint—that of the marketplace—is the second critical emphasis that an entrepreneur must incorporate into a business plan. Yet, although the actual value of this information is considered high, too many entrepreneurs tend to deemphasize in-depth marketing information in their business plans.[10] Establishing an actual market (determining who will buy the product or use the service) and documenting that the anticipated percentage of this market is appropriate for the venture's success are valuable criteria for the business plan.

The third viewpoint is related to the marketing emphasis just discussed. The investor's point of view is concentrated on the financial forecast. Sound financial projections are necessary if investors are to evaluate the worth of their investment. This is not to say that an entrepreneur should fill the business plan with spreadsheets of figures. In fact, many venture capital firms employ a "projection discount factor," which merely represents the belief of venture capitalists that successful new ventures usually reach approximately 50 percent of their projected financial goals.[11] However, a three- to five-year financial projection is essential for investors to use in making their judgment of a venture's future success.

These three viewpoints have been presented in order of decreasing significance to point out the emphasis needed in a well-conceived business plan. If they are addressed carefully in the plan, then the entrepreneur has prepared for what experts term the **five-minute reading**. The following six steps represent the typical business plan reading process that many venture capitalists use (less than one minute is devoted to each step):

Step 1: Determine the characteristics of the venture and its industry.

Step 2: Determine the financial structure of the plan (amount of debt or equity investment required).

Step 3: Read the latest balance sheet (to determine liquidity, net worth, and debt/equity).

Step 4: Determine the quality of entrepreneurs in the venture (sometimes *the* most important step).

Step 5: Establish the unique feature in this venture (find out what is different).

Step 6: Read over the entire plan lightly (this is when the entire package is paged through for a casual look at graphs, charts, exhibits, and other plan components).[12]

These steps provide insight into how the average business plan is read. It may seem somewhat unjust that so much of the entrepreneur's effort is put into a plan that is given only a five-minute reading. However, that's the nature of the process for many venture capitalists. Other financial or professional sources may devote more time to analyzing the plan. But keep in mind that venture capitalists read through numerous business plans; thus, knowing the steps in their reading process is valuable for developing any plan. Related to the process of venture capitalists is this updated version of an old quote that links entrepreneurs and venture capitalists: "The people who manage people manage people who manage things, *but* the people who manage money manage the people who manage people."[13]

12-5b Putting the Package Together

LO6 Emphasize the importance of coordinating the business plan segments

When presenting a business plan to potential investors, the entrepreneur must realize that the entire package is important. Presented next is a summary of key issues that the entrepreneur needs to watch for if his or her plan is going to be viewed successfully. A business plan gives financiers their first impressions of a company and its principals.

Potential investors expect the plan to look good, but not too good; to be the right length; to clearly and concisely explain (early on) all aspects of the company's business; and not to contain bad grammar and typographical or spelling errors.

Investors are looking for evidence that the principals treat their own property with care—and will likewise treat the investment carefully. In other words, form as well as content is important; investors know that good form reflects good content, and vice versa.

Among the format issues we think most important are the following:

Appearance—The binding and printing must not be sloppy; neither should the presentation be too lavish. A stapled compilation of photocopied pages usually looks amateurish, whereas bookbinding with typeset pages may arouse concern about excessive and inappropriate spending. A plastic spiral binding, holding together a pair of cover sheets of a single color, provides both a neat appearance and sufficient strength to withstand handling by a number of people without damage.

Length—A business plan should be no more than 20–25 pages long. The first draft will likely exceed that, but editing should produce a final version that fits within the 20-page ideal. Adherence to this length forces entrepreneurs to sharpen their ideas and results in a document that is likely to hold investors' attention.

Background details can be included in an additional volume. Entrepreneurs can make this material available to investors during the investigative period, after the initial expression of interest.

The Cover and Title Page—The cover should bear the name of the company, its address and phone number, and the month and year in which the plan is issued. Surprisingly, a large number of business plans are submitted to potential investors without return addresses or phone numbers. An interested investor wants to be able to contact a company easily to request further information or express an interest, either in the company or in some aspect of the plan.

Inside the front cover should be a well-designed title page on which the cover information is repeated and, in an upper or a lower corner, the "copy number" provided. Besides helping entrepreneurs keep track of plans in circulation, holding down the number of copies outstanding—usually to no more than 10—has a psychological advantage. After all, no investor likes to think that the prospective investment is shopworn.

The Executive Summary—The two to three pages immediately following the title page should concisely explain the company's current status, its products or services, the benefits to customers, the financial forecasts, the venture's objectives in three to seven years, the amount of financing needed, and how investors will benefit.

This is a tall order for a two-page summary, but it will either sell investors on reading the rest of the plan or convince them to forget the whole thing.

The Table of Contents—After the executive summary, include a well-designed table of contents. List each of the business plan's sections and mark the pages for each section.

An attractive appearance, an effective length, an executive summary, a table of contents, proper grammar, correct typing, and a cover page—all are important factors when putting together a complete package. These points often separate successful plans from unacceptable ones.

12-5c Guidelines to Remember

LO7 Review key recommendations by venture capital experts regarding a plan

The following points are a collection of recommendations by experts in venture capital and new-venture development.[14] These guidelines are presented as tips for successful business plan development. Entrepreneurs need to adhere to them to understand the importance of the various segments of the business plan they create, which will be discussed in the next section.

KEEP THE PLAN RESPECTABLY SHORT

Readers of business plans are important people who refuse to waste time. Therefore, entrepreneurs should explain the venture not only carefully and clearly but also concisely. (Ideally, the plan should be no more than 20–25 pages long, excluding the appendix.)

ORGANIZE AND PACKAGE THE PLAN APPROPRIATELY

A table of contents, an executive summary, an appendix, exhibits, graphs, proper grammar, a logical arrangement of segments, and overall neatness are elements critical to the effective presentation of a business plan.

ORIENT THE PLAN TOWARD THE FUTURE

Entrepreneurs should attempt to create an air of excitement in the plan by developing trends and forecasts that describe what the venture *intends* to do and what the opportunities are for the use of the product or service.

AVOID EXAGGERATION

Sales potentials, revenue estimates, and the venture's potential growth should not be inflated. Many times, a best-case, worst-case, and probable-case scenario should be developed for the plan. Documentation and research are vital to the plan's credibility. (See Table 12.1 for business plan phrases.)

TABLE 12.1   COMMON BUSINESS PLAN PHRASES: STATEMENT VERSUS REALITY

Statement	Reality
We conservatively project…	We read a book that said we had to be a $50 million company in five years, and we reverse-engineered the numbers.
We took our best guess and divided by 2.	We accidentally divided by 0.5.
We project a 10 percent margin.	We did not modify any of the assumptions in the business plan template that we downloaded from the Internet.
The project is 98 percent complete.	To complete the remaining 2 percent will take as long as it took to create the initial 98 percent but will cost twice as much.
Our business model is proven…	… if you take the evidence from the past week for the best of our 50 locations and extrapolate it for all the others.
We have a six-month lead.	We tried not to find out how many other people have a six-month lead.
We need only a 10 percent market share.	So do the other 50 entrants getting funded.
Customers are clamoring for our product.	We have not yet asked them to pay for it. Also, all of our current customers are relatives.
We are the low-cost producer.	We have not produced anything yet, but we are confident that we will be able to.
We have no competition.	Only IBM, Microsoft, Netscape, and Sun have announced plans to enter the business.
Our management team has a great deal of experience…	… consuming the product or service.
A select group of investors is considering the plan.	We mailed a copy of the plan to everyone in *Pratt's Guide*.
We seek a value-added investor.	We are looking for a passive, dumb-as-rocks investor.
If you invest on our terms, you will earn a 68 percent internal rate of return.	If everything that could ever conceivably go right does go right, you might get your money back.

Source: Adapted from William A. Sahlman, "How to Write a Great Business Plan" (July/August 1997): 106. Copyright © 1997 by the Harvard Business School Publishing. All rights reserved.

HIGHLIGHT CRITICAL RISKS

The critical-risks segment of the business plan is important in that it demonstrates the entrepreneur's ability to analyze potential problems and develop alternative courses of action.

GIVE EVIDENCE OF AN EFFECTIVE ENTREPRENEURIAL TEAM

The management segment of the business plan should clearly identify the skills of each key person as well as demonstrate how all such people can effectively work together as a team to manage the venture.

DO NOT OVER-DIVERSIFY

Focus the attention of the plan on one main opportunity for the venture. A new business should not attempt to create multiple markets or pursue multiple ventures until it has successfully developed one main strength.

IDENTIFY THE TARGET MARKET

Substantiate the marketability of the venture's product or service by identifying the particular customer niche being sought. This segment of the business plan is pivotal to the success of the other parts. Market research must be included to demonstrate how this market segment has been identified.

KEEP THE PLAN WRITTEN IN THE THIRD PERSON

Rather than continually stating "I," "we," or "us," the entrepreneur should phrase everything as "he," "she," "they," or "them." In other words, avoid personalizing the plan, and keep the writing objective.

CAPTURE THE READER'S INTEREST

Because of the numerous business plans submitted to investors and the small percentage of business plans funded, entrepreneurs need to capture the reader's interest right away by highlighting the uniqueness of the venture. Use the title page and executive summary as key tools to capture the reader's attention and create a desire to read more.

12-5d Questions to Be Answered

A well-written business plan is like a work of art: It's visually pleasing and makes a statement without saying a word. Unfortunately, the two are also alike in that they are worth money only if they're good. Researchers Donald F. Kuratko and Jeffrey S. Hornsby recommend the following key questions to consider when writing an effective business plan.

- *Is your plan organized so key facts leap out at the reader?* Appearances do count. Your plan is a representation of yourself, so don't expect an unorganized, less than acceptable plan to be your vehicle for obtaining funds.

- *Is your product/service and business mission clear and simple?* Your mission should state very simply the value that you will provide to your customers. It shouldn't take more than a paragraph.

- *Are you focused on the right things?* Determine what phase of the business you are really in, focus on the right tasks, and use your resources appropriately.

- *Who is your customer?* Does the plan describe the business's ideal customers and how you will reach them? Is your projected share of the market identified, reasonable, and supported?

- *Why will customers buy? How much better is your product/service?* Define the need for your product and provide references and testimonial support to enhance it. Try to be detailed in explaining how the customer will benefit from buying your product.

- *Do you have a competitive advantage?* Focus on differences and any unique qualities. Proprietary processes/technology and patentable items/ideals are good things to highlight as competitive strengths.

- *Do you have a favorable cost structure?* Proper gross margins are key. Does the break-even analysis take into consideration the dynamics of price and variable costs? Identify, if possible, any economics of scale that would be advantageous to the business.

- *Can the management team build a business?* Take a second look at the management team to see whether they have relevant experience in small business and in the industry. Acknowledge the fact that the team may need to evolve with the business.

- *How much money do you need?* Financial statements—including the income statement, cash-flow statement, and balance sheet—should be provided on a monthly basis for the first year and on a quarterly basis for the following two or three years.

- *How does your investor get a cash return?* Whether it's through a buyout or an initial public offering, make sure your plan clearly outlines this important question regarding a harvest strategy.[15]

These guidelines and questions have been presented to help entrepreneurs who are preparing to write a business plan. The following section analyzes the ten major segments of a business plan.

12-6 ELEMENTS OF A BUSINESS PLAN

LO8 Present a complete outline of an effective business plan

A detailed business plan usually includes anywhere from six to ten sections (depending on the idea, the industry, and the technical details). The ideal length of a plan is 25 pages, although—depending on the need for detail—the overall plan can range from 20 to more than 30 pages if an appendix is included.[16] Table 12.2 provides an outline of a typical plan. The remainder of this section describes the specific parts of the plan. A complete business plan for Hydraulic Wind Power appears in Appendix 12A at the end of this chapter.

12-6a Executive Summary

Many people who read business plans (bankers, venture capitalists, investors) like to see a summary of the plan that features its most important parts. Such a summary gives a brief overview of what is to follow, helps put all of the information into perspective, and should be no longer than two to three pages. The summary should be written only after the entire business plan has been completed. In this way, particular phrases or descriptions from each segment can be identified for inclusion in the summary. Because the summary is the first—and sometimes the only—part of a plan that is read, it must present the quality of the entire report. The summary must be a clever snapshot of the complete plan.

The statements selected for a summary segment should briefly touch on the venture itself, the market opportunities, the financial needs and projections, and any special research or technology associated with the venture. This should be done in such a way that the evaluator or investor will choose to read on. If this information is not presented in a concise, competent manner, the reader may put aside the plan or simply conclude that the project does not warrant funding.

12-6b Business Description

First, the name of the venture should be identified, along with any special significance (e.g., family name, technical name). Second, the industry background should be presented in terms of current status and future trends. It is important to note any special industry developments that may affect the plan. If the company has an existing business or franchise, this is the appropriate place to discuss it. Third, the new venture should be thoroughly described, along with its proposed potential. All key terms should be defined and made comprehensible. Functional specifications or descriptions should be provided. Drawings and photographs also may be included.

Fourth, the potential advantages the new venture possesses over the competition should be discussed at length. This discussion may include patents, copyrights, and trademarks, as well as special technological or market advantages.

TABLE 12.2 COMPLETE OUTLINE OF A BUSINESS PLAN

Section I: Executive Summary

Section II: Business Description

A. General description of the business
B. Industry background
C. Goals and potential of the business and milestones (if any)
D. Uniqueness of product or service

Section III: Marketing

A. Research and analysis
   1. Target market (customers) identified
   2. Market size and trends
   3. Competition
   4. Estimated market share
B. Marketing plan
   1. Market strategy—sales and distribution
   2. Pricing
   3. Advertising and promotions

Section IV: Operations

A. Identify location: advantages
B. Specific operational procedures
C. Personnel needs and uses
D. Proximity to supplies

Section V: Management

A. Management team—key personnel
B. Legal structure—stock agreements, employment agreements, ownership
C. Board of directors, advisors, consultants

Section VI: Financial

A. Financial forecast
   1. Profit and loss
   2. Cash flow
   3. Break-even analysis
   4. Cost controls
   5. Budgeting plans

Section VII: Critical Risks

A. Potential problems
B. Obstacles and risks
C. Alternative courses of action

Section VIII: Harvest Strategy It stands for Initial Public Offering but it should be well understood.

A. Liquidity event (IPO or sale)
B. Continuity of business strategy
C. Identify successor

Section IX: Milestone Schedule

A. Timing and objectives
B. Deadlines and milestones
C. Relationship of events

Section X: Appendix or Bibliography

Source: Donald F. Kuratko, *The Complete Entrepreneurial Planning Guide* (Bloomington: Kelley School of Business, Indiana University, 2015).

12-6c   Marketing Segment

In the **marketing segment** of the plan, the entrepreneur must convince investors that a market exists, that sales projections *can be achieved,* and that the competition can be beaten.

This part of the plan is often one of the most difficult to prepare. It is also one of the most critical, because almost all subsequent sections of the plan depend on the sales estimates developed here. The projected sales levels—which are based on the market research and analysis—directly influence the size of the manufacturing operation, the marketing plan, and the amount of debt and equity capital required.

Most entrepreneurs have difficulty preparing and presenting market research and analyses that will convince investors the venture's sales estimates are accurate and attainable. The following are aspects of marketing that should be addressed when developing a comprehensive exposition of the market.

12-6d   Market Niche and Market Share

A **market niche** is a homogeneous group with common characteristics—that is, all the people who have a need for the newly proposed product or service. When describing this niche, the writer should address the bases of customer purchase decisions: price, quality, service, personal contacts, or some combination of these factors.

Next, a list of potential customers who have expressed interest in the product or service—together with an explanation for their interest—should be included. If it is an existing business, the current principal customers should be identified and the sales trend should be discussed. It is important to describe the overall potential of the market. Sales projections should be made for at least three years, and the major factors affecting market growth (industry trends, socioeconomic trends, governmental policy, and population shifts) should be discussed. A review of previous market trends should be included, and any differences between past and projected annual growth rates should be explained. The sources of all data and methods used to make projections should be indicated. Then, if any major customers are willing to make purchase commitments, they should be identified, and the extent of those commitments should be indicated. On the basis of the product or service advantages, the market size and trends, the customers, and the sales trends in prior years, the writer should estimate market share and sales in units and dollars for each of the next three years. The growth of the company's sales and its estimated market share should be related to the growth of the industry and the customer base.

COMPETITIVE ANALYSIS

The entrepreneur should make an attempt to assess the strengths and weaknesses of the competing products or services. Any sources used to evaluate the competition should be cited. This discussion should compare competing products or services on the basis of price, performance, service, warranties, and other pertinent features. It should include a short discussion of the current advantages and disadvantages of competing products and services, and why they are not meeting customer needs. Any knowledge of competitors' actions that could lead to new or improved products and an advantageous position also should be presented.

Finally, a review of competing companies should be included. Each competitor's share of the market, sales, and distribution and production capabilities should be discussed. Attention should be focused on profitability and the profit trend of each competitor. Who is the pricing leader? Who is the quality leader? Who is gaining? Who is losing? Have any companies entered or dropped out of the market in recent years?

MARKETING STRATEGY

The general marketing philosophy and approach of the company should be outlined in the **marketing strategy**. A marketing strategy should be developed from market research and evaluation data and should include a discussion of (1) the kinds of customer groups to be targeted by the initial intensive selling effort; (2) the customer groups to be targeted for later selling efforts; (3) methods of identifying and contacting potential customers in these groups; (4) the features of the product or service (quality, price, delivery, warranty, etc.) to be emphasized to generate sales; and (5) any innovative or unusual marketing concepts that will enhance customer acceptance (e.g., leasing where only sales were previously attempted).

This section also should indicate whether the product or service initially will be introduced nationally or regionally. Consideration also should be given to any seasonal trends and what can be done to promote contra-seasonal sales.

PRICING POLICY

The price must be "right" to penetrate the market, maintain a market position, and produce profits. A number of pricing strategies should be examined, and then one should be convincingly presented. This pricing policy should be compared with the policies of the major competitors. The gross profit margin between manufacturing and final sales costs should be discussed, and consideration should be given to whether this margin is large enough to allow for distribution, sales, warranty, and service expenses; for amortization of development and equipment costs; and for profit. Attention also should be given to justifying any price increases over competitive items on the basis of newness, quality, warranty, or service.

ADVERTISING PLAN

For manufactured products, the preparation of product sheets and promotional literature; the plans for trade show participation, trade magazine advertisements, and direct mailings; and the use of advertising agencies should be presented. For products and services in general, a discussion of the advertising and promotional campaign contemplated to introduce the product and the kinds of sales aids to be provided to dealers should be included. Additionally, the schedule and cost of promotion and advertising should be presented; if advertising will be a significant part of the expenses, an exhibit that shows how and when these costs will be incurred should be included.

These five subsets of the marketing segment are needed to detail the overall marketing plan, which should describe *what* is to be done, *how* it will be done, and *who* will do it.

12-6e Research, Design, and Development Segment

The extent of any research, design, and development in regard to cost, time, and special testing should be covered in this segment. Investors need to know the status of the project in terms of prototypes, lab tests, and scheduling delays. Note that this segment is applicable only if R&D is involved in the business plan.

To achieve a comprehensive section, the entrepreneur should have (or seek out) technical assistance in preparing a detailed discussion. Blueprints, sketches, drawings, and models often are important.

It is equally important to identify the design or development work that still needs to be done and to discuss possible difficulties or risks that may delay or alter the project. In this regard, a developmental budget that shows the costs associated with labor, materials consulting, research, design, and the like should be constructed and presented.

12-6f Operations Segment

This segment always should begin by describing the location of the new venture. The chosen site should be appropriate in terms of labor availability, wage rate, proximity to suppliers and customers, and community support. In addition, local taxes and zoning requirements should be sorted out, and the support of area banks for new ventures should be touched on.

Specific needs should be discussed in terms of how the enterprise actually operates and the facilities required to handle the new venture (plant, warehouse storage, and offices), as well as any equipment that needs to be acquired (special tooling, machinery, computers, and vehicles).

THE ENTREPRENEURIAL PROCESS

Common Business Planning Mistakes

Entrepreneurs endure uncertainty in most everything they do. From hiring the right employees to finding reliable suppliers, building a business requires an entrepreneur to handle significant pressure on a daily basis. Given the variability inherent in any new venture, a business plan is crucial for effective management. In spite of the importance of business planning, few activities are more daunting for entrepreneurs than formalizing their thoughts on paper. In order for entrepreneurs to stay driven to succeed, they have to remain optimistic, so the fear of discovering some insurmountable obstacle while planning leads some management teams to avoid the process altogether. Whether the business is a start-up or a well-established corporation, a business plan, when done correctly, serves as the company's blueprint to ensure that all parties involved are in agreement regarding the business's overarching purpose. In the business plan sections listed below we present some of the common mistakes that entrepreneurs make when developing their plan.

Overall Mistakes

- Entrepreneurs are unable to clearly articulate their vision in the plan.
- Entrepreneurs use acronyms and technical jargon without clearly explaining them early in the business plan.
- Entrepreneurs fail to provide sufficient details regarding the implementation of their strategy.
- Entrepreneurs ineffectively present the goals and objectives which are most important to the business's success.
- Entrepreneurs do not convincingly present the basis for their strategy.
- Entrepreneurs do not improve their plan based on the feedback from investors.

Executive Summary

- Entrepreneurs are not precise about their needs and capabilities.
- Entrepreneurs waste words with fillers and superfluous information.

Management

- Entrepreneurs forget to include their previous successes and or failures.
- Entrepreneurs dismiss the importance investors place on an experienced management team.

Marketing

- Entrepreneurs rely heavily on secondary market research rather than soliciting the opinions of their potential customers.
- Entrepreneurs claim the percent of the market their company will own without research support.

Financials

- Entrepreneurs overlook and, in turn, underestimate their cash-flow requirements.
- Entrepreneurs inflate or understate their margins in order to arrive at their ideal profitability.

Source: Adapted from Mark Henricks, "Build a Better Business Plan," *Entrepreneur* (February 2007). Retrieved June 21, 2008 from https://www.entrepreneur.com/startingabusiness/businessplans/article174002.html; Andrew J. Sherman, *Grow Fast, Grow Right: 12 Strategies to Achieve Breakthrough Business Growth* (Chicago: Kaplan Publishing, 2007), 20–26; and Jay Snider, "Don't Make These 5 Business Plan Mistakes," *Up and Running Blog*, http://upandrunning.bplans.com/2012/04/20/dont-make-these-5-business-plan-mistakes/, accessed May 29, 2012.

Other factors that might be considered are the suppliers (number and proximity) and the transportation costs involved in shipping materials. The labor supply, wage rates, and needed skilled positions also should be presented.

Finally, the cost data associated with any of the operation factors should be presented. The financial information used here can be applied later to the financial projections.

12-6g Management Segment

This segment identifies the key personnel, their positions and responsibilities, and the career experiences that qualify them for those particular roles. Complete résumés should be provided for each member of the management team. In this section, the entrepreneur's role in the venture should be clearly outlined. Finally, any advisors, consultants, or members of the board should be identified and discussed.

The structure of payment and ownership (stock agreements, consulting fees, and so on) should be described clearly in this section. In summary, the discussion should be sufficient so that investors can understand each of the following critical factors that have been presented: (1) organizational structure, (2) management team and critical personnel, (3) experience and technical capabilities of the personnel, (4) ownership structure and compensation agreements, and (5) board of directors and outside consultants and advisors.

12-6h Financial Segment

The financial segment of a business plan must demonstrate the potential viability of the undertaking. Three basic financial statements must be presented in this part of the plan: the pro forma balance sheet, the income statement, and the cash-flow statement.

THE PRO FORMA BALANCE SHEET

Pro forma means "projected," as opposed to actual. The pro forma balance sheet projects what the financial condition of the venture will be at a particular point in time. Pro forma balance sheets should be prepared at start-up, semiannually for the first years, and at the end of each of the first three years. The balance sheet details the assets required to support the projected level of operations and shows how these assets are to be financed (liabilities and equity). Investors will want to look at the projected balance sheets to determine if debt/equity ratios, working capital, current ratios, inventory turnover, and so on are within the acceptable limits required to justify the future financings projected for the venture.

THE INCOME STATEMENT

The income statement illustrates the projected operating results based on profit and loss. The sales forecast, which was developed in the marketing segment, is essential to this document. Once the sales forecast (earnings projection) is in place, production costs must be budgeted based on the level of activity needed to support the projected earnings. The materials, labor, service, and manufacturing overhead (fixed and variable) must be considered, in addition to such expenses as distribution, storage, advertising, discounts, and administrative and general expenses (salaries, legal and accounting, rent, utilities, and telephone).

THE CASH-FLOW STATEMENT

The cash-flow statement may be the most important document in new-venture creation, because it sets forth the amount and timing of expected cash inflows and outflows. This section of the business plan should be carefully constructed.

Given a level of projected sales and capital expenditures for a specific period, the cash-flow forecast will highlight the need for and the timing of additional financing and will indicate peak requirements for working capital. Management must decide how this additional financing is to be obtained, on what terms, and how it is to be repaid. The total amount of needed financing may be supplied from several sources: part by equity financing, part by bank loans, and the balance by short-term lines of credit from banks. This information becomes part of the final cash-flow forecast. A detailed cash flow, if understood properly, can direct the entrepreneur's attention to operating problems before serious cash crises arise.

In the financial segment, it is important to mention any assumptions used to prepare the figures. Nothing should be taken for granted. This segment also should include how the statements were prepared (by a professional certified public accountant or by the entrepreneur) and who will be in charge of managing the business's finances.

The final document that should be included in the financial segment is a break-even chart, which shows the level of sales (and production) needed to cover all costs. This includes costs that vary with the production level (manufacturing labor, materials, sales) and costs that do not change with production (rent, interest charges, executive salaries).

12-6i Critical-Risks Segment

In this segment, potential risks such as the following should be identified: effect of unfavorable trends in the industry, design or manufacturing costs that have gone over estimates, difficulties of long lead times encountered when purchasing parts or materials, and unplanned-for new competition.

In addition to these risks, it is wise to cover the what-ifs. For example, what if the competition cuts prices, the industry slumps, the market projections are wrong, the sales projections are not achieved, the patents do not come through, or the management team breaks up?

Finally, suggestions for alternative courses of action should be included. Certainly, delays, inaccurate projections, and industry slumps all can happen, and people reading the business plan will want to know that the entrepreneur recognizes these risks and has prepared for such critical events.

12-6j Harvest Strategy Segment

Every business plan should provide insights into the future harvest strategy. It is important for the entrepreneur to plan for a liquidity event as an exit strategy or for the orderly transition of the venture if the plan is to grow and develop it. This section needs to deal with such issues as management succession and investor exit strategies. In addition, some thought should be given to change management—that is, the orderly transfer of the company assets if ownership of the business changes; continuity of the business strategy during the transition; and designation of key individuals to run the business if the current management team changes. With foresight, entrepreneurs can keep their dreams alive, ensure the security of their investors, and usually strengthen their businesses in the process. For this reason, a harvest strategy is essential.

12-6k Milestone Schedule Segment

The **milestone schedule segment** provides investors with a timetable for the various activities to be accomplished. It is important to show that realistic time frames have been planned and that the interrelationship of events within these time boundaries is understood. Milestone scheduling is a step-by-step approach to illustrating accomplishments in a piecemeal fashion. These milestones can be established within any appropriate time frame, such as quarterly, monthly, or weekly. It is important, however, to coordinate the time frame not only with such early activities as product design and development, sales projections, establishment of the management team, production and operations scheduling, and market planning but with other activities as well:

- Incorporation of the venture
- Completion of design and development, completion of prototypes
- Hiring of sales representatives, product display at trade shows
- Signing up distributors and dealers
- Ordering production quantities of materials, receipt of first orders
- First sales and first deliveries (dates of maximum interest because they relate directly to the venture's credibility and need for capital)
- Payment of first accounts receivable (cash in)

THE ENTREPRENEURIAL PROCESS

Straying from Your Business Plan?

A well-written, thoughtful business plan is an important tool for any entrepreneur; however, even the most conservative strategy can fail to address some obstacles that are encountered between the inception of a concept and the eventual harvest of the business. One example of such a hurdle is when a business encounters an economic downturn. What is the appropriate strategy when the general economy has begun to falter, leading consumers to tuck away dollars that they would have otherwise spent at your business?

The answer is that there is not one solution for dealing with an ailing economy. Despite the need for a business plan, entrepreneurs often find that strict adherence to their plan is as dangerous as not having one at all. The key is to know when to stray from your plan. Following are steps to take when your plan does not effectively address the environment in which you find your business:

Partner together. Partnering with companies that offer complimentary products to your own is an effective way to share the responsibility of building the market. Not only can advertising expenses be split but you can also introduce consumer incentives that encourage crossover purchasing from customers who otherwise would not have bought from your company. A common strategy is to determine what purchases your customers are currently making at other establishments that are closely associated with their purchases at your business. For instance, if you own a coffee shop and your customers are regularly walking in with pastry purchases from a local bakery, a partnership with the bakery could be a logical fit. The key is to take advantage of the existing behavior of your customers rather than try to change it.

Communicate with customers. When times are lean, your existing customers are your lifeblood, so keeping them happy becomes increasingly important. If your marketing budget will not allow for extravagant advertising, shift your focus to working closely with your current customers. Often you will find that your customers are more than willing to share their perspective on your business, which could lead to easy and cheap modifications that will build loyalty. By keeping track of prospective customers, you will be in a better position to follow-up with them when times are slow. For instance, if your business involves providing quotes to potential customers,

make note of those who chose not to make a purchase. When speaking with them, you will get insight about why they went elsewhere, and your efforts might convince them to rethink doing business with you.

Remain flexible. When the economy slackens, consumers become more conservative with their purchases and are more inclined to base their shopping on price alone. The problem with cutting prices during an economic downturn is that consumers will expect them to remain low when the economy improves. One way to avoid having to resort to cost-cutting measures is by offering more for the same price. For instance, extending your business's hours to better accommodate your customers' schedules or offering free in-home estimates for service-related businesses are both quick measures to take that could help set your business apart from the competition.

Build networks. As an entrepreneur, the ability to network is an important skill, especially when your business begins to wane. One important forum for many new ventures is the local chamber of commerce. By interacting with local businesses, entrepreneurs can keep close tabs on what the local economic trends are as well as gain access to potential commercial customers. In addition, working with other businesses can help you locate resources in your community, such as local talent and sources of funding; moreover, having a group of fellow entrepreneurs can be useful for vetting ideas as well as for moral support.

This list is not meant to be exhaustive. The underlying theme is that entrepreneurs need to maintain the versatility that they had when first starting their businesses. Developing a strategy is important for entrepreneurs to effectively manage their business, and formally documenting that strategy is important for ensuring the continuity of their business; however, entrepreneurs who depend solely on their business plan to direct their business decisions run the risk of locking themselves into a strategy that could quickly become obsolete due to a shift in the environment. Planning is crucial for your business, but knowing when to change your plan is equally important.

Source: Adapted from Rich Sloan, "Bad Economy? Time to Get Aggressive," *Fortune Small Business*, March 3, 2008, http://money.cnn.com/2008/03/03/smbusiness/startup_nation.fsb/index.htm (accessed May 12, 2012).

These items are the types of activities that should be included in the milestone schedule segment. The more detailed the schedule, the more likely the entrepreneur will persuade potential investors that he or she has thought things out and is therefore a good risk.

12-6l Appendix and/or Bibliography Segment

The final segment is not mandatory, but it allows for additional documentation that is not appropriate in the main parts of the plan. Diagrams, blueprints, financial data, vitae of management team members, and any bibliographical information that supports the other segments of the plan are examples of material that can be included. It is up to the entrepreneur to decide which, if any, items to put into this segment. However, the material should be limited to relevant and supporting information.

Table 12.3 provides an important recap of the major segments of a business plan, using helpful hints as practical reminders for entrepreneurs. By reviewing this, entrepreneurs can gain a macro view of the planning process. Table 12.4 is a personal checklist that gives entrepreneurs the opportunity to evaluate their business plan for each segment. The step-by-step evaluation is based on coverage of the particular segment, clarity of its presentation, and completeness. While it is understood that business plans will vary in the titles and headings that are used (see Appendix 12A), it is still valuable to assess each of the complete segments to see if and how they are presented in the final business plan.

TABLE 12.3 HELPFUL HINTS FOR DEVELOPING THE BUSINESS PLAN

I. Executive Summary

- No more than three pages. This is the most crucial part of your plan because you must capture the reader's interest.
- What, how, why, where, and so on must be summarized.
- Complete this part after you have a finished business plan.

II. Business Description Segment

- The name of your business.
- A background of the industry with history of your company (if any) should be covered here.
- The potential of the new venture should be described clearly.
- Any uniqueness or distinctive features of this venture should be described clearly.

III. Marketing Segment

- Convince investors that sales projections and competition can be met.
- Use and disclose market studies.
- Identify target market, market position, and market share.
- Evaluate all competition and specifically cover why and how you will be better than your competitors. Identify all market sources and assistance used for this segment.
- Demonstrate pricing strategy. Your price must penetrate and maintain a market share to produce profits; thus, the lowest price is not necessarily the best price.
- Identify your advertising plans with cost estimates to validate proposed strategy.

IV. Operations Segment

- Describe the advantages of your location (zoning, tax laws, wage rates). List the production needs in terms of facilities (plant, storage, office space) and equipment (machinery, furnishings, supplies).
- Describe the specific operations of the venture.
- Indicate proximity to your suppliers.
- Mention the need and use of personnel in the operation.
- Provide estimates of operation costs—but be careful: Too many entrepreneurs underestimate their costs.

V. Management Segment

- Supply résumés of all key people in the management of your venture.
- Carefully describe the legal structure of your venture (sole proprietorship, partnership, or corporation).
- Cover the added assistance (if any) of advisors, consultants, and directors.
- Give information on how and how much everyone is to be compensated.

(Continued)

TABLE 12.3 HELPFUL HINTS FOR DEVELOPING THE BUSINESS PLAN *(Continued)*

VI. Financial Segment

- Give actual estimated statements.
- Describe the needed sources for your funds and the uses you intend for the money.
- Develop and present a budget.
- Create stages of financing for purposes of allowing evaluation by investors at various points.

VII. Critical-Risks Segment

- Discuss potential risks before investors point them out—e.g.,
  - *Price cutting by competitors*
  - *Any potentially unfavorable industry-wide trends*
  - *Design or manufacturing costs in excess of estimates*
  - *Sales projections not achieved*
  - *Product development schedule not met*
  - *Difficulties or long lead times encountered in the procurement of parts or raw materials Greater than expected innovation and development costs to stay competitive*
  - *Provide some alternative courses of action.*

VIII. Harvest Strategy Segment

- Outline a plan for a liquidity event—IPO or sale.
- Describe the plan for transition of leadership.
- Mention the preparations (insurance, trusts, and so on) needed for continuity of the business.

IX. Milestone Schedule Segment

- Develop a timetable or chart to demonstrate when each phase of the venture is to be completed. This shows the relationship of events and provides a deadline for accomplishment.

X. Appendix or Bibliography

Source: Donald F. Kuratko, *The Complete Entrepreneurial Planning Guide* (Bloomington: Kelley School of Business, Indiana University, 2015).

TABLE 12.4 BUSINESS PLAN ASSESSMENT: A COMPLETE EVALUATION TOOL

The Components

Presented here are ten components of a business plan. As you develop your business plan, you should assess each component. Be honest in your assessment, because the main purpose is to improve your business plan and increase your chances of success. For instance, if your goal is to obtain external financing, you will be asked to submit a complete business plan for your venture. The business plan will help a funding source to more adequately evaluate your business idea.

Assessment

Directions: The brief description of each component will help you write that section of your plan. After completing your plan, use the scale provided to assess each component.

5	4	3	2	1
Outstanding	Very Good	Good	Fair	Poor
thorough and complete in all areas	most areas covered but could use improvement in detail	some areas covered in detail but other areas missing	a few areas covered but very little detail	no written parts

(Continued)

TABLE 12.4   BUSINESS PLAN ASSESSMENT: A COMPLETE EVALUATION TOOL (*Continued*)

The Ten Components of a Business Plan

1. **Executive Summary**. This is the most important section because it has to convince the reader that the business will succeed. In no more than three pages, you should summarize the highlights of the rest of the plan. This means that the key elements of the following components should be mentioned.

   The executive summary must be able to stand on its own. It is not simply an introduction to the rest of the business plan but rather discusses who will purchase your product or service, what makes your business unique, and how you plan to grow in the future. Because this section summarizes the plan, it is often best to write it last.

	5	4	3	2	1
Rate this component:	├	┼	┼	┼	┤
	Outstanding	Very Good	Good	Fair	Poor

2. **Description of the Business**. This section should provide background information about your industry, a history of your company, a general description of your product or service, and your specific mission that you are trying to achieve. Your product or service should be described in terms of its unique qualities and value to the customer. Specific short-term and long-term objectives must be defined. You should clearly state what sales, market share, and profitability objectives you want your business to achieve.

Key Elements	Have you covered this in the plan?	Is the answer clear? (yes or no)	Is the answer complete? (yes or no)
a. What type of business will you have?			
b. What products or services will you sell?			
c. Why does it promise to be successful?			
d. What is the growth potential?			
e. How is it unique?			

	5	4	3	2	1
Rate this component:	├	┼	┼	┼	┤
	Outstanding	Very Good	Good	Fair	Poor

3. **Marketing**. There are two major parts to the marketing section. The first part is research and analysis. Here, you should explain who buys the product or service—in other words, identify your target market. Measure your market size and trends, and estimate the market share you expect. Be sure to include support for your sales projections. For example, if your figures are based on published marketing research data, be sure to cite the source. Do your best to make realistic and credible projections. Describe your competitors in considerable detail, identifying their strengths and weaknesses. Finally, explain how you will be better than your competitors.

   The second part is your marketing plan. This critical section should include your market strategy, sales and distribution, pricing, advertising, promotion, and public awareness efforts. Demonstrate how your pricing strategy will result in a profit. Identify your advertising plans, and include cost estimates to validate your proposed strategy.

Key Elements	Have you covered this in the plan?	Is the answer clear? (yes or no)	Is the answer complete? (yes or no)
a. Who will be your customers? (*target market*)			
b. How big is the market? (*number of customers*)			
c. Who will be your competitors?			

(Continued)

TABLE 12.4 BUSINESS PLAN ASSESSMENT: A COMPLETE EVALUATION TOOL (*Continued*)

Key Elements	Have you covered this in the plan?	Is the answer clear? (yes or no)	Is the answer complete? (yes or no)
d. How are their businesses prospering?			
e. How will you promote sales?			
f. What market share will you want?			
g. Do you have a pricing strategy?			
h. What advertising and promotional strategy will you use?			

Rate this component:

5	4	3	2	1
Outstanding	Very Good	Good	Fair	Poor

4. **Operations**. In this segment, you describe the actual operations and outline their advantages. Specific operational procedures, proximity to supplies, and personnel needs and uses should all be considered in this section.

Key Elements	Have you covered this in the plan?	Is the answer clear? (yes or no)	Is the answer complete? (yes or no)
a. Have you identified a specific location?			
b. Have you outlined the advantages of this location?			
c. Any specific operational procedures to be considered?			
d. What personnel needs are there?			
e. Will your suppliers be accessible?			

Rate this component:

5	4	3	2	1
Outstanding	Very Good	Good	Fair	Poor

5. **Management.** Start by describing the management team, their unique qualifications, and your plans to compensate them (including salaries, employment agreements, stock purchase plans, levels of ownership, and other considerations). Discuss how your organization is structured; consider including a diagram illustrating who reports to whom. Also include a discussion of the potential contribution of the board of directors, advisors, or consultants. Finally, carefully describe the legal structure of your venture (sole proprietorship, partnership, or corporation).

Key Elements	Have you covered this in the plan?	Is the answer clear? (yes or no)	Is the answer complete? (yes or no)
a. Who will manage the business?			
b. What qualifications do you have?			
c. How many employees will you have?			
d. What will they do?			
e. How much will you pay your employees and what type of benefits will you offer them?			

(*Continued*)

TABLE 12.4 BUSINESS PLAN ASSESSMENT: A COMPLETE EVALUATION TOOL (*Continued*)			

Key Elements	Have you covered this in the plan?	Is the answer clear? (yes or no)	Is the answer complete? (yes or no)
f. What consultants or specialists will you use?			
g. What legal form of ownership will you have?			
h. What regulations will affect your business?			

Rate this component:

5	4	3	2	1
Outstanding	Very Good	Good	Fair	Poor

6. **Financial**. Three key financial statements must be presented: a balance sheet, an income statement, and a cash-flow statement. These statements typically cover a one-year period. Be sure you state any assumptions and projections made when calculating the figures.

   Determine the stages at which your business will require external financing and identify the expected financing sources (both debt and equity sources). Also, clearly show what return on investment these sources will achieve by investing in your business. The final item to include is a break-even analysis. This analysis should show what level of sales will be required to cover all costs.

   If the work is done well, the financial statements should represent the actual financial achievements expected from your business plan. They also provide a standard by which to measure the actual results of operating your business. They are a very valuable tool to help you manage and control your business.

Key Elements	Have you covered this in the plan?	Is the answer clear? (yes or no)	Is the answer complete? (yes or no)
a. What is your total expected business income for the first year? Quarterly for the next two years? (*forecast*)			
b. What is your expected monthly cash flow during the first year?			
c. Have you included a method of paying yourself?			
d. What sales volume will you need to make a profit during the three years?			
e. What will be the break-even point?			
f. What are your projected assets, liabilities, and net worth?			
g. What are your total financial needs?			
h. What are your funding sources?			

Rate this component:

5	4	3	2	1
Outstanding	Very Good	Good	Fair	Poor

7. **Critical Risks.** Discuss potential risks before they happen. Examples include: price-cutting by competitors, potentially unfavorable industry-wide trends, design or manufacturing costs that could exceed estimates, and sales projections that are not achieved. The idea is to recognize risks and identify alternative courses of action. Your main objective is to show that you can anticipate and control (to a reasonable degree) your risks.

(Continued)

TABLE 12.4 BUSINESS PLAN ASSESSMENT: A COMPLETE EVALUATION TOOL *(Continued)*

Key Elements	Have you covered this in the plan?	Is the answer clear? (yes or no)	Is the answer complete? (yes or no)
a. What potential problems have you identified?			
b. Have you calculated the risks?			
c. What alternative courses of action exist?			

Rate this component:

5	4	3	2	1
Outstanding	Very Good	Good	Fair	Poor

8. **Harvest Strategy.** Establishing an exit out of a venture is hard work. A founder's protective feelings for an idea built from scratch make it tough to grapple with issues such as management succession and harvest strategies. With foresight, however, an entrepreneur can either keep the dream alive and ensure the security of his or her venture or establish a plan for a liquidity event such as an IPO or the sale of the venture. Thus, a written plan for succession of your business is essential.

Key Elements	Have you covered this in the plan?	Is the answer clear? (yes or no)	Is the answer complete? (yes or no)
a. Have you planned for the orderly transfer of the venture assets if a liquidity event is established such as an IPO or a sale?			
b. Is there a continuity of business strategy for an orderly transition if the venture is not looking for an exit?			

Rate this component:

5	4	3	2	1
Outstanding	Very Good	Good	Fair	Poor

9. **Milestone Schedule.** This section is an important segment of the business plan because it requires you to determine what tasks you need to accomplish to achieve your objectives. Milestones and deadlines should be established and monitored on an ongoing basis. Each milestone is related to all others, and together all of them provide a timely representation of how your objective is to be accomplished.

Key Elements	Have you covered this in the plan?	Is the answer clear? (yes or no)	Is the answer complete? (yes or no)
a. How have you set your objectives?			
b. Have you set deadlines for each stage of your growth?			

Rate this component:

5	4	3	2	1
Outstanding	Very Good	Good	Fair	Poor

10. **Appendix.** This section includes important background information that was not included in the other sections. It is where you would put such items as résumés of the management team, names of references and advisors, drawings, documents, licenses, agreements, and any materials that support the plan. You may also wish to add a bibliography of the sources from which you drew information.

Key Elements	Have you covered this in the plan?	Is the answer clear? (yes or no)	Is the answer complete? (yes or no)
a. Have you included any documents, drawings, agreements, or other materials needed to support the plan?			

(Continued)

TABLE 12.4   BUSINESS PLAN ASSESSMENT: A COMPLETE EVALUATION TOOL (*Continued*)

Key Elements	Have you covered this in the plan?	Is the answer clear? (yes or no)	Is the answer complete? (yes or no)
b. Are there any names of references, advisors, or technical sources you should include?			
c. Are there any other supporting documents?			

Rate this component:

5	4	3	2	1
Outstanding	Very Good	Good	Fair	Poor

Summary: Your Plan

Directions: For each of the business plan sections that you assessed earlier, circle the assigned points on this review sheet and then total the circled points.

Components	Points				
1. Executive summary	5	4	3	2	1
2. Description of the business	5	4	3	2	1
3. Marketing	5	4	3	2	1
4. Operations	5	4	3	2	1
5. Management	5	4	3	2	1
6. Financial	5	4	3	2	1
7. Critical risks	5	4	3	2	1
8. Harvest strategy	5	4	3	2	1
9. Milestone schedule	5	4	3	2	1
10. Appendix	5	4	3	2	1

Total Points: _____

Scoring:

50 pts. — Outstanding! The ideal business plan. Solid!

45–49 pts. — Very Good.

40–44 pts. — Good. The plan is sound, with a few areas that need to be polished.

35–39 pts. — Above Average. The plan has some good areas but needs improvement before presentation.

30–34 pts. — Average. Some areas are covered in detail, yet other areas show weakness.

20–29 pts. — Below Average. Most areas need greater detail and improvement.

Below 20 pts. — Poor. Plan needs to be researched and documented much better.

Source: Donald F. Kuratko, *The Complete Entrepreneurial Planning Guide* (Bloomington: Kelley School of Business, Indiana University, 2015).

12-7 UPDATING THE BUSINESS PLAN

LO9 Present some helpful hints for writing an effective business plan

The business plan should serve as a planning tool to help guide the start-up and execution of a new venture. Once the venture is started, the business plan is still a vital tool for planning continued growth and/or profitability. There are several reasons to update the business plan, including:

- **Financial Changes.** Update your plan on at least a yearly basis to project financials and plan for fiscal needs.
- **Additional Financing.** If continued capital is needed, an updated business plan needs to reflect the current numbers and not the ones projected before the venture was started.
- **Changes in the Market.** Changes in the customer base and competition should be tracked and strategized with regard to how they might affect your venture.
- **Launch of a New Product or Service.** Updating the business plan is an essential method to assess the feasibility of any proposed new product or service and determine its viability.
- **New Management Team.** Any new members of the management team should develop their own plan to initiate strategies for growth.
- **Reflect the New Reality.** Business plans are written based on estimated numbers and projections that may not be accurate after the venture has started. Business plans should be updated to reflect the new reality that the entrepreneur experiences.[17]

12-7a A Practical Example of a Business Plan

As we have stressed in this chapter, every new venture should have a business plan; however, many entrepreneurs have no idea about the details required for a complete business plan. At the end of this chapter there is the sample new venture story about CommuniteeWeb .com with its business plan included. Also, an example of an actual business plan prepared for potential and business plan funding competitions is included in Appendix 12A at the end of this chapter. The plan—entitled "Hydraulic Wind Power"—was prepared for actual financial support and also was presented at five national business plan competitions. Specific parts of a business plan discussed earlier in the chapter are illustrated in this detailed example. By carefully reviewing this business plan, you will gain a much better perspective of the final appearance that an entrepreneur's plan must have.

12-8 PRESENTATION OF THE BUSINESS PLAN: THE "PITCH"

LO10 Highlight points to remember in the presentation of a business plan

Once a business plan is prepared, the next major challenge is presenting the plan to either a single financial person or, in some parts of the country, a forum at which numerous financial investors have gathered.[18] The oral presentation—commonly known as an **elevator pitch** (because of the analogy of riding an elevator and having only two minutes to get your story told to another person in the elevator)—provides the chance to sell the business plan to potential investors.

The presentation should be organized, well prepared, interesting, and flexible. Entrepreneurs should develop an outline of the significant highlights that will capture the audience's interest. Although the outline should be followed, they also must feel free to add or remove certain bits of information as the presentation progresses—a memorized presentation lacks excitement, energy, and interest.

An entrepreneur should use the following steps to prepare an oral presentation:

- Know the outline thoroughly.
- Use keywords in the outline that help recall examples, visual aids, or other details.
- Rehearse the presentation to get a feel for its length.
- Be familiar with any equipment to be used in the presentation—use your own laptop.
- The day before, practice the complete presentation by moving through each slide.

12-8a Suggestions for Presentation

Entrepreneurs are naturally anxious to tell (and sell) their story. However, most venture capitalists agree that the content should be focused and the delivery should be sharp. In the content of the presentation, it is important to be brief and to the point, to summarize the critical factor or unique "hook" of your venture up front, and to use no more than 12–15 PowerPoint slides. Following are some key suggestions about the actual delivery of the pitch to prospective investors:

- Focus on the "pain" for which your venture will be the solution. Investors want to know exactly what problem is being solved by your venture. Pinpoint the target of your solution.
- Demonstrate the reachable market. Instead of a dramatic **potential market,** outline the immediate reachable group of customers that will be targeted.
- Explain the **business model.** How this venture is designed to make money is critical to investors. Demonstrating a clear method of getting to the market for sales will indicate a successful beginning to the new venture.
- Tout the management team. Every investor wants to know the skills and ability of the venture's team to deliver and operationalize the concept. Emphasize the experienced people on your team as well as any technical advisors who are on board.
- Explain your metrics. Rather than using generic assumptions such as the famous "1% rule" (when someone claims that he or she will simply get 1% of a huge market with no research to back the claim up), highlight the metrics that were used to calculate any revenue projections.
- **Motivate** the audience. The entire purpose of a venture pitch is to move the audience to the next step: another meeting to discuss everything in detail. Therefore, you must remember that enthusiasm is hugely important. The investors must believe that you are excited before they can be excited.
- Why *you* and why *now*? The final point must answer the daunting questions in the minds of the investors: Why are you the right venture, and why is this the right time for it to be launched? Be confident in yourself and your team. Always demonstrate a timeline to show the speed with which your venture plans to capture a significant market.[19]

12-8b What to Expect

Entrepreneurs should realize that the audience reviewing their business plan and listening to their pitch is usually cynical and sometimes antagonistic. Venture capital sources often pressure entrepreneurs to test their venture as well as their mettle. Thus, entrepreneurs must expect and prepare for a critical (and sometimes skeptical) audience of financial sources. When you make your pitch and submit your business plan, the venture capitalist will listen and then glance at the plan briefly before beginning any initial comments. No matter how good you think your venture plan is, an investor is not going to look at it and say, "This is the greatest business plan I've ever seen!" Do not expect enthusiastic acceptance or even polite praise. It's highly likely that the remarks will be critical, and even if they aren't, they'll seem that way. Don't panic. Even if it seems like an avalanche of objections, bear in mind that some of the best venture capital deals of all time faced the same opposition. Never expect results in 20 minutes. Each pitch will be a learning experience that will build your confidence for the next one.

Entrepreneurs must be prepared to handle questions from the evaluators and to learn from their criticism. They should never feel defeated but rather should make a commitment to improving the business plan for future review. Table 12.5 outlines some of the key questions that an entrepreneur might ask when his or her business plan is turned down. Entrepreneurs should use the answers to these questions to revise, rework, and improve their business plan. Remember that you are starting out on a journey more similar to a marathon than a sprint. The goal is not so much to succeed the *first* time as it is to *succeed.*[20]

TABLE 12.5 WHAT TO DO WHEN A VENTURE CAPITALIST TURNS YOU DOWN: TEN QUESTIONS

1. *Confirm the decision*: "That means you do not wish to participate at this time?"

2. *Sell for the future*: "Can we count you in for a second round of financing, after we've completed the first?"

3. *Find out why you were rejected*: "Why do you choose not to participate in this deal?" (Timing? Fit? All filled up?)

4. *Ask for advice*: "If you were in my position, how would you proceed?"

5. *Ask for suggestions*: "Can you suggest a source who invests in this kind of deal?"

6. *Get the name*: "Whom should I speak to when I'm there?"

7. *Find out why*: "Why do you suggest this firm, and why do you think this is the best person to speak to there?"

8. *Work on an introduction*: "Who would be the best person to introduce me?"

9. *Develop a reasonable excuse*: "Can I tell him that your decision to turn us down was based on _____?"

10. *Know your referral*: "What will you tell him when he or she calls?"

Source: Joseph R. Mancuso, *How to Write a Winning Business Plan* (Englewood Cliffs, NJ: Prentice Hall, 1985), 37. Reprinted with the permission of Simon & Schuster Adult Publishing Group. Copyright © 1985 by Prentice Hall, Inc.

SAMPLE NEW VENTURE AND BUSINESS PLAN

CommuniteeWeb.com: An Internet Firm's Effort to Survive

Introduction

Dan Pale, a 30-year-old CEO of an Internet start-up company, CommuniteeWeb.com,[*] was faced with the most important decision of his business career. After more than a year of operation that was funded with approximately $1.6 million in start-up capital, his company was experiencing difficult times. Pale and cofounder, Jim Mack, were faced with some tough decisions. A lack of cash flow to the business coupled with rapidly increasing debt was causing mounting financial pressures. Potential legal problems were also on the horizon. Sitting at his desk on June 8, 2001, Pale now ponders a decision to sign a funding agreement with Wall Street Venture Capital.

Formation of the Initial Business Concept: CommuniteeWeb.com

Dan Pale had talked about and researched the idea of a localized Internet portal for many months. In the fall of 1999, Pale—determined that the idea seemed technologically feasible—visited Jim Mack, owner of a financial planning firm in Seymour, Indiana. After three meetings, Mack agreed to join the venture. They contacted the Information and Communication Sciences' Applied Research Institute at Ball State University to conduct further research on the concept. In March 2000, CommuniteeWeb, Inc. was

officially established. Jim Mack served as the CEO and chairman of the board of directors, while Dan Pale served as the president/COO.

The basic idea behind the business concept was to localize the Internet. This would be done through a website that would allow users to narrow information found on the Web to a localized and specific geographic area. In turn, the website would then generate advertisements specific to the geographic area from which the user had originated his or her visit. The idea was to contain these capabilities within one national website. This site would also give users the ability to interact by posting stories about local sporting and news events.

Building the Organization and Its Product

Dan Pale recruited and hired a talented, young team at CommuniteeWeb. For several months, employees mined and categorized an extensive database of URLs and built a model for taking CommuniteeWeb.com to market. The firm used in-house software to locate, capture, and categorize these website addresses. Pale and Mack planned to take their concept of localized Internet utilization to market via franchising. Franchisees would buy the rights to sell CommuniteeWeb.com advertising (banner ads, e-mail marketing, pop-up ads) to specific territories. Each franchise would sell for $35,000 and would cover a geographic region populated by approximately 100,000 people. Pale and Mack expected to use the franchise fees to fund

---

*Case study data presented here, including the company name and URL, are fictional, but the study itself is based on a real enterprise.

CommuniteeWeb's further growth. The company planned on retaining ownership of the 50 largest metropolitan markets in the United States.

Jim Mack and Dan Pale initially estimated that the company would need $2 million in start-up equity. Raising this amount of money as an Internet start-up, especially in a small, Midwestern city, was not an easy task. Jim Mack tapped his extensive base of financial planning clients and raised nearly all of the company's angel capital. However, the fund-raising efforts proved to be quite costly. A great deal of money was spent promoting CommuniteeWeb to potential investors. The amount contributed by each investor averaged between $25,000 and $50,000. By mid-January 2001, the company had raised $1.6 million of its original $2 million target but had sold only two franchises. Pale and Mack developed the company's business plan for the sole purpose of attracting investors (see Appendix). CommuniteeWeb's business model and the projected financial forecasts seemed to change on a near-weekly basis, making it difficult to constantly update the business plan. Very few changes were ever made to the firm's original business plan. As the business model began to change, financial projections were hastily adapted, and the business plan was never adjusted accordingly. The firm's first set of pro forma financial statements estimated that revenues would exceed $1 billion within two years. After consulting venture capital firms and other dot-com businesses that had already been in operation, CommuniteeWeb reduced its estimations to a more conservative figure. The projected third-year revenues would be just over $160 million. The company's June 2001 projected financial statements business plan addendum shows the earnings estimates also had been scaled back even further (see Table 1).

Because the firm's historical financial statements had not been audited, communication with potential institutional investors and venture capitalists was difficult.

There was also the issue that Jim Mack never registered the distribution of equities for private placement with the Securities and Exchange Commission (SEC). Therefore, the legality of these securities could be in question. (The SEC provides Regulation D for selling stock to private parties. Rules 504a, 504, 505, and 506 cover the specific requirements.)

The Founders and the Management Team

Dan Pale's business career began at age 23 when he founded a clothing store that quickly grew to more than $1.2 million in annual sales. Pale was also co-owner of his family's business, a True Value hardware store and Just Ask Rental Center. In 1998, he

repositioned himself in telecommunications and took over management of WKBY-AM talk radio in Seymour, Indiana. In less than two years, he increased the station's revenue by 600 percent. He also helped position WKBY as the largest talk-format station in southern Indiana. He served in a management role in Indiana Regional Radio Partners, Inc., through April 2000.

Jim Mack was a certified financial planner and registered financial consultant. He had 13 years experience in the financial services industry. He was cofounder and president of the Financial Investors Group based in Seymour, Indiana, and had clients in 17 states. Mack hosted a weekly radio program at WKBY and was a contributor to *The Roaring 2000's Investor's Guide,* one of the *New York Times* business best sellers. He also served on the advisory board of the H. S. Dent Foundation and was a noted speaker in areas of business development and fundamental economic trends.

The rest of the management team was very young and energetic. Most of the team members were recent college graduates. The following were the original management team at CommuniteeWeb and their credentials as of spring 2001:[21]

Jeffrey Lehm
Director of Database Development and Technology   Lehm left his position as computer information systems regional program chair for Ivy Tech State College in Seymour, Indiana, to join CommuniteeWeb.

Michael Hunt
Chief Information Officer   Hunt completed his master's degree in information and communication sciences from Ball State University in December 2000.

Jonathan Lester
Director of Communications   Lester earned degrees in both advertising and marketing from Ball State University and is currently completing a master's degree in public relations.

Tony Baker
Director of Franchise Sales and Business Development   Baker was the director of marketing for the largest franchise of BD's Mongolian Barbecue restaurants.

Jim McDuffy
Director of Special Markets   McDuffy had more than 10 years of management experience in various business environments, ranging from the entertainment industry to Web development.

TABLE 1	FINANCIAL PROJECTIONS COMMUNITEEWEB, INC.		
Projected Profit and Loss 2002–2004			
Income Statement	**2002**	**2003**	**2004**
Sales	$1,761,201.00	$7,508,323.00	$26,240,359.00
Direct Cost of Sales	$1,190,785.00	$5,508,538.00	$ 8,817,481.00
Other	—	—	—
Total Cost of Sales	$1,190,785.00	$5,508,538.00	$ 8,817,481.00
Gross Margin	$ 570,416.00	$1,999,785.00	$17,422,878.00
Gross Margin %	32.39%	26.63%	66.40%
Operating Expenses			
Accountant Fees	$2,400.00	$2,700.00	$3,000.00
Attorney Fees	12,000.00	12,300.00	12,600.00
Commissions or Referrals	111,322.80	386,265.00	597,412.50
Equipment Leases	67,608.00	67,608.00	67,608.00
Insurance—General Liability, WC, etc.	1,344.00	1,644.00	1,944.00
Insurance—Auto	2,208.00	2,508.00	2,808.00
Internet Connection	4,254.00	4,554.00	4,854.00
Web Hosting and Security	24,000.00	24,300.00	24,600.00
Advertising/Marketing	18,250.00	75,083.00	93,854.04
Miscellaneous	6,000.00	6,300.00	6,600.00
Office Supplies	6,000.00	6,300.00	6,600.00
Professional Dev./Subscription/Membership Fees	2,400.00	2,700.00	3,000.00
Payroll	568,795.02	812,557.50	934,441.13
Payroll Burden	170,069.71	243,767.25	280,332.34
Rent	22,200.00	22,200.00	22,200.00
Telephone	21,600.00	22,680.00	23,760.00
Trade Shows	6,000.00	6,300.00	6,600.00
Travel	4,250.00	4,550.00	4,850.00
Utilities	6,000.00	6,300.00	6,600.00
Total Overhead	$1,056,701.53	$1,710,616.75	$2,103,664.01
Total Operating Expense	$2,247,486.53	$7,219,154.75	$10,921,145.01
Profit Before Interest and Taxes	$(486,285.53)	$ 289,168.25	$15,319,213.99
Interest Expense (Short-term)	—	—	—
Interest Expense (Long-term)	—	—	—
Taxes Incurred	0	0	4,940,000.00
Net Profit	$(486,286.00)	$289,168.00	$10,379,213.99

John Taylor

Director of Wireless Strategies/Research and Development   Taylor received his bachelor of arts in marketing from Ball State University with a double minor in Japanese and Asian studies. He was also pursuing a master's degree in information and communication sciences.

Troy Simon

Director of Indianapolis Operations   Simon completed his master's degree in information and communication sciences from Ball State University in 1998. Simon then served as a business development representative at Intelliseek, a leading provider in personalized Internet services.

Business, Industry, and Economic Conditions

The Internet had a significant impact on the global business climate between 1999 and 2001. By 2001, there were more than 160 million Internet users worldwide, and they were beginning to spend a significant amount of time online—averaging more than 18 hours connected monthly. Internet retailing had also become a dominant business force in the U.S. economy, as monthly Internet spending was approaching $4 billion, an average of $270 per consumer.[22]

The economic conditions during 2001 made it difficult for growing businesses, especially Internet-based, to obtain funding. The Internet boom of 1999 and 2000, during which Internet companies received equity investment at alarming rates, was definitely a thing of the past. Many venture capitalists had gone back to basic business fundamentals and only considered firms with sound business models and solid business plans. In addition, private investors were becoming more cautious because of the recent plunge ("tech wreck") of the NASDAQ stock market (see Figure 1).

The NASDAQ composite peaked at a value of $5,133 in March 2000. Since that point, the NASDAQ composite value had declined to its June 2001 level of $2,161.[23] According to emarketer.com, more than 555 Internet businesses worldwide closed in the first half of 2001.

Internet firms such as Citysearch.com, localbusiness.com, and cityworks.com, among others, began to make major cutbacks or ceased operations. Double Click, the largest online ad broker, continued to lose more than $100 million per quarter. In addition, most companies, including dot-coms, were cutting their advertising budgets across the board. Competitive Media Reporting estimated that 2001 advertising spending across all media would fall more than $102.4 billion from 2000 levels.[24] Although there still seemed to be interest in specialized and localized Internet ads, many industry factors were causing negative pressures on ad revenue–based business models. According to John Groth, CEO of BeaconVentureCapital (Bethesda, Maryland), the capital markets were not looking favorably on firms with the majority of revenues coming from Internet advertising sales.

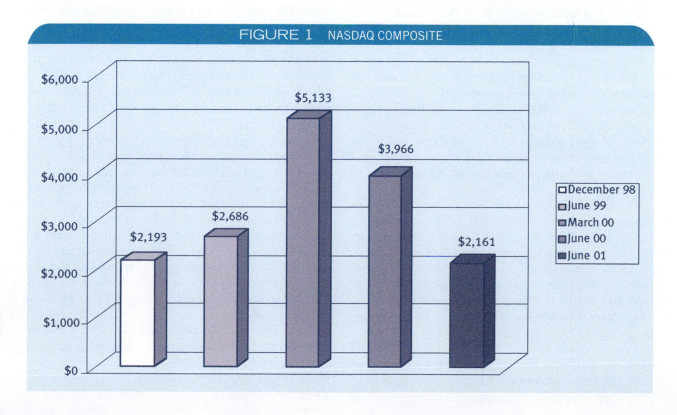

FIGURE 1   NASDAQ COMPOSITE

The Competitive Landscape

By June 2001, CommuniteeWeb faced competition from firms such as DigitalCity.com, OneMain.com, MyCity.com, Yahoo! Get Local, Visionvibes.com, Wowtown.com, URL-Surfer.com, Citysearch.com, megago.com, move.com, busyreceptionist.com, usaonline.com, switchboard.com, relocationcentral.com, MyWay.com, and numerous yellow pages websites, among others. CommuniteeWeb believed, however, that none of these sites truly provided local information across the nation. They contended that these sites were geared toward larger cities or were restricted to very small regions. Thus, CommuniteeWeb never viewed any of these competitors as major threats to the success of its business model. DigitalCity.com and Citysearch.com, however, were engaged in significant national advertising campaigns and had developed the greatest name recognition among localized Internet sites. CommuniteeWeb considered its main competitors to be local newspapers and radio stations. The firm saw these traditional media forms as its greatest rivals.

CommuniteeWeb.com in Operation

The CommuniteeWeb.com website was officially launched on January 28, 2001. Visitors to the site could read and post local news and sports stories, check the local weather forecast, and search for Uniform Resource Locators (URLs, or website addresses) tailored to specific locales and business categories. The URL searches used CommuniteeWeb's tool and its database, which by April 2001 included more than 200,000 URLs.

During the first few months of 2001, CommuniteeWeb was able to establish partnerships and alliances with several strong companies such as AT&T, Infospace.com, and Hargiss Communication. CommuniteeWeb, however, soon realized that many of these partners did not fit into its vision and broke all ties with most of these partners to pursue other partnerships with companies like LocaLine and valupage.com.

CommuniteeWeb continued to struggle to get its business concept off the ground. Tony Baker, the person hired as director of franchise sales, had managed to sell just two franchises, leaving Dan Pale and Jim Mack to contemplate their next move. They were faced with the immediate need to generate positive cash flow within the next two to three months.

CommuniteeWeb's workforce had peaked to approximately 175 employees in March 2001, causing the company to incur over $200,000 of payroll expenses. Pale and Mack had expected to sign more than 100 franchisees in the first year, but their efforts produced only failed prospects. Running short of

funds in April 2001, they imposed major cutbacks, leaving only 15 key employees and a monthly expenditure of about $75,000 (Table 2). Pale and Mack saw these cuts as a necessary move to keep their firm alive. With no incoming revenue, mounting debt, and a failing business model, they began to panic and felt that cutbacks across the board were their only option.

At this point, CommuniteeWeb had abandoned its original business plan and now focused on selling its website tools to Internet service providers (ISPs). They believed that CommuniteeWeb's tools could be used by the ISPs in their default browsers and portals (gateways). CommuniteeWeb would become their provider of local information and their "face" to users. However, the firm was forced to drop its URL database from its set of tools offered to ISPs, due to significant technical errors that reduced both the effectiveness and size (reduced to under 40,000 URLs) of the database. This was a major setback to CommuniteeWeb, but the company just did not have the financial resources needed to fix the database errors (see Table 3 for a timeline of critical events). To generate additional revenues, CommuniteeWeb also introduced a Web development division to its business. In addition, the company attempted to market itself as an ISP.

Mounting Financial Pressure and Internal Conflict

Jim Mack and Dan Pale recognized their financial crisis. They believed that CommuniteeWeb had only a few months to establish a positive cash flow. Mack planned to continue raising funds through his client base and personal network while Pale and his staff feverishly marketed their new business model to ISPs. Capital markets had become tighter and Mack seemingly had exhausted his personal resources. By the end of April 2001, Mack and Pale resorted to "bootstrapping" for short-term financing, pushing several of their own credit cards to their limits, delaying payments to most of the company's creditors, and falling more than $200,000 behind in remitting payroll taxes and employee withholdings to the Internal Revenue Service (IRS). The company had also accrued other debts in excess of $1 million (Table 4). Pale and Mack's personal debt had grown to more than $300,000. Employees also started to feel the pinch of the firm's cash flow problems as the issuance of paychecks was often delayed by as much as three to four weeks.

Amid the financial pressures, personal conflicts arose between Mack and the employees. Mack was often criticized for being too controlling. Key management personnel had questioned his desire to make all of the company's strategic decisions. Because of

TABLE 2   SUMMARY FINANCIAL INFORMATION AS PROVIDED BY MANAGEMENT

	March 2001	April 2001
Professional and consulting fees	$9,500	$2,000
Equipment lease and depreciation	19,000	3,000
Software/Connectivity/Hosting	35,000	—
Employee/Payroll expenses:		
CEO—Mack	10,000	6,250
President—Pale	10,000	5,000
Staff—Other	142,500	25,850
Contract labor—Mining	20,000	—
Taxes	14,300	3,265
Training	10,000	—
Other	2,600	2,500
Employee/Payroll expenses—total	209,400	42,865
Marketing expenses	20,050	5,000
Rent/Utilities	3,655	2,100
Website maintenance/design	14,000	13,000
Office supplies	4,000	3,100
Interest/Other	5,400	4,400
Total expenses	$320,005	$75,465

TABLE 3   TIMELINE OF CRITICAL EVENTS

- **January–February 2000**—Dan Pale researches the possibility of localizing the Internet.
- **February 2000**—Pale meets with Jim Mack of the Financial Investors Group to discuss the possibility of building a localized Internet portal.
- **March 2000**—Mack and Pale agree to start the business, which they name CommuniteeWeb. They incorporate as a C corporation and begin staffing the company.
- **April 2000–January 2001**—The large staff of "miners" collect and capture a comprehensive database of URLs.
- **January 28, 2001**—The website, http://www.CommuniteeWeb.com, is officially launched.
- **February–May 2001**—CommuniteeWeb management works on developing business relationships that will strengthen its position in the marketplace. The firm also works on raising equity and selling franchises.
- **April 2001**—Due to mounting financial pressures, Mack is forced to make major cutbacks in workforce and expenditures.
- **May 2001**—CommuniteeWeb changes its business model to sell its website tools to ISPs. The firm discontinues the use of its URL database. Mack steps down as CEO and chairman of the board, and Pale takes over as CEO. Mack remains on the board of directors.
- **June 2001**—CommuniteeWeb considers entering a deal with Wall Street Venture Capital of New York.

TABLE 4 BALANCE SHEET—FISCAL YEAR ENDING FEBRUARY 2002

Assets		
Current Assets		
Checking Account	$41.09	
Expense Account	237.11	
Client Fees Receivable	904.94	
Investments	50,000.00	
Total Current Assets		$51,183.14
Property and Equipment		
Furniture and Fixtures	$21,804.26	
Computer Equipment	257,960.30	
Leasehold Improvements	19,275.25	
Accum. Depreciation—Furniture	(7,014.80)	
Accum. Depreciation—Computer Equipment	(112,411.33)	
Accum. Depreciation—Leasehold	(6,203.74)	
Total Property and Equipment		$173,409.94
Total Assets		$224,593.08
Liabilities and Capital		
Current Liabilities		
Accounts Payable	$355,748.64	
Deductions Payable	785.71	
Federal Payroll Taxes Payable	266,406.50	
FUTA Tax Payable	4,450.64	
State Payroll Taxes Payable	32,715.16	
SUTA Payable	8,907.29	
Local Payroll Taxes Payable	7,630.73	
Employee Benefits Payable	18,705.47	
Total Current Liabilities		$695,350.14
Long-Term Liabilities		
Loan from Shareholder—Dan Pale	$304,929.20	
Loan from Shareholder—Jim Mack	68,500.00	
Long-Term Liabilities		$373,429.20
Total Liabilities		$1,068,779.34
Capital		
Treasury Stock	$(7,545.00)	
Paid-In Capital	1,892,008.68	
Retained Earnings	(1,017,263.51)	
Net Income	(1,711,386.43)	
Total Capital		$(844,186.26)
Total Liabilities and Capital		$224,593.08

Mack's constant changing of the business model, employees rarely knew the "latest" direction of the company. Conflict between Mack and Pale also began to surface. Mack and Pale often did not see "eye to eye" on strategic or financial issues. Pale felt as though Mack, the CEO, was taking control over the daily activities, which Pale considered his job as president and COO. In May 2001, due to the mounting conflicts and Mack's apparent mismanagement of the company, the board of directors removed Jim Mack as CEO and chairman of the board and appointed Pale as his replacement. Mack would remain on the board of directors but would relinquish all day-to-day operations of the company to Dan Pale. Mack maintained his role in raising capital for the company.

The Wall Street Venture Capital Deal

During the past several months of funding efforts, Mack and Pale had been working on developing a relationship with a relatively unknown firm named Wall Street Venture Capital from New York City. In June 2001, Pale and Mack capitalized on an invitation to present their business model to this venture capital firm. After seeing their presentation, Wall Street Venture Capital agreed to raise funding for CommuniteeWeb through a partnership. If CommuniteeWeb accepted the agreement, Wall Street Venture Capital would acquire 30 percent equity of the company, and CommuniteeWeb would be charged a $20,000 commitment fee. CommuniteeWeb would then be limited to raising an additional $500,000 outside of Wall Street Venture Capital during the next six months to fund current operations. Wall Street Venture Capital would agree to raise $5 million for CommuniteeWeb within six months, as well as position the firm for a buyout. CommuniteeWeb would also be able to use its relationship with Wall Street Venture Capital as leverage in meeting financial obligations to current investors and for forming new partnerships.

For almost two months, Jim Mack and Dan Pale attempted to investigate the viability of this New York–based venture capital firm. However, as of June 2001, Mack and Pale had been unable to establish whether or not Wall Street Venture Capital had a proven track record with multimillion-dollar start-up investing. Any information on the firm was hard to obtain. As an example, its website was not functional and the New York Chamber of Commerce did not have any information on the firm. When Mack and Pale asked the president of Wall Street Venture Capital, Joseph McElroys, to give documentation of the firm's successfully funded projects, the response was that most of Wall Street Venture Capital's deals were international and documentation was not readily available.

The Dilemma

Dan Pale now faces his toughest decision as CEO of CommuniteeWeb. He has the mounting pressures of sinking deeper and deeper into debt, risking more and more invested capital, and facing the legal issues associated with the debt to the IRS and the improper sale of securities. Pale is seriously considering entering the agreement with Wall Street Venture Capital. The following issues plague Pale as he considers his next move.

- *Federal Tax Liability*—The company owes the IRS an amount in excess of $200,000. The company has filed the IRS form 656 "Offer in Compromise" to settle this debt. There is no assurance that the IRS will accept this offer in compromise. The IRS may counteroffer or reject the offer completely. In this case, CommuniteeWeb may not have sufficient funds to pay the delinquent taxes, interest, and any penalties. Furthermore, the IRS can even foreclose on the company's assets if it chooses.

- *Indiana State Tax Liability*—The company owes the State of Indiana an amount in excess of $20,000. The company has entered into a payment agreement with the State of Indiana on this debt. If the company fails to make the required payments to the State of Indiana, the Indiana Department of Revenue could foreclose on the company's assets.

- *Securities Violations*—The company has previously sold investments in the company in excess of $1.6 million. The sale of these securities may not have been in compliance with all federal and state securities laws. They face the probability that a rescission offer would be made to all purchasers and that an action could be filed by the securities regulatory agencies. In addition, the company's officers could possibly face criminal charges for these SEC violations.

- *Failure to Make a Profit*—Since its inception in 2000, the company has been primarily involved in the research and development of its Internet technology and has had no chance to develop revenues. Currently, the company has not made a profit—and there is no future assurance it ever will. The company is operating with a "burn rate" (a popular term used to denote expenditures without sufficient revenue to at least approach a break-even point) and has yet to establish a working business model that can successfully show a profit. Much of the initial $1.6 million of raised capital was spent on developing the URL database, marketing franchises to potential buyers, and attracting potential investors.

Dan Pale needs to make a move to save his company. Taking into account all of these issues, the agreement with Wall Street Venture Capital may be the best choice—or is it?

APPENDIX: Business Plan

Executive Summary

CommuniteeWeb, Inc. is the Internet with local flavor and a personal touch. With CommuniteeWeb's unique search technology and full range of connectivity and other web-related solutions, it enables businesses, nonprofit organizations, and individuals to interact in a specific geographic locale via the Internet. People who use the CommuniteeWeb portal to search CommuniteeWeb's website database find content that is most relevant to them, from news and sports scores to classified ads and even a community calendar. The free, simple search process is based on the individual needs of each end user, which allows him or her to search for information, goods, and services in his or her hometown or almost any specific area without wading through the useless links that traditional search engines yield as results.

While optimizing localized Web searches for private citizens, CommuniteeWeb provides area businesses the same luxury for specific geographic areas. A business knows with reasonable certainty that someone who searches a specific location either lives in that community or plans to visit it. CommuniteeWeb enables businesses of all sizes to participate in Internet advertising. CommuniteeWeb's dynamic one-to-one marketing enables businesses to market toward specific geographic areas as well as to specific age groups, income ranges, and interests. To motivate end users to register, CommuniteeWeb offers them the free Local Rewards program. Registered members earn points for visiting local advertisers' sites. They can then redeem accumulated points for services and merchandise, or donate them to a local charity. Becoming a member is simple and free; in less than one minute, a user can join by providing basic geographic, demographic, and psychographic information. For example, a user may like music but have no interest in apparel. Businesses spend more than $2 billion per quarter on marketing on the World Wide Web, but they collect little to no information about end users. Local Rewards addresses that issue. CommuniteeWeb's Local Rewards program demonstrates yet another way that CommuniteeWeb provides a win-win scenario for businesses and residents of the communities it services.

CommuniteeWeb provides a human approach to the Internet. Through its franchise model, CommuniteeWeb will place community coordinators around the country in communities of all sizes. This provides a name and a face for people to call upon when things get confusing and technology changes, as it always does. CommuniteeWeb brings the Internet together for the individual and the community. CommuniteeWeb provides a customized browser that carries its name, Internet services from dial-up to high-speed connectivity solutions (through an alliance with AT&T), and Web design, hosting, and other related services (from alliances with various Web design firms).

Many companies have attempted to enter local communities from an Internet perspective. More than 20 companies have succeeded in tier-one cities that are defined as *metropolitan statistical areas* (MSAs); MSAs contain more than 1 million residents each and represent more than one-third of the U.S. population in 42 distinct areas. Companies that venture into tier-two and tier-three markets have failed from a global perspective. Individual community sites exist in these markets, but without continuity, they do nothing for commerce or community development in their respective areas. CommuniteeWeb is the platform that combines these communities, serving as the cord that provides individuality while binding communities together to provide true business relevance. CommuniteeWeb plans to corporately maintain these MSA market operations but will focus on initially proving its product through fully operational corporately owned test markets. CommuniteeWeb has partially funded the Indianapolis MSA as a test market and is seeking funding to start one corporately owned mid-market franchise each month, which started in April 2001.

CommuniteeWeb's success depends on a loyal number of users and massive name-brand recognition. CommuniteeWeb will employ three immediate strategies to gather these members and create product awareness. All three of these models provide built-in loyalty of membership as well as the opportunity for quick-start franchises. CommuniteeWeb will also allow select entrepreneurs to acquire franchise rights.

CommuniteeWeb will continue to franchise the business model in small-to-midsize markets nationwide. Franchisees can come from four different business backgrounds: (1) companies currently providing Internet service on a more local and/or regional basis; (2) traditional media outlets with built-in membership loyalty that provides a profitable alliance for both the company and CommuniteeWeb; (3) companies currently involved in website design; and (4) existing "specific community" websites with an identifiable user base.

CommuniteeWeb's main attack toward the franchise marketplace is through regional ISPs. CommuniteeWeb has found in its preliminary research that there are more than 600 regional ISPs in the Midwest that have less than 50,000 subscribers. CommuniteeWeb has also found that this will add very little to its current cost structure. These ISPs generally have somewhere around 5,000 subscribers, but they typically only generate approximately $2 per month toward their bottom line per customer. Communitee-Web's offer to these ISPs is simple: CommuniteeWeb will provide them with a CommuniteeWeb franchise in exchange for their conversion to the Communitee-Web system. This includes automatically registering their subscribers with CommuniteeWeb.com memberships, converting their subscribers' accounts to the CommuniteeWeb/AT&T virtual ISP, and selling CommuniteeWeb.com advertising in their markets. CommuniteeWeb has contacted more than 50 of these ISPs in Indiana alone and has gotten appointments with nearly all of them.

CommuniteeWeb is designed to be profitable by August 2001 and remain that way. The company uses Internet technology but is truly an interactive communications company focusing on dynamic one-to-one marketing.

Based on current Internet standards for usage and advertising, CommuniteeWeb can generate $15.60 per month per member. The business model and current plan calls for $2 million of initial investment with a positive cash flow of over $17 million in the second year of operations.

CommuniteeWeb has also recently seen the value of its unique URL database come to fruition. The database is proving to be highly marketable to thousands of websites at a monthly licensing fee of anywhere from $500 to $5,000.

CommuniteeWeb has more than 35 potential franchisees and has raised over $1,400,000. CommuniteeWeb is currently seeking an additional $600,000 in first-round funding and another $2 million in bridge financing. CommuniteeWeb is currently offering shares at $4 per share with the minimum investment of $25,000. That investment represents 6,250 voting-class shares controlling 1/8th percent (.00125) of the company.

The CommuniteeWeb Business Model

The CommuniteeWeb business model revolves around four main areas: members, community coordinators, content, and advertising. These four areas are simple in nature, but they drive the success of CommuniteeWeb.

Members

The most important aspect of CommuniteeWeb.com is membership. CommuniteeWeb has put a great deal of emphasis on the development of a dedicated user base. Member interaction through viewing advertisements, submitting content, and using the exclusive *CommuniteeWeb Directory*[25] drives the success of CommuniteeWeb. Members are encouraged to submit local content of interest to them.

Community Coordinators

Community coordinators, which exist both as franchisees and as MSA coordinators, provide a local "heartbeat" to the Internet for each community. These community coordinators and their sales force will have established relationships with community businesses, not-for-profits, and the general population, which allows for fast membership growth and accelerated advertising sales.

Content

Content—such as calendar events, local sports stories, local news stories, local press releases, and the *CommuniteeWeb Directory*—is what makes CommuniteeWeb.com an attractive, useful, informative, and successful website. CommuniteeWeb will provide the *CommuniteeWeb Directory* as well as localized content through news and sports stories, calendar events, and press releases, but members are encouraged to submit the bulk of this local content and represent their community on the Internet.

Advertising

Localized advertising is the main revenue engine of CommuniteeWeb.com. Very specifically targeted and localized advertising is what makes CommuniteeWeb's advertising system unique to the Internet. Local advertising will be utilized in the community section through promotional windows, CommuniteeWeb's *CommuniteeWeb Directory*, targeted e-mail marketing, and follow-up e-mail.

Strategic Alliances

CommuniteeWeb has developed several key technological and business relationships to better position itself in the marketplace.

AT&T: CommuniteeWeb has formed a strategic alliance with global communications giant AT&T in several areas. AT&T expects to better reach local markets through CommuniteeWeb, and CommuniteeWeb will utilize AT&T's resources to host the CommuniteeWeb.com website and provide private-labeled Internet connectivity services through a virtual ISP (VISP) system. This alliance will enable CommuniteeWeb to act as an ISP without having the initial capital expenses usually associated with launching local Internet services. Income from this alliance will come from every home or business that signs up for Internet access service. CommuniteeWeb's wholesale cost for dial-up accounts will be $13.95 per month. CommuniteeWeb plans to resell this service at a very competitive rate of $18.95 per month. This alliance should prove to be very powerful, given AT&T's position in the ISP market. AT&T is the world's largest and highest rated ISP.[26]

Hargiss Communication/Quad Entertainment: The proprietary Set Top Box that Hargiss Communication has developed is a hardware and software solution that provides "Movies On Demand," Internet access, games, digital cable TV, and a local guide to the surrounding area (through CommuniteeWeb) to hotel or resort amenities, hospitals, and homes. CommuniteeWeb has entered into a strategic partnership with Hargiss Communication to provide a local guide portal for their interface using the CommuniteeWeb index of local URLs and its local content. CommuniteeWeb currently has a 15 percent ownership in a new subsidiary company formed with Hargiss Communication, called Quad Entertainment, and will be an integral part of developing the Set Top Box business model. In addition, Jed Delke of CommuniteeWeb will serve as CEO of Quad Entertainment and CommuniteeWeb will occupy three of the six board of directors spots on the company.

InfoSpace.com: CommuniteeWeb has partnered with InfoSpace.com to increase the options and content that CommuniteeWeb can provide to members. InfoSpace is one of the largest information sources on the Web, thus providing a very powerful resource to CommuniteeWeb members. The information resources that InfoSpace provides enhance CommuniteeWeb's content, allowing CommuniteeWeb to concentrate on its core business. InfoSpace will provide these resources on contract through a co-branded system. CommuniteeWeb members will see the CommuniteeWeb website, color scheme, and structure when navigating the InfoSpace content through CommuniteeWeb.com. This partnership also provides CommuniteeWeb with a revenue source through the advertising revenue sharing model.

Legal, Professional, Accounting, and Technical Partners and Associates

Thomas Reardon, partner of James, Austin, Cooper, and Burr Law Offices, located in Seymour, Indiana, heads the legal counsel. Reardon's role is to help determine any specialized counsel that CommuniteeWeb will need along the business development process. In addition, CommuniteeWeb has partnered with franchise attorney Mark Jacoby of Indianapolis.

CommuniteeWeb will work with the Commercial Services Group of Crowe Chizek LLP for assistance with SEC and accounting issues. As a leading accounting and consulting organization, Crowe Chizek offers specialized services with a client-focused relationship culture. Crowe is the leading member firm of Howarth International, an international network of independent accounting and consulting firms, with more than 100 members and 400 offices in 372 cities throughout the world. Crowe Chizek's clients include IBM, Microsoft, Oracle, and Onyx Software. Specifically, Crowe Chizek will provide CommuniteeWeb assistance in finding an appropriate enterprise accounting package. They will also provide

independent audits of CommuniteeWeb's financial statements. Crowe Chizek will be able to provide consulting expertise should the need arise in the future. Four different individuals handle the accounting department. Donald Hager is chief advisor. He has contributed to acquisition planning and stock distribution. Jim Mack is serving in the capacity of controller. Gregory Borst, CPA, will handle current payroll and day-to-day taxation issues.

Technology Expertise—Internal and External

CommuniteeWeb has a team of highly educated and experienced database developers, programmers, and system architects. In addition, CommuniteeWeb has partnered with several higher-education institutions in the area. CommuniteeWeb has developed a dynamic site, which requires expertise from several different technology sectors. A commercially viable product was released on January 28, 2001, and is continuing to be built and improved. CommuniteeWeb has accomplished this mission by using its own talented employees and by contracting for services from Joseph A. Graves and Associates (JGA). Michael Hunt has led this team through the development phases and will continue to lead this team through continuous improvement phases. JGA has provided project management and programming expertise on different components of the site. Jeff Lehm has provided the database expertise.

Communiteeweb Associates

CommuniteeWeb has assembled a very talented, energetic, and enthusiastic group of entrepreneurial, business, and creative minds to drive this venture. Associate education backgrounds include marketing, entrepreneurship, political science, communication, journalism, and information sciences at both the undergraduate and graduate levels. Experiences include financial planning, retail management, franchise development, business development, education, and mass media management.

Officers, Board of Directors, Principals, and Significant Associates

James A. Mack, CFP, RFC
Chairman, Board of Directors and CEO
Jim Mack is a certified financial planner and registered financial consultant. Mack serves as president and cofounder of the Financial Investors Group, based in Seymour, Indiana, with clients in 17 states. He has spent 13 years in the financial services industry creating and evaluating business and succession

plans. He hosted a weekly radio show for five years and helped contribute to *The Roaring 2000s Investor: Strategies for the Life You Want.* Mack sits on the advisory board to the H. S. Dent Foundation and speaks nationally to thousands on business development concepts that focus on fundamental trends that drive the U.S. economy.

Daniel E. Pale

President Dan Pale has more than ten years of experience in retail business operations. At the age of 23, he started a retail clothing business that quickly grew to generate more than $1.2 million in sales per year. Pale also co-owns a True Value hardware store and a Just Ask Rental Center. In 1998, he entered the broadcast industry, taking over the management of WKBY Talk Radio in Seymour, Indiana. In less than two years, he increased station revenue by 600 percent and increased listenership, making the station the number one talk radio format in southern Indiana. He is also a member of the adjunct faculty at a local university's telecommunications program and— through April 2000—maintained a management role with Indiana Regional Radio Partners, Inc.

Greg Dent

Board of Directors Greg Dent is currently president and CEO of Healthx.com. Dent has more than 20 years of experience in the health care and technology industries. In 1987, Greg founded First Benefit Corp., a Midwest-based third-party administrator (TPA) that appeared in *Inc.* magazine's top 500 growth companies in 1991, 1992, and 1993. He also founded Qubic, a nationwide organization that comprises 12 independently owned TPAs. In 1993, First Benefit Corp. was acquired by CoreSource. In 1995, Dent founded a new company, Intermark, and began development of what is now the Healthx.com product. In 1998, the company officially became Healthx.com.

Dominic Mancino

Board of Directors A native of Southern California and a resident of Indiana for the past eight years, Dominic Mancino has been with AT&T for several years and works as a sales director for business services in Indiana. He comes with a wealth of industry knowledge, having worked within telecommunications for 20 years for companies like Western Electric and Pacific Bell. His responsibilities have taken him from sales and engineering to his current position as sales director. Mancino has consulted with companies all around the United States to define Internet strategies and the practical application of IP-based solutions for business development. Mancino is a graduate of Ricks College, which is now known as Brigham Young University of Idaho.

Dr. Nathan Walker

Board of Directors Nathan Walker was recently with the National Association of Broadcasters in Washington, DC, where he was vice president of television operations. He currently teaches courses in technology, business aspects, and regulatory issues at the Center for Information and Communication Sciences at Ball State University, along with serving as codirector of the Applied Research Institute. His work includes the development of the network, interactive kiosk system. Dr. Walker regularly consults with AT&T Bell Labs, U.S. West Advanced Technologies, Ameritech, McDonald's Corporation, and GTE Labs.

Sheri Waters

Board of Directors Sheri Waters is a motivational speaker, trainer, and coach. She is the president/owner of the Waters Connection, Inc., a Midwest-based national consulting firm that specializes in improving organizational performance through leadership development, sales and customer services coaching/ training, team building, and organizational development. Waters developed her expertise through years of service at Ameritech Corporation. Her responsibilities included training, developing, coaching, and supporting more than 3,000 senior managers and 4,000 associates in the Consumer Market Unit, which includes 17 Customer Care Centers across the states of Indiana, Illinois, Michigan, Wisconsin, and Ohio. Her most recent clients include Ameritech Consumer Services, Ameritech New Media, Cheap Tickets, Inc., and 21st Century Telecom, among others. Waters is a "Gold" member of the Indianapolis Chamber of Commerce.

Michael A. Marell

Board of Directors Mike Marell is the owner of Michael A. Marell & Associates, a consulting firm established to assist businesses in continuous improvement strategies using statistical methods. The firm uses many improvement methods, including the methods of Dr. W. Edwards Deming, Dr. Donald Wheeler, Dr. Genichi Taguchi, and William Conway. The firm's objective for its clients is to train and support them to make their business processes and customer services more effective. Marell was employed at Delco Remy Division of General Motors and Delphi Automotive Systems for more than 31 years in engineering, quality, and statistical assignments. For 18 years, Marell trained employees from all areas of the company to make improvements and to assist in the application of statistical process control, machine qualification, supplier development, design of experiments, and robust engineering. Marell is a licensed professional engineer and certified quality engineer.

William Vacarro, MD

Board of Directors William Vacarro has served the public through the practice of family medicine since 1973. Dr. Vacarro currently serves as the president and CEO of Community Hospital in Seymour, Indiana. Dr. Vacarro is on the board of directors for the Anderson Chamber of Commerce and the Corporation for Economic Development. Dr. Vacarro serves on the Executive Committee, Health Status Committee, and the Facilities and Technology Committee for the Madison Health Partners.

Dr. Michael Foster

Board of Directors Michael Foster received his bachelor's degree in accounting from the University of Wisconsin–Whitewater and his master's degree in guidance and counseling, also from Wisconsin–Whitewater. Dr. Foster went on to earn his doctoral degree in higher education from Indiana University in 1984. Since that time, Dr. Foster has consulted for several organizations, both for-profit and nonprofit in nature. Dr. Foster has also served since 1982 as a professor of management in Seymour University's School of Business. Dr. Foster served as the president and CEO of Marcon, Inc., in Seymour, Indiana, from 1995 to 1997.

Dr. Stephan Reece

Principal Stephan Reece is the codirector of the Applied Research Institute at Ball State University and an associate professor at the Center for Information and Communication Sciences, also at Ball State University. He was the owner of Communications and Digital Services, Inc., for ten years and engineered all system installations, data networks, and peripheral equipment (T-1, E&M, DID, voice processing, call sequencers, call accounting systems, CLID, ACDs, Centrex, ISDN services and products).

Jeffrey Lehm

Director of Database Development and Technology Jeff Lehm, as owner of Valcour Computer Group, Inc., constructed data management systems for government agencies and entities such as the Indiana Department of Workforce Development, and associations such as the National Free Flight Association. He is the Computer Information Systems regional program chair for Ivy Tech State College in Seymour, Indiana, and has extensive knowledge in database research and technology as it applies to the Internet. Lehm played an instrumental role in the development of the E-commerce Certification Program at Ivy Tech State College.

Michael Hunt

Chief Information Officer Michael Hunt is a 1995 graduate of Ball State University's Entrepreneurship and Small Business Management program. In addition, Hunt recently completed his master's degree in information and communication sciences at the Center for Information and Communication Sciences at Ball State University. Hunt contributed to the Network Integration Center (NIC), the Ball-Foster Unified Messaging Team, and the VPN Forum project. From 1995 to 1997, Hunt wrote the business plan and helped start Escapades, Inc., a family entertainment center in Marion, Indiana. After leaving Escapades in 1997, he worked at Knapp Supply Co., Inc., as the network administrator and purchasing agent.

Jonathan Lester

Director of Communications Jon Lester earned degrees in both advertising and marketing from Ball State University and is currently finishing a master's degree in public relations. As owner and operator of a successful advertising agency, JL Unlimited, Lester built a reputation within the small-to-midsize business market, winning several Addy Awards and Citations of Excellence. Clients include Alltrista; Community Hospitals, Indianapolis; and Community Hospital, Seymour, among others. Realizing the impact that the Internet is having on the advertising industry, Lester established webaxis, LLC—a high-end e-solutions provider—to coexist with his agency. Under his direction, webaxis has achieved several large strides in just under a year—a user window for controlling their e-environment (Executive Dashboard Systems), Web leasing financing, Perpetual Marketing Systems, and more.

Tony Baker

Director of Franchise Sales and Business Development Tony Baker was the director of marketing for the largest franchise of BD's Mongolian Barbeque restaurants, one of the fastest growing casual dining concepts in America. Baker strengthened and advanced the growth of BD's Mongolian Barbeque while spending less than 2 percent of its marketing budget on conventional advertising mediums. His local, or neighborhood, marketing techniques have brought franchises as much as 20 percent growth in sales in an industry that marvels at anything above 5 percent. Baker has designed and executed five record openings for franchisees. He has overseen marketing and operations for this $10 million franchise for three years.

Jim McDuffy

Director of Special Markets McDuffy has more than ten years of management experience in various business environments, ranging from the entertainment industry to Web development. He has served as lead developer and consultant for many

Web-based projects, including the Web strategy of Connecticut Electric, one of the world's largest suppliers of replacement circuit breakers. McDuffy's leadership enabled the Degerberg Academy in Chicago to grow to a 600 percent student increase during a four-year period, resulting in a national award from the United States Martial Arts Association in 1993. He studied theatre and filmmaking at Indiana University and worked in several production venues in Chicago between 1987 and 1997. McDuffy has also served as a radio personality, hosting a weekly computer talk show called "Computer Digest."

John Taylor
Director of Wireless Strategies/Research and Development
John Taylor received his bachelor of arts degree in marketing from Ball State University with a double minor in Japanese and Asian studies. He has demonstrated success in international relationship building, developing promotional material, marketing media, and project management. Taylor also recently completed his graduate degree at the Ball State University Center for Information and Communication Sciences. His project experience includes work with a leading wireless manufacturer and network hardware manufacturers and Web development for industry, nonprofit, and research organizations. His Web development portfolio includes the Applied Research Institute, the Virtual Private Network Forum, the Ohana Foundation, and the Institute for Wireless Innovation, among others.

Troy Simon
Director of Indianapolis Operations
Troy Simon is a 1997 graduate of Ball State University, where he earned a degree in corporate management and financial institutions as a scholar athlete. In December 1998, he completed his master's of science degree in information and communication sciences at the Center for Information and Communication Sciences, also at Ball State University. Simon then served as a business development representative at Intelliseek, a leading provider in personalized Internet services. He implemented more than 40 partnerships and created an estimated user count of 6 million. He brings knowledge of search technologies and experience in working with start-up companies to CommuniteeWeb.

Stock Distribution

The following chart details the stockholders in CommuniteeWeb and their ownership percentage. Five million shares have been authorized, and another 2.3 million shares are being held for future authorizations, issued as follows:

Owner	Number of Shares
Investors	2,300,000
Dan Pale	850,000
Jim Mack	850,000
Associates	600,000
Board of Directors	200,000
Stephan Reece	100,000
Nathan Walker	100,000

Of the 2.3 million investor shares, 1.8 million are being held for future placements and 500,000 are dedicated to the current placement.

It will be the practice of CommuniteeWeb to allow all employees to participate in stock ownership. Each of the directors has the opportunity to earn 50,000 options each year. The board of directors will determine the execution price on a year-by-year basis. For the year August 1, 2000 through July 31, 2001, the price will be $10 per share.

Each new full-time employee will receive 1,000 options at the same price provided to the directors.

Each board of directors member will receive 5,000 shares per year of participation.

Partners

Ball State University—Center for Information and Communication Sciences
Ball State University has contributed extensively to this project. More than 150 students at Ball State University have tested and developed concepts to further the scopes of the CommuniteeWeb website. Ball State also has elected to use CommuniteeWeb in a senior-level public relations curriculum. Six students initially were assigned to CommuniteeWeb to help in micro and macro development of the company. Their emphasis was in creating partnerships with local nonprofit and government organizations, as well as national firms. CommuniteeWeb has access to more than 150 undergraduate and graduate students from the Applied Research Institute Laboratory at Ball State University's Center for Information and Communication Sciences for research, testing, and employee recruitment. Present clients of the center include Ameritech, Cisco, Ericsson, First Consulting Group, Lucent, McDonald's, and Nortel.

Ivy Tech State College—Computer Science Laboratory
Ivy Tech State College has created an entire curriculum for a two-year degree to help provide assistance

in development as well as provide CommuniteeWeb with a long-term employee pool. Ivy Tech students, under the direction of professors and CommuniteeWeb staff, provide developmental solutions to assure that CommuniteeWeb is the most technologically advanced local Web portal.

CommuniteeWeb.com Exclusive Features

Geographically and Categorically Searchable Communiteeweb Directory

CommuniteeWeb's valuable directory of locally based websites is searchable by state, city, category, and subcategory. Searches by zip code and county are also planned for future search tool revisions. According to research conducted at the Center for Information and Communication Sciences at Ball State University, *no search index of this kind currently exists on the Internet.* Research has shown that the major local search engines today catalog only half of the URLs in existence. This would help to explain why just 6.86 percent of global website referrals are through traditional search engines. A poll recently taken by Roper Starch found that 71 percent of all users view their search engine experiences as being very frustrating.[27, 28] CommuniteeWeb gathers URLs in a unique manner that enables CommuniteeWeb to gather and catalog more URLs than any other search engine site. This "datamining" method of gathering URLs also enables CommuniteeWeb to screen the contents of the websites to *avoid any adult-oriented or other objectionable material.* The directory offers unique Web marketing opportunities for the future development of business-to-business and business-to-consumer sales.

Local Rewards Program

CommuniteeWeb has created a unique free membership program to businesses, nonprofit organizations, and individuals that accepts press releases, sports scores, editorials, birth announcements, calendar events, and more. The membership program will allow members to be rewarded with "Local Rewards" points for visiting advertisers' websites, interacting with promotions geared at driving traffic to a retailer's website and physical storefront location, and submitting content to CommuniteeWeb. Local Rewards points can then be redeemed in the CommuniteeWeb Online Prize Catalog to win products, services, merchandise, and more. The technology that powers this membership program will allow for advertising by specific geographic locations and demographic/ psychographic groupings with the delivery of targeted banner advertising to a viewer's interest. *This membership program has demonstrated click-through rates of more than 5,000 times the national average.*[29]

Communiteeweb.Com Unique Features

- An events community calendar for the display of event times, locations, and other information specific by location and category classification. End users can customize the calendar to display only those events that they have identified as important to them.

- A News and Sports section featuring national, state, and local content.

- Weather forecasts dynamically generated by CommuniteeWeb from data supplied by the National Weather Service. Forecasts can be viewed by geographic location and can be delivered daily via e-mail to the end user. The ABC affiliate weatherman for Indianapolis, Paul Poteet, will provide a human face to the site as the national forecaster on CommuniteeWeb.com.

- Direct links to local media sites with local radio and TV broadcast listings.

- A Web directory of community-based websites searchable by geographic location and keywords. The Web directory consists of the website name, categorization and subcategory listing, site description, and a direct link to the site.

Industry Background

Without a doubt, the world has been turned upside down since the Internet became commercialized in the early 1990s. An estimated 57 million people used the Internet in 1997, according to CyberAtlas. Internet usage grew to 200 million in 1999 and is expected to reach more than 300 million by the year 2005, which is approximately 5 percent of the world's population. Internet usage patterns are reported by CyberAtlas every month on their website.

A typical Internet user:

- Uses the Internet 19 times per month
- Views 671 pages per month
- Visits 11 unique sites per session
- Views an average of 36 pages per session

According to the Census Bureau, 80 percent of the people who use the Internet use it for e-mail or to find government, business, health, or education information. The next most sought-after information is news, weather, and sports. People access the Internet primarily through analog phone lines. The U.S. market for Internet service providers generated $32.5 billion in revenue in 2000, a 37 percent increase over 1999. Twelve million homes accessed the Internet through high-speed services in 2000. High-speed Internet access is expected to surpass dial-up services by the year 2005.[30]

Online Advertising Market

This newer medium has created another avenue for businesses to reach customers. Advertising on the Internet started with simple websites and links to a company's site from other websites. Online advertisements have become the way to reach customers on the Internet. Contrary to popular myth, online advertising is still growing at a significant rate. Internet advertising increased over 63 percent in the third quarter of 2000 compared to the third quarter of 1999.[31] In addition, online advertising revenues grew more than 53 percent in 2000. Those revenues from online advertisements exceeded $8 billion in 2000 and are expected to reach $32 billion by 2005.[32]

Market Analysis

Target Market

CommuniteeWeb is targeting its product to the baby boomer market, aged 35 to 54. This target group provides the best base to grow CommuniteeWeb into a profitable business. Demographics of this age group include:

- 83% Caucasian, 12% African American 50% male/female

- 70% married

- 30% attended or graduated from college

- 34% have an income above $75,000 76% work full-time

- more than 30% are in professional and/or managerial positions

  Internet usage:

- 66% have Internet access at home and/or work

- 15% use the Internet on a daily basis

- 9% use the Internet three to six times per week

- 52% prefer products that offer the latest technology

"Older" Internet users now constitute the fastest growing demographic group in the Internet market. Approximately 20 percent of U.S. Internet users are aged 45 to 64. This same group is on the Internet more often, stays on longer, and visits more sites than their younger counterparts. Baby boomers typically use the Internet to communicate with friends and family as well as to search for health- and lifestyle-related information.

CommuniteeWeb will reach this target market through key community influences. These influencing individuals include nonprofit organization leaders and constituents, public opinion leaders, and community coordinators (franchisees). CommuniteeWeb has developed an aggressive grassroots marketing plan that will drive membership through localized community influences. CommuniteeWeb's presence in each community will show these community leaders how their organizations and communities can benefit from CommuniteeWeb.com.[33]

Market Position

According to Media Metrix, baby boomers and seniors are the fastest growing section of the online population. Last year, this demographic grew by 18.4 percent and outpaced the 18- to 24-year-old demographic, which had a 17.5 percent growth rate. The report by Media Metrix also shows that this group stays online longer and views more pages. On average, they access the Internet 6.3 more days per month and stay logged on 235.7 minutes longer. Lifestyle and health-related sites are the most popular among the baby boomers. CommuniteeWeb will capture this market by catering to this demographic group's desire for localized lifestyle information. CommuniteeWeb is pursuing a franchise model for market penetration. This grassroots effort will help establish the heartbeat in a local community that has been lacking from most Internet websites.

Competition

CommuniteeWeb is positioning itself to be the premier local content provider and largest local search index in the world. Current attempts to localize content and services on the Web are being made by Internet service providers, search engines, media sites, local government, and others.

- Current attempts at providing this content and service have primarily been limited to only major market cities with populations above one million. America Online's Digital City, Yahoo!, Citysearch. com, and many others have maintained a narrow focus with limited community information and no content for small- to medium-size cities and towns.

- The competition for providing Internet services and e-commerce solutions is intense. *CommuniteeWeb's niche is the "human factor," putting real people in their own communities as a franchise owner.* Whereas most companies depend heavily on costly national advertising and direct mail campaigns, CommuniteeWeb will launch a grassroots effort that will provide the highest level of customer service available today.

The chart below details the competitive strengths and weaknesses of CommuniteeWeb's competition.

Marketing Plan

- Goal 1—To establish CommuniteeWeb as the leading supplier of local content and Internet-related services on the Web.
- Goal 2—To maintain and continually grow the world's deepest and most comprehensible index of local, regional, national, and global URLs in existence.
- Goal 3—To create the most extensive database of individuals classified geographically, demographically, and psychographically available on the Web.

Brand Evaluation

CommuniteeWeb is the first company on the Internet to compile all of the necessary tools that enable users to stay in touch with their local environment in such an in-depth manner. CommuniteeWeb makes all of these tools available in an easy-to-understand Web portal specifically designed to provide local content and services to individual communities.

Brand Awareness

CommuniteeWeb strives to be the decisive winner in providing a public forum and information source for specific communities and/or geographic regions. The website strives to relate reliable data and provide a place for community interaction on issues that are most important to individual families. "Community for You" will instantly be associated with family-friendly content and user-friendly navigation. "The community portal on the Web" is the branding stance CommuniteeWeb will take.

	CommuniteeWeb	OneMain	MyCity	DigitalCity	Yahoo!
Local Calendar	√				
Local News	√	√	√		
Local Sports	√		√		
Movie Times	√	√	√	√	√
Dining	√	√	√		
Maps	√	√	√	√	√
Local Advertisement	√		√		
Reward System	√	√			
Personalization	√	√	√	√	√

The company is a step ahead of its competition because of the focus on depth of information in conjunction with breadth of local information, interaction, and community services. Whereas others try to do a little of everything, CommuniteeWeb focuses on providing the most comprehensive source of content that is user perpetuated.

Customer Promise

"We strive to be your one stop comprehensive resource for providing insight into your local environment and in doing so, never creating a disappointing experience."

Consumer Market

In terms of target markets, CommuniteeWeb will focus its efforts on those markets it believes not only will benefit greatly from its technology but also will be the most receptive to its products and services, notably:

- Educational sector
- Corporate sector
- Small business sector
- Nonprofit sector
- Government

CommuniteeWeb market share will be achieved through:

- Grassroots efforts with the local franchisees
- Volunteers within each community helping the grassroots effort to take hold
- Direct competition in the marketplace
- Affiliations with other companies with dominant positions in their fields
- High-profile, local, regional, and national marketing and advertising campaigns

Technology Plan

CommuniteeWeb has developed and continues to further develop a dynamic site, which requires expertise from several different technology sectors. CommuniteeWeb has accomplished this mission by using its own talented employees and by contracting for services from JGA. Michael Hunt has led this team through the development phases and will continue to lead this team through continuous improvement phases. JGA has provided project management and programming expertise on different components of the website. Jeff Lehm has provided the databases expertise. A commercially viable product was released on January 28, 2001. This product is continuing to be built and improved.

- CommuniteeWeb will populate the directory database with more than one million URLs representing a broad range of community-based websites across the nation by April 1, 2001. This index will be the most comprehensive of its kind when compared to the Open Directory Project (approximately 300,000 URLs as of January 31, 2001) at www.dmoz.org. To accomplish this, CommuniteeWeb hired more than 100 full-time employees to harvest this data. A custom application was written to aid these data miners to ensure the quality and quantity of the information collected.

- The 100 full-time employees will be responsible for maintaining and adding new URLs after the initial population of the database has occurred. They will also be responsible for screening content that is submitted to our community pages.

The design, testing, and implementation of this website took place in approximately 12 weeks, starting October 17, 2000.

Financial Segment

Online Advertising—Per User Revenue

A typical Internet user accesses the Internet an average of 19 times per month, visits 17 unique sites per month, and views an average of 36 pages per session.[34] CommuniteeWeb has projected that a user of the site will visit it 15 times per month and view 6 pages on each of the 11 community sections (2 on the *CommuniteeWeb Directory*) per month. CommuniteeWeb has designed a website that has the capability to show a user five online advertisements per page. Each ad "impression" will result in an average of 3 cents of revenue. The result, coupled with 1 page of national advertising, is $15.60 in revenue from each member from online advertising. CommuniteeWeb has the ability to dynamically display advertising by geographic regions and in targeted categories of information. This will allow advertising customers to target not only a specific demographic but also a specific geographic region as small as a zip code. CommuniteeWeb has used these numbers to generate all of its monthly revenue projections.

At&T Internet Services

Dial-up access will continue to be the main method of accessing the Internet during the next few years. High-speed access subscription is increasing and is expected to take over the dial-up access market by the year 2005.[35] CommuniteeWeb is currently developing a high-speed Internet access program with AT&T. The alliance with AT&T will provide CommuniteeWeb with the ability to offer both dial-up access (short-term) and high-speed connectivity solutions (long-term) to the Internet. Franchisees will be able to sell dial-up access to users at $18.95 per month, which costs CommuniteeWeb $13.95 per month. CommuniteeWeb will have the luxury of a constant one-month cash float from revenues of this service through AT&T. CommuniteeWeb has projected that 5 percent of its members, in addition to an undetermined amount of nonmembers, will use CommuniteeWeb for Internet access.

Infospace.Com Advertising Revenues

Although CommuniteeWeb will outsource the InfoSpace content for a $5,000 monthly fee, CommuniteeWeb expects to recover and exceed this cost with advertising revenue gains once a member navigates the InfoSpace content through CommuniteeWeb.com. CommuniteeWeb will receive 35 percent of the banner advertising revenues on the co-branded pages once a unique visitor per day threshold of 10,000 is met.

Franchise Sales and Fees

Revenue from franchising is generated in two ways: (1) through a one-time fee for the sale of franchises, and (2) through a continuous revenue stream from fees charged to the franchise owner on a monthly basis. The average starting sale price for a franchise will be $35,000 per 100,000 capita. This price will increase as membership numbers are established in given areas. In other words, a market with an established membership will result in a larger investment for a potential franchisee. This is because CommuniteeWeb has already increased the value and potential of the market by providing an established membership, thus providing revenue existing streams to the franchisee. The sale of franchises will provide a great deal of revenue during the infancy and growth stage of the company. Each franchisee will also pay 12.5 percent of revenues as a royalty fee to CommuniteeWeb.

Quad Entertainment

Everyone who stays in a hotel or resort that is Hi-5 Set Top Box equipped will receive a free membership to CommuniteeWeb.com. Of the free memberships provided, CommuniteeWeb expects that 5 percent will continue to use CommuniteeWeb's website when they return home. The hotel and resort industry experiences a 67.5 percent utilization of the rooms available, and the average stay is 2.75 days. Given that there will be 40,000 rooms available, 27,000 will be occupied during a one-month period. Each of those rooms will accommodate 11 distinct visitors (30 days/2.75), resulting in 297,000 visitors and free memberships.[36] Five percent of those visitors, or 14,850, will continue to use CommuniteeWeb.com upon their return home. Revenue models for Internet access, the membership program, and normal website usage will apply to these end users as well. Revenue projections for the first month (starting in August 2001) are as follows:

Internet Access = $3,712($5.00 × 14,850 × 5%)
Online Advertising = $220,522($14.85 × 14,850)

Memberships will increase exponentially after the first month. Quad will continue to add boxes each month, and each box in place will provide CommuniteeWeb with two additional members per month.

Licensing of the CommuniteeWeb Directory

Another revenue opportunity has recently surfaced for CommuniteeWeb: CommuniteeWeb has taken offers to lease its database of categorized URLs. Through research and its contact with the CEO of MyCoupons.com, Randy Conrad, CommuniteeWeb has learned that there are more than 7,500 websites that would be willing to pay an average of more than $500 per month to lease the *CommuniteeWeb Directory* (as it exists today) in a co-branded environment. The directory is currently populated with more than 400,000 URLs—this number and the marketable value of the directory stand to increase drastically due to relationships that CommuniteeWeb has developed with NUOS and ListGuy. CommuniteeWeb is in the process of partnering with the two to further develop and market its database of URLs. ListGuy specializes in business mailing lists, has a database with more than 4 million URLs, and wishes to be the marketing and brokering arm of the *CommuniteeWeb Directory*. NUOS was started by two Harvard professors and has been very involved in the creation and maintenance of Dunn and Bradstreet's online database. They have more than 6 million URLs, which can be loaded into CommuniteeWeb's database. NUOS and ListGuy see value in merging the databases while utilizing CommuniteeWeb's expertise and search tool. Commission levels are still in negotiation, but CommuniteeWeb expects to retain 60 percent of the profits from this venture. (See the financial projection highlights that follows.)

Financial Projection Highlights (Corporate)

$ Millions	Year 1	Year 2	Year 3
Revenues	2.22	30.83	182.15
Net Income	(.41)	19.08	148.64
Cash Flow	2.87	19.08	148.64

Note: Net Income and Cash totals merely represent earning potential, as the majority of the positive cash flow and net profit earned will be utilized to further market the CommuniteeWeb name and product. Year 1 cash flow of $2.87 million includes $3.38 million in investment capital.

Milestone Schedule

Goal: 10 MSAs, 100 Franchises

CommuniteeWeb believes that the Midwest is the best market to penetrate using our "warm marketing" approach. We will use marketing dollars and the loyalty of the Midwest to attack the west and east coasts. Franchises Rollout—Year 1:

- Phase 1: 12 franchises by March 31, 2001
- Phase 2: 28 franchises by June 31, 2001
- Phase 3: 30 franchises by September 31, 2001
- Phase 4: 30 franchises by December 31, 2001

First-Year Franchise Rollout by Region:

- 40 franchises in Indiana, Illinois, and Michigan (Midwest)
- 20 franchises in California
- 20 franchises on East Coast

MSA Phase 1:

- Indianapolis—currently in operation
- Detroit—currently in operation

- Cleveland—currently in operation
- Louisville—April 1, 2001

CommuniteeWeb knows that a large part of the online community in the United States is located in the state of California. CommuniteeWeb's plan is to develop the three largest MSAs in California to capture this market early in our development. Silicon Valley is the cradle of many technology companies. This region's ability to duplicate CommuniteeWeb's concept and develop its own version is the primary reason California is in the second phase of the rollout. California also has 10 percent of the total population of the United States within its borders. CommuniteeWeb's marketing plans will reach more users more cost-effectively in this highly populated state. CommuniteeWeb will focus its marketing efforts on the MSAs. The marketing mediums in these MSAs are expected to bleed into the rest of the state.

MSA Phase 2:

- Los Angeles—April 1, 2001
- San Diego—March 1, 2001
- San Francisco—May 1, 2001

MSA Phase 3:

- New York—June 1, 2001
- Washington—July 1, 2001
- Philadelphia—August 1, 2001
- Boston—September 1, 2001

MSA Phase 4:

- Dallas—November 1, 2001
- Houston—December 1, 2001
- San Antonio—January 1, 2002

QUESTIONS

1. Should CommuniteeWeb utilize Wall Street Venture Capital as its primary funding source? If not, why, and what should the firm's next step be?

2. Assess the company's burn rate (cash expenditure without any notable cash inflow) and financial outlook.

3. What are some critical mistakes made by CommuniteeWeb?

4. Are there any ethical and/or legal concerns in this case?

5. What were some of the major reasons that CommuniteeWeb was having problems taking its business model to market?

6. What were some of the reasons that CommuniteeWeb was having trouble obtaining financing?

7. Evaluate the CommuniteeWeb business plan as an effective tool for raising capital.

SUMMARY

This chapter provided a thorough definition and examination of an effective business plan. The critical factors in planning and the pitfalls to be avoided were discussed. Indicators of these pitfalls and ways to avoid them also were presented.

Next, the benefits for both entrepreneurs and financial sources were reviewed. Developing a well-conceived plan was presented from the point of view of the audience for whom the plan is written. The typical six-step reading process of a business plan was presented to help entrepreneurs better understand how to put the business plan together. Ten guidelines in developing a business plan were provided, collated from the advice of experts in venture capital and new-business development.

The next section illustrated some of the major questions that must be answered in a complete and thorough business plan. The business plan was outlined, and every major segment was addressed and explained.

The chapter then presented some helpful hints for preparing a business plan, along with a self-analysis checklist for doing a careful critique of the plan before it is presented to investors.

Finally, the chapter closed with a review of how to present a business plan to an audience of venture capital sources. Some basic presentation tips were listed, together with a discussion of what to expect from the plan evaluators.

KEY TERMS

business model	management team	milestone schedule segment
business model canvas	market niche	pain
business plan	marketing segment	reachable market
elevator pitch	marketing strategy	
five-minute reading	metrics	

REVIEW AND DISCUSSION QUESTIONS

1. What is a business plan?
2. Describe each of the five planning pitfalls entrepreneurs often encounter.
3. Identify an indicator of each pitfall named in Question 2. What would you do about each?
4. Identify the benefits of a business plan (a) for an entrepreneur and (b) for financial sources.
5. What are the three major viewpoints to be considered when developing a business plan?
6. Describe the six-step process venture capitalists follow when reading a business plan.
7. What are some components to consider in the proper packaging of a plan?
8. Identify five of the ten guidelines to be used for preparing a business plan.

9. Briefly describe each of the major segments to be covered in a business plan.
10. Why is the summary segment of a business plan written last? Why not first?
11. What are five elements included in the marketing segment of a business plan?
12. What is the meaning of the term *critical risks*?
13. Describe each of the three financial statements that are mandatory for the financial segment of a business plan.
14. Why should a business plan be updated?
15. Outline some of the critical points to capture in an elevator pitch.

NOTES

1. Alexander Osterwalder and Yves Pigneur, *Business Model Generation: A Handbook for Visionaries, Game Changers, and Challengers* (Hoboken, NJ Wiley, 2010).

2. Adapted from ibid.

3. See Jeffrey A. Timmons, Andrew Zacharakis, and Stephen Spinelli, *Business Plans That Work* (New York: McGraw-Hill, 2004); Jan Brinckmann, Dietmar

Grichnik, and Diana Kapsa, "Should Entrepreneurs Plan or Just Storm the Castle? A Meta-Analysis on Contextual Factors Impacting the Business Planning–Performance Relationship in Small Firms," *Journal of Business Venturing* 25, no. 1 (2010): 24–40; and Anne Chwolka and Matthias G. Raith, "The Value of Business Planning Before Start-up—A Decision-Theoretical Perspective," *Journal of Business Venturing* 27, no. 3 (2012): 385–99.

4. James W. Henderson, *Obtaining Venture Financing* (Lexington, MA: Lexington Books, 1988), 13–14; see also Stephen C. Perry, "The Relationship Between Written Business Plans and the Failure of Small Businesses in the U.S.," *Journal of Small Business Management* 39, no. 3 (2001): 201–208; Gavin Cassar, "Are Individuals Entering Self-Employment Overly Optimistic? An Empirical Test of Plans and Projections on Nascent Entrepreneur Expectations," *Strategic Management Journal* 31, no. 8 (2010): 822–40; and Gerard George and Adam J. Bock, "The Business Model in Practice and Its Implications for Entrepreneurship Research," *Entrepreneurship Theory and Practice* 35, no. 1 (2011): 83–111.

5. Joseph R. Mancuso, *How to Write a Winning Business Plan* (Englewood Cliffs, NJ: Prentice Hall, 1985), 44.

6. See Donald F. Kuratko, "Demystifying the Business Plan Process: An Introductory Guide," *Small Business Forum* (Winter 1990/1991): 33–40.

7. Adapted from Henderson, *Obtaining Venture Financing*, 14–15; and Mancuso, *How to Write*, 43.

8. Henderson, *Obtaining Venture Financing*, 15.

9. Stanley R. Rich and David E. Gumpert, "How to Write a Winning Business Plan," *Harvard Business Review* 63, no. 2 (May/June 1985): 156–66; see also Colin Mason and Matthew Stark, "What Do Investors Look for in a Business Plan?" *International Small Business Journal* 22, no. 3 (2004): 227–48.

10. Gerald E. Hills, "Market Analysis in the Business Plan: Venture Capitalists' Perceptions," *Journal of Small Business Management* 23, no. 1 (January 1985): 38–46; see also Gerald E. Hills, Claes M. Hultman, and Morgan P. Miles, "The Evolution and Development of Entrepreneurial Marketing," *Journal of Small Business Management* 46, no. 1 (2008): 99–112.

11. Rich and Gumpert, "How to Write," 159.

12. Mancuso, *How to Write*, 52; see also Bruce R. Barringer, *Preparing Effective Business Plans: An Entrepreneurial Approach* 2nd ed. (Upper Saddle River, NJ: Pearson/Prentice Hall, 2015).

13. Mancuso, *How to Write*, 65.

14. These guidelines are adapted from Jeffrey A. Timmons, "A Business Plan Is More Than a Financing Device," *Harvard Business Review* 58, no. 2 (March/April 1980): 25–35; W. Keith Schilit, "How to Write a Winning Business Plan," *Business Horizons* 30,

no. 5 (September/October 1987): 13–22; William A. Sahlman, "How to Write a Great Business Plan," *Harvard Business Review* (July/August 1997): 98–108; and Donald F. Kuratko, *The Complete Entrepreneurial Planning Guide* (Bloomington: Kelley School of Business, Indiana University, 2015).

15. Donald F. Kuratko and Jeffrey S. Hornsby, *New Venture Management: The Entrepreneur's Roadmap* (Upper Saddle River, NJ: Pearson/Prentice Hall, 2009).

16. See Donald F. Kuratko, "Cutting Through the Business Plan Jungle," *Executive Female* (July/August 1993): 17–27; Andrew Burke, Stuart Fraser, and Francis J. Greene, "The Multiple Effects of Business Planning on New Venture Performance," *Journal of Management Studies* 47, no. 3 (2010): 391–415; Donald F. Kuratko, "The Business Plan," *Wiley Encyclopedia of Entrepreneurship* (West Sussex, UK: Wiley, 2014), Vol. 3; and Kuratko, *The Complete Entrepreneurial Planning Guide*.

17. Kuratko and Hornsby, *New Venture Management*.

18. For example, the Massachusetts Institute of Technology sponsors a business plan forum in Boston, and Plug and Play Tech Center in Silicon Valley provides numerous forums where new ideas are "pitched."

19. For more on venture "pitch" presentations, see Barringer, *Preparing Effective Business Plans*; and Andrew J. Sherman, *Start Fast and Start Right* (New York: Kaplan Publishing, 2007).

20. For excellent resources on business plan preparation and presentations, see Garage Technology Ventures at http://www.garage.com/resources.

21. See Appendix for more detailed management biographies.

22. http://www.clickz.com/stats/.

23. http://www.nasdaq.com.

24. http://www.emarketer.com.

25. See the "CommuniteeWeb.com Exclusive Features" section.

26. AT&T promotional literature.

27. "Banners Effective Even When People Don't Click," *Media* (January 2001): 7.

28. http://www.nua.com/surveys/.

29. Based on Media Rewards, LLC, and CommuniteeWeb research and beta testing.

30. http://www.clickz.com/stats/.

31. "Search Engines Refer Just 7% of Traffic," *Media* (January 2001): 6.

32. www.clickz.com/stats/.

33. EchoPoint Media Research—MRI Data.

34. http://www.clickz.com/stats/.

35. Ibid.

36. Hargiss Communication Business Plan.

12A-1 EXECUTIVE SUMMARY

12A-1a Overview

Hydraulic Wind Power, LLC (HWP) is a renewable energy company with a patent-pending technology that can make the production of wind energy more economically viable. Our highly efficient hydraulic drivetrain significantly reduces overall costs and increases total energy production. These benefits will allow turbines utilizing our technology to produce a cost of energy (COE) that is directly competitive with other energy sources (such as coal, nuclear, and hydroelectric, which have a COE of 3–5 cents per kWh).

Our goal is to be the industry expert in hydraulic drivetrains for land-based wind farm applications and provide alternative designs to current large wind turbines that improve the reliability, durability, and profitability of wind power. The company was formed on August 17, 2010 as an Indiana Limited Liability Company (LLC). The company also executed its exclusive licensing agreement with the Indiana University Research and Technology Corporation (IURTC) on the same date. The company is located at the Hoosier Hatchery in Bloomington, IN.

Contact information:
Hydraulic Wind Power, LLC
c/o Hoosier Hatchery
2719 E 10th St
Bloomington, IN 47408
info@hydraulicwindpower.com

Management:
Adam Johnson–CEO
Justin Otani–COO

Director of R&D:
Dr. Afshin Izadian

Business Advisors:
Dr. Donald F. Kuratko
Mark Long

Mark Need
Matt Rubin

Capital received to date:
$112,000

Capital seeking:
Series A of $1.8 million

Investors to-date:
Founders
Indiana University

12A-2 MARKET

In 2008, the U.S. gearbox market was over $4.5 billion, which is part of the larger $151.3 billion wind energy market.[1] Wind energy currently generates around 2 percent of U.S. electricity needs, but future growth is projected to substantially increase.[2] The U.S. Department of Energy released, in 2008, a plan to provide 20 percent of U.S. electricity through wind power by 2030.[3] A more recent analysis of wind integration in the eastern region of the United States drew similar conclusions.[4]

Despite the significant drop in demand for wind energy in 2010, U.S. wind energy seems to again be ramping up. The first-quarter of 2011 figures indicate that the industry seems poised for a renaissance. The under-construction figure is nearly twice the megawatts that the industry reported at this time in both 2009 and 2010; moreover, two-thirds of those megawatts are already locked in under long-term power purchase agreements with electric utilities, indicating an enduring industry that can endure a range of economic and policy conditions.[5]

However, wind energy still faces a number of key challenges that make improving the economic viability of wind critical to its future success. These challenges include:

The Low Price of Natural Gas At $35 a megawatt-hour, wind looked like a good deal back in 2007, when wholesale electric prices ranged between $45 and $85 per megawatt-hour. But the natural gas boom, plus the 2008 recession, drove prices under $30 by 2009, eliminating wind's financial edge. The price of natural gas has fallen by 77 percent since 2008, and the cost of producing electricity in gas plants is down 40 percent, due in part by advances in horizontal drilling and the effective (though highly controversial) technique of hydraulic fracturing, or fracking.[6]

The Instability of Production Tax Credits The renewable energy production tax credit (PTC), a credit of 2.1 cents per kilowatt-hour, is the primary federal incentive for wind energy and has been essential to the industry's growth. The wind energy industry faces two troubles regarding the PTC. First, the credit is continually extended for only one- and two-year terms, discouraging companies from making long-term, sizeable investments in wind power manufacturing and development. Second, in the current adverse financial climate, where demand for tax credits is limited, the PTC is providing little incentive to spur wind energy development. Also, NIMBY (Not In My Backyard) protests have made getting approval for a wind farm in the United States as difficult as getting it for a coal-fired plant.[7]

The Increasing Competition from Chinese Suppliers Chinese wind turbine producers have seen their market share rise dramatically in the past few years. Two of the top Chinese wind turbine producers now rank among the global top three manufacturers by megawatts of capacity sold. The rise has been fuelled by domestic demand for wind power, supported by the government target, and a requirement for 70 percent of wind turbine components to be manufactured locally. With their domestic market saturated and clear signs of overcapacity and upcoming consolidation, biggest Chinese producers have announced plans for international expansion.

12A-3 PROBLEM

Our alternative approach to capturing and transferring energy from the rotor to the generator is able to solve one of the largest and most expensive problems with current wind turbines. Most wind turbines currently utilize a gearbox-based design. These gearboxes are expensive, heavy, and fail often. Gearboxes need to be replaced on average about every 5–7 years and cost over $500,000 per replacement.[8] Our company's solution utilizes a hydraulic system in a unique configuration to eliminate gearboxes and significantly improves the reliability, durability, and profitability of wind turbines.

Gearbox failures account for the largest amounts of downtime, maintenance, and lost power production. These costly failures can total 15–20 percent of the price of the turbine.[9] The frequent maintenance requirements and multiple (costly) gearbox replacements have proven especially problematic for developers of large wind power production facilities. Most wind farm developments today have maintenance teams in place to maintain and replace gearboxes. Many economic models factor in total gearbox replacements every 5–7 years on each turbine.[10] The financial risk gearboxes represent is only somewhat mitigated by the large number of turbines in a major wind power production facility and developers' ability to amortize personnel, equipment, and consumables costs across a fleet of turbines.

Gearboxes are problematic by the very nature of the numerous moving parts and subsystems that are required for their operation and the demanding nature of the wind turbine application itself. It is generally accepted that the complexity and multiple moving parts involved in gearbox-driven designs are creating more opportunities for failure, more maintenance requirements, and costlier fixes.[11]

It is also not that surprising gearboxes have so many failures, especially if you compare them to car transmissions. A car transmission is functionally similar to a wind turbine's gearbox. Expecting a wind turbine's gearbox to last for 20 years of continuous operation would be like expecting a car's transmission to last for 4 million miles, which most would agree is an unreasonable expectation.[12]

The industry has attempted to solve these problems over the past two decades with wind turbine manufacturers, gear designers, bearing manufacturers, consultants, and lubrication engineers all working together to improve load prediction, design, fabrication, and operation. This collaboration has resulted in internationally recognized gearbox wind turbine design standards. However, despite reasonable adherence to these accepted design practices, wind turbine gearboxes have yet to achieve their design life goals of 20 years, with most systems requiring significant repair or overhaul well before the intended life is reached. The wind industry has reached a point where design practices for gearboxes do not result in sufficient life, and institutional barriers are hindering forward progress.[13]

12A-4 TECHNOLOGY

12A-4a Background

Since the acceptance of the gearbox-based configuration (which essentially won out during the 1990s as the dominant configuration and is used in most of today's modern wind turbines), despite their high costs and the high failure rates, U.S. wind turbine designers and manufacturers have proceeded only incrementally toward improvements in wind turbine design. These design and efficiency improvements are being achieved mostly by enlarging turbine size. The focus on incremental design changes have lessened design risk, however, as blades get longer, they challenge the ability of current designs and materials to support their own weight and withstand wind loads.[14]

One attempt by the industry to address these issues was the development of the direct drive system. The direct drive system was specifically designed to avoid the use of a gearbox. The system instead attaches the rotor directly to the generator and uses a costly variable speed electronic system to convert the erratic generation of electricity into a steady flow that can be fed into the power grid. These systems, in order to work, require the use of rare specialized permanent magnets. These specialized generator and variable speed electronic system make the direct drive system almost twice as expensive as the traditional gearbox design.

The required use of rare earth metals also serves as a significant barrier to the widespread adoption of these systems. Rare earths are elements needed in many high technology industries, including the manufacturing of wind turbines. China currently fulfills more than ninety percent of global demand for these elements, and last year, Beijing started to severely restrict its exports.[15] The cost and availability of these elements has limited the direct drive system's use to mostly offshore applications since these turbines' location makes them harder to repair and the larger units are able to generate enough power to justify the added costs.

12A-4b Opportunity

Some attempts at creating a hydraulic-based drivetrain comprising a pump and motor for main power transmission were attempted unsuccessfully in the early 1980s. Key problems that were identified were its inadequate capacity, efficiency, reliability, and lifespan of then-existing commercial hydraulic components. The lack of components specifically designed for the needs of efficient wind power generation ultimately led to the determination that these systems were not as commercially viable as the gearbox-based drivetrains. However, the advances over the past 30 years in pump manufacturing for the oil and gas industry and in fields such as materials science, fluid dynamics, and computational design tools have solved many of these issues and have reopened the door of opportunity for these past innovative drivetrain concepts.[16]

Traditional Gearbox Design

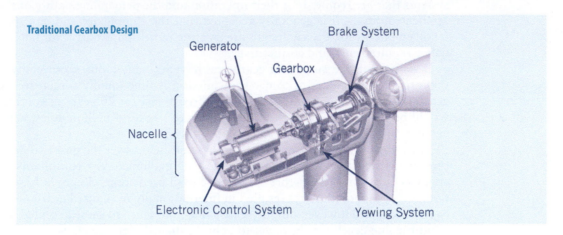

Evolution of Wind Turbine Designs over the Past 25 Years

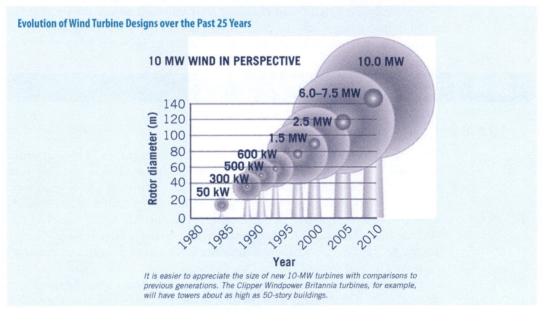

It is easier to appreciate the size of new 10-MW turbines with comparisons to previous generations. The Clipper Windpower Britannia turbines, for example, will have towers about as high as 50-story buildings.

Direct Drive Design

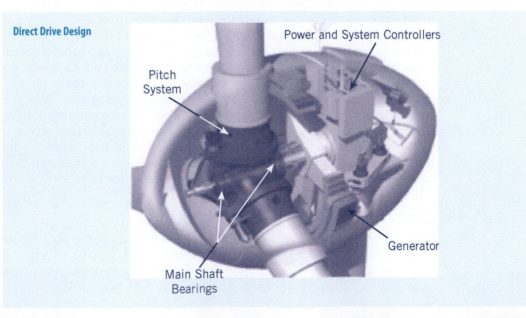

12A-5 OUR SOLUTION

Our company has created a unique solution to the problem of transferring energy by combining a novel hydraulic transmission system with a specialized closed loop control system. Hydraulic transmission systems (HTS) are well known as an exceptional means of power transmission for energy applications in manufacturing, automation, and heavy-duty vehicles.[17] The HTS developed by HWP allows the rotor to operate at variable speeds, enables the use of efficient hydraulic components, and enables the use of synchronous generators (without requiring costly variable speed electronic system).

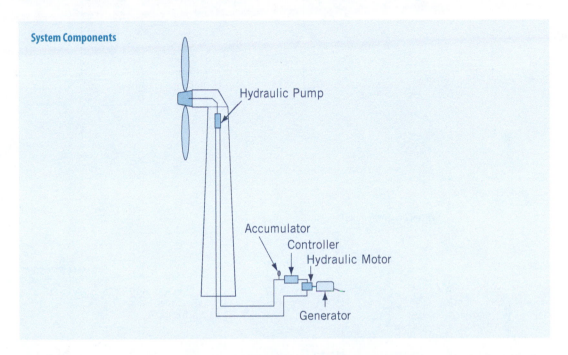

Operating at variable speeds increase the amount of energy captured, rotary hydraulics are extremely durable and highly efficient, and synchronous generators do not require a reactive magnetizing current and a reactive power compensation system (unlike induction generators, which are found in most current wind turbines), which reduce the efficiency of the system.

Utilizing our specialized closed loop control system, our drivetrain is able to maintain a constant frequency at the generator while it transfers energy captured by the rotor to a generator on the ground, and allows manufacturers to incorporate several turbines into a single centralized power generation unit (an ideal feature for wind farm applications).

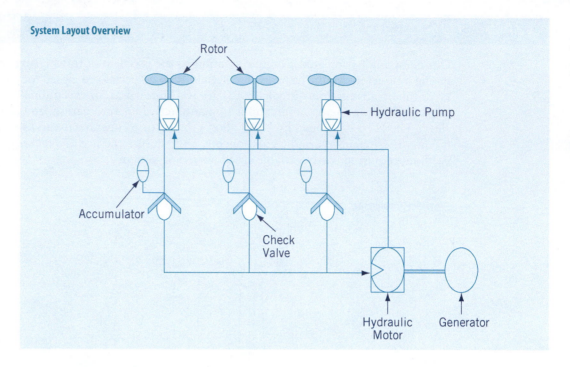

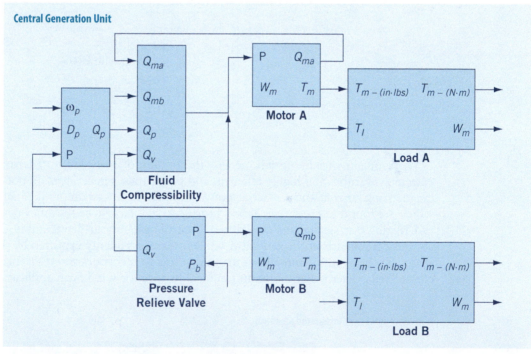

12A-5a Outside Validation

The company has received some initial feedback from the U.S. Department of Energy (DOE) on our technology. This feedback is highly encouraging and attests to the potential of the technology. The DOE did identify some areas of concern. However, the company has since worked hard to address these concerns and made substantial progress in the development of the technology. Dr. Izadian also has two peer-reviewed papers on the technology that have been accepted for publication (and are available upon request).

12A-5b Competitive Advantage

Rather than attempting to create a solution using abstract or untested technologies, our innovative control and energy conversion system leverages current industrial technologies and expertise to create a practical and effective solution. This also gives HWP a unique advantage because the manufacturing and distribution infrastructure already exists that would enable the rapid deployment of our system into new wind farm projects once the full-scale system is completed, tested, and proven.

Our system has a number of additional advantages when compared to traditional gear-box designs, direct drive designs, and alternative hydraulic designs. The combination of these advantages is expected to significantly reduce a turbine's COE. These advantages can be broken down into two key areas: efficiency advantages and cost advantages. These advantages are listed below:

Efficiency Advantages:

- Variable speed rotor
- Increased nominal speed; increased cut-out speed
- Reduced nacelle weight (also reduces costs)
- Improved generator efficiency and grid compatibility (also reduces costs)
- Elimination of large power electronics (also reduces costs)
- Enabled energy storage

Cost Advantages:

- Reduced downtime and repair costs
- Reduced Investor Risk
- Currently existing manufacturing infrastructure

Our system will enable manufacturers to provide developers a more reliable and durable turbine, while also increasing overall profitability. Acquiring a license in an existing and proven technology will also allow licensees to avoid the delays, risks, and costs inherent with in-house development. It reduces the lead-time needed to design and build new turbines and provides them access to an established component supply chain and supplier network.

12A-6 DEVELOPMENT PLAN

12A-6a Development Strategy

HWP has moved aggressively through the design and development of our hydraulic drive-train system and its associated technologies. The company has begun to establish industry partnerships with one wind farm development company and one large energy company. The company has also developed contacts with several other companies and organizations in the wind energy. We have identified four key phases for the development of the system and some alternative development options. These phases are:

- Small-scale model and simulation
- Medium-scale simulation; Large-scale simulation
- Full-scale build
- Medium build (alternative option)

SMALL-SCALE MODEL AND SIMULATION (COMPLETED)

The initial phase of development included the development of a mathematical model, a computer simulation, and a small-scale prototype of the system. The simultaneous development of these three different approaches has ensured the accuracy of the results and created a strong and reliable foundation for scaling up the system to a commercial size.

The result of this phase was the successful implementation of model-based control strategies for hydraulic wind energy harvesting systems that maintain a constant frequency at the generator. An energy transmission system for a wind turbine was mathematically modeled with one fixed displacement pump and two hydraulic motors. The obtained mathematical model was compared to the designed computer model using the SimHydraulic toolbox in Matlab/Simulink and the experimental results obtained from the small-scale prototype of the hydraulic system. The result was the experimental data from the small-scale prototype was equivalent to the simulated models and it illustrated that the gearless hydraulic power transfer system is an efficient and effective means of transferring energy.

MEDIUM-SCALE SIMULATION (IN-PROGRESS)

The company is currently in the process of scaling up the system into to a medium-size three tower system (approx. 100 kW per tower). Scaling the system to a medium-size system prior to a full-scale system is critical to ensuring the results of the small-scale designs are accurately translated into the system. This medium-size system can also be used as the basis for a fast and cost effective development project with an industry partner to demonstrate the viability of the technology. The goals of this phase are to accurately determine the effects of tower height on the system and the effect of distance of the system, to determine more accurate component specifications, and to further refine the COE calculations.

Errol Dogar, HWP's advisor and cofounder of American Tool & Machining, Inc., currently has an underutilized 4,000-square-foot facility on a one-acre lot in northwest Indianapolis that includes all necessary machine tools and 3-phase 480-volt power. With minor modifications, this building and lot is expected to be the base of operation for the prototype. This facility is fully capable of housing all needed equipment and personnel, as well as being able to do any needed machining, welding, assembly, and testing to successfully complete the medium-scale prototype phase of development. HWP's access to this facility is expected to reduce the cost of the medium scale prototype by roughly 60 percent.

The results of this actual size prototype will demonstrate the superior cost and maintenance aspects of our hydraulic system. In addition, it will also provide valuable information in identifying problem areas, and ways to improve the system. Once the concept is proven at realistic power levels, it will open up new sources of future funding as well as internal funding through retrofit sales and installations of medium-sized turbines.

LARGE-SCALE SIMULATIONS

After the development of the medium-size system, the company will continue to scale up the system into a full size system (1.5 MW per tower). This phase will include identifying new components, determining key technical and performance metrics, updating the COE analysis, identifying and quantifying expected improvements by area compared to existing technologies, updating the schedule and cost estimates, and completing a manufacturing cost analysis on new components. This phase will also include the exact designs for two-tower system that will be used for a full-scale build.

FULL-SCALE BUILD

HWP has identified two potential avenues for building a full-scale prototype based on the large-scale simulations and the medium prototype results. The company plans to develop a partnership with an industry partner that would allow the company to retrofit two larger towers with our system. The preconstruction needs for this initial system are projected to take about four months. The construction itself is expected to take an additional six months. During this period, HWP is expected to optimize the product and address any unanticipated challenges that may arise. HWP will then use the next six months to test the system under different wind conditions and use the data collected to complete our design of HWP's commercial six-tower integrated system.

12A-7 COMMERCIALIZATION PLAN

12A-7a Business Model

HWP is positioning itself to be the industry expert on hydraulic drivetrain systems for land-based wind farm applications. The company plans to emerge as an engineering design firm that will eventually expand on its core competency of designing hydraulic systems for wind turbines to also include construction, operations and maintenance, and supply chain

expertise and assistance for the systems we design. This will allow customers to quickly and seamlessly integrate our system into their products or development projects.

The company plans to commercialize our technology by securing licensing agreements for the use of our system. In exchange for an upfront licensing fee and a fixed royalty rate determined by gross sales on a per tower basis, HWP will provide manufacturers a complete product package. This package will include the right to build and sell turbines using our HTS and closed loop control system, component drawings and specifications, a bill of materials (parts list), supply chain development assistance, assembly and testing documentation, transportation and logistics documentation, field installation and commissioning procedures, operation and maintenance manuals, engineering consulting services, and a training program for manufacturing and service.

Customers will benefit by acquiring a license to an existing and proven technology. This allows licensees to avoid the delays, risks, and costs inherent with in-house development. HWP allows manufacturers to incorporate an innovative technology into their turbines, break-even faster, and make larger profits more quickly. It reduces the lead-time needed to design and build new turbines, and it will provide them access to an established component supply chain and supplier network. Licensees will also have access to professional high quality training and support from the development stage to full-scale implementation of the system.

As the premier experts on understanding and developing hydraulic drivetrains and related component (as opposed to expanding into blades or tower designs), the company expects to eventually expand our potential revenue streams (as our solution becomes more widely adopted) to also include operation and maintenance services, and additional consulting services.

12A-7b Entry Strategy

The company plans to pursue multiple strategies for marketing the company and bringing our technology to the market. These include establishing industry partnerships and building a number of relationships in the industry. Once the technology development phase nears completion, the company plans to leverage these relationships to establish a pilot program with either a turbine manufacturer or a wind farm developer. This pilot program is expected to involve the implementation of our system into a smaller wind farm development project or as a smaller part of a larger project. This initial project will help establish the acceptance of the technology within the market while minimizing the risk to the company's partners.

12A-7c Target Customers

HWP anticipates three different types of potential customers: current wind turbine manufacturers, wind farm developers, and hydraulic component manufacturers. The company will initially target current turbine manufacturers for its first licensees. Licensing directly to wind turbine manufacturers increases the company's influence in the value chain and its ability to enter the market quickly. These manufacturers have an expertise in wind turbine manufacturing and have already existing relationships with wind farm developers.

Alternatively, HWP will also seek to secure licensing agreements with wind farm developers and hydraulic component manufacturers. Wind farm development projects have high initial capital requirements and this has pushed wind farm developers to become increasingly vertically integrated in order to reduce these costs. Wind farm developers who manufacture their own turbines are also likely candidates to license our designs.

Our solution also represents a great opportunity for hydraulic component manufacturers to enter a new high-growth market. There are currently dozens of major hydraulics companies (including Caterpillar, Flowserve, Sulzer, and Eaton) that would possibly be interested in licensing HWP's technology. While the system is proprietary, the components that it uses are well known by these companies. Licensing our system to these manufacturers allows them access to a new market without them needing to look beyond their existing core competencies.

12A-7d Exit Strategy

The wind energy industry is characterized by a large number of strategic acquisitions. In 2010, there were 35 deals within North America, totaling $3.98 billion. Larger manufacturers have been quick to acquire smaller companies with improved technologies. For example, GE recently purchased Wind Tower Systems LLC to gain access to a technology for building tall towers more cheaply. HWP believes our alternative drivetrain system will make HWP a strong acquisition target for a larger manufacturer because of our technology's strong value proposition and ability to diversify a larger company's product portfolio.

12A-8 EXECUTIVE TEAM

12A-8a Start-Up Management

Interim Chief Executive Officer (CEO)–Adam Johnson (MBA) recently completed his MBA in entrepreneurship at the Indiana University Kelley School of Business. He has experience in the renewable energy sector working for a start-up, Microbial Energy Systems, and a background in finance, including working at Smith Barney Financial.

Chief Operating Officer (COO)–Justin Otani (JD/MBA) is currently completing his JD in business law and intellectual property at the Indiana University Maurer School of Law and his MBA in entrepreneurship and corporate finance at the Indiana University Kelley School of Business. He has experience working in the technology transfer office at Indiana University.

Director of R&D–Dr. Afshin Izadian is the inventor of HWP's technology and he is providing technical advice and development assistance to HWP. Dr. Izadian is an electrical engineering professor at Indiana University–Purdue University Indianapolis (IUPUI). He is also a research member at the Energy Center, Discovery Park–Purdue University, and a research faculty member at Richard Lugar Center for Renewable Energy.

12A-8b Advisory Board

The Advisory Board has a strong background in entrepreneurship, intellectual property, and bringing new technologies to the market. The Board provides assistance with our business plan and investor presentation, legal services, and general guidance on business development. The Advisory Board currently includes Dr. Donald F. Kuratko ("Dr. K"), Prof. Mark Need, and Mr. Matt Rubin. "Dr. K" is the Executive Director of the Johnson Center for Entrepreneurship and Innovation at Indiana University. Mark Need is the Director of the Elmore Entrepreneurship Law Clinic at Indiana University. Matt Rubin is a Business Development Manager for the Indiana University Research and Technology Corporation.

12A-9 RISKS

12A-9a Industry Risk

The renewable energy PTC, a credit of 2.1 cents per kilowatt-hour, is the primary federal incentive for wind energy and has been essential to the industry's growth. The wind energy industry faces two troubles regarding the PTC. First, the credit is continually extended for only one- and two-year terms, discouraging companies from making long-term, sizeable investments in wind power manufacturing and development. Second, in the current adverse financial climate, where demand for tax credits is limited, the PTC is providing little incentive to spur wind energy development.

Our system has the potential to make wind energy cost competitive without these government subsidies. This serves as a strong competitive advantage for our system. However, there is a risk that these PTCs may not be renewed prior to development and acceptance of HWP's system. If this occurs, it could result in a substantial decrease in demand for wind projects or investment in wind energy technologies, which could significantly slow the company's entry into the market. This risk is also mitigated because the wind turbine market is a global market, and even if this event occurs, the company will still be capable of commercializing our technology elsewhere.

12A-9b Alternative Technology Risks

Major turbine manufacturers have been working hard to make gearboxes more reliable. HWP recognizes the possibility that these companies may develop a more competitive solution to the gearbox problem. HWP feels that this risk is currently minimal considering the time and effort these companies have already incurred trying to improve current gearboxes. HWP strongly believes that our technology will be successful even if the lifetime of gearboxes is dramatically extended because of the decreases in initial capital costs, the decreases in turbine weight, and the decreases in costs of repairs when repairs are necessary.

12A-9c Hydraulic Fluid

Environmental concerns surrounding the use of hydraulic fluid is an area of potential concern. The company has already identified several environmentally friendly hydraulic fluids available in the market. Once the full-scale system is designed and analyzed, the optimal properties of a potential hydraulic fluid will be better known (viscosity, static pressure, vapor pressure, density, etc.). We anticipate that there will be an existing environmentally friendly fluid with these ideal properties. However, if there is not a fluid with the exact properties that would optimize the efficiency of the energy transferred, then it may require additional research into the development of fluid with the desired chemical properties.

12A-10 FINANCIAL SUMMARY

12A-10a Financials

The financial pro formas presented here are projections based in part on Windtec's success using a similar licensing model. HWP is confident in our ability to hit these revenue numbers when considering the advantages of the company's system over Windtec's gearbox-based systems. The company expects to sign their first licensing agreement within two years, but possibly earlier. HWP's goal is to close a Series A round of $1.8 million to fund technology development and prepare the company to build a full-scale prototype.

The funding will also allow the company to hire key personnel. After receiving the Series A round of funding, the company hopes to hire a Chief Technology Officer (CTO) and a Chief Executive Officer (CEO). The CTO will lead the charge in the development of our engineering team, and the CEO will be responsible for overseeing the management of the business and securing additional capital.

HWP believes bringing the technology development "in house" will be critical to the company's success. The company also anticipates needing to hire a Senior Electrical Engineer and Senior Control Systems Engineer in the first year. HWP also expects to hire a mechanical engineer and an electrical engineer in the second year. These engineers will be important as the company begins to prepare for the full-scale prototype build.

The company also anticipates closing a Series B round of $4 million to build a full-scale prototype. The financial projections are consistent with HWP partnering with a wind farm developer to retrofit two existing towers. However, this partnership could take on many different forms that could reduce the cost of this full-scale build significantly. The costs of parts include a contingency fund of $500,000 in year 3 and $250,000 in year 4 in case the company has any complications with the build. In addition to this spare parts contingency fund, the company never drops below $380,000 in cash. The extra cash will make sure the company will be able to survive even if unexpected complications or expenses occur.

HWP will not need to invest heavily in capital expenditures beyond the full-scale prototype because of the company's licensing strategy. This approach allows the company to be a long-term self-sustaining company and will eliminate the need for a third round of funding.

The company expects to be cash flow positive within three years. Most of the expenses beyond the full-scale prototype will be focused on continued R&D, as well as expanding and improving the engineering and sales teams.

Income Statement	Year 1	Year 2	Year 3	Year 4	Year 5
Licensing Fees		$ -	$ 500,000	$ 1,000,000	$ 3,000,000
Interest Revenue	$ 26,591	$ 112,886	$ 120,586	$ 91,472	$ 65,095
Royalties			$ 2,250,000	$ 10,500,000	$ 30,000,000
Other Revenue					
Total Revenue	$ 26,591	$ 112,886	$ 2,870,586	$ 11,591,472	$ 33,065,095
Pass-through Royalties	$ -	$ -	$ 1,125,000	$ 5,250,000	$ 15,000,000
Total Salaries	$ 450,000	$ 796,167	$ 1,061,050	$ 1,495,595	$ 2,724,341
Total IUPUI Expenses	$ 140,394	$ 140,394			
Outside Contractors	$ 100,000	$ 115,000	$ 132,250	$ 152,088	$ 174,901
Total Supplies for Initial Build		$ 1,310,122	$ 1,560,122	$ 375,000	$ 125,000
Construction Expenses for Initial Build		$ 500,000	$ 500,000		
Operating Expenses					
Total Operating Costs	$ 214,100	$ 161,385	$ 202,698	$ 300,805	$ 378,512
Total Costs	$ 904,494	$ 3,023,067	$ 4,581,119	$ 7,573,487	$ 18,402,753
EBT	$ (877,903)	$ (2,910,181)	$ (1,710,533)	$ 4,017,984	$ 14,662,342
Taxes (35%)	$ -	$ -	$ -	$ (1,406,295)	$ (5,131,820)
Net Income	**$ (877,903)**	**$ (2,910,181)**	**$ (1,710,533)**	**$ 2,611,690**	**$ 9,530,522**

*Please refer to exhibits for more detailed financial information

12-10b Exit

While our licensing model positions HWP to be a self-sustaining company, there is a strong likelihood the company will be acquired by a wind turbine manufacturer, hydraulic pump manufacturer, or wind farm developer. Therefore, based on an exit through acquisition in year 5, the company has a projected value of $162.8 million. This is based on a current industry standard of 11 times earnings before interest, taxes, depreciation, and amortization (EBITDA). Major companies have been quick to acquire smaller companies. This is evidenced by Mitsubishi Heavy Industries' (MHI) acquisition of Artemis IP and American.

Balance Sheet	Year 1	Year 2	Year 3	Year 4	Year 5
Assets					
Current Assets					
Cash	$ 943,075	$ 2,131,570	$ 386,284	$ 4,861,830	$ 19,851,153
Accounts Receivable		$ -	$ -	$ -	$ -
Total Assets	$ 943,075	$ 2,131,570	$ 386,284	$ 4,861,830	$ 19,851,153
Liabilities					
Current Liabilities					
Accounts Payable	$ 20,978	$ 119,653	$ 84,900	$ 242,462	$ 569,444
Total Liabilities	$ 20,978	$ 119,653	$ 84,900	$ 242,462	$ 569,444
Equity					
Capital Stock	$ 1,800,000	$ 5,800,000	$ 5,800,000	$ 5,800,000	$ 5,800,000
Retained Earnings	$ (877,903)	$ (3,788,083)	$ (5,498,616)	$ (1,480,632)	$ 13,181,710
Total Equity	$ 922,097	$ 2,011,917	$ 301,384	$ 4,319,368	$ 18,981,710
Total Liabilities & Equity	$ 943,075	$ 2,131,570	$ 386,284	$ 4,561,830	$ 19,551,153

Cash Flow Statement	Year 1	Year 2	Year 3	Year 4	Year 5
Net Income (Loss)	$ (877,903)	$ (2,910,181)	$ (1,710,533)	$ 4,017,984	$ 14,662,342
Working Capital Changes:					
Accounts Receivable (Increase)	$ -	$ -	$ -	$ 300,000	$ -
Accounts Payable (Increase)	$ 20,978	$ 98,676	($ 34,753)	$ 157,562	$ 326,982
Cash Used for Operations	$ (856,925)	$ (2,811,505)	$ (1,745,286)	$ 4,475,547	$ 14,989,323
Cash Used for Investments					
Cash from Financing Activities					
Capital Stock					
Change in Cash for Period	$ (856,925)	$ (2,811,505)	$ (1,745,286)	$ 4,475,547	$ 14,989,323
Cash: Beginning of Period	$ 1,800,000	$ 943,075	$ 2,131,570	$ 386,284	$ 4,861,830
Cash: End of Period	$ 943,075	$ 2,131,570	$ 386,284	$ 4,861,830	$ 19,851,153

*Please refer to exhibits for more detailed financial information

Series A Expected Financial Return					
Year 5 EBITA	14.8 (millions)				
Multiple	11				
Terminal Value	$ 162.8				
Series B	TV	IRR	Periods	DTV	
PV	$ 163	0.94	3.5	$ 16.15	
Investment	$ 4			25%	Series B Final Ownership
Retention Ratio	75%				
Series A	TV	IRR	Periods	DTV	
PV	$ 163	0.94	5	$ 6.00	
Investment	$ 1.8			30%	Series A Final Ownership
				40%	Series A Current Ownership

Ownership	Post A	Post-B	Series A Valuation			
Founders	45%	28%	Premoney	$	2.72	Series A
ICP	5%	10%	Series A	$	1.80	Cash-on-cash Return
Option Pool	10%	8%	Postmoney	$	4.52	27
Series A	40%	30%				Exit Return
Series B		25%				$48.83
Total	100%	100%				

Superconductor (AMSC) acquisition of Windtec. Details of the Artemis IP deal were not disclosed, but MHI committed over $160 million in a larger deal that included the acquisition. In the Windtec deal, AMSC acquired Windtec for $12.4 million in AMSC stock. Windtec also had a tremendous backlog of orders that it could not fill at the time.

APPENDIX

Use of Funds

	Growth Rate	Year 1	Year 2	Year 3	Year 4	Year 5
Salary Expense						
Chief Executive Officer	10%	$ 125,000	$ 137,500	$ 151,250	$ 166,375	$ 183,013
Adam Johnson, CFO	10%	$ 60,000	$ 80,000	$ 88,000	$ 96,800	$ 106,480
Justin Otani, COO	10%	$ 40,000	$ 80,000	$ 88,000	$ 96,800	$ 106,480
Chief Technology Officer	10%	$ 100,000	$ 110,000	$ 121,000	$ 133,100	$ 133,100
Senior Electrical Engineer	10%	$ 75,000	$ 100,000	$ 110,000	$ 121,000	$ 121,000
Senior Control Systems Engineer	10%	$ 50,000	$ 100,000	$ 110,000	$ 121,000	$ 121,000
Junior Mechanical Engineer	10%		$ 50,000	$ 55,000	$ 60,500	$ 66,550
Junior Electrical Engineer	10%		$ 50,000	$ 55,000	$ 60,500	$ 66,550
Sales Manager	10%		$ 23,333	$ 70,000	$ 77,000	$ 84,700
Sales Manager	10%		$ 23,333	$ 70,000	$ 77,000	$ 84,700
Other Salaries	240%		$ 42,000	$ 142,800	$ 485,520	$ 1,650,768
Total Salaries		$ 450,000	$ 796,167	$ 1,061,050	$ 1,167,155	$ 1,283,871
IUPUI						
Principal Investigator		$ 6,590	$ 6,590			
Co-Principal Investigator		$ 4,000	$ 4,000			
Two Postdoctoral Fellows		$ 36,000	$ 36,000			
Two Graduate Research Assistants		$ 14,400	$ 14,400			
IUPUI Salaries		$ 60,990	$ 60,990			
		$ 0	$ 0			
Fringe Benefits/Payroll Benefits		0	0			
PI/Co PI		$ 2,783	$ 2,783			
Two Graduate Research Assistants		$ 2,278	$ 2,278			
Postdoctoral Fellows		$ 15,120	$ 15,120			
Total IUPUI Benefits		$ 20,181	$ 20,181			
		$ 0	$ 0			

Use of Funds (*Continued*)

	Growth Rate	Year 1	Year 2	Year 3	Year 4	Year 5
Graduate Student Fee Remission		$ 11,000	$ 11,000			
		$ 0	$ 0			
Supplies/Materials		0	0			
One Synchronous Motor		0	0			
Computing Systems		0	0			
Replacement Parts		0	0			
Total IUPUI Supplies/ Materials		$ 2,500	$ 2,501			
		$ 0	$ 1			
IUPUI Indirect Costs		$ 45,723	$ 45,723			
Total IUPUI		$ 140,394	$ 140,394			
Outside Contractors						
Engineer Consulting	15%	$ 100,000	$ 115,000	$ 132,250	$ 152,088	$ 174,901
Supplies for Initial Build						
Low speed shafts			$ 195,000			
CV Joints			$ 12,000			
Bearings			$ 70,200			
Brake			$ 17,550			
Yaw Drive & Bearing			$ 75,000			
Control/Safety System			$ 204,750			
Mainframe			$ 420,000			
Electrical Connection			$ 274,743			
Large Hydraulic Pump			$ 180,000			
Generator			$ 300,000			
Hydraulic Tank			$ 21,000			
Bypass Valves			$ 60,000			
Electric Control Shut off Val.			$ 45,000			
Check Valves			$ 30,000			
Pressure Relief Valves			$ 30,000			
Reduced Size Power Conv.			$ 90,000			
Flow Control Valve			$ 30,000			

(*Continued*)

Use of Funds (Continued)

	Growth Rate	Year 1	Year 2	Year 3	Year 4	Year 5
Pressure Booster Pump			$ 24,000			
Piping			$ 36,000			
Secondary Generator			$ 225,000			
Hydraulic Pump			$ 120,000			
Accumulator			$ 60,000			
Spare Parts			$ 100,000	$ 500,000	$ 250,000	
Total Supplies for Initial Build			$ 2,620,243	$ 500,000	$ 250,000	
Construction Costs for Initial Build			$ 1,000,000			
Operating Costs						
	8%					
Payroll Processing Fees		$ 2,000	$ 3,000	$ 3,000	$ 3,000	$ 3,000
Office Rent	5%		$ 15,000	$ 15,750	$ 15,750	$ 15,750
Fringe Benefits	35%	$ 6,000	$ 12,000	$ 16,200	$ 21,870	$ 29,525
Travel – Related Expenses	15%	$ 30,000	$ 34,500	$ 39,675	$ 45,626	$ 52,470
Trade Shows	15%	$ 4,000	$ 4,600	$ 5,290	$ 6,084	$ 6,996
Brochures & Publications	15%	$ 2,000	$ 2,300	$ 2,645	$ 3,042	$ 3,498
Market Research	15%	$ 5,000	$ 5,750	$ 6,613	$ 7,604	$ 8,745
Postage	15%	$ 500	$ 575	$ 661	$ 760	$ 875
Cell Phones	15%	$ 1,500	$ 1,725	$ 1,984	$ 2,281	$ 2,624
Legal Fees	15%	$ 10,000	$ 11,500	$ 13,225	$ 15,209	$ 17,490
Other Professional Fees	15%	$ 10,000	$ 11,500	$ 13,225	$ 15,209	$ 17,490
Website Development and Upkeep		$ 20,000	$ 1,500	$ 1,500	$ 1,500	$ 1,500
Dues & Subscriptions	15%	$ 900	$ 1,035	$ 1,190	$ 1,369	$ 1,574
Patent Costs		$ 80,000	$ 15,000	$ 30,000	$ 100,000	$ 150,000
Computers and Software (SimHydraulics)	18,200	13,800	20,000	25,000	25,000	
Office Equipment & Supplies	15%	$ 7,000	$ 8,050	$ 9,258	$ 10,646	$ 12,243
Telephone & Utility Expenses	15%	$ 3,000	$ 3,450	$ 3,968	$ 4,563	$ 5,247
Accounting Services	15%	$ 4,000	$ 4,600	$ 5,290	$ 6,084	$ 6,996
Miscellaneous	15%	$ 10,000	$ 11,500	$ 13,225	$ 15,209	$ 17,490
Total Operating Costs		$ 214,100	$ 161,385	$ 202,698	$ 300,805	$ 378,512
Total Cost		$ 904,494	$ 4,833,188	$ 1,895,998	$ 1,870,047	$ 1,837,283

Income Statement (Year 1):

Income Statement	1	2	3	4	5	6	7	8	9	10	11	12	Year 1
Licensing Revenue													
Interest Revenue	$ 3,159	$ 2,819	$ 2,698	$ 2,575	$ 2,453	$ 2,330	$ 2,207	$ 1,961	$ 1,784	$ 1,660	$ 1,535	$ 1,410	$ 26,591
Royalties													
Other Revenue													
Total Revenue	$ 3,159	$ 2,819	$ 2,698	$ 2,575	$ 2,453	$ 2,330	$ 2,207	$ 1,961	$ 1,784	$ 1,660	$ 1,535	$ 1,410	$ 26,591
Licensing Expense													
Labor & Related Costs													
Chief Executive Officer	$ 10,417	$ 10,417	$ 10,417	10,417	10,417	10,417	10,417	10,417	10,417	10,417	10,417	10,417	$ 125,000
Adam Johnson, CFO	$ 5,000	$ 5,000	$ 5,000	5,000	5,000	5,000	5,000	5,000	5,000	5,000	5,000	5,000	$ 60,000
Justin Otani, COO	$ 3,333	$ 3,333	$ 3,333	3,333	3,333	3,333	3,333	3,333	3,333	3,333	3,333	3,333	$ 40,000
Chief Technology Officer	$ 8,333	$ 8,333	$ 8,333	8,333	8,333	8,333	8,333	8,333	8,333	8,333	8,333	8,333	$ 100,000
Senior Electrical Engineer	$ 0	$ 0	$ 0	8,333	8,333	8,333	8,333	8,333	8,333	8,333	8,333	8,333	$ 75,000
Senior Control Systems Engineer	$ 0	$ 0	$ 0	0	0	0	8,333	8,333	8,333	8,333	8,333	8,333	$ 50,000
Junior Mechanical Engineer	$ 0	$ 0	$ 0	0	0	0	0	0	0	0	0	0	$ -
Junior Electrical Engineer	$ 0	$ 0	$ 0	0	0	0	0	0	0	0	0	0	$ -
Sales Manager	$ 0	$ 0	$ 0	0	0	0	0	0	0	0	0	0	$ -
Sales Manager	$ 0	$ 0	$ 0	0	0	0	0	0	0	0	0	0	$ -
Other Salaries	0	0	0	0	0	0	0	0	0	0	0	0	$ -
Total Salaries	$ 27,083	$ 27,083	$ 27,083	35,417	35,417	35,417	43,750	43,750	43,750	43,750	43,750	43,750	$ 450,000
Total IUPUI Expenses	$ 140,394												
Outside Contractors	$ 8,333	$ 8,333	$ 8,333	8,333	8,333	8,333	8,333	8,333	8,333	8,333	8,333	8,333	$ 100,000
Total Supplies for Initial Build													
Construction Costs for Initial Build													

(Continued)

Income Statement (Year 1): *(Continued)*

Income Statement	1	2	3	4	5	6	7	8	9	10	11	12	Year 1
Operating Expenses													
Payroll Processing Fees	$ 167	$ 167	$ 167	$ 167	$ 167	$ 167	$ 167	$ 167	$ 167	$ 167	$ 167	$ 167	$ 2,000
Office Rent	$ -	$ -	$ -	$ -	$ -	$ -	$ -	$ -	$ -	$ -	$ -	$ -	$ -
Fringe Benefits	$ 500	$ 500	$ 500	$ 500	$ 500	$ 500	$ 500	$ 500	$ 500	$ 500	$ 500	$ 500	$ 6,000
Travel - Related Expenses	$ 2,500	$ 2,500	$ 2,500	$ 2,500	$ 2,500	$ 2,500	$ 2,500	$ 2,500	$ 2,500	$ 2,500	$ 2,500	$ 2,500	$ 30,000
Trade Shows	$ 333	$ 333	$ 333	$ 333	$ 333	$ 333	$ 333	$ 333	$ 333	$ 333	$ 333	$ 333	$ 4,000
Brochures & Publications	$ 167	$ 167	$ 167	$ 167	$ 167	$ 167	$ 167	$ 167	$ 167	$ 167	$ 167	$ 167	$ 2,000
Market Research	$ 417	$ 417	$ 417	$ 417	$ 417	$ 417	$ 417	$ 417	$ 417	$ 417	$ 417	$ 417	$ 5,000
Postage	$ 42	$ 42	$ 42	$ 42	$ 42	$ 42	$ 42	$ 42	$ 42	$ 42	$ 42	$ 42	$ 500
Cell Phones	$ 125	$ 125	$ 125	$ 125	$ 125	$ 125	$ 125	$ 125	$ 125	$ 125	$ 125	$ 125	$ 1,500
Legal Fees	$ 833	$ 833	$ 833	$ 833	$ 833	$ 833	$ 833	$ 833	$ 833	$ 833	$ 833	$ 833	$ 10,000
Other Professional Fees	$ 833	$ 833	$ 833	$ 833	$ 833	$ 833	$ 833	$ 833	$ 833	$ 833	$ 833	$ 833	$ 10,000
Website Development	$ 1,667	$ 1,667	$ 1,667	$ 1,667	$ 1,667	$ 1,667	$ 1,667	$ 1,667	$ 1,667	$ 1,667	$ 1,667	$ 1,667	$ 20,000
Dues & Subscriptions	$ 75	$ 75	$ 75	$ 75	$ 75	$ 75	$ 75	$ 75	$ 75	$ 75	$ 75	$ 75	$ 900
Patent Costs	$ 6,667	$ 6,667	$ 6,667	$ 6,667	$ 6,667	$ 6,667	$ 6,667	$ 6,667	$ 6,667	$ 6,667	$ 6,667	$ 6,667	$ 80,000
Computers and Software (SimHydraulics)	$ 1,517	$ 1,517	$ 1,517	$ 1,517	$ 1,517	$ 1,517	$ 1,517	$ 1,517	$ 1,517	$ 1,517	$ 1,517	$ 1,517	$ 18,200
Office Equipment & supplies	$ 583	$ 583	$ 583	$ 583	$ 583	$ 583	$ 583	$ 583	$ 583	$ 583	$ 583	$ 583	$ 7,000
Telephone & Utility Expenses	$ 250	$ 250	$ 250	$ 250	$ 250	$ 250	$ 250	$ 250	$ 250	$ 250	$ 250	$ 250	$ 3,000
Accounting Services	$ 333	$ 333	$ 333	$ 333	$ 333	$ 333	$ 333	$ 333	$ 333	$ 333	$ 333	$ 333	$ 4,000
Miscellaneous	$ 833	$ 833	$ 833	$ 833	$ 833	$ 833	$ 833	$ 833	$ 833	$ 833	$ 833	$ 833	$ 10,000
Total Operating Costs	$ 17,842	$ 17,842	$ 17,842	$ 17,842	$ 17,842	$ 17,842	$ 17,842	$ 17,842	$ 17,842	$ 17,842	$ 17,842	$ 17,842	$ 214,100
Total Costs	$ 193,652	$ 17,842	$ 53,258	$ 61,592	$ 61,592	$ 61,592	$ 69,925	$ 69,925	$ 69,925	$ 69,925	$ 69,925	$ 69,925	$ 904,494
Net Income (EBT)	$ (190,493)	$ -	$ (50,561)	$ (59,016)	$ (59,139)	$ (59,261)	$ (67,718)	$ (67,964)	$ (68,141)	$ (68,265)	$ (68,390)	$ (68,515)	$ (877,903)

Balance Sheet (Year 1):

Balance Sheet	1	2	3	4	5	6	7	8	9	10	11	12	Year 1
Assets													
Current Assets													
Cash	$ 1,667,603	$ 1,575,046	$ 1,524,485	$ 1,467,969	$ 1,408,830	$ 1,349,569	$ 1,284,351	$ 1,216,387	$ 1,148,246	$ 1,079,980	$ 1,011,590	$ 943,075	$ 943,075
Accounts Receivable													
Total Assets	$ 1,667,603	$ 1,575,046	$ 1,524,485	$ 1,467,969	$ 1,408,830	$ 1,349,569	$ 1,284,351	$ 1,216,387	$ 1,148,246	$ 1,079,980	$ 1,011,590	$ 943,075	$ 943,075
Liabilities													
Current Liabilities													
Accounts Payable	$ 58,096	$ 15,978	$ 15,978	$ 18,478	$ 18,478	$ 18,478	$ 20,978	$ 20,978	$ 20,978	$ 20,978	$ 20,978	$ 20,978	$ 20,978
Total Liabilities	$ 58,096	$ 15,978	$ 15,978	$ 18,478	$ 18,478	$ 18,478	$ 20,978	$ 20,978	$ 20,978	$ 20,978	$ 20,978	$ 20,978	$ 20,978
Equity													
Capital stock	$ 1,800,000	$ 1,800,000	$ 1,800,000	$ 1,800,000	$ 1,800,000	$ 1,800,000	$ 1,800,000	$ 1,800,000	$ 1,800,000	$ 1,800,000	$ 1,800,000	$ 1,800,000	$ 1,800,000
Retained Earnings	$ (190,493)	$ (240,932)	$ (291,492)	$ (350,509)	$ (409,647)	$ (468,909)	$ (536,627)	$ (604,591)	$ (672,732)	$ (740,997)	$ (809,387)	$ (877,903)	$ (877,903)
Total Equity	$ 1,609,507	$ 1,559,068	$ 1,508,508	$ 1,449,491	$ 1,390,353	$ 1,331,091	$ 1,263,373	$ 1,195,409	$ 1,127,268	$ 1,059,003	$ 990,613	$ 922,097	$ 922,097
Total Liabilities & Equity	$ 1,667,603	$ 1,575,046	$ 1,524,485	$ 1,467,969	$ 1,408,830	$ 1,349,569	$ 1,284,351	$ 1,216,387	$ 1,148,246	$ 1,079,980	$ 1,011,590	$ 943,075	$ 943,075

Cash Flow (Year 1):

Cash Flow Statement	1	2	3	4	5	6	7	8	9	10	11	12	Year 1
Net Income (Loss)	$ (190,493)	$ (50,439)	$ (50,561)	$ (59,016)	$ (59,139)	$ (59,261)	$ (67,718)	$ (67,964)	$ (68,141)	$ (68,265)	$ (68,390)	$ (68,515)	$ (877,903)
Working Capital Changes:													
Accounts Receivable (Increase)	$ -	$ -	$ -	$ -	$ -	$ -	$ -	$ -	$ -	$ -	$ -	$ -	$ -
Accounts Payable (Increase)	$ 58,096	$ (42,118)	$ 0	$ 2,500	$ 0	$ 2,500	$ 0	$ 0	$ 0	$ 0	$ 0	$ 0	$ 20,978
Cash Used for Operations	$ (132,397)	$ (92,557)	$ (50,561)	$ (56,516)	$ (59,139)	$ (59,261)	$ (65,218)	$ (67,964)	$ (68,141)	$ (68,265)	$ (68,390)	$ (68,515)	$ (856,925)
Cash Used for Investments													
Cash from Financing Activities													
Capital Stock	$ 1,800,000												$ 1,800,000
Change in Cash for Period	$ 1,667,603	$ (92,557)	$ (50,561)	$ (56,516)	$ (59,139)	$ (59,261)	$ (65,218)	$ (67,964)	$ (68,141)	$ (68,265)	$ (68,390)	$ (68,515)	$ 943,075
Cash: Beginning of Period	$ 0	$ 1,667,603	$ 1,575,046	$ 1,524,485	$ 1,467,969	$ 1,408,830	$ 1,349,569	$ 1,284,351	$ 1,216,387	$ 1,148,246	$ 1,079,980	$ 1,011,590	$ 0
Cash: End of Period	$ 1,667,603	$ 1,575,046	$ 1,524,485	$ 1,467,969	$ 1,408,830	$ 1,349,569	$ 1,284,351	$ 1,216,387	$ 1,148,246	$ 1,079,980	$ 1,011,590	$ 943,075	$ 943,075

Income Statement (Year 2):

Income Statement	13	14	15	16	17	18	19	20	21	22	23	24	Year 2
Licensing Revenue													$ -
Interest Revenue	$ 1,210	$ 978	$ 745	$ 13,030	$ 12,815	$ 12,599	$ 12,400	$ 12,208	$ 12,016	$ 11,822	$ 11,629	$ 11,434	$ 112,886
Royalties													
Other Revenue													
Total Revenue	$ 1,210	$ 978	$ 745	$ 13,030	$ 12,815	$ 12,599	$ 12,400	$ 12,208	$ 12,016	$ 11,822	$ 11,629	$ 11,434	$ 112,886
Licensing Expense													
Labor & Related Costs													
Chief Executive Officer	$ 11,458	$ 11,458	$ 11,458	$ 11,458	$ 11,458	$ 11,458	$ 11,458	$ 11,458	$ 11,458	$ 11,458	$ 11,458	$ 11,458	$ 137,500
Adam Johnson, CFO	$ 6,667	$ 6,667	$ 6,667	$ 6,667	$ 6,667	$ 6,667	$ 6,667	$ 6,667	$ 6,667	$ 6,667	$ 6,667	$ 6,667	$ 80,000
Justin Otani, COO	$ 6,667	$ 6,667	$ 6,667	$ 6,667	$ 6,667	$ 6,667	$ 6,667	$ 6,667	$ 6,667	$ 6,667	$ 6,667	$ 6,667	$ 80,000
Chief Technology Officer	$ 9,167	$ 9,167	$ 9,167	$ 9,167	$ 9,167	$ 9,167	$ 9,167	$ 9,167	$ 9,167	$ 9,167	$ 9,167	$ 9,167	$ 110,000
Senior Electrical Engineer	$ 8,333	$ 8,333	$ 8,333	$ 8,333	$ 8,333	$ 8,333	$ 8,333	$ 8,333	$ 8,333	$ 8,333	$ 8,333	$ 8,333	$ 100,000
Senior Control Systems Engineer	$ 8,333	$ 8,333	$ 8,333	$ 8,333	$ 8,333	$ 8,333	$ 8,333	$ 8,333	$ 8,333	$ 8,333	$ 8,333	$ 8,333	$ 100,000
Junior Mechanical Engineer	$ 4,167	$ 4,167	$ 4,167	$ 4,167	$ 4,167	$ 4,167	$ 4,167	$ 4,167	$ 4,167	$ 4,167	$ 4,167	$ 4,167	$ 50,000
Junior Electrical Engineer	$ 4,167	$ 4,167	$ 4,167	$ 4,167	$ 4,167	$ 4,167	$ 4,167	$ 4,167	$ 4,167	$ 4,167	$ 4,167	$ 4,167	$ 50,000
Sales Manager	$ 0	$ 0	$ 0	$ 0	$ 0	$ 0	$ 0	$ 0	$ 5,833	$ 5,833	$ 5,833	$ 5,833	$ 23,333
Sales Manager	$ 0	$ 0	$ 0	$ 0	$ 0	$ 0	$ 0	$ 0	$ 5,833	$ 5,833	$ 5,833	$ 5,833	$ 23,333
Other Salaries	$ 3,500	$ 3,500	$ 3,500	$ 3,500	$ 3,500	$ 3,500	$ 3,500	$ 3,500	$ 3,500	$ 3,500	$ 3,500	$ 3,500	$ 42,000
Total Salaries	$ 62,458	$ 62,458	$ 62,458	$ 62,458	$ 62,458	$ 62,458	$ 62,458	$ 62,458	$ 74,125	$ 74,125	$ 74,125	$ 74,125	$ 796,167
Total IUPUI Expenses	$ 140,394												$ 140,394
Outside Contractors	$ 9,583	$ 9,583	$ 9,583	$ 9,583	$ 9,583	$ 9,583	$ 9,583	$ 9,583	$ 9,583	$ 9,583	$ 9,583	$ 9,583	$ 115,000
Total Supplies for Initial Build							$ 218,354	$ 218,354	$ 218,354	$ 218,354	$ 218,354	$ 218,354	$ 1,310,122
Construction Costs for Initial Build							$ 83,333	$ 83,333	$ 83,333	$ 83,333	$ 83,333	$ 83,333	$ 500,000

(Continued)

Income Statement (Year 2): (Continued)

Income Statement	13	14	15	16	17	18	19	20	21	22	23	24	Year 2
Operating Expenses													
Payroll Processing Fees	$ 250	$ 250	$ 250	$ 250	$ 250	$ 250	$ 250	$ 250	$ 250	$ 250	$ 250	$ 250	$ 3,000
Office Rent	$ 1,250	$ 1,250	$ 1,250	$ 1,250	$ 1,250	$ 1,250	$ 1,250	$ 1,250	$ 1,250	$ 1,250	$ 1,250	$ 1,250	$ 15,000
Fringe Benefits	$ 1,000	$ 1,000	$ 1,000	$ 1,000	$ 1,000	$ 1,000	$ 1,000	$ 1,000	$ 1,000	$ 1,000	$ 1,000	$ 1,000	$ 12,000
Travel - Related Expenses	$ 2,875	$ 2,875	$ 2,875	$ 2,875	$ 2,875	$ 2,875	$ 2,875	$ 2,875	$ 2,875	$ 2,875	$ 2,875	$ 2,875	$ 34,500
Trade Shows	$ 383	$ 383	$ 383	$ 383	$ 383	$ 383	$ 383	$ 383	$ 383	$ 383	$ 383	$ 383	$ 4,600
Brochures & Publications	$ 192	$ 192	$ 192	$ 192	$ 192	$ 192	$ 192	$ 192	$ 192	$ 192	$ 192	$ 192	$ 2,300
Market Research	$ 479	$ 479	$ 479	$ 479	$ 479	$ 479	$ 479	$ 479	$ 479	$ 479	$ 479	$ 479	$ 5,750
Postage	$ 48	$ 48	$ 48	$ 48	$ 48	$ 48	$ 48	$ 48	$ 48	$ 48	$ 48	$ 48	$ 575
Cell Phones	$ 144	$ 144	$ 144	$ 144	$ 144	$ 144	$ 144	$ 144	$ 144	$ 144	$ 144	$ 144	$ 1,725
Legal Fees	$ 958	$ 958	$ 958	$ 958	$ 958	$ 958	$ 958	$ 958	$ 958	$ 958	$ 958	$ 958	$ 11,500
Other Professional Fees	$ 958	$ 958	$ 958	$ 958	$ 958	$ 958	$ 958	$ 958	$ 958	$ 958	$ 958	$ 958	$ 11,500
Website Development	$ 125	$ 125	$ 125	$ 125	$ 125	$ 125	$ 125	$ 125	$ 125	$ 125	$ 125	$ 125	$ 1,500
Dues & Subscriptions	$ 86	$ 86	$ 86	$ 86	$ 86	$ 86	$ 86	$ 86	$ 86	$ 86	$ 86	$ 86	$ 1,035
Patent Costs	$ 1,250	$ 1,250	$ 1,250	$ 1,250	$ 1,250	$ 1,250	$ 1,250	$ 1,250	$ 1,250	$ 1,250	$ 1,250	$ 1,250	$ 15,000
Computers and Software (SimHydraulics)	$ 1,150	$ 1,150	$ 1,150	$ 1,150	$ 1,150	$ 1,150	$ 1,150	$ 1,150	$ 1,150	$ 1,150	$ 1,150	$ 1,150	$ 13,800
Office Equipment & Supplies	$ 671	$ 671	$ 671	$ 671	$ 671	$ 671	$ 671	$ 671	$ 671	$ 671	$ 671	$ 671	$ 8,050
Telephone & Utility Expenses	$ 288	$ 288	$ 288	$ 288	$ 288	$ 288	$ 288	$ 288	$ 288	$ 288	$ 288	$ 288	$ 3,450
Accounting Services	$ 383	$ 383	$ 383	$ 383	$ 383	$ 383	$ 383	$ 383	$ 383	$ 383	$ 383	$ 383	$ 4,600
Miscellaneous	$ 958	$ 958	$ 958	$ 958	$ 958	$ 958	$ 958	$ 958	$ 958	$ 958	$ 958	$ 958	$ 11,500
Total Operating Costs	$ 13,449	$ 13,449	$ 13,449	$ 13,449	$ 13,449	$ 13,449	$ 13,449	$ 13,449	$ 13,449	$ 13,449	$ 13,449	$ 13,449	$ 161,385
Total Costs	$ 225,884	$ 85,490	$ 85,490	$ 85,490	$ 85,490	$ 85,490	$ 387,177	$ 387,177	$ 398,844	$ 398,844	$ 398,844	$ 398,844	$ 3,023,067
Net Income (EBT)	$ (224,674)	$ (84,513)	$ (84,746)	$ (72,460)	$ (72,675)	$ (72,891)	$ (374,777)	$ (374,969)	$ (386,828)	$ (387,022)	$ (387,215)	$ (387,410)	$ (2,910,181)

Balance Sheet (Year 2):

Balance Sheet	13	14	15	16	17	18	19	20	21	22	23	24	Year 2
Assets													
Current Assets													
Cash	$ 765,188	$ 638,557	$ 553,812	4,481,351	4,408,676	$ 4,335,785	4,051,514	3,676,545	3,293,216	2,906,195	2,518,979	$ 2,131,570	$ 2,131,570
Accounts Receivable						$ -	$ -	$ -	$ -	$ -	$ -	$ -	$ -
Total Assets	$ 765,188	$ 638,557	$ 553,812	4,481,351	4,408,676	$ 4,335,785	4,051,514	3,676,545	3,293,216	2,906,195	2,518,979	$ 2,131,570	$ 2,131,570
Liabilities													
Current Liabilities													
Accounts Payable	$ 67,765	$ 25,647	25,647	25,647	25,647	$ 25,647	116,153	116,153	119,653	119,653	119,653	$ 119,653	119,653
Total Liabilities	$ 67,765	$ 25,647	25,647	25,647	25,647	$ 25,647	116,153	116,153	119,653	119,653	119,653	$ 119,653	119,653
Equity													
Capital Stock	$ 1,800,000	1,800,000	5,800,000	5,800,000	5,800,000	5,800,000	5,800,000	5,800,000	5,800,000	5,800,000	5,800,000	5,800,000	5,800,000
Retained Earnings	$(1,102,577)	$(1,187,090)	$(1,271,835)	$(1,344,296)	$(1,416,971)	$(1,489,862)	$(1,864,640)	$(2,239,609)	$(2,626,437)	$(3,013,459)	$(3,400,674)	$(3,788,083)	$(3,788,083)
Total Equity	$ 697,423	$ 612,910	4,528,165	4,455,704	4,383,029	$ 4,310,138	3,935,360	3,560,391	3,173,563	2,786,541	2,399,326	$ 2,011,917	2,011,917
Total Liabilities & Equity	$ 765,188	$ 638,557	4,553,812	4,481,351	4,408,676	$ 4,335,785	4,051,514	3,676,545	3,293,216	2,906,195	2,518,979	$ 2,131,570	2,131,570

Cash Flow (Year 2):

Cash Flow Statement	13	14	15	16	17	18	19	20	21	22	23	24	Year 2
Net Income (Loss)	$ (224,674)	$ (84,513)	$ (84,746)	$ (72,460)	$ (72,675)	$ (72,891)	$ (374,777)	$ (374,969)	$ (386,828)	$ (387,022)	$ (387,215)	$ (387,410)	$ (2,910,181)
Working Capital Changes:													
Accounts Receivable (Increase)	$ -	$ -	-	-	$ -	$ -	$ -	$ -	$ -	$ -	$ -	$ -	-
Accounts Payable (Increase)	$ 46,788	($42,118)	$ 0	0	$ 0	$ 0	$ 90,506	$ 0	$ 3,500	$ 0	$ 0	$ 0	98,676
Cash Used for Operations	$ (177,886)	$ (126,631)	$ (84,746)	$ (72,460)	$ (72,675)	$ (72,891)	$ (284,271)	$ (374,969)	$ (383,328)	$ (387,022)	$ (387,215)	$ (387,410)	$ (2,811,505)
Cash Used for Investments													
Cash from Financing Activities													
Capital Stock				$ 4,000,000									
Change in Cash for Period	$ (177,886)	$ (126,631)	$ (84,746)	$ 3,927,540	$ (72,675)	$ (72,891)	$ (284,271)	$ (374,969)	$ (383,328)	$ (387,022)	$ (387,215)	$ (387,410)	$ (2,811,505)
Cash: Beginning of Period	$ 943,075	$ 765,188	$ 638,557	$ 553,812	$ 4,481,351	$ 4,408,676	$ 4,335,785	$ 4,051,514	$ 3,676,545	$ 3,293,216	$ 2,906,195	$ 2,518,979	$ 943,075
Cash: End of Period	$ 765,188	$ 638,557	$ 553,812	$ 4,481,351	$ 4,408,676	$ 4,335,785	$ 4,051,514	$ 3,676,545	$ 3,293,216	$ 2,906,195	$ 2,518,979	$ 2,131,570	$ 2,131,570

Income Statement (Year 3):

Income Statement	25	26	27	28	29	30	31	32	33	34	35	36	Year 3
Licensing Revenue	$ 500,000												$ 500,000
Interest Revenue	$ 11,228	11,016	10,803	10,590	10,375	10,161	$ 9,945	9,729	9,512	9,294	9,076	$ 8,857	$ 120,586
Royalties	$ 125,000	125,000	125,000	125,000	125,000	125,000	$ 250,000	250,000	250,000	250,000	250,000	$ 250,000	$ 2,250,000
Other Revenue													
Total Revenue	$ 636,228	136,016	135,803	135,590	135,375	135,161	$ 259,945	259,729	259,512	259,294	259,076	$ 258,857	$ 2,870,586
Licensing Expense	$ 62,500	62,500	62,500	62,500	62,500	62,500	$ 125,000	125,000	125,000	125,000	125,000	$ 125,000	$ 1,125,000
Labor & Related Costs													
Chief Executive Officer	$ 12,604	12,604	12,604	12,604	12,604	12,604	$ 12,604	12,604	12,604	12,604	12,604	$ 12,604	$ 151,250
Adam Johnson, CFO	$ 7,333	7,333	7,333	7,333	7,333	7,333	$ 7,333	7,333	7,333	7,333	7,333	$ 7,333	$ 88,000
Justin Otani, COO	$ 7,333	7,333	7,333	7,333	7,333	7,333	$ 7,333	7,333	7,333	7,333	7,333	$ 7,333	$ 88,000
Chief Technology Officer	$ 10,083	10,083	10,083	10,083	10,083	10,083	$ 10,083	10,083	10,083	10,083	10,083	$ 10,083	$ 121,000
Senior Electrical Engineer	$ 9,167	9,167	9,167	9,167	9,167	9,167	$ 9,167	9,167	9,167	9,167	9,167	$ 9,167	$ 110,000
Senior Control Systems Engineer	$ 9,167	9,167	9,167	9,167	9,167	9,167	$ 9,167	9,167	9,167	9,167	9,167	$ 9,167	$ 110,000
Junior Mechanical Engineer	$ 4,583	4,583	4,583	4,583	4,583	4,583	$ 4,583	4,583	4,583	4,583	4,583	$ 4,583	$ 55,000
Junior Electrical Engineer	$ 4,583	4,583	4,583	4,583	4,583	4,583	$ 4,583	4,583	4,583	4,583	4,583	$ 4,583	$ 55,000
Sales Manager	$ 5,833	5,833	5,833	5,833	5,833	5,833	$ 5,833	5,833	5,833	5,833	5,833	$ 5,833	$ 70,000
Sales Manager	$ 5,833	5,833	5,833	5,833	5,833	5,833	$ 5,833	5,833	5,833	5,833	5,833	$ 5,833	$ 70,000
Other Salaries	$ 11,900	11,900	11,900	11,900	11,900	11,900	$ 11,900	11,900	11,900	11,900	11,900	$ 11,900	$ 142,800
Total Salaries	$ 88,421	88,421	88,421	88,421	88,421	88,421	$ 88,421	88,421	88,421	88,421	88,421	$ 88,421	$ 1,061,050
Total IUPUI Expenses													
Outside Contractors	$ 11,021	11,021	11,021	11,021	11,021	11,021	$ 11,021	11,021	11,021	11,021	11,021	$ 11,021	$ 132,250
Total Supplies for Initial Build	$ 218,354	218,354	218,354	218,354	218,354	218,354	$ 41,667	41,667	41,667	41,667	41,667	$ 41,667	$ 1,560,124
Construction Costs for Initial Build	$ 83,333	83,333	83,333	83,333	83,333	83,333							$ 500,000

(Continued)

Income Statement (Year 3): *(Continued)*

APPENDIX 12A   Hydraulic Wind Power, LLC

Income Statement	25	26	27	28	29	30	31	32	33	34	35	36	Year 3
Operating Expenses													
Payroll Processing Fees	$ 250	$ 250	$ 250	$ 250	$ 250	$ 250	$ 250	$ 250	$ 250	$ 250	$ 250	$ 250	$ 3,000
Office Rent	$ 1,313	$ 1,313	$ 1,313	$ 1,313	$ 1,313	$ 1,313	$ 1,313	$ 1,313	$ 1,313	$ 1,313	$ 1,313	$ 1,313	$ 15,750
Fringe Benefits	$ 1,350	$ 1,350	$ 1,350	$ 1,350	$ 1,350	$ 1,350	$ 1,350	$ 1,350	$ 1,350	$ 1,350	$ 1,350	$ 1,350	$ 16,200
Travel - Related Expenses	$ 3,306	$ 3,306	$ 3,306	$ 3,306	$ 3,306	$ 3,306	$ 3,306	$ 3,306	$ 3,306	$ 3,306	$ 3,306	$ 3,306	$ 39,675
Trade Shows	$ 441	$ 441	$ 441	$ 441	$ 441	$ 441	$ 441	$ 441	$ 441	$ 441	$ 441	$ 441	$ 5,290
Brochures & Publications	$ 220	$ 220	$ 220	$ 220	$ 220	$ 220	$ 220	$ 220	$ 220	$ 220	$ 220	$ 220	$ 2,645
Market Research	$ 551	$ 551	$ 551	$ 551	$ 551	$ 551	$ 551	$ 551	$ 551	$ 551	$ 551	$ 551	$ 6,613
Postage	$ 55	$ 55	$ 55	$ 55	$ 55	$ 55	$ 55	$ 55	$ 55	$ 55	$ 55	$ 55	$ 661
Cell Phones	$ 165	$ 165	$ 165	$ 165	$ 165	$ 165	$ 165	$ 165	$ 165	$ 165	$ 165	$ 165	$ 1,984
Legal Fees	$ 1,102	$ 1,102	$ 1,102	$ 1,102	$ 1,102	$ 1,102	$ 1,102	$ 1,102	$ 1,102	$ 1,102	$ 1,102	$ 1,102	$ 13,225
Other Professional Fees	$ 1,102	$ 1,102	$ 1,102	$ 1,102	$ 1,102	$ 1,102	$ 1,102	$ 1,102	$ 1,102	$ 1,102	$ 1,102	$ 1,102	$ 13,225
Website Development	$ 125	$ 125	$ 125	$ 125	$ 125	$ 125	$ 125	$ 125	$ 125	$ 125	$ 125	$ 125	$ 1,500
Dues & Subscriptions	$ 99	$ 99	$ 99	$ 99	$ 99	$ 99	$ 99	$ 99	$ 99	$ 99	$ 99	$ 99	$ 1,190
Patent Costs	$ 2,500	$ 2,500	$ 2,500	$ 2,500	$ 2,500	$ 2,500	$ 2,500	$ 2,500	$ 2,500	$ 2,500	$ 2,500	$ 2,500	$ 30,000
Computers and Software (SimHydraulics)	$ 1,667	$ 1,667	$ 1,667	$ 1,667	$ 1,667	$ 1,667	$ 1,667	$ 1,667	$ 1,667	$ 1,667	$ 1,667	$ 1,667	$ 20,000
Office Equipment & Supplies	$ 771	$ 771	$ 771	$ 771	$ 771	$ 771	$ 771	$ 771	$ 771	$ 771	$ 771	$ 771	$ 9,258
Telephone & Utility Expenses	$ 331	$ 331	$ 331	$ 331	$ 331	$ 331	$ 331	$ 331	$ 331	$ 331	$ 331	$ 331	$ 3,968
Accounting Services	$ 441	$ 441	$ 441	$ 441	$ 441	$ 441	$ 441	$ 441	$ 441	$ 441	$ 441	$ 441	$ 5,290
Miscellaneous	$ 1,102	$ 1,102	$ 1,102	$ 1,102	$ 1,102	$ 1,102	$ 1,102	$ 1,102	$ 1,102	$ 1,102	$ 1,102	$ 1,102	$ 13,225
Total Operating Costs	$ 16,891	$ 16,891	$ 16,891	$ 16,891	$ 16,891	$ 16,891	$ 16,891	$ 16,891	$ 16,891	$ 16,891	$ 16,891	$ 16,891	$ 202,698
Total Costs	$ 480,520	$ 480,520	$ 480,520	$ 480,520	$ 480,520	$ 480,520	$ 283,000	$ 283,000	$ 283,000	$ 283,000	$ 283,000	$ 283,000	$ 4,581,121
Net Income (EBT)	$ 155,708	$ (344,504)	$ (344,717)	$ (344,930)	$ (345,145)	$ (345,359)	$ (23,055)	$ (23,271)	$ (23,488)	$ (23,706)	$ (23,924)	$ (24,143)	$ (1,710,535)

Balance Sheet (Year 3):

Balance Sheet	25	26	27	28	29	30	31	32	33	34	35	36	Year 3
Assets													
Current Assets													
Cash	$ 2,461,780	$ 1,967,276	$ 1,622,559	$ 1,277,629	$ 932,484	$ 587,125	$ 504,814	$ 481,543	$ 458,054	$ 434,349	$ 410,425	$ 386,282	
Accounts Receivable	$ 150,000												$ -
Total Assets	$ 2,611,780	$ 1,967,276	$ 1,622,559	$ 1,277,629	$ 932,484	$ 587,125	$ 504,814	$ 481,543	$ 458,054	$ 434,349	$ 410,425	$ 386,282	
Liabilities													
Current Liabilities													
Accounts Payable	$ 144,156	144,156	144,156	144,156	144,156	144,156	84,900	84,900	84,900	84,900	84,900	84,900	
Total Liabilities	$ 144,156	144,156	144,156	144,156	144,156	144,156	84,900	84,900	84,900	84,900	84,900	84,900	
Equity													
Capital Stock	$ 5,800,000	$ 5,800,000	$ 5,800,000	$ 5,800,000	$ 5,800,000	$ 5,800,000	$ 5,800,000	$ 5,800,000	$ 5,800,000	$ 5,800,000	$ 5,800,000	$ 5,800,000	
Retained Earnings	$(3,632,376)	$(3,976,880)	$(4,321,597)	$(4,666,527)	$(5,011,672)	$(5,357,031)	$(5,380,086)	$(5,403,358)	$(5,426,846)	$(5,450,551)	$(5,474,475)	$(5,498,618)	
Total Equity	$ 2,167,624	$ 1,823,120	$ 1,478,403	$ 1,133,473	$ 788,328	$ 442,969	$ 419,914	$ 396,642	$ 373,154	$ 349,449	$ 325,525	$ 301,382	
Total Liabilities & Equity	$ 2,311,780	$ 1,967,276	$ 1,622,559	$ 1,277,629	$ 932,484	$ 587,125	$ 504,814	$ 481,543	$ 458,054	$ 434,349	$ 410,425	$ 386,282	

Cash Flow (Year 3):

Cash Flow Statement	25	26	27	28	29	30	31	32	33	34	35	36	Year 3
Net Income (Loss)	$ 155,708	$ (344,504)	$ (344,717)	$ (344,930)	$ (345,145)	$ (345,359)	$ (23,055)	$ (23,271)	$ (23,488)	$ (23,706)	$ (23,924)	$ (24,143)	$ (1,710,535)
Working Capital Changes:													
Accounts Receivable (Increase)	$ 150,000	$ (150,000)	- $	- $	- $	- $	- $	- $	- $	- $	- $	- $	- $
Accounts Payable (Increase)	$ 24,503	0 $	0 $	0 $	0 $	0 $	$ (59,256)	0 $	0 $	0 $	0 $	0 $	$ (34,753)
Cash Used for Operations	$ 330,211	$ (494,504)	$ (344,717)	$ (344,930)	$ (345,145)	$ (345,359)	$ (82,311)	$ (23,271)	$ (23,488)	$ (23,706)	$ (23,924)	$ (24,143)	$ (1,745,288)
Cash Used for Investments													
Cash from Financing Activities													
Capital Stock													
Change in Cash for Period	$ 330,211	$ (494,504)	$ (344,717)	$ (344,930)	$ (345,145)	$(345,359)	$ (82,311)	$ (23,271)	$ (23,488)	$ (23,706)	$ (23,924)	$ (24,143)	$ (1,745,288)
Cash: Beginning of Period	$ 2,131,570	$ 2,461,780	$ 1,967,276	$ 1,622,559	$1,277,629	$ 932,484	$ 587,125	$ 504,814	$ 481,543	$ 458,054	$ 434,349	$ 410,425	$ 2,131,570
Cash: End of Period	$ 2,461,780	$ 1,967,276	$ 1,622,559	$ 1,277,629	$ 932,484	$ 587,125	$ 504,814	$ 481,543	$ 458,054	$ 434,349	$ 410,425	$ 386,282	$ 386,282

Income Statement (Year 4):

Income Statement	37	38	39	40	41	42	43	44	45	46	47	48	Year 4
Licensing Revenue	$1,000,000												$ 1,000,000
Interest Revenue	$ 8,661.32	$8,474.94	$8,287.78	$8,099.83	$ 7,911.08	$ 7,721.55	$ 7,531.22	$ 7,340.10	$ 7,148.46	$ 6,956.82	$ 6,765.19	$ 6,573.55	$ 91,471.83
Royalties	$ 500,000	$ 500,000	$ 500,000	$ 750,000	$ 750,000	$ 750,000	$ 1,000,000	$ 1,000,000	$ 1,000,000	$ 1,250,000	$ 1,250,000	$ 1,250,000	$ 10,500,000
Other Revenue													
Total Revenue	$1,508,661	$ 508,475	$ 508,288	$ 758,100	$ 757,911	$ 757,722	$1,007,531	$1,007,340	$1,007,148	$ 1,256,957	$ 1,256,765	$ 1,256,574	$ 11,591,472
Licensing Expense	$ 250,000	$ 250,000	$ 250,000	$ 375,000	$ 375,000	$ 375,000	$ 500,000	$ 500,000	$ 500,000	$ 625,000	$ 625,000	$ 625,000	$ 5,250,000
Labor & Related Costs													
Chief Executive Officer	$ 13,865	$ 13,865	$ 13,865	$ 13,865	$ 13,865	$ 13,865	$ 13,865	$ 13,865	$ 13,865	$ 13,865	$ 13,865	$ 13,865	166,375
Adam Johnson, CFO	$ 8,067	$ 8,067	$ 8,067	$ 8,067	$ 8,067	$ 8,067	$ 8,067	$ 8,067	$ 8,067	$ 8,067	$ 8,067	$ 8,067	96,800
Justin Otani, COO	$ 8,067	$ 8,067	$ 8,067	$ 8,067	$ 8,067	$ 8,067	$ 8,067	$ 8,067	$ 8,067	$ 8,067	$ 8,067	$ 8,067	96,800
Chief Technology Officer	$ 11,092	$ 11,092	$ 11,092	$ 11,092	$ 11,092	$ 11,092	$ 11,092	$ 11,092	$ 11,092	$ 11,092	$ 11,092	$ 11,092	133,100
Senior Electrical Engineer	$ 10,083	$ 10,083	$ 10,083	$ 10,083	$ 10,083	$ 10,083	$ 10,083	$ 10,083	$ 10,083	$ 10,083	$ 10,083	$ 10,083	121,000
Senior Control Systems Engineer	$ 10,083	$ 10,083	$ 10,083	$ 10,083	$ 10,083	$ 10,083	$ 10,083	$ 10,083	$ 10,083	$ 10,083	$ 10,083	$ 10,083	121,000
Junior Mechanical Engineer	$ 5,042	$ 5,042	$ 5,042	$ 5,042	$ 5,042	$ 5,042	$ 5,042	$ 5,042	$ 5,042	$ 5,042	$ 5,042	$ 5,042	60,500
Junior Electrical Engineer	$ 5,042	$ 5,042	$ 5,042	$ 5,042	$ 5,042	$ 5,042	$ 5,042	$ 5,042	$ 5,042	$ 5,042	$ 5,042	$ 5,042	60,500
Sales Manager	$ 6,417	$ 6,417	$ 6,417	$ 6,417	$ 6,417	$ 6,417	$ 6,417	$ 6,417	$ 6,417	$ 6,417	$ 6,417	$ 6,417	77,000
Sales Manager	$ 6,417	$ 6,417	$ 6,417	$ 6,417	$ 6,417	$ 6,417	$ 6,417	$ 6,417	$ 6,417	$ 6,417	$ 6,417	$ 6,417	77,000
Other Salaries	$ 40,460	$ 40,460	$ 40,460	$ 40,460	$ 40,460	$ 40,460	$ 40,460	$ 40,460	$ 40,460	$ 40,460	$ 40,460	$ 40,460	485,520
Total Salaries	$ 124,633	$ 124,633	$ 124,633	$ 124,633	$ 124,633	$ 124,633	$ 124,633	$ 124,633	$ 124,633	$ 124,633	$ 124,633	$ 124,633	1,495,595
Total IUPUI Expenses													
Outside Contractors	$ 12,674	$ 12,674	$ 12,674	$ 12,674	$ 12,674	$ 12,674	$ 12,674	$ 12,674	$ 12,674	$ 12,674	$ 12,674	$ 12,674	152,088
Total Supplies for Initial Build	$ 41,667	$ 41,667	$ 41,667	$ 41,667	$ 41,667	$ 41,667	$ 20,833	$ 20,833	$ 20,833	$ 20,833	$ 20,833	$ 20,833	375,000
Construction Costs for Initial Build													

(Continued)

Income Statement (Year 4): *(Continued)*

Income Statement	37	38	39	40	41	42	43	44	45	46	47	48	Year 4
Operating Expenses													
Payroll Processing Fees	$ 250	$ 250	$ 250	$ 250	$ 250	$ 250	$ 250	$ 250	$ 250	$ 250	$ 250	$ 250	$ 3,000
Office Rent	$ 1,313	$ 1,313	$ 1,313	$ 1,313	$ 1,313	$ 1,313	$ 1,313	$ 1,313	$ 1,313	$ 1,313	$ 1,313	$ 1,313	$ 15,750
Fringe Benefits	$ 1,823	$ 1,823	$ 1,823	$ 1,823	$ 1,823	$ 1,823	$ 1,823	$ 1,823	$ 1,823	$ 1,823	$ 1,823	$ 1,823	$ 21,870
Travel - Related Expenses	$ 3,802	$ 3,802	$ 3,802	$ 3,802	$ 3,802	$ 3,802	$ 3,802	$ 3,802	$ 3,802	$ 3,802	$ 3,802	$ 3,802	$ 45,626
Trade Shows	$ 507	$ 507	$ 507	$ 507	$ 507	$ 507	$ 507	$ 507	$ 507	$ 507	$ 507	$ 507	$ 6,084
Brochures & Publications	$ 253	$ 253	$ 253	$ 253	$ 253	$ 253	$ 253	$ 253	$ 253	$ 253	$ 253	$ 253	$ 3,042
Market Research	$ 634	$ 634	$ 634	$ 634	$ 634	$ 634	$ 634	$ 634	$ 634	$ 634	$ 634	$ 634	$ 7,604
Postage	$ 63	$ 63	$ 63	$ 63	$ 63	$ 63	$ 63	$ 63	$ 63	$ 63	$ 63	$ 63	$ 760
Cell Phones	$ 190	$ 190	$ 190	$ 190	$ 190	$ 190	$ 190	$ 190	$ 190	$ 190	$ 190	$ 190	$ 2,281
Legal Fees	$ 1,267	$ 1,267	$ 1,267	$ 1,267	$ 1,267	$ 1,267	$ 1,267	$ 1,267	$ 1,267	$ 1,267	$ 1,267	$ 1,267	$ 15,209
Other Professional Fees	$ 1,267	$ 1,267	$ 1,267	$ 1,267	$ 1,267	$ 1,267	$ 1,267	$ 1,267	$ 1,267	$ 1,267	$ 1,267	$ 1,267	$ 15,209
Website Development	$ 125	$ 125	$ 125	$ 125	$ 125	$ 125	$ 125	$ 125	$ 125	$ 125	$ 125	$ 125	$ 1,500
Dues & Subscriptions	$ 114	$ 114	$ 114	$ 114	$ 114	$ 114	$ 114	$ 114	$ 114	$ 114	$ 114	$ 114	$ 1,369
Patent Costs	$ 8,333	$ 8,333	$ 8,333	$ 8,333	$ 8,333	$ 8,333	$ 8,333	$ 8,333	$ 8,333	$ 8,333	$ 8,333	$ 8,333	$ 100,000
Computers and Software (SimHydraulics)	$ 2,083	$ 2,083	$ 2,083	$ 2,083	$ 2,083	$ 2,083	$ 2,083	$ 2,083	$ 2,083	$ 2,083	$ 2,083	$ 2,083	$ 25,000
Office Equipment & Supplies	$ 887	$ 887	$ 887	$ 887	$ 887	$ 887	$ 887	$ 887	$ 887	$ 887	$ 887	$ 887	$ 10,646
Telephone & Utility Expenses	$ 380	$ 380	$ 380	$ 380	$ 380	$ 380	$ 380	$ 380	$ 380	$ 380	$ 380	$ 380	$ 4,563
Accounting Services	$ 507	$ 507	$ 507	$ 507	$ 507	$ 507	$ 507	$ 507	$ 507	$ 507	$ 507	$ 507	$ 6,084
Miscellaneous	$ 1,267	$ 1,267	$ 1,267	$ 1,267	$ 1,267	$ 1,267	$ 1,267	$ 1,267	$ 1,267	$ 1,267	$ 1,267	$ 1,267	$ 15,209
Total Operating Costs	$ 25,067	$ 25,067	$ 25,067	$ 25,067	$ 25,067	$ 25,067	$ 25,067	$ 25,067	$ 25,067	$ 25,067	$ 25,067	$ 25,067	$ 300,805
Total Costs	$ 1,054,620	$ 454,041	$ 454,041	$ 579,041	$ 579,041	$ 579,041	$ 683,207	$ 683,207	$ 683,207	$ 808,207	$ 808,207	$ 808,207	$ 7,573,487
Net Income (EBT)		$ 54,434	$ 54,247	$ 179,059	$ 178,870	$ 178,681	$ 324,324	$ 324,133	$ 323,942	$ 448,750	$ 448,558	$ 448,367	$ 4,017,984

Balance Sheet (Year 4):

Balance Sheet	37	38	39	40	41	42	43	44	45	46	47	48	Year 4
Assets													
Current Assets													
Cash	$ 1,792,214	$ 1,546,648	$ 1,600,895	$ 1,817,454	$ 1,996,324	$ 2,175,005	$ 2,530,579	$ 2,854,712	$ 3,178,653	$ 3,664,903	$ 4,113,461	$ 4,561,828	$ 4,561,828
Accounts Receivable	$ 300,000											$ -	$ -
Total Assets	$ 2,092,214	$ 1,546,648	$ 1,600,895	$ 1,817,454	$ 1,996,324	$ 2,175,005	$ 2,530,579	$ 2,854,712	$ 3,178,653	$ 3,664,903	$ 4,113,461	$ 4,561,828	$ 4,561,828
Liabilities													
Current Liabilities													
Accounts Payable	$ 136,212	$ 136,212	$ 136,212	$ 173,712	$ 173,712	$ 173,712	$ 204,962	$ 204,962	$ 204,962	$ 242,462	$ 242,462	$ 242,462	$ 242,462
Total Liabilities	$ 136,212	$ 136,212	$ 136,212	$ 173,712	$ 173,712	$ 173,712	$ 204,962	$ 204,962	$ 204,962	$ 242,462	$ 242,462	$ 242,462	$ 242,462
Equity													
Capital Stock	$ 5,800,000	$ 5,800,000	$ 5,800,000	$ 5,800,000	$ 5,800,000	$ 5,800,000	$ 5,800,000	$ 5,800,000	$ 5,800,000	$ 5,800,000	$ 5,800,000	$ 5,800,000	$ 5,800,000
Retained Earnings	$(4,443,998)	$(4,389,564)	$(4,335,317)	$(4,156,258)	$(3,977,388)	$(3,798,708)	$(3,474,383)	$(3,150,250)	$(2,826,309)	$(2,377,559)	$(1,929,001)	$(1,480,634)	$(1,480,634)
Total Equity	$ 1,356,002	$ 1,410,436	$ 1,464,683	$ 1,643,742	$ 1,822,612	$ 2,001,292	$ 2,325,617	$ 2,649,750	$ 2,973,691	$ 3,422,441	$ 3,870,999	$ 4,319,366	$ 4,319,366
Total Liabilities & Equity	$ 1,492,214	$ 1,546,648	$ 1,600,895	$ 1,817,454	$ 1,996,324	$ 2,175,005	$ 2,530,579	$ 2,854,712	$ 3,178,653	$ 3,664,903	$ 4,113,461	$ 4,561,828	$ 4,561,828

Cash Flow (Year 4):

Cash Flow Statement	37	38	39	40	41	42	43	44	45	46	47	48	Year 4
Net Income (Loss)	$1,054,620	$ 54,434	$ 54,247	$ 179,059	$ 178,870	$ 178,681	$ 324,324	$ 324,133	$ 323,942	$ 448,750	$ 448,558	$ 448,367	$ 4,017,984
Working Capital Changes:													
Accounts Receivable (Increase)	$ 300,000	$ (300,000)	$ -	$ -	$ -	$ -	$ -	$ -	$ -	$ -	$ -	$ -	$ -
Accounts Payable (Increase)	$ 51,312	$ -	$ -	$ 37,500	$ -	$ -	$ 31,250	$ -	$ -	$ 37,500	$ -	$ -	$ 157,562
Cash Used for Operations	$1,405,933	$ (245,566)	$ 54,247	$ 216,559	$ 178,870	$ 178,681	$ 355,574	$ 324,133	$ 323,942	$ 486,250	$ 448,558	$ 448,367	$ 4,175,546
Cash Used for Investments													
Cash from Financing Activities													
Capital Stock													
Change in Cash for Period	$1,405,933	$ (245,566)	$ 54,247	$ 216,559	$ 178,870	$ 178,681	$ 355,574	$ 324,133	$ 323,942	$ 486,250	$ 448,558	$ 448,367	$ 4,175,546
Cash: Beginning of Period	$ 386,282	$1,792,214	$1,546,648	$1,600,895	$1,817,454	$1,996,324	$2,175,005	$2,530,579	$2,854,712	$3,178,653	$3,664,903	$4,113,461	$ 386,282
Cash End of Period	$1,792,214	$1,546,648	$1,600,895	$1,817,454	$1,996,324	$2,175,005	$2,530,579	$2,854,712	$3,178,653	$3,664,903	$4,113,461	$4,561,828	$4,561,828

Income Statement (Year 5):

Income Statement	49	50	51	52	53	54	55	56	57	58	59	60	Year 5
Licensing Revenue	$ 3,000,000												$ 3,000,000
Interest Revenue	$ 6,393	$ 6,217	$ 6,041	$ 5,865	$ 5,689	$ 5,513	$ 5,337	$ 5,161	$ 4,984	$ 4,808	$ 4,632	$ 4,456	$ 65,095
Royalties	$ 1,750,000	$ 1,750,000	$ 1,750,000	$ 2,250,000	$ 2,250,000	$ 2,250,000	$ 2,750,000	$ 2,750,000	$ 2,750,000	$ 3,250,000	$ 3,250,000	$ 3,250,000	$ 30,000,000
Other Revenue													
Total Revenue	$ 4,756,393	$ 1,756,217	$ 1,756,041	$ 2,255,865	$ 2,255,689	$ 2,255,513	$ 2,755,337	$ 2,755,161	$ 2,754,984	$ 3,254,808	$ 3,254,632	$ 3,254,456	$ 33,065,095
Licensing Expense	$ 875,000	$ 875,000	$ 875,000	$ 1,125,000	$ 1,125,000	$ 1,125,000	$ 1,375,000	$ 1,375,000	$ 1,375,000	$ 1,625,000	$ 1,625,000	$ 1,625,000	$ 15,000,000
Labor & Related Costs													
Chief Executive Officer	$ 15,251	$ 15,251	$ 15,251	$ 15,251	$ 15,251	$ 15,251	$ 15,251	$ 15,251	$ 15,251	$ 15,251	$ 15,251	$ 15,251	$ 183,013
Adam Johnson, CFO	$ 8,873	$ 8,873	$ 8,873	$ 8,873	$ 8,873	$ 8,873	$ 8,873	$ 8,873	$ 8,873	$ 8,873	$ 8,873	$ 8,873	$ 106,480
Justin Otani, COO	$ 8,873	$ 8,873	$ 8,873	$ 8,873	$ 8,873	$ 8,873	$ 8,873	$ 8,873	$ 8,873	$ 8,873	$ 8,873	$ 8,873	$ 106,480
Chief Technology Officer	$ 11,092	$ 11,092	$ 11,092	$ 11,092	$ 11,092	$ 11,092	$ 11,092	$ 11,092	$ 11,092	$ 11,092	$ 11,092	$ 11,092	$ 133,100
Senior Electrical Engineer	$ 10,083	$ 10,083	$ 10,083	$ 10,083	$ 10,083	$ 10,083	$ 10,083	$ 10,083	$ 10,083	$ 10,083	$ 10,083	$ 10,083	$ 121,000
Senior Control Systems Engineer	$ 10,083	$ 10,083	$ 10,083	$ 10,083	$ 10,083	$ 10,083	$ 10,083	$ 10,083	$ 10,083	$ 10,083	$ 10,083	$ 10,083	$ 121,000
Junior Mechanical Engineer	$ 5,546	$ 5,546	$ 5,546	$ 5,546	$ 5,546	$ 5,546	$ 5,546	$ 5,546	$ 5,546	$ 5,546	$ 5,546	$ 5,546	$ 66,550
Junior Electrical Engineer	$ 5,546	$ 5,546	$ 5,546	$ 5,546	$ 5,546	$ 5,546	$ 5,546	$ 5,546	$ 5,546	$ 5,546	$ 5,546	$ 5,546	$ 66,550
Sales Manager	$ 7,058	$ 7,058	$ 7,058	$ 7,058	$ 7,058	$ 7,058	$ 7,058	$ 7,058	$ 7,058	$ 7,058	$ 7,058	$ 7,058	$ 84,700
Sales Manager	$ 7,058	$ 7,058	$ 7,058	$ 7,058	$ 7,058	$ 7,058	$ 7,058	$ 7,058	$ 7,058	$ 7,058	$ 7,058	$ 7,058	$ 84,700
Other Salaries	$ 137,564	$ 137,564	$ 137,564	$ 137,564	$ 137,564	$ 137,564	$ 137,564	$ 137,564	$ 137,564	$ 137,564	$ 137,564	$ 137,564	$ 1,650,768
Total Salaries	$ 227,028	$ 227,028	$ 227,028	$ 227,028	$ 227,028	$ 227,028	$ 227,028	$ 227,028	$ 227,028	$ 227,028	$ 227,028	$ 227,028	$ 2,724,341
Total IUPUI Expenses													
Outside Contractors	$ 14,575	$ 14,575	$ 14,575	$ 14,575	$ 14,575	$ 14,575	$ 14,575	$ 14,575	$ 14,575	$ 14,575	$ 14,575	$ 14,575	$ 174,901
Total Supplies for Initial Build	$ 20,833	$ 20,833	$ 20,833	$ 20,833	$ 20,833	$ 20,833							$ 124,998
Construction Costs for Initial Build													

(Continued)

Income Statement (Year 5): *(Continued)*

Income Statement	49	50	51	52	53	54	55	56	57	58	59	60	Year 5
Operating Expenses													
Payroll Processing Fees	$ 250	$ 250	$ 250	$ 250	$ 250	$ 250	$ 250	$ 250	$ 250	$ 250	$ 250	$ 250	$ 3,000
Office Rent	$ 1,313	$ 1,313	$ 1,313	$ 1,313	$ 1,313	$ 1,313	$ 1,313	$ 1,313	$ 1,313	$ 1,313	$ 1,313	$ 1,313	$ 15,750
Fringe Benefits	$ 2,460	$ 2,460	$ 2,460	$ 2,460	$ 2,460	$ 2,460	$ 2,460	$ 2,460	$ 2,460	$ 2,460	$ 2,460	$ 2,460	$ 29,525
Travel - Related Expenses	$ 4,373	$ 4,373	$ 4,373	$ 4,373	$ 4,373	$ 4,373	$ 4,373	$ 4,373	$ 4,373	$ 4,373	$ 4,373	$ 4,373	$ 52,470
Trade Shows	$ 583	$ 583	$ 583	$ 583	$ 583	$ 583	$ 583	$ 583	$ 583	$ 583	$ 583	$ 583	$ 6,996
Brochures & Publications	$ 292	$ 292	$ 292	$ 292	$ 292	$ 292	$ 292	$ 292	$ 292	$ 292	$ 292	$ 292	$ 3,498
Market Research	$ 729	$ 729	$ 729	$ 729	$ 729	$ 729	$ 729	$ 729	$ 729	$ 729	$ 729	$ 729	$ 8,745
Postage	$ 73	$ 73	$ 73	$ 73	$ 73	$ 73	$ 73	$ 73	$ 73	$ 73	$ 73	$ 73	$ 875
Cell Phones	$ 219	$ 219	$ 219	$ 219	$ 219	$ 219	$ 219	$ 219	$ 219	$ 219	$ 219	$ 219	$ 2,624
Legal Fees	$ 1,458	$ 1,458	$ 1,458	$ 1,458	$ 1,458	$ 1,458	$ 1,458	$ 1,458	$ 1,458	$ 1,458	$ 1,458	$ 1,458	$ 17,490
Other Professional Fees	$ 1,458	$ 1,458	$ 1,458	$ 1,458	$ 1,458	$ 1,458	$ 1,458	$ 1,458	$ 1,458	$ 1,458	$ 1,458	$ 1,458	$ 17,490
Website Development	$ 125	$ 125	$ 125	$ 125	$ 125	$ 125	$ 125	$ 125	$ 125	$ 125	$ 125	$ 125	$ 1,500
Dues & Subscriptions	$ 131	$ 131	$ 131	$ 131	$ 131	$ 131	$ 131	$ 131	$ 131	$ 131	$ 131	$ 131	$ 1,574
Patent Costs	$ 12,500	$ 12,500	$ 12,500	$ 12,500	$ 12,500	$ 12,500	$ 12,500	$ 12,500	$ 12,500	$ 12,500	$ 12,500	$ 12,500	$ 150,000
Computers and Software (SimHydraulics)	$ 2,083	$ 2,083	$ 2,083	$ 2,083	$ 2,083	$ 2,083	$ 2,083	$ 2,083	$ 2,083	$ 2,083	$ 2,083	$ 2,083	$ 25,000
Office Equipment & Supplies	$ 1,020	$ 1,020	$ 1,020	$ 1,020	$ 1,020	$ 1,020	$ 1,020	$ 1,020	$ 1,020	$ 1,020	$ 1,020	$ 1,020	$ 12,243
Telephone & Utility Expenses	$ 437	$ 437	$ 437	$ 437	$ 437	$ 437	$ 437	$ 437	$ 437	$ 437	$ 437	$ 437	$ 5,247
Accounting Services	$ 583	$ 583	$ 583	$ 583	$ 583	$ 583	$ 583	$ 583	$ 583	$ 583	$ 583	$ 583	$ 6,996
Miscellaneous	$ 1,458	$ 1,458	$ 1,458	$ 1,458	$ 1,458	$ 1,458	$ 1,458	$ 1,458	$ 1,458	$ 1,458	$ 1,458	$ 1,458	$ 17,490
Total Operating Costs	$ 31,543	$ 31,543	$ 31,543	$ 31,543	$ 31,543	$ 31,543	$ 31,543	$ 31,543	$ 31,543	$ 31,543	$ 31,543	$ 31,543	$ 378,512
Total Costs	$ 1,168,979	$ 1,168,979	$ 1,168,979	$ 1,418,979	$ 1,418,979	$ 1,418,979	$ 1,648,146	$ 1,648,146	$ 1,648,146	$ 1,898,146	$ 1,898,146	$ 1,898,146	$ 18,402,751
Net Income (EBT)	$ 3,587,414	$ 587,238	$ 587,062	$ 836,886	$ 836,710	$ 836,533	$ 1,107,190	$ 1,107,014	$ 1,106,838	$ 1,356,662	$ 1,356,486	$ 1,356,310	$ 14,662,344

Balance Sheet (Year 5):

Balance Sheet	49	50	51	52	53	54	55	56	57	58	59	60	Year 5
Assets													
Current Assets													
Cash	$ 9,157,473	$8,844,711	$ 9,431,773	$10,343,658	$11,180,368	$ 12,016,901	$13,192,842	$14,299,856	$ 15,406,695	$16,838,357	$ 18,194,843	$ 19,551,153	$ 19,551,153
Accounts Receivable	$ 900,000												$ -
Total Assets	$10,057,473	$8,844,711	$ 9,431,773	$10,343,658	$11,180,368	$ 12,016,901	$13,192,842	$14,299,856	$ 15,406,695	$16,838,357	$ 18,194,843	$ 19,551,153	$ 19,551,153
Liabilities													
Current Liabilities													
Accounts Payable	$ 350,694	$ 350,694	$ 350,694	$ 425,694	$ 425,694	$ 425,694	$ 494,444	$ 494,444	$ 494,444	$ 569,444	$ 569,444	$ 569,444	569,444
Total Liabilities	$ 350,694	$ 350,694	$ 350,694	$ 425,694	$ 425,694	$ 425,694	$ 494,444	$ 494,444	$ 494,444	$ 569,444	$ 569,444	$ 569,444	569,444
Equity													
Capital Stock	$ 5,800,000	$ 5,800,000	$ 5,800,000	$ 5,800,000	$ 5,800,000	$ 5,800,000	$ 5,800,000	$ 5,800,000	$ 5,800,000	$ 5,800,000	$ 5,800,000	$ 5,800,000	$ 5,800,000
Retained Earnings	$ 2,106,780	$ 2,694,017	$ 3,281,079	$ 4,117,965	$ 4,954,674	$ 5,791,208	6,898,398	8,005,412	9,112,251	$10,468,913	$ 11,825,399	13,181,710	13,181,710
Total Equity	$ 7,906,780	$8,494,017	$ 8,494,017	$ 9,081,079	$9,917,965	$10,754,674	$11,591,208	$12,698,398	$13,805,412	$14,912,251	$16,268,913	$ 17,625,399	$18,981,710	$18,981,710
Total Liabilities &	$ 8,257,473	$8,844,711	$ 9,431,773	$10,343,658	$11,180,368	$ 12,016,901	$13,192,842	$14,299,856	$ 15,406,695	$16,838,357	$ 18,194,843	$ 19,551,153	$ 19,551,153

Cash Flow (Year 5):

Cash Flow Statement	49	50	51	52	53	54	55	56	57	58	59	60	Year 5
Net Income (Loss)	$ 3,587,414	$ 587,238	$ 587,062	$ 836,886	$ 836,710	$ 836,533	$ 1,107,190	$ 1,107,014	$ 1,106,838	$ 1,356,662	$ 1,356,486	$ 1,356,310	$ 14,662,344
Working Capital Changes:													
Accounts Receivable (Increase)	$ 900,000	$ (900,000)	$ -	$ -	$ -	$ -	$ -	$ -	$ -	$ -	$ -	$ -	-
Accounts Payable (Increase)	$ 108,232	$ -	$ -	75,000	$ -	$ -	68,750	$ -	$ -	75,000	$ -	$ -	326,982
Cash Used for Operations	$ 4,595,645	$ (312,762)	$ 587,062	911,886	836,710	836,533	1,175,941	1,107,014	1,106,838	1,431,662	1,356,486	1,356,310	14,989,325
Cash Used for Investments													
Cash from Financing Activities													
Capital Stock													
Change in Cash for Period	$ 4,595,645	$ (312,762)	$ 587,062	911,886	836,710	836,533	1,175,941	1,107,014	1,106,838	1,431,662	1,356,486	1,356,310	14,989,325
Cash: Beginning of Period	$ 4,561,828	$ 9,157,473	$ 8,844,711	9,431,773	$ 10,343,658	$ 11,180,368	$ 12,016,901	$ 13,192,842	$ 14,299,856	$ 15,406,695	$ 16,838,357	$ 18,194,843	4,561,828
Cash: End of Period	$ 9,157,473	$ 8,844,711	$ 9,431,773	$ 10,343,658	$ 11,180,368	$ 12,016,901	$ 13,192,842	$ 14,299,856	$ 15,406,695	$ 16,838,357	$ 18,194,843	$ 19,551,153	19,551,153

NOTES

1. SBI–Wind Power Market: Turbine Components & Subcomponents and Demand in the U.S. and the World (www.sbireports.com)

2. Global Wind Energy Council (http://www.gwec.net/index.php?id=121)

3. www.20percentwind.org

4. NREL 2010: Eastern Wind Integration and Transmission Study (http://www.nrel.gov/wind/systemsintegration/ewits.html)

5. Center for Environmental Innovation and Leadership (CEIL) (http://www.ceileadership.org/index.php/energy-efficiency-and-renewable-energy/2693-uswind-industry-reports-enduring-growth-in-first-quarter-of-2011)

6. http://m.wired.com/magazine/2012/01/ff_solyndra/all/1

7. Ibid.

8. (http://www.allbusiness.com/energy-utilities/utilitiesindustry-electric-power-power/11716155-1.html) and (http://www.nrel.gov/features/20090417_wind.html)

9. *Renewable Energy World,* September 2008.

10. The Gearbox Problem–July 2009 (http://getmore.northernpower.com/downloads/the-gearbox-problem.pdf)

11. Ibid.

12. Ibid.

13. Improving Wind Turbine Gearbox Reliability–2007 (http://www.nrel.gov/wind/pdfs/41548.pdf)

14. SBI–Wind Power Market: Turbine Components & Subcomponents and Demand in the U.S. and the World (www.sbireports.com)

15. *Bridges Trade BioRes* 11, no. 14 (July 25, 2011).

16. Department of Energy, *Advanced Wind Turbine Drivetrain Concepts* (2010).

17. K. Dasgupta, "Analysis of a hydrostatic transmission system using a low speed high torque motor," *Mechanism and Machine Theory* 35 (Oct. 2000): 1481–99.

PART 4

Growth Strategies for Entrepreneurial Ventures

CHAPTER 13

Strategic Entrepreneurial Growth

Entrepreneurial Thought

Without continual growth and progress, such words as improvement, achievement, and success have no meaning.

—Benjamin Franklin Founding Father of the United States

There are no great limits to growth because there are no limits of human intelligence, imagination, and wonder.

—Ronald W. Reagan 40th President of the United States

13-1 STRATEGIC PLANNING AND EMERGING FIRMS

LO1 Introduce the importance of strategic planning with emerging firms

Although most entrepreneurs do some form of planning, it often tends to be informal and unsystematic.[1] The actual need for systematic planning varies with the nature, size, and structure of the business. In other words, a small two-person operation may successfully use informal planning because little complexity is involved. But an emerging venture that is rapidly expanding with constant increases in personnel and market operations will need to formalize its planning because a great deal of complexity exists.

An entrepreneur's planning will need to shift from an informal to a formal systematic style for other reasons. First is the degree of uncertainty with which the venture is attempting to become established and to grow. With greater levels of uncertainty, entrepreneurs have a stronger need to deal with the challenges that face their venture, and a more formal planning effort can help them to do this. Second, the strength of the competition (in both numbers and quality of competitors) will add to the importance of more systematic planning in order for a new venture to monitor its operations and objectives more closely.[2] Finally, the amount and type of experience the entrepreneur has may be a factor in deciding the extent of formal planning. A lack of adequate experience, either technological or business, may constrain the entrepreneur's understanding and thus necessitate formal planning to help determine future paths for the organization. It is only through this type of planning that entrepreneurs can manage entrepreneurial growth.

13-2 THE NATURE OF STRATEGIC PLANNING

LO2 Delve into the nature of strategic planning

Strategic planning is the formulation of long-range plans for the effective management of environmental opportunities and threats in light of a venture's strengths and weaknesses. It includes defining the venture's mission, specifying achievable objectives, developing strategies, and setting policy guidelines. Dynamic in nature, the strategic management process (see Figure 13.1) is the full set of commitments, decisions, and actions required for a firm to achieve strategic competitiveness and earn above-average returns. Relevant strategic inputs derived from analyses of the internal and external environments are necessary for effective strategy formulation and implementation. In turn, effective strategic actions are a prerequisite to achieving the desired outcomes of strategic competitiveness and above-average returns. Thus, the strategic management process is used to match the conditions of an ever-changing market and competitive structure with a firm's continuously evolving resources, capabilities, and core competencies (the sources of strategic inputs). Effective strategic actions that take place in the context of carefully integrated strategy formulation and implementation actions result in desired strategic outcomes.[3] Thus, strategic planning is the primary step in determining the future direction of a business. The "best" strategic plan will be influenced by many factors, among them the abilities of the entrepreneur, the complexity of the venture, and the nature of the industry. Yet, whatever the specific situation, five basic steps must be followed in strategic planning:

1. Examine the internal and external environments of the venture (strengths, weaknesses, opportunities, threats).
2. Formulate the venture's long-range and short-range strategies (mission, objectives, strategies, policies).
3. Implement the strategic plan (programs, budgets, procedures).
4. Evaluate the performance of the strategy.
5. Take follow-up action through continuous feedback.

Figure 13.1 illustrates these basic steps in a flow diagram.

The first step—examining the environment—can be one of the most critical for an emerging venture. Analyses of its external and internal environments provide a firm with the information required to develop its strategic intent and strategic mission. As shown in Figure 13.1, strategic intent and strategic mission influence strategy formulation and implementation actions. A clear review of a venture's internal and external factors is needed, and both sets of factors must be considered when performing an environmental analysis.

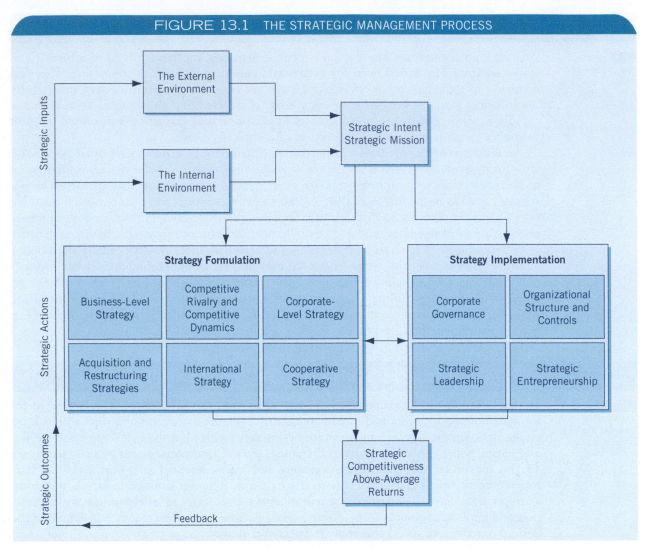

FIGURE 13.1 THE STRATEGIC MANAGEMENT PROCESS

Source: Michael A. Hitt, R. Duane Ireland, and Robert E. Hoskisson, *Strategic Management*, 11th ed., © 2015 Cengage Learning.

This analysis is often called a **SWOT analysis**; SWOT is an acronym for a venture's internal *strengths* and *weaknesses* and its external *opportunities* and *threats*. The analysis should include not only the external factors most likely to occur and to have a serious impact on the company but also the internal factors most likely to affect the implementation of present and future strategic decisions. By focusing on this analysis, an emerging venture can proceed through the other steps of formulation, implementation, evaluation, and feedback.[4]

The greatest value of the strategic planning process is the "strategic thinking" it promotes among business owners. Although strategic thinking is not always articulated formally, it synthesizes the intuition and creativity of an entrepreneur into a vision for the future.[5]

13-2a The Lack of Strategic Planning

The importance of new ventures to the economy is substantial in terms of innovation, employment, and sales, and effective planning can help these new firms survive and grow. Unfortunately, research has shown a distinct lack of planning on the part of new ventures. Five reasons for the lack of strategic planning have been found:

1. **Time scarcity.** Entrepreneurs report that their time is scarce and difficult to allocate to planning in the face of day-to-day operating schedules.

2. **Lack of knowledge.** Entrepreneurs have minimal exposure to, and knowledge of, the planning process. They are uncertain of the components of the process and the sequence

of those components. The entrepreneurs also are unfamiliar with many planning information sources and how they can be used.

3. **Lack of expertise/skills.** Entrepreneurs typically are generalists, and they often lack the specialized expertise necessary for the planning process.

4. **Lack of trust and openness.** Entrepreneurs are highly sensitive and guarded about their businesses and the decisions that affect them. Consequently, they are hesitant to formulate a strategic plan that requires participation by employees or outside consultants.

5. **Perception of high cost.** Entrepreneurs perceive the cost associated with planning to be very high. This fear of expensive planning causes many business owners to avoid or ignore planning as a viable process.[6]

In addition to these reasons, other factors have been reported as difficulties of the planning process. For example, both high-performing and low-performing small ventures have problems with long-range planning. Both time and expense are major obstacles. Additionally, low-performing firms report that a poor planning climate, inexperienced managers, and unfavorable economic conditions are problems. Quite obviously, strategic planning is no easy chore for new ventures. On the other hand, many benefits can be gained from such planning.

13-2b The Value of Strategic Planning

Does strategic planning pay off? Research shows it does. A number of studies have focused on the impact of planning on entrepreneurial firms.[7] These studies support the contention that strategic planning is of value to a venture. Most of the studies imply—if they do not directly state—that planning influences a venture's survival. In one study of 70,000 failed firms, lack of planning was identified as a major cause of failure,[8] and still another investigation demonstrated that firms engaged in strategic planning outperformed those that did not use such planning.[9] A study of 220 small firms further established the importance of selecting an appropriate strategy (niche strategy) for a venture to build distinctive competence and a sustainable competitive advantage.[10] Another research study examined the dynamic effects of strategies on company performance in the software industry and found that, when focus or differentiation strategies were established, performance by those firms was enhanced.[11] Finally, there was a study that examined 253 smaller firms to determine the relationship between performance and planning sophistication. The study classified companies into the following categories:

Category I: No written plan (101 firms, or 39.9 percent)
Category II: Moderately sophisticated planning, including a written plan and/or some quantified objectives, some specific plans and budgets, identification of some factors in the external environment, and procedures for anticipating or detecting differences between the plan and actual performance (89 firms, or 35.2 percent).
Category III: Sophisticated planning, including a written plan with all of the following: some quantified objectives, some specific plans and budgets, identification of some factors in the external environment, and procedures for anticipating or detecting differences between the plan and actual performance (63 firms, or 24.9 percent).

The results demonstrated that more than 88 percent of firms with Category II or Category III planning performed at or above the industry average, compared with only 40 percent of those firms with Category I planning.[12]

In summary, all of the research indicates that emerging firms that engage in strategic planning are more effective than those that do not. Most important, the studies emphasize the significance of the planning process, rather than merely the plans, as a key to successful performance.[13]

13-2c Fatal Visions in Strategic Planning

The actual execution of a strategy is almost as important as the strategy itself. Many entrepreneurs make unintentional errors when they apply a specific strategy to their own specific venture. Competitive situations differ, and the particular application of known strategies must be tailored to those unique situations.

Researcher Michael E. Porter has noted five fatal mistakes entrepreneurs continually fall prey to in their attempt to implement a strategy.[14] Outlined next are these flaws and their explanations.

- *Fatal Vision #1: Misunderstanding industry attractiveness.* Too many entrepreneurs associate attractive industries with those that are growing the fastest, appear to be glamorous, or use the fanciest technology. This is wrong, because attractive industries have high barriers to entry and the fewest substitutes. The more high-tech or high-glamour a business is, the more likely a lot of new competitors will enter and make it unprofitable.

- *Fatal Vision #2: No real competitive advantage.* Some entrepreneurs merely copy or imitate the strategy of their competitors. That may be an easy tactic, and it is certainly less risky, but it means that an entrepreneur has no competitive advantage. To succeed, new ventures must develop unique ways to compete.

- *Fatal Vision #3: Pursuing an unattainable competitive position.* Many aggressive entrepreneurs pursue a position of dominance in a fast-growing industry. However, they are so busy getting off the ground and finding people to buy their products that they forget what will happen if the venture succeeds. For example, a successful software program will be imitated quickly; therefore, the advantage it alone gives cannot be sustained. Real competitive advantage in software comes from servicing and supporting buyers, providing regular upgrades, and getting a company online with customers so their computer departments depend on the organization. That creates barriers to entry. Sometimes, small companies simply cannot sustain an advantage.

- *Fatal Vision #4: Compromising strategy for growth.* A careful balance must exist between growth and the competitive strategy that makes a new venture successful. If an entrepreneur sacrifices his or her venture's unique strategy in order to have fast growth, then the venture may grow out of business. Although fast growth can be tempting in certain industries, it is imperative that entrepreneurs also maintain and grow their strategic advantage.

- *Fatal Vision #5: Failure to explicitly communicate the venture's strategy to employees.* It is essential for every entrepreneur to clearly communicate the company's strategy to every employee. Never assume that employees already know the strategy. Always be explicit.

According to Porter, "One of the fundamental benefits of developing a strategy is that it creates unity, or consistency of action, throughout a company. Every department in the organization works toward the same objectives. But if people do not know what the objectives are, how can they work toward them? If they do not have a clear sense that low cost, say, is your ultimate aim, then all their day-to-day actions are not going to be reinforcing that goal. In any company, employees are making critical choices every minute. An explicit strategy will help them make the right ones."[15]

13-2d Entrepreneurial and Strategic Actions

Entrepreneurship and strategic management are both dynamic processes concerned with firm performance. Strategic management calls for firms to establish and exploit competitive advantages within a particular environmental context. Entrepreneurship promotes the search for competitive advantages through product, process, and market innovations. A new venture typically is created to pursue the marketplace promise from innovations.

Researchers R. Duane Ireland, Michael A. Hitt, S. Michael Camp, and Donald L. Sexton argue that entrepreneurial and strategic actions often are intended to find new market or competitive space for a firm to create wealth. Firms try to find fundamentally new ways of doing business that will disrupt an industry's existing competitive rules, leading to the development of new business models that create new competitive life forms. The degree to which a firm acts entrepreneurially in terms of innovativeness, risk-taking, and proactivity is related to dimensions of strategic management. Within these commonalties between

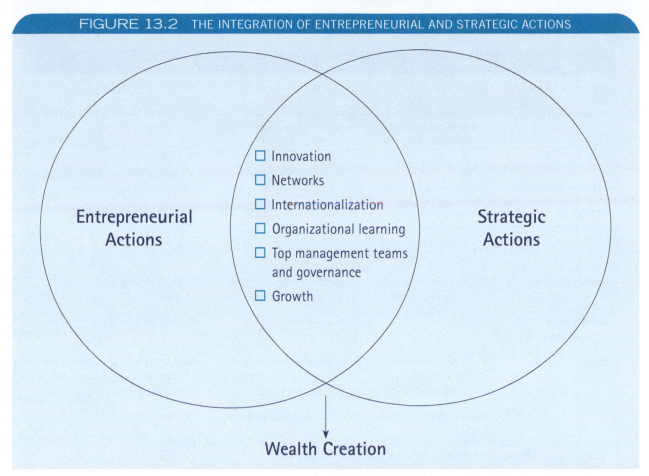

FIGURE 13.2   THE INTEGRATION OF ENTREPRENEURIAL AND STRATEGIC ACTIONS

Source: R. Duane Ireland, Michael A. Hitt, S. Michael Camp, and Donald L. Sexton, "Integrating Entrepreneurship and Strategic Management Actions to Create Firm Wealth," *Academy of Management Executive* 15, no. 1 (February 2001): 51.

entrepreneurship and strategic management are specific domains of innovation, networks, internationalization, organizational learning, top management teams and governance, and growth (see Figure 13.2). Understanding the critical intersections of these specific domains allow entrepreneurs to increase their knowledge, which in turn leads to higher quality entrepreneurial and strategic actions.[16]

13-2e Strategic Positioning: The Entrepreneurial Edge

Strategic competition can be thought of as the process of perceiving new positions that attract customers from established positions or draw new customers into the market. In principle, incumbents and entrepreneurs face the same challenges in finding new strategic positions. In practice, entrepreneurs often have the edge.

Strategic positionings often are not obvious, and finding them requires creativity and insight. Entrepreneurs frequently discover unique positions that have been available but simply overlooked by established competitors. In addition, entrepreneurial ventures can prosper by occupying a position that a competitor once held but has ceded through years of imitation and straddling.

Fundamental approaches to strategic positioning include establishing and defending a defensible position, leveraging resources to dominate a market, and pursuing opportunities to establish new markets (see Table 13.1). Entrepreneurs must understand that the pursuit of opportunities provides the best choice for capitalizing on change.

Most commonly, new positions open up because of change: New customer groups or purchase occasions arise; new needs emerge as societies evolve; new distribution channels

	Position	Leverage	Opportunities
Strategic Logic	Establish position	Leverage resources	Pursue opportunities
Strategic Steps	Identify an attractive market Locate a defensible position Fortify and defend	Establish a vision Build resources Leverage across markets	Jump into the confusion Keep moving Seize opportunities Finish strong
Strategic Question	Where should we be?	What should we be?	How should we proceed?
Source of Advantage	Unique, valuable position with tightly integrated activity system	Unique, valuable, inimitable resources	Key processes and unique simple rules
Works Best in	Slowly changing, well-structured markets	Moderately changing, well-structured markets	Rapidly changing, ambiguous markets
Duration of Advantage	Sustained	Sustained	Unpredictable
Risk	It will be too difficult to alter position as conditions change Profitability	Company will be too slow to build new resources as conditions change Long-term dominance	Managers will be too tentative in executing on promising opportunities Growth

TABLE 13.1   STRATEGIC APPROACHES: POSITION, LEVERAGE, OPPORTUNITIES

Source: From "Strategy as Simple Rules," by Kathleen M. Eisenhardt and Donald N. Sull (January 2001): 109. Copyright © 2001 by the Harvard Business School Publishing. All rights reserved.

appear; new technologies develop; new machinery or information systems become available. When such changes happen, entrepreneurial ventures unencumbered by long histories in the industry can often more easily perceive the potential for a new way of competing. Unlike incumbents, these organizations can be more flexible because they face no tradeoffs with their existing activities.[17]

13-2f An Entrepreneurial Strategy Matrix Model

Based on the structure of traditional strategy matrices (such as the Boston Consulting Group [BCG] matrix) that have been used for portfolio analysis, researchers Matthew C. Sonfield and Robert N. Lussier developed an **entrepreneurial strategy matrix** that measures risk and innovation.[18] For the purpose of this matrix, **innovation** is defined as the creation of something new and different. In terms of measurement, the newer and more different the proposed product or service is, the higher it would be scored on a measurement scale.

Risk is defined as the probability of major financial loss. What are the chances of the entrepreneurial venture failing? How serious would be the resulting financial loss? Whereas many ways exist to increase innovation, reducing risk largely focuses on financial factors, with a secondary consideration of self-image and ego.

The model allows even the most inexperienced entrepreneurs to characterize their new or existing venture situations and identify appropriate strategies. The model places innovation on the vertical axis and risk on the horizontal axis. It denotes the levels of these two variables by using I and R for high levels and i and r for low levels (see Figure 13.3).

The value of the entrepreneurial strategy matrix is that it suggests appropriate avenues for different entrepreneurs. When the entrepreneur identifies the cell that best describes the

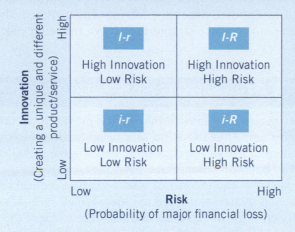

FIGURE 13.3   THE ENTREPRENEURIAL STRATEGY MATRIX: INDEPENDENT VARIABLES

Source: Matthew C. Sonfield and Robert N. Lussier, "The Entrepreneurial Strategic Matrix: A Model for New and Ongoing Ventures." Reprinted with permission from *Business Horizons*, May/June 1997, by the trustees at Indiana University, Kelley School of Business.

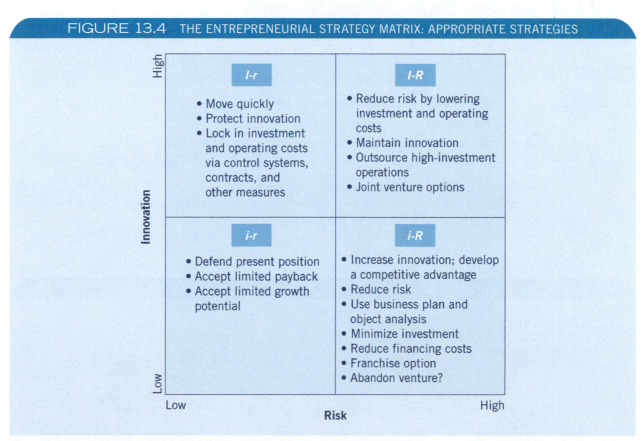

FIGURE 13.4   THE ENTREPRENEURIAL STRATEGY MATRIX: APPROPRIATE STRATEGIES

Source: Matthew C. Sonfield and Robert N. Lussier, "The Entrepreneurial Strategic Matrix: A Model for New and Ongoing Ventures." Reprinted with permission from *Business Horizons*, 40, no. 3 (May/June) 1997, by the trustees at Indiana University, Kelley School of Business.

new or existing venture being contemplated, then certain strategies are indicated as more likely to be effective (see Figure 13.4).

It should be obvious that certain cells are more advantageous than others. A high-innovation/low-risk venture is certainly preferable to a low-innovation/high-risk one. Yet, for every venture found in *I-r*, large numbers of ventures can be found in *i-R*. Risk is more common than innovativeness in the business world.

The strategic implications of the matrix are twofold. First, entrepreneurs will find certain cells preferable to others, and one set of appropriate strategies involves moving from one cell to another. Second, such movement is not always possible for an entrepreneur, so the appropriate strategies involve reducing risk and increasing innovation within a cell.

13-3 MANAGING ENTREPRENEURIAL GROWTH

LO3 Examine the challenges of managing entrepreneurial growth

Managing entrepreneurial growth may be the most critical tactic for the future success of business enterprises. After initiation of a new venture, the entrepreneur needs to develop an understanding of management change. This is a great challenge, because it often encompasses the art of balancing mobile and dynamic factors.[19]

Thus, the survival and growth of a new venture require that the entrepreneur possess both strategic and tactical skills and abilities. Which specific skills and abilities are needed depend in part on the venture's current development; Figure 13.5 illustrates the typical venture life cycle. Managing growth can be a formidable challenge to the successful development of any venture.

13-3a Venture Development Stages

LO4 Discuss the five stages of a typical venture life cycle: development, start-up, growth, stabilization, and innovation or decline

As noted, Figure 13.5 represents the traditional life-cycle stages of an enterprise. These stages include new-venture development, start-up activities, growth, stabilization, and innovation or decline. Other authors describe these stages in different terms. For example, Alfred Chandler identifies the following stages in a firm's evolution:

1. Initial expansion and accumulation of resources
2. Rationalization of the use of resources
3. Expansion into new markets to assure the continued use of resources
4. Development of new structures to ensure continuing mobilization of resources[20]

These four phases are, in effect, the same major stages illustrated in Figure 13.5, with the exception of stabilization. In short, authors generally agree regarding a venture's life cycle. Presented next are the five major stages.

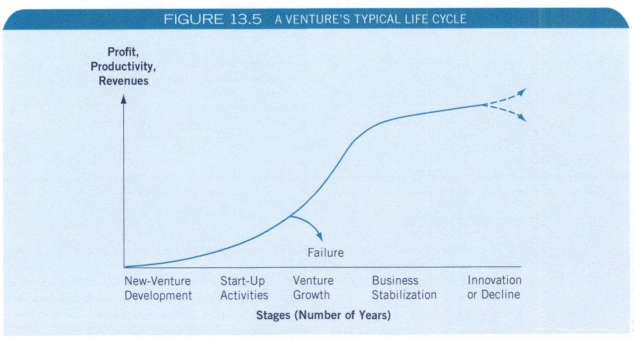

FIGURE 13.5   A VENTURE'S TYPICAL LIFE CYCLE

Profit, Productivity, Revenues

Failure

New-Venture Development | Start-Up Activities | Venture Growth | Business Stabilization | Innovation or Decline

Stages (Number of Years)

© Cengage Learning

NEW-VENTURE DEVELOPMENT

The first stage, new-venture development, consists of activities associated with the initial formulation of the venture. This initial phase is the foundation of the entrepreneurial process and requires creativity and assessment. In addition to the accumulation and expansion of resources, this is a creativity, assessment, and networking stage for initial entrepreneurial strategy formulation. The enterprise's general philosophy, mission, scope, and direction are determined during this stage.

START-UP ACTIVITIES

The second stage, start-up activities, encompasses the foundation work needed to create a formal business plan, search for capital, carry out marketing activities, and develop an effective entrepreneurial team. These activities typically demand an aggressive entrepreneurial strategy with maximum efforts devoted to launching the venture. This stage is similar to Chandler's description of the rationalization of the use of resources. It is typified by strategic and operational planning steps designed to identify the firm's competitive advantage and uncover funding sources. Marketing and financial considerations tend to be paramount during this stage.[21]

GROWTH

The growth stage often requires major changes in entrepreneurial strategy. Competition and other market forces call for the reformulation of strategies. For example, some firms find themselves "growing out" of business because they are unable to cope with the growth of their ventures. Highly creative entrepreneurs sometimes are unable, or unwilling, to meet the administrative challenges that accompany this growth stage. As a result, they leave the enterprise and move on to other ventures.

   This growth stage presents newer and more substantial problems than those the entrepreneur faced during the start-up stage.[22] These newer challenges force the entrepreneur into developing a different set of skills while maintaining an "entrepreneurial perspective" for the organization.[23] The growth stage is a transition from entrepreneurial one-person leadership to managerial team-oriented leadership.

BUSINESS STABILIZATION

The stabilization stage is a result of both market conditions and the entrepreneur's efforts. During this stage, a number of developments commonly occur, including increased competition, consumer indifference to the entrepreneur's good(s) or service(s), and saturation of the market with a host of "me too" look-alikes. Sales often begin to stabilize, and the entrepreneur must start to think about where the enterprise will go during the next three to five years. This stage is often a "swing" stage in that it precedes the period when the firm either swings into higher gear and greater profitability or swings toward decline and failure. During this stage, innovation is often critical to future success.

INNOVATION OR DECLINE

Firms that fail to innovate will die. Financially successful enterprises often will try to acquire other innovative firms, thereby ensuring their own growth. Also, many firms will work on new product/service development to complement current offerings.

   All of a venture's life-cycle stages are important strategic points, and each requires a different set of strategies. However, this chapter concentrates specifically on the growth stage because entrepreneurs often ignore it. This happens not because of incompetence but rather because of the almost hypnotic effect a successful growth stage can cause. We shall now examine the key factors that affect the ability to manage this stage.

13-3b Transitioning from Entrepreneurial to Managerial

The transitions between stages of a venture are complemented (or in some cases inhibited) by the entrepreneur's ability to make a transition in style. A key transition occurs during the growth stage of a venture when the entrepreneur shifts into a managerial style. This is not easy to do. As researchers Charles W. Hofer and Ram Charan have noted, "Among the different transitions that are possible, probably the most difficult to achieve and also perhaps the most important for organizational development is that of moving from a one-person, entrepreneurially managed firm to one run by a functionally organized, professional management team."[24]

A number of problems can occur during this transition, especially if the enterprise is characterized by factors such as (1) a highly centralized decision-making system, (2) an overdependence on one or two key individuals, (3) an inadequate repertoire of managerial skills and training, and (4) a paternalistic atmosphere.[25] Although these characteristics often are effective for the new venture's start-up and initial survival, they pose a threat to the firm's development during the growth stage. Quite often, these characteristics inhibit development by detracting from the entrepreneur's ability to manage the growth stage successfully.

BALANCING THE FOCUS: ENTREPRENEURIAL VERSUS MANAGERIAL

When managing the growth stage, entrepreneurs must remember two important points. First, an adaptive firm needs to retain certain entrepreneurial characteristics to encourage innovation and creativity. Second, the entrepreneur needs to translate this spirit of innovation and creativity to his or her personnel while personally making a transition toward a more managerial style.[26] This critical entrepreneur/manager balance is extremely difficult to achieve. Although every firm wants to be as innovative, flexible, and creative as Apple, Google, and Facebook, there are thousands of new restaurants, Internet businesses, retail stores, and high-tech ventures that presumably have tried to be innovative and grow but have failed.

Remaining entrepreneurial while making the transition to some of the more administrative traits is vital to the successful growth of a venture. Table 13.2 provides a framework for comparing the entrepreneurial and administrative characteristics and pressures relative to five major factors: strategic orientation, commitment to seize opportunities, commitment of resources, control of resources, and management structure. Each of these five areas is critical to the balance needed to manage entrepreneurially. At the two ends of the continuum (from entrepreneurial focus to administrative focus) are specific points of view. One study characterized these using a question format.

The Entrepreneur's Point of View

- Where is the opportunity?
- How do I capitalize on it?
- What resources do I need?
- How do I gain control over them?
- What structure is best?

The Administrative Point of View

- What resources do I control?
- What structure determines our organization's relationship to its market?
- How can I minimize the impact of others on my ability to perform?
- What opportunity is appropriate?[27]

The logic behind the variance in the direction of these questions can be presented in a number of different ways. For example, the commitment of resources in the entrepreneurial frame of mind responds to changing environmental needs, whereas the managerial point of view is focused on the reduction of risk. In the control of resources, entrepreneurs will avoid ownership because of the risk of obsolescence and the need for more flexibility, whereas managers will view ownership as a means to accomplish efficiency and stability. In terms of structure, the entrepreneurial emphasis is placed on a need for flexibility and independence, whereas the administrative focus is placed on ensuring integration with a complexity of tasks, a desire for order, and controlled reward systems.

These examples of differences in focus help establish the important issues involved at both ends of the managerial spectrum. Each point of view—entrepreneurial and

TABLE 13.2   THE ENTREPRENEURIAL CULTURE VERSUS THE ADMINISTRATIVE CULTURE

	Entrepreneurial Focus		Administrative Focus	
	Characteristics	Pressures	Characteristics	Pressures
Strategic Orientation	Driven by perception of opportunity	Diminishing opportunities Rapidly changing technology, consumer economics, social values, and political rules	Driven by controlled resources	Social contracts Performance measurement criteria Planning systems and cycles
Commitment to Seize Opportunities	Revolutionary, with short duration	Action orientation Narrow decision windows Acceptance of reasonable risks Few decision constituencies	Evolutionary, with long duration	Acknowledgement of multiple constituencies Negotiation about strategic course Risk reduction Coordination with existing resource base
Commitment of Resources	Many stages, with minimal exposure at each stage	Lack of predictable resource needs Lack of control over the environment Social demands for appropriate use of resources Foreign competition Demands for more efficient use	A single stage, with complete commitment out of decision	Need to reduce risk Incentive compensation Turnover in managers Capital budgeting systems Formal planning systems
Control of Resources	Episodic use or rent of required resources	Increased resource specialization Long resource life compared with need Risk of obsolescence Risk inherent in the identified opportunity Inflexibility of permanent commitment to resources	Ownership or employment of required resources	Power, status, and financial rewards Coordination of activity Efficiency measures Inertia and cost of change Industry structures
Management Structure	Flat, with multiple informal networks	Coordination of key noncontrolled resources Challenge to hierarchy Employees' desire for independence	Hierarchy	Need for clearly defined authority and responsibility Organizational culture Reward systems Management theory

Source: An exhibit from "The Heart of Entrepreneurship," by Howard H. Stevenson and David E. Gumpert, March/April 1985, 89. Copyright © 1985 by the President and Fellows of Harvard College. All rights reserved.

administrative—has important considerations that need to be balanced if effective growth is going to take place.

13-3c Understanding the Growth Stage

The growth stage often signals the beginning of a metamorphosis from a personal venture to a group-structured operation. Domination by the lead entrepreneur gives way to a team approach based heavily on coordination and flexibility.

KEY FACTORS DURING THE GROWTH STAGE

LO6 Identify the key factors that play a major role during the growth stage

Entrepreneurs must understand four key factors about the specific managerial actions that are necessary during the growth stage. These factors are control, responsibility, tolerance of failure, and change.

Control   Growth creates problems in command and control. When dealing with these problems, entrepreneurs need to answer three critical questions: (1) Does the control system imply trust? (2) Does the resource allocation system imply trust? (3) Is it easier to ask permission than to ask forgiveness? These questions reveal a great deal about the control of a venture. If they are answered with "yes," the venture is moving toward a good blend of control and participation. If they are answered with "no," the reasons for each negative response should be closely examined.

Responsibility   As the company grows, the distinction between authority and responsibility becomes more apparent. This is because authority always can be delegated, but it is most important to create a sense of responsibility. This action establishes flexibility, innovation, and a supportive environment. People tend to look beyond the job alone if a sense of responsibility is developed, so the growth stage is better served by the innovative activity and shared responsibility of all of the firm's members.

Tolerance of Failure   Even if a venture has avoided the initial start-up pitfalls and has expanded to the growth stage, it is still important to maintain a tolerance of failure. The level of failure the entrepreneur experienced and learned from at the start of the venture should be the same level expected, tolerated, and learned from in the growth stage. Although no firm should seek failure, to continually innovate and grow it should tolerate a certain degree of failure as opposed to punishing it.

Three distinct forms of failure should be distinguished:

- **Moral failure.** This form of failure is a violation of internal trust. Because the firm is based on mutual expectations and trust, this violation is a serious failure that can result in negative consequences.

- **Personal failure.** This form of failure is brought about by a lack of skill or application. Usually, responsibility for this form of failure is shared by the firm and the individual. Normally, therefore, an attempt is made to remedy the situation in a mutually beneficial way.

- **Uncontrollable failure.** This form of failure is caused by external factors and is the most difficult to prepare for or deal with. Resource limitations, strategic direction, and market changes are examples of forces outside the control of employees. Top management must carefully analyze the context of this form of failure and work to prevent its recurrence.

Change   Planning, operations, and implementation are all subject to continual changes as the venture moves through the growth stage and beyond. Retaining an innovative and opportunistic posture during growth requires a sense of change and variation from the norm. Entrepreneurs must realize, however, that change holds many implications for the enterprise in terms of resources, people, and structure. It is therefore important during growth that the flexibility regarding change be preserved. This allows for faster managerial response to environmental conditions.

13-3d Managing Paradox and Contradiction

LO7 Discuss the complex management of paradox and contradiction

When a venture experiences surges in growth, a number of structural factors begin to present multiple challenges. Entrepreneurs constantly struggle over whether to organize these factors—such as cultural elements, staffing and development of personnel, and appraisal and rewards—in a rigid, bureaucratic design or a flexible, organic design.

Research has shown that new-venture managers experiencing growth, particularly in emerging industries, need to adopt flexible, organic structures.[28] Rigid, bureaucratic structures are best suited for mature, stabilized companies. Thus, the cultural elements need to follow a flexible design of autonomy, risk taking, and entrepreneurship. This type of culture is a renewal of the entrepreneur's original force that created the venture. Although the entrepreneur's focus makes a transition toward a more administrative style, as mentioned earlier, the culture of the organization must be permeated with a constant renewal of the virtues of innovation and entrepreneurship.

When entrepreneurs design a flexible structure for high growth, they must realize that a number of contradictory forces are at work in certain other structural factors. Consider the following.

BUREAUCRATIZATION VERSUS DECENTRALIZATION

Increased hiring stimulates bureaucracy: Firms formalize procedures as staffing doubles and triples. Employee participation and autonomy decline, and internal labor markets develop. Tied to growth, however, is also an increased diversity in product offering that favors less formalized decision processes, greater decentralization, and the recognition that the firm's existing human resources lack the necessary skills to manage the broadening portfolio.

ENVIRONMENT VERSUS STRATEGY

High environmental turbulence and competitive conditions favor company cultures that support risk taking, autonomy, and employee participation in decision-making. Firms confront competitors, however, through strategies whose implementation depends on the design of formal systems that inhibit risk taking and autonomy.

STRATEGIC EMPHASES: QUALITY VERSUS COST VERSUS INNOVATION

Rapidly growing firms strive to simultaneously control costs, enhance product quality, and improve product offerings. Minimizing costs and undercutting competitors' product prices, however, are best achieved by traditional hierarchical systems of decision-making and evaluations. Yet, these strategies conflict with the kinds of autonomous processes most likely to encourage the pursuit of product quality and innovation.[29]

These factors emphasize the importance of managing paradox and contradiction. Growth involves the multiple challenges of (1) the stresses and strains induced by attempts to control costs while simultaneously enhancing quality and creating new products to maintain competitive parity and (2) centralizing to retain control while simultaneously decentralizing to encourage the contributions of autonomous, self-managed professionals to the embryonic corporate culture. Rapidly growing firms are challenged to strike a balance among these multiple pulls when designing their managerial systems.

13-3e Confronting the Growth Wall

LO8 Introduce the steps useful for breaking through the growth wall

In attempting to develop a managerial ability to deal with venture growth, many entrepreneurial owners confront a **growth wall** that seems too gigantic to overcome. Thus, they are unable to begin the process of handling the challenges that growth brings about.

Researchers have identified a number of fundamental changes that confront rapid-growth firms, including instant size increases, a sense of infallibility, internal turmoil, and extraordinary resource needs. In addressing these changes that can build a growth wall, successful growth-oriented firms have exhibited a few consistent themes:

- The entrepreneur is able to envision and anticipate the firm as a larger entity.
- The team needed for tomorrow is hired and developed today.

THE ENTREPRENEURIAL PROCESS

From Entrepreneur to Manager

For many entrepreneurs, one of the most difficult tasks is to make the successful transition from a creative, task-juggling entrepreneur to a business-skill-applying manager. A number of top entrepreneurs have been successful in this challenging transition while others have faltered. Most of the time the success always relates to the entrepreneur's ability to grow and develop his or her workforce. Today there are key management strategies that entrepreneurs should keep in mind when confronting the challenge of enhancing the abilities of their employees while growing their ventures.

There are effective human resource management practices that entrepreneurs need to develop and improve as they expand and grow their ventures. In many firms, the owner must personally handle all human resource practices, and, thus, inefficiencies may occur due to the amount of other activities the owner performs. This situation creates the danger that small entrepreneurs might fail to recognize or understand critical issues regarding human resources.

Researchers Jeffrey S. Hornsby and Donald F. Kuratko point out that dealing with the human resource issue may be the most critical challenge confronting entrepreneurs in the twenty-first century. In a number of studies they conducted on entrepreneurs' views of the human resource challenge, they found a number of critical issues that remain constant no matter how fast the business grows. Issues such as the availability and retention of quality workers, technology in the workplace, motivation of the workforce, and employee morale are considered to be foremost in the minds of most entrepreneurs seeking to manage a growing firm.

In trying to constantly improve employee performance two control-related areas warrant the entrepreneur's attention. The first is the link between pay and performance. The second is the spirit of teamwork.

The Pay-Performance Link: One of the most common causes of poor morale can be tied to the pay/performance link. Do those who do the best work receive the highest salaries? In many growing ventures, all salaries are kept secret. Only the owner and the respective employee know how much the employee makes. Over time, however, raises usually are given to those who stay, and they are not uniform; some people get more money than others. This can create a morale problem when employees feel that raises are arbitrary and are not tied to performance. When this is the case, two things can happen. First, those who can make more money by going elsewhere will take advantage of such employment opportunities. Second, those who stay will do less work, reasoning that "I may not be paid what I'm worth, but I'm not putting forth as much effort as I used to, either." So, it is imperative that the entrepreneur-manager try to tie raises to performance whenever possible. Not everyone's job is quantifiable. It may be easy to evaluate a salesperson's performance simply by looking at how much the person has sold, but a software developer's performance may call for a highly subjective evaluation. This is why some kind of evaluation system should be used. In addition the entrepreneur-manager needs to remain alert to locally competitive salaries. Some businesses are unable to match the salaries of other employers, but they must

come close or risk losing key personnel. Overall, however, few people leave their jobs just because of dissatisfaction with their pay. In many cases, that is just one of the reasons. Another is dissatisfaction with the work environment, as when it has no feeling of teamwork, so personnel simply do not like it there.

Develop Teamwork: Although some entrepreneur-managers believe they encourage teamwork, they actually promote competition. For example, the owner who goes overboard in praising and rewarding the best salesperson soon will find the other salespeople working to undermine that individual. The result is infighting among the personnel. The best way is to ensure real teamwork is developing is to reward those who are team players and, most important of all, to reprimand (and, in some cases, fire) those who refuse to cooperate for the overall good.

Remember the work climate is most important among younger employees today. People want to find fulfillment in their jobs. Research shows that attending to the psychological side of the work environment, including aspects such as a feeling of importance, creating an opportunity to do meaningful work, and the belief that workers are contributing to the business, is often more important to employees than salary and working conditions. When these good feelings are present, morale tends to be high and performance good.

As one shining example of those issues, author Carmine Gallo, in his book **The Innovation Secrets of Steve Jobs**, outlines a number of significant managing principles that emanated from Apple founder and CEO, Steve Jobs. Here are a few that apply to the challenge of employee motivation:

- *Help people find what they love in their work.* If people do what they love, motivation and performance are never questioned.
- *Put a dent in the universe.* Inspire your workforce to develop a sense of meaning in their performance as it relates to what the firm is trying to accomplish. Develop a sense of purpose in everyone's job.
- *Sell dreams not products.* Everyone wants to work at something significant in this world. Create a dream that is bigger than the entire workforce.
- *Say no to 1,000 things.* Remain focused on the simplicity of what can be done. Avoid the temptation to "add on" constantly and keep everyone aimed on the few areas of excellence.
- *Master the message.* Communicate with your employees continuously. Use stories and examples to make them understand the true message you intend for the atmosphere of the venture.

As you peruse the list you can see how they relate to creating a unique and significant experience for the employees of a growing firm. Once an entrepreneur can understand and execute effectively on the challenge of human resources then the transition from entrepreneur to manager becomes a more successful one.

Source: © Cengage Learning

- The original core vision of the firm is constantly and zealously reinforced.
- New "big-company" processes are introduced gradually as supplements to, rather than replacements for, existing approaches.
- Hierarchy is minimized.
- Employees hold a financial stake in the firm.[30]

These themes are important for entrepreneurs to keep in mind as they develop their abilities to manage growth.

One researcher found that internal constraints such as lack of growth capital, limited spans of control, and loss of entrepreneurial vitality occur in growth firms that struggle to survive versus those that successfully achieve high growth. In addition, fundamental differences exist in the firms' approach to environmental changes and trends.[31] Thus, a few key steps are recommended for breaking through the inability to handle environmental changes or trends. These include: *creating a growth task force* to organize and interpret the environmental data, to identify the venture's strengths and weaknesses, to brainstorm new ideas that leverage the firm's strengths, and to recommend key ideas that should be developed further; *planning for growth* with strategies to resolve the stagnation, a set of potential results, and identification of the necessary resources; *maintaining a growth culture* that encourages and rewards a growth-oriented attitude; and *developing an outside board of advisors* to become an integral part of the venture's growth. This board should help determine, design, and implement an organizational structure to enhance the desire for growth.[32]

13-4 BUILDING AN ENTREPRENEURIAL COMPANY IN THE TWENTY-FIRST CENTURY

LO9 Explore the elements of building an entrepreneurial company

The pace and magnitude of change continues to accelerate in the second decade of the twenty-first century; having the evolution and transformation of entrepreneurial firms match this pace is critical. How to build dynamic capabilities that are differentiated from those of the emerging competitors is the major challenge for growing firms that seek to adapt to the changing landscape. Two ways of building dynamic capabilities are internal (utilization of the creativity and knowledge from employees) and external[33] (the search for external competencies to complement the firm's existing capabilities).[34] The trend toward globalization, the advent of new technology, and the information movement are all examples of forces in this new millennium that are causing firms to examine their cultures, structures, and systems for flexibility and adaptability. Innovation and entrepreneurial thinking are essential elements in the strategies of growing ventures.

It has been noted that entrepreneurs (1) perceive an opportunity, (2) pursue this opportunity, and (3) believe that success of the venture is possible.[35] This belief is often due to the uniqueness of the idea, the strength of the product, or some special knowledge or skill the entrepreneur possesses. These same factors must be translated into the organization itself as the venture grows.

13-4a The Entrepreneurial Mind-Set

It is important for the venture's manager to maintain an entrepreneurial frame of mind. Figure 13.6 illustrates the danger of entrepreneurs evolving into bureaucrats who in turn stifle innovation. Table 13.3 provides a delineation of the differences between a managerial mind-set versus an entrepreneurial mind-set from the perspective of decision-making assumptions, values, beliefs, and approaches to problems.

In some cases, success will affect an entrepreneur's willingness to change and innovate. This is particularly true when the enterprise has developed a sense of complacency and the entrepreneur likes this environment: The person does not want to change. In fact, some entrepreneurs will create a bureaucratic environment in which orders are issued from the top down and change initiated at the lower levels is not tolerated.[36] As a result, no one in the venture is willing (or encouraged) to become innovative or entrepreneurial, because the owner/founder stifles such activity.

FIGURE 13.6 THE ENTREPRENEURIAL MIND-SET

Future Goals

	Change	Status Quo
Possible	Entrepreneur	Satisfied manager
Blocked	Frustrated manager	Classic bureaucrat

Perceived Capability

© Cengage Learning

TABLE 13.3 THE MANAGERIAL VERSUS THE ENTREPRENEURIAL MIND-SET

	Managerial Mind-Set	Entrepreneurial Mind-Set
Decision-Making Assumptions	The past is the best predictor of the future. Most business decisions can be quantified.	A new idea or an insight from a unique experience is likely to provide the best estimate of emerging trends.
Values	The best decisions are those based on quantitative analyses. Rigorous analyses are highly valued for making critical decisions.	New insights and real-world experiences are more highly valued than results based on historical data.
Beliefs	Law of large numbers: Chaos and uncertainty can be resolved by systematically analyzing the right data.	Law of small numbers: A single incident or several isolated incidents quickly become pivotal for making decisions regarding future trends.
Approach to Problems	Problems represent an unfortunate turn of events that threaten financial projections. Problems must be resolved with substantiated analyses.	Problems represent an opportunity to detect emerging changes and possibly new business opportunities.

Source: Mike Wright, Robert E. Hoskisson, and Lowell W. Busenitz, "Firm Rebirth: Buyouts as Facilitators of Strategic Growth and Entrepreneurship," *Academy of Management Executive* 15, no. 1 (2001): 114.

One study found that the entrepreneur directly affects the firm's growth orientation as measured by profitability goals, product/market goals, human resource goals, and flexibility goals.[37] If the entrepreneur hopes to maintain the creative climate that helped launch the venture in the first place, specific steps or measures must be taken.

13-4b Key Elements for an Entrepreneurial Firm

It is important for entrepreneurs to establish a business that remains flexible beyond start-up. An entrepreneurial firm increases opportunity for its employees, initiates change, and instills a desire to be innovative. Entrepreneurs can build this type of firm in several ways.[38]

The following are not inflexible rules, but they do enhance a venture's chance of remaining adaptive and innovative both through and beyond the growth stage.

SHARE THE ENTREPRENEUR'S VISION

The entrepreneur's vision must be permeated throughout the organization for employees to understand the company's direction and share in the responsibility for its growth. The entrepreneur can communicate the vision directly to the employees through meetings, conversations, or seminars. It also can be shared through symbolic events or activities such as social gatherings, recognition events, and displays. Whatever the format, having shared vision allows the venture's personnel to catch the dream and become an integral part of creating the future.[39]

INCREASE THE PERCEPTION OF OPPORTUNITY

This can be accomplished with careful job design. The work should have defined objectives for which people will be responsible. Each level of the hierarchy should be kept informed of its role in producing the final output of the product or service. This often is known as "staying close to the customer." Another way to increase the perception of opportunity is through a careful coordination and integration of the functional areas. This allows employees in different functional areas to work together as a cohesive whole.

INSTITUTIONALIZE CHANGE AS THE VENTURE'S GOAL

This entails a preference for innovation and change rather than preservation of the status quo. If opportunity is to be perceived, the environment of the enterprise must not only encourage it but also establish it as a goal. Within this context, a desire for opportunity can exist if resources are made available and departmental barriers are reduced.

INSTILL THE DESIRE TO BE INNOVATIVE

The desire of personnel to pursue opportunity must be carefully nurtured. Words alone will not create the innovative climate.[40] Specific steps, such as the following, should be taken.

A Reward System   Explicit forms of recognition should be given to individuals who pursue innovative opportunities. For example, bonuses, awards, salary advances, and promotions should be tied directly to the innovative attempts of personnel.

An Environment That Allows for Failure   The fear of failure must be minimized by the general recognition that often many attempts are needed before a success is achieved. This does not imply that failure is sought or desired. However, learning from failure, as opposed to expecting punishment for it, is promoted. When this type of environment exists, people become willing to accept the challenge of change and innovation.

Flexible Operations   Flexibility creates the possibility of change taking place and having a positive effect. If a venture remains too rigidly tied to plans or strategies, it will not be responsive to new technologies, customer changes, or environmental shifts. Innovation will not take place because it will not "fit in."

The Development of Venture Teams   In order for the environment to foster innovation, venture teams and team performance goals need to be established. These must not be just work groups but visionary, committed teams that have the authority to create new directions, set new standards, and challenge the status quo.[41]

13-5 UNIQUE MANAGERIAL CONCERNS OF GROWING VENTURES

LO10 Identify the unique managerial concerns with growth businesses

Emerging businesses differ in many ways from larger, more structured businesses. Several unique managerial concerns involve growing businesses in particular. These concerns may seem insignificant to the operation of a large business, but often they become important to emerging entrepreneurs.

13-5a The Distinctiveness of Size

The distinction of *smallness* gives emerging businesses certain disadvantages. The limited market, for example, restricts a small firm. Because a small size limits a company's ability to geographically extend throughout a region or state, the firm must recognize and service its available market. Another disadvantage is the higher ordering costs that burden many small firms. Because they do not order large lots of inventory from suppliers, small businesses usually do not receive quantity discounts and must pay higher prices. Finally, a smaller staff forces small firms to accept less specialization of labor. Thus, employees and managers are expected to perform numerous functions.

However, the distinction of small size is not all bad, and the advantages to smallness should be recognized and capitalized on. One advantage is greater flexibility. In smaller ventures, decisions can be made and implemented immediately, without the input of committees and the delay of bureaucratic layers. Production, marketing, and service are all areas that can be adjusted quickly for a competitive advantage over larger businesses in the same field. A second advantage is constant communication with the community.[42] An entrepreneur lives in the community and is personally involved in its affairs. The special insight of this involvement allows the entrepreneur to adjust products or services to suit the specific needs or desires of the particular community. This leads to the third and probably most important advantage of closeness to the customer: the ability to offer personal service. The personal service that an entrepreneur can provide is one of the key elements of success today. Major corporations work feverishly to duplicate or imitate the idea of personal service. Because the opportunity to provide personal service is an advantage that emerging firms possess by nature of their size, it *must* be capitalized on.

13-5b The One-Person-Band Syndrome

Most entrepreneurs start their businesses alone or with a few family members or close associates. In effect, the business *is* the entrepreneur and the entrepreneur is the business.[43] However, a danger arises if the entrepreneur refuses to relinquish any authority as the emerging business grows. The one-person-band syndrome exists when an entrepreneur fails to delegate responsibility to employees, thereby retaining *all* decision-making authority. One study revealed that most planning in entrepreneurial firms is done by the owner alone, as are other operational activities.[44] This syndrome often is derived from the same pattern of independence that helped start the business in the first place. However, the owner who continues to perform as a one-person band can restrict the growth of the firm, because the owner's ability is limited. How can proper planning for the business be accomplished if the owner is immersed in daily operations? Thus, the entrepreneur must recognize the importance of delegation. If the owner can break away from the natural tendency to do *everything,* then the business will benefit from a wider array of that person's abilities.

13-5c Time Management

Effective time management is not exclusively a challenge to entrepreneurs. However, limited size and staff force the entrepreneur to face this challenge most diligently. It has been said a person never will *find* time to do anything but must, in fact, *make* time. In other words, entrepreneurs should learn to use time as a resource and not allow time to use them.[45] To perform daily managerial activities in the most time-efficient manner, owner/managers should follow four critical steps:

1. **Assessment.** The business owner should analyze his or her daily activities and rank them in order of importance. (A written list on a notepad is recommended.)

2. **Prioritization.** The owner should divide and categorize the day's activities based on his or her ability to devote the necessary time to the task that day. In other words, the owner should avoid a procrastination of duties.

3. **Creation of procedures.** Repetitive daily activities can be handled easily by an employee if instructions are provided. This organizing of tasks can be a major timesaver for the owner that would allow the fourth and last step to be put into effect.

4. **Delegation.** Delegation can be accomplished after the owner creates procedures for various jobs. As mentioned in the description of the one-person-band syndrome, delegation is a critical skill entrepreneurs need to develop.

All of these steps in effective time management require self-discipline on the part of entrepreneurs.

13-5d Community Pressures

Proximity to the community was mentioned earlier as a size advantage for small emerging ventures. However, unlike major corporations with public relations departments, the entrepreneur is involved with community activities directly. The community presents unique pressure to emerging entrepreneurs in three ways: participation, leadership, and donations.

Each of these expectations from the community requires entrepreneurs to plan and budget carefully. Many community members believe that the entrepreneur has "excess" time because he or she owns the business. They also believe that the owner has leadership abilities needed for various community activities. Although the latter may be true, the owner usually does not have excess time. Therefore, entrepreneurs need to plan carefully the activities they believe would be most beneficial. One consideration is the amount of advertising or recognition the business will receive for the owner's participation. When the owner can justify his or her community involvement, both the business and the community benefit.

Financial donations also require careful analysis and budgeting. Again, because consumers have access to the entrepreneur (as opposed to the chief executive officer of a major corporation), he or she may be inundated with requests for donations to charitable and community organizations. Although each organization may have a worthy cause, the entrepreneur cannot support every one and remain financially healthy. Thus, the owner needs to decide which of the organizations to assist and to budget a predetermined amount of money for annual donations. Any other solicitations for money must be placed in writing and submitted to the entrepreneur for consideration. This is the only way entrepreneurs can avoid giving constant cash donations without careful budget consideration.

The critical fact to remember is that time and money are extremely valuable resources for an entrepreneur. They should be budgeted in a meaningful way. Therefore, entrepreneurs need to analyze their community involvement and to continuously reassess the costs versus the benefits.[46]

13-5e Continuous Learning

A final unique concern for the entrepreneur is continuous learning. All of the previously mentioned concerns leave very little time for owners to maintain or improve their managerial and entrepreneurial knowledge. However, the environment of the twenty-first century has produced dramatic changes that can affect the procedures, processes, programs, philosophy, or even the product of a growing business. The ancient Greek philosopher Epictetus once said, "It is impossible for a man to learn what he thinks he already knows." This quote illustrates the need for entrepreneurs to dedicate time to learning new techniques and principles for their businesses. Trade associations, seminars, conferences, publications, and college courses all provide opportunities for entrepreneurs to continue their entrepreneurial education. Staying abreast of industry changes is another way that entrepreneurs can maintain a competitive edge.

13-6 ACHIEVING ENTREPRENEURIAL LEADERSHIP IN THE NEW MILLENNIUM

Entrepreneurial leadership may be the most critical element in the management of high growth ventures. Terms such as *visionary* and *strategic* have been used when describing different types of leaders. Table 13.4 provides a comprehensive description of strategic leaders, visionary leaders, and managerial leaders. Research has demonstrated that the concept behind strategic leadership is the most effective in growing organizations.[47] Researchers R. Duane Ireland and Michael A. Hitt identified some of the most important concepts in effective strategic

TABLE 13.4 STRATEGIC, VISIONARY, AND MANAGERIAL LEADERSHIP

Strategic Leaders

√ synergistic combination of managerial and visionary leadership

√ emphasis on ethical behavior and value-based decisions

√ oversee operating (day-to-day) and strategic (long-term) responsibilities

√ formulate and implement strategies for immediate impact and preservation of long-term goals to enhance organizational survival, growth, and long-term viability

√ have strong, positive expectations of the performance they expect from their superiors, peers, subordinates, and themselves

√ use strategic controls and financial controls, with emphasis on strategic controls

√ use, and interchange, tacit and explicit knowledge on individual and organizational levels

√ use linear and nonlinear thinking patterns

√ believe in strategic choice, that is, their choices make a difference in their organizations and environment

Visionary Leaders	Managerial Leaders
√ are proactive, shape ideas, change the way people think about what is desirable, possible, and necessary	√ are reactive; adopt passive attitudes toward goals; goals arise out of necessities, not desires and dreams; goals based on past
√ work to develop choices, fresh approaches to long-standing problems; work from high-risk positions	√ view work as an enabling process involving some combination of ideas and people interacting to establish strategies
√ are concerned with ideas; relate to people in intuitive and empathetic ways	√ relate to people according to their roles in the decision-making process
√ feel separate from their environment; work in, but do not belong to, organizations; sense of who they are does not depend on work	√ see themselves as conservators and regulators of existing order; sense of who they are depends on their role in organization
√ influence attitudes and opinions of others within the organization	√ influence actions and decisions of those with whom they work
√ concerned with insuring future of organization, especially through development and management of people	√ involved in situations and contexts characteristic of day-to-day activities
√ more embedded in complexity, ambiguity, and information overload; engage in multifunctional, integrative tasks	√ concerned with, and more comfortable in, functional areas of responsibilities
√ know less than their functional area experts	√ expert in their functional area
√ more likely to make decisions based on values	√ less likely to make value-based decisions
√ more willing to invest in innovation, human capital, and creating and maintaining an effective culture to ensure long-term viability	√ engage in, and support, short-term, least-cost behavior to enhance financial performance figures
√ focus on tacit knowledge and develop strategies as communal forms of tacit knowledge that promote enactment of a vision	√ focus on managing the exchange and combination of explicit knowledge and ensuring compliance to standard operating procedures
√ utilize nonlinear thinking	√ utilize linear thinking
√ believe in strategic choice, that is, their choices make a difference in their organizations and environment	√ believe in determinism, that is, the choices they make are determined by their internal and external environments

Source: W. Glenn Rowe, "Creating Wealth in Organizations: The Role of Strategic Leadership," *Academy of Management Executive* 15, no. 1 (2001): 82.

leadership.[48] This type of leadership can be classified as **entrepreneurial leadership**, which arises when an entrepreneur attempts to manage a fast-paced, growth-oriented company.[49]

Entrepreneurial leadership can be defined as the entrepreneur's ability to anticipate, envision, maintain flexibility, think strategically, and work with others to initiate changes that will create a viable future for the organization. If these leadership processes are difficult for competitors to understand—and, hence, to imitate—the firm will create a competitive advantage.

Today's fast-paced economy has created a new competitive landscape—one in which events change constantly and unpredictably. These changes are revolutionary in nature—that is, they happen swiftly and are relentless in their frequency, affecting virtually all parts of an organization simultaneously. The ambiguity that results from revolutionary changes challenges firms and their strategic abilities to increase the speed of the decision-making processes through which strategies are formulated and implemented.[50]

Growth-oriented firms need to adopt a new competitive mind-set—one in which flexibility, speed, innovation, and strategic leadership are valued highly. With this mind-set, firms can identify and completely exploit opportunities that emerge in the new competitive landscape. These opportunities surface primarily because of the disequilibrium that is created by continuous changes (especially technological changes). More specifically, although uncertainty and disequilibrium often result in seemingly hostile and intensely rivalrous conditions, these conditions may simultaneously yield significant product-driven growth opportunities. Through effective entrepreneurial leadership, growth firms can adapt their behaviors and exploit such opportunities.[51]

SUMMARY

Although many ways of strategically planning a venture exist, all have one common element: Each is an extension of the entrepreneur's vision—each takes the owner's concept of the business and puts it into action. Entrepreneurs may not use strategic planning for many reasons, among them scarcity of time, lack of knowledge about how to plan, lack of expertise in the planning process, and lack of trust in others.

A number of benefits to strategic planning exist. In particular, studies have shown that small firms that use this process tend to have better financial performance than those that do not. Other benefits include more efficient resource allocation, improved competitive position, higher employee morale, and more rapid decision-making.

The challenges of managing entrepreneurial growth were then examined. A typical life cycle of a venture has five stages: development, start-up, growth, stabilization, and innovation or decline. This chapter focused on ways to maintain an entrepreneurial frame of mind while making the necessary adjustments to deal with the growth phase. The balance of entrepreneurial and managerial approaches was reviewed in this section. This balance was demonstrated by considering five major factors: strategic orientation, commitment to seize opportunities, commitment of resources, control of resources, and management structure. This differentiation of major factors is important for analyzing aspects of the venture that need either more administrative or more entrepreneurial emphasis.

The chapter then examined the importance of a venture's growth stage. Underscoring the metamorphosis a venture goes through, four factors were discussed: control, responsibility, tolerance of failure, and change. In addition, the challenge of managing paradox and contradiction was presented.

The elements involved in building an entrepreneurial firm were then discussed. When building the desired entrepreneurial firm, entrepreneurs need to be concerned with three important responsibilities: (1) increasing the perception of opportunity, (2) institutionalizing change as the venture's goals, and (3) instilling the desire to be innovative. In addition, the unique managerial concerns of growing ventures were outlined for entrepreneurs.

Finally, the concept of entrepreneurial leadership was introduced as a way for entrepreneurs to anticipate, envision, maintain flexibility, think strategically, and work with others to initiate changes that will create a viable future for the growth-oriented venture.

KEY TERMS

entrepreneurial firm	lack of trust and openness	start-up activities
entrepreneurial leadership	life-cycle stages	strategic planning
entrepreneurial strategy matrix	moral failure	strategic positioning
growth stage	new-venture development	SWOT analysis
growth wall	one-person-band syndrome	time scarcity
innovation	perception of high cost	uncontrollable failure
lack of expertise/skills	personal failure	
lack of knowledge	stabilization stage	

REVIEW AND DISCUSSION QUESTIONS

1. In what way does an entrepreneur's vision affect the company's strategic plan?

2. How is the strategic plan of an engineer/scientist entrepreneur likely to be different from that of an entrepreneur whose primary strength is in the manufacturing area? Be complete in your answer.

3. Give three reasons why many entrepreneurs do not like to formulate strategic plans.

4. Does strategic planning really pay off for entrepreneurial ventures?

5. Describe the entrepreneurial strategy matrix and explain why it is effective for entrepreneurs.

6. Briefly identify and describe the stages of development for a new venture.

7. Firms that fail to innovate will die. What does this statement mean in the context of new ventures?

8. How can entrepreneurs build an entrepreneurial firm? Be complete in your answer.

9. Successful ventures balance entrepreneurial characteristics with managerial style. What does this statement mean?

10. Comparing the entrepreneurial focus with the administrative focus involves five major areas of consideration. What are these areas?

11. Identify and describe the four key factors that need to be considered during the growth stage.

12. What is meant by managing paradox and contradiction?

13. Identify five unique managerial concerns of growing businesses.

14. Define the one-person-band syndrome.

15. Explain the concept of entrepreneurial leadership.

NOTES

1. Amar Bhide, "How Entrepreneurs Craft Strategies That Work," *Harvard Business Review* 72, no. 2 (March/April 1994): 150–61; and Marc Gruber, "Uncovering the Value of Planning in New Venture Creation: A Process and Contingency Perspective," *Journal of Business Venturing* 22, no. 6 (2007): 782–807.

2. Scott Shane and Frédéric Delmar, "Planning for the Market: Business Planning before Marketing and the Continuation of Organizing Efforts," *Journal of Business Venturing* 19, no. 6 (November 2004): 767–85.

3. Michael A. Hitt, R. Duane Ireland, and Robert E. Hoskisson, *Strategic Management: Competitiveness and Globalization,* 11th ed. (Mason, OH: Cengage Learning, 2015).

4. See James R. Lang, Roger J. Calantone, and Donald Gudmundson, "Small Firm Information Seeking as a Response to Environmental Threats and Opportunities," *Journal of Small Business Management* 35, no. 1, (1997): 11–23; Reginald M. Beal, "Competing Effectively: Environmental Scanning, Competitive Strategy, and Organizational Performance in Small Manufacturing Firms," *Journal of Small Business Management* 38, no. 1 (2000): 27–47; and Andreea N. Kiss and Pamela S. Barr, "New Venture strategic Adaptation:

The Interplay of Belief Structures and Industry Context," *Strategic Management Journal*, 36, no. 8 (2015): 1245–63.

5. Henry Mintzberg, "The Fall and Rise of Strategic Planning," *Harvard Business Review* 72, no. 1 (January/February 1994): 107–14.

6. Charles H. Matthews and Susanne G. Scott, "Uncertainty and Planning in Small and Entrepreneurial Firms: An Empirical Assessment," *Journal of Small Business Management* 33, no. 4 (1995): 34–52; and Sigal Haber and Arie Reichel, "The Cumulative Nature of the Entrepreneurial Process: The Contribution of Human Capital, Planning, and Environmental Resources to Small Venture Performance," *Journal of Business Venturing* 22, no. 1 (2007): 119–45.

7. John W. Mullins and David Forlani, "Missing the Boat or Sinking the Boat: A Study of New Venture Decision Making," *Journal of Business Venturing* 20, no. 1 (January 2005): 47–69; and Michael D. Ensley, Craig L. Pearce, and Keith M. Hmieleski, "The Moderating Effect of Environmental Dynamism on the Relationship Between Entrepreneur Leadership Behavior and New Venture Performance," *Journal of Business Venturing* 21, no. 2 (2006): 243–63.

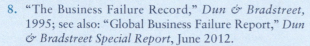

8. "The Business Failure Record," *Dun & Bradstreet,* 1995; see also: "Global Business Failure Report," *Dun & Bradstreet Special Report*, June 2012.

9. Richard B. Robinson, "The Importance of Outsiders in Small Firm Strategic Planning," *Academy of Management Journal* 25, no. 2 (March 1982): 80–93.

10. A. Bakr Ibrahim, "Strategy Types and Small Firm's Performance: An Empirical Investigation," *Journal of Small Business Strategy* 4, no. 1 (Spring 1991): 13–22.

11. Elaine Mosakowski, "A Resource-Based Perspective on the Dynamic Strategy—Performance Relationship: An Empirical Examination of the Focus and Differentiation Strategies in Entrepreneurial Firms," *Journal of Management* 19, no. 4 (1993): 819–39.

12. Leslie W. Rue and Nabil A. Ibrahim, "The Relationship Between Planning Sophistication and Performance in Small Business," *Journal of Small Business Management* 36, no. 4, (1998): 24–32.

13. Charles R. Schwenk and Charles B. Shrader, "Effects of Formal Strategic Planning on Financial Performance in Small Firms: A Meta Analysis," *Entrepreneurship Theory and Practice* 17, no. 3 (Spring 1993): 53–64; see also Philip D. Olson and Donald W. Bokor, "Strategy Process—Content Interaction: Effects on Growth Performance in Small, Startup Firms," *Journal of Small Business Management* 33, no. 1 (1995): 34–44; and Patrice Perry-Rivers, "Stratification, Economic Adversity, and Entrepreneurial Launch: The Effect of Resource Position on Entrepreneurial Strategy," *Entrepreneurship Theory and Practice,* (2015): in press.

14. Michael E. Porter, "Knowing Your Place—How to Assess the Attractiveness of Your Industry and Your Company's Position in It," *Inc.* (September 1991): 90–94.

15. Ibid., 93.

16. R. Duane Ireland, Michael A. Hitt, S. Michael Camp, and Donald L. Sexton, "Integrating Entrepreneurship and Strategic Management Actions to Create Firm Wealth," *Academy of Management Executive* 15, no. 1 (February 2001): 49–63.

17. Michael E. Porter, "What Is Strategy?" *Harvard Business Review* 74, no. 5 (November/December 1996): 61–78.

18. Matthew C. Sonfield and Robert N. Lussier, "The Entrepreneurial Strategy Matrix: A Model for New and Ongoing Ventures," *Business Horizons* 40, no. 3 (May/June 1997): 73–77.

19. Hyung Rok Yim, "Quality Shock vs. Market Shock: Lessons from Recently Established Rapidly Growing U.S. Startups," *Journal of Business Venturing* 23, no. 2 (2008): 141–64; Alexander McKelvie and Johan Wiklund, "Advancing Firm Growth Research: A Focus on Growth Mode Instead of Growth Rate," *Entrepreneurship Theory and Practice* 34, no. 2 (2010): 261–88; and Lorraine M. Uhlaner, André van Stel, Valérie Duplat, and Haibo Zhou, "Disentangling the Effects of Organizational Capabilities, Innovation and Firm size on SME Sales Growth," *Small Business Economics* 41, no. 3, (2013): 581–607.

20. Alfred Chandler, *Strategy and Structure* (Cambridge: MIT Press, 1962); see also Enno Masurel and Kees van Montfort, "Life Cycle Characteristics of Small Professional Service Firms," *Journal of Small Business Management* 44, no. 3 (2006): 461–73.

21. Jeffrey G. Covin, Dennis P. Slevin, and Michael B. Heeley, "Pioneers and Followers: Competitive Tactics, Environment, and Firm Growth," *Journal of Business Venturing* 15, no. 2 (2000): 175–210; and Brandon A. Mueller, Varkey K. Titus, Jr., Jeffrey G. Covin, and Dennis P. Slevin, "Pioneering Orientation and Firm Growth: Knowing When and to What Degree Pioneering Makes Sense," *Journal of Management* 38, no. 5 (2012): 1517–49.

22. David E. Terpstra and Philip D. Olson, "Entrepreneurial Start-up and Growth: A Classification of Problems," *Entrepreneurship Theory and Practice* 17, no. 3, (1993): 5–20; and Bret Golan, "Achieving Growth and Responsiveness: Process Management and Market Orientation in Small Firms," *Journal of Small Business Management* 44, no. 3 (2006): 369–85.

23. See Michael H. Morris, Nola N. Miyasaki, Craig R. Watters, and Susan M. Coombes, "The Dilemma of Growth: Understanding Venture Size Choices of Women Entrepreneurs," *Journal of Small Business Management* 44, no. 2 (2006): 221–44; and Donald F. Kuratko and Michael H. Morris, *Entrepreneurship & Leadership* (Cheltenham, UK: Edward Elgar Publishing, 2013).

24. Charles W. Hofer and Ram Charan, "The Transition to Professional Management: Mission Impossible?" *American Journal of Small Business* 9, no. 1 (Summer 1984): 1–11; and Morten T. Hansen, Nitin Nohria, and Thomas Tierney, "What's Your Strategy for Managing Knowledge?" *Harvard Business Review* 77, no. 2 (1999): 106–16.

25. Shaker A. Zahra, "The Changing Rules of Global Competitiveness in the 21st Century," *Academy of Management Executive* 13, no. 1 (1999): 36–42.

26. Howard H. Stevenson and Jose Carlos Jarillo-Mossi, "Preserving Entrepreneurship as Companies Grow," *Journal of Business Strategy* 7, no. 1 (Summer 1986): 10; Jonathan Rowe, "Turning Darkness into Light: Strategic Thinking for Entrepreneurial Managers," *Engineering Management* 16, no. 4 (2006): 42–45; and Steven W. Bradley, Johan Wiklund, and Dean A. Shepherd, "Swinging a Double-edged Sword: The Effect of Slack on Entrepreneurial Management and Growth," *Journal of Business Venturing* 26, no. 6 (2011): 537–54.

27. Jill Kickul and Lisa K. Gundry, "Prospecting for Strategic Advantage: The Proactive Entrepreneurial Personality and Small Firm Innovation," *Journal of Small Business Management* 40, no. 2 (2002): 85–97.

28. Lanny Herron and Richard B. Robinson, Jr., "A Structural Model of the Effects of Entrepreneurial Characteristics on Venture Performance," *Journal of Business Venturing* 8, no. 3 (May 1993): 281–94; Alvarez, S.A. and Barney, J.B, "How Do Entrepreneurs Organize Firms Under Conditions of Uncertainty?" *Journal*

of Management 31, no. 5 (2005): 776–93; Daniel V. Holland and Dean A. Shepherd, "Deciding to Persist: Adversity, Values, and Entrepreneurs' Decision Policies," *Entrepreneurship Theory and Practice* 37, no. 2 (2013): 331–58.

29. Donald F. Kuratko, Jeffrey S. Hornsby, and Laura M. Corso, "Building an Adaptive Firm," *Small Business Forum* 14, no. 1 (Spring 1996): 41–48; and Jonathan T. Eckhardt and Scott A. Shane, "Industry Changes in Technology and Complementary Assets and the Creation of High-Growth Firms," *Journal of Business Venturing* 26, no. 4 (2011): 412–30.

30. Steven H. Hanks and L. R. McCarrey, "Beyond Survival: Reshaping Entrepreneurial Vision in Successful Growing Ventures," *Journal of Small Business Strategy* 4, no. 1 (Spring 1993): 1–12; Joern H. Block, Karsten Kohn, Danny Miller, and Katrin Ullrich, "Necessity Entrepreneurship and Competitive Strategy," *Small Business Economics* 44, no. 1 (2015): 37–54.

31. See Sanjay Prasad Thakur, "Size of Investment, Opportunity Choice, and Human Resources in New Venture Growth: Some Typologies," *Journal of Business Venturing* 14, no. 3 (May 1999): 283–309; and Massimo G. Colombo and Luca Grilli, "On Growth Drivers of High-Tech Start-ups: Exploring the Role of Founders' Human Capital and Venture Capital," *Journal of Business Venturing* 25, no. 6 (2010): 610–26.

32. Jon R. Katzenbach and Douglas K. Smith, "The Discipline of Teams," *Harvard Business Review* 70, no. 2 (March/April 1993): 111–20; Alexander L. M. Dingee, Brian Haslett, and Leonard E. Smollen, "Characteristics of a Successful Entrepreneurial Management Team," in *Annual Editions 00/01* (Guilford, CT: Dushkin/McGraw-Hill, 2000/2001), 71–75; and G. Page West III, "Collective Cognitions: When Entrepreneurial Teams, Not Individuals, Make Decisions," *Entrepreneurship Theory and Practice* 31, no. 1 (2007): 77–102.

33. Hofer and Charan, 3; see also William Lowell, "An Entrepreneur's Journey to the Next Level," *Small Business Forum* 14, no. 1 (Spring 1996): 68–74.

34. Hofer and Charan, 4.

35. John B. Miner, "Entrepreneurs, High Growth Entrepreneurs, and Managers: Contrasting and Overlapping Motivational Patterns," *Journal of Business Venturing* 5, no. 4 (July 1990): 221–234; and Michael J. Roberts, "Managing Growth," in *New Business Ventures and the Entrepreneur* (New York: Irwin/McGraw-Hill, 1999), 460–64.

36. Howard H. Stevenson and David E. Gumpert, "The Heart of Entrepreneurship," *Harvard Business Review* 63, no. 2 (March/April 1985): 86–87; Jesper B. Sorensen, "Bureaucracy and Entrepreneurship: Workplace Effects on Entrepreneurial Entry," *Administrative Science Quarterly* 52, no. 3 (2007): 387–412.

37. Jeffrey G. Covin and Dennis P. Slevin, "New Venture Strategic Posture, Structure, and Performance: An Industry Life Cycle Analysis," *Journal of Business Venturing* 5, no. 4, (March 1990): 123–33; see also Jeffrey G. Covin, Kimberly M. Green, and Dennis P. Slevin, "Strategic Process Effects on the Entrepreneurial Orientation-Sales Growth Rate Relationships," *Entrepreneurship Theory and Practice* 30, no. 1 (2006): 57–82.

38. Charles J. Fombrun and Stefan Wally, "Structuring Small Firms for Rapid Growth," *Journal of Business Venturing* 4, no. 2 (March 1989): 107–22; Donna J. Kelley and Mark P. Rice, "Advantage Beyond Founding: The Strategic Use of Technologies," *Journal of Business Venturing* 17, no. 1 (2002): 41–58; see also Andrew J. Sherman, *Grow Fast Grow Right* (Chicago: Kaplan, 2007).

39. Donald C. Hambrick and Lynn M. Crozier, "Stumblers and Stars in the Management of Rapid Growth," *Journal of Business Venturing* 1, no. 1 (January 1985): 31–45.

40. Richard L. Osborne, "Second Phase Entrepreneurship: Breaking Through the Growth Wall," *Business Horizons* 37, no. 1 (January/February 1994): 80–86.

41. Ibid., 82–85.

42. See Jerry R. Cornwell, "The Entrepreneur as a Building Block for Community," *Journal of Developmental Entrepreneurship* 3, no. 2 (Fall/Winter 1998): 141–48; and Ana María Peredo and James J. Chrisman, "Toward a Theory of Community-Based Enterprise," *Academy of Management Review* 31, no. 2 (2006): 309–28.

43. David E. Gumpert and David P. Boyd, "The Loneliness of the Small Business Owner," *Harvard Business Review* 62, no. 5 (November/December 1984): 19–24.

44. Douglas W. Naffziger and Donald F. Kuratko, "An Investigation into the Prevalence of Planning in Small Business," *Journal of Business and Entrepreneurship* 3, no. 2 (October 1991): 99–110; see also Marjorie A. Lyles, Inga S. Baird, J. Burdeane Orris, and Donald F. Kuratko, "Formalized Planning in Small Business: Increasing Strategic Choices," *Journal of Small Business Management* 31, no. 1 (1993): 38–50.

45. Charles R. Hobbs, "Time Power," *Small Business Reports* (January 1990): 46–55; Jack Falvey, "New and Improved Time Management," *Small Business Reports* (July 1990): 14–17; and Julie Morgenstern, *Time Management from the Inside Out: The Foolproof System for Taking Control of Your Schedule—and Your Life* 2nd ed. (New York: Henry Holt/Owl Books, 2004).

46. Terry L. Besser, "Community Involvement and the Perception of Success Among Small Business Operators in Small Towns," *Journal of Small Business Management* 37, no. 4, (October 1999): 16–29; and Rhonda Walker Mack, "Event Sponsorship: An Exploratory Study of Small Business Objectives, Practices, and Perceptions," *Journal of Small Business Management* 37, no. 3 (July 1999): 25–30.

47. W. Glenn Rowe, "Creating Wealth in Organizations: The Role of Strategic Leadership," *Academy of Management Executive* 15, no. 1 (2001): 81–94.

48. R. Duane Ireland and Michael A. Hitt, "Achieving and Maintaining Strategic Competitiveness in the 21st

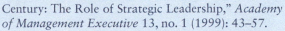

Century: The Role of Strategic Leadership," *Academy of Management Executive* 13, no. 1 (1999): 43–57.

49. Michael A. Hitt, R. Duane Ireland, S. Michael Camp, and Donald L. Sexton, "Strategic Entrepreneurship: Entrepreneurial Strategies for Wealth Creation," *Strategic Management Journal* 22, no. 6 (2001): 479–92; see also John L. Thompson, "A Strategic Perspective of Entrepreneurship," *International Journal of Entrepreneurial Behavior & Research* 5, no. 6 (1999): 279–96; Catherine M. Daily, Patricia P. McDougall, Jeffrey G. Covin and Dan R. Dalton, "Governance and Strategic Leadership in Entrepreneurial Firms," *Journal of Management* 28, no. 3 (2002): 387–412; and Kuratko and Morris, *Entrepreneurship & Leadership*.

50. E. H. Kessler and A. K. Chakrabarti, "Innovation Speed: A Conceptual Model of Context, Antecedents, and Outcomes," *Academy of Management Review* 21 (1996): 1143–91; Kathleen M. Eisenhardt, Nathan R. Furr and Christopher B. Bingham, "Microfoundations of Performance: Balancing Efficiency and Flexibility in Dynamic Environments," *Organization Science* 21, no. 6 (2005): 1263–73; and Donald F. Kuratko, "The Entrepreneurial Imperative of the 21st Century," *Business Horizons* 52, no. 5 (2009): 421–28.

51. Donald F. Kuratko, R. Duane Ireland, and Jeffrey S. Hornsby, "Improving Firm Performance Through Entrepreneurial Actions: Acordia's Corporate Entrepreneurship Strategy," *Academy of Management Executive* 15, no. 4 (2001): 60–71; V. Gupta, Ian C. MacMillan and G. Surie, "Entrepreneurial Leadership: Developing and Measuring a Cross-Cultural Construct," *Journal of Business Venturing* 19, no. 2 (2004): 241–60.

CHAPTER 14

Valuation of Entrepreneurial Ventures

LEARNING OBJECTIVES

1 To explain the importance of valuation

2 To examine the underlying issues involved in the acquisition process

3 To describe the basic elements of due diligence

4 To outline the various aspects of analyzing a business

5 To present the major points to consider when establishing a firm's value

6 To highlight the available methods of valuing a venture

7 To examine the three principal methods currently used in business valuations

8 To consider additional factors that affect a venture's valuation

Entrepreneurial Thought

Market transactions are often not observable for assets such as privately held businesses. Thus, fair market value must be estimated. An estimate of fair market value is usually subjective due to the circumstances of place, time, the existence of comparable precedents, and the evaluation principles of each involved person. Opinions on value are always based upon subjective interpretation of available information at the time of assessment.

—Definition of Fair Market Value from Wikipedia.com

14-1 THE IMPORTANCE OF BUSINESS VALUATION

LO1 Explain the importance of valuation

Every entrepreneur should be able to calculate the value of his or her business and also should be able to determine the value of a competitor's operation. Such **business valuation** is essential in the following situations:

- Buying or selling a business, division, or major asset
- Establishing an employee stock option plan (ESOP) or profit-sharing plan for employees
- Raising growth capital through stock warrants or convertible loans
- Determining inheritance tax liability (potential estate tax liability)
- Giving a gift of stock to family members
- Structuring a buy/sell agreement with stockholders
- Attempting to buy out a partner
- Going public with the company or privately placing the stock

Equally important is the entrepreneur's desire to know the real value of the venture. This valuation can provide a scorecard for periodically tracking the increases or decreases in the business's value.[1]

14-2 UNDERLYING ISSUES WHEN ACQUIRING A VENTURE

LO2 Examine the underlying issues involved in the acquisition process

As we demonstrated in Chapter 6, acquisition of a venture is one pathway to entering the entrepreneurial arena. Because one of the main reasons a valuation would take place with a venture is that it is being sold, we will examine a few more points concerning acquisition of a venture. Three issues underlie the proper valuation of a venture set to be acquired: (1) the differing goals of a buyer and seller, (2) the emotional bias of the seller, and (3) the reasons for the acquisition.

14-2a Goals of the Buyer and Seller

It is important to remember one's reasons for valuing an enterprise. Both major parties to the transaction, buyer and seller, will assign different values to the enterprise because of their basic objectives. The seller will attempt to establish the highest possible value for the business and will not heed the realistic considerations of the market, the environment, or the economy. To the seller, the enterprise may represent a lifetime investment—or at the very least one that took a lot of effort. The buyer, on the other hand, will try to determine the lowest possible price to be paid. The enterprise is regarded as an investment for the buyer, and he or she must assess the profit potential. As a result, a pessimistic view often is taken. An understanding of both positions in the valuation process is important.

14-2b Emotional Bias

The second issue in valuing a business is the **emotional bias** of the seller. Whenever someone starts a venture, nurtures it through early growth, and makes it a profitable business, the person tends to believe that the enterprise is worth a great deal more than outsiders believe it is worth. Entrepreneurs therefore must try to be as objective as possible in determining a fair value for the enterprise (realizing that this fair amount will be negotiable).

14-2c Reasons for the Acquisition

The third issue in valuing a business is the reason an entrepreneur's business is being acquired. The following are some of the most common reasons for acquisition:

- Developing more growth-phase products by acquiring a firm that has developed new products in the company's industry
- Increasing the number of customers by acquiring a firm whose current customers will broaden substantially the company's customer base

- Increasing market share by acquiring a firm in the company's industry
- Improving or changing distribution channels by acquiring a firm with recognized superiority in the company's current distribution channel
- Expanding the product line by acquiring a firm whose products complement and complete the company's product line
- Developing or improving customer service operations by acquiring a firm with an established service operation, as well as a customer service network that includes the company's products
- Reducing operating leverage and increasing absorption of fixed costs by acquiring a firm that has a lower degree of operating leverage and can absorb the company's fixed costs
- Using idle or excess plant capacity by acquiring a firm that can operate in the company's current plant facilities
- Integrating vertically, either backward or forward, by acquiring a firm that is a supplier or distributor
- Reducing inventory levels by acquiring a firm that is a customer (but not an end user) and adjusting the company's inventory levels to match the acquired firm's orders
- Reducing indirect operating costs by acquiring a firm that will allow elimination of duplicate operating costs (e.g., warehousing and distribution)
- Reducing fixed costs by acquiring a firm that will permit elimination of duplicate fixed costs (e.g., corporate and staff functional groups)[2]

In summary, it is important that the entrepreneur and all other parties involved objectively view the firm's operations and potential. An evaluation of the following points can assist in this process:

- A firm's potential to pay for itself during a reasonable period of time
- The difficulties the new owners face during the transition period
- The amount of security or risk involved in the transaction; changes in interest rates
- The effect on the company's value if a turnaround is required
- The number of potential buyers
- Current managers' intentions to remain with the firm
- The taxes associated with the purchase or sale of an enterprise[3]

14-3 DUE DILIGENCE

LO3 Describe the basic elements of due diligence

When considering the acquisition of a venture, an entrepreneur should perform a complete **due diligence**, which means a thorough analysis of every facet of the existing business. Table 14.1 provides a due diligence outline that is used to assess the viability of a firm's business plan. Notice how each major segment is analyzed by applying specific questions to that part.

TABLE 14.1 PERFORMING DUE DILIGENCE

Understanding the key questions to ask in a due diligence evaluation may be a critical step for any entrepreneur considering an acquisition. Provided here are those questions that impact each of the major sections analyzed in a potential candidate for acquisition.

I. **Industry Analysis**

  A. General industry questions

   1. What are the chief characteristics of the industry (economic, technological, political, social, change)?

   2. How does the plan address these? How is the proposed venture impacted by these?

(Continued)

TABLE 14.1   PERFORMING DUE DILIGENCE (*Continued*)

3. How attractive is the industry in terms of its prospects for above-average profitability?

4. What has the industry growth rate been for the past five years and what is it projected to be for the next five? Give specific support or justification for these projections.

5. Have there been any recent transactions in the industry, such as IPOs, LBOs, private placements, mergers, or acquisitions? Describe the transactions and provide a brief explanation of the financial arrangements of each transaction.

  B. Competitive environment questions

    1. What competitive forces (entry barriers, substitutes, power of buyers and suppliers—rivalry is addressed in next section) are at work in the industry and how strong are they?

    2. Has the plan identified the competitive environment and how the company will fit into that environment, including the degree of market saturation?

    3. Calculate total market available in dollars.

  C. Primary Competitor Analysis

    1. Compare and contrast *major* competitors along core competitive dimensions, including:

Product/Service	First mover
Pricing	Market share
Distribution	Technology
Marketing	Financial backing
Strategic Partnerships	Financial performance

    2. Calculate market share available for this firm not already captured by competitors (dollars and users). Is this enough market share to achieve the financial projections in the plan?

    3. Which companies are in the strongest/weakest competitive position?

    4. Who will likely make what competitive moves next?

    5. What key factors will determine competitive success or failure?

II. Target Market Analysis

  A. Describe the target market: size, scope, growth, growth potential, demand drivers, price sensitivity, sales cycle.

  B. What is the need or want that the company is satisfying?

  C. What are the barriers that will keep competitors from copying this venture's product or service? What market inefficiencies exist?

  D. How strong are competitive forces (rivalry, substitutes) within this target market?

  E. What has the growth rate of the target market been for the past five years and what is it projected to be for the next five? Provide support/justification for these projections.

III. Venture Analysis

  A. Value proposition

    1. What does the venture do, and how does it provide value to its customers and investors?

  B. Management team

    1. Does this team have what it takes to make this venture a success?

    2. Is success dependent on one key person? If so, is this recognized and dealt with in the plan (succession, key man replacement, etc.)?

    3. Employee gaps? Plans to address gaps?

  C. Business model

    1. How does the company make money?

    2. How and when does it plan to be profitable?

    3. Does the plan follow a demonstrated success formula? For example, discuss similar companies in terms of size (revenues/employees), operations, revenue model, and/or business model. These companies could be direct competitors or similar firms that are not in the same market, but instead just a similar type of company/model.

TABLE 14.1 PERFORMING DUE DILIGENCE (*Continued*)

D. Strategy

1. How does the venture plan on achieving success in its business model?

2. What other strategic approaches might work well in this situation?

E. Marketing plan

1. How will the venture convert prospects into customers?

2. Who makes the customer's purchase decisions? When and how are the decisions made? What dimensions are critical to the customer in making the decisions? Is the plan specific in defining their strategy in this area?

3. Does the venture have a base of current customers?

F. Operations

1. Does the venture's operating plan make sense in terms of supporting its strategy and business model?

IV. **Situation Analysis**

A. What are the company's strengths, weaknesses, opportunities, and threats?

B. Look at your competitor analysis; is the company competitive on cost? Is it differentiated compared to competitors? How?

C. How strong is the company's competitive position? Are there entry barriers that protect the company? What key strategic factors support this proposition? Which ones are counter to its success?

D. What strategic issues does the company face?

V. **Financial Analysis**

A. Ratio analysis: liquidity, solvency, profitability, viability.

B. Compare projected growth rates versus historical industry growth rates. State why this company will be able to sustain the projected rate above that of its industry. If it is determined that the projections are too optimistic, what can be expected?

C. Valuation

1. Calculate pre-money valuation. What supports this valuation (number of shares, price per share, current audited balance sheet/accepted revenue multiples, etc.)?

2. Triangulate this valuation by (1) comparing the P/E ratios or revenue multiples of similar companies and (2) discounting the company's cash flow projections.

D. Other financial considerations:

1. Start-up cash spent or needed

2. Current cash "burn rate"

3. Cash needed for years 1 to 5

4. Five-year revenues

5. Five-year profits

6. Breakeven:

   a. Revenues

   b. Timeline

E. Additional considerations:

1. Accuracy

2. Abnormalities. Is the budget in line or out of hand? Is the accounting correct?

3. Needed assumptions

   a. Is the plan well written? Is it concise and to the point?

   b. Can the "layperson" understand it?

   c. Is the idea viable?

(Continued)

TABLE 14.1   PERFORMING DUE DILIGENCE (*Continued*)

    d. Is this appropriate for venture investing? Can we expect enough growth? What is the risk/reward relationship?

    e. Other

Appendices

    A. Are there resources and/or a bibliography listed to check?

    B. Is there any other detailed support for particular sections of the plan?

© Cengage Learning

The entrepreneur also may apply a more general approach to better assess the viability of the potential purchase; however, one critical area that always needs to be addressed is *the future trends of the business*, which require an overall look at the particular industry trends and how this business will fit into them. In addition, the financial health of the business needs to be projected, and *how much capital is needed to buy the venture* must be determined; this step requires understanding that the final purchase price is not the only factor that needs to be taken into consideration. Repairs, new inventory, opening expenses, and working capital are just a few of the additional costs that should be considered. Figure 14.1 illustrates how to calculate the total amount needed to buy a business venture.[4]

FIGURE 14.1   TOTAL AMOUNT NEEDED TO BUY A BUSINESS

Family Living Expenses	From last paycheck to takeover day	$ _____
	Moving expense	_____
	For three months after takeover day	_____
Purchase Price	Total amount (or down payment plus three monthly installments)	_____
Sales Tax	On purchased furniture and equipment	_____
Professional Services	Escrow, accounting, legal	_____
Deposits, Prepayments, Licenses	Last month's rent (first month's rent in Operating Expense below)	_____
	Utility deposits	_____
	Sales tax deposit	_____
	Business licenses	_____
	Insurance premiums	_____
Takeover Announcements	Newspaper advertising	_____
	Mail announcements	_____
	Exterior sign changes	_____
	New stationery and forms	_____
New Inventory		_____
New Fixtures and Equipment		_____
Remodeling and Redecorating		_____
Three Months' Operating Expense	Including loan repayments	_____
Reserve to Carry Customer Accounts		_____
Cash	Petty cash, change, etc.	_____
	Total $	_____

© Cengage Learning

Note: Money for living and business expenses for at least three months should be set aside in a bank savings account and not used for any other purpose. This is a cushion to help get through the start-up period with a minimum of worry. If expense money for a longer period can be provided, it will add to peace of mind and help the buyer concentrate on building the business.

14-4 ANALYZING THE BUSINESS

LO4 Outline the various aspects of analyzing a business

When analyzing small, closely held businesses, entrepreneurs should not make comparisons with larger corporations. Many factors distinguish these types of corporations, and valuation factors that have no effect on large firms may be significantly important to smaller enterprises. For example, many closely held ventures have the following shortcomings:

- *Lack of management depth*. The degrees of skills, versatility, and competence are limited.
- Undercapitalization. The amount of equity investment is usually low (often indicating a high level of debt).
- *Insufficient controls*. Because of the lack of available management and extra capital, measures in place for monitoring and controlling operations are usually limited.
- Divergent goals. The entrepreneur often has a vision for the venture that differs from the investors' goals or stockholders' desires, thus causing internal conflicts in the firm.

These weaknesses indicate the need for careful analysis of the small business.

The checklist in Table 14.2, which is patterned after the information required for an effective business plan (see Chapter 12), provides a concise method for examining the various factors that differentiate one firm from another.

TABLE 14.2 CHECKLIST FOR ANALYZING A BUSINESS

History of the Business

The original name of business and any subsequent name changes

Date company was founded

Names of all subsidiaries and divisions; when they were formed and their function

States where company is incorporated

States where company is licensed to do business as a foreign corporation

Review of corporate charter, bylaws, and minutes

Company's original line of business and any subsequent changes

Market and Competition

Company's major business and market

Description of major projects

Sales literature on products

Growth potential of major markets in which company operates

Name, size, and market position of principal competitors

How does company's product differ from that of the competition?

Company's market niche

Information on brand, trade, and product names

Sales pattern of product lines—that is, are sales seasonal or cyclical?

Review of any statistical information available on the market—for example, trade associations, government reports, and Wall Street reports

Comparative product pricing

Gross profit margin on each product line (analyze sales growth and profit changes for three years)

Concentration of government business

Research and development expenditures—historical and projected

Sales and Distribution

How does company sell—own sales force or through manufacturer representatives?

Compensation of sales force

(Continued)

TABLE 14.2   CHECKLIST FOR ANALYZING A BUSINESS (*Continued*)

Details on advertising methods and expenditures

Details on branch sales offices, if any

Details on standard sales terms, discounts offered, and return and allowance policies

Are any sales made on consignment?

Does company warehouse its inventory?

If company uses distributors, how are they paid, and what are their responsibilities?
(For example, do they provide warranty services?)

Are company's products distributed nationwide or in a certain geographic area?

Names and addresses of company's principal customers

Sales volume of principal customers by product line for last few years

How long have customers been buying from company?

Credit rating of principal customers

Historical bad-debt experience of company

Details on private-label business, if any

Do sales terms involve any maintenance agreements?

Do sales terms offer any express or implied warranties?

Has company experienced any product liability problems?

Does company lease, as well as sell, any of its products?

What is the percentage of foreign business? How is this business sold, financed, and delivered?

Have any new products come on the market that would make company's products obsolete or less competitive?

Have any big customers been lost? If so, why?

Size and nature of market—fragmented or controlled by large companies?

Manufacturing

Full list of all manufacturing facilities

Are facilities owned or leased?

Does company manufacture from basic raw materials, or is it an assembly-type operation?

Types and availability of materials required to manufacture the product

Time length of production cycle

Does company make a standard shelf-type product, manufacture to specification, or both?

How is quality control handled in the factory?

What is the accounting system for work in process?

Are any licenses needed to manufacture product?

What is the present sales capacity based on current manufacturing equipment?

Does company have a proprietary manufacturing process?

What is company's safety record in its factory operations?

Do any problems with Occupational Safety and Health Administration (OSHA) or federal or state environmental regulations exist?

What is stability of company's supplier relationships?

Employees

Total number of employees by function

Does a union exist? If not, what is the probability of unionization? If a union exists, what have been its historical relations with company?

Any strikes or work stoppages?

Details on local labor market

Details on company's wage and personnel policies

(*Continued*)

TABLE 14.2 CHECKLIST FOR ANALYZING A BUSINESS (*Continued*)

Is employee level fixed, or can workforce be varied easily in terms of business volume?

What is company's historical labor turnover, especially in key management?

Analysis of working conditions

Analysis of general employee morale

Has the company ever been cited for a federal violation—for example, OSHA, Pregnancy Discrimination Act, Fair Labor Practices?

What are fringe benefits, vacation time, sick leave, and so on?

Physical Facilities

List of all company-used facilities, giving location, square footage, and cost

Which facilities are owned? Which leased?

What is present condition of all facilities, including machinery and equipment?

If any facilities are leased, what are the details of expiration term, cost, renewal options, and so forth?

Are current facilities adequate for current and projected needs?

Will any major problems occur if expansion is needed?

Is adequate insurance maintained?

Are facilities adequately protected against casualty loss, such as fire damage, through sprinkler systems, burglar alarms, or other measures?

Are facilities modern and functional for work process and employees?

Are facilities air conditioned and do they have adequate electric, heat, gas, water, and sanitary service?

Are facilities easily accessible to required transportation?

What is cost, net book value, and replacement value for company-owned buildings and equipment?

Ownership

List of all current owners of the company's common and preferred stock, by class if applicable

List of all individuals and the number of their shares exercisable under stock option and warrant agreements with prices and expiration dates

Breakdown of ownership by shares and percentage: actual and pro forma (assuming warrants and stock options exercised)

Does common stock have preemptive rights or liquidation or dividend preference?

Do the shares carry an investment letter?

Do restrictions on the transferability of the shares or on their use as collateral exist?

Do any buy/sell agreements exist?

Does an employee stock ownership plan or stock bonus plan exist?

Are the shares fully paid for?

Are any shareholders' agreements outstanding?

Has any stock been sold below par or stated value?

Does cumulative voting exist?

With respect to the principal owner's stock, have any shares been gifted or placed in a trust?

How many shares does the principal stockholder own directly and beneficially (including family)?

If all stock options and warrants are exercised, will the principal stockholder still control 51 percent of the company?

If a business is being bought or sold, what percentage of the total outstanding shares is needed for approval?

Financial

Three years of financial statements

• Current ratio and net quick ratio

• Net working capital and net quick assets

(*Continued*)

TABLE 14.2 CHECKLIST FOR ANALYZING A BUSINESS (*Continued*)

- Total debt as a percentage of stockholder's equity
- Source and application of funds schedules

Analysis of the company's basic liquidity and turnover ratios

- Cash as a percent of current liabilities
- Accounts receivable and inventory turnovers
- Age of accounts payable
- Sales to net working capital

If company has subsidiaries (or divisions), consolidating statements of profit and loss

Verification of the cash balance and maximum and minimum cash balances needed throughout year

If company owns marketable securities, what is their degree of liquidity (salability) and current market values?

Age of all accounts and notes receivable, any customer concentration, and the adequacy of bad debt reserve

Cost basis for recording inventories and any inventory reserves; age of inventory and relation to cost of sales (turnover)

Details on all fixed assets, including date of purchase, original cost, accumulated depreciation, and replacement value

Current market appraisals on all fixed assets, real estate, and machinery and equipment

Analysis of any prepaid expenses or deferred charges as to nature and as to amortization in or advance to affiliates; comparison of true value to book value; financial statements

Personal financial statements of principal stockholders

If company carries any goodwill or intangible items, such as patents or trademarks, what is their true value (to extent possible)? Does company have any intangible assets of value not carried on books (such as mailing lists in a publishing operation)?

Analysis of all current liabilities, including age of accounts payable and details of all bank debt and lines of credit, including interest rate, term, and collateral; loan agreements

Details on all long-term debt by creditor, including loan agreement covenants that may affect future operations

Do any contingent liabilities or other outstanding commitments, such as long-term supplier agreements exist?

Details on franchise, lease, and royalty agreements

Income statement accounts for at least three years and analysis of any significant percentage variances, that is, cost of sales as percent of sales

Company's tax returns—do they differ from its financial statements? Which years still may be open for audit?

Three-year projection of income and cash flow for reasonableness of future sales and profits and to establish financing needs

Pension, profit-sharing, and stock bonus plans for contractual commitments and unfunded past-service liability costs

Management

Details on all officers and directors—length of service, age, business background, compensation, and fringe benefits

Ownership positions: number of shares, stock options, and warrants

Similar details on other nonofficer/nondirector key management

Organizational chart

What compensation-type fringe benefits are offered to key management: bonuses, retirement-plan stock bonuses, company-paid insurance, deferred compensation?

What is management's reputation in its industry?

Does management have any personal interests in any other businesses? Does it have any other conflicts of interest?

Does key management devote 100 percent of its time to the business?

Any employment contracts—amount of salary, length of time, other terms

Has key management agreed to a noncompete clause and agreed not to divulge privileged information obtained while employed with company?

14-5 ESTABLISHING A FIRM'S VALUE

LO5 Present the major points to consider when establishing a firm's value

After using the checklist in Table 14.2, the entrepreneur can begin to examine the various methods used to valuate a business. The establishment of an actual value is more of an art than a science—estimations, assumptions, and projections are all part of the process. The quantified figures are calculated based, in part, on such hidden values and costs as goodwill, personal expenses, family members on the payroll, planned losses, and the like.[5]

Several traditional valuation methods are presented here, each using a particular approach that covers these hidden values and costs. Employing these methods will provide the entrepreneur with a general understanding of how the financial analysis of a firm works. Remember, also, that many of these methods are used concurrently and that the *final* value determination will be the actual price agreed on by the buyer and seller.

14-5a Valuation Methods

LO6 Highlight the available methods of valuing a venture

Table 14.3 lists the various methods that may be used for business valuation. Each method is described and key points about them are presented. In this section, specific attention will be concentrated on the three methods that are considered the principal measures used in current business valuations: (1) adjusted tangible assets (balance sheet values), (2) price/earnings (multiple earnings value), and (3) discounted future earnings.

TABLE 14.3 METHODS FOR VENTURE VALUATION

Method	Description/Explanation	Notes/Key Points
Fixed price	Two or more owners set initial value based on what owners "think" business is worth	Inaccuracies exist due to personal estimates
	Uses figures from any one or a combination of methods	Should allow periodic update
	Common for buy/sell agreements	
Book value (known as balance sheet method) 1. Tangible 2. Adjusted tangible	1. *Tangible book value*: Set by the business's balance sheet Reflects net worth of the firm Total assets less total liabilities (adjusted for intangible assets) 2. *Adjusted tangible book value*: Uses book value approach Reflects fair market value for certain assets Upward/downward adjustments in plant and equipment, inventory, and bad debt reserves	Some assets also appreciate or depreciate substantially, thus not an accurate valuation Adjustments in assets eliminate some of the inaccuracies and reflect a fair market value of each asset
Multiple of earnings	Net income capitalized using a price/earnings ratio (net income multiplied by P/E number) 15% capitalization rate often used (equivalent to a P/E multiple of 6.7, which is 1 divided by 0.15) High-growth businesses use lower capitalization rate (e.g., 5%, which is a multiple of 20) Stable businesses use higher capitalization rate (e.g., 10%, which is a multiple of 10) Derived value divided by number of outstanding shares to obtain per-share value	Capitalization rates vary as to firm's growth; thus, estimates or P/E used must be taken from similar publicly traded corporation

(Continued)

TABLE 14.3   METHODS FOR VENTURE VALUATION *(Continued)*

Method	Description/Explanation	Notes/Key Points
Price/earnings ratio (P/E)	Similar to a return-on-investment approach Determined by price of common stock divided by after-tax earnings Closely held firms must multiply net income by an appropriate multiple, usually derived from similar publicly traded corporations Sensitive to market conditions (prices of stocks)	More common with public corporations Market conditions (stock prices) affect this ratio
Discounted future earnings (discounted cash flow)	Attempts to establish future earning power in current dollars Projects future earnings (five years), calculates present value using a then discounted rate Based on projected "timing" of future income	Based on premise that cash flow is most important factor Effective method if (1) business being valued needs to generate a return greater than investment and (2) only cash receipts can provide the money for reinvesting in growth
Return on investment (ROI)	Net profit divided by investment Provides an earnings ratio Need to calculate probabilities of future earnings Combination of return ratio, present value tables, and weighted probabilities	Will *not* establish a value for the business Does not provide projected future earnings
Replacement value	Based on value of each asset if it had to be *replaced* at current cost Firm's worth calculated as if building from "scratch" Inflation and annual depreciation of assets are considered in raising the value above reported book value Does *not* reflect earning power or intangible assets	Useful for selling a company that's seeking to break into a new line of business Fails to consider earnings potential Does not include intangible assets (goodwill, patents, and so on)
Liquidation value	Assumes business ceases operation Sells assets and pays off liabilities Net amount after payment of all liabilities is distributed to shareholders Reflects "bottom value" of a firm Indicates amount of money that could be borrowed on a secured basis Tends to favor seller since all assets are valued as if converted to cash	Assumes each division of assets sold separately at auction Effective in giving absolute bottom value below which a firm should liquidate rather than sell
Excess earnings	Developed by the U.S. Treasury to determine a firm's intangible assets (for income tax purposes) Intent is for use only when no better method available Internal Revenue Service refers to this method as a last resort Method does not include intangibles with estimated useful lives (i.e., patents, copyrights)	Method of last resort (if no other method available) Very seldom used
Market value	Needs a "known" price paid for a similar business Difficult to find recent comparisons Methods of sale may differ—installment versus cash Should be used only as a reference point	Valuable only as a reference point Difficult to find recent, similar firms that have been sold

ADJUSTED TANGIBLE BOOK VALUE

LO7 Examine the three principal methods currently used in business valuations

A common method of valuing a business is to compute its net worth as the difference between total assets and total liabilities. However, it is important to adjust for certain assets in order to assess true economic worth, because inflation and depreciation affect the value of some assets.

In the computation of the **adjusted tangible book value**, goodwill, patents, deferred financing costs, and other intangible assets are considered with the other assets and deducted from or added to net worth. This upward or downward adjustment reflects the excess of the fair market value of each asset above or below the value reported on the balance sheet. Following is an example:

	Book Value	Fair Market Value
Inventory	$100,000	$125,000
Plant and Equipment	400,000	600,000
Other Intangibles		(50,000)
	—	—
	$500,000	$675,000

Excess = $175,000

Remember that in industry comparisons of adjusted values, only assets used in the actual operation of the business are included.

Other significant balance sheet and income statement adjustments include (1) bad debt reserves; (2) low-interest, long-term debt securities; (3) investments in affiliates; and (4) loans and advances to officers, employees, or other companies. Additionally, earnings should be adjusted. Only true earnings derived from the operations of the business should be considered. One-time items (from the sale of a company division or asset, for example) should be excluded. Also, if the company has been using a net operational loss carry forward, so its pretax income has not been fully taxed, this also should be considered.

Upward (or downward) income and balance sheet adjustments should be made for any unusually large bad-debt or inventory write-off, and for certain accounting practices, such as accelerated versus straight-line depreciation.

PRICE/EARNINGS RATIO (MULTIPLE OF EARNINGS) METHOD

The **price/earnings ratio (P/E)** is a common method used for valuing publicly held corporations. The valuation is determined by dividing the market price of the common stock by the earnings per share. A company with 100,000 shares of common stock and a net income of $100,000 would have earnings per share of $1. If the stock price rose to $5 per share, the P/E would be 5 ($5 divided by $1). Additionally, since the company has 100,000 shares of common stock, the valuation of the enterprise now would be $500,000 (100,000 shares × $5).

The primary advantage of a price/earnings approach is its simplicity. However, this advantage applies only to publicly traded corporations. Closely held companies do not have prices in the open market for their stock and thus must rely on the use of a multiple derived by comparing the firm to similar public corporations. This approach has four major drawbacks:[6]

1. The stock of a private company is not publicly traded. It is illiquid and may actually be restricted from sale (that is, not registered with the Securities and Exchange Commission). Thus, any P/E multiple usually must, by definition, be subjective and lower than the multiple commanded by comparable publicly traded stocks.

2. The stated net income of a private company may not truly reflect its actual earning power. To avoid or defer paying taxes, most business owners prefer to keep pretax income down. In addition, the closely held business may be "overspending" on fringe benefits instituted primarily for the owner's benefit.

3. Common stock that is bought and sold in the public market normally reflects only a small portion of the business's total ownership. The sale of a large controlling block of stock (typical of closely held businesses) demands a premium.

4. It is very difficult to find a truly comparable publicly held company, even in the same industry. Growth rates, competition, dividend payments, and financial profiles (liquidity and leverage) rarely will be the same.

When applied to a closely held firm, the following is an example of how the multiple-of-earnings method could be used:

Shares of common stock = 100,000

2015 net income = $100,000

15% capitalization rate assumed = 6.7 price/earnings multiple

(derived by dividing 1 by 15 and multiplying

the result by 100)

Price per share = $6.70

Value of company = 100,000 × $6.70 = $670,000

DISCOUNTED EARNINGS METHOD

Most analysts agree that the real value of any venture is its potential earning power. The discounted earnings method, more than any other, determines the firm's true value. One example of a pricing formula that uses earning power as well as adjusted tangible book value is illustrated in Figure 14.2.

The idea behind discounting the firm's cash flows is that dollars earned in the future (based on projections) are worth less than dollars earned today (due to the loss of purchasing power). With this in mind, the "timing" of projected income or cash flows is a critical factor.

THE ENTREPRENEURIAL PROCESS

The Valuation of Facebook: Real or Fantasy??

In May of 2012 the amazingly successful social networking site, Facebook, had a starting valuation of more than $100 billion. Some investors paid as much as $45 a share for Facebook on opening day, which, for a few moments at least, valued the company at more than $133 billion. That was equivalent to the valuation of Amazon.com and exceeded the valuation of Hewlett-Packard and Dell combined. Experts argued that the valuation was too high for a company that posted $1 billion in profit on revenue of $3.7 billion in 2011.

Most valuation experts agreed that a $50 billion valuation would have been more in line with the company's true earnings potential. That valuation would have made the original stock price closer to $20. But the fact that Facebook had many advertisers and built a huge following on their platform provided a solid foundation to build a growth business.

In the initial public offering, Facebook raised $16 billion. Facebook's stock price was introduced at over 100 times historical earnings versus Apple's stock price, which is 14 times historical earnings. Even with that extremely high price, numerous investors figured that the stock price would soar even higher because Facebook is the leader in social networking with almost 1 billion users (one in seven people on the planet).

When a software error on Nasdaq OMX U.S. exchange delayed the start of trading by 30 minutes, claims of "selective disclosure" leading up to the IPO about Facebook's slowing revenue growth cast the company in controversy. Then perceptions among some investors were that the stock had been overpriced from the beginning.

Facebook's stock price began to tumble as concerns surfaced about the social network's long-term business prospects and an overpriced initial offering. At one point the stock price fell 10 percent to a low of $28.65. Since the opening day stock price of $38 (with some investors paying $45), the eight-year-old company lost approximately $25 billion in value.

Some analysts predict that the challenges of earning money off smartphone and tablet users may cause difficulties for Facebook in securing large advertisers, where the majority of its revenue is found. Will Facebook have the metrics to prove profitability and growth in the future? Only time (and the market) will tell.

Source: Adapted from: Larry Magid, "Facebook's Real Value Has Nothing to Do with Its Stock Price," 5/30/2012 *Forbes* (May 30, 2012), http://www.forbes.com/sites/larrymagid/2012/05/30/facebooks-real-value-has-nothing-to-do-with-itsstock-price (accessed May 31, 2012); Alistair Barr and Edwin Chan, "Facebook Shares Plumb New Depths, Valuation Questioned," Reuters (May 29, 2012), http://www.reuters.com/article/2012/05/30/us-facebook-shares-idUS-BRE84S0VR20120530 (accessed May 31, 2012).

FIGURE 14.2   THE PRICING FORMULA

The following step-by-step process outlines the traditional pricing formula used when calculating the value of a business:

Step 1.   Determine the adjusted tangible net worth of the business. (The total market value of all current and long-term assets less liabilities.)

Step 2.   Estimate how much the buyer could earn annually with an amount equal to the value of the tangible net worth invested elsewhere.

Step 3.   Add to this a salary normal for an owner-operator of the business. This combined figure provides a reasonable estimate of the income the buyer can earn elsewhere with the investment and effort involved in working in the business.

Step 4.   Determine the average annual net earnings of the business (net profit before subtracting owner's salary) over the past few years.

This is before income taxes, to make it comparable with earnings from other sources or by individuals in different tax brackets. (The tax implications of alternative investments should be carefully considered.)

This trend of earnings is a key factor. Have they been rising steadily, falling steadily, remaining constant, or fluctuating widely? The earnings figure should be adjusted to reflect these trends.

Step 5.   Subtract the total of earning power (2) and reasonable salary (3) from this average net earnings figure (4). This gives the extra earning power of the business.

Step 6.   Use this extra earnings figure to estimate the value of the intangibles. This is done by multiplying the extra earnings by what is termed the "years-of-profit" figure.

This "years-of-profit" multiplier pivots on these points. How unique are the intangibles offered by the firm? How long would it take to set up a similar business and bring it to this stage of development? What expenses and risks would be involved? What is the price of goodwill in similar firms? Will the seller be signing an agreement with a covenant not to compete?

If the business is well-established, a factor of five or more might be used, especially if the firm has a valuable name, patent, or location. A multiplier of three might be reasonable for a moderately seasoned firm. A younger but profitable firm might merely have a one-year profit figure.

Step 7.   Final price equals adjusted tangible net worth plus value of intangibles (extra earnings times "years of profit").

Example	Enterprise X	Enterprise Y
1. Adjusted value of tangible net worth (assets less liabilities)	2,000,000	2,000,000
2. Earning power at 8%[a] of an amount equal to the adjusted tangible net worth, if invested in a comparable risk business	160,000	160,000
3. Reasonable salary for owner-operator in the business	50,000	50,000
4. Net earnings of the business over recent years (net profit before subtracting owner's salary)	255,000	209,000
5. Extra earning power of the business (line 4 minus lines 2 and 3)	45,000	(1,000)
6. Value of intangibles—using three-year profit figure for moderately well-established firm (3 times line 5)	135,000	0
7. Final price (lines 1 and 6)	2,135,000	2,000,000 (or less)

With *Enterprise X*, the seller receives a value for goodwill because the business is moderately well established and earning more than the buyer could earn elsewhere with similar risks and effort.

With *Enterprise Y*, the seller receives no value for goodwill because the business, even though it may have existed for a considerable time, is not earning as much as the buyer could through outside investment and effort. In fact, the buyer may feel that even an investment of $2,000,000—the current appraised value of net assets—is too much because it cannot earn sufficient return.

[a]This is an arbitrary figure, used for illustration. A reasonable figure depends on the stability and relative risks of the business and the investment picture generally. The rate of return should be similar to that which could be earned elsewhere with the same approximate risk.

THE ENTREPRENEURIAL PROCESS

Knowing a Venture's Pre-Money and Post-Money Valuation

Even though the final valuation of any venture is the final price at which a willing buyer and seller agree upon for a venture, the world of venture capital is filled with terms and procedures in valuation that may seem confusing. Let's examine two of the key terms and methods that are typical in today's venture capital market for new ventures seeking to be valued.

Pre-Money versus Post-Money Valuation: This terminology is in reference to the money that a venture investor puts into the new venture. In other words, it is the timing of the valuation. Both pre-money and post-money are valuation measures of new ventures. Pre-money refers to a venture's value **before** it receives outside financing, while post-money refers to its value **after** it gets outside funds. It is important to know which is being referred to as they are critical concepts in valuation.

In simpler terms, the valuation is based on either "before" the investor puts the money in or "after" the investor puts the money in the venture. For example, a $2.5 million investment based on a $10 million valuation must be clarified. An entrepreneur may assume that the venture investor now owns 25 percent of the company. However, that depends on whether the $10 million valuation is pre-money or post-money. If the investor is basing the valuation on the addition of the $2.5 million, then that means the pre-money valuation would have been $7.5 million. That allows the venture investor to now own 33 percent of the venture. If the valuation of $10 million is considered pre-money, then with the addition of the $10 million, the venture investor would then own 25 percent.

So, the pre-money value plus the investment equals the post-money value. Or to put it another way, the post-money value minus the investment equals the pre-money value. It may sound simple but it is extremely important to be aware of in any negotiation for the value of a new venture. Here are the formal equations for pre-money valuation and post-money valuation:

1. Pre-money Valuation Post-money Valuation Venture Capital Investment

2. Post-money Valuation Venture Capital Investment/Venture Capital Ownership Percentage

Using these equations, we can provide one more example. A venture capital firm provides a $4 million investment at a $6 million pre-money valuation. To determine how much the start-up venture gives up in exchange for the $4 million, use equation (1) from above:

$6 million = Post-money valuation − $4 million, and solving for Post-money valuation (Post-money = Pre-money + Investment) gives us $10 million. Next, use equation (2) from above to find the Venture Capital firm's percentage: $10 million = $4 million/Venture Capital Firm Ownership Percentage (VCFOP), solving for VCFOP (VCFOP = $4 million divided into the $10 million) equals 40 percent.

The key to working with any venture capital investor is to understand the terminology associated with their valuation techniques.

© Cengage Learning

Basically, the discounted earnings method for calculating the value of a venture uses a four-step process:

1. **Expected cash flow is estimated.** For long-established firms, historical data are effective indicators, although adjustments should be made when available data indicate that future cash flows will change.

2. **An appropriate discount rate is determined.** The buyer's viewpoint has to be considered in the calculation of this rate. The buyer and seller often disagree, because each requires a particular rate of return and will view the risks differently. Another point the seller often overlooks is that the buyer will have other investment opportunities to consider. The appropriate rate, therefore, must be weighed against these factors.

3. **A reasonable life expectancy of the business must be determined.** All firms have a life cycle that depends on such factors as whether the business is one product/one market or multiproduct/multimarket.

4. **The firm's value is then determined** by discounting the estimated cash flow by the appropriate discount rate over the expected life of the business.[7]

14-6 TERM SHEETS IN VENTURE VALUATION

Whenever investors are examining a venture for potential infusion of capital, the value of the venture comes into play. This always involves what is called the **term sheet**. This document outlines the material terms and conditions of a venture agreement. (See Appendix 14-A at the end of this chapter for a complete sample term sheet.) After a *term sheet* has been executed, it guides legal counsel in the preparation of a proposed final agreement. It then guides, but is not necessarily binding, the final terms of the agreement.

Term sheets are very similar to **letters of intent (LOIs)** in that they are both preliminary, mostly nonbinding documents meant to record two or more parties' intentions to enter into a future agreement based on specified (but incomplete or preliminary) terms. Many LOIs, however, contain provisions that are binding, such as nondisclosure agreements, a covenant to negotiate in good faith, or a "stand-still" provision that promises exclusive rights to negotiate.

The purposes of an LOI may be:

- To clarify the key points of a complex transaction for the convenience of the parties
- To declare officially that the parties are currently negotiating
- To provide safeguards in case a deal collapses during negotiation

The difference between a term sheet and an LOI is slight and mostly a matter of style: An LOI is typically written in letter form and focuses on the intentions; a term sheet skips most of the formalities and lists deal terms in bullet-point format. To help clarify the concepts of term sheets in the valuation process, we present the following terminology that is common in these documents.

Price/Valuation The value of a company is what drives the price investors will pay for a piece of the action. The information used to determine valuation comes out of the due diligence process and has to do with the strength of the management team, market potential, the sustainable advantage of the product/service, and potential financial returns. Another way to look at valuation is how much money it will take to make the company a success. In the end, the value of a company is the price at which a willing buyer and seller can complete a transaction.

Fully Diluted Ownership and valuation is typically calculated on a **fully diluted** basis. This means that all securities (including preferred stock, options, and warrants) that can result in additional common shares are counted in determining the total amount of shares outstanding for the purposes of determining ownership or valuation.

Type of Security Investors typically receive convertible preferred stock in exchange for making the investment in a new venture. This type of stock has priority over common stock if the company is acquired or liquidated and assets are distributed. The higher priority of the preferred stock justifies a higher price, compared to the price paid by founders for common stock. *Convertible* means that the shares may be exchanged for a fixed number of common shares.

Liquidation Preference When the company is sold or liquidated, the preferred stockholders will receive a certain fixed amount before any assets are distributed to the common stockholders; this is known as **liquidation preference**. A *participating preferred* stockholder not only will receive the fixed amount but will also share in any additional amounts distributed to common stock.

Dividend Preference Dividends are paid first to preferred stock and then to common stock. This dividend may be cumulative, so that it accrues from year to year until paid in full—or noncumulative and discretionary.

Redemption Preferred stock may be redeemed or retired, either at the option of the company or the investors, or on a mandatory basis—frequently at some premium over the initial purchase price of the stock. One reason why venture firms want this right is due to the finite life of each investment partnership managed by the firm.

Conversion Rights Preferred stock may be converted into common stock at a certain conversion price, generally whenever the stockholder chooses. Conversion may also happen automatically in response to certain events, such as when the company goes public.

Antidilution Protection The conversion price of the preferred stock is subject to adjustment for certain diluting events, such as stock splits or stock dividends; this is known as **antidilution protection**. The conversion price is typically subject to *price protection*, which is an adjustment based on future sales of stock at prices below the conversion price. Price protection can take many forms. One form is called *ratchet* protection, which lowers the conversion price to the price at which any new stock is sold, no matter the number of shares. Another form is broad-based *weighted average* protection, which adjusts the conversion price according to a formula that incorporates the number of new shares being issued and their price. In many cases, a certain number of shares are exempted from this protection to cover anticipated assurances to key employees, consultants, and directors.

Voting Rights Preferred stock has a number of votes equal to the number of shares of common stock into which it is convertible. Preferred stock usually has special voting rights, such as the right to elect one or more of the company's directors, or to approve certain types of corporate actions, such as amending the articles of incorporation or creating a new series of preferred stock.

Right of First Refusal Holders of preferred stock typically have the right to purchase additional shares when issued by the company, up to their current aggregate ownership percentage.

Co-Sale Right Founders will often enter into a co-sale agreement with investors. A co-sale right gives investors some protection against founders selling their interest to a third party by giving investors the right to sell some of their stock as part of such a sale.

Registration Rights Registration rights are generally given to preferred investors as part of their investment. These rights provide investors liquidity by allowing them to require the company to register their shares for sale to the public—either as part of an offering already planned by the company (called piggyback rights), or in a separate offering initiated at the investors' request (called demand rights).

Vesting on Founders' Stock A percentage of founders' stock, which decreases over time, can be purchased by the company at cost if a founder leaves the company. This protects investors against founders leaving the company after it gets funded.[8]

14-7 ADDITIONAL FACTORS IN THE VALUATION PROCESS

LO8 Consider additional factors that affect a venture's valuation

After reviewing these valuation methods, the entrepreneur needs to remember that additional factors intervene in the valuation process and should be given consideration. Presented next are three factors that may influence the final valuation of the venture.

14-7a Avoiding Start-Up Costs

Some buyers are willing to pay more for a business than what the valuation methods illustrate its worth to be. This is because buyers often are trying to avoid the costs associated with start-up and are willing to pay a little more for an existing firm. The higher price they pay will be still less than actual start-up costs and also avoids the problems associated with working to establish a clientele. Thus, for some buyers, a known commodity may command a higher price.

14-7b Accuracy of Projections

The sales and earnings of a venture are always projected on the basis of historical financial and economic data. Short histories, fluctuating markets, and uncertain environments are all reasons for buyers to keep projections in perspective. It is critical that they examine the trends, fluctuations, or patterns involved in projections for sales revenues (higher prices or more customers?), market potential (optimistic or realistic assumptions?), and earnings potential (accurate cost/revenue/market data?), because each area has specific factors that need to be either understood or measured for the accuracy of the projection.

14-7c Control Factor

The degree of control, or **control factor**, an owner legally has over the firm can affect its valuation. If the owner's interest is 100 percent or such that the complete operation of the firm is under his or her influence, then that value is equal to the enterprise's value. If the owner does not possess such control, then the value is less. For example, buying out a 49 percent shareholder will not be effective in controlling a 51 percent shareholder. Also, two 49 percent shareholders are equal until a 2 percent "swing vote" shareholder makes a move. Obviously, minority interests also must be discounted due to lack of liquidity—a minority interest in a privately held corporation is difficult to sell. Overall, it is important to look at the control factor as another facet in the purchase of any interest in a firm.

SUMMARY

Entrepreneurs need to understand how to valuate a business for either purchase or sale. Many would like to know the value of their businesses. Sometimes this is strictly for informational purposes, and other times it is for selling the operation. In either case, a number of ways of valuing an enterprise exist.

The first step is to analyze the business's overall operations, with a view to acquiring a comprehensive understanding of the firm's strong and weak points. Table 14.2 provided a checklist for this purpose. The second step is to establish a value for the firm. Table 14.3 set forth 10 methods for the valuation of a venture. Three of the most commonly used are (1) adjusted tangible assets, (2) P/E (multiple of earnings), and (3) discounted future earnings.

The adjusted tangible book value method computes the value of the business by revaluing the assets and then subtracting the liabilities. This is a fairly simple, straightforward process.

The P/E method divides the market price of the common stock by the earnings per share and then multiplies by the number of shares issued. For example, a company with a price/earnings multiple of 10 and 100,000 shares of stock would be valued at $1 million.

The discounted earnings method takes the estimated cash flows for a predetermined number of years and discounts these sums back to the present using an appropriate discount rate. This is one of the most popular methods of valuing a business. Other factors to consider for valuing a business include start-up costs, accuracy of projections, and the control factor.

KEY TERMS

adjusted tangible book value	divergent goals	liquidation preference
antidilution protection	due diligence	price/earnings ratio (P/E)
business valuation	emotional bias	term sheet
control factor	fully diluted	undercapitalization
discounted earnings method	letter of intent (LOI)	

REVIEW AND DISCUSSION QUESTIONS

1. Identify and discuss the three underlying issues in the evaluation of a business.

2. Define the term *due diligence*. How is it applied to the acquisition of an existing venture?

3. To analyze a business, what types of questions or concerns should the entrepreneur address in the following areas: history of the business, market and competition, sales and distribution, management, and finances?

4. One of the most popular methods of business valuation is the adjusted tangible book value. Describe how this method works.

5. Explain how the P/E method of valuation works. Give an example.

6. What are the steps involved in using the discounted earnings method? Give an example.

7. How do the following methods of valuing a venture work: fixed price, multiple of earnings, return on investment, replacement value, liquidation value, excess earnings, and market value? In each case, give an example.

8. Explain why the following are important factors to consider when valuing a business: start-up costs, accuracy of projections, and degree of control.

NOTES

1. See, for example, W. G. Sanders and S. Bovie, "Sorting Things Out: Valuation of New Firms in Uncertain Markets," *Strategic Management Journal* 25, no. 2 (February 2004): 167–86; and Saikat Chaudhuri and Behnam Tabrizi, "Capturing the Real Value in High-Tech Acquisitions," *Harvard Business Review* 77, no. 4 (September/October 1999): 123–30.

2. "Acquisition Strategies—Part 1," *Small Business Reports* (January 1987): 34, reprinted with permission from *Small Business Reports*; see also Laurence Capron, "The Long-Term Performance of Horizontal Acquisitions," *Strategic Management Journal* 20, no. 11 (November 1999): 987–1018; and Mark Humphery-Jenner, "Takeover Defenses, Innovation, and Value Creation: Evidence from Acquisition Decisions," *Strategic Management Journal* 35, no. 5 (2014): 668–90.

3. "Valuing a Closely Held Business," *Small Business Report* (November 1986): 30–31; see also Hal B. Heaton, "Valuing Small Businesses: The Cost of Capital," *Appraisal Journal* 66, no. 1 (January 1998): 11–16; Alan Mitchell, "How Much Is Your Company Really Worth?" *Management Today* (January 1999): 68–70; Patrick L. Anderson, "The Value of Private Businesses in the United States," *Business Economics* 44 (2009): 87–108; and Stever Robins, "How to Value a Business?" *Entrepreneur*, January 11, 2004 (accessed January 12, 2015).

4. For additional insights, see Ted S. Front, "How to Be a Smart Buyer," *D & B Reports* (March/April 1990): 56–58; and Alfred Rappaport and Mark L. Sirower, "Stock or Cash? The Trade-Offs for Buyers and Sellers in Mergers and Acquisitions," *Harvard Business Review* 77, no. 5 (November/December 1999): 147–58.

5. Gary R. Trugman, *Understanding Business Valuation: A Practical Guide to Valuing Small to Medium-Sized Businesses* (New York: American Institute of Certified Public Accountants, 1998); and Robert W. Pricer and Alec C. Johnson, "The Accuracy of Valuation Methods in Predicting the Selling Price of Small Firms," *Journal of Small Business Management* 35, no. 4 (October 1997): 24–35; see also Wayne Lonergan, *The Valuation of Businesses, Shares and Other Equity* (Australia: Allen & Unwin, 2003).

6. Adapted from Albert N. Link and Michael B. Boger, *The Art and Science of Business Valuation* (Westport, CT: Quorum Books, 1999); and Stanley J. Feldman, "Business Valuation 101: The Five Myths of Valuing a Private Business," *SCORE*, May 10, 2011 (accessed January 12, 2015).

7. "Valuing a Closely Held Business," 34; see also: "3 Ways to Value a Business for Sale," National Federation of Independent Business (NFIB) September 23, 2013 (accesed January 12, 2015); and Ed Powers, "5 Key Numbers a Buyout Firm Uses to Value Your Company," *Inc.* January 31, 2014.

8. Justin J. Camp, *Venture Capital Due Diligence* (New York: Wiley & Sons, 2002); see also John B. Vinturella and Suzanne M. Erickson, *Raising Entrepreneurial Capital* (Burlington, MA: Elsevier, 2004).

This sample document is the work product of a coalition of attorneys who specialize in venture capital financings, working under the auspices of the National Venture Capital Association (NVCA). See the NVCA website for a list of the Working Group members. This document is intended to serve as a starting point only, and should be tailored to meet your specific requirements. This document should not be construed as legal advice for any particular facts or circumstances. Note that this sample presents an array of (often mutually exclusive) options with respect to particular deal provisions.

This Term Sheet summarizes the principal terms of the Series A Preferred Stock Financing of [_____], Inc., a [Delaware] corporation (the "**Company**"). In consideration of the time and expense devoted and to be devoted by the Investors with respect to this investment, the No Shop/Confidentiality and Counsel and Expenses provisions of this Term Sheet shall be binding obligations of the Company whether or not the financing is consummated. No other legally binding obligations will be created until definitive agreements are executed and delivered by all parties. This Term Sheet is not a commitment to invest, and is conditioned on the completion of due diligence, legal review and documentation that is satisfactory to the Investors. This Term Sheet shall be governed in all respects by the laws of the [State of Delaware].

Offering Terms

Closing Date:	As soon as practicable following the Company's acceptance of this Term Sheet and satisfaction of the Conditions to Closing (the "Closing"). [*provide for multiple closings if applicable*]
Investors:	Investor No. 1: [_____] shares ([_____]%), $[_____]
	Investor No. 2: [_____] shares ([_____]%), $[_____]
	[as well other investors mutually agreed upon by Investors and the Company]
Amount Raised:	$[_____], [including $[_____] from the conversion of principal [and interest] on bridge notes].[1]
Price Per Share:	$[_____] per share (based on the capitalization of the Company set forth below) (the "Original Purchase Price").
Pre-Money Valuation:	The Original Purchase Price is based upon a fully-diluted pre-money valuation of $[_____] and a fully diluted post-money valuation of $[_____] (including an employee pool representing [_____] % of the fully diluted post-money capitalization).
Capitalization:	The Company's capital structure before and after the Closing is set forth below:

Security	Pre-Financing		Post-Financing	
	# of Shares	%	# of Shares	%
Common – Founders				
Common – Employee				
Stock Pool				
Issued				
Unissued				
[Common – Warrants]				
Series A Preferred				
Total				

Charter[2]

Dividends:

[*Alternative 1*: Dividends will be paid on the Series A Preferred on an as converted basis when, as, and if paid on the Common Stock]

[*Alternative 2*: Non-cumulative dividends will be paid on the Series A Preferred in an amount equal to $[_____] per share of Series A Preferred when and if declared by the Board.]

[*Alternative 3*: The Series A Preferred will carry an annual [_____]% cumulative dividend [compounded annually], payable upon a liquidation or redemption. For any other dividends or distributions, participation with Common Stock on an as-converted basis.][3]

Liquidation Preference:

In the event of any liquidation, dissolution, or winding up of the Company, the proceeds shall be paid as follows:

[*Alternative 1 (non-participating Preferred Stock)*: First pay [one] times the Original Purchase Price [plus accrued dividends] [plus declared and unpaid dividends] on each share of Series A Preferred. The balance of any proceeds shall be distributed to holders of Common Stock.]

[*Alternative 2 (full participating Preferred Stock)*: First pay [one] times the Original Purchase Price [plus accrued dividends] [plus declared and unpaid dividends] on each share of Series A Preferred. Thereafter, the Series A Preferred participates with the Common Stock on an as-converted basis.]

[*Alternative 3 (cap on Preferred Stock participation rights)*: First pay [one] times the Original Purchase Price [plus accrued dividends] [plus declared and unpaid dividends] on each share of Series A Preferred. Thereafter, Series A Preferred participates with Common Stock on an as-converted basis until the holders of Series A Preferred receive an aggregate of [_____] times the Original Purchase Price.] A merger or consolidation (other than one in which stockholders of the Company own a majority by voting power of the outstanding shares of the surviving or acquiring corporation) and a sale, lease, transfer, or other disposition of all or substantially all of the assets of the Company will be treated as a liquidation preferences described above [unless the holders of [_____]% of the Series A Preferred elect otherwise].

Voting Rights:

The Series A Preferred Stock shall vote together with the Common Stock on an as-converted basis, and not as a separate class, except (i) the Series A Preferred as a class shall be entitled to elect [_____] [()] members of the Board (the "Series A Directors"), (ii) as provided under "Protective Provisions" below or (iii) as required by law. The Company's Certificate of Incorporation will-provide that the number of authorized shares of Common Stock may be increased or decreased with the approval of a majority of the Preferred and Common Stock, voting together as a single class, and without a separate class vote by the Common Stock.[4]

Protective Provisions:

So long as [*insert fixed number, or %, or "any"*] shares of Series A Preferred are outstanding, the Company will not, without the written consent of the holders of at least [_____]% of the Company's Series A Preferred, either directly or by amendment, merger, consolidation, or otherwise:

(i) liquidate, dissolve, or wind up the affairs of the Company, or effect any Deemed Liquidation Event; (ii) amend, alter, or repeal any provision of the Certificate of Incorporation or Bylaws [in a manner adverse to the Series A Preferred];[5] (iii) create or authorize the creation of or issue any other security convertible into or exercisable for any equity security, having rights, preferences, or privileges senior to or on parity with the Series A Preferred, or increase the authorized number of shares of Series A Preferred; (iv) purchase or redeem or pay any dividend on any capital stock prior to the Series A Preferred [other than stock repurchased from former employees or consultants in connection with the cessation of their employment/services, at the lower of fair market value or cost;] [other than as approved by the Board, including the approval of [_____] Series A Director(s)]; or (v) create or authorize the creation of any debt security [if the Company's aggregate indebtedness would exceed $[_____] [other than equipment leases or bank lines of credit][other than debt with no equity feature][unless such debt security has received the prior approval of the Board of Directors, including the approval of [_____] Series A Director (s)]; (vi) increase or decrease the size of the Board of Directors.

Optional Conversion:

The Series A Preferred initially converts 1:1 to Common Stock at any time at option of holder, subject to adjustments for stock dividends, splits, combinations, and similar events and as described below under "Anti-dilution Provisions."

Anti-dilution Provisions:

In the event that the Company issues additional securities at a purchase price less than the current Series A Preferred conversion price, such conversion price shall be adjusted in accordance with the following formula:

[*Alternative 1*: "Typical" weighted average:

$$CP2 = CP1 * (A + B)/(A + C)$$

$CP2$ = New Series A Conversion Price

$CP1$ = Series A Conversion Price in effect immediately prior to new issue

A = Number of shares of Common Stock deemed to be outstanding immediately prior to new issue (includes all shares of stock, all shares of outstanding common outstanding preferred stock on an as-converted basis, and all outstanding options on an as-exercised basis; and does not include any convertible securities converting into this round of financing)

B = Aggregate consideration received by the Corporation with respect to the new issue divided by $CP1$

C = Number of shares of stock issued in the subject transaction]

[*Alternative 2*: Full-ratchet — the conversion price will be reduced to the price at which the new shares are issued.]

[*Alternative 3*: No price-based anti-dilution protection.]

The following issuances shall not trigger anti-dilution adjustment:[6]

(i) securities issuable upon conversion of any of the Series A Preferred, or as a dividend or distribution on the Series A Preferred; (ii) securities issued upon the conversion of any debenture, warrant, option, or other convertible security; (iii) Common Stock issuable upon a stock split, stock dividend, or any subdivision of shares of Common Stock; and (iv) shares of Common Stock (or options to purchase such shares of Common Stock) issued or issuable to employees or directors of, or consultants to, the Company pursuant to any plan approved by the

Company's Board of Directors [including at least [_____] Series A Director(s)] [(v) shares of Common Stock issued or issuable to banks, equipment lessors pursuant to a debt financing, equipment leasing, or real property leasing transaction approved by the Board of Directors of the Corporation [including at least [_____] Series A Director(s)].

Mandatory Conversion:	Each share of Series A Preferred will automatically be converted into Common Stock at the then applicable conversion rate in the event of the closing of a [firm commitment] underwritten public offering with a price of [_____] times the Original Purchase Price (subject to adjustments for stock dividends, splits, combinations, and similar events) and [net/gross] proceeds to the Company of not less than $[_____] (a "QPO"), or (ii) upon the written consent of the holders of [_____]% of the Series A Preferred.[7]
Pay-to-Play:	[Unless the holders of [_____]% of the Series A elect otherwise,] on any subsequent down round all [Major] Investors are required to participate to the full extent of their participation rights (as described below under "Investor Rights Agreement — Right to Participate Pro Rata in Future Rounds"), unless the participation requirement is waived for all [Major] Investors by the Board [(including vote of [a majority of] the Series A Director[s])]. All shares of Series A Preferred[8] of any [Major] Investor failing to do so will automatically [lose anti-dilution rights] [lose right to participate in future rounds] [convert to Common Stock and lose the right to a Board seat if applicable].[9]
Redemption Rights:[10]	The Series A Preferred shall be redeemable from funds legally available for distribution at the option of holders of at least [_____]% of the Series A Preferred commencing any time after the fifth anniversary of the Closing at a price equal to the Original Purchase Price [plus all accrued but unpaid dividends]. Redemption shall occur in three equal annual portions. Upon a redemption request from the holders of the required percentage of the Series A Preferred, all Series A Preferred shares shall be redeemed [(except for any Series A holders who affirmatively opt-out)].[11]

Stock Purchase Agreement

Representations and Warranties:	Standard representations and warranties by the Company. [Representations and warranties by Founders regarding [technology ownership, etc.].[12]
Conditions to Closing:	Standard conditions to Closing, which shall include, among other things, satisfactory completion of financial and legal due diligence, qualification of the shares under applicable Blue Sky laws, the filing of a Certificate of Incorporation establishing the rights and preferences of the Series A Preferred, and an opinion of counsel to the Company.
Counsel and Expenses:	[Investor/Company] counsel to draft closing documents. Company to pay all legal and administrative costs of the financing [at Closing], including reasonable fees (not to exceed $[_____]) and expenses of Investor counsel [unless the transaction is not completed because the Investors withdraw their commitment without cause].[13]

Company Counsel: [_____
_____
_____]

Investor Counsel: [_____
_____]

Investor Rights Agreement

Registration Rights:

Registrable Securities:	All shares of Common Stock issuable upon conversion of the Series A Preferred and [any other Common Stock held by the Investors] will be deemed "Registrable Securities."[14]

Demand Registration: Upon earliest of (i) [three–five] years after the Closing; or (ii) [six] months following an initial public offering ("IPO"), persons holding [_____]% of the Registrable Securities may request [one][two] (consummated) registrations by the Company of their shares. The aggregate offering price for such registration may not be less than $[5–10] million. A registration will count for this purpose only if (i) all Registrable Securities requested to be registered are registered and (ii) it is closed, or withdrawn at the request of the Investors (other than as a result of a material adverse change to the Company).

Registration on Form S-3: The holders of [10–30]% of the Registrable Securities will have the right to require the Company to register on Form S-3, if available for use by the Company, Registrable Securities for an aggregate offering price of at least $[1–5 million]. There will be no limit on the aggregate number of such Form S-3 registrations, provided that there are no more than [two] per year.

Piggyback Registration: The holders of Registrable Securities will be entitled to "piggyback" registration rights on all registration statements of the Company, subject to the right, however, of the Company and its underwriters to reduce the number of shares proposed to be registered to a minimum of [30]% on a pro rata basis and to complete reduction on an IPO at the underwriter's discretion. In all events, the shares to be registered by holders of Registrable Securities will be reduced only after all other stockholders' shares are reduced.

Expenses: The registration expenses (exclusive of stock transfer taxes, underwriting discounts, and commissions) will be borne by the Company. The Company will also pay the reasonable fees and expenses [not to exceed $] of one special counsel to represent all the participating stockholders.

Lock-up: Investors shall agree in connection with the IPO, if requested by the managing underwriter, not to sell or transfer any shares of Common Stock of the Company [(excluding shares acquired in or following the IPO)] for a period of up to 180 days following the IPO (provided all directors and officers of the Company and [1–5]% stockholders agree to the same lockup). Such lockup agreement shall provide that any discretionary waiver or termination of the restrictions of such agreements by the Company or representatives of the underwriters shall apply to [Major] Investors, pro rata, based on the number of shares held. A "Major Investor" means any Investor who purchases at least $[_____] of Series A Preferred.

Termination: Earlier of [5] years after IPO, upon a Deemed Liquidation Event, or when all shares of an Investor are eligible to be sold without restriction under Rule 144(k) within any 90-day period. No future registration rights may be granted without consent of the holders of a [majority] of the Registrable Securities unless subordinate to the Investor's rights.

Management and Information Rights: A Management Rights letter from the Company, in a form reasonably acceptable to the Investors, will be delivered prior to Closing to each Investor that requests one.[15]

Any Major Investor [(who is not a competitor)] will be granted access to Company facilities and personnel during normal business hours and with reasonable advance notification. The Company will deliver to such Major Investor (i) annual, quarterly, [and monthly] financial statements, and other information as determined by the Board; (ii) 30 days prior to the end of each fiscal year, a comprehensive operating budget forecasting the Company's revenues, expenses, and cash position on a month-to-month basis for the upcoming fiscal year; and (iii) promptly following the end of each quarter an up-to-date capitalization table, certified by the CFO.

Right to Participate Pro Rata in Future Rounds:	All [Major] Investors shall have a pro rata right, based on their percentage equity ownership in the Company (assuming the conversion of all outstanding Preferred Stock into Common Stock and the exercise of all options outstanding under the Company's stock plans), to participate in subsequent issuances of equity securities of the Company (excluding those issuances listed at the end of the "Anti-dilution Provisions" section of this Term Sheet and issuances in connection with acquisitions by the Company). In addition, should any [Major] Investor choose not to purchase its full pro rata share, the remaining [Major] Investors shall have the right to purchase the remaining pro rata shares.
Matters Requiring	[So long as [_____]% of the originally issued Series A Preferred remains outstanding] the Company will not, without Board approval, which approval must include the affirmative vote of [_____] of the Series A Director(s):
Investor Director Approval:	(i) make any loan or advance to, or own any stock or other securities of, any subsidiary or other corporation, partnership, or other entity unless it is wholly owned by the Company; (ii) make any loan or advance to any person, including any employee or director, except advances and similar expenditures in the ordinary course of business or under the terms of a employee stock or option plan approved by the Board of Directors; the Company or any subsidiary arising in the ordinary course of business; (iv) make any investment other than investments in prime commercial paper, money market funds, certificates of deposit in any United States bank having a net worth in excess of $100,000,000, or obligations issued or guaranteed by the United States of America, in each case having a maturity not in excess of [two years]; (v) incur any aggregate indebtedness in excess of $[_____] that is not already included in a Board-approved budget, other than trade credit incurred in the ordinary course of business; (vi) enter into or be a party to any transaction with any director, officer, or employee of the Company or any "associate" (as defined in Rule 12b-2 promulgated under the Exchange Act) of any such person [except transactions resulting in payments to or by the Company in an amount less than $[60,000] per year], [or transactions made in the ordinary course of business and pursuant to reasonable requirements of the Company's business and upon fair and reasonable terms that are approved by a majority of the Board of Directors]; [16] (vii) hire, fire, or change the compensation of the executive officers, including approving any option plans; (viii) change the principal business of the Company, enter new lines of business, or exit the current line of business; or (ix) sell, transfer, license, pledge, or encumber technology or intellectual property, other than licenses granted in the ordinary course of business.
Noncompetition and Non-Solicitation and Agreements:[17]	Each Founder and key employee will enter into a [one] year noncompetition and non-solicitation agreement in a form reasonably acceptable to the Investors.
Nondisclosure and Developments Agreement:	Each current and former Founder, employee, and consultant with access to Company confidential information/trade secrets will enter into a nondisclosure and proprietary rights assignment agreement in a form reasonably acceptable to the Investors.
Board Matters:	Each Board Committee shall include at least one Series A Director. The Board of Directors shall meet at least [monthly][quarterly], unless otherwise agreed by a vote of the majority of Directors.

The Company will bind D & O insurance with a carrier and in an amount satisfactory to the Board of Directors. In the event the Company merges with another entity and is not the surviving corporation, or transfers all of its assets, proper provisions shall be made so that successors of the Company assume Company's obligations with respect to indemnification of Directors.

Employee Stock Options:

All employee options to vest as follows: [25% after one year, with remaining vesting monthly over next 36 months].

[Immediately prior to the Series A Preferred Stock investment, [_____] shares will be added to the option pool creating an unallocated option pool of [_____] shares.]

Key Person Insurance:

Company to acquire life insurance on Founders [*name each Founder*] in an amount satisfactory to the Board. Proceeds payable to the Company.

[IPO Directed Shares:[18]

To the extent permitted by applicable law and SEC policy, upon an IPO consummated one year after Closing, Company to use reasonable best efforts to cause underwriters to designate [10]% of the offering as directed shares, 50% of which shall be allocated by Major Investors.]

[QSB Stock:

Company shall use reasonable best efforts to cause its capital stock to constitute Qualified Small Business Stock unless the Board determines that such qualification is inconsistent with the best interests of the Company.]

Termination:

All rights under the Investor Rights Agreement, other than registration rights, shall terminate upon the earlier of an IPO, a Deemed Liquidation Event, or a transfer of more than 50% of Company's voting power.

Right of First Refusal/Co-Sale Agreement and Voting Agreement

Right of First Refusal/Right of Co-Sale (Take-Me-Along):

Company first and Investors second (to the extent assigned by the Board of Directors) have a right of first refusal with respect to any shares of capital stock of the Company proposed to be sold by Founders [and employees holding greater than [1]% of Company Common Stock (assuming conversion of Preferred Stock)], with a right of oversubscription for Investors of shares unsubscribed by the other Investors. Before any such person may sell Common Stock, he will give the Investors an opportunity to participate in such sale on a basis proportionate to the amount of securities held by the seller and those held by the participating Investors.[19]

Board of Directors:

At the initial Closing, the Board shall consist of [_____] members comprised of (i) [*Name*] as [the representative designated by [_____], as the lead Investor, (ii) [*Name*] as the representative designated by the remaining Investors, (iii) [*Name*] as the representative designated by the Founders, (iv) the person then serving as the Chief Executive Officer of the Company, and (v) [_____] person (s) who are not employed by the Company and who are mutually acceptable [to the Founders and Investors][to the other directors].

Drag Along:

Holders of Preferred Stock and the Founders [and all current and future holders of greater than [1]% of Common Stock (assuming conversion of Preferred Stock and whether then held or subject to the exercise of options)] shall be required to enter into an agreement with the Investors that provides that such stockholders will vote their shares in favor of a Deemed Liquidation Event or transaction in which 50% or more of the voting power of the Company is transferred, approved by [the Board of Directors] [and the holders of a [majority][super majority] of the outstanding shares of Preferred Stock, on an as-converted basis].

Termination:	All rights under the Right of First Refusal/Co-Sale and Voting Agreements shall terminate upon an IPO, a Deemed Liquidation Event, or a transfer of more than 50% of Company's voting power.

Other Matters

Founders' Stock:	All Founders to own stock outright subject to Company right to buy-back at cost. Buyback right for [_____]% for first [12 months] after Closing; thereafter, right lapses in equal [monthly] increments over following [_____] months.
[Existing Preferred Stock:[20]	The terms set forth below for the Series [_____] Stock are subject to a review of the rights, preferences and restrictions for the existing Preferred Stock. Any changes necessary to conform the existing Preferred Stock to this term sheet will be made at the Closing.]
No Shop/ Confidentiality:	The Company agrees to work in good faith expeditiously toward a closing. The Company and the Founders agree that they will not, for a period of [six] weeks from the date these terms are accepted, take any action to solicit, initiate, encourage, or assist the submission of any proposal, negotiation, or offer from any person or entity other than the Investors relating to the sale or issuance, of any of the capital stock of the Company [or the acquisition, sale, lease, license, or other disposition of the Company or any material part of the stock or assets of the Company] and shall notify the Investors promptly of any inquiries by any third parties in regards to the foregoing. [In the event that the Company breaches this no-shop obligation and, prior to [_____], closes any of the above-referenced transactions [without providing the Investors the opportunity to invest on the same terms as the other parties to such transaction], then the Company shall pay to the Investors $[_____] upon the closing of any such transaction as liquidated damages.][21] The Company will not disclose the terms of this Term Sheet to any person other than officers, members of the Board of Directors, and the Company's accountants and attorneys and other potential Investors acceptable to [_____], as lead Investor, without the written consent of the Investors.
Expiration:	This Term Sheet expires on [_____, 200] if not accepted by the Company by that date.

EXECUTED THIS [_____] DAY OF [_____], 200[_____].

[SIGNATURE BLOCKS]

NOTES

1. Modify this provision to account for staged investments or investments dependent on the achievement of milestones by the Company.

2. The Charter is a public document, filed with the [Delaware] Secretary of State, that establishes all of the rights, preferences, privileges, and restrictions of the Preferred Stock. Note that if the Preferred Stock does not have rights, preferences, and privileges materially superior to the Common Stock, then (after Closing) the Company cannot defensibly grant Common Stock options priced at a discount to the Preferred Stock.

3. In some cases, accrued and unpaid dividends are payable on conversion as well as upon a liquidation event.

Most typically, however, dividends are not paid if the preferred is converted. Another alternative is to give the Company the option to pay accrued and unpaid dividends in cash or in common shares valued at fair market value. The latter are referred to as "PIK" (payment-in-kind) dividends.

4. For California corporations, one cannot "opt out" of the statutory requirement of a separate class vote by Common Stockholders to authorize shares of Common Stock.

5. Note that, as a matter of background law, Section 242(b)(2) of the Delaware General Corporation Law provides that if any proposed charter amendment would

adversely alter the rights, preferences, and powers of one series of Preferred Stock, but not similarly adversely alter the entire class of all Preferred Stock, then the holders of that series are entitled to a separate series vote on the amendment.

6. Note that additional exclusions are frequently negotiated, such as issuances in connection with equipment leasing and commercial borrowing.

7. The per-share test ensures that the investor achieves a significant return on investment before the Company can go public. Also consider allowing a non-QPO to become a QPO if an adjustment is made to the Conversion Price for the benefit of the investor, so that the investor does not have the power to block a public offering.

8. Alternatively, this provision could apply on a proportionate basis (e.g., if Investor plays for ½ of pro rata share, receives ½ of antidilution adjustment).

9. If the punishment for failure to participate is losing some but not all rights of the Preferred (e.g., anything other than a forced conversion to common), the Charter will need to have so-called "blank check preferred" provisions at least to the extent necessary to enable the Board to issue a "shadow" class of preferred with diminished rights in the event an investor fails to participate. Note that, as a drafting matter, it is far easier to simply have (some or all of) the preferred convert to common.

10. Redemption rights allow Investors to force the Company to redeem their shares at cost [plus a small guaranteed rate of return (e.g., dividends)]. In practice, redemption rights are not often used; however, they do provide a form of exit and some possible leverage over the Company. While it is possible that the right to receive dividends on redemption could give rise to a Code Section 305 "deemed dividend" problem, many tax practitioners take the view that if the liquidation preference provisions in the Charter are drafted to provide that, on conversion, the holder receives the greater of its liquidation preference or its as-converted amount (as provided in the NVCA model Certificate of Incorporation), then there is no Section 305 issue.

11. Due to statutory restrictions, it is unlikely that the Company will be legally permitted to redeem in the very circumstances where investors most want it (the so-called "sideways situation"), investors will sometimes request that certain penalty provisions take effect where redemption has been requested but the Company's available cash flow does not permit such redemption—for example the redemption amount shall be paid in the form of a one-year note to each unredeemed holder of Series A Preferred, and the holders of a majority of the Series A Preferred shall be entitled to elect a majority of the Company's Board of Directors until such amounts are paid in full.

12. Note that, while it is not at all uncommon in East Coast deals to require the Founders to personally rep and warrant (at least as to certain key matters, and usually only in the Series A round), such Founders reps are rarely found in West Coast deals.

13. The bracketed text should be deleted if this section is not designated in the introductory paragraph as one of the sections that is binding upon the Company regardless of whether the financing is consummated.

14. Note that Founders/management sometimes also seek registration rights.

15. See commentary in introduction to NVCA model Managements Rights Letter, explaining purpose of such letter.

16. Note that Section 402 of the Sarbanes-Oxley Act of 2003 would require repayment of any loans in full prior to the Company filing a registration statement for an IPO.

17. Note that noncompete restrictions (other than in connection with the sale of a business) are prohibited in California, and may not be enforceable in other jurisdictions, as well. In addition, some investors do not require such agreements for fear that employees will request additional consideration in exchange for signing a Noncompete/Nonsolicit (and indeed the agreement may arguably be invalid absent such additional consideration—although having an employee sign a noncompete contemporaneous with hiring constitutes adequate consideration). Others take the view that it should be up to the Board on a case-by-case basis to determine whether any particular key employee is required to sign such an agreement. Noncompetes typically have a one-year duration, although state law may permit up to two years.

18. SEC Staff examiners have taken position that, if contractual right to friends and family shares was granted less than 12 months prior to filing of registration statement, this will be considered an "offer" made prematurely before filing of IPO prospectus. So, investors need to agree to drop shares from offering if that would hold up the IPO. While some documents provide for alternative parallel private placement where the IPO does occur within 12 months, such a parallel private placement could raise integration issues and negatively impact the IPO. Hence, such an alternative is not provided for here.

19. Certain exceptions are typically negotiated, for example, estate planning or *de minimis* transfers.

20. Necessary only if this is a later round of financing, and not the initial Series A round.

21. It is unusual to provide for such "breakup" fees in connection with a venture capital financing, but might be something to consider where there is a substantial possibility the Company may be sold prior to consummation of the financing (e.g., a later-stage deal).

CHAPTER 15

Harvesting the Entrepreneurial Venture

LEARNING OBJECTIVES

1 To present the concept of "harvest" as a plan for the future

2 To examine the key factors in the management succession of a venture

3 To identify and describe some of the most important sources of succession

4 To discuss the potential impact of recent legislation on family business succession

5 To relate the ways to develop a succession strategy

6 To examine the specifics of an IPO as a potential harvest strategy

7 To present "selling out" as a final alternative in the harvest strategy

Entrepreneurial Thought

In the agrarian mindset there is an ideal and defined window to bring a harvest to the marketplace. If you do it too soon, the product will not yet be ripe. Nobody will buy it. If you're too late, then there will be rotting, spoilage, and waste. Why can't we take that same approach with today's entrepreneurial ventures?

—Andrew J. Sherman *Harvesting Intangible Assets*

15-1 HARVESTING THE VENTURE: A FOCUS ON THE FUTURE

LO1 Present the concept of "harvest" as a plan for the future

Entrepreneurs must realize that the eventual success of their venture will lead them to a decision concerning the future operation and management of the business. A *harvest plan* defines how and when owners and investors will realize an actual cash return on their investment. Note that "harvest" does not mean that the challenges and responsibility of the entrepreneur are over. There are challenging decisions to be made. It may be a decision regarding managerial control and succession for successful continued operations as a privately held firm.[1] It may be a desire to initiate a liquidity event, through which the venture is able to generate a significant amount of cash for investors. It may be that the venture has grown to a stage at which the possibility of an initial public offering (IPO), which we discussed in Chapter 8, is a reality. Or it may be that the most realistic opportunity is selling the business. In any of these situations, the entrepreneur is confronted with a myriad of choices and possibilities. Although it is impossible for this chapter to answer all of the questions that an entrepreneur faces at this point, because each venture presents a unique set of circumstances, it is the goal of this final chapter to review some of the more common challenges that confront entrepreneurs during this stage. Thus, we examine the challenge of a management succession strategy and the two most notable harvest strategies for ventures: the IPO and the sale of the venture.

15-2 THE MANAGEMENT SUCCESSION STRATEGY

LO2 Examine the key factors in the management succession of a venture

Research shows that many privately held firms go out of existence after 10 years; only 3 of 10 survive into a second generation. More significantly, only 16 percent of all privately held enterprises make it to a third generation.[2] The average life expectancy for a privately held business is 24 years, which is also the average tenure for the founders of a business.[3] One of the major problems most privately held businesses face is the lack of preparation for passing managerial control to the next generation. The cruel fact is that one generation succeeds the other with biological inevitability, yet most privately held firms never formulate succession plans.

Management succession, which involves the transition of managerial decision-making in a firm, is one of the greatest challenges confronting owners and entrepreneurs in privately held businesses. At first glance, succession would not seem to be a major problem. All an owner has to do is designate which heir will inherit the operation or, better yet, train one (or more) of them to take over the business during the founder's lifetime. Unfortunately, this is easier said than done—a number of problems exist. One of the major ones is the owner. To a large degree, the owner is the business; the individual's personality and talents make the operation what it is. If this person were to be removed from the picture, the company might be unable to continue. Additionally, this individual may not want to be removed. So, if the owner/manager begins to have health problems or is unable to manage effectively, he or she may still hang on. The owner often views any outside attempt to get him or her to step aside as greedy efforts to plunder the operation for personal gain. What's more, the owner and family members may feel anxiety about death, because discussing the topic of death conjures up a negative image in everyone's mind.

Other barriers to succession include sibling rivalry, family members' fear of losing status, or a complete aversion to death for fear of loss or abandonment.[4] Table 15.1 provides a list of barriers to succession attributed to the owner and to the family.

The basic rule for privately held businesses is this: The owner should develop a succession plan. Because many people want to keep the business in their families, decisions have to be made regarding heirs. This is often psychologically difficult. Choosing an heir can be like buying a cemetery plot—it is an admission of one's mortality. Owners who refuse to face the succession issue, however, place an unnecessary burden on those whom they leave behind. Successor problems are not insurmountable. For our consideration of these problems, the best place to begin is with an identification of the key factors in succession.

TABLE 15.1	BARRIERS TO SUCCESSION PLANNING IN PRIVATELY HELD BUSINESSES
Founder/Owner	**Family**
Death anxiety	Death as taboo
Company as symbol	• Discussion is a hostile act
• Loss of identity	• Fear of loss/abandonment
• Concern about legacy	Fear of sibling rivalry
Dilemma of choice	Change of spouse's position
• Fiction of equality	
Generational envy	
• Loss of power	

Source: Manfred F. R. Kets de Vries, "The Dynamics of Family-Controlled Firms: The Good News and the Bad News," *Organizational Dynamics* (Winter 1993): 68.

15-3 KEY FACTORS IN SUCCESSION

It has been said that the concept of "smooth succession" in a privately held business is a contradiction of terms. This contradiction is because succession is a highly charged emotional issue that requires not only structural changes but cultural changes as well.[5] Family succession includes the transfer of ethics, values, and traditions, along with the actual business itself. The "family business" and the "business family" are two distinct components that must be dealt with and disentangled if progress toward succession is to be made.[6]

A number of considerations affect the succession issue.[7] One way to examine them is in terms of pressures and interests inside the firm and outside the firm. Another way is to examine forcing events. A third way is to examine the sources of succession. Finally, we will discuss the legal restrictions that may affect succession decisions.

15-3a Succession Pressures and Interests inside the Firm

Two types of succession pressures originate within privately held businesses (see Figure 15.1). One comes from family members; the other comes from nonfamily employees.[8]

FAMILY MEMBERS

When members of the family are also employees, a number of succession-type problems can arise. One is that the family members may want to keep the business in existence so that they and their families will be able to manage it. Sometimes this results in the members wanting to get, or increase, control over operations. Another common development is pressure on the owner/manager to designate an heir. A third possible development is rivalry among the various branches of the family. For example, each of the owner's children may feel that the owner should put him or her (or one of his or her children) in charge of the operation. Given that only one of the family branches can win this fight, the rivalry can lead to the sale or bankruptcy of the business.[9]

NONFAMILY EMPLOYEES

Nonfamily employees sometimes put pressure on the owner/manager in an effort to protect their personal interests. For example, long-term employees often think that the owner should give them an opportunity to buy a stake in the company, or they believe that they should be

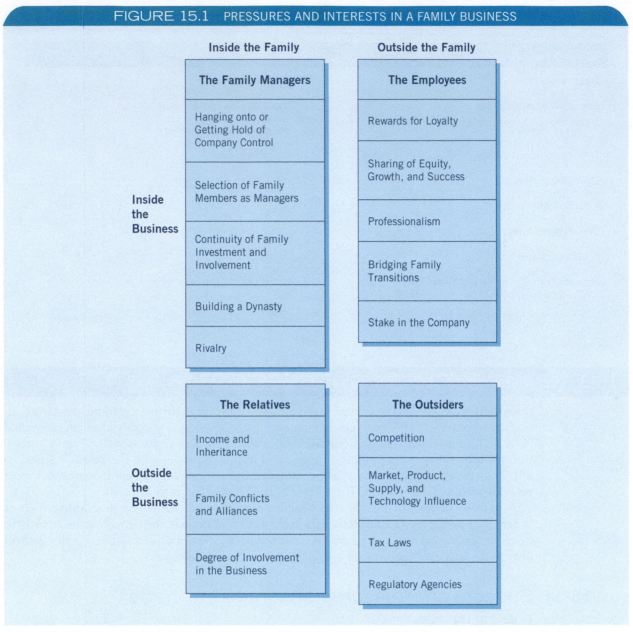

FIGURE 15.1   PRESSURES AND INTERESTS IN A FAMILY BUSINESS

	Inside the Family	Outside the Family
Inside the Business	**The Family Managers** Hanging onto or Getting Hold of Company Control Selection of Family Members as Managers Continuity of Family Investment and Involvement Building a Dynasty Rivalry	**The Employees** Rewards for Loyalty Sharing of Equity, Growth, and Success Professionalism Bridging Family Transitions Stake in the Company
Outside the Business	**The Relatives** Income and Inheritance Family Conflicts and Alliances Degree of Involvement in the Business	**The Outsiders** Competition Market, Product, Supply, and Technology Influence Tax Laws Regulatory Agencies

Source: Adapted and reprinted by permission of the *Harvard Business Review*. An Exhibit from "Transferring Power in the Family Business," by Louis B. Barnes and Simon A. Hershon (July/August 1976): 106. Copyright © 1976 by the President and Fellows of Harvard College; all rights reserved.

given a percentage of the business in the owner's will. Such hopes and expectations are often conveyed to the owner and can result in pressure for some form of succession plan. Moreover, to the extent that the nonfamily employees are critical to the enterprise's success, these demands cannot be ignored. The owner must reach some accommodation with these people if the business is to survive.

15-3b Succession Pressures and Interests Outside the Firm

Outside the firm, both family members and nonfamily elements exert pressure on and hold interest in the firm's succession.

FAMILY MEMBERS

Even when family members do not play an active role in the business, they can apply pressure. Quite often these individuals are interested in ensuring that they inherit part of the operation, and they will put pressure on the owner/manager toward achieving that end. In some cases, they pressure to get involved in the business. Some family members will pressure the owner/manager to hire them. Quite often these appeals are resisted on the grounds of the firm not needing additional personnel or needing someone with specific expertise (sales ability or technical skills), and thus the owner sidesteps the request.

NONFAMILY ELEMENTS

Another major source of pressure comes from external environmental factors. One of these is competitors who continually change strategy and force the owner/manager to adjust to new market considerations. Other factors include customers, technology, and new-product development. These forces continually change, and the entrepreneur must respond to them. Tax laws, regulatory agencies, and trends in management practices constitute still other elements with which the owner/manager must contend.[10] Depending on the situation, any of these sources of pressure can prove troublesome.

Figure 15.2 illustrates the distinction of family and business issues in a systems model. At the interface of the family and business systems, both the family and the business respond to disruptions in their regular transaction patterns. These disruptions may come from outside the family and business or from within them. Outside sources of disruption include public policy changes, economic upheavals, and technological innovation. Inside sources of disruption include marriage, birth, death, and divorce of family members. These disruptions may

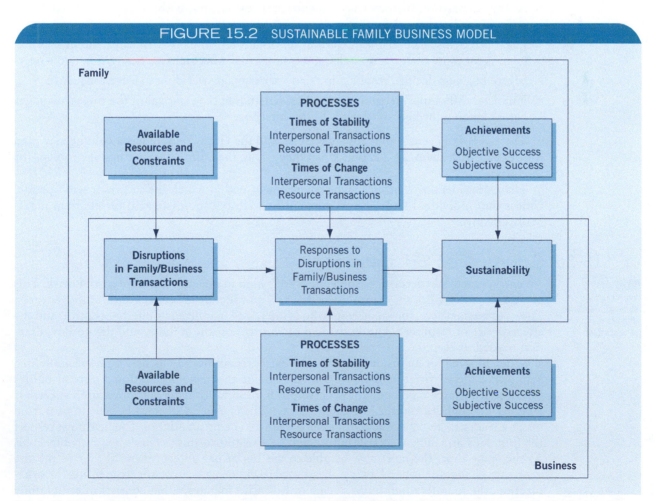

FIGURE 15.2   SUSTAINABLE FAMILY BUSINESS MODEL

Source: Kathryn Stafford, Karen A. Duncan, Sharon Dane, and Mary Winter, "A Research Model of Sustainable Family Business," *Family Business Review* 12, no. 3 (September 1999): 197–208.

be either good or bad. In either case, they require a response from both the family and the business.

The extent of overlap between the family and business systems will vary from family business to family business. In privately held businesses, where the prevailing orientation is to keep the family and the business separate, there is little overlap—diagrammatically, this case is illustrated by a small area of interface between the two systems. Conversely, in privately held businesses characterized by great overlap, the area of interface between the family and business systems is considerable.

Sustainability results from the confluence of family success, business success, and appropriate responses to disruptions. In other words, sustainability requires consideration of the family as well as the business. It also requires consideration of the ability of the family and business to cooperate in responding to disruptions in a way that does not impede the success of either.[11]

15-3c Forcing Events

Forcing events are those happenings that cause the replacement of the owner/manager. These events require the entrepreneur to step aside and let someone else direct the operation. The following are typical examples:

- Death, resulting in the heirs immediately having to find a successor to run the operation
- Illness or some other form of nonterminal physical incapacitation
- Mental or psychological breakdown, resulting in the individual having to withdraw from the business
- Abrupt departure, such as when an entrepreneur decides, with no advance warning, to retire immediately
- Legal problems, such as incarceration for violation of the law (if this period of confinement is for more than a few weeks, succession usually becomes necessary, if in name only)
- Severe business decline, resulting in the owner/manager deciding to leave the helm
- Financial difficulties, resulting in lenders demanding the removal of the owner/manager before lending the necessary funds to the enterprise

These types of events often are unforeseen, and the family seldom has a contingency plan for dealing with them. As a result, when they occur, they often create a major problem for the business.

These considerations influence the environment within which the successor will operate. Unless that individual and the environment fit well, the successor will be less than maximally effective.

15-3d Sources of Succession

LO3 Identify and describe some of the most important sources of succession

An **entrepreneurial successor** is someone who is high in ingenuity, creativity, and drive. This person often provides the critical ideas for new-product development and future ventures. The **managerial successor** is someone who is interested in efficiency, internal control, and the effective use of resources. This individual often provides the stability and day-to-day direction needed to keep the enterprise going.

When looking for an inside successor, the entrepreneur usually focuses on a son, daughter, nephew, or niece, with the intent of gradually giving the person operational responsibilities followed by strategic power and ownership. An important factor in the venture's success is whether the founder and the heir can get along. The entrepreneur must be able to turn from being a leader to being a coach, from being a doer to being an advisor. The heir must respect the founder's attachment to the venture and be sensitive to this person's possessive feelings. At the same time, the heir must be able to use his or her entrepreneurial flair to initiate necessary changes.[12] When looking ahead toward choosing a successor from inside the organization, the founder often trains a team of executive managers that consists of both family

TABLE 15.2   COMPARISON OF ENTRY STRATEGIES FOR SUCCESSION IN PRIVATELY HELD BUSINESSES

	Advantages	Disadvantages
Early Entry Strategy	Intimate familiarity with the nature of the business and employees is acquired.	Conflict results when the owner has difficulty with teaching or relinquishing control to the successor.
	Skills specifically required by the business are developed.	Normal mistakes tend to be viewed as incompetence in the successor.
	Exposure to others in the business facilitates acceptance and the achievement of credibility.	Knowledge of the environment is limited, and risks of inbreeding are incurred.
	Strong relationships with constituents are readily established.	
Delayed Entry Strategy	The successor's skills are judged with greater objectivity.	Specific expertise and understanding of the organization's key success factors and culture may be lacking.
	The development of self-confidence and growth independent of familial influence are achieved.	Set patterns of outside activity may conflict with those prevailing in the family firm.
	Outside success establishes credibility and serves as a basis for accepting the successor as a competent executive.	Resentment may result when successors are advanced ahead of long-term employees.
	Perspective of the business environment is broadened.	

Source: Jeffrey A. Barach, Joseph Ganitsky, James A. Carson, and Benjamin A. Doochin, "Entry of the Next Generation: Strategic Challenge for Family Firms," Journal of Small Business Management 26, no. 2 (April 1988): 53.

and nonfamily members. This enables the individual to build an experienced management team capable of producing a successor. The founder assumes that, in time, a natural leader will emerge from the group.[13]

Two key strategies center on the entry of the inside younger generation and when the "power" actually changes hands. Table 15.2 illustrates the advantages and disadvantages of the early entry strategy versus the delayed entry strategy. The main question is the ability of the successor to gain credibility with the firm's employees. The actual transfer of power is a critical issue in the implementation of any succession plan.[14]

If the founder looks for a family member outside the firm, he or she usually prefers to have the heir first work for someone else. The hope is that the individual will make his or her initial mistakes early on, before assuming the family business reins.

Sometimes the founder will look for a nonfamily outsider to be the successor, perhaps only temporarily. The entrepreneur may not see an immediate successor inside the firm and may decide to hire a professional manager, at least on an interim basis, while waiting for an heir to mature and take over.

Another form of nonfamily outsider is the specialist who is experienced in getting ventures out of financial difficulty. The founder usually gives the specialist total control, and this person later hands the rejuvenated venture to another leader.

Still another nonfamily approach is for the founder to find a person with the right talents and to bring this individual into the venture as an assistant, with the understanding that he or she will eventually become president and owner of the venture. No heirs may exist, or perhaps no eligible family member is interested.

THE ENTREPRENEURIAL PROCESS

Harvesting a Business Online

Selling a business, also known as harvesting a business, is normally a time-consuming, stressful experience for entrepreneurs. Between the due diligence performed by the buyer and the emotional distress felt by the entrepreneur as a result of leaving the business, the sales process is far more involved than selling a car or even a house. Employees have to be considered, financial statements have to be organized and analyzed, and the entrepreneur has to figure out what to do after the business is sold.

Purchasing a business is a complex procedure, which is difficult to simplify; however, companies looking to facilitate the buying and selling of businesses are gaining in popularity. These companies are offering online services designed to match entrepreneurs with potential buyers. The objective is to provide greater visibility for businesses to eliminate much of the anxiety felt by entrepreneurs, which results from completing the most difficult part of the process: locating an interested party.

Business brokers have been around for decades. Most, if not all, brokers now have websites with directories of businesses currently for sale, not unlike those provided by realtors. These brokers usually keep their lists private and limit their scope to a given region. The new services are planning to differentiate themselves by providing global listings to maximize exposure for entrepreneurs and to entice buyers to frequent their sites. In addition, these sites will offer the added functionality of broadcasting their listings to popular search services such as Craigslist and Google.

BizTrader.com, one such company, is an all-inclusive provider for anyone looking to buy, sell, or value a small business. The company has received positive feedback from existing brokerage agencies, a fact that it attributes to hiring a chief operating officer with experience running operations for online real estate services. Many similarities exist between the tasks of brokering businesses and selling real estate—a fact that BizTrader.com has successfully exploited.

Another similar site is BizBuySell.com, which has been in business since 1996. The company boasts that it has 45,000 companies listed at any given time. Its first mover advantage has positioned it as the industry leader. Although the site does not offer the same global exposure that BizTrader.com

is promoting, the size of BizBuySell.com allow it to provide greater value than any new service could.

Both BizTrader.com and BizBuySell.com provide valuable functionality for entrepreneurs. The fees are variable depending upon the services provided. The primary purpose of each of these websites is to provide small business with a platform to list their businesses for sale. Both websites also provide ancillary services, such as helping entrepreneurs find financing opportunities and assisting with business valuations. The broker fee for BizTrader.com is $49 per month with free membership. It also provides two pricing options for selling business ads. The standard option is free for 30 days with limited capabilities. However, a valuation is included. BizTrader.com's premium option for advertising requires a onetime fee of $59 and is available until the business is sold. It has increased capabilities and will publish the ad on ten different websites. The broker plans for BizBuySell.com start at $59.95 per month. Purchasing an ad to sell a business has a starting price of $49.95 per month with free distribution on 150 or more partner websites. BizBuySell.com provides valuation reports ranging from $19.95–$59.95, contingent on how many businesses are being analyzed in the report.

As online advertising becomes increasingly important to businesses, newspaper classified ads are waning in popularity. The success of the Internet as a forum to promote businesses is largely attributed to the opportunity it provides for entrepreneurs to more effectively promote their businesses at a reduced cost.

Although some experts strongly encourage entrepreneurs to focus their resources on Internet postings, entrepreneurs who have sold their businesses tend to utilize all available channels. The notion that more is better certainly applies when selling a business, and online services such as BizBuySell.com and BizTrader.com serve to increase the resources at entrepreneurs' disposal.

Source: Adapted from Konstantin Shishkin, "Selling Your Business? Click Here," *Fortune Small Business*, April 14, 2008, http://money.cnn.com/2008/04/14/smbusiness/biztrader.fsb/index.htm (accessed April 17, 2008); and the company websites http://www.biztrader.com and http://www.bizbuysell.com (accessed January 30, 2015).

15-3e Legal Restrictions

LO4 Discuss the potential impact of recent legislation on family business succession

The first source for succession often is family and in-house personnel prospects. However, such traditions of succession practices in privately held businesses were challenged in the *Oakland Scavenger Company* case.

This suit was brought in 1984 by a group of black and Hispanic workers at the California-based **Oakland Scavenger Company** (a garbage collection firm), who complained of employment discrimination because of their race. The U.S. District Court of Northern California dismissed the suit on the basis that it had no relation to antidiscrimination laws. However, the U.S. Court of Appeals for the Ninth Circuit reviewed the decision and held that "nepotistic concerns cannot supersede the nation's paramount goal of equal economic opportunity for all."[15]

According to Oakland Scavenger's legal brief, the question focused on the Fifth Amendment versus Title VII of the 1964 Civil Rights Act: If discrimination overrides the protection of life, liberty, and property from unreasonable interference from the state, then the rights of parents to leave their property and business to anyone can be abolished. This decision can have a major effect on the management succession plans of privately held businesses.

The case was appealed to the Supreme Court. However, before the Court could make a ruling, the Oakland Scavenger Company was purchased by Waste Management Corporation, and an out-of-court $8 million settlement was reached. The settlement allocated sums of at least $50,000 to 16 black and Hispanic plaintiffs, depending on their length of service, and also provided for payments to a class of more than 400 black and Hispanic workers Oakland Scavenger employed after January 10, 1972.[16]

As K. Peter Stalland, legal representative for the National Family Business Council, has stated, "The effect this case can have on small business is tremendous. It means, conceivably, that almost any small business can be sued by an employee of a different ethnic origin than the owner, based upon not being accorded the same treatment as a son or daughter. The precedent is dangerous."[17] Thus, nepotism is something that now must be considered seriously in light of the legal ramifications.

The Oakland Scavenger case has started a movement that is sure to result in more guidelines and limitations for family employment, and privately held businesses will have to be aware of this challenge when preparing succession plans. (See "Entrepreneurship in Practice: Legal Concerns Regarding Nepotism" for more on this topic.)

15-4 DEVELOPING A SUCCESSION STRATEGY

 Relate the ways to develop a succession strategy

Developing a succession strategy involves several important steps: (1) understanding the contextual aspects, (2) identifying successor qualities, and (3) developing a written succession plan.[18]

15-4a Understanding Contextual Aspects of Succession

The five key aspects that must be considered for an effective succession follow.

TIME

The earlier the entrepreneur begins to plan for a successor, the better the chances of finding the right person. The biggest problem the owner faces is the prospect of events that force immediate action and result in inadequate time to find the best replacement.

TYPE OF VENTURE

Some entrepreneurs are easy to replace; some cannot be replaced. To a large degree, this is determined by the type of venture. An entrepreneur who is the idea person in a high-tech operation is going to be difficult to replace. The same is true for an entrepreneur whose personal business contacts throughout the industry are the key factors for the venture's success. On the other hand, a person running an operation that requires a minimum of knowledge or expertise usually can be replaced without much trouble.

CAPABILITIES OF MANAGERS

The skills, desires, and abilities of the replacement will dictate the future potential and direction of the enterprise. As the industry matures, the demands made on the entrepreneur also may change. Industries where high tech is the name of the game often go through a change in which marketing becomes increasingly important. A technologically skilled entrepreneur with an understanding of marketing, or with the ability to develop an orientation in this direction, will be more valuable to the enterprise than will a technologically skilled entrepreneur with no marketing interest or background.

ENTREPRENEUR'S VISION

Most entrepreneurs have expectations, hopes, and desires for their organization. A successor—it is hoped—will share this vision, except, of course, in cases where the entrepreneur's plans have gotten the organization in trouble and a new vision is needed. Examples are plentiful today because of the huge increase in life sciences ventures, high-technology ventures, and other emerging technologies in which the founding entrepreneur possesses the initial vision to launch the company but lacks the managerial experience to grow the venture. Outside executive experience is sought because the board of directors may feel that a more managerial, day-to-day entrepreneurial manager is needed to replace the highly conceptual, analytical entrepreneur who founded the company.

ENVIRONMENTAL FACTORS

Sometimes a successor is needed because the business environment changes and a parallel change is needed at the top. An example is Edwin Land of Polaroid. Although his technological creativity had made the venture successful, Land eventually had to step aside for someone with more marketing skills. In some cases, owners have had to allow financial types to assume control of the venture because internal efficiency was more critical to short-run survival than was market effectiveness.

15-4b Identifying Successor Qualities

Successors should possess many qualities or characteristics. Depending on the situation, some will be more important than others. In most cases, however, all will have some degree of importance. Some of the most common of these successor qualities are sufficient knowledge of the business or a good position (especially marketing or finance) from which to acquire this knowledge within an acceptable time frame; fundamental honesty and capability; good health; energy, alertness, and perception; enthusiasm about the enterprise; personality compatible with the business; high degree of perseverance; stability and maturity; reasonable amount of aggressiveness; thoroughness and a proper respect for detail; problem-solving ability; resourcefulness; ability to plan and organize; talent to develop people; personality of a starter and a finisher; and appropriate agreement with the owner's philosophy about the business.[19]

15-4c Writing a Succession Strategy

These elements prepare the entrepreneur to develop a management continuity strategy and policy. A written policy can be established using one of the following strategies.

1. The owner controls the *management continuity strategy* entirely. This is very common, yet legal advice is still needed and recommended.

2. The owner consults with selected family members. Here, the legal advisor helps to establish a *liaison* between family and owner in constructing the succession mechanism.

3. The owner works with professional advisors. This is an actual board of advisors from various professional disciplines and industries that works with the owner to establish the mechanism for succession (sometimes referred to as a "quasi-board").[20]

4. The owner works with family involvement. This alternative allows the core family (blood members and spouses) to actively participate in and influence the decisions regarding succession.

If the owner is still reasonably healthy and the firm is in a viable condition, the following additional actions should be considered.

5. The owner formulates **buy/sell agreements** at the very outset of the company, or soon thereafter, and whenever a major change occurs. This is also the time to consider an appropriate insurance policy on key individuals that would provide the cash needed to acquire the equity of the deceased.

6. The owner considers **employee stock ownership plans (ESOPs)**. If the owner has no immediate successor in mind and respects the loyalty and competence of his or her

employees, then an appropriate ESOP might be the best solution for passing control of the enterprise. After the owner's death, the employees could decide on the management hierarchy.

7. The owner sells or liquidates the business when losing enthusiasm for it but is still physically able to go on. This could provide the capital to launch another business. Whatever the owner's plans, the firm would be sold before it fails due to disinterest.

8. The owner sells or liquidates after discovering a terminal illness but still has time for the orderly transfer of management or ownership.[21]

Legal advice is beneficial for all of these strategies, but of greater benefit is having advisors (legal or otherwise) who understand the succession issues and are able to recommend a course of action.

Entrepreneurial founders of privately held businesses often reject thoughts of succession. However, neither ignorance nor denial will change the inevitable. It is therefore crucial for entrepreneurs to design a plan for succession very carefully. Such plans prevent today's flourishing privately held businesses from becoming a statistic of diminishing family dynasties.

CONSIDER OUTSIDE HELP

Promotion from within is a morale-building philosophy. Sometimes, however, it is a mistake. When the top person does a poor job, does promoting the next individual in line solve the problem? The latter may be the owner/manager's clone. Conversely, consider family-owned businesses that start to outgrow the managerial ability of the top person. Does anyone in the firm *really* have the requisite skills to manage the operation? The questions that must be answered are: How can the business be effectively run, and who has the ability to do it? Sometimes answering these questions calls for an outside person. Privately held businesses also face the ever-present ego factor. Does the owner/manager have the wisdom to step aside and the courage to let someone else make strategic decisions? Or is the desire for control so great that the owner prefers to run the risks associated with personally managing the operation? The lesson is clear to the dispassionate observer; unfortunately, it is one that many owners have had to learn the hard way.[22]

15-5 THE EXIT STRATEGY: LIQUIDITY EVENTS

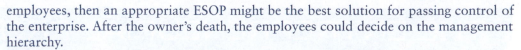

It is true that most entrepreneurs are focused on launching and growing their ventures rather than the plan for exiting the venture in the years to come. However, an exit strategy is always of prime importance to outside investors. Investors' commitment to capital will always reside on the confidence that they will recover their initial investment with a healthy profit. Entrepreneurs need to be aware that an exit strategy *for* the venture may mean the entrepreneur's exit *from* the venture as well.

An **exit strategy** is defined as that component of the business plan where an entrepreneur describes a method by which investors can realize a tangible return on their investment. The questions of "how much," "when," and "how" need to be addressed. Investors always want to convert their share of the investment into a more "liquid" form, known as a **liquidity event**, which refers to the positioning of the venture for the realization of a cash return for the owners and the investors. This "event" is most often achieved through an IPO or complete sale of the venture. In either scenario, the entrepreneur must seek professional advice and legal counsel due to the significant regulations and legal parameters involved. For our purposes, we delve into the basic concepts involved with each of these liquidity events.

15-5a The Initial Public Offering (IPO)

LO6 Examine the specifics of an IPO as a potential harvest strategy

As we covered in Chapter 8, many entrepreneurs have sought capital through the public markets. Just to reiterate, the term **initial public offering (IPO)** is used to represent the registered public offering of a company's securities for the first time. As we illustrated in Chapter 8, there is tremendous volatility that exists within the stock market and entrepreneurs should be aware of the concerns that confront them when they pursue the

THE ENTREPRENEURIAL PROCESS

Using Buy/Sell Agreements

Many entrepreneurs owe their continued success to the combined skills of two or more owners. But did any owner, at the inception of the venture, contemplate involuntarily continuing the business with a co-owner's children? With a co-owner's ex-spouse? With a co-owner's creditors? Probably not. But smart entrepreneurs plan ahead, in order to deal with issues of control that may unpredictably arise by virtue of one of the "Four *Ds*": Disability, Death, Dissolution, and Debtorship. Should a co-owner become disabled, die, be involved in a marital dissolution, or have assets seized by his or her creditors, ownership of his or her interest in the business may be in jeopardy of transfer to one or more third parties. Fortunately, it is possible (and imperative) that the parties take the steps necessary to assure that the transfer of any ownership interest in the business is carried out in a way that protects the future of the business, the ownership interests of remaining shareholders, and the financial security of the departing owner's family. A buy/sell agreement can provide just such protection. It ensures that, in the event of one of these "triggering events," interest in a closely held business is transferred in a manner that is advantageous to all involved parties. This type of agreement can be designed to make certain the following:

1. The remaining shareholder(s) has(have) the first right to retain the ownership interest.

2. The departing owner (or beneficiaries) receives a fair market price for the ownership interest.

3. Lawsuits and disputes that could threaten the company's existence are avoided.

4. Funds are available to purchase the ownership interest.

Legal counsel is necessary to ensure that a buy/sell agreement addresses all of the unique circumstances of a particular company.

The two basic types of agreements are the crosspurchase agreement, in which the shareholders are obligated to purchase the departing owner's stock, and the redemption agreement, in which the company is obligated to purchase the departing owner's stock. Each case has certain advantages, disadvantages, and tax implications that need to be considered, and some agreements include "blended" options and obligations for such purchases. Thus, both a lawyer and a tax accountant should be consulted.

Source: Thomas Owens, "Buy–Sell Agreements," *Small Business Reports* (January 1991): 57–61; and Mark E. Need, Elmore Entrepreneurship Law Clinic Director, Indiana University–Bloomington, 2015.

IPO market. Many entrepreneurs already have begun to recognize some of the complex requirements involved with going public.[23] Table 15.3 provides a complete illustration of the steps involved with an IPO.

The Securities and Exchange Commission (SEC) requires the filing of a registration statement that includes a complete prospectus on the company. The SEC then reviews the registration, ensuring that full disclosure is made before giving permission to proceed. (See Table 15.4 for a presentation of the registration process.)

The prospectus must disclose fully all pertinent information about a company and must present a fair representation of the firm's true prospects. All negative information must be clearly highlighted and explained. Some of the specific, detailed information that must be presented follows.

- History and nature of the company
- Capital structure Description of any material contracts
- Description of securities being registered
- Salaries and security holdings of major officers and directors and the price they paid for
- holdings
- Underwriting arrangements
- Estimate and use of net proceeds
- Audited financial statements
- Information about the competition with an estimation of the chances of the company's survival

TABLE 15.3   THE IPO PROCESS

The entire initial public offering process is at once fast-moving and highly structured, governed by an interlocking set of federal and state laws and regulations and self-regulatory organization rules. Each member of the IPO team has specific responsibilities to fulfill; however, the company ultimately calls the plays for the team.

The following steps in the IPO process apply to both U.S. and non-U.S. companies.

Present proposal to the board. The IPO process begins with management making a presentation to the company's board of directors, complete with business plan and financial projections, proposing their company enter the public market. The board should consider the proposal carefully.

Restate financial statements and refocus the company *(applies only to companies not in compliance with U.S. GAAP).* If the board approves the proposal to go public, the company's books and records should be reviewed for the past two to three years. Financial statements should be restated to adhere to GAAP in order for them to be certified. Any intracompany transactions, compensation arrangements, and relationships involving management or the board that are customary to a private enterprise—but improper for a public company— must be eliminated and the statements appropriately restated. Also, companies should consider whether any outside affiliations (operations tangential to the company's core business) will be perceived negatively by the market.

Find an underwriter and execute a "letter of intent." At this point, a company should select an underwriter, if it has not already engaged one. A company's relationship with an underwriter should then be formalized through a mutual "letter of intent," outlining fees, ranges for stock price and number of shares, and certain other conditions.

Draft prospectus. After a letter of intent is executed, the IPO attorneys can begin work on the prospectus.

Respond to due diligence. The next step is to ask your investment banker and accountant to begin an elaborate investigation of your company (the due diligence process). Your underwriter will examine your company's management, operations, financial conditions, performance, competitive position, and business plan. Other factors open to scrutiny are your labor force, suppliers, customers, creditors, and any other parties that have a bearing on the viability of the company as a public entity and could affect the proper, truthful, adequate disclosure of its condition in the prospectus. The accounting firm will examine financial information and such specific documents as contracts, billings, and receipts to ensure the accuracy and adequacy of financial statements.

Select a financial printer. Your company should select an experienced financial printer—one that is familiar with SEC regulations governing the graphic presentation of a prospectus and has the facilities to print sufficient quantities under severe time constraints.

Assemble the syndicate. After the preliminary prospectus has been filed with the SEC and is available for circulation among potential investors, your underwriter should assemble the "syndicate," consisting of additional investment bankers who will place portions of the offering to achieve the desired distribution. Your underwriter should also accumulate "indications of interest"—solicited through its efforts as well as those of the syndicate—from institutions and brokers that have approached their clients. These indications give assurance that the IPO is viable and help to determine the final number of shares to be offered and the allocations to investors.

Perform the road show. Next, your company and your investment banker should design and perform the "road show," a series of meetings held with potential investors and analysts in key cities across the country and, if appropriate, overseas. The road show has become increasingly important not only to communicate key information to investors but also to display the managerial talent and expertise that will be leading the company.

Prepare, revise, and print the prospectus. In the meantime, the preliminary prospectus should have been prepared and revised according to SEC and NASDR (National Association of Securities Dealers Regulations) comments. Upon completion of these revisions, the company can expect NASDR to issue a letter stating that it has no objections to the underwriting compensation, terms, and arrangements, and the SEC to indicate its intent to declare their registration effective. The preliminary prospectus should be circulated to potential investors at least two days before the effective date; then the final version of the prospectus can be printed.

Price the offering. Just before the underwriting agreement is signed, on the day before the registration becomes effective and sales begin, the offering is priced. The investment banker should recommend a price per share for management's approval, taking into account the company's financial performance and

(Continued)

TABLE 15.3 THE IPO PROCESS (*Continued*)

competitive prospects, the stock price of comparable companies, general stock market conditions, and the success of the road show and ensuing expressions of interest. While the company will want to price the offering as high as possible, an offering that does not sell or sell completely will not be in its best interest or in the interest of the investors who find the share price declining in the market immediately after their initial purchase. In fact, investors look for at least a modest increase in the market price to reassure them about their investment decision.

Determine the offering size. The investment banking team should also consult with management regarding the offering size, taking into consideration how much capital the company needs to raise, the desired degree of corporate control, and investor demand. Often, the more shares outstanding, the greater the liquidity of the stock, which will increase institutional interest.

Source: Adapted from *Going Public* (New York: The NASDAQ Stock Market, Inc., 2005), 5–9; updated for accuracy February, 2015.

TABLE 15.4 THE REGISTRATION PROCESS

Event	Participants	Agenda	Timetable
Preliminary meeting to discuss issue	President, VP Finance, independent accountants, underwriters, counsel	Discuss financial needs; introduce and select type of issue to meet needs	1 July (begin)
Form selection	Management, counsel	Select appropriate form for use in registration statement	3 July (3 days)
Initial meeting of working group	President, VP Finance, independent accountants, underwriter, counsel for underwriter, company counsel	Assign specific duties to each person in the working group; discuss underwriting problems with this issue; discuss accounting problems with the issue	8 July (8 days)
Second meeting of working group	Same as for initial meeting	Review work assignments; prepare presentation to board of directors	22 July (22 days)
Meeting of board of directors	Board of directors, members of working group	Approve proposed issue and increase of debt or equity; authorize preparation of materials	26 July (26 days)
Meeting of company counsel with underwriters	Company counsel, counsel for underwriters, underwriters	Discuss underwriting terms and blue-sky problems	30 July (30 days)
Meeting of working group	Members of working group review collected material and examine discrepancies		6 August (37 days)
Prefiling conference with SEC staff	Working group members, SEC staff, other experts as needed	Review proposed registration and associated problems: legal, financial, operative	9 August (40 days)
Additional meetings of working group	Members of working group	Prepare final registration statement and prospectuses	12–30 August (61 days)

(Continued)

TABLE 15.4   THE REGISTRATION PROCESS (*Continued*)

Event	Participants	Agenda	Timetable
Meeting with board of directors	Board of directors, members of working group	Approve registration statement and prospectuses; discuss related topics and problems	6 September (68 days)
Meeting of working group	Members of working group	Draft final corrected registration statement	10 September (72 days)
Filing registration statement with SEC	Company counsel or representative and SEC staff	File registration statement and pay fee	12 September (74 days)
Distribution of "red herring" prospectus	Underwriters	Publicize offering	16 September (78 days)
Receipt of letter of comments	Members of working group	Relate deficiencies in registration statement	15 October (107 days)
Meeting of working group	Members of working group	Correct deficiencies and submit amendments	21 October (113 days)
Due diligence meeting	Management representatives, independent accountants, company counsel, underwriter's counsel, underwriters, other professionals as needed	Exchange final information and discuss pertinent problems relating to underwriting and issue	24 October (116 days)
Pricing amendment	Management, underwriters	Add the amounts for the actual price, underwriter's discount or commission, and net proceeds to company to the amended registration statement	25 October (117 days)
Notice of acceptance	SEC staff	Report from SEC staff on acceptance status of price-amended registration statement	28 October (120 days)
Statement becomes effective			30 October (122 days)

Source: From K. Fred Skousen, *An Introduction to the SEC*, 5th ed. © 1991 Cengage Learning; see also. K Fred Skousen, Steven Glover, **and** Douglas Prawitt, *An Introduction to Corporate Governance and the SEC* (Mason, OH: Cengage Learning, 2004).

Some of the more important disclosure requirements for annual reports follow.

- Audited financial statements that include the balance sheets for the past two years and income and funds statements for the past three years
- Five years of selected financial data
- Management's discussion and analysis of financial conditions and results of operations
- A brief description of the business
- Line-of-business disclosures for the past three fiscal years

- Identification of directors and executive officers, with the principal occupation and employer of each
- Identification of the principal market in which the firm's securities are traded
- Range of market prices and dividends for each quarter of the two most recent fiscal years
- An offer to provide a free copy of the 10-K report to shareholders on written request unless the annual report complies with Form 10-K disclosure requirements[24]

Some of the forms the SEC requires follow.

- Form S-1 (information contained in the prospectus and other additional financial data)
- Form 10-Q (quarterly financial statements and a summary of all important events that took place during the three-month period)
- Form 8-K (a report of unscheduled material events or corporate changes deemed important to the shareholder and filed with the SEC within 15 days of the end of a month in which a significant material event transpired)
- Proxy statements (information given in connection with proxy solicitation)[25]

Entrepreneurs who pursue the public securities route should be prepared for these reporting requirements, disclosure statements, and the shared control and ownership with outside shareholders.

15-6 COMPLETE SALE OF THE VENTURE

LO7 Present "selling out" as a final alternative in the harvest strategy

After considering the various succession ideas presented in this chapter, as well as the potential for an IPO, many privately held business entrepreneurs choose a **harvest strategy** that involves complete sale of the venture. If this becomes the proper choice for an entrepreneur (keep in mind that it may be the best decision for an entrepreneur who has no interested family members or key employees), then the owner needs to review some important considerations. The idea of "selling out" actually should be viewed in the positive sense of "harvesting the investment."

Entrepreneurs consider selling their venture for numerous reasons. Based on 1,000 business owners surveyed, some of the motivations are (1) boredom and burnout, (2) lack of operating and growth capital, (3) no heirs to leave the business to, (4) desire for liquidity, (5) aging and health problems, and (6) desire to pursue other interests.[26]

Whether it is due to a career shift, poor health, a desire to start another venture, or retirement, many entrepreneurs face the sellout option during their entrepreneurial lifetime. This harvesting strategy needs to be carefully prepared in order to obtain the adequate financial rewards.[27]

15-6a Steps for Selling a Business

There are generally eight recommended steps for the proper preparation, development, and realization of the sale of a venture.[28]

STEP 1: PREPARE A FINANCIAL ANALYSIS

The purpose of such an analysis is to define priorities and forecast the next few years of the business. These fundamental questions must be answered:

- What will executive and other workforce requirements be, and how will we pay for them?
- If the market potential is so limited that goals cannot be attained, should we plan an acquisition or develop new products to meet targets for sales and profits?
- Must we raise outside capital for continued growth? How much and when?

STEP 2: SEGREGATE ASSETS

Tax accountants and lawyers may suggest the following steps to reduce taxes:

- Place real estate in a separate corporation, owned individually or by members of the family.

- Establish a leasing subsidiary with title to machinery and rolling stock. You can then lease this property to the operating company.

- Give some or all of the owner's shares to heirs when values are low, but have the owner retain voting rights. Thus, when a sale is made, part or all of the proceeds can go directly to another generation without double taxation.

- Hold management's salaries and fringe benefits at reasonable levels to maximize profits.

STEP 3: VALUE THE BUSINESS

The various methods used to valuate a venture were discussed in Chapter 14. Obviously, establishing the valuation of a company constitutes a most important step in its sale.

STEP 4: IDENTIFY THE APPROPRIATE TIMING

Knowing when to offer a business for sale is a critical factor. Timing can be everything. A few suggestions follow:

- Sell when business profits show a strong upward trend.
- Sell when the management team is complete and experienced.
- Sell when the business cycle is on the upswing, with potential buyers in the right mood and holding excess capital or credit for acquisitions.
- Sell when you are convinced that your company's future will be bright.

STEP 5: PUBLICIZE THE OFFER TO SELL

A short prospectus on the company that provides enough information to interest potential investors should be prepared. This prospectus should be circulated through the proper professional channels: bankers, accountants, lawyers, consultants, and business brokers.

STEP 6: FINALIZE THE PROSPECTIVE BUYERS

Inquiries need to be made in the trade concerning the prospective buyers. Characters and managerial reputation should be assessed to find the best buyer.

STEP 7: REMAIN INVOLVED THROUGH THE CLOSING

Meeting with the final potential buyers helps to eliminate areas of misunderstanding and to negotiate the major requirements more effectively. Also, the involvement of professionals such as attorneys and accountants usually precludes any major problems arising at the closing.

STEP 8: COMMUNICATE AFTER THE SALE

Problems between the new owner and the remaining management team need to be resolved to build a solid transition. Communication between the seller and the buyer and between the buyer and the current management personnel is a key step.

In addition to these eight steps, an entrepreneur must be aware of the tax implications that arise from the sale of a business. For professional advice, a tax accountant specializing in business valuations and sales should be consulted.

The eight steps outlined here, combined with the information on valuation in Chapter 14, will help entrepreneurs harvest their ventures. The steps provide a clear framework within which entrepreneurs can structure a fair negotiation leading to a sale. If the purpose of a valuation is to sell the business, then the entrepreneur must plan ahead and follow through with each step.

SUMMARY

This chapter focused on the harvesting of the venture. Beginning with the issue of management succession as one of the greatest challenges for entrepreneurs, a number of considerations that affect succession were discussed. Using privately held firms as the focal point in this chapter, key issues such as family and nonfamily members—both within and outside the firm—were identified to show the unique pressures on the entrepreneur. Some family members will want to be put in charge of the operation; others simply want a stake in the enterprise.

Two types of successors exist: An entrepreneurial successor provides innovative ideas for new-product development, whereas a managerial successor provides stability for day-to-day operations. An entrepreneur may search inside or outside the family as well as inside or outside the business. The actual transfer of power is a critical issue, and the timing of entry for a successor can be strategic.

The Oakland Scavenger Company case revealed how legal concerns now exist about the hiring of only family members. Nepotism has been challenged in the courts on the basis of discrimination.

Developing a succession plan involves understanding these important contextual aspects: time, type of venture, capabilities of managers, the entrepreneur's vision, and environmental factors. Also, forcing events may require the implementation of a succession plan, regardless of whether or not the firm is ready to implement one. This is why it is so important to identify successor qualities and carry out the succession plan.

The chapter closed with a discussion of the entrepreneur's decision to sell out. The process was viewed as a method to "harvest" the investment, and eight specific steps were presented for entrepreneurs to follow.

KEY TERMS

buy/sell agreements
delayed entry strategy
early entry strategy
employee stock ownership plans (ESOPs)

entrepreneurial successor
exit strategy
forcing events
harvest strategy
initial public offering (IPO)

liquidity event
management succession
managerial successor
nepotism
Oakland Scavenger Company

REVIEW AND DISCUSSION QUESTIONS

1. What are the potential choices for an entrepreneur to examine as the venture matures?

2. A number of barriers to succession in privately held businesses exist. Using Table 15.1, identify some of the key barriers.

3. What pressures do entrepreneurs sometimes face from inside the family? (Use Figure 15.1 in your answer.)

4. What pressures do entrepreneurs sometimes face from outside the family? (Use Figure 15.1 in your answer.)

5. An entrepreneur can make a number of choices regarding a successor. Using Table 15.2 as a guide, discuss each of these choices.

6. How might the Oakland Scavenger case affect succession decisions in small businesses?

7. What are three of the contextual aspects that must be considered in an effective succession plan?

8. In what way can forcing events cause the replacement of an owner/manager? Cite three examples.

9. What are five qualities or characteristics successors should possess?

10. Why do entrepreneurs look forward to the day when they can take their company public?

11. What eight steps should be followed to harvest a business? Discuss each of these steps.

NOTES

1. Tammi S. Feltham, Glenn Feltham, and James J. Barnett, "The Dependence of Family Businesses on a Single Decision-Maker," *Journal of Small Business Management* 43, no. 1 (January 2005): 1–15; see also Timothy Bates, "Analysis of Young, Small Firms that Have Closed: Delineating Successful from Unsuccessful Closures," *Journal of Business Venturing* 20, no. 3 (May 2005): 343–58.

2. John L. Ward, *Keeping the Family Business Healthy* (San Francisco: Jossey-Bass, 1987), 1–2.

3. Richard Beckhard and W. Gibb Dyer, Jr., "Managing Continuity in the Family-Owned Business," *Organizational Dynamics* 12, no. 1 (Summer 1983): 7–8.

4. Manfred F. R. Kets de Vries, "The Dynamics of Family-Controlled Firms: The Good News and the Bad News," *Organizational Dynamics* 21, no. 3 (Winter 1993): 59–71; and Richard A. Cosier and Michael Harvey, "The Hidden Strengths in Family Business: Functional Conflict," *Family Business Review* 11, no. 1 (March 1998): 75–79.

5. Peter Davis, "Realizing the Potential of the Family Business," *Organizational Dynamics* 12, no. 1 (Summer 1983): 53–54; and Thomas Hubler, "Ten Most Prevalent Obstacles to Family Business Succession Planning," *Family Business Review* 12, no. 2 (June 1999): 117–22.

6. Michael D. Ensley and Allison W. Pearson, "An Exploratory Comparison of the Behavioral Dynamics of Top Management Teams in Family and Nonfamily New Ventures: Cohesion, Conflict, Potency, and Consensus," *Entrepreneurship Theory and Practice* 29, no. 3 (May 2005): 267–84; Paul Westhead and Carole Howorth, "Ownership and Management Issues Associated with Family Firm Performance and Company Objectives," *Family Business Review* 19 (2006): 301–16; and Michael H. Morris, Jeffrey A. Allen, Donald F. Kuratko and David Brannon, "Experiencing Family Business Creation: Differences Between Founders, Nonfamily Managers, and Founders of Nonfamily Firms," *Entrepreneurship Theory and Practice* 34, no. 6 (2010): 1057–84.

7. See Donald F. Kuratko, "Understanding the Succession Challenge in Family Business," *Entrepreneurship, Innovation, and Change* 4, no. 3 (September 1995): 185–91; see also Heather A. Haveman and Mukti V. Khaire, "Survival Beyond Succession? The Contingent Impact of Founder Succession on Organizational Failure," *Journal of Business Venturing* 19, no. 3 (May 2004): 437–63.

8. See Neil C. Churchill and Kenneth J. Hatten, "Non-Market-Based Transfers of Wealth and Power: A Research Framework for Family Business," *American Journal of Small Business* 12, no. 2 (Fall 1987): 53–66; and Timothy P. Blumentritt, Andrew D. Keyt, and Joseph H. Astrachan, "Creating an Environment for Successful Nonfamily CEOs: An Exploratory Study of Good Principals," *Family Business Review* 20 (2007): 321–36.

9. Peter S. Davis and Paula D. Harveston, "The Influence of Family on the Family Business Succession Process: A Multi-Generational Perspective," *Entrepreneurship Theory and Practice* 22, no. 3 (Spring 1998): 31–54; Eleni T. Stavrou, "Succession in Family Business: Exploring the Effects of Demographic Factors on Offspring Intentions to Join and Take Over the Business," *Journal of Small Business Management* 37, no. 3 (1999): 43–61; and Sue Birley, "Attitudes of Owner-Managers' Children Toward Family and Business Issues," *Entrepreneurship Theory and Practice* 26, no. 3 (2002): 5–19.

10. See Donald F. Kuratko, Helga B. Foss, and Lucinda L. Van Alst, "IRS Estate Freeze Rules: Implications for Family Business Succession Planning," *Family Business Review* 7, no. 1 (Spring 1994): 61–72; and Joseph H. Astrachan and Roger Tutterow, "The Effect of Estate Taxes on Family Business: Survey Results," *Family Business Review* 9, no. 3 (Fall 1996): 303–14.

11. Shaker A. Zahra, James C. Hayton, and Carlo Salvato, "Entrepreneurship in Family vs. Nonfamily Firms: A Resource-Based Analysis of the Effect of Organizational Culture," *Entrepreneurship Theory and Practice* 28, no. 4 (Summer 2004): 363–82; and Matthew W. Rutherford, Lori A. Muse, and Sharon L. Oswald, "A New Perspective on the Developmental Model for Family Business," *Family Business Review* 19 (2007): 317–33.

12. For an interesting perspective, see Kathryn Stafford, Karen A. Duncan, Sharon Dane, and Mary Winter, "A Research Model of Sustainable Family Business," *Family Business Review* 12, no. 3 (September 1999): 197–208; see also Lucia Naldi, Mattias Nordqvist, Karin Sjöberg, and Johan Wiklund, "Entrepreneurial Orientation, Risk Taking, and Performance in Family Firms," *Family Business Review* 20 (2007): 33–48; and Shaker A. Zahra, "Harvesting Family Firms' Organizational Social Capital: A Relational Perspective," *Journal of Management Studies* 47, no. 2 (2010): 345–66.

13. See Kevin C. Seymour, "Intergenerational Relationships in the Family Firm: The Effect on Leadership Succession," *Family Business Review* 6, no. 3 (Fall 1993): 263–82; Eleni T. Stavrou and Paul Michael Swiercz, "Securing the Future of Family Enterprise: A Model of Offspring Intentions to Join the Business," *Entrepreneurship Theory and Practice* 22, no. 2 (Winter 1998): 19–40; and James P. Marshall, Ritch Sorenson, Keith Brigham, Elizabeth Wieling, Alan Reifman, and Richard S. Wampler, "The Paradox for the Family Firm CEO: Owner Age Relationship to Succession-Related Processes and Plans," *Journal of Business Venturing* 21, no. 3 (2006): 348–68.

14. Jeffrey A. Barach, Joseph Ganitsky, James A. Carson, and Benjamin A. Doochin, "Entry of the Next Generation: Strategic Challenge for Family Firms," *Journal of Small Business Management* 26, no. 2 (1988): 49–56; see also Matthew W. Rutherford, Donald F. Kuratko, and Daniel T. Holt, "Examining the Link Between

Familiness and Performance: Can the F-PEC Untangle the Family Business Theory Jungle?" *Entrepreneurship Theory and Practice* 32, no. 6: 1089–109; and Daniel T. Holt, Matthew W. Rutherford, and Donald F. Kuratko, "Advancing the Field of Family Business Research: Further Testing the Measurement Properties of the F-PEC," *Family Business Review* 23, no. 1 (2010): 76–88.

15. "Nepotism on Trial," *Inc.*, July 1984, 29.

16. David Graulich, "You Can't Always Pay What You Want," *Family Business* (February 1990): 16–19.

17. "Feuding Families," *Inc.*, January 1985, 38.

18. Donald F. Kuratko and Richard M. Hodgetts, "Succession Strategies for Family Businesses," *Management Advisor* (Spring 1989): 22–30; see also Mark Fischetti, *The Family Business Succession Handbook* (Philadelphia: Family Business, 1997).

19. James J. Chrisman, Jess H. Chua, and Pramodita Sharma, "Important Attributes of Successors in Family Business: An Exploratory Study," *Family Business Review* 11, no. 1 (March 1998): 19–34; and Franz W. Kellermanns, Kimberly A. Eddleston, Tim Barnett, and Allison Pearson, "An Exploratory Study of Family Member Characteristics and Involvement: Effects on Entrepreneurial Behavior in the Family Firm," *Family Business Review* 21 (2008): 1–14.

20. Adapted from Harold W. Fox, "Quasi-Boards: Useful Small Business Confidants," *Harvard Business Review* 60, no. 1 (January/February 1982): 64–72.

21. Glenn R. Ayres, "Rough Family Justice: Equity in Family Business Succession Planning," *Family Business Review* 3, no. 1 (Spring 1990): 3–22; Ronald E. Berenbeim, "How Business Families Manage the Transition from Owner to Professional Management," *Family Business Review* 3, no. 1 (Spring 1990): 69–110; and Michael H. Morris, Roy O. Williams, Jeffrey A. Allen, and Ramon A. Avila, "Correlates of Success in Family Business Transitions," *Journal of Business Venturing* 12, no. 5 (1997): 385–402.

22. Johannes H. M. Welsch, "The Impact of Family Ownership and Involvement on the Process of Management Succession," *Family Business Review* 6, no. 1 (Spring 1993): 31–54; and Veroniek Collewaert, "Angel Investors' and Entrepreneurs' Intentions to Exit Their Ventures: A Conflict Perspective," *Entrepreneurship Theory and Practice* 36, no. 4 (2012): 753–79.

23. See *Going Public* (New York: The NASDAQ Stock Market, Inc., 2005), 5–9; see also Richard C. Dorf and Thomas H. Byers, *Technology Ventures: From Idea to Enterprise*, 2nd ed. (New York: McGraw-Hill, 2008); and Moren Lévesque, Nitin Joglekar, and Jane Davies, "A Comparison of Revenue Growth at Recent-IPO and Established Firms: The Influence of SG&A, R&D and COGS," *Journal of Business Venturing* 27, no. 1 (2012): 47–61.

24. K. Fred Skousen, *An Introduction to the SEC*, 5th ed. (Mason, OH: Thomson/South-Western), 157; see also Catherine M. Daily, S. Travis Certo, and Dan R. Dalton, "Investment Bankers and IPO Pricing: Does Prospectus Information Matter?" *Journal of Business Venturing* 20, no. 1 (January 2005): 93–11; and Ning Gao and Bharat A. Jain, "Founder Management and the Market for Corporate Control for IPO Firms: The Moderating Effect of the Power Structure of the Firm," *Journal of Business Venturing* 27, no. 1 (2012): 112–26.

25. For a complete listing, see Skousen, *An Introduction to the SEC*, 60; see also Andrew J. Sherman, *Raising Capital* (New York: AMACOM, 2005).

26. James Fox and Steven Elek, "Selling Your Company," *Small Business Reports* (May 1992): 49–58; see also John B. Vinturella and Suzanne M. Erickson, *Raising Entrepreneurial Capital* (Burlington, MA: Elsevier, 2004); and Andrew J. Sherman, *Harvesting Intangible Assets* (New York: AMACOM, 2012).

27. See Donald Reinardy and Catherine Stover, "I Want to Sell My Business. Where Do I Begin?" *Small Business Forum* (Fall 1991): 1–24; see also J. William Petty, "Harvesting Firm Value: Process and Results," *Entrepreneurship 2000* (Chicago: Upstart, 1997), 71–94; Dawn R. DeTienne, "Entrepreneurial Exit as a Critical Component of the Entrepreneurial Process: Theoretical Development," *Journal of Business Venturing* 25, no. 2 (2010): 203–15; and Karl Wennberg, Johan Wiklund, Dawn R. DeTienne, and Melissa S. Cardon, "Reconceptualizing Entrepreneurial Exit: Divergent Exit Routes and Their Drivers," *Journal of Business Venturing* 25, no. 4 (2010): 361–75.

28. From the *Harvard Business Review*, "Packaging Your Business for Sale," by Charles O'Conor, March/April 1985, 52–58. Copyright © 1985 by the President and Fellows of Harvard College; all rights reserved; see also Michael S. Long, *Valuing the Closely Held Firm* (Oxford: Oxford University Press, 2008); and James C. Brau, Ninon K. Sutton, and Nile W. Hatch, "Dual-Track versus Single-Track Sell-Outs: An Empirical Analysis of Competing Harvest Strategies," *Journal of Business Venturing* 25, no. 4 (2010): 389–402.

GLOSSARY

Abandonment Nonuse of a trademark for two consecutive years without justification or a statement regarding abandonment of the trademark.

Accounts payable Liabilities incurred by a business when goods or supplies are purchased on credit.

Accounts receivable Claims of a business against its customers for unpaid balances from the sale of merchandise or the performance of services.

Accounts receivable financing Short-term financing that involves either the pledge of receivables as collateral for a loan or the outright sale of receivables. (See also Factoring.)

Accredited purchaser A category used in Regulation D that includes institutional investors; any person who buys at least $150,000 of the offered security and whose net worth is in excess of $1 million; a person whose individual income was greater than $200,000 in each of the last two years; directors, partners, or executive officers selling securities; and certain tax-exempt organizations with more than $500,000 in assets.

Adjusted tangible book value A common method of valuing a business by computing its net worth as the difference between total assets and total liabilities.

Administrative expenses Operating expenses not directly related to selling or borrowing.

Advertising model Generates revenue by selling advertisements against the traffic of the site.

Affiliate model Generates revenue by driving traffic, leads, or sales to another, affiliated company's website.

Angel capital Investments in new ventures that come from wealthy individuals referred to as "business angels."

Antidilution protection The conversion price of the preferred stock is subject to adjustment for certain diluting events, such as stock splits or stock dividends. The conversion price is typically subject to "price protection," which is an adjustment based on future sales of stock at prices below the conversion price.

Appositional relationship A relationship among things and people existing in the world in relation to other things and other people.

B corporation A legal structure that expands corporate accountability to make decisions that are good for society, not just shareholders. B corporations' performance standards enable consumers to support businesses that align with their values.

Balance sheet A financial statement that reports the assets, liabilities, and owners' equity in the venture at a particular point in time.

Bankruptcy A legal process for insolvent debtors who are unable to pay debts as they become due. For business, this includes Chapters 7, 11, and 13 of the federal bankruptcy code.

Bankruptcy Act Federal law that provides for specific procedures in handling insolvent debtors.

Benefit corporation It is exactly the same as traditional corporations except for a few specific elements that make them more socially sustainable enterprises: purpose, accountability, transparency.

Better widget strategies Innovation that encompasses new or existing markets.

Blog monitoring Analysing blog content to identify prominent terms or themes.

Bootlegging Secretly working on new ideas on company time as well as on personal time.

Bootstrapping The art of doing more with less.

Break-even analysis A technique commonly used to assess expected product profitability, which helps to determine how many units must be sold to break even at a particular selling price.

Budget A statement of estimated income and expenses over a specified period of time.

Business angel Wealthy people in the United States looking for investment opportunities.

Business broker Professionals specializing in business opportunities often can provide leads and assistance in finding a venture for sale.

Business model How a venture is designed to make money, demonstrating a clear method of getting to the market for sales.

Business model canvas A structured brainstorming tool for entrepreneurs to use to define and understand the strategic focus and the questions that need to be answered for each of the nine business building blocks.

Business plan The written document that details a proposed venture. It must illustrate current status, expected needs, and projected results of the new business.

Business valuation The calculated value of the business, used to track its increases or decreases.

Buy/sell agreements Agreements designed to handle situations in which one (or more) of the entrepreneurs wants to sell her interest in the venture.

Cancellation proceedings A third party's challenge to the trademark's distinctiveness within five years of its issuance.

Capital budgeting A budgeting process used to determine investment decisions. It relies heavily on an evaluation of cash inflows.

Career risk Whether an entrepreneur will be able to find a job or go back to an old job if his or her venture fails.

Cash Coins, currency, and checks on hand. It also includes money the business has in its checking and savings accounts.

Cash-flow budget A budget that provides an overview of inflows and outflows of cash during a specified period of time.

Cash-flow statement A financial statement that sets forth the amount and timing of actual and/or expected cash inflows and outflows.

Champion Within the context of corporate entrepreneurship, this is a person with an innovative vision and the ability to share it.

Claims A series of short paragraphs, each of which identifies a particular feature or combination of features, protected by a patent.

Cleaning-out procedure The failure of a trademark owner to file an affidavit stating that it is in use or justifying its lack of use within six years of registration.

Code of conduct A statement of ethical practices or guidelines to which an enterprise adheres.

Cognition It refers to mental processes. These processes include attention, remembering, producing and understanding language, solving problems, and making decisions.

Cognitive adaptability The ability to be dynamic, flexible, and self-regulating in one's cognitions given dynamic and uncertain task environments.

Collective entrepreneurship Individual skills integrated into a group wherein the collective capacity to innovate becomes something greater than the sum of its parts.

Company's profitability The amount of net profit a company produces after expenses.

Comprehensive feasibility approach A systematic analysis incorporating external factors.

Consumer pricing Combining penetration and competitive pricing to gain market share.

Consumer-driven philosophy A marketing philosophy that relies on research to discover consumer preferences, desires, and needs before production actually begins. (See also **Production-driven philosophy** and **Sales-driven philosophy**).

Contribution margin approach A common approach to break-even analysis, determined by calculating the difference between the selling price and the variable cost per unit.

Control factor The degree of control an owner legally has over the firm can affect its valuation.

Copyright A legal protection that provides exclusive rights to creative individuals for the protection of their literary or artistic productions.

Corporate entrepreneurship A new "corporate revolution" taking place due to the infusion of entrepreneurial thinking into bureaucratic structures.

Corporate Entrepreneurship Assessment Instrument (CEAI) A questionnaire designed to measure the key entrepreneurial climate factors.

Corporate venturing The adding of new businesses (or portions of new businesses via equity investments) to the corporation. This can be accomplished through three implementation modes: internal corporate venturing, cooperative corporate venturing, and external corporate venturing.

Corporation An entity legally separate from the individuals who own it, created by the authority of state laws, and usually formed when a transfer of money or property by prospective shareholders takes place in exchange for capital stock in the corporation.

Corridor principle States that with every venture launched, new and unintended opportunities arise.

Creative process The four phases of creative development: background or knowledge accumulation, incubation process, idea experience, and evaluation or implementation.

Creativity The generation of ideas that results in an improvement in the efficiency or effectiveness of a system.

Critical factors Important new-venture assessments.

Crowdfunding It is a twenty-first century phenomenon. Commercial lenders are not always willing to make loans to unproven enterprises, leaving entrepreneurs desperate for funding to seek new loan options.

Customer availability Having customers available before a venture starts.

Dark side of entrepreneurship A destructive side that exists within the energetic drive of successful entrepreneurs.

Debt financing Borrowing money for short- or long-term periods for working capital or for purchasing property and equipment.

Debtor-in-possession When a debtor involved in a Chapter 11 proceeding continues to operate the business.

Delayed entry strategy A succession strategy that encourages the younger generation to enter the business at a later age to gain experience outside the family held firm.

Demand-oriented pricing A flexible strategy that bases pricing decisions on the demand level for the product.

Design-centered entrepreneurship In essence, the entrepreneur applies design methods in four action stages of developing an opportunity: Ideation; market engagement; business model.

Design methodology Takes an initial concept idea and develops a proof of concept that elicits feedback from relevant stakeholders.

Diaspora networks They are relationships among ethnic groups that share cultural and social norms.

Direct public offering (DPO) It eases the regulations for the reports and statements required for selling stock to private parties—friends, employees, customers, relatives, and local professionals.

Discounted earnings method A method that determines the true value of the firm with a pricing formula that includes earning power as well as adjusted tangible book value.

Displacement school of thought A school of entrepreneurial thought that focuses on group phenomena such as the political, cultural, and economic environments.

Divergent goals When the entrepreneur has a vision for the venture that differs from the investors' goals or stockholders' desires, thus causing internal conflicts in the firm.

Due diligence A thorough analysis of every facet of the existing business.

Duplication A basic type of innovation that involves the replication of an already existing product, service, or process.

Dynamic states model A network of relationships and systems that convert opportunity tension into value for a venture's customers, generating new resources that maintain the dynamic state.

Early entry strategy A succession strategy that encourages the younger generation to enter the business at an early age to gain experience.

Ecopreneurship Environmental entrepreneurship with entrepreneurial actions contributing to preserving the natural environment, including the Earth, biodiversity, and ecosystems.

Ecovision Leadership style for innovative organizations. Encourages open and flexible structures that encompass the employees, the organization, and the environment, with attention to evolving social demands.

Either/or thinking People often get bogged down with striving for an unreasonable amount of certainty in their lives. But the creative person learns to accept a reasonable amount of ambiguity in his or her work and life.

Elevator pitch The brief oral presentation for selling a business plan to potential investors (named for the analogy of riding an elevator and having only two minutes to get your story told to another person in the elevator).

Emotional bias The tendency to believe an enterprise is worth a great deal more than outsiders believe it is worth.

Employee stock ownership plans (ESOPs) Passing control of the enterprise to the employees if the owner has no immediate successor in mind.

Entrepreneur An innovator or developer who recognizes and seizes opportunities; converts these opportunities into workable/marketable ideas; adds value through time, effort, money, or skills; assumes the risks of the competitive marketplace to implement these ideas; and realizes the rewards from these efforts.

Entrepreneurial behaviour An entrepreneur's decision to initiate the new venture formation process.

Entrepreneurial cognition The knowledge structures that people use to make assessments, judgments, or decisions involving opportunity evaluation, venture creation, and growth.

Entrepreneurial discipline Entrepreneurship is based upon the same principles, whether the entrepreneur is an existing large institution or an individual starting his or her new venture singlehanded.

Entrepreneurial experience Entrepreneurs emerge as a function of the novel, idiosyncratic, and experiential nature of the venture creation process involving three parallel, interactive phenomena: emergence of the opportunity, emergence of the venture, and emergence of the entrepreneur.

Entrepreneurial firm It increases opportunity for its employees, initiates change, and instills a desire to be innovative.

Entrepreneurial leadership An entrepreneur's ability to anticipate, envision, maintain flexibility, think strategically, and work with others to initiate changes that will create a viable future for the organization.

Entrepreneurial mind-set All the characteristics and elements that compose the entrepreneurial potential in every individual.

Entrepreneurial motivation The willingness of an entrepreneur to sustain his or her entrepreneurial behavior.

Entrepreneurial persistence An entrepreneur's choice to continue with an entrepreneurial opportunity regardless of counterinfluences or other enticing alternatives.

Entrepreneurial Revolution The tremendous increase in entrepreneurial business and entrepreneurial thinking that has developed during the last 20 years. This revolution will be as powerful to the twenty-first century as the Industrial Revolution was to the twentieth century (if not more!).

Entrepreneurial strategy matrix Measures risk and innovation.

Entrepreneurial successor A successor to a venture who is highly gifted with ingenuity, creativity, and drive.

Entrepreneurial trait school of thought A school of entrepreneurial thought that focuses on identifying traits that appear common to successful entrepreneurs.

Entrepreneurship A dynamic process of vision, change, and creation. It requires an application of energy and passion toward the creation and implementation of new ideas and creative solutions. Essential ingredients include the willingness to take calculated risks—in terms of time, equity, or career; the ability to formulate an effective venture team; the creative skill to marshal needed resources; the fundamental skill of building a solid business plan; and, finally, the vision to recognize opportunity where others see chaos, contradiction, and confusion.

Environmental school of thought A school of entrepreneurial thought that focuses on the external factors and forces—values, mores, and institutions—that surround a potential entrepreneur's lifestyle.

Equity financing The sale of some ownership in a venture in order to gain capital for start-up.

Ethics A set of principles prescribing a behavioral code that explains what is good and right or bad and wrong.

European Union (EU) The EU is an economic and political union of 27 member states which are located primarily in Europe.

Exit strategy That component of the business plan where an entrepreneur describes a method by which investors can realize a tangible return on their investment.

Expenses An expired cost; any item or class of cost of (or loss from) carrying on an activity; a present or past expenditure defraying a present operating cost or representing an irrecoverable cost or loss; an item of capital expenditures written down or off; or a term often used with some qualifying expression denoting function, organization, or time, such as a selling expense, factory expense, or monthly expense.

Exporting It is the shipping of a domestically produced good to a foreign destination for consumption. Exporting is important for entrepreneurs because it often means increased market potential.

Extension A basic type of innovation that involves extending the life of a product, service, or process already in existence.

External locus of control A point of view in which external processes are sometimes beyond the control of the individual entrepreneur.

External problems Related to customer contact, market knowledge, marketing planning, location, pricing, product considerations, competitors, and expansion.

Factoring The sale of accounts receivable.

Failure A venture not being able to survive as caused by inexperience or incompetent management.

Failure prediction model Based on financial data from newly founded ventures; assumes the financial failure process is characterized by too much initial indebtedness and too little revenue financing.

Fair use doctrine An exception to copyright protection that allows limited use of copyrighted materials.

Family and social risk Starting a new venture uses much of the entrepreneur's energy and time. Entrepreneurs who are married, and especially those with children, expose their families to the risks of an incomplete family experience and the possibility of permanent emotional scars. In addition, old friends may vanish slowly because of missed get togethers.

Feasibility criteria approach A criteria selection list from which entrepreneurs can gain insights into the viability of their venture.

Finance companies Asset-based lenders that lend money against assets such as receivables, inventory, and equipment.

Financial expense The interest expense on long-term loans. Many companies also include their interest expense on short-term obligations as part of their financial expense.

Financial risk The money or resources at stake for a new venture.

Financial/capital school of thought A school of entrepreneurial thought that focuses on the ways entrepreneurs seek seed capital and growth funds.

Five-minute reading A six-step process that venture capitalists use when they are reviewing a business plan for potential investment.

Fixed assets Land, building, equipment, and other assets expected to remain with the firm for an extended period.

Fixed cost A cost that does not change in response to changes in activity for a given period of time.

Forcing events Happenings that cause the replacement of the owner/manager.

Framework of frameworks Allows for the entrepreneurship theory to move forward identifying the static and dynamic elements of new theories, typologies, or frameworks.

Franchise Any arrangement in which the owner of a trademark, trade name, or copyright has licensed others to use it to sell goods or services.

Franchise Disclosure Document (FDD) A legal disclosure document that must now be presented to prospective buyers of franchises in the presale disclosure process in the United States. It was originally known as the Uniform Franchise Offering Circular (UFOC).

Franchise fee The initial amount of money needed to purchase a franchise.

Franchisee An individual who purchases and operates a franchise.

Franchisor An individual (or company) who offers to sell or license his operation in the form of a franchise.

Franchisor control The franchisor generally exercises a fair amount of control over the operation in order to achieve a degree of uniformity.

Freemium model Generates revenue by offering a basic service for free while charging for a premium service with advanced features to paying members.

Fully diluted All securities—including preferred stock, options, and warrants—that can result in additional common shares are counted in determining the total amount of shares outstanding for the purposes of determining ownership or valuation.

Functional perspective Viewing things and people in terms of how they can be used to satisfy one's needs and to help complete a project.

Gazelle A business establishment with at least 20 percent sales growth every year, starting with a base of at least $100,000.

Generic meaning Allowance of a trademark to represent a general grouping of products or services (for example, Kleenex has come to represent tissue).

Global entrepreneurs An entrepreneur who relies on global (international) networks for resources, design, and distribution.

Goodwill The amount of value created by an owner of a business in terms of his or her time, effort, and public image with the business itself.

Great chef strategies The skills or special talents of one or more individuals around whom a venture is built.

Grief recovery The traditional process of recovering from grief involves focusing on the particular loss to construct an account that explains why the loss occurred.

Growth of sales The growth pattern anticipated for new-venture sales and profits.

Growth stage The third stage of a new venture life cycle, typically involving activities related to reformulating strategy in the light of competition.

Growth stage The third stage of a new venture life cycle, typically involving activities related to reformulating strategy in the light of competition.

Growth wall A psychological wall against change that prevents entrepreneurs from developing a managerial ability to deal with venture growth.

Guerrilla marketing Applying nonconventional tactics and unorthodox practices to marketing research.

Harvest strategy A strategy of how and when the owners and investors will realize an actual cash return on their investment in a venture.

High-growth venture When sales and profit growth are expected to be significant enough to attract venture capital money and funds raised through public or private placements.

Horizontal analysis Looks at financial statements and ratios over time.

Importing It is buying and shipping foreign-produced goods for domestic consumption.

Income statement A financial document that reports the sales, expenses, and profits of the enterprise over a specified period (usually one year).

Incongruities Whenever a gap or difference exists between expectations and reality.

Incremental innovation The systematic evolution of a product or service into newer or larger markets.

Individualize An aspect of global social media strategy directing customized messages to different users based on location, taste preferences, and shopping habits.

Informal risk capitalist Wealthy people in the United States are looking for investment opportunities; they are referred to as business angels or informal risk capitalists.

Infringement budget A realistic budget for prosecuting violations of the patent.

Initial public offering (IPO) A corporation's raising of capital through the sale of securities on the public markets.

Initiate An aspect of global social media strategy creating user-generated content in order to start a meaningful dialogue between different consumers as they communicate online.

Innovation team (I-Team) An internal corporate team formulated for the purpose of creating new innovations for the organization.

Innovation The process by which entrepreneurs convert opportunities into marketable ideas.

Insolvent debtor Those who are unable to pay debts as they become due.

Integrate An aspect of global social media strategy inserting the application into the daily life of the user by offering incentives, prizes, or discounts.

Intellectual property right Provides protection such as patents, trademarks, or copyrights against infringement by others.

Interactive learning Learning ideas within an innovative environment that cut across traditional, functional lines in the organization.

Internal locus of control The viewpoint in which the potential entrepreneur has the ability or control to direct or adjust the outcome of each major influence.

Internal problems Involve adequate capital, cash flow, facilities/equipment, inventory control, human resources, leadership, organizational structure, and accounting systems.

Internal rate of return (IRR) A capital-budgeting technique that involves discounting future cash flows to the present at a rate that makes the net present value of the project equal to zero.

International alliances Another alternative available to the entrepreneur in the international arena. There are three main types of these strategic alliances: informal international cooperative alliances; formal international cooperative alliances (ICAs); and international joint ventures.

Intracapital Special capital set aside for the corporate entrepreneur to use whenever investment money is needed for further research ideas.

Intrapreneurship Entrepreneurial activities that receive organizational sanction and resource commitments for the purpose of innovative results within an established corporation (see also **Corporate entrepreneurship**).

Invention A basic type of innovation that involves the creation of a new product, service, or process that is often novel or untried.

Inventory Merchandise held by the company for resale to customers.

Involve An aspect of global social media strategy engaging the user interactively with a type of a story or game.

Joint venture Occurs when two or more firms analyze the benefits of creating a relationship, pool their resources, and create a new entity to undertake productive economic activity.

L3C A low-profit, limited liability company that facilitates investments in socially beneficial, for-profit ventures. L3C has an explicit primary charitable mission and only a secondary profit concern. Unlike a charity, an L3C is free to distribute the profits, after taxes, to owners or investors.

Lack of expertise/skills When smallbusiness managers lack the specialized expertise/skills necessary for the planning process.

Lack of knowledge Small-firm owners/managers' uncertainty about the components of the planning process and their sequence due to minimal exposure to, and knowledge of, the process itself.

Lack of trust and openness When small firm owners/managers are highly sensitive and guarded about their businesses and the decisions that affect them.

Lean start-up methodology Provides a scientific approach to creating early venture concepts and delivers a desired product to customers' hands faster. It is hypothesis-driven and entrepreneurs must work to gather and *incorporate* customer feedback early and often.

Learning curve concept The time needed for new methods or procedures to be learned and mastered.

Left brain The part of the brain that helps an individual analyze, verbalize, and use rational approaches to problem solving. (See also **Right brain**.)

Legal restraint of trade A legal document signed by the seller of a business that restricts him or her from operating in the same business for a reasonable amount of time and within a reasonable geographic jurisdiction.

Letter of intent (LOI) Nonbinding document meant to record two or more parties' intentions to enter into a future agreement based on specified (but incomplete or preliminary) terms. Many LOIs contain provisions that are binding, such as nondisclosure agreements, a covenant to negotiate in good faith, or a "stand-still" provision promising exclusive rights to negotiate.

Liabilities The debts of a business, incurred either through normal operations or through the process of obtaining funds to finance operations. (See also **Short-term liabilities** and **Longterm liabilities**).

Licensing A business arrangement in which the manufacturer of a product (or a firm with proprietary rights over technology or trademarks) grants permission to a group or an individual to manufacture that product in return for specified royalties or other payments.

Life-cycle stages The typical life cycle through which a venture progresses, including venture development, startup, growth, stabilization, and innovation or decline.

Lifestyle venture A small venture in which the primary driving forces include independence, autonomy, and control.

Limited liability company (LLC) A hybrid form of business enterprise that offers the limited liability of a corporation but the tax advantages of a partnership.

Limited liability limited partnership (LLLP) A variant of the limited partnership. An LLLP has elected limited liability status for all of its partners, including general partners.

Limited liability partnership (LLP) A form of partnership that allows professionals the tax benefits of a partnership while avoiding personal liability for the malpractice of other partners. If a professional group organizes as an LLP, innocent partners are not personally liable for the wrongdoing of the other partners.

Limited partnership A form of company organization that permits capital investment without responsibility for management *and* without liability for losses beyond the initial investment.

Liquidation See Bankruptcy.

Liquidation preference When the company is sold or liquidated, the preferred stockholders will receive a certain fixed amount before any assets are distributed to the common stockholders.

Liquidity event The positioning of the venture for the realization of a cash return for the owners and the investors. This "event" is most often achieved through an initial public offering or complete sale of the venture.

Loan payable The current instalment on a long-term debt that must be paid this year.

Long-term liabilities Business debts that are not due and payable within the next 12 months.

Loss leader pricing Pricing the product below cost in an attempt to attract customers to other products.

Macro view of entrepreneurship A broad array of factors that relate to success or failure in contemporary entrepreneurial ventures.

Macroiteration In design-centered entrepreneurship it is moving from one particular action stage back to a previous stage for further development.

Management succession The transition of managerial decision making in a firm, one of the greatest challenges that confronts owners and entrepreneurs in family businesses.

Management team The founders of a new venture who plan on managing the company, as well as any advisors, consultants, or members of the board.

Managerial successor A successor to a venture who is interested in efficiency, internal control, and the effective use of resources.

Market A group of consumers (potential customers) who have purchasing power and unsatisfied needs. (See also **Market niche** and **Niche**).

Market niche A homogeneous group of consumers with common characteristics.

Market segmentation The segment of a business plan that describes aspects of the market such as the target market, the market size and trends, the competition, estimated market share, market strategy, pricing, and advertising and promotion.

Marketability Assembling and analyzing relevant information about a new venture to judge its potential success.

Marketing research A gathering of information about a particular market, followed by an analysis of that information.

Marketing segment The segment of a business plan that describes aspects of the market such as the target market, the market size and trends, the competition, estimated market share, market strategy, pricing, and advertising and promotion.

Marketing strategy The general marketing philosophy of the company should be outlined to include the kinds of customer groups to be targeted by the initial intensive selling effort; the customer groups to be targeted for later selling efforts; methods of identifying and contracting potential customers in these groups; the features of the product or service (quality, price, delivery, warranty) to be emphasized to generate sales; and innovative or unusual marketing concepts that will enhance customer acceptance.

Market-rich countries Countries have something that others need, thus forming the basis of an interdependent international trade system.

Metacognitive model Integrates the combined effects of entrepreneurial motivation and context, toward the development of metacognitive strategies applied to information processing within an entrepreneurial environment.

Metrics Assumptions and calculations used for any revenue projections.

Micro view of entrepreneurship Examines the factors specific to entrepreneurship and part of the internal locus of control.

Microiteration In design-centered entrepreneurship it is iterating within each action stage to improve the outcome.

Milestone schedule segment The section of a business plan that provides investors with timetables for the accomplishment of various activities such as completion of prototypes, hiring of sales representatives, receipt of first orders, initial deliveries, and receipt of first accounts receivable payments.

Minimum viable product (MVP) This is the early version of the product that enables a full turn on the feedback loop with a minimum of effort.

Mixed costs A blend of fixed and variable costs.

Mobile marketing It allows for an even higher level of individualized company-to-consumer communication by directing customized messages to different users based on location, taste preferences, and shopping habits.

Moral failure This form of failure is a violation of internal trust.

Mountain gap strategies Identifying major market segments as well as interstice (in-between) markets that arise from larger markets.

Muddling mind-sets When creative thinking is blocked or impeded.

Nepotism The hiring of relatives in preference to other, more qualified candidates.

Net income The excess of revenue over expenses during a particular period.

Net present value (NPV) method A capital-budgeting technique used to evaluate an investment that involves a determination of future cash flows and a discounting of these flows to arrive at a present value of these future dollars.

New-new approach A start up approach to business in which the concept is a brand new idea to the marketplace.

New-old approach A start up approach to business in which the concept provides a new angle to something that already exists in the marketplace.

New-venture development The first stage of a venture's life cycle that involves activities such as creativity and venture assessment.

Non-compete agreement An agreement that the previous owner will refrain from conducting the same business within a reasonable distance for a period of at least five years.

North American Free Trade Agreement (NAFTA) An international agreement among Canada, Mexico, and the United States that eliminates trade barriers among the three nations.

Note payable Promissory notes given as tangible recognition of a supplier's claim or notes given in connection with an acquisition of funds, such as for a bank loan.

Oakland Scavenger Company A garbage collection firm based in California that was involved in a legal dispute over nepotism in a family business.

One-person-band syndrome Exists when an entrepreneur fails to delegate responsibility to employees, thereby retaining all decision-making authority.

Operating budget A budget that sets forth the projected sales forecast and expenses for an upcoming period.

Operating expenses The major expenses, exclusive of costs of goods sold, in generating revenue.

Opportunity identification The ability to recognize a viable business opportunity within a variety of good ideas.

Owners' equity What remains after the firm's liabilities are subtracted from its assets.

Pain The nickname that venture capitalists use for exactly what problem is being solved by your venture.

Partnership An association of two or more persons acting as co-owners of a business for profit.

Patent An intellectual property right granted to an inventor, giving him or her the exclusive right to make, use, or sell an invention for a limited time period (usually 20 years).

Patent and trademark office An office of the federal government through which all patent and trademark applications are filed.

Payback method A capital-budgeting technique used to determine the length of time required to pay back an original investment.

Peer-to-peer lending (P2P) Commonly abbreviated as P2PL is the practice of lending money to unrelated individuals, or "peers," without going through a bank or other traditional financial institution. Also known as "debt-based crowdfunding" this lending takes place online on peer-to-peer lending companies' websites using various different lending platforms.

Penetration Setting prices at such a low level that products are sold at a loss. Allows quick gains in market share by setting a price below competitors' prices.

Perception of high cost When smallbusiness owners perceive the cost associated with planning to be very high.

Personal failure A form of failure brought about by a lack of skill or application.

Pivot A structured course correction designed to test a new fundamental hypothesis about the product, strategy, and engine of growth.

Political risks They include unstable governments, disruptions caused by territorial conflicts, wars, regionalism, illegal occupation, and political ideological differences.

Prepaid expenses Expenses the firm already has paid but that have not yet been used.

Price/earnings ratio (P/E) A method of valuing a business that divides the price of the common stock in the market by the earnings per share and multiplies the result by the number of shares of stock issued.

Primary data New data that are often collected using observational or questioning methods.

Private placement A method of raising capital through securities; often used by small ventures.

Pro forma statements Projection of a firm's financial position during a future period (pro forma income statement) or on a future date (pro forma balance sheet).

Probability thinking Relying on probability to make decisions in the struggle to achieve security.

Product availability The availability of a salable good or service at the time the venture opens its doors.

Production-driven philosophy A market philosophy based on the principle of producing efficiently and letting sales take care of themselves. (See also **Consumer-driven philosophy** and **Sales-driven philosophy**).

Profit trend A venture's ability to generate a profit over a sustained period.

Prototyping A physical representation of the venture that captures the essence of an idea in a form that can be shared with others for communication and feedback that closes the gap between concept and reality.

Psychic risk The great psychological impact on and the well-being of the entrepreneur who creates a new venture.

Qualitative research It needs far less sample size as it involves the researcher into the process and is able to delve deeper into the questions with the respondents.

Quantitative research It involves empirical assessments that work from numerical measurements and analytical approaches to compare the results in some way.

Radical innovation The inaugural breakthroughs launched from experimentation and determined vision that are not necessarily managed but must be recognized and nurtured.

Rationalizations What managers use to justify questionable conduct.

Ratios Designed to show relationships among financial statement accounts.

Reachable market The immediate reachable group of customers that will be targeted by a new venture.

Regulation D Regulation and exemption for reports and statements required for selling stock to private parties based on the amount of money being raised.

Resource-rich countries Countries have something that others need, thus forming the basis of an interdependent international trade system.

Retained earnings The accumulated net income over the life of the corporation to date.

Revenues The gross sales made by a business during a particular period under review.

Revised Uniform Limited Partnership Act (RULPA) An act that governs limited partnerships and contains 11 articles and 64 sections of guidelines covering areas such as (1) general provisions, (2) formation, (3) limited partners, (4) general partners, (5) finance, (6) distributions and withdrawals, (7) assignment of partnership interest, (8) dissolution, (9) foreign limited partnerships, (10) derivative actions, and (11) miscellaneous.

Right brain The part of the brain that helps an individual understand analogies, imagine things, and synthesize information. (See also **Left brain**.)

Risk Involves uncertain outcomes or events. The higher the rewards, the greater the risk entrepreneurs usually face.

Risk versus reward Examine overall gains and losses to point out the importance of getting an adequate return on the amount of money risked.

Role assertion Unethical acts involving managers/entrepreneurs who represent the firm and who rationalize that they are in a position to help the firm's longrun interests.

Role distortion Unethical acts committed on the basis that they are "for the firm" even though they are not, and involving managers/entrepreneurs who commit individual acts and rationalize that they are in the firm's longrun interests.

Role failure Unethical acts against the firm involving a person failing to perform his or her managerial role, including superficial performance appraisals (not being totally honest) and not confronting someone who is cheating on expense accounts.

S corporation Formerly termed a Subchapter S corporation, an **S corporation** takes its name from Subchapter S of the Internal Revenue Code, under which a business can seek to avoid the imposition of income taxes at the corporate level, yet retain some of the benefits of a corporate form (especially the limited liability).

Sales forecast The process of projecting future sales by applying statistical techniques to historical sales figures.

Sales-driven philosophy A marketing philosophy that focuses on personal selling and advertising to persuade customers to buy the company's output. (See also **Consumer-driven philosophy** and **Product-driven philosophy**).

Secondary data Data that have already been compiled. Examples are periodicals, articles, trade association information, governmental publications, and company records.

Security hunting Common mental habit that inhibits creativity and innovation by hindering creative thought processes.

Shared value It is a transformation of business thinking recognizing societal weaknesses that create internal costs for firms (e.g., wasted energy, accidents, inadequacies in education).

Short-term liabilities (current liabilities) Business debts that must be paid during the coming 12 months (also called *current liabilities*).

Simple linear regression A technique in which a linear equation states the relationship among three variables used to estimate the sales forecast.

Skimming Deliberately setting a high price to maximize short-term profits.

Skunk Works A highly innovative enterprise that uses groups functioning outside traditional lines of authority.

Small profitable venture A venture in which the entrepreneur does not want venture sales to become so large that he or she must relinquish equity or ownership position and thus give up control over cash flows and profits, which it is hoped will be substantial.

Social cognition theory Cognition is used to refer to the mental functions, mental processes (thoughts), and mental states of intelligent humans. Social cognition theory introduces the idea of knowledge structures—mental models (cognitions) that are ordered in such a way as to optimize personal effectiveness within given situations—to the study of entrepreneurship.

Social entrepreneurship A new form of entrepreneurship that exhibits characteristics of nonprofits, government, and businesses; it applies traditional (private-sector) entrepreneurship's focus on innovation, risk taking, and large-scale transformation to social problem solving.

Social impact investing Raising funds for socially motivated causes.

Social media marketing It describes the use of these tools for marketing purposes. The most common social media marketing tools include Twitter, blogs, LinkedIn, Facebook, Flickr, and YouTube.

Social value Contribution to the welfare or well-being in a given community.

Sole proprietorship A business that is owned and operated by one person. The enterprise has no existence apart from its owner. This individual has a right to all of the profits and bears all of the liability for the debts and obligations of the business.

Sophisticated investor Wealthy individuals who invest more or less regularly in new and early- and latestage ventures. They are knowledgeable about the technical and commercial opportunities and risks of the businesses in which they invest.

Specification The text of a patent; it may include any accompanying illustrations.

Stabilization stage The fourth stage of a new-venture life cycle, typified by increased competition, consumer indifference to the entrepreneur's good (s) or service(s), and saturation of the market with a host of "me too" lookalikes. During this stage, the entrepreneur begins planning the venture's direction for the next three to five years.

Start-up activities The second stage of a new-venture life cycle, encompassing the foundation work needed to create a formal business plan, search for capital, carry out marketing activities, and develop an effective entrepreneurial team.

Start-up problems A perceived problem area in the start-up phase of a new venture, such as lack of business training, difficulty obtaining lines of credit, and inexperience in financial planning.

Stereotyping Refers to averages that people fabricate and then, ironically, base decisions on as if they were entities existing in the real world.

Strategic entrepreneurship The exhibition of large-scale or otherwise highly consequential innovations that are adopted in the firm's pursuit of competitive advantage. Using strategic entrepreneurship approaches, innovation can be in any of five areas: the firm's strategy, product offerings, served markets, internal organization (i.e., structure, processes, and capabilities), or business model.

Strategic formulation school of thought A school of entrepreneurial thought that focuses on the planning process used in successful venture formulation.

Strategic planning The primary step in determining the future direction of a business influenced by the abilities of the entrepreneur, the complexity of the venture, and the nature of the industry.

Strategic positioning The process of perceiving new positions that attract customers from established positions or draw new customers into the market.

Stress A function of discrepancies between a person's expectations and ability to meet demands, as well as discrepancies between the individual's expectations and personality. If a person is unable to fulfill role demands, then stress occurs.

Subscription model Generates revenue by requiring users to pay a fee (generally monthly or yearly) to access a product or service.

Sustainable entrepreneurship It focused on the preservation of nature, life support, and community in the pursuit of perceived opportunities to bring into existence future products, processes, and services for gain, where gain is broadly construed to include economic and noneconomic gains to individuals, the economy, and society.

SWOT analysis A strategic analysis that refers to strengths, weaknesses, opportunities, and threats.

Synthesis A basic type of innovation that involves combining existing concepts and factors into a new formulation.

Taxes payable Liabilities owed to the government—federal, state, and local.

Technical feasibility Producing a product or service that will satisfy the expectations of potential customers.

Term sheet Document that outlines the material terms and conditions of a venture agreement and lists deal terms in bullet-point format.

Time scarcity Lack of time and the difficulty of allocating time for planning in the face of continual day-today operating problems.

Top management support When upper level managers in a corporation can concentrate on helping individuals within the system develop more entrepreneurial behavior.

Trade credit Credit given by a supplier who sells goods on account. A common arrangement calls for the bill to be settled within 30 to 90 days.

Trade secrets Customer lists, plans, research and development, pricing information, marketing techniques, and production techniques. Generally, anything that makes an individual company unique and has value to a competitor could be a trade secret.

Trademark A distinctive name, mark, symbol, or motto identified with a company's product(s).

Triple bottom line (TBL) An accounting framework that goes beyond the traditional measures of profit, return on investment, and shareholder value to include environmental and social dimensions.

Uncontrollable failure Form of failure caused by external factors that are outside the control of employees, such as resource limitations, strategic direction, and market changes.

Undercapitalization The amount of equity investment is usually low (often indicating a high level of debt).

Uniqueness Special characteristics and/or design concepts that draw the customer to the venture and should provide performance or service superior to competitive offerings.

Unlimited liability The individual proprietor is personally responsible for all business debts. This liability extends to *all* of the proprietor's assets.

Unscrupulous practices Business practices that are devoid of ethics and seek personal gain at any cost.

Upside gain and downside loss Within the financial capital domain, this is the best possible gain weighed against the worst loss possible. (See also **Risk vs. reward**.)

Validated learning A process in which one learns by trying out an initial idea and then measuring it to substantiate the effect.

Variable cost A cost that changes in the same direction as, and in direct proportion to, changes in operating activity.

Venture capitalist Individuals who provide a full range of financial services for new or growing ventures, such as capital for start-ups and expansions, marketing research, management consulting, assistance with negotiating technical agreements, and assistance with employee recruitment and development of employee agreements.

Venture opportunity school of thought A school of entrepreneurial thought that focuses on the search for idea sources, on concept development, and on implementation of venture opportunities.

Vertical analysis The application of ratio analysis to one set of financial statements.

Virtual goods model Generates revenue by charging users for virtual goods, such as upgrades, points, or gifts, on a website or in a game.

Water well strategies The ability to gather or harness special resources (land, labor, capital, raw materials) over the long term.

World Trade Organization (WTO) The umbrella organization governing the international trading system. Its job is to oversee international trade arrangements, but, contrary to popular belief, the WTO does not replace the General Agreement on Tariffs and Trade (GATT).

NAME INDEX

SUBJECT INDEX